VARIORUM COLLECTED STUDIES SERIES

Image and Value in the
Graeco-Roman World

Dr Richard Gordon

Richard Gordon

Image and Value in the
Graeco-Roman World

Studies in Mithraism and Religious Art

ASHGATE
VARIORUM

This edition copyright © 1996 by Richard Gordon

Published in the Variorum Collected Studies Series by

Ashgate Publishing Limited
Gower House, Croft Road,
Aldershot, Hampshire
GU11 3HR
Great Britain

Ashgate Publishing Company
Suite 420
101 Cherry Street
Burlington, VT 05401-4405
USA

Ashgate website: http://www.ashgate.com

Reprinted 2003

ISBN 0-86078-608-0

British Library Cataloguing-in-Publication Data
Gordon, Richard.
Image and Value in the Graeco-Roman World: Studies in Mithraism and
Religious Art. (Variorum Collected Studies Series: CS551).
1. Art, Classical–Religious aspects. 2. Classical antiquities. 3. Mithraism.
4. Art and Religion–Greece.
I. Title.
292

US Library of Congress CIP Data
Gordon, R.L. (Richard Lindsay).
Image and Value in the Graeco-Roman World / Richard Gordon.
p. cm. – (Collected Studies Series; CS551).
Includes index (cloth: alk. paper).
1. Mithraism. 2. Mithraism in art. 3. Art and religion– Rome. 4. Rome–
Antiquities. 5. Excavations (Archaeology)–Rome. 6. Rome–Religion.
I. Title. II. Series: Collected Studies Series; CS551.
BL1585. G67   1996   96-8972
299'. 15–dc20   CIP

The paper used in this publication meets the minimum requirements of the
American National Standard for Information Sciences – Permanence of
Paper for Printed Library Materials, ANSI Z39.48–1984. ∞ ™

Printed in Great Britain by Biddles Limited, Guildford and King's Lynn

VARIORUM COLLECTED STUDIES SERIES CS551

CONTENTS

> This volume contains xii + 338 pages

PREFACE

All but one of the nine essays collected in this volume explore a rather ill-defined no-man's-land between archaeology on the one hand and aspects of Graeco-Roman religion on the other. For many, such a no-man's-land does not exist, since the two disciplines simply complement one another. For me too the monuments are the indispensable starting-point of any enquiry. But whereas others are most interested in using archaeological monuments singly or in series as illustrations or commentaries on beliefs or practices known from texts, taking the existence of both monument and cult for granted, as a lapsed Scottish Presbyterian with a particular fondness for Roman Catholic religious art I have always had more of an eye for the place of religious art in the construction of the religious enterprise than for the Realien of religious belief. This focus upon the how of religious belief rather than its matter owes something to David Martin, whose seminar at the London School of Economics I attended occasionally in 1966–67. At that time there was a vogue for a primitive version of constructionism, and I vividly remember the high hopes I had on opening a book on *The Social Construction of Reality* by Peter Berger and Thomas Luckmann, and how swiftly they were dashed. But if 'reality' itself could not possibly be socially constructed as they claimed, it seemed to me no less certainly the case that religion was, if not 'socially' constructed (whatever that might mean), at least an enterprise of the human imagination, one of whose major features was the objectivity – reality in that sense – it claimed for itself. It is not that I am indifferent to the possible emotional meanings of religion but that these seem to me purely superficial matters as far as the historian of religion is concerned – so obvious that they do not require discussion. Above all, they do not exhaust the possible implications of the notion 'religious meaning'.

During much of the period that I wrote these essays – all but one date from between 1971 and 1980 – I was thus on the look-out for ways of representing to oneself the modes by which religious art contributes to the instantiation of the imaginary world that is the religious world, at a level beyond the simply obvious. It was at this time that I became interested in the early work of anthropologists such as Clifford Geertz, Mary Douglas, Dan Sperber and Pierre Bourdieu, all of whom provided substance for my eclecticism. In focusing on the possibilities of the term evocation, I was trying to do justice both to the thought that at any historical point a religious world appears to the believer/practitioner as a given, and that he or she must be free to change or adapt that given in the construction of personal existential meanings – that indeed religious practice is only meaningful insofar as it is internalised. It is this awareness of the subterranean, inchoate, inexpressible quality of lived religious belief that makes me diffident about many of the generalisations and fixed ideas that are alone able to support scholars through the writing of grand historical accounts of Graeco-Roman religion.

Except in the case of the earliest essay (no. III), written from a thoroughly Weberian perspective, my main underlying questions have thus been two. First, what is the place of representation in the construction of the religious world as objectively existent? It seems likely from Jaś (John) Elsner's recent *Art and the Roman Viewer* (1995) that this issue will now become more topical, though I am not convinced that it can satisfactorily be answered solely from the theoretical perspective of the 'viewer' (which is to my mind too vacant a construction to serve as a starting-point). Can we step back from ancient religious 'art' sufficiently to see it as element in a larger project of construction? Second, if we conceive of representation as a 'practice through which things take on meaning and value' (M. J. Shapiro, *The Politics of Representation*, 1988, p.xi), how exactly are such meanings and values connoted or implied by the representation? Here one can only work on a small canvass, and for purely contingent reasons (the study of Mithraism, when I came to it in 1968 or so, in connection with a quite different problem, seemed in such a mess that it needed some abrasive cleanser), I have mostly worked on this apparently minor topic. Minor it may be, but its interest from my perspective is that it offers a case of a more or less private religious world, one peculiar even in the context of Graeco-Roman civic religiosity, one moreover in which the almost complete absence of relevant literary interpretation and exegesis throws the would-be interpreter *faute de mieux* onto the surviving monuments, both figurative and architectural. Mithraism has therefore for me a synecdochic relation to the wider problems of Graeco-Roman religion. But it is not merely for that reason that I take a wide view of 'representation', since I also wish to raise doubts about the appropriateness of our art-historical category of 'naturalism' and its apparently obvious antithesis 'symbolism'.

These perspectives explain why my cast on the study of Mithraism may seem rather peculiar, why there is no extended comment here upon *the* meaning of the scene in which Mithras kills the bull, and why I have in principle preferred to investigate how it made sense rather than in precise terms the sense it made. I say in principle because there certainly are occasions when I have lost sight of what on reflection I understand as the the main task and turned to something uncomfortably like the usual archaeological practice of identification and exegesis. On the central issue of the sense the Mysteries of Mithras offered, I would now say that they sought to combine a theodicy of (relative) good fortune with a 'utopian' story (to use the term of J.Z. Smith, *Drudgery Divine*, 1992) about the possibility of individual salvation. This indeed is the burden of a book I am currently writing with R.L. Beck, in which we return to many of the issues I raise in these pages. But it is precisely this issue on which there is unlikely to be much agreement among scholars.

In trying to relate the discourse of the Mysteries of Mithras to wider issues in the Graeco-Roman world, I have often turned to the body of ideas associated with what is now known as the Centre Louis Gernet, the group of scholars that includes J-P. Vernant, P. Vidal-Naquet and M. Detienne. Their perspectives and assumptions, which I was able to absorb at first hand during six months spent in Paris in 1967–8, were nothing less than revelatory to anyone who had experienced a Classical education in England during the early 1960s. The historicism represented by a Walter Burkert, however intelligently and learnedly prosecuted, has never been able to compete with this early influence: for me, the historical is simply one (secondary) option among explanatory choices. My interest in ancient animals as 'good to think' was aroused by Vernant and Detienne's *Les ruses de l'intelligence* (1974) much more directly than by Lévi-Strauss' *La pensée sauvage* (1962). It may be that I have little critical distance to these ideas: even when I read the works of their younger followers, such as Pauline Schmitt Pantel's *La cité au banquet* (1992), I find the categories and procedures they use so wholly familiar that they seem simply to be common-sense. Certainly in these essays it did not occur to me to raise questions, which anyone now writing would of course raise, about the category religion as applied to the ancient world, or the rôle attributed to the practice of sacrifice. My view of the category mystery is also decidedly conservative, perhaps even romantic; but, though the present trend is towards deflation of the notion, there still seems to me some merit in looking at the mode within which the meanings of 'mystery cults' were presented.

It would not have occurred to me that these essays might still have some wider interest had it not been for a suggestion from Robin Cormack, who introduced me to John Smedley of Ashgate Publishing. Without their direct intervention, this collection would not have come into being. Although most of the work on Mithraism republished here was written before my close co-operation with Roger Beck, I can no longer imagine what it was like to work without benefit of his stimulation, advice and insight; I sometimes think our joint book has been in progress so long because we cannot bear to bring the co-operation to a close. Being convinced that no one would want to read what I write, I am also most grateful for the support of two American scholars, Richard Brilliant and John Gager, who have encouraged me to think differently. Virtually all of these papers were written while I was a member of the School of European Studies at the University of East Anglia at Norwich, where the ancient world was my sole province, and where lively colleagues soon made me dreadfully conscious of knowing nothing about modern history or literary criticism; in such an environment the barriers that keep most of us on the strait path of disciplinary virtue had little meaning and no attraction – I learned all the time.

Ilmmünster
April 1996

RICHARD GORDON

ACKNOWLEDGEMENTS

Grateful acknowledgement is made to the following institutions and publishers for the permission to reproduce the essays included in this volume: Basil Blackwell Publishers, Oxford (for essay I); The Pennsylvania State University Press (II); the Academic Press Ltd (III); Alan Sutton Publishing Ltd., Gloucester and Newnham College, Cambridge (IV); and Routledge, London and Henley on Thames (V, VI, VII, VIII & IX).

PUBLISHER'S NOTE

The articles in this volume, as in all others in the Collected Studies Series, have not been given a new, continuous pagination. In order to avoid confusion, and to facilitate their use where these same studies have been referred to elsewhere, the original pagination has been maintained wherever possible.

Each article has been given a Roman number in order of appearance, as listed in the Contents. This number is repeated on each page and is quoted in the index entries.

THE REAL AND THE IMAGINARY:

Production and Religion in the Graeco-Roman World

The inheritance of Winckelmann lies heavy on the sub-discipline called History of Classical Art. So much so that it was contemptuously – and despairingly – accused of having abandoned entirely the historical vocation by Ranuccio Bianchi Bandinelli in 1966.[1] For him, the subject had become lost in the effort of systematic pigeonholing (the creation of categories solely by the observer) or in the pursuit of 'fictitious problems' such as the originality of Roman art (a problem created by the Romantic category of sincerity). Since that time there has been some recognition of alternatives, especially among the Italian pupils of Bianchi Bandinelli writing in the *Dialoghi di Archeologia*, and in odd books, the most impressive of which is Dieter Metzler's *Porträt und Gesellschaft* (Münster, 1971).[2] But in general it may not unfairly be remarked that the history of classical art, as a discipline, has succeeded only in fusing connoisseurship – the connoisseur defined by Panofsky as 'the collector, museum curator or expert who deliberately limits his contribution to scholarship to identifying works of art with respect to date, provenance and authorship, and to evaluating them with respect to quality and condition'[3] – with iconography, the identification of motifs recognized as carriers of a secondary or conventional meaning.[4] We still regularly find the casual employment of 'explanatory' categories such as the 'evolution' of one style into another, the notion of 'influence' to deal with the problem of change, an unquestioning opposition between 'great creative masters' and 'imitators' or 'pupils', and a studious avoidance of the really difficult problems: the nature of the constraints, motives, meanings and options, in relation not only to ancient craftsmen but to the societies in which they worked and lived.[5] The ostensible reason for this failure is of course that there is no evidence for such matters; but evidence is a function not so much of matter as of questions. If the appropriate questions were asked, more appropriate answers might be forthcoming. If only ancient art were as dead as ancient Greek or ancient history, things might be different. Or again, they might not: mummies are mummies.

Now Bianchi Bandinelli's alternative to the intellectual stances which he criticized was a Marxist approach to the history of classical art: 'Car la culture artistique de

THE REAL AND THE IMAGINARY: PRODUCTION AND RELIGION IN THE GRAECO-ROMAN WORLD

l'Antiquité présente des caractéristiques et un développement général particulièrement favorables à démontrer la fécondité d'une analyse qui considère l'oeuvre d'art non pas comme le résultat uniquement d'une intuition ou d'une émotion (plus ou moins conscient) de l'artiste ou bien la conséquence des idées qui circulaient dans la culture de son temps, mais aussi et fondamentalement un des aspects des conditions matérielles et des rapports de production qui dominaient les artistes et les liaient à ceux qui les chargeaient de l'exécution des oeuvres. Par ces conditions est nourri et déterminé le génie particulier de l'artiste.'[6] As a corrective, that sentiment is no doubt admirable; yet the project is in practice impossible. For without much more in the way of theory it is impossible to move from the examination of the conditions of material production, or that of the relations between craftsmen and patrons, to the study of the particular forms or particular innovations which Bianchi Bandinelli himself later on (p. 272) declares to be the central problems for the art historian. And it is clear that in his own work Bianchi Bandinelli never resolved this dilemma, but teetered constantly between grand generalization and a discussion of particulars that was indistinguishable from the work of those whom he criticized. We find exactly the same ambivalence in Marxist discussion of literary problems, an ambivalence which ends up by producing not an effective critique of what non-Marxists do but a completely different subject. And if this difficulty is only just being transcended in literary criticism, one cannot say that the same is true of the history of art.[7]

The rapid dissemination of some at least of Sir Ernst Gombrich's observations on 'mental sets' among historians of classical art testifies to a general dissatisfaction with older accounts of the development of Greek art in particular. Because the thesis had an obvious bearing upon already recognized – indeed formulaic – problems, and could readily be assimilated into an aestheticist framework (indeed that work was done already by Gombrich himself), its success was assured. But 'scheme' and 'correction' are only new fig-leaves, not a pair of trousers; new names for an old problem, not a solution or an explanation. Whiggish history still stalks the *gestaltpsychologisch* shades; and 'value-free' cognitivism is too jaded a mule to bear the weight of a claimed unique human value in Greek illusionism. The very notion of 'correction' presupposes what ought to be part of the problem, namely the source of the norms which suggested or 'determined' alterations A, B, C rather than A_1, B_1, C_1, to say nothing of the exclusion of alterations X, Y, Z. And 'schema' is an ideal-type of such lofty circumstance that one is unsure whether its linguistic analogue might be language, speech (performance), writing, genre, mode or trope. As a correlative pair, they seem to be predicated upon an implied opposition between form and content, an opposition generally abandoned in the study of other arts and certainly in history. If Marxist art history has not taken us very far, it does not look as if aesthetic cognitivism will either.

If it is not foolish to make such criticisms, it is certainly foolhardy. For they are likely to promise yet another anti-climax. And criticism generates its own like-minded children. But I have no competing New View on offer, and I have no desire to be, or to appear to be, prescriptive. Such interest as I have in current scholarship in the history of classical art derives from a desire to understand the relation between the religious art of the Graeco-Roman world and the culture in which it was made. Connoisseurship and iconography, the social conditions of the material production of artefacts, the relationship between norm and form are all legitimate procedures and perspectives. But their products can only be equivalent to their questions. And none of them seems of very much help in answering the sort of questions about ancient religious art which interest me. Quite apart from their theoretical failings, they are sets of questions each of which can address the problem of religious art only, as it were, in passing.

One way of illustrating this is to take the question of classification. Everyone knows that the Elder Pliny's 'Chapters on the History of Art' in fact form part of what is for us an entirely different topic, the taxonomy and technology of metal and stone in books 34-6 of the *Historia Naturalis*. But so to muddle chemistry, metallurgy, mining, pharmacy, domestic hygiene and the history of Art is simply incomprehensible to us. And scholars have obligingly removed the embarrassment by publishing the 'art history' abstracted from the rest: which imperceptibly generates an assumption that the ancient world enjoyed something called 'Art History'. Insensibly, and doubtless for the best motives, we palm our classifications off on to the ancient world. Now this might of course be inconsequential. But I do not think it is. Part of our conception of art history is that it should be 'true'; the positivist genius is to scent out the misconceptions and misrepresentations of sources, with the aid of archaeology and epigraphy. 'Misconceptions' then become bricks to hurl at sources, rather than evidence in their own right, whether of values, automatic associations of ideas or of cognitive procedures. Being 'purely conventional',[8] Pliny's scheme for the use of bronze, furniture – statues of gods – statues of men (34.9; 15), simply drops out of sight, his or his source's motives for believing it being of no interest whatever. Was it a concern for 'art history' that prompted Pliny to begin his 'historical' treatment of (bronze) sculpture with Pheidias' Zeus at Olympia?[9] Or for the facts, which caused him to pick out Julius Caesar and Augustus as those primarily responsible for the *auctoritas* of painting at Rome (35.26-7)?

A further consequence of this sleight-of-hand is evident in translation. Although Pausanias (for example) often uses the expression *agalma* (statue) with the divinity's name in the genitive (e.g. *Aphroditēs agalma*, 3.18.8), he more often puts simply the divinity's name, as in the same passage: *hupo men dē tōi prōtōi tripodi Aphroditēs agalma hestēken, Artemis de hupo tōi deuterōi.* This is duly translated by H. Stuart Jones: 'The first tripod is supported by an image of Aphrodite, the second by one of Artemis.'[10] Now in English, it looks simply quaint to say 'Artemis' and refer to a statue: we do not believe in Greek divinities but we do believe in art-historical classifications, and we take Pausanias to 'mean' what we would say: '*an* Artemis'. Nor is it enough to point out that neither Greek nor Latin used the indefinite article; for there would be nothing simpler than for Pausanias to have put *Artemidos de hupo tōi deuterōi.* That would have shown that he was conscious of a semantic difficulty in applying the name of the divinity to the statue, conceived as the product of technique. In fact, it is English which reveals the greater discomfort. Where Pausanias can say of Pheidas' Wooden Horse at Delphi, *eisi de Athēna te kai Apollōn, kai anēr tōn stratēgēsantōn Miltiadēs*, we have to say '(the statues) represent Athena and Apollo, and one human figure, that of Miltiades the

7

general'.[11] It is we who introduce the concept of 'representation', where Pausanias says 'they are . . .'.

This feature of ancient 'failure' to distinguish between god and statue at the linguistic level is naturally referred to 'popular' conceptions of art. The muddleheaded non-specialists looked only for 'realism', miraculous qualities and value expressed in price, which are evidently vulgar errors.[12] It can at once be assumed that craftsmen's own theoretical–practical writings, and the lucubrations of ancient philosophers and rhetoricians, constitute a 'more important' aspect of ancient thinking about art. But the notion of 'importance' conceals more than it reveals. For it is in effect being suggested that the sheer familiarity of vulgar notions, as well as their 'non-intellectual quality', permits us to discount them. And so a book such as J. J. Pollitt's *The Ancient View of Greek Art* ends up by excluding as 'uninteresting' precisely those modes of apprehension of art which were socially most important, important not only because they were shared by patrons but because they constituted the frame of the craftsmen's own understanding of the significance, and indeed the value, of what they produced. The existence of practical-technical writings by men such as Polycleitus, Pasiteles and Parrhasius, which represent merely an extension of the ordinary reproduction of craft rules within the family and workshop, suggests, by their very limitation of scope, the ease with which Graeco-Roman art accepted that wider frame of meaning, and its correlative constraints.[13] Art was a 'problem' only to philosophers.

Since 'popular' conceptions of art are defined as 'uninteresting', because vulgar and superficial, they have no history by definition, since dull things are merely existential givens. This attitude legitimates another equally interesting exclusion from Pollitt's book.[14] For it contains virtually nothing – in spite of its title – on archaic myths about the crafts and craftsmanship, and on Daedalus and his family in particular. For Pollitt, Greek thinking about art began with what he finds himself able to think of as 'art history', or at least forms of self-consciousness which appear to be similar to our own. It is only natural to find that myth has been classified out as a mode of self-consciousness: it is, after all, 'myth' (and vulgar, and unsophisticated). But, as Françoise Frontisi-Ducroux has pointed out,[15] the myths of Daedalus are concerned precisely with the preoccupations of 'popular' attitudes to art: with the role of special skills, with 'problematic' production, with finding the appropriate classification for the craftsman in society, with the strange and marvellous capacity of the human imagination to 'create' in the manner of Nature or divinity. That such problems are not of interest to most historians of classical art is a comment on the present conception of the subject, not an apt reply to their un-importance.

That Daedalus' statues, like Hephaestus' handiwork, could move of themselves in spite of being inanimate makes it clear that in the Archaic period sculpture and doubtless other artefacts were seen neither as inert matter nor as humans or animals; they required special classification. In this respect they did not differ from other products of human know-how, from houses to hunting; and predictably 'histories' of ancient art treated the subject in the language of technology, with its 'inventions', 'revelations', and 'refinements'. Painting, sculpture and the other arts 'made progress' unless they were prevented from doing so by *moral* impediments, just as human technology did,[16] and indeed Greek or Roman civilization as a whole. At the same time, the apparently effortless superiority of Daedalus over ordinary craftsmen marked a boundary: the limits of human endeavour were set beforehand. The products of craft, though troubling to classify, were marked off as permissible precisely because they were inanimate: they could be distinguished – always – from natural creatures by possessing no life. Others of Daedalus' feats, the statue of a cow which permitted Pasiphäe's bestiality, the wings on which he and Icarus flew to Sicily, mark points of excess. The problem of the *exact* boundary between permissible and impermissible became one of intense interest throughout the entire history of Classical Art. In an important sense, the myths about Daedalus defined the terms of ancient art until (I suppose) Christian culture was able to impose rather different conditions for the boundary between the permissible and the illicit.

This perspective may have interest for us in two different ways. In the first place, it provides a rationale for that allegedly 'spontaneous' or 'natural' Greek drift towards illusionism, because illusionism is one obvious way of dicing with the impermissible, of going *beyond* the already permitted towards the Daedalic goal. But of course it is obvious that the frontier is deep and long; the gambling-points are innumerable. One point is naturally the improvement of merely 'reproductive' capacity, of anatomical authenticity; another is to pursue another kind of *alētheia/veritas*, as Lysippus did: 'There is no Latin name for the *summetria* which he observed utterly scrupulously, substituting a new and unprecedented scheme for the "square" figures of earlier sculptors. He often used to say that they made men as they were, he as they appeared to be' (Pliny, *HN* 34.65).[17] Another might be Kanakhos' ingenious device which enabled his Apollo in the Didymaion at Branchidae to move in some way while holding a stag (Pliny, *HN* 34.75).[18] Another might be the choice to paint scenes of 'low life', 'barbers' shops, cobblers' stalls, asses, things to eat and all that' (Pliny, *HN* 35.112 of Piraeieus the *rhuparographos*). Another, to paint an Athena whose 'eyes are turned to the spectator no matter where he looks from' (*HN* 35.120). Another, to succeed with a painted snake of enormous proportions in preventing the birds from keeping Lepidus awake at night (*HN* 35.121). There is no need to go on. The momentum towards illusionism in Graeco-Roman art was neither univocal nor consistent: we are just making up a pretty story if we write its history so as to prove that it was either. For 'illusionism' is a rag-bag category, not a concept capable of specification. It has no 'laws', and no single direction. But perhaps we can treat it as a unitary phenomenon in relation to the shifting frontier of the 'permissible' and the 'impermissible', Daedalus' legacy.

The second point is this. An indispensable counterpart to the craftsmen's own negotiation of this frontier was the verbal negotiation of it by their audiences. Both sides understood the enterprise, its rules, its habitual and its extreme possibilities. Many of the metaphors (which eventually became catachrestic) by which the Greeks referred to statues are instructive in this connection. The word *zōon*, which first appears in extant Greek literature in the fifth century B.C., means primarily 'living thing', including human beings conceived in their biological aspect or in opposition to inanimate matter. But Herodotus also uses it to mean 'image' or 'representation', whether carved or painted; it is as though we could say, when talking of a statue of a god in a temple, for example, 'There is a creature inside the temple'. The word forms the root of ordinary Greek words for 'painter' and 'to paint' (*zōgraphos, zōgraphein*) while words connected with the other meaning tended to be marked phonemically by the addition of a short –o–: zōo–. There was also a word, used especially for statues of the human male (*anēr*, stem *andr*–), *andrias*, whose semantic motivation is equally clear: the thing is a man but not a man.[19] A third, *eikōn*, is derived from a word *eikō, which in Homer is already doubtful between the sense 'be like' and that of 'seem'. By the fourth century it could be used casually to mean 'something imaginary', 'something which exists only in the mind'. As I have said, all these words became catachrestic: their early ambiguity became as imperceptible as the metaphor of the eye of a needle for us. But the ambiguity of human representation continued to be signalled in many other ways. The statue of Artemis on Chios made by the school of 'Melas' in the sixth century was supposed to change its expression: when one entered it looked severe (*tristem*), when one departed, glad[20] (Pliny, *HN* 36.13). Pythagoras' lame figure (? Philoctetes) at Syracuse could make the spectator feel that he himself was suffering from the wound (Pliny, *HN* 34.59: *cuius ulceris dolorem sentire etiam spectantes videntur*). Many literary treatments of sculpture and other art-forms play insistently on the trope: a well-known epigram on Myron's statue of the runner Ladas is founded upon the conceit in the first line, which plays on the homonymity of statue and athlete (both of course called Ladas), qualifies this ambiguous creature as *empnoōs* ('with the breath inside', so catachrestically 'alive'), and addresses him/it in the vocative, 'as if' it could attend.[21] In Propertius' single-line mention of one of Myron's groups, four cattle round an altar (2.31.7), the ambiguity is heavily stressed: *quattuor artifices, vivida signa, boves*. Talking about bronze statues, Dio Chrysostom (37.10) bothers to observe that though they may have wings, they cannot be moved. Leochares made a statue of the rape of Ganymede, in which the eagle was 'conscious of the prize he had in Ganymede and of him to whom he bore him' (Pliny, *HN* 34.79).[22] Citations of this kind could be almost indefinitely multiplied.

Yet clichés are only boring to those who imagine that only the 'interesting' can be profitable. The obvious point that we have here a continuous series of metaphors and antitheses registering the ambiguous status of the art object (and especially sculptures and painted figures) suggests to me a 'deliberate' refusal on the part of the majority in the ancient world to take the 'sensible' way out adopted by different philosophical traditions, particularly Platonism and Stoicism: the development of a theory of the imagination. The abstention from catachresis, the continued insistence upon the metaphors, are surely to be explained by reference to the legacy of Daedalus. The metaphors are utterly self-conscious: but they all, in different measure, gamble with the impermissible. They at once assert and deny that statues or painted figures are alive. 'Living' is broken down into its denotations: breath, sight, feelings, movement, skin-sheen, facial expression. So far as one or two of these denotations may be taken as 'sufficient' evidence of 'life', the images live. But the whole inventory is never present, and the attempt to pass into the realm of the impermissible always fails. The clichés are a genuine form of cultural negotiation of boundaries, of human self-definition.

THE REAL AND THE IMAGINARY: PRODUCTION AND RELIGION IN THE GRAECO-ROMAN WORLD

If even 'secular' sculpture and painting suffer misrepresentation because of the tacit assumption on the part of historians of classical art that ancient classifications are readily translatable, religious sculpture and painting probably suffer more. For evidently it would be as absurd to suppose that one can meaningfully rank Agorakritos' Aphrodite, which Varro esteemed above all other statues (Pliny, *HN* 36.17), above the meanest ex-voto from Caere or Myrrhina, as to rank inscriptions according to the beauty of their cutting and letter-forms. It is of course possible, but it is pointless. Moreover, to do so is in practice to claim that aesthetic criteria have privilege as a means of 'understanding', which in turn legitimates neglect of alternative classifications. The 'experts' on ancient religious art are art historians, not historians of religion. And when the two disciplines confront each other in the same book, such as in Franz Cumont's *Recherches sur le symbolisme funéraire des Romains* (1942), or Robert Turcan's *Les sarcophages romains à représentations dionysiaques* (1966), incompatible perspectives simply take turns, they do not meet. Connoisseurship sometimes, and sometimes iconography, hold sway. Their joint rule proposes the obvious and 'serious' questions. And the exclusive appropriateness of those questions seems to be legitimate since they relate closely to the classifications of religious art already current among the Romans. For in the process of cultural borrowing between Greece and Rome in which the Romans ransacked the hellenistic world for art objects, there occurred an important reclassification of Greek religious art: it became 'art' not an 'offering'.[23] Nor was it obvious to the Romans, especially the troops, that religious art, or even art more generally, should be classified as 'booty', rather than as something to be smashed *in situ*.[24] It seems to have taken some time for the Romans to realize that art-works could be sold at the auction of the booty after a victory, that there was a 'market' in art (cf. the story about L. Mummius and the sack of Corinth[25]). But there was a particular value in depriving a conquered city of its religious sculpture and painting, since this action 'removed' its gods, in much the same way that the traditional Roman practice of *evocatio* removed the power of a divinity from the enemy to the Romans. And there is a surprising amount of evidence that Roman generals did indeed, especially in the second century B.C., deliberately remove important cult-statues.[26] But although some religious sculptures and paintings were in turn consecrated in Roman temples, many more items of Greek religious art entered private collections, such as those of Pompey, Caesar, Augustus, Asinius Pollio and M. Agrippa, or those of Hellenistic kings, such as the Attalids of Pergamum. Divested of their proper context, they could easily be reclassified so as to be appropriate material for 'art history'.

Such a perspective enables modern art historians to ignore a great deal of evidence about alternative ancient classifications of religious artefacts: they can be dismissed as 'popular', as '*ben trovato* stories', as 'fiction'. The same concentration upon form compels us to draw a binary opposition between 'iconic' and 'aniconic' forms of religious representation, and to treat them as though they were completely at odds with each other; but they are so only when that opposition is taken as a privileged classification.[27] But, as symbols, stones and carved marble, lumps of metal and cast bronze, all 'work' in the same way: both sorts of image invoke elements from the 'encyclopaedia' of kept knowledge, are themselves organized by selection from the encyclopaedia using certain criteria of relevance; and both provoke new connotations which in turn enter the encyclopaedia as kept knowledge. Neither form of symbol is in itself more or less capable of specificity of 'meaning', a meaning which is in each case controlled not by the object but by those who use it. And it is evident that the control will be more determinate in a very small, relatively integrated society, or in a small, coherent institution within a large one, than in a society where evocations are made unpredictable by the development of quite sharply different social roles, themselves the consequence of the division of labour and the differential acquisition of material goods and social power. Even in a small society dissonant evocations may be encouraged by special rules concerning the acquisition of knowledge and by borrowing from neighbours, and with the development of the complex state, whether industrial or pre-industrial, it becomes less possible, as well as less necessary, to perform the endless acts of evocation-sorting which ensure ideological coherence (in the sense that one can properly reconstruct its 'system') in a small-scale society.

By the Archaic period, which is the first point (notwithstanding the 'Mycenaean origins of Greek religion') at which we can say that we know anything interesting about Greek religion, Greek society was already sharply differentiated both 'horizontally', in terms of status, and 'vertically', in that each developing *polis* effectively created its own structure of meanings and social relationships. As fast as the presumed common cultural matrix (deriving from the distant common 'tribal' past of the Greeks) broke down into linguistic, social, political and cultural diversity, so fast were ideological, that is consciously created, substitutes developed: the institutionalization of Homer's epic poetry; the claim that poets were 'masters of truth',[28] who mediated privileged meanings which, because written, could transcend the frontiers of the *polis*; the institutionalization of relationships between the aristocracies of different *poleis*, in guest-friendship, marriage with foreign women, and above all the games; the appearance of 'wise men' and new kinds of religious specialists who could be imported to write laws and cleanse pollution; and, not least I think, new representations of divinity.[29]

The classical Greeks believed that in the old days it was usual in Greece to pay the divine honours later paid to statues of gods to unshaped stones.[30] Whatever the historians of religion make of this belief, I shall remark here simply that, as far as the belief itself is concerned, it is 'pseudohistory' not 'history'. The serialization of the relationship unshaped stones/anthropomorphic statues offers an explanation of the co-existence of two (apparently) different representations of divinity in the Archaic and Classical periods – and indeed beyond, down to the very end of the Roman Empire. Pausanias' stress upon the fact that the forms of honour paid were the same in each case makes it clear that the two modes, aniconic and iconic, were not conceived in opposition to each other.[31] Now it is obvious that the emergence of a new preferred mode of representation of divinity in the Archaic period has nothing to do with some novel thrust towards 'anthropomorphism'. For the complexity of the representation of the gods as 'people' evident in the earliest literature known to us, the *Iliad* and the *Odyssey* and Hesiod's *Theogony* and *Works and Days* (conventionally dated in the eighth century B.C.), to say nothing of the sharp differences of conception within and between these poems, imply an already long habit of 'anthropomorphism'. The complexity of the corpus of myths suggests the same. But where the aniconic image is utterly particular, non-generalizable and non-reproducible, the iconic image is 'universal': it can generate as many forms as need to be conceived. But it does so at the price of a choice: it must concentrate upon one aspect of Greek conceptions of divinity, that gods were (like) people. Consequently, such a choice suppresses other current evocations available in the relevant 'encyclopaedia', which can only be evoked by special attention. The solution was found in the notion of 'attribute', which can be seen as a deliberate attempt to escape from the closure of evocation involved in the iconic choice.[32] The use of costly materials, gold, silver, ivory, for statues of gods suggests an attempt to extend the range of overt evocation still further, associating the statue with the semantic cluster connected with 'gleaming' or 'brightness' that is so marked a feature of Greek conceptions of divinity.[33] It also permits further evocations and introduces new themes: the theme of hiding *versus* revelation (the gods are *epiphaneis* but live on Olympos; 'are' rivers, trees, caves but also 'in' them; and so on) because metal is found in the earth and has to be made manifest; the theme of purity and perfection, because such metals have to be smelted and refined; the theme of *mētis*, the cunning which supports Zeus' rule over the world but which is also necessary to the cunning artificer; and the theme of illusion, of which the gods are masters.

If we understand the existence of statues of the gods in Greece (and, *mutatis mutandis*, in Rome) as a deliberate choice in pursuit of a particular good in the Archaic period, that of reproducibility, motivated by essentially 'non-religious' ends, it becomes clear that the choice involved losses as well as gains. In so far as certain 'losses' came to be recognized as such, they could be retrieved. Statues came to be designed more 'adequately', so as to be capable of evoking a more adequate range of meaning. Personal evocations could then be represented 'objectively' and so acquire a more than personal status. There is an instructive story in this connection about Pericles, which is doubtless untrue but therefore interesting. Plutarch (*Perikles* 13) says that one of Pericles' favourite slaves fell off the roof of the Propylaia on the Acropolis and was dangerously ill. Pericles had a dream in which Athena prescribed a cure, which was duly administered. The slave recovered, and Pericles had the sculptor Pyrrhus erect a statue in bronze of Athena *Hugieia*, Athena 'Good-health'. The generalization of the personal evocation is clear from the actual inscription, which we happen to possess, for it does not mention Pericles at all: *Athēnaioi tēi Athēnaiai tēi Hugieiai*.[34] In this way, the very use of art as a mode of 'realizing' the divine world permitted constant innovation of a shareable kind. The statues, reliefs and paintings come to serve as the visible, noted entries, whether as 'headwords' or as 'derived senses', in the lexicon of religious meanings. Not only do they make possible the generalization of personal evocations, they also provide the illusion of coherence, just as the dictionary provides the illusion that words have, at any one point in time, 'settled significations'.

Statues and pictures of gods permit another allusion to the relevant encyclopaedia of divinity, however. How big is a god? Now that looks like a question as silly as that medieval conundrum which exercised many good minds, 'How many angels can stand on the head of a pin?' But of course neither question is in the slightest silly. The issue in the medieval period was in fact crucial: what is the relationship between the material and the spiritual? And the issue of the size of the gods is raised frequently by Homer, when he insists on the physical appearance of a god who chooses to turn into a 'human being' for some purpose, or when he describes the size of the river Skamander against whom Achilles fights, or that of Ares laid low by Pallas Athene.[35] One of the features of gods is that they can pass the barrier constructed by the oppositions formed/shapeless, limited/unlimited, visible/invisible, great/small. As a range of artificial objects, statues of gods permitted the Greeks to register this aspect of the 'otherness' of the gods by playing precisely on this issue of size. And I raise the issue of play quite deliberately, for it helps us to understand a repeated theme in Greek discussions of divine statues. When Strabo is describing Pheidias' statue of Zeus at Olympia, he writes: '[the statue] is of such colossal size that, although the temple is very large, the craftsman seems to have failed to observe proportion, and has represented the god seated but almost touching the roof with his head, thus creating the impression that should he rise and stand upright he would push the temple roof off'.[36] I take it that Pheidias incorporated a deliberate allusion to the puzzle over the gods' ability to transcend human polarities into his design: Zeus is in the temple, but also not – he does not 'fit'. And we have some confirmation of this in what Strabo, quite innocently, goes on to say about Pheidias' inspiration for the design. For Pheidias was supposed to have told his fellow-contractor (and brother) Panainos that his *paradeigma* (the technical word for an architect's plan or the sculptor's model) was the lines of Homer (*Iliad*, 1, 528–30):

> He spoke, the son of Kronos, and nodded his head with the dark brows,
> and the immortally anointed hair of the great god
> swept from his divine head, and all Olympos was shaken,[37]

which explicitly refer to Zeus' superordinate might in physical terms. In his description of Antikyra, Pausanias mentions a statue of Artemis by Praxiteles (10.37.1), and says: 'it holds a torch in the right hand and a quiver hangs from the shoulder; beside it, on the left is a dog. In size, the statue is larger than the largest woman.'[38] Except on the assumption that size of statues of gods was an issue, this seems an absurd remark to make. The play derives from the very choice of the human form: gods are appropriately given human form. Human form demands a certain size. To make a god larger than that 'means' something – that gods both are and are not 'human'. Martial (9.44) describes in an epigram a famous miniature statue of Heracles (the Heracles *epitrapezios*), and deliberately draws attention to the contrast between the tiny image and Hercules' 'size': *exiguo magnus in aere deus* (line 2). Again the literary conceit (and there are many others) is instructive precisely because it is utterly conventional – yet not what we would call a cliché. The conceit remains a conceit with point. A slightly different example is given by Pliny in his passage on colossal statues in bronze as instances of 'audacity' (34.39–47). He mentions of Lysippus' Zeus at Tarentum that it was so perfectly balanced that although it could be turned round by a touch of the hand, it could not be blown over by the wind (34.40). Even the colossus, which has made its choice of god's size only too explicit, subverts that choice by refusing to be equally, or rather commensurately, heavy. But if the colossus is 'light' it could be blown away by the wind, so it must be anchored to a pillar. The sheer frivolity of the popular story suggests some self-conscious play of this kind. And the play remains revealing whether we suppose it to have originated with Lysippos or to have been picked up locally by some periegete.[39]

The problem of the appropriate size of statues resonates of course in the case of human statues as well. Several commentators found it amusing that Lucius Accius, the Republican poet, set up a large statue of himself in the temple of the Camenae (the Roman Muses) 'although he was a very small man' (Pliny, *HN* 34.19). Pliny quite casually notes that the statues set up in the forum of those who had been killed *iniuria* while on public service (*HN* 34.23–4) were only three feet high, and evidently finds the fact in need of explanation: *haec videlicet mensura honorata tunc erat*.[40] But perhaps appearance was a more important issue: the Greeks believed that originally 'the ancients did not make statues (*effigies*) of individual men unless they deserved immortality by some distinction, at first through a victory in the sacred games (especially at Olympia) . . .' (Pliny, *HN* 34.17). In the rest of this passage 'honour' is measured by likeness: those who had won three times were granted statues *ex membris ipsorum similitudine expressa*.[41] The well-known anecdote about Lysistratus, the brother of Lysippus of Sicyon, that he was the first to strive for literal exactitude in portraits, even to taking plaster-casts of the living face, while earlier sculptors had attempted to make likenesses as beautiful as possible (Pliny, *HN* 35.153), reveals an identical opposition between 'like' and 'unlike'. But what was a god like? There are some revealing stories here. We have already seen how Pheidias was supposed to have discovered his *paradeigma* for the Zeus at Olympia.[42] After the horse-headed *agalma* of Black Demeter in the cave in Mount Elaion near Phigaleia had been destroyed by fire, Onatas (first half of the fifth century) was commissioned by the Phigaleians to make a new one. They had been warned by a famine to reinstitute the discontinued worship of the goddess. Onatas was supposed to have found some picture or copy of the old statue which he used as his model for his bronze statue; but his most important inspiration, 'it is said', was the sight of the goddess in dreams (Paus. 8.42.7).[43] Praxiteles' Cnidian Aphrodite was believed to have been made *dea favente ipsa*, even though the famous anecdote included the information that Praxiteles had made two at the same time, one clothed and the other nude, and was selling them on the open market (Pliny, *HN* 36.20–1). The sculptural convention for Silenus was legitimated by the discovery of a complete statue of the god inside a block of Parian marble that was being split by wedges (Pliny, *HN* 36.14).[44]

But there might be other influences at work on the craftsman. Thrasymedes of Paros was allegedly prevented from representing his Asclepius for the temple at Epidaurus with a beard by the protests of Dionysius I of Syracuse. Quite reasonably, he pointed out that it was improper to represent Asclepius with a beard since his father, Apollo, did not have one (Cicero, *Nat. Deor.* 3.83).[45] The proper relationship between father: son:: age: youth would be disturbed by making the son aged = bearded. But the most important constraint lay in the fact that craftsmen were usually obliged to compete for public contracts, just as the Athenian tragedians could only present their plays if they were selected by the responsible board of magistrates.[46] Quite apart from local-boy loyalties, which allegedly allowed Alkamenes to win the competition for an Aphrodite against Agorakritos (Pliny, *HN* 36.17), this must have meant that generalized criteria of appropriateness, especially *semnotēs, megaloprepeia, megalophrosunē, haplotēs, eurhuthmia*, were demanded of any statue of a god for a public temple.[47] Of course such criteria altered over time, and were understood in different parts of the Greek world very differently, and if you did not win the competition, you might turn your Aphrodite into a Nemesis and get someone else to buy it (as Agorakritos did); but these constraints upon experimentation were not less important than the constraints upon craftsmen imposed by the familial and workshop organization of art-production in the ancient world.

Yet competition need not be seen simply as a constraint upon craftsmen. The public recognition of a successful statue, especially in the case of a cult-statue for an important temple, legitimated this particular concatenation of choices, and helped turn image into god. A story about the Daedalic sculptors Dipoinos and Skyllis (traditionally, sixth century B.C.) is instructive. Pliny (*HN* 36.9-10) says that after they had been awarded the contract for statues of Apollo, Artemis, Heracles and Athena by the people of Sicyon, a dispute arose over payment (or some *iniuria*, at least). The sculptors went off in dudgeon to Aetolia. Sicyon was attacked by the terrible twins *fames . . . ac sterilitas* (*limos* and *loimos*), an invariable sign of divine anger. On consulting the Delphic oracle, they were told to permit the two sculptors to finish the statues, and then their troubles would be over. Without the images, there could be no cult of the gods. Indeed, much more was done to further the (conscious) pretence that statues *were* gods. They might be clothed in fine robes, like the new statue of Artemis at Brauron by Praxiteles.[48] Only temple servants were allowed to touch them, except in the case of an appeal for sanctuary when the rule might be broken: the rule-breakage itself confirmed the rule, since it initiated a direct assertion of divine protection for the suppliant.[49] Well-known anecdotes made it true that gods punished those who committed sacrilege against their images (it would be interesting to know what interpretations were offered when a statue of Dionysus fell off the acropolis at Athens in a high wind: Plutarch, *Vit. Anton.* 60).[50] One of the most interesting fantasies in the ancient world involved sexual relations with statues of gods (and of humans): a predictable acting-out of neurotic symptoms, if it ever occurred, but no less interesting as an image of total self-pollution if it did not.[51] All this was clearly fictional though: people believed simultaneously that statues were gods and that they were not. After mentioning that Zeus had sent Pheidias a sign that his statue at Olympia was pleasing, Pausanias wanders on to mention that the floor in front of the statue was of black marble, and that it was bordered by a little wall of white marble which helped contain the oil which dripped from the statue. The oil helped prevent the ivory of the statue from splitting.[52] Statues could be melted down, or altered to represent some other god; temple inventories catalogue them indiscriminately with other temple property.

THE REAL AND THE IMAGINARY: PRODUCTION AND RELIGION IN THE GRAECO-ROMAN WORLD

I would argue, then, that the game of 'let's pretend they are gods' which the Greeks (and the Romans) played with their statues and other representations of divinity is even more perceptible than the gambling with the frontier between the permissible and the impermissible to which I have referred earlier primarily in connection with the representation of human beings. There the problem centres on how far human beings can usurp the creative prerogatives of the gods (a game played also by poets, law-givers, hellenistic kings and Roman Emperors); here the issue is the viability of an entire set of symbolic meanings. In what follows, I propose to discuss three different ways in which Graeco-Roman religious art helped validate what remained recognizably the same 'world-view' over a period of more than a thousand years in spite of very considerable changes in political and social structure, in cosmological theory, representations of the self and the content of the generally available 'encyclopaedia'.

Let me return to a point made earlier in passing (p. 13), concerning the role of religious representations in 'realizing' the imaginary world of divinity. Since the publication of John Skorupski's Symbol and Theory (Cambridge, 1976), we may be allowed to distance ourselves from the 'classic' Durkheimian view of religion, even if one values the work of neo-Durkheimians such as Mary Douglas. The alternative is some form of intellectualism; and, among those on offer, the most helpful for my immediate argument is the cognitivism of Clifford Geertz.[53] Without abandoning ourselves to simple-minded relativism,[54] we may agree that reality is made actual and granted significance by the individual subject not privately but by means of extensively overlapped congeries of related ideas, which we call codes. These codes are not merely mental ('ideas') but are cues for action: for the most part being alive is not an existential thrust after self-affirmation, but a constant, unselfconscious enactment of quite familiar routines, in which idea and action are inseparable. Entire tracts of our lives are passed at the level at which four o'clock means tea. Such codes are shared, and we rarely remember learning them or adapting them; and they are shared at the widest by a linguistic community, at the narrowest by a single family. The most central, and successful, codes are the ones we suppose to be universal, screwed into the fabric of reality. When these are threatened we respond emotionally, in indignation, fear, anger or violence.

For the cognitivist, religion is one of the central and most important codes in a society. That is not, of course, to say that it is in any way autonomous, since it is linked in all sorts of ways to others, alimentary, reproductive, linguistic codes for example. But it is central (especially in a traditional society) inasmuch as it articulates for its adherents the scope and nature of power, both 'vertically' between us and the divine world and 'horizontally' between men. It represents to believers a diagram of possible forms of power, and accounts for the limits of power as conceived by the society at any given point in its history; but it also provides access to power. For religion is evidently not simply a matter of seeing and believing (nor of believing and seeing). It must be inscribed in action. Just as there is no sense in a society's possessing an alimentary code, the whole gamut of rules about eating – times, places, objects, satisfactions – if all its inhabitants live on Luft and Liebe; so there is no point in religion if it has no consequences in action.

We may illustrate these points in relation to Graeco-Roman sacrifice. At one level, the ritual is a special case of wider rules concerning prestations in the ancient world, in which the giving of gifts both between status-equals and between social-unequals was a central mode of social intercourse, status-affirmation and claim to status. The prestation in sacrifice is modelled upon the pattern of 'exchange' between status-unequals, in which the social inferior offers whatever he 'can' (labour, services, respect, votes, enthusiasm) in return for what it is appropriate for the social superior to bestow on him (food, clothes, job, protection at law, a place in the world). Every exchange re-enacts the status-relation and reaffirms it, but real results ensue in the form of non-symbolic goods.[55] This reciprocal structuring of unequal social relations remained the dominant mode throughout Graeco-Roman antiquity (though it did not apply to slaves, foreigners, women or children). In sacrifice of a public nature, demanded by the ritual calendar (itself simply an aspect of another code, the social organization and regulation of time), the gift is 'appropriate' in eactly the same way as the social inferior's gift is appropriate: sex, colour, condition and preparation of the animal are all prescribed. Just as there is no problem in the real world in arranging an appropriate exchange, so there is not here.[56] Fulfilment of men's side of the reciprocal relation guarantees, in normal circumstances, the appropriate returns from the gods, ranging from the maintenance of social/ritual/ reproductive order to good fortune for a new warship. The gods know their duty, just as properly brought up social superiors do. But, if etiquette is not followed (the more complex the system and the more valued the exchange, the more complex the etiquette), the exchange does not take place. A system of signs, of extreme complexity, was devised in order to diagnose what had gone wrong if the exchange failed, or to prevent it from going wrong: oracles; various kinds of mantic procedures with bones, pebbles, birds, animal parts and peculiar behaviour in the natural world; soothsaying; prophecy under possession. This system effected a disentangling of confused wires; when they were straightened out the reciprocal exchange would work again. No one ever doubted that in the ancient world, apart perhaps from the Cynics. The sacrificial system thus enforced the moral code, of which 'etiquette' in the narrow sense was a sign.

The sacrificial system also patterned the social world in a different way. Access to the role of sacrificer (the agent of mediation) differed depending on the context. Public priesthoods were invariably reserved for members of the élite (and even women, in the hellenistic world, if they were rich enough). But heads of families were responsible for the domestic cult; and 'deviant' cults, such as that of Dionysus and increasing numbers of others, offered sacrificial roles even to the humble. There were exclusively male and exclusively female festivals; and many joint ones, in which women were seen and not heard. Since the system was enormously adaptable, it could be enlarged to meet many kinds of new needs while forgotten needs could be quietly dropped out. Hellenistic kings and Roman Emperors could be sacrificed for and even to ('as though' they were gods); the *Flamen Dialis* might die away without being noticed, even if his rituals continued to be performed. Because sacrifice involved the cooking and eating of meat according to certain rules, it was both parasitic upon and confirmatory of wider alimentary rules. This involved not only a definition of man by contrast to gods above and animals below, but also the assertion of the relationship between eating, labour, marriage, sex, reproduction and death.[57] New religions tended to claim legitimacy by denying some at least of these 'obvious' connections. They thus opened up new forms of access to divinity; the religious 'expert', the possessor of new power, is the correlate at the level of religious structures of the socially mobile within the context of an increasingly complex division of labour, specialization of function and new roles in the 'real' world.

Knowing 'how to act' as a member of a community in the ancient world, then, was inseparable (with the exception of an insignificant number of individuals) from the practice-and-belief of religion. It offered a highly complex structure of meaning with almost endless ramifications, which was capable of a high degree of innovation and adaptation. It both patterned and sanctioned action, both positively and negatively. But it is obvious that the realization of religion is not merely a matter of action; linguistic utterance is also important. Of course we may understand speaking as a form of action, and quite appropriately; but here I want to insist upon the role of language as an enabler of human fictions (parallel with the replicative and imitative actions in religion). Forming grammatical sentences, and using a small stock of principles – inversion, negation, substitution and analogy – anyone in any language can make utterances which are meaningful but do not 'refer' to anything that has been seen or experienced or classified. Fantasies cannot be predicted but their logic can generally be reconstructed. Normally, however, the fantasist uses aspects of known classifications and associations in order to create a complex new account of experience; the fantasist is each of us in our capacity to be private sense-makers. Freud's account of the case of 'Dora' is a perfect example of this private sense-making. Making use of common metaphorical meanings of words (and anyone for whom German is a second or third language is forcibly made aware that he could not have made such a construction, since the words have no such complex evocative power for him), Dora produced what is in a sense a highly satisfactory interpretation of aspects of her experience, threading together remarks, actions, sights, tactile sensations.[58] The case (and we are all in the same case) is a perfect example of Dan Sperber's principle of evocation at work.[59]

Although we all have this capacity, and presumably the constant habit, much more work has been done on shared fantasies; but of course once one introduces the notion of sharing, the word 'fantasy' becomes less appropriate. Shareable accounts of experience must be both more enduring and more firmly structured even if they are constructed in fundamentally the same manner. Semantically, a language taken as a whole at a point in time represents a rough index of the stock of classifications and categories available in a community; though it of course contains obsolete categories, and all the contents of individual consciousness cannot be semantically represented. By an instructive economy, no language contains more than a tiny number of names for the names of its categories: all languages regularly fuse *signifié* and *signifiant*. Reification, that is, is a device not a disease. By another principle of economy that is no less ideological, all languages contain means of lessening the number of operative categories: the two principal means are metaphor and abstraction. The first works by creating relationships by analogy between discrete categories, so that we have 'eyes' all over the place, not just in heads, for example. Metaphor is thus a strategy for imposing higher-level order upon experience. Abstraction involves the creation of new categories which subsume ('denote') indefinite numbers of particulars. This enables us to say 'dog' instead of knowing the name of each dog or even knowing lower-level abstractions, such as the species or strains of dogs.

We can perhaps understand religion, in this context, as a specialized sub-system of language focused upon the category 'power'. It is the elaboration of a taxonomy of power. Of course the taxonomy is not self-sufficient: it is a classification-system overlaid (or perhaps underlaid) upon others. This is particularly clear in the case of the Greek and Roman understanding of nature: there were categories of the type 'the tree outside my backdoor which I like sitting under in the evening'; 'olive-tree'; 'tree'. But there were also categories concerned with another aspect of trees, their capacity to grow and live, their power to be alive. These categories also proceed from the particular to the general: the power of this tree; Tree-Nymphs; Pan. The classification of the power of trees allocates them to different spheres of power: wild trees are opposed to domesticated trees; hot trees to cold trees: wet trees to dry trees. At a more abstract level, the system of Olympian gods in Greece presents an enormously elaborate taxonomy of power whose character we are only just beginning to understand.[60] The taxonomy is partly calqued upon human capacities and abilities, but its specific character is constituted by the deliberate negation of human limitations: a complex definition of what it is to be human is constructed by a fantastic elaboration of what it is to be not-human, an elaboration which also proceeds in a 'downwards' direction, in relation to the animal world.[61] All three worlds, divine, human and animal are related by a complex process of definition by similarity and opposition, and in turn opposed as a group to inanimate things.

Religion then can be seen as a way of naming powers and, by the act of classification, asserting and denying relationships between 'aspects' of powers. It is a characteristically human intellectual enterprise. I have already observed that reification is no less character-istic of language than are metaphor and abstraction. Classifications turn into realities; the names of things 'are' the things. The taxonomy of powers easily turns into a popula-tion of 'people', though of course it need not do so: those strange forms of religion that so fascinated the nineteenth century, 'animism', 'fetishism' and the rest, are examples of taxonomies of powers that reject this option, and had to be called 'primitive' simply because they were different. Once that happens, it is a simple step to reinforce that choice by representing the powers *as* people, on condition that one 'reserves' the classification – they are people, but they are also not. While such a system remains intact, no one is in danger of making the category mistake of thinking that 'people' are people. Once it begins to break down, easy mileage can be got out of the deliberate category mistake, as the philosophical critics of Graeco-Roman paganism, and the Christian apologists, discovered.

But the act of representation involves another fundamental human necessity, labour and production. One of the many merits of Marx's view of human labour is that he sets it uncompromisingly in relation to Nature: 'Labour is, in the first place, a process in which both man and Nature participate, and in which man of his own accord starts, regulates and controls the material re-actions between himself and Nature. He opposes himself to Nature as one of her own forces, setting in motion arms and legs, head and hands, the natural forces of his body, in order to appropriate Nature's productions in a form adapted to his own wants. By thus acting on the external world and changing it, he at the same time changes his own nature.'[62] In labour, the conceptual opposition between Nature and Culture is necessarily denied; moreover, the 'subject is present in the object inasmuch as it materializes certain goals of the subject'.[63] I am not here concerned to discuss Marx's notion that in capitalist society the use-value of artistic products becomes secondary to their commodity-value, whereas in earlier periods the use-value was somehow primary (the 'fetishism' of art is immediately apparent in the ancient world, for example[64]), nor to discuss the more general problems connected with his notion of 'free, creative labour'. But Marx's aesthetics are valuable in so far as they stress, against Kant, the relationship between art and labour as different manifestations of man's creative capacity: 'truly creative artistic production becomes the antithesis of capitalist material production, but not of all forms of social production . . . .'[65]

In the products both of ordinary labour and of the artist conception is translated into artefact, into an object, which exists independently of those intentions. An idea is concretized, but in such a way that the object transcends the idea: the object does not merely 'betray' the intentions which formed it, it provides the objective basis for further acts of signification. Its meaning is no longer confined to the intention of the maker, which has no special privilege and may, in a given society, have no privilege at all. (It is for this reason, of course, that it becomes necessary to study the social role of the artist.) All societies classify the products of labour which they know in different ways. The principles of classification are to be established empirically therefore; they are not 'obvious'. But they are likely to be both systematic and related to other classification-sets. And the system of classification sets the rules for the making of labour-products. 'Form' can then be understood as the consequence of a complex of epistemological decisions, which themselves rely upon prior classifications. Established form, habitual form, then becomes a mnemonic of those epistemological decisions. Exactly the same is true of habitual actions which do not produce a literal shape-in-the-world.

Making, then, involves knowing. Making is the process of literally reifying knowledge; it is an act of translation. This objectified knowledge alters the world in a patterned and systematic way. In the special case of religious art (a tiny sub-system of the totality of human making) the objectification of the taxonomy of power, subject as it is to the wider rules of making in a given society, conditions in turn the taxonomy which created it. Because each object embodies choices, it opens up some further possibilities while foreclosing others. Religious art becomes itself a generative source of evocation. Dreams and visions are based upon representations of gods. The Cross becomes a densely polyvalent sign. At the same time, the freedom of the maker is constrained by the knowledge which he is making, a knowledge which does not derive from himself. Many others in his society know, even if they do not know how to make. There is of course a negotiation here: just as poets in the ancient world, and especially in the Archaic and Classical periods, claimed privileged knowledge by appealing to the inspiration of the Muses, so many craftsmen claimed privilege through 'wisdom'.[66] But that is only a negotiation, not an assertion of artistic 'freedom'. The really important hierarchy of privilege in the ancient world, in this context, was ordered by the network of temples. Some religious representations were more important than others because of the prestige of the temple in which they were put up, and within that little system, according to their size and placing within or on the temple. The great temples set the pattern of representation for lesser ones, as well as for private votive offerings. The central cult statues endured for centuries, privileged patterns of divinity. Unless there was a fire, or a sack, they need never be replaced.[67] The history of privileged cult-representations can be read as the constant search for new 'outlets' – new cities, the hellenization of barbarian lands, new cults, imperial religious 'policy', all provided such outlets. These 'exceptional' privileged forms constituted the paraded and famous limits, the zenith of the game of let's pretend they are gods. Less privileged forms entered the humdrum world of ordinary use and unnoticed familiarity: they had their uses, but only religious nuts like Theophrastus' Superstitious Man would dream of treating them in the special way reserved for the privileged images.[68]

We may then regard the making of religious images in the ancient world as a component of the process of realizing the imaginary, through action, speech and making. The religious mode in each case is merely a fraction of the total activity of these three kinds in any society, though privileged because of its central concern with the taxonomy of power and access to it. My second perspective relates to the notion of production in rather a different way.

We owe to an anonymous commentator in *The Economist* (18–24 November 1978, p. 52) an expression which deserves domestication: the 99·9 per cent democracy, to be found in those one-party states in which it is obligatory to vote, the party counts the vote, and the government owns the newspapers. The more consumptive the democracy, the louder it prattles. Likewise, the more intellectuals talk about the 'value' (beyond price, of course) of art and culture, the more they show themselves the victims of that economism which opposes 'real' value to 'symbolic' value. To defend the interests of one side of the polarity is also to defend the polarity, to lose oneself unselfconsciously in the ideology. It would be more effective to abandon the polarity; but that is just what we cannot do, since our culture depends upon it. The inescapability of the polarity makes it extremely difficult for us to understand the role of 'symbolic capital' in non-capitalist, and especially traditional, societies.[69] In the case of the ancient world, economic and social historians urge us constantly to uncover the 'real' relationships and processes, and by implication ignore the 'symbolic' aspects of ancient social and economic life, which are 'just ideology'. We thus turn the ancient world into yet another economist garden. There is only one kind of rationality. . . .

As an honour society, the Graeco-Roman world spent quite as much labour and time on symbolic capital accumulation as it did upon what we would call real capital accumulation. Capable of a very low rate of production, it squandered freely the only commodity in endless supply: time. The generalized purpose of life was to do what we should call 'nothing' – sitting around, talking to one's friends, a bit of physical exercise;

in between, to inspect one's property, give presents and orders, help out or e's dependents, arrange marriages, loan money. In a crisis, one might have to speak in public or fight, but not very often. In general the poor aspired to this ideal of leisure, but occupied themselves even so with a version of the same lifestyle: there was after all very little to do for most of the year in the fields, and just as little in the cities. Public life was the focus of the accumulation of maximal amounts of symbolic capital.[70] Faithful to these ideals, the élite consistently despised the representatives of 'rational economic man', those who broke the honour code by being *evidently* interested in profit, who accumulated without dispersing, who engaged in commerce rather than exchange. In short, the reality of production was socially repressed. In such a framework, art necessarily has particular interest. Even for us it is 'useless' (and we defend it by appealing to its symbolic value). Perhaps the ancient world valued precisely its uselessness?

One of Pliny's silly little grumbles concerns the disappearance of small pictures, *tabulae* (35.118). 'No artists', he says, 'enjoy a real glory unless they have painted easel pictures, and here the wisdom of past generations claims our greater respect. They did not decorate walls to be seen only by their owners, nor houses that must always remain in one place and could not be carried away in case of fire. Protogenes was content with a cottage in his little garden, and no fresco was to be seen in the house of Apelles. It was not yet men's pleasure to dye whole surfaces of wall; Art laboured for the cities, and the painter was *res communis terrarum*.' The small size of *tabulae*, their transportability, is turned into a moral virtue: they can be enjoyed by everybody. The creaking theme of ancient *simplicitas* is surely used to make a point about symbolic capital: as useless public delights *tabulae* had a value which is denied when paintings are made for private individuals. As public delights they form symbolic capital for those who bestowed them upon the collectivity; they are bench marks of the public competition between those who can afford to give such things to their city. Now the notion that art should really be public property was widespread only when large private collections began to be built up by hellenistic kings and wealthy Roman aristocrats.[71] Such men gained double profit: they increased their own symbolic (and real) capital by proving that they were tasteful; and they further increased their symbolic capital by bestowing odd works of art on cities. Instructively, Pliny expresses surprise that Tiberius, a well-known boor (*minime comis imperator*: *HN* 35.28), should have paid six million sesterces for a painting by Parrhasios and have kept it in *his bedroom*.[72] He expects everyone to see the point: all that money for *nothing*?

The famous story about Apelles' visit to Parrhasios at Rhodes illustrates another aspect of the same topic (Pliny, *HN* 35.81–3). The competition was perfect, because perfectly useless. First Apelles drew a perfect line; then Parrhasios another even more perfect (on top); and Apelles won the zero-sum game by drawing the most perfect line on top of that. Aware of their almost instant acquisition of symbolic capital, they 'agreed to hand down the painting just as it was to posterity, a marvel to all, but especially to artists'. And posterity snapped it up. As Pliny mourns, after its destruction by fire: 'Formerly we might look on it; its wide surface disclosed nothing save lines which eluded the sight, and among the numerous works by excellent painters it was like an empty

THE REAL AND THE IMAGINARY: PRODUCTION AND RELIGION IN THE GRAECO-ROMAN WORLD

space: which was precisely what lent it its attraction and its nobility surpassing every other work ([*tabulam*] *allicientem omnique opere nobiliorem*).' Even the language of symbolic capital accumulation is used. The emptiest painting conceivable is worth most – not money, but *value*. It was not only patrons who competed for art, it was the artists themselves. Apelles used to hang his pictures on a balcony, so that people could criticize them and he could improve them 'regarding the public as more accurate critics than himself' (*HN* 35.84). Just so were men in Sparta, that republic of honour, elected to the *Gerousia* by the loudness of the acclamation that greeted them in the Apella. The same Apelles was paid for a portrait of Alexander in the Temple of Artemis at Ephesus twenty talents, not counted out in coin, but *weighed* (Pliny, *HN* 35.92). For as we know, great artists are indifferent to mere details about money. To have counted would have been mercenary. 'Real' value and symbolic value are bedfellows, not enemies.[73] One final lie by Pliny is worth noting. It was the Macedonian Pamphilus, who made plain his status by refusing to teach anyone painting for less than a talent, who brought it about that in the fourth century B.C. painting on wooden tablets was the first subject taught freeborn boys. 'It was at any rate had in such honour that at all times the freeborn, and later on persons of distinction practised it, while by a standing prohibition no slaves might ever acquire it, and this is why neither in painting nor in statuary are there any celebrated works by artists who had been slaves' (*HN* 35.77). Well, of course: nothing so conspicuously useless as art could be entrusted to *slaves*, who by definition could not compete in the honour stakes. Slaves could paint, cast bronze, sculpture marble, and did all the time; but their art did not 'exist'. It was classified out. The history of art in the ancient world is the history of the accumulation of symbolic capital, by cities, patrons and craftsmen. It is our art history that busies itself with the painters of pots.

But we must return to religion. That well-known ancient lover of art and beauty, Pericles, is recorded by Thucydides (2.13) as having said something about Pheidias' Athena *Parthenos* that we should find rather odd. For he lists its forty talents of pure gold among the financial reserves of Athens for the war against Sparta. Indeed, the fact that the gold was easily detachable had already been useful: he was supposed to have told Pheidias' accusers in his trial for peculation to take the gold off and weigh it (Plutarch, *Perikles* 31). In other words, the statue did duty, or might do duty, as a bank: the city could get a loan from it.[74] Symbolic capital, invested at vast expense in toil and time,[75] could be converted back into 'real' capital.[76] Many cities, when hard up, sold off their public statues and pictures to make money for their debts; but symbolic value might weigh even heavier than need, as King Nicomedes of Bithynia discovered when the people of Knidos refused to sell him their nude Aphrodite by Praxiteles even for the value of their public debt to the Romans (Pliny, *HN* 36.20). But the major value of representations of the gods, even costly ones, was not their renegotiability into 'real' value. It lay in the storing up of an increasing weight of symbolic value, which could be 'cashed' in times of emergency, drought, famine, plague and other collective disasters.[77] The long time-span between dedication (the initial gift) and request amply concealed the intentionality of the exchange; the 'economic' function of the gift is socially repressed. Ancient cities were stuffed with these enduring banks of symbolic capital, 'vertical' capital jostling with 'horizontal' capital, statues of gods with statues of honourable men: in Pliny's day there were supposed still to be 73,000 bronzes on Rhodes, and 'at least as many' at Athens, Olympia and Delphi (Pliny, *HN* 34.36, quoting his contemporary C. Licinius Mucianus). And when they were removed to Rome, as so many of them were, they simply entered into a similar relationship: symbolic capital is hard to get rid of. And because the gods *were* the 'nature of things', the necessity of divine representations helped in turn to conceal from the ancient world what it knew and did not know, that art is useless. And so it could go on fuelling the game of honour, the useless centre of Graeco-Roman consciousness.

My third point picks up several points made earlier, about paradox, play and meaning. A great deal of anthropological energy has gone into the investigation of boundaries and rules and classifications recently. And not without justification. Such preoccupations have been enormously helpful in studying pollution fears, witchcraft, status assignation, alimentation and a range of other phenomena. But as Pierre Bourdieu has argued, this perspective neglects not only the lived, habitual aspect of rules which turns them into modes of knowing-how-to-act (that is, uses them positively not merely negatively) but also the energy expended on concealing, and changing, rules. Because 'being' is for us a static and not a dynamic category, the study of rules and boundaries, which define being, tends towards a sclerotic view of human self-definition. We need a new word for 'being-in-action': 'aming'? In the case of religious representations in antiquity, their static quality, their status as objects-in-the-world, surreptitiously legitimates the art-historical perspective, which naturally deals with them merely as objects. The museographic mind is not even aware of the arbitrariness of this classification. That perspective defines the enquiry. It constitutes the only possible enquiry. If, that is, one wishes to be a real art historian. And, as I have said, there *seem* to be classifications in the ancient world itself sufficiently similar to legitimate it also for us. Let me call the religious representation so conceived a *re*presentation. What would a *R*epresentation be? A representation-in-action, used, manipulated, given signification, re-presented.[78] That is, a working representation, a social phenomenon. It is only from that perspective that we can break the vicious oppositions which dominate most study of ancient religious art, Art versus Life, Form versus Content, Meaning versus Use, Excellence versus Vulgarity.

As a representation, a statue or picture of a god (and of a man, woman or dog) negates fluidity, movement, dissolution. It negates essential aspects of 'aming'. But, as a reproduction, it asserts other aspects of that same aming. It is of the essence of the representation that it denies in order to assert. It is a sort of logical puzzle. But then, so are gods. They are here and not here, seen and invisible, human and not human, just and unjust, ordered and disorderly, powerful and weak. They combine every contrary. They are impossible but actual. As representations, statues and pictures of gods indeed *represent* them. They are true illusions, pictures of a world we cannot know. And we can understand the development of ancient illusionism as a means of making truer illusions, more adequate pictures, by dint of a whole series of devices, as I have observed (p. 9 above). But as a Representation, the statue or picture of a god goes beyond the paradoxes of which it is the meeting-point; it generates new meanings from them.[79] 'Les oeuvres individuelles sont toutes des mythes en puissance, mais c'est leur adoption sur le mode collectif qui actualise, le cas échéant, leur "mythisme"', observes Lévi-Strauss of myth,[80] and the same is true of representations/Representations.

It is simple enough to see how religious images reproduce structures (which are of course also structures of 'meaning'). I have already said something about that reproductive capacity. There is of course more to be said. The geography of statues and other representations is itself an organizing structure, and itself part of a wider geography of the sacred: there are central and peripheral representations, 'high' ones and 'low' ones, private ones and public ones; some are known all over Greece or Italy, others familiar only to local peasants. As permanent fixtures, representations assert the immanence of divinity, they reproduce the repetitious aspect of ritual (both repetition *in* rituals and the repetition *of* rituals year by year). Like language, they deny flux and change; they guarantee that tomorrow will be the same as yesterday, mingling life and death, growth and decay. They are repositories of collective and individual symbolic capital. They evoke the appropriate myths, commentaries and tales of the encylopaedia, with their complex encoding of rules, statements and interdictions. They are the weight of the past.

But there is also another side to them. Rituals contain not only repetition but also discontinuity, disparity, jokes. The search for structure has always to be compromised by awareness of anti-structure. And we have seen that the ancient world was only too aware of the ambiguous status of religious representations. As potent things-in-the-world, representations are the victim of a multiplicity of private evocations, which cannot be censored; they enter dreams and fantasies, and thus legitimate actions, including religious innovation. As jokes, they constitute standing doubts about the collective project of sensemaking of which they are the product.[81] As artefacts made by human hands they are subject to the very decay and change which they negate as divine representations; they can be honoured and dishonoured, subject to men's whims. The meanings they construct constantly leak away.

Innovation, doubting and decay may be seen as three modes of escape from the actual. They are all at work all the time; but in the Representation that effect of the non-actual is effectively repressed. Only the reproductive aspect is highlighted. That is evident not only in the ritual incorporation of religious images into ceremonies, processions and private votive activity, all of which are repetitious, but in the 'deliberate' limitation of thought about such images, the general refusal to 'think' about art. Aestheticism is hostile to the Representation. The boringness of what Pollitt calls 'popular' attitudes towards what we call art is part of a much wider phenomenon in traditional societies, the social repression of the reality of production, and not only the production of things-in-the-world but of new ideas, of disconcertion, of the alternative. The ancient world in general refused to see what is so obvious to us about its art, that it contains many styles, constant historical development of choices. Having separated the Daedalic from 'our' art (as 'primitive'), they saw art as simply playing with equally appropriate possibilities, 'solemnity', 'true appearance', the infusion of 'life', 'thoughts', 'feelings', all of which had their advantages. The technological perspective in terms of which the technical history of art was written legitimated the idea that techniques, having been discovered, never needed to change. The history of art, from this perspective, was simply part of the listing of *prōtoi heuretai*, the 'first discoverers'.[82] When we say, 'Bell invented the telephone' we are quite aware that if Bell were alive now he would find the modern technology of telecommunications quite bewildering, just as we are aware that Bell's was only one of a number of similar machines that worked on slightly different principles. But no such dynamic view of technology existed in the ancient world. The renegotiation of the frontier between Nature and Culture was discontinuous, impromptu, the result of 'inspiration', 'revelation' or 'chance'. The history of technology was represented as a series of moments, not a process. And the focus of ancient 'art history' upon discrete 'moments', its anecdotal mode, is the analogue of that perspective upon technology as a whole. The attitude is both an expression and the foundation of *longue durée* in the ancient world.[83]

The refusal of aestheticism, then, permitted the ancient world to inscribe art into the nature of things. Its decay was equally in the nature of things, a consequence of moral failure on the part of the society which used it. I have already mentioned Pliny's complaint about the growth of private collections, and its harmful effect upon the relation between the collectivity and the producers of art works. But the people of Rome could still hit back, and save art. The Emperor Tiberius conceived such a passion for Lysippus' statue of a man scraping himself with a strigil, which M. Agrippa had dedicated in front of his baths behind the Pantheon, that he removed it to his *cubiculum* (again!): *cum quidem tanta populi Romani contumacia fuit ut theatri clamoribus reponi apoxyomenon flagitaverit princepsque quamquam adamatum reposuerit.*[84] Both chance and nature might protect art from such vulgarity: the Emperor Caius was prevented from removing two famous figures, of Atalanta and Helen, from a ruined temple in Lanuvium by the fact that they were on stucco (Pliny, *HN* 35.18); lightning struck the monstrous portrait of Nero painted on linen, 120 feet long, and burned it, together with the gardens of Maius (*HN* 35.51). Moral decay caused the loss of techniques produced by the moral superiority of the past: 'The truth is that the aim of the artist, as of everyone else in our times, is to gain money, not fame as in the old days, when the noblest of their nation thought art one of the paths to glory, and ascribed it even to the gods. The process of founding bronze is so completely lost that for generations even fortune has not been able to secure the results formerly ensured by skill' (Pliny, *HN* 34.5). Perhaps the Roman passion for copying has a moral basis too, and is not merely a testament to their vulgarity?

As usual, social lies are more important than 'truth'. The moral view of artistic production is simply one aspect of a wider and deliberate miscognition of the nature of production in traditional society. As representations, statues and pictures of gods were subject to that miscognition. But as Representations they played a crucial part in the legitimation of that view of production, inasmuch as traditional religion was a central element in the miscognizing world-view.[85] They privileged continuity and inertia over flux and flow. Yet power obviously transcends every human effort of control and manipulation; at best we make up stories about it *ex post facto*. As paradoxes, divine representations are jokes, threats to the process of miscognition. The ideology is always running to keep up. Lucian (*Eikones*, 6) made his Panthea of elements from the most perfect statues. Her smile he borrowed from Kalamis' famous statue of Aphrodite *Sōsandra* ('Saviour of Males') at the entrance to the Athenian Acropolis. *To meidiama semnon kai lelēthos.* 'Majestic and secret': the language of symbolic capital accumulation rubs against the language of privacy, of the doubtful, of the unknown. The totems of continuity and inertia rightly smile. For we are always deceived.[86]

NOTES

1 R. Bianchi Bandinelli, 'Quelques réflexions à propos des rapports entre archéologie et l'histoire de l'art, *Mélanges offerts à K. Michałowski* (Warsawa, 1966), pp. 261–74. On other aspects of Winckelmann's legacy, see Nikolaus Himmelmann, *Utopische Vergangenheit: Archäologie und moderne Kultur* (Berlin, 1976).

2 See, for example, the review by M. I. Finley, 'In lieblicher Bläue . . .', *Arion* NS 3.1 (1976), pp. 79–93. Among articles from *Dialoghi di Archeologia*, one may cite Patrizio Pensabene, 'Considerazioni sul transporto di manufatti marmorei in età imperiale a Roma e in altri centri occidentali', *DA* 6 (1972), pp. 317–62; Clara Gallini, 'Che cosa intendere per ellenizzazione. Problemi di metodo', *DA* 7 (1973), pp. 175–91; Giuseppe Pucci, 'La produzione della ceramica aretina. Note sull' "industria" nella prima età imperiale romana', *DA* 7 (1973), pp. 255–93. Not, of course, that they necessarily carry conviction.

3 Erwin Panofsky, 'The history of art as a humanistic discipline', in *Meaning in the Visual Arts* (Doubleday ed., 1955), pp. 1–25 at p. 19.

4 Erwin Panofsky, 'Iconography and iconology: an introduction to the study of Renaissance art', in *Meaning*, pp. 26–54 at p. 29.

5 I do not of course wish to imply, any more than Panofsky, that there is no legitimate place for connoisseurship and iconography. But inasmuch as in themselves they provide no sort of theory, art historians, in trying to move beyond the categories they offer (as they constantly

do, simply in order to write 'history'), are faced with the choice between received or common-sense ideas about change and the obligation to elaborate specific theories. Almost invariably, it is the first option that is chosen.

6 Bianchi Bandinelli, 'Quelques réflexions . . .', p. 269.

7 For new developments in Marxist literary criticism, see Terry Eagleton, *Criticism and Ideology: a study in Marxist literary theory* (London, 1976), and Rosalind Coward and J. Ellis, *Language and Materialism: developments in semiology and the theory of the subject* (London, 1977).

8 See K. Jex-Blake and E. Sellers, *The Elder Pliny's Chapters in the History of Art* (London, 1896), p. 9: Note to line 21; more generally (and more recently), note J. J. Pollitt, *The Ancient View of Greek Art* (New Haven and London, 1974), p. 73 [Students' edition]: 'The value of the information (often demonstrably erroneous, occasionally absurd) contained in the *Natural History* depends on the source from which it is derived . . .'.

9 The Latin is instructive: *Iove Olympio facto* (*HN* 34.49) means 'with (or by) his Olympian [Zeus]'. Pliny is rather embarrassed at beginning his account of bronze sculpture with one made, as he remarks, of ivory and gold; but the expression *Iuppiter Olympius* tells us all. Bronze sculpture 'starts' with the most renowned sculpture of the highest god. Not a very art-historical perspective of course, which presumably led Detlefsen to read *Olympiae* ('at Olympia') with the inferior manuscripts.

10 H. Stuart Jones, *Select Passages from Ancient Writers illustrative of the History of Greek Sculpture* (London, 1895, repr. Chicago, 1966), p. 26, no. 37. The Loeb translation of Pausanias (by a different Jones) gives 'an Artemis'. Some other examples in Pausanias: 1.20.3; 1.22.8; 1.24.8; 2.10.3; 3.18.8; 5.20.2-3; 5.23.1; 5.25.12; 5.26.2 and 6; 5.27.8; 6.18.1; 8.42.7; 9.10.2; 10.9.7; 10.19.4. Cf. A. Schubart, 'Die Wörter *agalma, eikōn, xoanon, andrias* und *verwandte*, in ihren verschiedenen beziehungen, Nach Pausanias', *Philologus* 24 (1866), pp. 561-87.

11 Stuart Jones, *Select Passages*, pp. 96-7 no. 128 (Pausanias, 10.10.1). Other writers, especially Pliny, use the same terminology, which certainly sometimes seems to approximate to our way of putting the matter, e.g. *HN* 34.54 *aliam Minervam*; 36.15 *Veneremque eius*. But Cicero's delicacy is instructive (*ND* 1.30 *laudamus Vulcanum eum, quem fecit Alcamenes*).

12 J. J. Pollitt, *The Ancient View*, pp. 63-6.

13 See Alison Burford, *Craftsmen in Greek and Roman Society* (London, 1972), pp. 124-35. For what can be reconstructed about such craftsmen's writing, see H. L. Urlichs, *Über Griechische Kunstschrift-steller* (Würzburg, 1887).

14 I take Pollitt's book once more because it might have been extremely good. It is a great pity that its conception of the task is so narrow. The rejection of 'popular' beliefs about art condemns it to a discussion of allegedly 'interesting' views, those of rhetoricians and philosophers especially, which demonstrably had virtually no influence upon the actual making of ancient art. Consequently, it cannot hope to persuade art historians that it is important to know something about 'ancient attitudes' towards art, which is the formal purpose of the book.

15 F. Frontisi-Ducroux, *Dédale: mythologie de l'artisan en Grèce ancienne* (Paris, 1975); note also the Telchines: M. Detienne, *Les Ruses de l'intelligence* (Paris, 1974), pp. 242-58.

16 See further below, pp. 26-7.

17 On *summetria* and *alētheia/veritas*, see Pollitt, *The Ancient View*, pp. 160-2, 170-82.

18 The text is corrupt, and it seems clear that Pliny did not fully understand what his source said. The different editions of Pliny diverge hopelessly in their interpretations, and it is best to say no more than I have said here.
  Another obvious device was to adulterate metal so as to make it more capitable of representing some physical state, as Silanion added silver to bronze to make his statue of Jocasta look as though it were consuming away in death (Plutarch, *Quaest. conv.* 5.1.2) or Aristonides iron, to make a statue blush (Pliny, *HN* 34.140).

19 E. Benveniste, 'Le sens du mot *kolossos*', *Rev. phil.*, Ser. 3, 6 (1932), pp. 118-35 quotes approvingly (p. 132) Kretschmer's idea that *andrias* connoted originally 'little man' and was a diminutive. None of the passages quoted seems to me in the least persuasive: philology would help itself by permitting the notion of semantic motivation to become more generally known. Quite exceptionally, in Egypt, *andrias* was used to mean 'statue of god'.
  J.-P. Vernant, 'Figuration de l'invisible et catégorie psychologique du double', in *Mythe et Pensée chez les Grecs* (ed. 4, Paris, 1971), 2, pp. 65-78, and Jean Ducat, 'Fonction de la statue dans la Grèce archaïque: *kouros* et *kolossos*', *BCH* 100 (1976), pp. 239-51 have both drawn attention to the ambiguity of early statues; I think the point can be made much more widely.

20 The manuscripts differ, but Mayhoff is probably right to read *exhilaratum*, 'brightened', 'cheered'.

21 *Anthol. Planud.* 54, 54a (Loeb, Vol. 5, p. 188). Stuart Jones' translation (*Select passages*, no. 92a) coyly refuses the ambiguity by translating *empnoë Lada*, 'O Ladas, instinct with life', which derives from our way of regarding the ambiguity of representational art. The epigram continues with another metaphor, this time from coin-making: as bronze, the statue can no doubt be 'stamped', but here the whole body (*epi panti . . . sōmati*) is stamped with 'eagerness for the crown at Olympia' (lines 3-4). No. 92b (= 54a) pursues the trope slightly differently: the play is on the denotation 'breath' contained in *empnoë*, and so 'speed' (of wind, panting etc.).

22 The conceit is probably derived from an epigrammatic tradition: cf. Le Bonniec (Budé ed.), p. 76 and note 5 to 34.79 on pp. 256–7. Dio's point may also be; it certainly recurs in Callistratus, *Imag.* 3.2 (424K).

23 The primary sense of *agalma* was 'offering to a god' (cf. Benveniste, 'Le sens . . .', p. 131) although in Homer and in fifth-century poetry it can mean metaphorically 'delight', 'glory'. By the hellenistic period, its dominant meaning was 'cult statue of a god' (or, rarely, a king's statue) and was regularly opposed to *eikōn*, which finally acquired the technical sense of 'image of the emperor'. See L. Robert, 'Recherches épigraphiques', *REA* 62 (1960), pp. 316–18; *Hellenica* XI–XII (1960), p. 124, n. 2. But it is also found quite loosely to mean 'piece of sculpture', 'picture' and even 'image' in the sense of 'something imagined'.

24 Presumably, the sentiments hostile to the fashion for removing Greek art from conquered cities which Livy (34.4.1–4) puts into Cato's mouth were widespread. 'Cato' makes a telling point about whether the Roman gods will continue to 'work' if they are replaced or put alongside new kinds of representation. Cf. Pliny's 'conservative' defence of old images in clay (*HN* 35.157–8): 'We have no reason to be ashamed of the men who worshipped deities of clay, and would not, even for their gods, change gold and silver into images. . . . The admirable execution of these figures, their artistic merits and their durability make them more worthy of honour than gold, and they are at any rate more innocent.'

25 There were in fact several stories. According to Polybius, the soldiers were using paintings as dice-boards, and Philopoemen offered Mummius 100 talents to assign one of them, by Aristeides, to Attalus (ap. Strabo, 8.6.23, 381C). Pliny, *HN* 35.24, relates that Mummius was so amazed at the offer, that he decided to take it back to Rome even though he could see nothing in it; this version is elaborated by Velleius Paterculus, 1.13.4, where Mummius simply tells the men in charge of the embarkation and transportation of the art-works that they must be careful; if any were damaged, new ones would have to be made.

26 For example, Livy 6.29.8–9 (Praeneste, 381/0 B.C.); 9.44.16 (Samnites, 305 B.C.); Pliny, *HN* 34.34 (Volsinii, 264); 34.40 (Tarentum, 209); Livy 35.40.1–3 (Syracuse, 211); 26.34.12 (Capua, 211); Polybius 21.30.9 (Ambracia, 187); Plutarch, *Aemilius Paullus* 33 (Pydna, 168); Pausanias 7.16.7–8 (Corinth, 146). The resentment which might be stirred up by the removal of an important cult-statue is vividly caught by one of Cicero's accounts of Verres' activities in Sicily (2 *Verr.* 4.94–5: temple of Heracles in Agrigentum). For others, see J. J. Pollitt, *The Art of Rome: sources and documents* (Englewood Cliffs, 1966), pp. 66–74.

27 The following passage, from Silvana Fasce, *Eros: la figura e il culto* (Genova, 1977), p. 120, provides an instructive illustration of the consequences of this opposition: 'In una forma di religiosità primitiva le contraddizioni possono rimanere, perchè ciascun elemento, preso isolatamente, ha un senso o un interesse, che viene considerato indipendente dal problema della sua coerenza nella relazione con gli altri dati del culto e della credenza religiosa. Se in generale le diverse caratteristiche individuabili nelle rappresentazioni di una stessa divinità possono dipendere o da una varietà del racconto mitico o da una originaria mancanza di individuazzione . . .; il dio (Eros) . . . ha conservato alcuni aspetti del culto arcaico, al punto da non essere individualizzato in una precisa figura divina.'

28 See Marcel Detienne, *Les Maîtres de vérité dans la Grèce archaïque* (Paris, 1967).

29 Cf. Louis Gernet and A. Boulanger, *Le Génie grec dans la religion* (Paris, 1932), pp. 236–41; indeed, Gernet's whole section on 'Les représentations' is instructive (pp. 233–88).

30 Pausanias, 7.22.4: 'At a more remote period, all the Greeks worshipped unshaped stones instead of statues'; the Greek says 'paid honour to'.

31 I do not therefore share Edwyn Bevan's view that iconism meant that 'the images were now held not only to be a means of communication with the gods, but to give information about them' (*Holy Images: an enquiry into idolatry and image-worship in ancient paganism and Christianity* [London, 1940], p. 16). The opposition is too facile, though it seems likely, from

the debates under the Empire, that the two modes came to be opposed by intellectuals: see Ch. Clerc, *Les théories relatives aux cultes des images chez les auteurs grecs du IIme siècle après J-C.* (Paris, 1915/1920), pp. 10–21; and E. Benveniste, 'Le sens . . .', pp. 126–7.

32 I think therefore that Pausanias' evident interest in attributes may be motivated by more than his periegetical vocation. Some examples picked at random: 1.24.3 (Athena Parthenos); 1.33.2 and 7 (Nemesis); 1.40.4 (Zeus); 2.10.3 (Asclepius); 2.10.4 (Aphrodite); 2.17.4 (Hera); 5.20.3 (Pluto); 5.25.12 (Heracles); 5.27.8 (Hermes); 7.18.9 (Artemis); 9.16.1 (Tyche); 9.16.1 (Eirene); 10.13.10 (Phalanthos); Pliny, *HN* 34.59 (Apollo). Occasionally specific innovations are noticed: Paus. 4.30.6 (the *polos* and cornucopia of the Tyche of Smyrna); 2.30.1 (first representation of Hekate as triform); Schol. on Aristophanes, *Birds* 573 (wings on Nike and Erotes). And the reverse, omission of usual attributes: Paus. 5.26.6; Schol. on Aeschines, Tim. 747R, etc. For the slow growth in complexity of attributes of Artemis at Ephesus, see Robert Fleischer, *Artemis von Ephesos und verwandte Kultstatuen aus Anatolien und Syrien:* EPROER 35 (Leiden, 1973), pp. 46–114.

33 See for example C. Rowe, 'Conceptions of colour and colour symbolism in the ancient world', *Eranos Jb.* 41 (1972), 327–64. It will be remembered that official sacrifices took place at dawn, facing east: Brigitta Bergquist, 'The Archaic Greek Temenos: a study of structure and function', *Skrifter utgivna av Svenska Inst. i Athen,* in 4°, 13 (Lund, 1967) pp. 109–14. The gods 'themselves' become bright: see L. Robert on the use of precious metals for statues, 'Recherches épigraphiques', *REA* 32 (1960), pp. 318–19; also K. Scott, 'The significance of statues in precious metals in Emperor worship', *TAPhA* 62 (1931), pp. 101–23.

34 'The Athenians to Athena Goodhealth': *IG* I. 335 (signed by Pyrrhos). A slightly different story is given by Pliny, *HN* 22.44. The usual explanation is that Pericles' private votive was paid for and dedicated publicly. The story legitimates a particular image, then; for we happen to know that Athena Hygieia was known in Athens by

the late sixth century B.C.: M. P. Nilsson, *Geschichte der griechischen Religion³* (München, 1967), I, pp. 440, 784.

35 For example, *Iliad* 21.406–8; cf. 5.864–7 (Ares); 21.233 ff. (Skamander).

36 Strabo, 8.3.30 (353C).

37 Strabo, 8.3.30 (354C). The translation is by Richmond Lattimore. The same anecdote precisely is quoted by Dio Chrysostom, *Or.* 12.25–6 and by Valerius Maximus, 3.7.4. Plutarch, *Aemilius Paullus* 28.2 also knows it. Note also Macrobius' attibution to Pheidias himself that 'from the eyebrows and the hair he had gathered the whole face of Zeus' (*Saturn.* 5.13.23). The sculpture on the base seems also to have been inspired by epic poetry, the Homeric Hymns: L. R. Farnell, *The Cults of the Greek States* (5 vols, Oxford, 1896–1909), I, p. 130.

38 The word used, *megethos*, does not simply refer to height; it includes bulk or 'scale'.

39 Such a story reminds us of the habit of chaining statues to prevent them from getting away: see most recently, R. Merkelbach, 'Gefesselte Götter', *Antaios* 12 (1971), 549–65.

40 'This must have been the height then esteemed.' This little note is instructively omitted from Pollitt's translation of the passage (*The Art of Rome*, p. 22): for us, the size of a statue is an 'artistic' decision.

I may note another curious passage of Pliny (*HN* 34.27), in connection with the practice of putting statues on columns. He says, 'The point of [using] columns was that [the statues] were elevated above ordinary mortals, which is the purpose also of the new-fangled arches [they use now]'. This is closely related to a well-known passage in Lucian, *Huper tōn eikonōn* 11, which implicitly opposes permissible size of statues of Olympic victors to the lack of limit for divine statues.

41 The passage has excited a large literature since Lessing, most of which is concerned with whether what Pliny says is 'true'. It is not *that* which matters. For the practice of putting up such statues, see E. N. Gardiner, *Athletics of the Ancient World* (Oxford, 1930), pp. 58–68.

42 Zeus sent a sign confirming the legitimacy of the statue: a thunderbolt fell into the ground nearby, at a spot marked by a hydria when Pausanias saw it. The

I

legitimacy of statues was frequently marked by the portents they gave out, sweating blood, moving and so on: see Ch. Clerc, *Les théories* . . ., pp. 37–49; Bevan, *Holy Images*, pp. 25–6. Even so, the most 'marvellous' statues were the Colossus of Memnon.

43 Frazer gives a description of the cave, as visible in the late nineteenth century, in his edition, vol. 4, pp. 406–7. Nothing is known of the statue Onatas made in this manner.

44 The story was traditional: Cicero has a parallel one, about which he is as sceptical as Pliny, concerning a figure of Pan discovered by some stone-cutters on Chios (*De Div.* 1.13.23). Some images of course had special privilege, either because they fell from heaven, like Artemis of Ephesus (R. Fleischer, *Artemis*, p. 125) or emerged from a hill-top like Athena Polias (Nilsson, *GGR*³ I, 438); or because they were created by special intervention of the deity (*eikones acheiropoiētai*): E. von Dobschütz, *Christusbilder* (Texte und Untersuchungen, NF 3, 18 [1899]), pp. 270–1. Such claims of course caused a great fuss: Bevan, *Holy Images*, pp. 46–83; Joh. Geffcken, 'Der Bilderstreit des heidnischen Altertums', *ARW* 19 (1916–19), pp. 286–315; Gerhart B. Ladner, 'The concept of the image in the Greek Fathers and the Byzantine Iconoclastic Controversy', *Dumbarton Oaks Papers* 7 (1953), pp. 1–34. In passage after passage, pagan and Christian, the tensions are played with.

45 Cicero tells the story, as does Valerius Maximus, 1.1.3, as a demonstration of Dionysius' wickedness (see Pease, *ad loc.*). But tyrants mark margins.

46 This is certainly the impression several casual stories suggest: Pliny, *HN* 36.16–17; 34.53; also an inscription relating to Paionios of Mende: *Syll.*³ I, 80. Such competitions must be distinguished from 'purely' honorific competitions, such as those between potters at Athens. On both, see Alison Burford, *Craftsmen*, p. 211.

47 For the terms, see Pollitt, *The Ancient View*, pp. 143–54, 242–4.

48 Paus. 1.23.7 with Frazer's note. The practice was very common, cf. P. Stengel, *Die griechischen Kultusaltertümer* (München, 1920), pp. 27–8; W. Pfister, *RE* (1922) s.v. *Kultus*, cols. 2142–3.

49 Both temple and statue were generally kept closed, except in the case of temples which were tourist attractions. But there were all kinds of variations to the rules for entry: Stengel, *Kultusalterthümer*, p. 28; Pfister, *RE*, s.v. *Kultus*, cols. 2139–42. It may be worth pointing out that one of the words for a cult-statue, *hedos*, seems originally to have meant 'god's seat', first meaning the *temenos*, later the statue: Benveniste, 'Le sens . . .', p. 131. On supplication rules, J. Gould, 'Hiketeia', *JHS* 93 (1973), pp. 74–103 (though he does not mention a case involving a statue).

50 See Clerc, *Les théories*, pp. 50–4; Kurt Latte, *Heiliges Recht* (Tübingen, 1920), pp. 83–8.

51 The best-known incident occurs in Lucian, *Erotes* 13–17 cf. *Eikones* 4 and Val. Max. 8.11.4; the object of the fantasy (and deed) being the Cnidian Aphrodite. Predictably, intercourse is *per anum*.

52 Paus. 5.10.2. He also mentions, while on the subject, that the Athena Parthenos was treated with water, and that the presence of a well underneath the Asclepius at Epidaurus kept it moist. Similar treatment was given to Artemis at Ephesus.

53 Clifford Geertz, 'Religion as a cultural system', *Anthropological Approaches to the Study of Religion* (ASA Monographs, 3), ed. M. Banton (London, 1966), pp. 1–46; cf. Fredrik Barth, *Ritual and Knowledge among the Baktaman of New Guinea* (New Haven/Oslo, 1975); Alfred Gell, *Metamorphosis of the Cassowaries* (London, 1975); Irving Goldman, *The Mouth of Heaven: an introduction to Kwakiutl religious thought* (New York/London, 1975).

54 See the able defence of some form of monism by Ernest Gellner, *The Legitimation of Belief* (Cambridge, 1974).

55 Cf. A. R. Hands, *Charities and Social Aid in Greece and Rome* (London, 1968), pp. 26–61.

56 Pierre Bourdieu, *Outline of a Theory of Practice* (= *Esquisse d'une théorie de la pratique*, 1972) (Cambridge, 1977), p. 171, suggests that we should not project the countergift retrospectively into the project of the gift; because this has the 'effect of transforming into mechanical sequences of obligatory acts the at once risky and necessary improvisation of the everyday

strategies which owe their infinite complexity to the fact that the giver's undeclared calculation must reckon with the receiver's undeclared calculation, and hence satisfy his expectations without appearing to know what they are'. I agree in principle; but the emergence of proto-class structures enforces much stricter relations of unequal exchange – so that the norms are even enforced in law. And as a paradigm of unequal exchange, one might expect religion to express this ideal more clearly than one could ever find in life.

57 J.-P. Vernant, 'Le mythe prométhéen chez Hésiode, in *Mythe et société en Grèce ancienne* (Paris, 1974), pp. 177–94; 'Sacrifice et alimentation humaine à propos du *Prométhée* d'Hésiode', *Annali della Scuola Normale Superiore di Pisa*, Cl. Lett. e Fil., Ser. III, 7.3 (1977), pp. 905–40; P. Vidal-Naquet, 'Valeurs religieuses et mythiques de la Terre et du Sacrifice dans l'Odyssée', *Annales, ESC*, 25 (1970), pp. 1278–97.

58 'Fragment of an analysis of a case of Hysteria ("Dora")', Standard edition, 7, pp. 1–122.

59 *Rethinking Symbolism* (= *Le symbolisme en général*, 1974) (Cambridge, 1975), pp. 85–149.

60 Cf. J.-P. Vernant and M. Detienne, *Les ruses de l'intelligence* (Paris, 1974) (E.T., Hassocks, Sussex, 1978); for Rome, G. Dumézil, *La Religion romaine archaïque* (Paris, 1966) (E.T., Chicago and London, 2 vols, 1970).

61 M. Detienne, 'Ronger la tête de ses parents', in *Dionysos mis à mort* (Paris, 1977), pp. 135–60.

62 *Capital*, I, part III, ch. 7 (Foreign Languages Publ. House, Moscow, 1971), p. 177.

63 Adolfo Sánchez Vásquez, *Art and Society: essays in Marxist aesthetics* (= *Las ideas estéticas de Marx*, Mexico City, 1965) (London, 1973), p. 185.

64 And of the most blatant kind: Nero was so fond of Strongylion's statue of an Amazon, because it had such beautiful legs, that he had it carried around everywhere with him (Pliny, *HN* 34.82); he also admired a statue of Alexander as a boy so much that he wanted to mark it with his favour, and had it ruinously gilded (*HN* 34.63); Tiberius too

conceived 'passions' for works of art – and so did Augustus (*HN* 35.131). But fetishism in the ordinary art-world sense is equally marked in the astonishing prices paid, for paintings especially.

65 Sánchez Vásquez, *Art and Society*, p. 187.

66 Apart from Onatas' inscription at Olympia recorded by Paus. 5.25.8, 'Many are the works of Onatas, *sophos* . . .', and *IG* 11.5. 147 (Achermos, sixth century B.C.), we have the evidence of the Daedalic tradition: Frontisi-Ducroux, *Dédale*, pp. 193–216 et passim. It is too easy to accept the Aristotelian equation between *sophia* and *technē* and suppose that it applies equally to the Archaic and early Classical periods, as Alison Burford, *Craftsmen*, p. 207, does (and she is not loathe to translate *sophia* in Achermos' inscription 'technical knowhow'). What are all the stories about Pheidias concerned with if not a capacity greater than *technē*? The entire second half of Dio Chrysostom's *Or.* 12, is extremely instructive (sections 45–85).

67 The Artemis at Ephesus was claimed to have survived seven destructions of the temple unscathed (R. Fleischer, *Artemis*, pp. 124–5), and there are a number of other stories of miraculous preservation. But it seems clear that in the Classical period there was a gradual process of installing 'modern' statues alongside, and at the expense of, older images, *xoana*.

68 Theophrastus, *Characters* 28 (Jebb). New cults, which often could not afford expensive cult-furniture, devised special ways of making their icons significant: by using curtains and lighting-effects; by reducing their number; by using 'informative' reliefs of a kind quite different from traditional reliefs in design and intention. The adoption of new cult-icons is thus motivated, especially during the Empire, in a way that is rarely seen, quite apart from their character as 'public' votives in a private space.

69 Pierre Bourdieu, *Outline*, 171–83, to whom, with M. I. Finley, *The Ancient Economy* (Berkeley and London, 1973), what follows is heavily indebted.

70 And, in the Roman Republic, increasingly of real capital, through the expansion of empire. But the predominant use of such real capital was symbolic since it fuelled the increasingly intense competition for

victory in the zero-sum game of Roman aristocratic politics – an ineluctable pressure that destroyed the fictional consensus on which the aristocracy's dominance rested.

71 M. Agrippa wrote a famous speech arguing that art should be public property. But, as Pliny aptly remarks (*HN* 35.26), that did not prevent him from collecting too.

72 *cubiculo suo inclusit*: *HN* 35.70. I take *cubiculum* to mean 'bedroom', although it might refer to the emperor's private box in the theatre.

73 For other dazzling triumphs, see Pliny, *HN* 35.62 (Zeuxis) and 35.55 (Boularchos). Craftsmen were always boasting about their unsurpassed *technē*: Burford, *Craftsmen*, pp. 208–12. This of course recalls the 'quality records' of athletes.

74 Temple treasuries regularly functioned as banks, both state and private.

75 It took fifteen years actually to build the Parthenon; the combined cost of temple, statue and the Propylaia may have been around 2,000 talents, the temple itself costing perhaps 700–800: R. Meiggs and D. Lewis, *A Selection of Greek Historical Inscriptions to the End of the Fifth Century B.C.* (Oxford, 1969), pp. 164–5; and in general, M. Robertson, *A History of Greek Art* (Cambridge, 1975), I, pp. 292–322.

76 'Insult politics' demanded that statues erected to men, or to emperors, who later became undesirable, should be melted down, their remaining symbolic value being to signal the social disappearance of the *persona non grata*: cf. Pliny, *HN* 34.27; 30, etc.). Hence Pliny's surprise (33.12) that there should still be three statues of Hannibal in Rome.

77 This of course was only the most dramatic use: divine statues were 'cashed' constantly inasmuch as the divine world organizes the production of crops, ensures fertility of animals and humans, preserves the order of the heavens and the cycle of the seasons, keeps the land dry and the sea wet, the hot hot and the straight straight.

Individuals had a little banking system of their own in votives.

78 I have borrowed this device from Elizabeth Tonkin, 'Masks and powers', unpublished paper presented to a colloque on Symbolism, University of Birmingham, April 1978.

79 Of course 'it' generates nothing, as Sperber observes: 'Symbolicity is not a property either of objects or of acts, but of conceptual representations that describe or interpret them' (*Rethinking Symbolism*, p. 112).

80 *L'homme nu* (Mythologiques, 4) (Paris, 1971), p. 560.

81 Mary Douglas, 'Jokes' in *Implicit Meanings: Essays in Anthropology* (London, 1975), pp. 90–114.

82 A. Kleingünther, *Prōtos heuretēs: Philologus*, Suppl. 26 (1933); cf. Thomas Cole, *Democritus and the Sources of Greek Anthropology* (Philological Monographs, 25: American Philological Association, 1967) and Alison Burford, *Craftsmen*, pp. 189–98.

83 See M. I. Finley, 'Technical innovation and economic progress in the Ancient World', *Economic History Review*, 2nd series, 18 (1965), pp. 29–45; *The Ancient Economy*, pp. 62–122; H. W. Pleket, 'Technology and society in the Graeco-Roman World', *Acta Historiae Neerlandica* 2 (1967), pp. 1–25.

84 'The populace of Rome resented this so deeply that they raised an outcry in the theatre, demanding the restitution of the *apoxuomenos*. Which the Emperor did, though he had set his heart on the thing': Pliny, *HN* 34.62. Such negotiations between Emperor and people were commonplace; see Z. Yavetz, *Plebs and Princeps* (Oxford, 1968).

85 See P. Bourdieu, 'Génèse et structure du champs religieux', *Rev. fr. de sociologie*, 12 (3) (1971), pp. 318–35.

86 I wish to express my warm thanks to Simon Price not merely for criticizing this article but helping to remedy my dismal knowledge of the relevant bibliography.

II

The Moment of Death:
Art and the Ritual of Greek Sacrifice

FOR the historian of religion, representations of ritual have generally an uncomplicated status: They are documents that can be used to clarify matters of fact when other evidence, generally of a literary or textual order, fails. This is certainly so in relation to Greek sacrifice. Such use of iconographic evidence is scarcely art-historical, but it is frequently indispensable. A striking case in point is the recent publication by Jean-Louis Durand of a black-figure amphora in the museum at Viterbo, which shows seven strong young men bodily lifting a bovine quadruped—bull or steer—by the legs; an eighth man hauls on a rope round its muzzle while a ninth extends his hands in the air. The only fully clothed figure is represented directly beneath the animal, thrusting a long butcher's knife into its throat.[1] The recognition of this vase painting immediately resolved a long-standing dispute over the meaning of several similar phrases occasionally found in Athenian ephebic inscriptions and elsewhere of the type, "At the Mysteries also they lifted up the cattle at Eleusis for sacrifice."[2]

Once we have resolved such matters of fact, however, other considerations become pressing. What other kinds of information about sacrifice might representations give us? Are there stereotyped scenes which occur regularly? What selection from the numerous "moments," or separable units of action, was made in the iconography? Are these selections correlated with the emphases of other textual evidence for sacrifice? What is the pattern of exclusion: Why should some moments never, or very rarely, be chosen for representation? Conversely, why should there be numerous representations of "moments" that seem quite trivial, especially nonritual preparations such as giving water to the victims to drink? By asking these and other questions we enter a difficult realm, which is neither that of the philologist concerned with the *Realien* of antiquity nor that of the art historian concerned with the iconography—or even the iconology—of individual artistic creations. All the same, in themselves the questions seem perfectly natural, and a start has been made, particularly by J.-L. Durand, to answer them in the case of Athenian vase painting of the classical period.[3] But much more work remains to be done, especially at the theoretical level.

The general problem, then, concerns the relation between the preferred or dominant set of images representing sacrifice at a given time or place and the ideological roles of sacrifice in the religious systems of the Greek world.[4] Before discussing this issue explicitly, however, three preliminary points need to be made, all arising out of the fundamental politico-religious organization of the Greek world, and above all the refusal to permit the development of a professional full-time priesthood.

This absence in the first place inhibited the development of complex rituals of any great elaborateness, which are common where priestly castes exist. The great majority of civic rituals were simply

Reprinted from *Acts of the XXVIth Congress for the History of Art (Washington, 11–16 August 1986), World Art: Themes of Unity in Diversity*, ed. I. Lavin et al. (Univeristy Park, PA: The Pennsylvania State University Press, 1989), pp. 567–573. Copyright © 1989 by The Pennsylvania State University Press. Reproduced by permission.

variations on the theme of procession-with-sacrifice. Blood sacrifice conducted on behalf of the state was, in general, almost identical to blood sacrifice performed by heads of families or by the members of dining-groups and other fraternities. At all times and in all places "eccentric" rituals can be found, which bore virtually no relationship in formal terms to what we may call normative public sacrifice. But in general civic sacrifice was not in the least arcane.

Moreover, except to a limited degree in the Roman Principate, it never occurred to anyone to develop an authoritative iconography of ritual. States might commission elaborate religious buildings, including narrative friezes (such as the Parthenon frieze showing the procession at the Panathenaic festival), but the combination of a decentralized religious system together with the material and social conditions of art- or craft-production meant that the major determinants of the system of religious representation were implicit or unconscious rather than the relatively explicit rules of an ecclesiastical or other institutional patron. One of the major difficulties in attempting to sketch the nature of the system (if it deserves to be called that) of representations of ritual is the markedly individual character of choices of subject, treatment, and overall conception. This is true especially in relation to Athenian vase painting.

Third, sacrifice never received an explicit theology or rationale. The standard response to (our) question, "Why do you perform this ritual?" would be, "Because our forefathers established it." Even when relatively objective and even critical intellectual inquiry developed, from the mid-fifth century B.C.E., it proved impossible to develop a more than superficial account of the meanings established by such rituals.[5] Religious expertise lay not in the hands of intellectuals but elsewhere. Most obviously, there were the local exegetes of religious law and tradition who were concerned only with particular rules and customs, generally in a prescriptive mode. Then there were ritual professionals—in the case of public sacrifice, the butchers who did the actual killing, the cooking, and the carving, and who were in the historical period, it seems, invariably slaves. Finally, there were the poets who composed hymns for ritual use.[6] Each of these groups was concerned with a quite different level of religious or ritual knowledge. Only the poets were in a position to produce any sort of synthetic account of the implications of sacrifice. But invariably the means chosen was a reflection on myth, and to a modern eye much more remained unstated in such a mode than could be made explicit.[7]

In short, sacrifice in the Greek world was an embedded institution, which could not be disengaged from its social contexts by anyone in antiquity until the advent of Christianity. It is certainly true that the idiom of the sacrificial rules—what kinds of animals could be killed, how they should be cooked, what parts could be eaten and by whom—was used to express rejection or criticism of dominant norms of social life. The best example of this criticism is the imagery of the Dionysiac cult, with its frenzied women devotees, who are sometimes represented as tearing wild animals apart. This imagery is simply one imaginable antithesis of the rules for civic sacrifice, which takes place within the city itself and not in the mountains, in which (at least iconographically) only men could be sacrificants, where (at least normally) only domestic animals could be slaughtered, and where the ideal social comportment was solemn, grave, and reverent. But such use of cultural rules is quite different from the critical examination of an embedded institution.[8]

One way of placing Greek representations of sacrifice is to ask what they were used for: before they are icons, they are objects. It is important to understand that representations of sacrifice in the Greek world did not, for the most part, belong to an autonomous category. We should rather place them in a much wider category, that of commemorative or mnemonic devices. The institution of sacrifice can itself be said to be based on memory, both the social memory encapsulated in the ritual calendar or "sacred laws," and the personal or collective recollection of vows undertaken under particular circumstances. It seems to have been usual in the Greco-Roman world for placards to be carried in the sacrificial procession publicizing the purpose of the sacrifice.[9] But there were several ways of making a more permanent record of so signal an act of piety. One was to hang on the walls of the temple the head of the sacrificial victim, which gradually lost flesh and skin to become a mere skull. There is an excellent iconographic example of this practice on an Orestes-Iphigeneia sarcophagus now in the Munich Glyptothek: The shrine of Artemis Taurica (to whom, according to the myth, captured human beings were sacrificed) is represented as a grove containing an image of the goddess, in which the trees are decked with severed human heads.[10] Another way of commemorating a sacrifice was to hang the hide of the sacrificial animal, once it had been skinned, on the walls of the temple. These hides became excellent material for mythic and ritual elaboration.[11] One example is the rule that those who wished to receive an oracle from Amphiaraus at Oropus, in Boeotia, had to sleep on the skin of the ram which they had sacrificed to purify themselves.[12]

Art, however, provided another idiom in which a record of piety might be made. A neat compromise between an actual skull and a mere painting of a skull is provided by an unusual stele from Castro (Thespiae), now in the museum at Thebes, erected by a dining-group in honor of Zeus Karaios. On the front is a carving in bas-relief of a *bucranion* (the clean skull of a bovine quadruped); on the lateral faces, the skull and the lower jaw of a wild boar, again in relief. The monument is evidently the record of a double sacrifice, one domestic, one wild, to this Boeotian city-Zeus who was at the same time a god of the mountain.[13] In an important sense, it is no less an image of sacrifice than the more obvious images showing sacrificants, victims, and altars. But it substitutes for the actual remains of the sacrificial animals images of them which will endure much longer. In time, the device of substituting images of *bucrania* for the actual victims came to have its own connotations. Once the device decorates altars and friezes, as it does in the Hellenistic period, it stands for the continuity of piety in a particular spot without reference to individual sacrificial offerings. The image can generalize where the object itself particularizes.[14]

The commemorative function of representations of sacrifice is expressed in numerous other ways, progressively distanced from immediate reference to actuality. For example, the sacred groves frequently found in the vicinity of temples, where the timber could never be felled, seem to have been decorated with great numbers of small painted wooden or terra-cotta plaques (*pinakes*), sometimes at least representing scenes of sacrifice, dedicated by sacrificants. In this case, reference to the physical remains of a sacrifice is suppressed in order to recapture, or re-present, the historical scene—or rather an ideal or stereotyped version of it.[15] Alternatively, and particularly in the Hellenistic period, marble reliefs—the frame carved to suggest a civic temple—might be set up in a sanctuary on individual pillars: Dozens were found in the temples of Asclepius in Athens and the Piraeus; many others are known from other sanctuaries, for example, that of Artemis at Brauron.[16] Typically, these reliefs provide a self-conscious interpretation of the intention or hope that lies behind the sacrifice. At the center stands the altar. On one side of it appears the divinity, or a divine group, represented as attentive and concerned. On the other side, on a much smaller scale, stand the human dedicants looking toward them. The only unmistakable reference to the act of sacrifice is the victim, usually represented in a very inconspicuous manner. The most elaborate example of this form of commemoration is the well-known "Family Sacrifice" relief now in the Munich Glyptothek (Fig. 1).[17] A variant upon this expensive type of commemoration is offered by the gold, silver, and bronze plaques found recently at Mesembria (Nessebre, Thrace), which were apparently nailed to some wooden structure: They show similar processions and condensed allusions to sacrifice to Cybele, the Mother of the Gods.[18]

The last variant on the commemorative image which should be noted here is the commemorative-normative image. The type here is the procession, representations of which occur from the mid-sixth century at Athens, generally in relation to the Panathenaic festival.[19] In commemorating a specific event, such images also prescribe its repetition.

Understood simply as commemorations, then, representations of sacrifice operated in a number of different ways. Already it is clear that image and function are interdependent. But there is a large class of representations of sacrifice which is in no obvious sense commemorative: those on Greek, and especially Athenian, vases of the archaic and classical periods. These are usually understood as part of a wider class of "images of everyday life" even if they have peculiarities which make them unreliable as evidence for actual rituals.[20] What I wish to urge is that this deficiency or unreliability may itself offer important evidence of the ways in which the religious system, in alliance with visual imagery, was able to create implicit meanings. In effect, I understand the imagery of sacrifice as a kind of commentary upon the practice of sacrifice. I distinguish two major forms of commentary.

The first constitutes an implicit answer to the question, Why do we perform this ritual? Three types of answer can be discerned: (1) Because the gods perform a type of sacrifice. Iconographically there are several variants upon this claim. The earliest is the representation of divinities, above all Apollo, offering libation from a *phiale*, generally over an altar, which is usually shown as blood-stained.[21] Although libation is not exclusively associated with blood sacrifice, it was the normal preliminary act; the blood-stained altar provides a metonymic association with the human institution—which discreetly avoids the obvious challenge, How can gods sacrifice, and to whom?[22] The gods might also be represented as taking part in acts apparently of sacrifice in this world, especially on black-figure vases of the latter part of the sixth century B.C.E.[23] The commonest trope here is the goddess of Victory playing the part of a servant, holding vessels or pouring wine into the *phiale* during the cooking of the meat on spits.[24] By around 400 B.C.E. there developed at Athens a special form of this trope, Nike performing a bull-sacrifice without assistance—all alone she forces the bull to remain still, raises its head by force, and cuts the carotids.[25] (2) Sacrifice could also be legitimated by referring it to the heroic period: There are numerous representations of heroes, and especially Herakles, in various stages of blood-sacrifice, above all cooking or carving.[26] The implicit claim here is that sacrifice is performed because of its grounding in the past, it is an act that does indeed belong to *ta patria*, the customs of our fathers. (3) We have already noted the emergence in the fourth century of images which link the divine world to the human world by means of a central altar. A claim is here being made that the institution of sacrifice is indeed successful in its asserted objective, to link this world with the Other World. Such images do double work: They record an act of piety, testifying to the power of the divinity to aid, but they also supply a reassuring answer to the underlying question, What is the point of sacrifice? We have not merely to do with the development of a consciousness of personal dependence upon particular divinities.[27]

We may term the second type of commentary *social:* It suggests the value or meaning of sacrifice by concentrating upon those elements which could most easily be understood as contributing to collective solidarity—a sort of Durkheimianism *avant la lettre*.

Actual sacrifices were presumably chaotic and unpredictable affairs, with children wandering about, passing distractions, and many kinds of disorganization. Moreover, there were disgusting aspects to them: the guts of the animals (and in state sacrifices there were often dozens of animals) to be disposed of, the flies to brush away, the smell of blood and raw meat. Art could dispense with all these realities and provide prescriptive images to convey the "real" atmosphere of piety, reverence, and order, which in actuality was surely not present. In a sense the images showed the Greeks what sacrifice was.

Moreover, the artist or craftsman was forced to make choices among possible scenes to be represented. The images thus provide us with an important indication of the unconscious emphases of Greek society in relation to sacrificial ritual. The character of this selection will be clearer if I list the separable "moments"—perhaps ideally simplified—of Greek "Olympian" sacrifice. We may distinguish eleven:[28] (1) The procession to the altar with the victims adorned with wool fillets and sometimes crowns. (2) The ritual turn around the altar to the right. (3) The initial libation and ritual question to the participants. (4) The sacrificant dips his hands into the holy water and sprinkles the victim, and scatters barley-ears over it. (5) Prayer to relevant divinities are offered by sacrificant. (6) Hairs are cut from the victim's forehead and burned on the altar fire. (7) The animal's throat is cut (with or without stunning) and the blood collected in a special dish; meanwhile, the flautist plays. (8) When the animal is more or less bled, the liver is inspected (at public sacrifices); otherwise the butcher proceeds to joint the carcass. (9) Portions of the meat are assigned to gods and various categories of humans. (10) The butcher or his assistants cook the innards (heart, lungs, liver) on spits while the sacrificant or an assistant pours wine over them from the libation vessel. (11) The innards are eaten by the participants.

Of these "moments" only three are at all common in the iconography: procession, jointing the carcass, cookery on spits. These may in fact be reduced to two, since butchery and cookery were two phases of the reduction of the sacrificial animal to mere food.[29] The only other stereotyped representation is a synthetic one, in which all the participants are frozen at an unspecifiable moment when nothing is happening at all.[30] This straightforward bias toward procession and butchery/cooking constitutes an implied commentary upon the value of sacrifice to the community. The procession represents an idealized social order. Civic life is based on public decorum, as opposed to the relative disorder of domestic life on the one hand, and the "natural" incoherence of the world beyond the pasture-land. The representation of the sacrificial procession asserts an ideal of gravity whose highest form appears here. In the case of butchery/cookery, the festive meaning of sacrifice comes to the fore: The laboriousness and the unpleasantness of the business is painted out in order to convey the "real" meaning, which is the collective pleasure taken in the feast.[31]

Oddly enough, however, the act of eating the sacrificial meat seems never to be represented. The "real" meanings are conveyed indirectly, by metonymic association. One has already to know the ritual perfectly before the images can produce their inner meaning. The representations are no less "embedded" than the institution they comment upon. And to our eyes the strangest exclusion is that of the representation of the death of the victim, which, apart from the Nike-stereotype (by definition, a nonhuman achievement), is shown only on fourth-century and Hellenistic gems.[32]

What I have said about metonymic association, of course, suggests that one explanation of this iconographic silence lies in the implications of what *is* represented: procession and butchery. The third, "frozen," representational type alludes to the moment of death even more strongly, though, so far as I know, the knife is only once depicted in the sacrificant's hand.[33] There cannot have been any general repugnance against depictions of death: The sacrificial death of Iphigeneia at Aulis is often represented with cheerful bloodthirstiness.

It is more satisfactory, I think, to recall here the fact that religious systems are fictional, and that, as with all fictions, numerous techniques are necessary to make the fiction convincing. One of the best is to interweave the banal with the problematic or opaque. Banality is beneath notice, is entirely natural; and the most successful ideological constructs are those we notice least. But religious structures need to be constantly revised to be adequate to experience, and here enigma is invaluable. It prompts the expansion of the system by the provision of imaginative answers to insoluble problems. An excellent example is Plutarch's question, Why do we not use salt when boiling up the guts at sacrifices? Perhaps the best explanation of the Greek iconographic silence on the moment of death is to be found precisely here: that ultimately sacrifice acquires its power through its unintelligibility.

NOTES

1. J-L. Durand and A. Schnapp, "Boucherie sacrificielle et chasses initiatiques," in *La Cité des images*, préf. J.-P. Vernant (Lausanne/Paris, 1984), 54–55, fig. 83.

2. See, e.g., H. von Fritze, "Zum griechischen Opferritual," *Jahrbuch des Deutschen Archäologischen Instituts* 13 (1903), 58–59; P. Stengel, *Opferbräuchen der Griechen* (Leipzig/Berlin, 1910), 105–112; L. Ziehen, s. v. "Opfer," *Paulys Real-Encyclo-*

pädie, 18, 35 (1939), 610–611; J. Rudhardt, *Notions fondamentales de la pensée religieuse . . . dans la Grèce classique* (Geneva, 1958), 261–262.

3. The traditional philological view is still represented, for example, by W. Burkert, *Greek Religion in the Archaic and Classical Periods* (1977, ET 1985), 6: "Paintings of ritual scenes which offer an insight into the reality of the cult are compara-

tively rare but exceptionally important." Compare J.-L. Durand, "Figurativo e processo rituale," *Dialoghi di Archeologia* n.s. 1 (1979), 16–31 (though Durand's work is sometimes quite fanciful, it is always stimulating); J. Fallot, "Mythe, art et philosophie en Grèce," *Quaderni di Storia* 6 (1980), 331–349.

4. Rudhardt 1958 (as in note 2) rightly stresses that it is impossible to define the unity of Greek sacrificial practice in any simple manner. In this paper I am concerned only with forms of sacrifice denoted by words derived from the root *thu-*.

5. The first known attempt to describe the meaning of blood-sacrifice in a relatively objective manner is Theophrastus's in his lost work, *On Piety*: "Sacrifice to the gods should be undertaken for three reasons: to honour them, to give thanks or to ask for benefits" (*ap.* Porphyry, *de abstinentia* 2, 24; W. Pötscher, *Theophrastus' Peri eusebeias* [Leiden, 1964]).

6. On the exegetes, F. Jacoby, *Atthis* (Oxford, 1949), 8–51; on Philochorus, idem, *Fragmente der griechischen Historiker*, no. 328, IIIb Suppl. (2 vols.). On the sacrificial butchers, G. Berthiaume, *Les Rôles du mageiros* (Leiden, 1982).

7. Hesiod is the poet upon whom the best work in this connection has been done: J.-P. Vernant, "Sacrifice et alimentation humaine à propos du Prométhée d'Hésiode," *Annali della Scuola Normale di Pisa* 7 (1977), 905–940.

8. For the Dionysiac inversion, see M. Daraki, "Aspects du sacrifice dionysiaque," *Revue de l'histoire des religions* 197 (1980), 131–157. Women could of course sometimes legitimately act as sacrificants: the best-known example is the widespread festival of the Thesmophoria.

9. P. Veyne, "Titulus praelatus: offrande, solennisation et publicité dans les ex-voto gréco-romains," *Revue archéologique* 1983), 2, 281–300.

10. D. Ohly, *Glyptothek München: griechische und römische Skulpturen* (Munich, 1972), 104–105 (no plate), c. 130–140 C.E. On human sacrifice in the cult of Artemis Taurica, A. Henrichs, "Human sacrifice in Greek religion," *Le Sacrifice dans l'antiquité*, ed. O. Reverdin and J. Rudhardt, Entretiens Fondation Hardt (Vandoeuvres, 1980), 195–242.

11. J. Pley, *De lanae in antiquorum ritibus usu* (Gieszen, 1911). The hide might alternatively be offered to a presiding magistrate (e.g., Xenophon, *Anabasis* 4.8.26) or to the priest: F. Puttkammer, *Quo modo Graeci victimarum carnes distribuerunt*, diss. (Königsberg, 1912), 30–31, 65–68.

12. Pausanias 1.34.5, with Frazer's note *ad loc.*, 2, 476.

13. Published by A. de Ridder, *Bulletin de correspondance hellénique* 46 (1922), 262, no. 88, fig. 37, but first accurately identified by A. Plassart, *BCH* 52 (1926), 399, no. 17; K. Demakopoulou and D. Konsola, *Guide to the Archaeological Museum of Thebes* (Athens, 1981), 79, no. 154 (?third century B.C.E.). Almost nothing is known of the cult of this Zeus; for the sacrifice of other wild animals, see L. Ziehen (as in note 2), 589–591.

14. On archaic and classical Athenian vases, *bucrania* signify loosely "sanctuary," as on the bell krater in Boston, MFA 95.25: Caskey-Beazley, *Attic Vase Paintings in the Museum of Fine Arts* 3 (1963), no. 167, pl. CI. In general, Ch. Börker, "Bukranion und Bukephalion," *Archäologische Anzeiger* 90 (1975), 244–250; P. Righetti, "Altari cilindrici a bucrani e festoni in Grecia," *Xenia* 3 (1982), 49–70.

15. *Anthol. Palatina* 6.221.10; Veyne (as in note 9), 288–289.

16. K. Vierniesel, *Hellenistische Votivreliefs* (1956); G. Neumann, *Probleme des griechische Weihreliefs* (Tübingen, 1979). The Asclepius reliefs are still best studied in the old catalogue of the National Museum in Athens by Svoronos-Barth.

17. The precise significance of this monument remains enigmatic; see E. Thiemann, *Hellenistische Vatergottheiten* (Münster, 1959), 93–100; and W. Hornbostel, *Sarapis* (Leiden, 1973), 356, n. 1, for quite different, yet equally plausible, arguments.

18. A. Vavritsas, "Anaskaphè Mesèmbrias Thrakès," *Praktika* (Athens) (1971 [1973]), 119–123; idem, *To Ergon* (1973), 50–58, figs. 42–44; H. W. Catling, *JHS Archaeological Reports* 20, (1973–1974), 28.

19. The earliest is perhaps a bf lekanis in the British Museum, B 80: Walters, *Catalogue of Vases* 2, (1893), 76–77 = CVA GB 2 BM 2 pl. 7.4b (III H e), c. 540 B.C.E., which represents schematically on part of the rim a Panathenaic procession toward the statue of Athena Promachos.

20. A. Rumpf, "Attische Feste—Attische Vasen," *Bonner Jahrbücher* 161 (1961), 208–214.

21. See, for example, the rf hydria from Caere now in the Kunsthistorisches Museum, Vienna, inv. no. IV 3739, 490–80 B.C.E. = *Götter, Heroen, Menschen: Sonderausstellung, Wien, 1974*, ed. K. Gschwantler and W. Oberleitner (Vienna, 1974), no. 42, pl. 10 (Artemis pouring wine into Apollo's libation-dish, over a bloodstained altar). Particularly interesting is a neck-amphora in the Ashmolean, Oxford (1924. 3): on face A, Nike pours wine from an oenochoe for Zeus's libation over a bloodstained altar; on face B is an athlete with his friend (CVA GB 3 Oxford 1 pl. 15. 3–4). The notion that there is a mythical narrative behind such a scene is quite superfluous. "Bloodying the altar" was an important aspect of *thu*-sacrifice: J. H. Waszink, s.v. "Blut," *Reallexicon für Antike und Christentum* 2 (1954), 461.

22. There has been a lively discussion over the meaning of such images ("Spendende Götter") since A. Furtwängler, "Zwei Thongefässe aus Athen," *Athenische Mitteilungen* 6.(1881), 117. The best résumé is W. Fuchs, "Attisches Weihrelief im Vatikan," *Römische Mitteilungen* 68 (1961), 176–179. There is much to commend the commonsense view of A. Fairbanks, *Greek Gods and Heroes*, 3d ed., (Cambridge, Mass., 1927), 23: "Apparently the act of worship was idealized by representing the gods as engaged in worship."

23. For instance, two vases in the British Museum: (1) bf amphora from Vulci, B 195 = CVA GB4 BM 3, pl. 37. 2b (III H e): procession of gods, from l., Dionysus with kantharos; Apollo playing lyre, behind him a bull; in front, Hermes, who looks back; (2) bf amphora, B 167 = CVA GB 4 BM 3, pl. 34. 1a (III H e): from r., Hermes playing lyre, with goat; Herakles playing double flute, with bull alongside; at end, ?Iolaus (cf. pl. 34. 1b, analogous, but with Silenoi).

24. See rf bell krater in Kunsthistorisches Museum, Vienna, inv. no. 1144 (Herakles sacrificing): Nike stands to right of altar, with the incense and the *kanoun*; rf stamnos in British Museum from Cerveteri, E 456, cf. 455 ("Diomedes" sacrificing): Nike pours wine onto flames on altar from her oenochoe (= CVA GB 4 BM 3 pl. 24. 3a,c).

25. For the significance, see N. Kunisch, *Die stiertötende Nike*, diss. (Munich, 1964), 9–19.

26. E. Hooker, "The Sanctuary and Altar of Chryse in Attic rf Vase Paintings," *Journal of Hellenic Studies* 70 (1950), 35–41; also *Hommes, dieux et héros de la Grèce* (Expos. Rouen, October 1982–January 1983), 250–251, no. 103 on Louvre, F 338 (bf olpe): Herakles holding a spit vertically over altar; and the Gallatin lekythos, C. H. E. Haspels, *Attic bf lekythoi*, pl. 32 Id (also pl. 33 Ic): Herakles at altar with acolyte and old man.

27. For personal dependence in the Hellenistic period, see H. W. Pleket, "Godsdienstgeschiedenis als mentaliteitsgeschiedenis," *Lampas* 12 (1979), 126–151.

28. The best account is that of J. Rudhardt 1958, 256–265. I exclude the preparation of the altar, the purchase and preparation of the animal, and the filling of the basket containing the barley-grains, the crown(s), the *sphageion* (the dish for collecting the blood), and the knife.

29. M. Detienne, "Il coltello da carne," *Dialoghi di Archeologia*, n.s. 1 (1979), 6–16; J.-L. Durand in Detienne and J.-P. Vernant, *La Cuisine du sacrifice en pays grec* (Paris, 1979), chap. 3.

30. The best examples are the Herakles scenes studied by Hooker (as in note 26): the figures are ideally hieratic and solemn.

31. Rudhardt 1958, 293–295; Durand and Schnapp 1984, 46–66; also G. E. Rizza, "Una nuova pelike a figure rosse e lo 'splanchnoptes' di Styppax," *Annuario della Scuola archeologica di Atene* 37–38, n.s. 21–22 (1959–1960), 321–345.

32. Apart from the Viterbo bf amphora (see note 1), a possible exception is the rf hydria, perhaps from Caere, in the National Museum, Copenhagen (13567) discussed by K. Friis Johansen, *Opuscula Romana* 4 (1962), 71–78, pls. I, III, IV: the *boutupos* swings a double axe at the ready while his assistant holds the *sphageion* and knife; the best illustration is J. M. Hemelrijk, *Caeretan Hydriae* (Mainz, 1984), 1, 29–30, pl. 68.

On gems, the usual representation is the so-called "rural sacrifice," in which one figure, usually old, kills the victim, a kid, piglet, or lamb, in front of a statue of Priapus: e.g., P. Fossing, *Thorvaldsen Museum: Catalogue of the Engraved Gems* (Copenhagen/London, 1929), no. 942, pl. XII.

33. On an Apulian rf bell krater, mid-fourth century, in the British Museum, F 66: Walters, *Catalogue of Vases* 4 (1986), 44 pl. I (face a) = Trendall-Cambitoglou, *RF Vases of Apulia*, 8/18. A few other representations of knives at the ready are listed by Friis Johansen 1962, 76, n. 4, but none concerns the civic sacrifice of bovine quadrupeds, the paradigmatic form.

FIG. 1. Hellenistic votive relief, the "Family sacrifice," second century B.C.E. Munich, Glyptothek

MITHRAISM AND ROMAN SOCIETY:
Social factors in the explanation of religious change in the Roman Empire

For more than a hundred years the problem of religious change has exercised historians of Roman religion. Not infrequently a contrast has been drawn between the wholesome agrarian body of archaic Roman religion and the successive waves of foreign cults, culminating in Christianity, which engulfed it.[1] The preoccupation with the uniquely Roman has diverted attention from two fundamental points: that the religion of any society is not an internally coherent set of rituals and beliefs practised and held by all its members, but rather a loose federation of beliefs only partly expressed in a series of cult institutions.[2] Second, given that a central function of religion is the formulation and inculcation of important integrative values, the means employed must change as the society's internal and external relations alter. The religious change may vary from the relatively trivial, the adoption of a new means of divination, or a variant to a 'charter' myth to extreme attempts to re-create a culture under stress. That a given innovation happens to come from outside a given culture is relatively trivial[3]: it is more significant that an additional cult is being provided so that the religious system as a whole can continue its integrating function.

During the Republic (and indeed afterwards) the aristocracy organized in the Senate maintained detailed supervision of worship by arguing that as a whole the different kinds of divine being promoted the welfare of the entire people, on condition that they received proper treatment. Religious innovation was actually institutionalized by the device of *evocatio* (the bribery of an enemy god to desert his own side) and the practice of referring to a collection of oracles, the Sibylline Books, in a crisis of disconfirmation.[4] The introduction of foreign cults was frequently motivated by aristocratic rivalry.[5] Typically, the new deities introduced with senatorial permission arrived as single gods, or a pair of gods, in the form of an image: in Italy they were worshipped either with their own traditional ritual, often by imported professionals, or with a doctored Roman ritual. But they came without any elaborate priesthood or body of doctrine: if they were not introduced for reasons of state, they provided new technological or therapeutic rituals. They neither offered nor occasioned any change in the unsophisticated 'irrational' traditional theodicy, whereby the individual's significance was determined by the collectivity's needs.[6]

With Polybius, we can feel astonishment at the rapidity of Rome's

conquest of the Mediterranean between 202 and 146 B.C. But both politic-
ally and culturally it was for the aristocracy an ambiguous triumph. Politic-
ally it meant increased competition, with the stakes wildly increased;
culturally, it meant contact with Greece and hellenized Asia Minor, on a
much larger scale than previous contacts with the Greek cities of Italy and
Sicily. For the first time, the Senate found itself unable to control religious
innovation to its own satisfaction. The social changes produced in Italy by
the conquest produced in turn a demand for a new rationale for anomic
events, a demand which Greek religious and philosophical culture seemed
capable of fulfilling. A characteristic development of archaic Greek religiosity
had been the elaboration of a new theodicy which helped to explain such
anomic events by offering compensation in an afterlife; and the cultural
contact stimulated by Alexander the Great's conquests produced a number
of new cults embodying such a theodicy. (At the same time, Stoic and Cynic
philosophy offered a much more nearly rational account of the same problems.) These cults are usually referred to as 'mystery religions'.[7] Some of them
undoubtedly developed out of existing rituals of salvation and of intensifica-
tion, and their secret ceremonies were probably borrowed from rituals of
passage. While many of these cults were invented and maintained by individuals, some, and these the most important in terms of adherents,[8] were
developments of specific cults of Egypt, Asia Minor and Greece. They arrived
in Italy sporadically from the second century B.C. It should be clear therefore that although conceptually[9] they form a single problem, historically
they presented themselves as an insidious addition to existing cult institutions: in only one case, that of the Bacchanals in 186 B.C. and later, was
repressive action violent. Mithraism, that is a cult of Mithras claiming Persian
origin and described as a 'Mystery', was the last such cult to appear in the
West, in the middle of the second century A.D., long after the appearance of
Christianity.[10] At that time, cult buildings and inscriptions appear simultaneously in several different parts of the Empire, in Italy, Northern Gaul,
Germany, Pannonia Superior and Spain (which perhaps presupposes, as
in the case of Christianity, an earlier period without specific cult-buildings.
But as will become clear, the cult building is far more significant in
Mithraism than in Christianity).

It has been well observed that ' "saviour gods" and mysteries
probably did not bulk so large in the life of the first century A.D. as in
modern study'.[11] But this particular form of religious change has attracted
an enormous amount of scholarly attention, mostly because of the supposed
link with Christianity. Generally, the function of the cults has been represented in terms of the individual and his isolation. The situation of the individual is dramatized in order to explain the 'rise' of the mystery cults, of
the growth of belief in Fate, of cult associations. There is discerned a flight
from the world, a failure of nerve caused by the social and political changes
in hellenistic Greece and then in Rome. This approach, reminiscent of the
work of Erich Fromm on the present century, has its origins in the traditional preoccupations of the history of religions school: and it is apparently
responsible for the refusal in a recent discussion of the religious culture of

the period A.D. 160–320 to use inscriptional evidence or deal with 'external forms of worship' on the grounds that 'these seldom tell us much about the underlying personal experience'.[12]

The theory is attractive because of its simplicity. But it remains plausible only when the concept of mystery religion is very highly generalized, when we confine ourselves to the formula that they provided a theodicy which legitimated the existing order by referring it to another plane of existence, and so were able to reduce perceived discontinuities. Yet this kind of generalization will not help to explain the peculiarities of the distribution of each of these cults; nor will it help us to understand their role as 'established sects' (to use a modern analogy). Was the reinterpretation of human life provided by the mystery cults intended as a permanent 'conversion', or was it simply an occasional reassurance? If the first, what measures ensured belief? How do we explain their provision of an alternative theodicy which simply co-existed with the less explicit explanations of the human condition provided by other and more traditional cult institutions patronized by a given individual? What were the social assumptions of mystery cults, and their attitude towards the wider society? Did they tend to be used for more complex purposes than the solution of personal crises? The only way to study the functions of these cults when they cease to be 'deviant' and become routinized is to examine their organization, the relation between this and the belief-system, the relative emphasis upon different parts of the system, the social teaching. Information about their social catchment may then become useful in a way previously unthinkable.[13]

Granted that one possible function of mystery religions was to solve individual problems of identity, a function particularly characteristic of their early history in the East and in Italy, how can the problem of their routinization be approached? One way would be to concentrate on their social catchment, and discuss the relation of local (and Imperial) élites to the cult priesthoods: this is probably the most rewarding approach for the cult of the Magna Mater and Attis.[14] It might also be helpful to discuss the relation between the type of subsidiary cult organizations which were developed, and the various kinds of professional and private corporations (*collegia*) common in towns.[15] But the most rewarding examination is probably of the type of social relation, both towards the god(s) and toward fellow-worshippers, which these religions presupposed. This also raises the Troeltschian question of the interpretation they made of their adherents' social relations generally, their obligations in the outside world, their hostility or assent to external norms. And whether this interpretation is critical or compliant, examination of the relation between the culture of the outside society and the culture of the religious organization is likely to increase our understanding of the latter.[16]

This paper approaches one of the mystery religions, Mithraism, with these questions in mind. No one of these suggestions makes possible a satisfactory interpretation of the relation between the cult and the wider society. They can all make a contribution. The nature of much of the evidence, derived as it is from the assertions of Christian apologists no less than the ambiguous results of frequently inadequate excavation, means that no detailed study of change is possible. One can only hope to draw attention to a few factors so as to outline an 'ideal' cult as it existed between about A.D. 150 and 300 There is no discussion of the reasons for the sudden appearance of the cult in the West in the second century: that is a different problem. I have tried first to characterize the type of social relation, the concept of self and the personal style sanctioned by Mithraism, and then to show to what extent this is confirmed by our impression of the religion's social catchment. The normal relation to the god was strictly formal. This formality is mirrored in the organization of the religious community, which differs in important ways from that found in other mystery cults. The evidence for the social catchment shows that the social experience of what one may call the 'typical' Mithraist was precisely formal, authoritarian, ritualist. Relations in the religious community, both divine and human, were structured in the same way, and with many of the same explicit values. There is no possibility of discussing Mithraism as a response to some form of deprivation: we find simply a confirmation or reiteration of ordinary social experience. This has two implications. On the one hand, the religion sanctions an attitude of acceptance of the outside world, and can thus be seen as an economical agent of social control. On the other hand, the considerable scope for religious leadership offered by Mithraism provided yet another opportunity for the comparatively successful in social groups which had no *a priori* hostility to new cults to display their status and achievements; and the cult's high evaluation of spiritual mobility permitted these men to believe in the propriety of their success. The identification of Mithraism with the main agents of Roman power, the army and the Imperial administration, seems to have prevented its expansion among the civilian population of the Greek East, traditionally indifferent or even hostile to Roman culture; while long-romanized areas of the West with little contact with the army had greater élite stability and required no new symbolic confirmation of success. In so far as the cult constituted a means of social control, especially in complex organizations, it is to be seen as fulfilling a traditional and highly conscious function of Roman religion; and its stringent and determinate social ideal prefigures the social fixity of the Late Empire.

I. First of all, some distinctions must be drawn between Mithraism and other mystery cults found in the West. Mithra was the Iranian god of light, justice and the contract.[17] His cult was one of the last to arrive in the Western part of the Roman Empire from the hellenized East (however much modification it experienced in the West). It has already been observed that innovations in Roman religion, in the third century B.C. and later, tended to be either simple or complex. The latter implied the greater threat to the status quo. Typically, they demanded conversion—though not an exclusive adherence—and special ritual lustration. In return they promised secret religious knowledge, which was sometimes expressed in the notion of 'rebirth'. Initiation was not synonymous with belief in the relevant god(s) in several of these religions, but a further and rather exclusive step.

The main differences between these other mysteries and Mithraism relate
to the mythical role of the central god, to the concept of rebirth, and to the
cult organization or 'church order'.

Other familiar mysteries, for example the cults of Isis, of Cybele (at least
by the second century A.D.), of Demeter at Eleusis,[18] possessed a myth which
described the birth of a god or goddess from the chief female deity, its
subsequent death and some form of revival. This myth was probably
expounded as a paradigm of human life, and plant life too. All the mysteries
of this type presented a theodicy which legitimated the present by offering
compensation in the afterlife, and they were all to some extent ethically
normative, though they apparently lacked adequate sanctions and 'after-
care'. The Mithraic 'charter' myth was very different.[19] The god Mithras,
creator and father of all,[20] struggled with a white cosmic bull, which he
finally overcame and killed. From the bull came all plant-life—especially
that useful to men—and probably also animal life. Mithras was conceived
as creator in so far as his action released creative energy into the cosmos.
No doubt the early versions of the cult in Asia Minor went no further:
Mithras before his introduction into the West was probably simply an
aspect of the sun god associated with the maintenance of fertility.[21] There
was no death of Mithras, no female divinity, no justification for annual
ceremonies retelling and re-enacting the myth. But in the West the killing
of the bull became the means of 'rebirth' and 'salvation' for men, presumably because the giving of life in the beginning was considered an allegory
of the granting of life to sinful men.[22] There were probably no divinities
worshipped by Mithraists superior to Mithras in honour and power, although there was a deity representing the passage of time, and the ordinary
Greek pantheon was somehow integrated into the myth.

The relation between the act of creation and salvation has already been
referred to. This in fact raises a number of important questions. One of these
concerns the difference in Mithraic theodicy. Although there is no good
reason to suppose that the cult was narrowly dualist in the sense that it
believed in the exactly equivalent power of good and evil in the world,[23]
sin seems nevertheless to have been the universal human condition prior
to salvation by Mithras. There were two aspects to this saving. First the
individual must repent, and be purged of sin by baptism[24]: this represents
primary initiation. But it was merely the prelude to a complete structured
religious life. It is here that we find the second significant difference from
other mysteries. Ordinarily, there were two ways of penetrating more
deeply into the different kinds of religious experience offered by these cults.
The less sophisticated offered one or two further initiations—probably
never more—the last of which exhausted their religious content. They might
be offered on successive days or with a minimum interval of a few weeks:
examples might be the Eleusinian mysteries, the cult of the Samothracian
Kabeiroi, the mysteries of Glykon opportunistically invented by Alexander
of Abonoteichos.[25] An example of the alternative is the cult of Isis as
described in Book XI of Apuleius's *Metamorphoses*. Here initiation was
unusual and expensive, a concern only of the deeply committed. Ordinary

worship consisted in semi-public sacrifices and processions conducted by a specialized priesthood and organized religious fraternities. In the former type, initiation is a *communal* experience, in the latter highly private and personal: it followed a long course of instruction, fasting and continence. But it could also be repeated several times at least, the same ritual providing ever-deeper insight into the nature of the deity. But the point remains that repeated initiation was only permitted, it was not a normal means of maintaining commitment.

In effect Mithraism combined these two methods of providing more intense religious experience. Mithraists believed that the human soul descended from heaven either at birth or at some earlier point.[26] But there was an incompatibility between the incorporeal soul and the material body. The central claim of Mithraism was that belief in Mithras permitted the soul to escape from the sublunar world during the lifetime of the individual upon earth. The overt aim of the cult in fact was to permit the soul to rise from the earth, through the seven planetary spheres that ring the earth, until it reached the sphere of Saturn (the highest in Mithraic cosmology). It is quite uncertain what its fate was believed to be thereafter, but presumably (after death?) it eventually reached the sphere of the fixed stars. What is characteristic of Mithraic theodicy is the emphasis placed upon decision between good and evil in this world, and the exemplification of this choice by one's gradual spiritual progress—while yet alive—through the planetary spheres. We have here a significant shift of emphasis from the pattern of simple other-worldly compensation found in other mysteries.

The means by which this ascent was achieved introduces the third main difference. Each Mithraic fraternity or cell was divided into seven grades, and the religious progress of each member of the cell was marked by his grade. Entry into a higher grade demanded special preparation, apparently consisting of self-discipline as well as religious lore, and a fresh initiation with special symbolism to illustrate the duties and nature of the new grade. But each grade was not only a deepening of religious experience, it was also the external sign of the soul's ascent up the planetary ladder. Grades and planets were paired in an ascending sequence: the grade *Raven* with Mercury, *Bridegroom* with Venus, *Soldier* with Mars, *Lion* with Jupiter, *Persian* with the Moon, *Runner in the race of the Sun* (or *Messenger of the Sun*) with the Sun, *Father* with Saturn. Advancement in the cult symbolized on earth, in the holy society, the unseen journey of the soul away from the earth. There is no room in Mithraism for doubt about salvation.

There are two more points to be made about the organization of the cult. The seven grades were justified in a most unusual way in that they were counterparts of the planets: the geography of the cosmos is mirrored in the structure of the cult, which is itself a chart of the members' religious progress. Other mysteries had grades, but they had no claim to be modelled upon the structure of the cosmos—they were not necessary in that sense, they were simply convenient. And although other cults had many officials of different significance[27] they did not claim that there was any connexion between one's religious progress and one's official function as Keyholder,

Basket-carrier or Dooropener: these were in no sense indicators of one's religious virtuosity. Indeed, the very notion of religious progress seems to have been largely unfamiliar to any of these cults apart from Mithraism and Christianity.

The second point concerns the exclusion of women. Although cults which excluded one or other of the sexes were known in the traditional religions of Greece and Rome, they did so as constituents of an entire religious system in which male and female had different but complementary roles in various circumstances.[28] Although some mystery cults took care to segregate the sexes, none is known to have been totally exclusive like Mithraism. But this was no Albigensian rejection of sexuality as such: many Mithraists invoke the god's protection for their families and household, and there are at least 14 cases of one or more sons being associated with their father in the cult.[29] Perhaps the situation was analogous (in this respect) to that in Islam, in which the existence of women is acknowledged, though they are of no religious significance and must be kept firmly subordinate.[30] Perhaps it is also worth remarking that one of the most frequent sacral rules regulating admission to cults was precisely sexual abstinence for a period, so that exclusion of one sex might be seen as an extreme effort to ensure ritual purity; and that there is a curious analogy in the refusal of the Roman army to countenance the legal marriage of soldiers until about A.D. 195, a symbolic expression of the separation of camp and home. The religious life of Mithraism was more closely modelled on the values of the camp than of the domestic hearth.

Although it is necessary to point out various distinctions between the cult of Mithras and other analogous cults, there is an important quality which Mithras shares with other major gods both new and traditional—his ability to assist the believer in everyday life. Mithras was pre-eminently an energetic god. This is demonstrated most clearly by the nature of the votive offerings dedicated to him. These are either items of cult-furniture—the cult-relief with the standard representation of Mithras in the act of killing the cosmic bull, or a statue of one of the other deities[31]—or simple stone altars and plaques. In each case, they normally bear an inscription giving the name of the believer and the god to whom the votive is given. Many explicitly thank the god for something he has done. For example: 'To the Unconquerable God Mithras: L. Pius Paulus gave (this altar) as a gift to fulfil a vow. L. Iustinus Augurius, Father (of the Mithraic community), also called Melitus, officiated at the ceremony'[32]. This implies that Paulus promised the god to spend a certain sum on an altar in Mithras's honour on condition that Mithras helped him in some immediate crisis, or perhaps to achieve some long-term ambition. The god has duly performed his part of the bargain (at least to Paulus's satisfaction), and the inscription is our more or less informative record of this religious transaction. In this respect at least Mithraism shares in the generally instrumental nature of Roman religion with its very highly developed contractual relation to the gods.[33] Other surviving votives actually explain why the votive was undertaken—to escape drowning or some other sudden death, to procure a particular benefit for some relation, or for a master or patron in the case of a slave or freedman.[34] Votives may also be precautionary in that they pay cash down as it were so as to secure future benefits.

The votive offerings therefore are one important indication that Mithras was felt to be a successful and helpful god. They are proofs of his efficacy as well as showing that it was considered part of his function to assist in daily problems. He was no mere object of philosophical speculation. Another confirmation is provided by his direct communication with adherents, either in a dream (or vision)—perhaps interpreted by the Father of the community—or by means of a sign or omen.[35] Direct communication of this sort could solve any kind of human problem. The cult's ethical rigorism was tempered by Mithras's willingness to help his adherents *in persona propria.*

Perhaps the best method of characterizing Mithraism is to draw attention to some of its main themes, which can be divided into pairs for analysis. The first dual theme is that of Good and Evil. Although the standard Western epithets for Mithras, 'invincible', 'holy', do not make specific mention of his goodness or of his justice,[36] yet his creation of life in the world, his saving of sinful men, the cult's persistent emphasis upon light and brightness, the specific symbolism of fire, water and honey, all these help to define Mithras's moral character.[37] The evidence does not permit a definite statement of the nature of the opposition between Good and Evil in Mithraic thought, nor of the manner in which it came about that the soul's prime duty was to evacuate the world which Mithras created; nor do we know whether Evil was conceived as a personal entity or as merely the consequence of human choice. But the struggle of the Mithraist against evil for the release of his soul was carefully structured. Initiation into each grade included ritual purification, whose precise form was related to the supposed nature of the new grade: for instance, because the grade Lion (the fourth) was identified with Jupiter, the planet whose Greek name was Phaethon, it was reasonable to invest the grade with fire symbolism. It is associated with the colour red, with the sacred shovel used in the burning of sacrifices and other offerings, and with Jupiter's thunderbolt.[38] According to Tertullian, the grade was considered 'as a symbol of the dry and fiery principle in Nature'.[39] This symbolism was taken quite literally, for when it came to finding an apt means of cleansing would-be Lions, it was obvious that water (presumably the ordinary method) would be incompatible with their fiery nature. The only suitable substance, being analogous to water as a liquid and as a pure substance, but yet not water, was honey. And this was therefore used.[40] But because the lion and the fire are both destructive, the symbolic nature of the grade Lion suggested its function within the economy of the Mithraic community-special responsibility for sinfulness within the group. This seems to be the significance of the opaque sentence painted on the wall of the Mithraeum beneath the Church of Santa Prisca on the Aventine in Rome: '*Accipe thuricremos pater, accipe sancte Leones,/per quos thuradamus, per quos consumimur ipsi*' which seems to mean 'Father/receive those who burn incense, holy one receive the Lions, through whom we offer incense, by whom we ourselves are consumed'.[41]

The idea that each grade was specially responsible for some area of concern, and therefore, by implication, specially antagonistic to the relevant manifestation of evil, is supported by Porphyry's observation that the spreading of honey over members of the grade Persian was done not because they were connected with fire but because they protected natural produce (plants and fruit): the honey is a symbol of their quality as protectors.[42] Thus the manifestation of evil (in this case sterility) with which the Mithraist is particularly concerned, is closely related to his position within the community and so to his spiritual progress: the struggle is proportionate to one's presumed strength. So although our detailed knowledge of the Mithraic imagery of evil is very small, it is possible to see how the conflict was articulated in this crucial matter of escape from the world.

The existence of evil in the world necessitated struggle to escape its power. This theme, which more generally one may call that of energy, can be set against the theme of wisdom. Mithras is an energetic god, active, unconquerable, unsurpassable. Only by heroic labour is he able to overcome the bull and thereby institute his saving relationship to mankind. He is brilliant and youthful, readily intervening in favour of his adherents. In imitation, Mithraists were required to keep themselves continuously from wrongdoing,[43] to strive against evil and so mount the rungs of the planetary ladder. This is no short-term religious commitment, but, at least in principle, a life-long journey. In its grade-structure Mithraism provided, alone of the 'oriental religions', the institutional support for such a commitment. Yet energy alone was insufficient. One also required understanding of secret wisdom[44]; without that, the significance of each grade was unintelligible and the entire effort to no purpose. The attainment of wisdom was an object of particular ambition in fact. Although the details of this lore escape us, it must have comprised an account of Mithras's achievements, perhaps newly allegorized for each grade; an account of the human condition and the urgency of escape in the spirit; and a mass of symbols and correspondences of the kind already mentioned in relation to the grades Lion and Persian. It would be false to suppose that because all this sounds uninspiring to the unbelieving modern, there must have been other spectacular revelations.[45] If the mumbo-jumbo of a foreign cult is not terrifying because devilish, it is likely to be simply pathetic. Having declared its hand (Mithras' saving action) in order to stimulate conversion, Mithraism, like mainstream Christianity, had only the religious life to offer, the slow gathering of true wisdom.

Both learning and effort were indispensable to advancement in the cult. It is certain that many adherents never reached the highest grades (though we do not know whether that presented an eschatological problem), but for those who did the rewards were considerable. This brings us to the last pair of themes, power and escape. Power is not used here to refer to specifically religious power. So far as we know, there were no 'holy men' in Mithraism, which was a closed, secret and retiring religion—hardly the field for personal miraculous feats. Every Mithraic cell was a small face-to-face organization, in which relations of authority were clearly defined and sanctioned by religious belief. The Father (or the senior Father in some cases) was by virtue of his grade the wisest, most ascetic, most free from sin, least earth-bound of the cell's membership.[46] He therefore had the moral right to exercise authority—a convenient use of the circular argument. The symbols associated with the grade Father express this authority quite strikingly: we find the staff, the ring, Mithras' 'phrygian cap' and Saturn's sickle, all found in other contexts to express the idea of rule, depicted in the Mithraeum *di Felicissimo* at Ostia[47]; and in Rome itself (Santa Prisca) the Father is shown sitting on a throne to receive homage from representatives of the other grades.[48]

From the Father's point of view, all the initiates were equally subordinate to his authority. This is one of the implications of the term 'brothers' occasionally employed to describe a group of Mithraists.[49] The Father decided whom to admit to the cult, supervised many of the rituals including the dedication of votive-offerings, was responsible with some assistance for all initiations and grade promotions. In fact he was the outstanding figure in each cell.[50] The counterpart of his authority is the grade system, which established the social and religious identity (within the cult) of every member, prescribed his ritual behaviour, and set limits upon his access to complete purity and full knowledge. Each step up the planetary ladder required commitment, special preparation, symbolic withdrawal (asceticism and suffering) and a new purification. Promotion was desirable but difficult. There is little room here for a personal religious style: behaviour and sentiment is prescribed, not a matter of free invention. Glossolalia, ecstatic trance, prophetic utterance, anything that differentiates the individual from his grade equals or superiors but cannot be controlled by them—all this is excluded. Though Mithras might appear to an initiate in a vision, the significance of the vision apparently had to be interpreted by the Father: at any rate there is no evidence that a vision might be made the sanction for behavioural unorthodoxy.[51] Social constraints in Mithraism were tightly drawn—and the social constraints are the social expression, the organizational expression, of the religious ideal. The Mithraist of the sacred paintings is young, strong, unbearded, the image of social conformity, not of marginality. He accepted a slow, methodical, long-term commitment, for which the religious organization is designed to provide continuous support, so as to ensure his spiritual promotion. And promotion was achieved only by acceptance of and submission to authority.

For some, therefore, Mithraism was closely concerned with the issue of power (and so of coercion).[52] Yet attainment of power in the community involved by its very nature escape from the constraints of the world: the gratification of Fatherhood lay in the success of the flight as much as in the domination of his religious subordinates. The theme of escape is important for two reasons. It confirms what has just been said about Mithraic religious style: this is no Aristean soul-journey concerned with geophysical irregularity and botanical rarity[53], but a serious, indeed desperate, undertaking. But there is also a quaint literalism about escape in Mithraism: it permitted a kind of denial of death. If the body is corporeal and material, then it is merely a hindrance to the soul's ascent; and once the soul has escaped from the world then there can be no great interest in the fate of the body. It is no coincidence that Mithraism has no funerary symbolism, no statues of the dead, no gravestones. There are no Mithraic sarcophagi, no pious hopes for immortality.[54] The only two funerary inscriptions which certainly concern Mithraists are more impressed with the fact that they were priests (Fathers) than with their eschatological hopes.[55]

II. The emphasis in Mithraism upon escape from the world naturally raises the question of how far the cult is comparable to a sect in Christianity, and whether the standard explanation of alienation or some form of deprivation is relevant here.[56] In some respects, Mithraism certainly reminds one of a Christian sect in a pluralistic society: it was a minority movement, secluded from the rest of society, with distinctive teaching and aims; it possessed a distinctive ethic; the leaders were unprofessional; its claim to authenticity lay in its 'historical' origins in the teachings of Zoroaster, who as a Magus could vouch for all beliefs and practices. But there are several reasons for rejecting such a comparison. First, a polytheistic society generally has a far more lax attitude towards religious innovation than a Christian one—there is no need for the typically self-conscious and defensive attitude of the sect, because there is no concept of exclusive revelation. The intermittent opposition towards exotic cults shown by the Senate in the late Republic and early Empire has more to do with their being unroman and uncontrolled than with their doctrines or beliefs. The secrecy of Mithraism was not forced upon it by the disapproval of the wider society. Secondly, Mithraism was not exclusive in the sense that it demanded prior rejection of other traditional gods—on the contrary they were an important part of the belief-system. Nor was it totalitarian by seeking to organize as many aspects as possible of the lives of adherents. Third, some of the motifs usually held to characterize a sect are in this case simply evidence of the difference between modern and Roman culture: it was rather unusual to find professional priests in the Roman Empire except in those provinces in which a hieratic form of society had existed before the arrival of the Romans.[57] Ordinarily a priesthood was a temporary part-time office whose function was as much to confirm or claim social status as to serve the god.[58] More significantly, Mithraism's emphasis upon escape was a theme pursued increasingly not only in religion but in philosophy: the revival of Platonism in the first, and particularly the second, century A.D. is very relevant to the detailed form of Mithraic escape. But the most important argument against the classification of Mithraism as a sect is its entire cast and intention. Although some modern sects, for instance Christian Science, are conformist and accept the values of the wider society, characteristically they are also 'instrumentalist'—they offer a way of succeeding in terms which the world will recognize.[59] Mithraism is not overtly instrumentalist—at least in principle—but it is equally far from being totally 'mystic-religious'. The cult demanded a readiness in all its members, of whatever social rank, to be dignified, restrained, morally righteous; to submit to the authority of superior grades, but especially that of the Father; to approve of such authority as rational and necessary, justified by superior wisdom, commitment and experience. The stringency and definiteness of this social ideal is paralleled by the Mithraic urgency to define the unknown, to chart the soul's journey and its dangers, to remove the element of risk that inheres for instance in all Christian notions of salvation except that of sects like the Free Spirit.[60] Mithraism was indeed a 'mystery', but its social ideal is precisely that of the wider society, just as its narrowly religious ideal is parallel to an important contemporary religious and philosophical aim. But it is possible to be more specific than this, and to suggest that Mithraism was to be found typically in circles which even by the standards of the Empire were particularly authoritarian and status-conscious, and that as a consequence the theory of deprivation must be replaced by a theory of replication.[61]

Our only evidence for the social catchment of Mithraism between A.D. 150 and 300 is the votive inscriptions. As a means of analysis they are clearly quite inadequate either for a synchronic or diachronic description. But they do have some uses. One is that by their mere physical distribution they show that Mithraism was to be found primarily in Italy (31 per cent of known dedicators, 18 per cent in Rome itself) and in the Rhine-Danube frontier provinces (49 per cent of known dedicators). And except in areas with very few inscriptions of any kind, particularly Syria and Egypt where the stone is lacking, this is a reasonable indication of relative significance. The second point is that although very little can be made of the comparatively (in terms of their probable proportion of the population) small number of private slaves, the almost total absence of Senators, Equestrians (except a few in military posts)[62] and decurions (outside the Danube area)[63] does require explanation, simply because for these groups the expense of erecting inscriptions was comparatively insignificant, and anyway constituted one dimension of their social pre-eminence. Again, the fact that 81 of the 210 (38 per cent) of dedicators whose status in the outside world is known were soldiers of the rank of centurion or below[64], must be compared with the much smaller numbers of soldiers recorded as members of other mystery cults with the exception of the Syrian cult of Jupiter Optimus Maximus Dolichenus which had a distinctly military cast.[65] Although we can have no real idea of the relative proportions of Mithraists who were soldiers (and their relatives?) to others in the frontier areas, the mere existence of so many dedications means that any discussion of the social catchment of Mithraism must begin with the army.[66] The dedications also imply that members of the Imperial administrative service and private slaves were important in the cult's membership, both in the northern provinces and in Italy.[67]

In the most tentative terms, it can hardly be coincidental that Mithraists were often legionary soldiers, Imperial slaves and private slaves. In each of these situations submission to authority and acceptance of a particular role in an organization, whether the army, administration or private household, were at a premium. At the same time, promotion was possible in each case: the condition of submissiveness was tempered by the hope of advancement for those found suitable. (Of course it is precisely this possibility which confirms the excellence of authority and stabilizes the organization.) Each of these considerations is important in discussing the role of Mithraism here. Essentially the argument that follows is that the symbolic or 'cultural' and social structures of Mithraism replicate the basic symbolic and social structures of all these organizations (but particularly of the army), and that the type of social experience constructed by Mithraists by order of the god is the replica of their 'ordinary' social experience, but without the irrationalities and contradictions of that experience. That they choose such replication rather than a more effervescent religious style, or a more manipulationist one, implies acceptance of their 'ordinary' experience in spite of its difficulties.[68] In effect, Mithraism can be seen as a fairly sophisticated contribution to the maintenance of social control, one element in the apparatus of normative controls open to such organizations. What is interesting about its role here is that it was never part of official cult practice[69] either in the public organizations or in private households[70] but was maintained by the intermediate members of the hierarchy. In the case of private households, the typical leader seems to have been the freedman.[71]

III. 'Organizations have only limited control over the powers they apply and the involvement of lower participants. The exercise of power depends on the resources the organization can recruit and the licence it is allowed in utilizing them.'[72] This familiar modern problem was rather unfamiliar in antiquity: the army and the Imperial administration were virtually the only large-scale organizations of the Roman Empire. Their nearest parallels were not industrial organizations but the private households of the wealthy, although these were incomparably smaller in scale. These two organizations therefore posed particular problems of control for the Emperor and the Senators and Equestrians who found themselves from time to time involved with them. The solutions they found fall into the same categories, coercive, utilitarian and normative, as those employed today. In the case of the army, there was a considerable body of rationalized experience which purported to show how control should be maintained. Much of this experience took the form of anecdotes from the glorious military past, chiefly of the Republican expansion. Its more sober expression is represented for us chiefly in a handbook, the *Epitome Rei Militaris* by Flavius Vegetius Renatus. Although this was actually composed in the late fourth century A.D. for the instruction of the Emperor, much of its content dates from an earlier period, especially the second century A.D.[73] In any case, what is of interest in this connexion is not so much the detailed institutional arrangements as Vegetius' constant emphasis upon the psychology of troops, military values, the difficulty of troop control and management. One can trace this concern as far back as the Elder Cato's manual early in the second century B.C.

Vegetius assumes throughout that what soldiers feel and think, not only

before battle but also in ordinary life in peacetime[74], is of the first importance. He continually stresses the danger of mutiny (that is the total collapse
of all the available means of compliance) and suggests a number of ways to
prevent it.[75] Essentially, the advice is that battles are won not by glorious
indiscipline but by training: 'In every battle it is not so much superiority
of numbers and plain guts as skill and practice that wins the victory.'[76]
That involved hard physical exercise and arms drill; it also, at the normative
level, implied emphasis upon, even veneration of, the virtue of discipline.[77]
A constituent of discipline was obedience[78], symbolically reinforced by the
military oath to the emperor: 'The soldiers swear to do all that they are
called upon to do by the Emperor to the best of their ability; never to
desert the colours; never to refuse to meet death for the Roman State.'[79]
The consequence of disobedience is brutal punishment: one of the commander's desirable qualities is 'severitas', sternness.[80] The finely tuned
system of allowances, in money and kind, according to grade, as well as the
opportunity for financial exploitation of subordinates, illustrates the role
of utilitarian coercion.

But it is normative control which is of most importance here, although
naturally in practice the three types are inextricably linked. This complex
of values sketched above is the ideological instrument by means of which
Vegetius expects control of the army to be maintained. It does not need
to be remarked that the Roman army in reality frequently mutinied, sometimes fled before the enemy, was often slovenly and drunk: indeed, to judge
from the Roman historians, was exceedingly badly behaved. But it is no
less clear that these values were in fact constantly reiterated in the army,
that they provided the ideals against which to judge achievement, that
they formed the stuff of pre-battle harangues and the rhetoric of the parade-
ground.[81] As an element of social control, they must be taken seriously.

A rather similar value-system is observable in the Imperial administrative service, but as it were, *sotto voce*. Physical strength was not important
here, but obedience, diligence, training and moral excellence have their
place.[82] Unfortunately we possess nothing like Vegetius for the administrative service and such evidence as there is has to be rather overworked.
But there exist one or two testimonials for Imperial freedmen and others
which describe them as hardworking and careful, obedient and familiar
with their duties. Loyalty, modesty, honesty and impartiality are also
offered as reasons for official approval of such men.[83] Again, although there
is not much reason to suppose that the bureaucracy was actually imbued
with such virtues (any more than other pre-industrial bureaucracies) as
elements of the official value system they afforded reasons for promotion
(at least at the verbal level, given the role of patronage), and so ensured
a measure of control. It is no surprise to find honesty and diligence the
most regarded virtues, loss of revenue and duplication of work being the
administrative service's chief headaches.

Although the private household cannot compare in complexity with
these organizations, it presented quite similar problems of control on a
smaller scale: most dramatically, the slaves of a household could protect

their master—or murder him. Pliny's tense phrase, 'All of a sudden there were his slaves ringing him . . .' catches that permanent fear very well.[84] Of course, slaves did not often kill their masters: but the law tried to compel a man's slaves to protect him by enforcing the death penalty upon the entire household in the event of the master's murder by a slave.[85] Fear of one's own household was only part of a more general fear, of course (perhaps a little faded in the Empire) of slave revolt, which might itself merge into 'social' banditry. Gladiators were indeed a dangerous luxury. In this sense, slavery constituted a permanent threat to order in the ancient world.[86] But it did not need murder and revolt to remind the Romans that slaves were an ambiguous form of labour and that coercive and utilitarian forms of control were in themselves inadequate: the slave has so many ways of making life disagreeable.[87] So a predictable set of ideas appeared, to persuade the slave to love his servitude, quite apart from the (far-off) promise of freedom. Of this complex, loyalty is the most important, the subject of a mass of edifying tales. But honesty, bravery, a sense of duty, co-operation, identification with the interests of the master, all these are stressed in the literature.[88] The extent to which such virtues would be expected of a given individual would obviously depend on his function in the household and its various centres of authority: the potential variation here is very large. Again this is an 'official' ideology—indeed most familiar to us from philosophical writings—but it represents a necessary modification of the naked coercive relation, necessary even in Larcius Macedo's household.

To some extent these three sets of values are specific to the purpose of the three different organizations, but they share an emphasis upon commitment, subordination to legitimate authority and formality. Conformity to them enabled the individual to make himself acceptable to his superiors and so to adjust more positively to the situation in which he found himself. From the point of view of the organization, these values constitute an attempt to increase control over their subordinate members without increasing investment in, say, cash or overseers—they help to cut down unit costs as it were.

The values promoted by Mithraism as necessary to the religious life, as a means of making oneself acceptable to Mithras, were closely parallel to the values noted in these three types of organization. This we may call the 'cultural' parallelism between the religion and the society from which many of its adherents came. Values that have considerable functional importance in the maintenance of control in large-scale organizations are here applied to very small face-to-face groups: the point is that they are incongruous in relation to the real problem of the maintenance of control in such groups. Although they are particularly close to the specifically military values, there is no reason to argue that Mithraism was in some sense peculiarly 'military'. Perseverance or endurance, as in Mithras so in the initiate, is implied by a phrase painted on the wall of the Santa Prisca Mithraeum, 'And I have borne upon my shoulders the commands of the gods, to their fulfilment'; training and discipline by the concept of a special struggle by each grade against a particular evil; self-denial by the story in Tertullian of the initiate's refusal of a crown.[89] Fair-dealing, truthfulness and honesty are presupposed by the general demand that Mithraists should be just in their dealings, and by the highly developed sense of sin, both in word and deed.[90] Above all, there is obedience, both to the god and to the hierarchy. Many dedications record that they were prompted by the god's own intervention: failure to obey would be unerringly punished.[91] The Father's religious authority has been noted above.[92]

There are also some other less important parallels to be found. Just as the army permitted a man time to find his feet, Mithraism had a probationary period.[93] Army and cult demanded the swearing of an oath of admission, to emphasize the gulf that separated the new life from the old.[94] The corporate unity of army, administration and slave *familia* were all stressed, underlining the significance of the collectivity over the individual: likewise, Mithraic groups expressed their communal feeling. One mystical name for themselves was 'those linked by the handshake'; as a group, they were 'jointly bound by the oath'.[95] Sacred robes and the entire secret ritual of course served to maintain this social boundary.

The organizational parallels scarcely need to be pointed out. They concern not only the way in which the organizations, both secular and religious, are stratified so as to create a variety of quite closely determined grades whose purpose is to define the individual's prescribed functions, duties and rights; but also the emphasis upon improving one's position within the organization. Here a contrast can be drawn between the secular and the religious organizations. In 'real' life it was the sheer contradictoriness and brutality of one's lot that prompted the desire for escape—which only meant the opportunity to exploit one's subordinates in the same way that one had been exploited oneself, whereas in the religious organization promotion had quite a different rationale. And it not only had a rationale, but the process of promotion was dependent only upon one's application and devotion: commitment was rewarded in a direct manner most uncharacteristic of the 'real' world. The brutality and drudgery of the private's life, expressed most dramatically in the periodic mutinies[96], produced a quite general desire for promotion into some higher rank which afforded escape from permitted and illegal impositions by various superiors.[97] Since this desire on the part of the soldiers coincided with a desire on the part of senior officers for patronage (promotion seems to have been based entirely on patronage), we find a gradually increasing number of intermediate ranks whose virtue—it cannot have been efficiency—was surely the partial refuge they afforded from the full weight of arbitrary imposition. The nature of the work of the Imperial administrative service was less arduous, but the profits from seniority seem to have been considerable: ingenuity in the invention of forms of peculation was no doubt a matter of quiet pride.[98] In the case of Imperial slaves, the hope of freedom (which has been shown to have been a condition for the more senior jobs[99]) must also have been important. Although private households had no such elaborately formal structure, from comparative evidence it is clear that a complex pecking order, responsive to different sources of authority, existed, and promotion consisted in transfer to 'superior' tasks and access to the ear of the departmental boss—a partly informal system in fact.[100] Again, the financial rewards from plum jobs, such as door-keeper and chamberlain, could be very considerable. But the main point to be made about each of these types of organization is that, in spite of the existence of a set of values which could be invoked on the occasion of promotion, there might be very little real justification for such invocation: it might well be simply a decent rationalisation of a quite different process of selection. The man who conscientiously trained himself in the military virtues proclaimed by Vegetius might still find himself a private after his 20 years if he had no influential father, no cash and no taste for sycophancy. The informal system of patronage thus conflicted with the overt value system. Because in Mithraism the ambition of escaping from the world depended more upon commitment to the god and his commands than upon the whim of the Father (even though as a human system it involved relations of authority and prestige) the religion represented a much more rational system than the 'real' world organization.

Mithraism can then be seen as divine replication of 'ordinary' social experience: the fundamental constraint of the social ideal was the point at which religion and life intersected. To this extent the religion can also be seen as a confirmation of such a social ideal, and so as an element in the apparatus of normative control. But to have adopted the cult (which always remained secret and attractive only to a minority) officially would have been to destroy this function of the cult: it could never then have confirmed the 'real' world from outside nor provided a reconciliation for those disaffected or disappointed but not to the point of mutiny or outright opposition.[101] Instead the cult was permitted to exist alongside the traditional religious practices of the army and the household, which, while containing explicit sanctions against opposition, had neither the ideological nor the organizational effectiveness of Mithraism in this respect.

It is easy to understand that Mithraism's acceptance, indeed reinforcement, of hierarchy and authority should have acted as a theodicy of good fortune, in the sense of a religious explanation of good fortune. This function must be seen as the corollary of its function of social control in these same organizations. 'The fortunate is seldom satisfied with the fact of his being fortunate. Beyond this he needs to know that he has a right to his good fortune. He wants to be convinced that he "deserves" it, and above all, that he deserves it in comparison with others. He wishes to be allowed the belief that the less fortunate also merely experiences his due.'[102] It is impossible to generalize about the extent to which centurions in the army tended to dominate the higher ranks of Mithraism in the northern provinces, because we know the social status of only one or two Fathers in these areas: the number of grade references known here is insignificant in comparison with those known in Italy (19 against 66), though the proportion of Fathers to other grades recorded is very similar (84 per cent against 80 per cent). But as far as the evidence of the inscriptions goes for military membership alone, we know that 18 (22 per cent) were centurions, 35 (44 per cent) occupied one of the many ranks between that of junior centurion and private, and only 28 (35 per cent) (including men of whom we only know that they were retired) privates. This must be set beside the general consideration that wealth and social significance in the outside world were not devoid of value in the religious world. A good deal of nonsense has been talked about the egalitarian functions of the cult, as though the status differences of the outside world were simply forgotten in the religious context. That is surely no more true of Mithraism than of early Christianity.[103] The idea of an ordinary private soldier lording it over his, or any centurion, is absurd: it would have meant an enduring reversal of proper social relations impossible not only (but particularly) in the army but in the society of the Empire more generally. If we make allowance for the odd charismatic figure, we may assume that the social status of the senior Father provided a rough index of the social composition of a community. (It is clear that in general, centurions were particularly committed to the maintenance of the system which they had learned to operate: in mutinies they frequently alone opposed the rioting soldiers just as they were usually the main target of their men's hatred.[104])

As Ostia, the port of Rome, and in Rome itself, it is possible to be a little more precise about Mithraism's role as a theodicy of good fortune; 15 Mithraea have been found in the area of Ostia already excavated. Their foundations date from about A.D. 150 to about 260. Three of the four earliest were constructed in existing buildings, none in private houses. Although one or two Ostian Mithraists of the second and early-third centuries were at least minor worthies of the town, 16 of the 32 names known from the inscriptions are Greek; 11 of these 16 were Roman citizens, either freedmen or descendants of freedmen, and there is some reason to suppose that 3 of the 15 Latin names belonged to freedmen; 9 of the 20 men known to have been Roman citizens are expressly mentioned as Fathers or priests, against 2 of the 12 others. The impression given by these figures is that the men most likely to hold high office in the cult in Ostia, as well as the most lavish donors, were freedmen, or their descendants. In Rome this predominance is rather less marked: of the 81 names certainly associated with the cult, only 33 are Greek. Of these 19 were citizens according to the explicit evidence of their names. But only 5 of these were certainly freedmen, together with 3 with Latin names. Only 2 certain Fathers admit to being freedmen. But since possession of a Greek *cognomen* is *prima facie* evidence of origin in the Eastern part of the Empire, even if at some remove[105], it is still reasonable to associate devotion to Mithraism with a consciousness of achieved status, just as the excessively large representation of freedmen and Greek names in funerary inscriptions of the first two centuries A.D. may point in the same direction.[106]

But Mithraism was not able to perform a similar function for the governing élite, either at the local level or in the Senatorial and Equestrian orders. Each of these was committed to the maintenance of the traditional cults which had for so long preserved the Roman state and their own cities. J. Beaujeu has remarked on the very slight attraction of mystery religions for the known members of the Senate in the second century A.D., as opposed to the cultus of individual new gods in the familiar Roman manner.[107] The two partial exceptions to this generalization in the case of Mithraism are significant. The first concerns the decurions and *Augustales* (who together constituted local city élites) known to have been Mithraists. Twenty-two of these are known, 18 of them from the 'military' provinces; 16 of these 18 are from the Danubian provinces, generally the least urbanized and Romanized of the Empire, and in which it was common for veterans and serving soldiers to be appointed to local town councils—the town itself generally owing its existence to an original Roman fort or camp.[108] Although only one such case is known for certain, it is likely that these men's knowledge of Mithraism was owed directly or indirectly to the presence of the army.[109] The existence of the cult naturally presupposes the possibility of becoming familiar with it.

The second exception is the group of senior officers, almost all of Equestrian rank, in command of army units on the frontier and elsewhere and who made dedications to Mithras during their tenure.[110] It is probable that such men first came into contact with the religion when they arrived to command a unit in which the religion was already known, but then realized its possible contribution to the maintenance of discipline. Very few of them seem to have been more committed than this: there is certainly no reason to think that the slow penetration of Mithraism into upper-class circles in Rome, which we see an accomplished fact in the fourth-century pagan reaction against Christianity, was derived from this military familiarity: for the most part that was a self-conscious piece of opportunism.[111]

There were rather two factors which contributed to Mithraism's assimilation into what the fourth century regarded as traditional Roman religion. There is first the interest of many educated men in secret learning from the East, from Egypt, India, Babylonia, Israel, Persia, which seems to have become increasingly fashionable in the second and third centuries A.D.[112] In the case of Persia no distinction was made between various beliefs associated with the Magi, which circulated in Greek under the names of Zoroaster and Ostanes, and properly Mithraic beliefs: Porphyry in the third century, for instance, uses such material indiscriminately.[113] Mithraism was of interest in this connexion because it preached a unique cosmology with the authority of the Magi, as was supposed, at a time of quite general interest in such arcane matters.[114] It could thus appear intellectually respectable even to philosophers. The second factor is that as pagan members of the Roman aristocracy sought support for their opposition to Christianity— which was really only a symbol of the monstrous and distressing change in their own fortunes and prestige—they sought to redefine the traditional religion which both pagan sceptics and Christian apologists found so easy to mock. One way of doing this was to show that polytheism was really a kind of monotheism; another was to improve existing mystery religions to demonstrate their similarity to Christianity—the way had already been pointed out by Christian apologists.[115] Mithras thus joined Isis, the Magna Mater, Hecate, Demeter and Liber Pater in this factitious revival. But it is significant that virtually all of the 16 fourth-century Senators known to have been Mithraists were senior Fathers, just as they held the chief positions in the other cults: perhaps it is no coincidence that these men were as much interested in maintaining their position over against the itinerant Imperial court and its current favourites as in mere religious traditionalism.[116]

In spite of its Persian origins, Mithraism thus became utterly Roman, a mainstay of the old order.[117] But this was only the culmination of a long development, which is of interest in two ways. It has always been puzzling that a religion which apparently owed so much to Asia Minor should have left so few traces in its homeland.[118] But this could be explained if the cult had been largely developed in the West as an amalgam of items from several sources (together of course with much original invention) and so was only known, in a developed form, in the East as a proselytized *Roman* religion, Roman in the sense that it was imported by Westerners, generally on Imperial business. It scarcely needs to be pointed out that no Roman cult had much success in the East. Roman religion was virtually non-exportable here, except for the Imperial cult, largely because of the combination of cultural contempt and political distaste which the East tended to feel towards Rome, however much local aristocracies might admire and cooperate.[119] Mithraism seems to have succeeded here usually where things Roman were an ordinary part of life, in the army especially. Even so, the evidence is limited to Dura-Europos (whose cult-buildings seem to be borrowed from the Danube style) and a handful of other sites.[120]

Dura raises the second point. All the men immediately responsible for the first Mithraeum were officers of the local gendarmerie raised to police the caravan routes. Unless the foundation of this Mithraeum in A.D. 168 is mere coincidence, it is tempting to suppose that knowledge of the developed cult had reached Dura at the time of Lucius Verus's Parthian expedition of 162–6, when troops from the Rhine and Danube legions were employed.[121] The proximity of Dura to Parthia (it had been occupied by the Parthians before Verus's expedition) provided the material for the odd changes and idiosyncrasies we find there, such as the use of *Magus*.[122] Knowledge of Mithraism in Dura was probably an element of the military culture of Rome: it was part of their experience of Romanization, of cooperation with the Imperial power. A similar consideration applies to the native provincials in the West who became Mithraists. The religion was one of many elements of Roman culture, which they accepted because of its social importance in the military environment in which they lived. In the provinces in which the military was not important, native provincials (never numerous in the inscriptions[123]) disappear almost entirely. Because the religion was not a characteristic part of Roman culture in these areas (most of Gaul, Spain, North Africa and Italy) there was neither point nor institutional support for adherence to Mithraism. Where Roman culture had become familiar before the rise of Mithraism, and where local élites had little connexion with the army, we do not find the cult.

In the northern provinces, therefore, Mithraism seems to have played a role as mediator of Roman values. One can apply that point to the army also, faced as it was with a continuous problem of acculturation. As recruitment became more exclusively provincial, symbols such as the bestowal of a Roman name, the insistence upon Latin as the *lingua franca* of legions and auxiliary units, became more and more important. The role of the official army cults in this attempt has been pointed out by the editors of the military religious calendar found at Dura.[124] Once the correspondence between the values and social assumptions of Mithraism with those of the army have been pointed out, as well as the role of officers of junior grades, it becomes much less plausible to see Mithraism with Ramsay MacMullen as evidence of the barbarization of the army, alongside the introduction of foreign units into the army without even the pretence of Roman organization.[125] This view is based on a misunderstanding of the origins of Mithraism, and ignores totally its intellectual content. More important, it fails to appreciate the role of the religion as a confirmation of the social structure of the army, and as a partial resolution of its contradictions. The encouragement of Mithraism by senior officers (even if they were not themselves members) implies a conscious realization of this point.

IV. We can now return to the general problem of routinization. The crucial point is the complexity of Mithraism and its effort to maintain the adherence of the convert. It was able to perform different functions for men in several different social situations, and of course its functions changed over time. It obtained commitment by focusing on the individual's choice between good and evil. The institutions of the cult maintained and deepened this commitment. But the religion was always world-affirming rather than world-denying. The world is not evil itself: it had been made by Mithras and saved by his action. The rejection of the world implied by the ascent of the planetary ladder was not violent: the position was more like that of Plotinus, the third-century Neoplatonist. He rejected the gnostic position that escape is made imperative because of the total and necessary corruption of this world: for Plotinus, the existence of the One is the imperative which demands ecstatic philosophical union—the emphasis is upon the understanding, not upon the escape.[126] On the other hand, no doubt the ambiguity of the Mithraic position did permit different views about the importance of escape. Historically and analytically, the primary role of Mithraism in complex organizations was its externalization of values central to the maintenance of control, and its sanction of them. Its provision of a parallel but rational social system, the opportunities provided for religious leadership and conspicuous religious expenditure by the comparatively successful, its contribution to acculturation in the army, slave households and among provincials, its intellectual possibilities for the pagan reaction, are some of the relations later established between cult and society.

The point does not need to be laboured any further. To highlight the narrowly 'religious' elements in Mithraism does not get us very far. 'Mithraism' is of course not only a system of teaching about a god and the experience of the individual soul, but an organization, a social teaching, a cultural system that not only explains experience but patterns it. It is this aspect of

113

the cult which transforms it from a mere series of 'mystery ideas' into a meaningful personal choice. While the arguments over the details of myth, origins and cultus must continue, we must be clear about what they cannot help us to do. Perhaps the concept of routinization offers a way of reformulating the problems concerning the mystery cults in the Roman Empire. Until that is done, we will have to go on believing in the *'mutation psychologique'*[127] which suitably paved the way for the adoption of Christianity.

NOTES

I would like to thank Professors M. I. Finley and A. Momigliano for helpful criticism of my work.

1. This attitude is particularly marked in the early literature: L. Krahner, *Grundlinien zur Geschichte der Verfalls der Römische Staatsreligion bis auf die Zeit des August*: Gymnasium-Programm Halle, 1837; W. Ward Fowler, *The Roman Festivals*, London, 1908, pp. 341–4; id. *The Religious Experience of the Roman people*, London, 1911, p. 342; G. Wissowa, *Religion und Kultus der Römer*, ed. 2, Munich, 1912, pp. 60–102. But a form of it is still apparent in two good recent histories, K. Latte, *Römische Religionsgeschichte*, Munich, 1960, pp. 25–35, 251–93, 327–59; J. Bayet, *Histoire politique et psychologique de la Religion romaine*, ed. 2, Paris, 1969, pp. 144–68.

2. A. F. C. Wallace, *Religion—an Anthropological View*, New York, 1966, pp. 52–96, esp. 78.

3. Though R. Horton, 'A Definition of Religion and its Uses', *Journal of the Royal Anthropological Institute*, 90, 1960, pp. 201–26, points out on pp. 215–7 that the precise borrowings made by one culture from among the mass of material known and available outside can be useful for an estimate of the nature of the problems perceived by the borrowers.

4. Cf. V. Basanoff, *Evocatio*, Paris, 1947; W. Hoffmann, *Wandel und Herkunft der Sibyllinischen Bücher in Rom*, Diss. Leipzig, 1933.

5. The best example is perhaps the introduction of the Magna Mater into Rome in 204 B.C.: cf. Th. Köves, 'Zum Empfang der Magna Mater in Rom', *Historia* 12, 1963, pp. 321–47 (esp. Part I). More generally, J. North, *The Interrelation of State Religion and Politics in Roman Public Life from the end of the second Punic War* . . . (D.Phil. Oxford, 1968, unpubl.).

6. P. L. Berger, *The Social Reality of Religion*, London, 1969, pp. 53–80 extends the fundamental discussion of theodicy by M. Weber, *The Sociology of Religion* (trans. Fischoff), London, 1966, pp. 138–50. For the terms, Wallace, op. cit., pp. 108–26.

7. R. Pettazzoni, *I Misteri*, Bologna, 1924, and A. D. Nock, *Conversion*, Oxford, 1933, are in their quite different ways probably the best synthetic works on classical and later mystery cults.

8. The notion of adherence to these cults ranges from occasional participation in public festivals to repeated initiation at considerable personal expense. The oriental mystery cults were a novel creation on the basis of old cults made possible only by cultural contact with Greeks: C. Schneider, 'Die grieschischen Grundlagen der hellenistischen Religionsgeschichte', *Archiv für Religionswissenschaft*, 36, 1939, pp. 300 ff.

9. But the continuing attempt to impose a common form and intention upon the bizarre variety of these cults gains unity at the expense of truth.

10. There is no adequate evidence to support the frequently repeated opinion given authority by F. Cumont, *Textes et Monuments relatifs aux Mystères de Mithra I*, Brussels, 1899, pp. 243–5, that the cult of Mithra reached Rome during the late Republic. Although there are a handful of inscriptions which are to be dated between about A.D. 90 and 130, they do not compel belief in Mithraic *mysteries* at this date.

11. A. D. Nock, *Early Gentile Christianity and its Hellenistic Background*, Harper Torchbook ed., New York 1964 (but first published in *Essays on the Trinity and the Incarnation*, ed. A. E. J. Rawlinson, London, 1928), p. 29.

12. E. R. Dodds, *Pagan and Christian in an Age of Anxiety*, Cambridge, 1968, pp. 2–3. For a critique of Fromm and his methods, J. A. C. Brown, *Freud and the Post-Freudians*, Harmsworth, 1961, pp. 145–160.

13. The work of E. Troeltsch on the Social Teaching of Early Christianity has inspired a good deal of work in this sense upon Christianity. It is curious that this tradition has scarcely touched work on the mystery cults, which have been dominated by a narrower concern with the 'history of religions'.

14. J. Toutain, *Les Cultes paiens dans l'Empire reomain* II, Paris, 1911, pp. 105 ff.; S. Gsell, 'Autel romain de Zana', *Comptes Rendus de l'Academie . . . des Inscriptions*, 1931, pp. 251–69; R. Duthoy, *Taurobolium*, Leiden, 1969, pp. 92–101. G. S. R. Thomas of the University of Tübingen is preparing a full study of this type.

15. On the lines of D. Fishwick, 'Hastiferi', *Journal of Roman Studies*, LVII, 1967, pp. 142–60.

16. Roland Robertson, *The Sociological Interpretation of Religion*, London, 1970, chap. 6.

17. Mithra (Miθρō, nominative) is the Avestan form; Mithras or Mithres the Latin and Greek forms. On Mithra in Iran, see I. Gershevitch, *The Avestan Hymn to Mithra*, Cambridge, 1959; F. B. J. Kuiper, 'Remarks on the Avestan Hymn to Mithra', *Indo-Iranian Journal*, 5, 1961–2, pp. 36–60; M. Boyce, 'On Mithra's Part in Zoroastrianism', *Bulletin of the School of Oriental and African Studies*, 32, 1969, pp. 10–34.

18. P. de Grandmaison, 'Dieux morts et ressuscités', *Revue Scientifique de Religion*, 17, 1927, pp. 97–136; G. Bertram, s.v. 'Auferstehung', *Reallexicon für Antike und Christentum* I, 1950, pp. 919–30 are typical. But it is clear that this belief was by no means necessary to the vague concept 'mystery': P. Lambrechts, 'Over Griekse en Oosterse Mysteriegodsdiensten: de zgn. Adonismysteries': *Mededelingen van de konink. Vlaamse Akad. voor Wetenschappen, Letteren en Schone Kunst van België; Kl. Lettere*, XVI.1, 1954.

19. This point was made by Nock, 'The Genius of Mithraism', *Journal of Roman Studies*, XXVII, 1937, pp. 108–13, which is perhaps the best short characterization of the cult. Cf. id., *Cambridge Ancient History*, XII, pp. 429–30.

20. As creator, Porphyry, *De Antro Nympharum* 6: he is also described as Demiurge of the cosmos there (the precise formulation is presumably due to Neoplatonic influence). In Neoplatonism 'demiurge' is not necessarily a subordinate divinity. Mithras is occasionally associated with Zeus in invocations, which also implies sovereignty.

21. One of Mithras's commonest cult titles is *'Deus Sol Invictus Mithras'*; both *Sol Invictus* (Unconquered Sun) and *Invictus (Deus) Mithras* appear separately in the cult. Sol Invictus is also the cult-title of several Syrian high gods. The theme of the sun as creator of life (in some sense) is as old as Anaxagoras: Diels-Kranz, *Fragmente der Vorsokratiker* II (ed. 5), 15A117, p. 32. cf. R. M. Jones, 'Posidonius and Solar Eschatology', *Classical Philology*, 27, 1932, pp. 116 ff. who criticizes F. Cumont, *'La Théologie solaire du Paganisme Romaine'*, Mémoires présentés par divers Savants . . XII.2, 1913, pp. 447–79. The possibility of an earlier pre-mystery cult of Mithras is mentioned by Nock, *Early Gentile Christianity*, p. 29.

22. The only explicit mention of salvation in Mithraism appears in a fragment of a cult-hymn (?) painted on the wall of the Santa Prisca Mithraeum in Rome: *'et nos servasti eternali sanguine fuso'*: 'and you have saved us by shedding the undying blood': of course the *'eternali'* may be proleptic. See now C. C. van Essen and M. J. Vermaseren: *The Excavations in the Mithraeum of Santa Prisca*, Leiden, 1965, pp. 217–21 (which goes too far).

23. As Sasanian Zoroastrianism came to do: R. C. Zaehner, *Zurvan, A Zoroastrian Dilemma*, Oxford, 1955, pp. 7–53 (without commitment to his general thesis however). The existence of five dedications to Areimanios in Western Mithraism does not of course prove that this deity was conceptually or functionally the Ahriman of Zoroastrianism as Cumont thought (e.g. in *Les Religions Orientales dans le Paganisme romain* [ed. 4], Paris, 1929, pp. 141–4).

24. Himerius, *Or.* XLI.1 (but cf. 8). Tertullian supposed that lustration should imply repentance in *De Praescr.Haer.* 40.3 (which does not refer to Mithraism however); cf. *De Baptismo* 5. Porphyry (*De Antr.Nymph.* 15) also presupposes some sort of repentance.

25. Eleusis: P. Roussel, 'Initiation préalable et le symbole éleusinien', *Bulletin de Corres-pondance Hellenique*, 54, 1930, pp. 51–74; Kabeiroi: B. Hemberg, *Die Kabiren*, Uppsala, 1950, pp. 116–20; Glykon: Lucian, *Alexander-pseudomantis*, 38–9; cf. Nock, *Classical Quarterly*, 22, 1928, pp. 160–2; O. Weinreich, 'Alexandros der Lugen-prophet und seiner Stellung in der Religiosität des II Jahrhdts.n.Chr.', *Neue Jahrbücher für Kl.Altertum, Geschichte und Deutsche Literatur*, 24, 47, 1921, pp. 129–151, esp. pp. 147–8.

26. Origen, *Contra Celsum* VI.22; Porphyry, *De Ant.Nymph.* 6. cf. Nonnus Mythographus, *Comment. in Greg.Orationem contra Iulianum* I.6 (=Migne, *Patrol.Graeca* XXXVI. p. 989). Porphyry's statements in *De Abstinenta* IV.16 about metempsychosis are not reliable, and there is no evidence for Cumont's assertions in *Textes et Monuments*, I, pp. 38–41, 309–10. For the development of views on the soul in the Empire, see Cumont, *Afterlife in Roman Paganism*, New Haven, 1922 and *Lux Perpetua*, Paris, 1949, pp. 157–88, 343–84.

27. The most extreme case is perhaps that of the Dionysiac group from Torrenova: F. Cumont-A. Vogliano, *American Journal of Archaeology*, 37, 1939, pp. 213–70, which boasted about 20 different offices; the Isiac groups at Delos had a bewildering variety of officials: cf. L. Vidman, *Sylloge inscriptionum religionis Isiacae*, Berlin, 1968, index of officials, some at least derived from customary temple organization in Egypt.

28. L. R. Farnell, 'Sociological hypotheses concerning the position of women in ancient religion', *Archiv für Religionswissenschaft*, 7, 1904, pp. 70–94.

29. The formula for protection of one's family is '*pro se et suis*'. For sons, see M. J. Vermaseren, *Corpus inscriptionum . . . religionis mithriacae* (*CIMRM*), The Hague, 1956–60, nos. 473–4, 510, 526, 715, 730, 863, 911, 1009, 1165, 1434, 1524, 1728, 1766 (and possibly 313, 518, 687, 1717). 2007 asks protection for wife and son.

30. R. Levy, *The Social Structure of Islam* (ed. 2), Cambridge, 1965, pp. 91–134. This attitude reaches its perfect absurdity in the comment by Farîd al-Dîn 'Attâr quoted on p. 132, on female sainthood: . . . 'a woman on the path of God becomes a man, she cannot be called a woman'. Little, *The Mende of Sierra Leone* (ed. 2), London, 1967, pp. 169–70, suggested that one motive for the popularity of Islam among chiefs and other wealthy people in Mende society is the extra control it affords over polygynous households given to adultery.

31. We possess dedications to Cautes and Cautopates, Mithras' two acolytes, to the Sun, to Areimanius, to Mercury, Hercules, Oceanus, Caelus, a few local fertility goddesses and in the fourth century to Hecate. Statues of all of these have been found (with the possible exception of Areimanius).

32. *CIMRM* 413 (assuming that Melitus is a *signum*: but we may have a parallel to *CIMRM* 527, in which case Melitus would be Augurius' assistant).

33. Public cult: Wissowa, *RuK*², pp. 381–5; Latte *RRG* pp. 46–7; private: A. de Marchi, *Il Culto Privato di Roma antica*, Milan, 1896–1903, I. pp. 271 ff. The Maya had a similar emphasis: J. E. S. Thompson, *Maya History and Religion*, Oklahoma, 1970, pp. 170–2.

34. Drowning: *CIMRM* 568 (but probably not Mithraic); unspecified: 658, 691; for blessings on the whole Mithraic community.: ?1017, 1783, ?1787, 1788; for a master 747, ?2173; for Caesar by an Imperial slave or freedman: ?626, 754, 1438, ?1476, 1529, ?1659, 1661; for a patron by a freedman: 407, 1408, 1428, 1760, 1778, 1936–7, 2011, 2150; 333(1) may be added if it is genuine; for an owner by his *vicarius*: 1533, 1588?, 2029. In *CIMRM* 275 a master and slave join together in a votive.

35. Vision: 214, ?502, 527, 704, 1385, 1490, 1497, ?1710, 1778, 1805, 2030, perhaps 2075 and 2143. A probably non-visual command: 213, 423, 497, 1013, 1063=5, 1455, ?1970; 1229 and 1251 are indeterminable. On this mode of communication, Nock, 'Studies in the Graeco-Roman Beliefs of the Empire', *Journal of Hellenic Studies*, 45, 1925, pp. 95–8. He stresses that this implies a deeper sense of the superiority of the gods: but it surely also implies that the gods are just as available to human need as ever. The frequency of such visitations seems to me to contrast rather sharply with E. R. Dodds' description (op. cit., chap. 1) of the devaluation of the

cosmos in the early Christian centuries and the accompanying withdrawal of divinity from the world. We must distinguish the philosophical model of reality from the assumptions upon which relations with the gods both in public and private were ordinarily based.

36. *CIMRM* 18, from Tyana in Cappadocia 'To the just God Mithras', probably owes its formulation to the important Anatolian cult of the Sun's justice (cf. I. W. MacPherson, *Annual of the British School at Athens*, 49, 1954, p. 12, no. 2; L. Robert, *Anatolia*, 3, 1958, pp. 114–5) rather than to a genuine Mazdean sentiment: Cumont only used the inscription opportunistically as evidence for the West (*TMM* I p. 308 n. 7). On the Iranian link between Mithra and Avštāt, Gershevitch, op. cit., pp. 286 ff.

37. Cumont, *TMM* I p. 308, uses doubtful evidence to demonstrate the goodness of Mithras in the West.

38. Red: some of the Lions in the procession at Santa Prisca have red cloaks (van Essen and Vermaseren, *Excavations*, p. 156)—though it is also found with the highest grades (ibid.) and once with the lowest (p. 169). Fire-shovel: G. Becatti, *I Mitrei di Ostia*, Rome, 1954, pp. 109–10. Cf. the figure in the Mitreo degli Animali (ibid. *Tav.* XVII) and at Santa Prisca (*Excavations*, p. 156 no. 4, pl. LX). An actual example is known from Carrawburgh: I. A. Richmond and M. Gillam, *Archaeologia Aeliana*[4], 29, 1951, pp. 84, 87. Thunderbolt: this is the third symbol of the grade in the Mitreo di Felicissimo: Becatti op. cit., pp. 109–10. Brightness is another symbol: the grade is called *habros* at Dura (*Report of the Eighth and Ninth Seasons*, New Haven, 1937, no. 856, p. 120) one of whose meanings is 'shining' or 'bright'—exactly the association of Phaethon.

39. *Adv.Marcionem* 1.13.4: written about 207 according to the usual estimate. Cf. T. D. Barnes, *Tertullian*, Oxford, 1971, p. 47.

40. Porphyry, *De Antro Nymph*. 15.

41. *Excavations*, pp. 224–32, esp. 226–7. There is a graffito at Dura which may refer to the same belief, since it runs, 'fiery wind, ?holy lustration for the Magi also' (*Dura Report*, p. 126–7 no. 865; but note the reading of W. Vollgraff, *Meded.Kon. Nederl. Akad.Wetenskapen*, 18/8, 1955, p. 127).

42. Porphyry, ibid. This is confirmed by the grade symbol in di Felicissimo, a *harpe* or sickle, which is not the symbol of the hero Perseus.

43. This is shown by the insistence upon 'dikaiopraxia', 'righteous dealing' in ordinary life (Justin Martyr, *Dial.cum Tryph*. 70.1) and by the repeated lustrations: Porph. *De Antro*. 15: 'When they pour honey instead of water into the hands of those being initiated as Lions (as a lustration), they bid (the initiates) keep their hands pure from every thing evil, harmful and baneful . . . they also purify their tongues with honey to purge them of everything sinful'. One may perhaps add the word used at Dura of the grade Soldier—'akeraios', 'pure' or 'blameless' (*Dura Report* no. 857).

44. As is clear from the insistence of (Ambrosiaster) *Quaest.vet.nov.Test*. 114 upon the profound folly and ignorance of those '*qui se sapientes appellant*'. The claim that Mithraism was founded by Zoroaster, the archmagus, implies the same concern for wisdom (Porph. *De Abstin*. IV. 16; *De Antr*. 6). Note too Origen, *Contra Celsum* I.12: 'What I have said about the Egyptian wise men and common people can also be seen in the case of the Persians; among them there are mysteries which are explained rationally by the learned among them, but which are taken in their external significance by rather superficial minds and by the common people among them. The same may be said of the Syrians and Indians, and of all who have both myths and interpretative writings' (trans. Chadwick).

45. I imagine that the belief that the taurobolium was practised in Mithraism, and that there was a doctrine of final conflagration and judgment of the dead, stems from this passion for excitement. My point is well made by Lucius in Apuleius, *Metamorphoses* XI: everything is seen from his point of view—he is totally absorbed: yet nothing spectacular occurred. Cf. V. W. Turner, *The Ritual Process*, London, 1969, pp. 20–37; A. van Gennep, *The Rites of Passage*, 1908=Eng. trans. London, 1960, pp. 79 f.

46. Cf. the use of superlatives with this grade: *CIMRM* 423 '*dignissimus*'; 1821 '*pientissimus*'. I have the impression that the superlative is often used in association with bishops in the Christian inscriptions in Asia Minor.
47. Staff: the 'magi' at Dura also hold staffs (*Report*, pp. 110–11); on its significance, de Waele, *RE²*, III, 1929, cols. 1901–4. The ring is generally considered to be a sacrificial dish cf. Marshall, *RE A*1, 1914, pp. 833–41. The 'phrygian cap' is in fact an emblem of royalty and divinity: J. H. Young, 'Commagenian Tiaras, Royal and Divine', *American Journal of Archaeology*, 68, 1964, pp. 29 ff.; sickle: M. Leglay, *Saturne Africain; Histoire*, Paris, 1960, pp. 142–6.
48. *Excavations*, p. 169; power is also in the hands of the next grade, Heliodromus, who has an orb, and wears a radiate crown in some representations.
49. Cumont, *TMM*, I, p. 318 and *Mystères de Mithra* (ed. 3), Brussels, 1913, pp. 159, 201 exaggerates the frequency of this: *CIMRM* 1267 is the only probable example. The usage is common to many cult associations and corporations.
50. Father as intermediary: *CIMRM* 377, 647. There are some purely honorary inscriptions for Fathers: 54, 67, 225, 235, 911. In 23 cases the Father is mentioned *honoris causa* but also as a kind of dating.
51. For the functions of glossolalia: V. H. Hines, 'Pentecostal glossolalia: towards a functional interpretation': *Journal for the Scientific Study of Religion*, 8, 1969, pp. 211–26 cf. P. Ennis, 'Ecstasy and everyday life', ibid. 6, 1967, pp. 40–8.
52. The rewards presumably spilled over into 'secular' life too as they did for the Christian Polycarp: Eusebius, *Hist. Eccl.* IV.15.30.
53. J. D. P. Bolton, *Aristeas of Proconnesus*, Oxford, 1962, pp. 142–75.
54. This is in striking contrast to most other mysteries in the Imperial period. The odd graves found near the Mithraea at Saalburg, Gross Krotzenburg and Stockstadt I in Germany are by no means certainly to be associated with the cult; and if they could be shown to be, that would only reiterate the point.
55. *CIMRM* 511 (which is also for his wife and household); 708 (also for wife). 730 is a dedication to Mithras '*ob memor(iam) patris sui ex colleg(a)*'.
56. C. Y. Glock, 'The role of deprivation in the origin and evolution of religious groups', in R. Lee and M. E. Marty (eds), *Religion and Society in Tension*, Chicago, 1964, pp. 245–56. Mary Douglas, *Natural Symbols*, London, 1970, pp. 5–6 has recently criticized this model, though her own solution is too ambitious. My discussion is indebted to B. Wilson, *Sects and Society*, London, 1964, pp. 326 ff. (which I do not think has been improved on).
57. A full study of types of priesthoods (and of religious leadership) is badly required for the classical world. But see W. G. A. Otto, *Priester und Tempel in hellenistischen Ägypten*, 2 vols, Leipzig–Berlin, 1905–08; M. I. Rostovtzeff, *Social and Economic History of the Hellenistic World*, Oxford, 1941, I, pp. 503–7 etc.; J. and L. Robert, *La Carie*, II, Paris, 1954, pp. 294 ff.
58. P. Stengel, *Die griechische Kultusaltertümer*, (ed. 3), Munich, 1920, pp. 31–48.
59. B. Wilson, op. cit., pp. 331ff, 347–50. For the term 'mystic-religious', J. Jackson and R. Jobling, 'Towards an Analysis of Contemporary Cults', in *A Sociological Yearbook of Religion in Britain*, I, London, 1968, ed. D. Martin, pp. 94–105 on pp. 97–8. A similar polarity is suggested more generally by R. Horton, art. cit.
60. N. Cohn, *The Pursuit of the Millennium*, (ed. 2), London, 1970, pp. 146 ff. and Appendix; H. Grundmann, '*La mistica tedesca nei suoi riflessi popolari: il beghinismo*': *Storia del Medioevo*, Vol. II of Proceedings of the Tenth International Congress of Historical Sciences, Florence, 1955, pp. 467–84.
61. For the term replication, Mary Douglas, op. cit., pp. 81 ff.
62. The Equestrians were members of the second rank within the Roman system of estates, dependent directly upon the Emperor (and senatorial patronage) for employment within the higher ranks of the military and civil administration. At all times a proportion of Equites did not enter imperial service: the sense in which the rank can be said to be hereditary is disputed.
63. Decurions formed the third estate (they were included in the category of legally privileged under the criminal law), and were usually members of local landed

families who administered the internal government of cities which had been granted a measure of autonomy. The minimum wealth qualification was often one quarter of that for the Equites, and from early in the Empire they were responsible for ensuring the delivery of taxes to the administration.

64. The Roman army was rather differently organized from modern ones. The important point is that centurions were not the equivalent of modern N.C.O.s, but were the senior permanent officers of the legion (though some of their superiors, of equestrian rank, did follow military careers): Septimius Severus (193–209) made them eligible for Equestrian rank on retirement. They were minutely organized in order of seniority, and had large opportunities for amassing wealth.

65. J. Toutain, *Cultes paiens* (op. cit.) II, pp. 25–7 (which does not support his pp. 22–3), 103–111; P. Merlat, *Essai sur le Culte de Jupiter Dolichenus*, Paris, 1960, pp. 10 ff.

66. One cannot simply assume with C. H. Moore, 'The distribution of the oriental cults in the Gauls and Germanies', *Transactions of the American Philological Association* 38, 1907, pp. 142–3, that all those who do not mention their social status are not soldiers; nor can one be so certain that 'a large majority of the devotees of Mithras (in these provinces) were civilians', ibid., p. 195.

67. 29% of Mithraists whose status is known (46 men) in the Northern and Eastern provinces were slaves or freedmen of the Emperor or of private individuals. This is the second largest group of the same status. The figure rises to 68% (35 men) of the much smaller total of known statuses in the 'civilian' provinces (Italy, Spain, Gaul).

68. There were cults—admitted into the official list—which did permit a temporary, 'therapeutic', inversion of ordinary discipline in the army. The Saturnalia is well known, but the Rosaliae signorum seems to have had a similar role: A. S. Hoey, 'Rosaliae Signorum', *Harvard Theological Review*, 30, 1937, pp. 15–35.

69. A. S. Hoey, 'Official Policy towards Oriental Cults in the Roman Army': pp. *T. A. Ph. A.* 70, 1939, pp. 456–81, esp. pp. 458 f., 468 f.

70. Although the construction of Mithraea in large private houses (the earliest in Rome is S. Clemente, at the end of the second century) implies recognition by owners of the value of the cult: but it does not seem to permit the inference that the owners themselves were initiates, of which there is no evidence until the mid-third century.

71. See below p. 109. It is important to remember that freedmen might still play an important part in their patron's household.

72. A. Etzioni, *A Comparative Analysis of Complex Organizations*, New York, 1961, p. 13.

73. Cf. D. Schenk, *Flavius Vegetius Renatus: Die Quellen der Epitome Rei militaris*, Klio Beiheft 22, Leipzig, 1930, pp. 8 ff., 26 ff. (whose conclusions have been corrected slightly by later work).

74. Vegetius does not distinguish the two problems, though they do deserve quite different treatment: Etzioni, op. cit., pp. 56 ff.

75. Veget. I.7; II.9; III.4; 9–12; it was also a commonplace among historians, e.g. Tacitus, *Histories* IV.26; Pliny, *Letters* VIII.14.7. The modern literature on this subject is extraordinarily meagre.

76. Veget. I. title; I.1; 8; 9; III praef. Cf. Tacitus, *Annals* XIII.35–6.

77. Veget. I.8; 13; 28; II.3; 12; 18, etc.; Frontinus, *Strategems* 4.1.1; 15; 23; Josephus, *Jewish War* III.5.7. Typical encomia of discipline: Valerius Maximus, *Epitome* II.7 praef. (and *passim*); Livy 45.37; I praef. 9–12 and see R. W. Davies, 'Fronto, Hadrian and the Roman Army', *Latomus*, 27, 1968, pp. 75–95.

78. Veget. II.9; 19; III.4–6; Cassius Dio, *Histories* 41.33.2–4; Tacitus, *Ann.* XV.17; *Hist.* I.83.2; 84.1–2.

79. Veget. II.5. For other versions see R. Watson, *The Roman Soldier*, London, 1969, pp. 144–50; J. F. Gilliam on Dura Pap. Inv. 9: *Yale Classical Studies*, XI, 1950, p. 233.

80. Veget. II.9; I.23; III.4; 10. Cf. Cassius Dio, 41.29.3. For(ideal?) military punishments, Polybius, *Histories*, VI.37–8.

81. For example: Hadrian's speeches at Lambaesis, *C.I.L.* VIII.2532+18042 etc. (*C.I.L.* VIII index p. 404 s.v. 18042); *C.I.L.* XVI. no. 17 line 5 (not a formula); Pap. Yale 1528=*Sammelbuch* V.8247 lines 20 ff.; *P. Mich.* VIII. 468 col. II.35–8; Pliny, *Letters* VI.31.4–6; Tacitus, *Hist.* I.84, 2; II.21.4; 82.1; III.3.1; 27.3 etc.

These values were undoubtedly assimilated to some extent. Etzioni (p. 57) remarks that such purely normative means to compliance are more likely to be successful before battle than in peacetime, when coercive and utilitarian methods become necessary.

82. See generally, M. Weber, Bureaucracy (in *From Max Weber*, ed. H. H. Gerth and C. W. Mills, London, 1949), p. 198—which is applicable to ancient bureaucracies too in spite of their tendency towards irrationalism.

83. The material is very scattered, but see H-G. Pflaum, *Les Procurateurs équestres sous le Haut-Empire romain*, Paris, 1950, pp. 197–208 (mostly on equestrian administrative virtues though); and C. W. Keyes in *American Journal of Philology*, 56, 1935, pp. 21 ff.

84. Pliny, *Epistles*, III.14.4 (Larcius Macedo). Cf. Plutarch, *Life of Cato Maior* 5.

85. *Digest* 29.5.19 (Modestinus)—notice that self-sacrifice even was demanded: '*obiectu corporis*'. Under the Empire (by the SC Silanianum of A.D. 10 and an SC Claudianum of A.D. 57: Tac. *Ann.* XIII 32.1) the Republican rule was made more severe. Pedanius Secundus (Tac. *Ann.* XIV.42–4) is only the best known case.

86. Cf. M. Capozza, *Movimenti servili nel mondo Romano in età repubblicana* I, Rome, 1966, on 501–148 B.C. (much of the material is merely exemplary of course: a good example of historical mythology); J. Vogt, 'Zur Struktur der antiken Sklavenkriege', pp. 20–60 of his *Sklaverei und Humanität*: Historia Einzelschrift, 8, 1965, (with reservations); R. MacMullen, *Enemies of the Roman Order*, Cambridge, Mass., 1966, Appendix B, pp. 255–68. The bandit Bulla is said to have attracted imperial slaves (presumably engaged in agriculture) in his career in Italy, *c.* A.D. 205–7: Cassius Dio, 76.10.5 (Boissevain).

87. As has been observed for the Southern States: Raymond and Alice Bauer, 'Day to Day Resistance to Slavery', *Journal of Negro History*, 27, 1942, pp. 401 ff.

88. The important texts are: Valerius Maximus, *Epitome* VI.8; Macrobius, *Saturnalia* I.11.16–46; Seneca, *De Beneficiis* III.17–28: though Epictetus for example has much material. Cf. J. Vogt, 'Sklaventreue', ibid. pp. 83–96. One function of Christianity was to reinforce these values: H. Gülzow, *Christentum und Sklaverei*, Bonn, 1969, pp. 57 ff., 101 ff.

89. The dipinto: *Excavations*, pp. 204–5; cf. line 7 (pp. 200–2); crown: Tertullian, *De Corona* 15.

90. See note 43 above.

91. There is no direct evidence of this in Mithraism, but note the well-known case of Zoilus of Aspendus (*Pap. Soc. Ital.* IV (1917) 435=A. Longo, *Aretalogie*, Genova, 1969, no. 62, p. 103), and the many Galatian inscriptions mentioning punishment by a local sun-god: M.A.M.A. IV nos. 279–82 for example (1933). R. Pettazzoni, 'Confession of sins in the Classics', *Harvard Theological Review*, 30, 1937, pp. 1–14 at pp. 3–4.

92. See above pp. 15–16.

93. Vegetius I.7; Tertullian, *De Corona* 15.4.

94. Note 79; Tertullian, ibid. Naturally this can be seen as an essential step in the process of separation from the outside world and commitment to the 'enclosed' one: van Gennep, op. cit., pp. 84 ff.

95. 'Syndexi': Firmicus Maternus, *De Errore Profanarum Religionum* 5.2; *CIMRM* 423; and several times at Dura, *CIMRM* 54, 60, 65. Cf. Tacitus, *Hist.* I.51.1. 'Consecranei', 'consacrati': *CIMRM* 876; cf. Firm. Mat. ibid. 'Syndexi' seems to be a term confined to Mithraism.

96. There is no general discussion in the modern literature, but note, for the Republic, W. S. Messer, 'Mutiny in the Roman Army: The Republic', *Classical Philology*, 15, 1920, pp. 158–75, which is quite unsophisticated; and the thesis of P. A. Brunt, 'The Army and the Land in the Roman Revolution', *Journal of Roman Studies*, lii, 1962, pp. 69–86. Concern under the Empire seems to be confined to the army as Kingmaker, which is peripheral to this subject.

97. A good example is *Pap. Mich.* VIII (1951) p. 465 (A.D. 107, Apollinaris at Bostra) lines 14 ff.: 'I thank Sarapis and Good Fortune that while all the others are worn out breaking stones all day, I sit around doing nothing as a Principalis'. Cf. ibid. 466,

lines 18–24; *Pap. Lund.* II.i.5; and the remark of Tacitus about Aufidienus Rufus, *'vetus operis ac laboris et eo inmitior quia toleraverat'* (*Annals* I.20).

98. It is noticeable that the group of Mithraic slaves and freedmen from the imperial administrative service gave more lavishly to the god (in terms of cult furniture) than any other group.

99. P. R. C. Weaver, in *Proceedings of the Cambridge Philological Society*, NS 10, 1964, pp. 74–92.

100. Compare J. J. Hecht, *The Domestic Servant Class in 18th century England*, London, 1956, pp. 35–70, 177–99.

101. The religion both externalizes the organizational values (makes them more explicit) and justifies disappointment by (i) referring to a higher plane of meaning, (ii) offering a parallel but rational social system.

102. Max Weber, 'The Social Psychology of the World Religions', in *From Max Weber* (op. cit.) p. 271.

103. H. Kreissig, 'Zur sozialen Zusammensetzung der frühchristl. Gemeinden im ersten Jhdt.' *Eirene*, 6, 1967, pp. 91–100; E. A. Judge, *Social Pattern of the Christian Groups in the first Century*, London, 1960, pp. 49–61.

104. Loyalty in mutiny: Tacitus, *Hist.* III.31.1–2; 54.3; IV.59; I.56.1; 59.1; 80.2; II.19.1–2; 60.1; *Annals* II.81.2; Plutarch, *Otho* 3.5 for example. A new Emperor might review their appointments: Tac. *Hist.* III.8.3; 44. As a target for hatred: Tac. *Ann.* I.20, 27, 32, though a centurion like Sirpicus might be protected: ibid. 23.

105. H. Thylander, *Etude sur l'Epigraphie latine*, Lund, 1952, pp. 134–85; I. Kajanto, 'The Significance of Non-Latin Cognomina', *Latomus*, 27, 1968, pp. 517–34.

106. L. R. Taylor, 'Freedmen and Freeborn in the Epitaphs of Imperial Rome', *American Journal of Philology*, 82, 1961, pp. 113–32.

107. J. Beaujeu, 'La Religion de la Classe sénatoriale à l'Epoque des Antonins', *Hommages à Jean Bayet*, Collection Latomus 70, Brussels, 1964, pp. 54–75.

108. T. Nagy, 'Quelques aspects de la Romanisation dans la Pannonie orientale', VIII Congrès international d'Archéologie classique, Paris, 1965, pp. 375–81; A. Mócsy, *Gesellschaft und Romanisation in der Provinz Moesia Superior*, Amsterdam–Budapest 1970; id.s.v. Pannonia, *RE* Suppl. IX, 1962, cols. 596–610; soldiers on town councils: R. MacMullen, *Soldier and Civilian in the Later Roman Empire*, Cambridge, Mass., 1962, pp. 103–9.

109. *CIMRM* 2222; 11 of the 16 relevant inscriptions are from towns in which there was a legionary garrison.

110. There are only three men of senatorial rank known to have made dedications to Mithras before A.D. 300, all between 180 and 220 and all in the army or closely connected with it. (There are one or two others who dedicate to Sol Invictus however.) The numbers of Equestrians for any one province are hardly significant except in Britain where there are nine known: two acting legionary commanders (Africa and Pannonia); two men in charge of isolated auxiliary units (Africa and Dacia); two or three men second-in-command of such units (Syria, Mauretania, Germany) and a commander of legionary vexillations probably in A.D. 264–5 (Pannonia). All these are early- and mid-third century.

111. This goes against the standard view, which is that these men were important carriers of the cult: it is worth remarking that except for two of the commanders of forts in Britain, not one of these wealthy men says that he provided the least piece of cult furniture (which contrasts with the fourth century position).

112. Again, this development has received virtually no specific treatment by modern scholars, except in the excesses of men such as H. H. Schaeder, J. Bidez, F. Cumont, R. Reitzenstein, whose primary intentions were rather different.

113. *De Abstinentia* IV.16 (using Euboulus); similarly Origen, *Contra Celsum* I.12; VI.21–2 etc. This was partly of course because the western Mithraists claimed that their religion was founded by Zoroaster (Porph. *De Antro* 6).

114. Nock, *The Genius of Mithraism* (art. cit.) pp. 110–11.

115. M. H. Shepherd, 'The Early Apologists and Christian Worship', *Journal of Religion*, 18, 1938, pp. 60–79; more work needs to be done on the changes introduced by the

pagan reaction into the mystery cults: see A. D. Nock, *Sallustius, Concerning the Gods and the Universe*, Cambridge, 1924, pp. cii–iii.

116. See for example, A. Alföldi, *A Conflict of Ideas in the Late Roman Empire*, Oxford, 1952.

117. It is worth noting Diocletian's fulminations against Manichaeism as a filthy new religion in *Mos. et Rom. Leg. Collatio* XV.3.2–3 (= FIRA II², p. 580). Diocletian and his co-emperors made a dedication to Mithras at Carnuntum in Pannonia Superior in about 307 (after Diocletian's retirement in fact), which is evidence of the strength of the cult there (though this is only one of a long series of dedications by these emperors to the sun): *CIMRM* 1698.

118. 'Erstaunlich gering' as M. P. Nilsson, *Geschichte der Griechische Religionn* II, ed. 2, Munich, 1961, p. 670 remarks. Both F. Cumont, 'Mithra en Asie Mineure', *Studies for W. H. Buckler*, Manchester, 1939, pp. 65–75, and E. Will, *Le Relief Cultuel Greco-Romain*, Paris, 1955, pp. 144–69 argued from the iconography and from Plutarch *Life of Pompey* 24 that the absence of remains was simply coincidental. Different solutions have been offered by F. Saxl, *Mithras: Typengeschichtliche Untersuchungen*, Berlin, 1931—influence of Greek art and ideas; Nock, art. cit.—creation by a single man on the basis of Greco-Iranian speculation; S. Wikander, 'Etudes sur les mystères de Mithra': *Årsbok vetenskaps Soc. i Lund* 1950, 1951, pp. 5–46—not really Iranian at all, but perhaps Balkan; R. Merkelbach, 'Die Cosmogonie der Mithrasmysterien', *Eranos Jahrbücher*, 34, 1965, pp. 219–55 (Iranian basis conflated with straight borrowing from the Timaeus of Plato by a genius). I agree largely with Nock: one may compare the genesis of Manichaeism; or the African church founded by John Marauke (M. Aquina, 'The People of the Spirit: an Independent Church in Rhodesia', *Africa*, 37, 1967, pp. 203–18).

119. See the collection of material in H. Fuchs, *Der geistige Widerstand gegen Rom* (ed. 2), Munster, 1938 = 1964. Of course this must not be exaggerated: one has only to think of gladiators. Yet the range of things which the educated pro-Romans found to praise is curiously narrow and predictable: J. Palm, *Rom, Römertum und Imperium in der gr. Literatur der Kaiserzeit*: Acta Reg. Soc. Hum. Lit. Lundinensis 57 (Lund, 1959).

120. Mithraea II and III at Dura were actually built inside the military compound, and most of the graffiti are by 'Roman' soldiers apparently: *Report*, p. 88: there are only three other sites known in Syria before the fourth century.

121. F. Cumont, *Fouilles de Dura-Europos*, 1922–3 (Paris, 1926), pp. LIII–IV. cf. S.H.A. *vit. Veri* 7.5–8 with T. D. Barnes, 'Hadrian and Lucius Verus', *Journal of Roman Studies*, 57, 1967, pp. 65–79 at pp. 71–2.

122. *Report*, pp. 83 ff.

123. I count 28 (possibly up to 35) such names, excluding the four benefactors at Dura I. About 85% of these are in 'military' areas. 5(7) soldiers who were clearly locally recruited made Mithraic dedications on this criterion. There are no certainly native names in Britain, Africa or Spain, though some of the Latin names there may conceal first-generation citizens.

124. A. S. Hoey, *The Feriale Duranum* (with R. O. Fink, W. F. Snyder), *Yale Classical Studies*, VII, 1940, pp. 202–210.

125. MacMullen, *Soldier and Civilian* (op. cit.) pp. 96–7: he seems to see the cult as though it were as alien as the Osroenians he passes on to next.

126. Plotinus, *Enneads* II.9.5 ff. esp. 8–9; A. H. Armstrong in *The Cambridge History of Later Greek and Early Mediaeval Philosophy*, Cambridge, 1967, pp. 250–63. J. M. Rist, 'Plotinus on Matter and Evil', *Phronesis*, 6, 1961, 154–66 shows that Plotinus differed from the gnostics principally in the type of dualism he admitted.

127. J. Bayet, *Histoire . . . de la religion romaine* (op. cit.) pp. 231–7.

AUTHORITY, SALVATION AND MYSTERY IN THE MYSTERIES OF MITHRAS[1]

One of the characteristic devices of the non-traditional religions of the Graeco-Roman world was secrecy. Reticence was not merely a means of self-protection: it was an essential part of their appeal. Secrecy contrasted with the public character of the dominant civic cults intimately associated with the cultural and political power of the elite. One means of justifying such secrecy was to make a distinction between (oral) myths, taken as the common property of a people, and interpretative writings, the property of the wise. Truth was taken as a commodity made precious by its rarity; meanings devised by individual ingenuity could easily be imposed upon a self-elected community; commentary, and the writings which enshrined it, could become the guardians of exclusivity. In the Roman Empire, the type of such religious apartheid was held to be Egypt, 'where the Egyptian wise men who have studied their traditional writings give profound philosophical interpretations of what they regard as divine, while the common people hear certain myths of which they are proud, although they do not understand the meaning' (Origen, *Contra Celsum* 1, 12).[2] But the same was believed to be true of Persia, where there were supposed to be 'mysteries (*teletai*) which are cultivated rationally (*logikōs*) by the learned among them, but which are taken in their external significance (*sumbolikōs*) by ordinary people there and by rather superficial minds' (*ibid.*).[3] To be initiated into a mystery cult in the Roman Empire was to make a claim to the power granted by secret knowledge. Ideally, such knowledge was also ancient, revealed by certain 'wise nations', whether Greek or barbarian – by the Egyptians, Assyrians, Indians, Persians, Odrysians, Samothracians, Eleusinians, Druids, Getae and others.[4] The very existence of this power depended upon the norm of public knowledge and acknowledgement which grounded the civic religions of antiquity.

The historian of the Mysteries of Mithras is thus faced with a double difficulty. There is first the physical destruction of material artefacts and interpretative writings. This loss can indeed to some extent be made good by sensitive use of idiosyncratic, or unusual monuments – there is a very marked tendency in the later monuments,. especially of the mid third century, towards greater explicitness. But even sensitivity is no substitute for direct evidence; and no modern interpretation can avoid constant appeal to a tangled network of usually implicit assumptions about what is 'credible' or 'plausible'. The second difficulty is less obvious. One implication of a distinction between the wise and the vulgar is that any given element in the religion may have had a different rationale according to the position of the initiate in the hierarchy of seven grades. In that event, there would not in any simple sense be *a* theology or 'true doctrine' to reconstruct: there would be an articulation over time of different, and perhaps inconsistent or contradictory, meanings.[5] Moreover, it seems likely that the personal evocations of individual initiators or 'theologians' differed from place to place, and certainly over time, albeit within the ground rules fixed for us by the shared motifs of the monuments. Implicit associations are essential in a religion at whose centre lies a claim to an enigmatic truth, that life is death and death is life. Even if we possessed the voluminous writings on the Mysteries by Euboulos and Pallas, we might well not feel that we had any firmer grasp of 'the essence' of the belief system. What we would have would be a splendid insight into the imaginative possibilities opened up by a self-consciously 'foreign' religion ever eager to prove its legitimacy through the ingenuity of its demonstrations.[6]

However that may be, it has always been tempting to believe that the loss of material was not complete and that there was somewhere a key to the opacity of the iconography. Franz Cumont, the founder of the modern study of the Mysteries, believed he had found such a key in the sacred books of Persian Zoroastrianism.[7] For a half century, despite the considerable objections that could have been levelled against it, this theory won more or less universal acceptance. Its chief weakness, however, was that it explained at once too much and too little. It proposed too precise an identity between individual elements of Zoroastrianism, especially divinities, and evidence from the Mysteries, proposals which evidently were extremely problematic. But the theory was also unable to provide a clear interpretation of the main thrust of the Mysteries, their character as a religion, their appeal to adherents.[8] Now that it has been generally abandoned, the quest for *the* key to the iconography has been vigorously renewed.[9] An unruly crowd of competing Mysteries has tumbled into the ring, each starting with a different understanding of the character of the problem, and each confident that there is *an* answer, taking in my view insufficient account both of the inherent limitations of the type of evidence we possess and of the type of religious structure under discussion.[10]

It is here, I think, that we may learn from the example of Jocelyn Toynbee. Although her own published contribution to the study of the Mysteries was small, she retained a close interest in the field all her life, as Hugh Plommer's bookplate for her eightieth birthday suggests.[11] Her work was distinguished by independence of judgement, a scrupulous regard for evidence and a minute familiarity with the iconography. She was dismissive of easy distinctions and inferences, sharp with nonsense. Her posthumously published account of the Walbrook temple combines an eye for telling detail with a wide knowledge of appropriate contexts for comparison.[12] In a word, she never allowed the undoubted thrill of the speculative hunt to overwhelm her sense of what the evidence would bear. A volume dedicated by Newnham College to Jocelyn Toynbee's memory provides a fine opportunity to make more widely available recent developments in the study of the iconography of the Mysteries within the wider context of the craft-production of the Graeco-Roman world. My principal concern is not so much with the positive doctrines of the religion as with the manner in which a specific type of effective, salvific 'knowledge' was constructed and maintained.

The Mysteries claimed to have been founded by the *magos* Zoroaster: 'Zoroaster was the first to dedicate a natural cave in honour of Mithras', observes Porphyry, quoting Euboulus (*de antro nympharum* 6).[13] This appeal to a named founder suggests at once a self-conscious distance from the cults traditionally constitutive of civic piety in the Graeco-Roman world. Whereas civic piety refused history by appealing to the authority of 'the ancestors', the Mysteries accepted a specific foundation in time and space – but an extremely remote time, and in a place quite outside the confines of the Graeco-Roman world. This claim to have been founded by Zoroaster should be understood, of course, not as a genuinely historical claim but as an ideological one. To have been founded 'out there' permitted any distance that might be judged desirable between the norms and claims of the Mysteries and those of the ordinary Graeco-Roman world beyond. But it also implies an acknowledgement of the need for authority, inasmuch as Zoroaster was an already accepted facet of the history of 'philosophy' in one strand of Graeco-Roman historiography when the Mysteries began to spread around 100 A.D. in the western Empire.

To have been founded by the Persian *magos* was not, however, the religion's only means of claiming the right to be heard in the market of interesting experiences. There were several others, to some of which I wish to draw attention here.

The Mysteries delighted in their strangeness, as anyone can attest who has visited one of the accessible underground temples in Rome (San Clemente, the temple in the garden of the Palazzo Barberini, Santa Prisca) or the most impressive painted shrines, those at S. Maria Capua Vetere near Naples [Cover plate] and the vaulted room at Marino in the Alban Hills.[14] This emphatic strangeness is another feature of the cult's self-conscious claim to authority. 'Strangeness' announced at least a superficial rejection of current public norms in religion, whatever deeper consistency there may have been between the values of the Mysteries and the wider world within which they spread. But as an 'illegitimate' – new, non-traditional, non-civic-religion in the Roman Empire, the Mysteries faced a characteristic difficulty. On the one hand, they had to convince potential adherents of the special nature of the message and the effectiveness of the means offered; on the other, they had to operate within a world of pre-established expectations and assumptions.

The actual origins of the Mysteries are more or less completely unknown to us: the surviving evidence is simply not adequate for anything but guesswork. Despite the existence of undoubtedly Iranian elements, of which the most obvious – and superficial – are the words *nama* (which means Hail! in Old Persian) and *nabarze* (which means 'victorious'), the dominant impression is of eclecticism.[15] Whatever their ultimate or remotest origins in the break-up of Persian institutions in hellenistic Anatolia, the Mysteries as a developed religion were constructed from ideas borrowed from different sources and mixed into a bricolage.[16] Three aspects of this bricolage concern me here.

The first is the use by the Mysteries of current lore about the structure of the heavens, lore which was not generally known – commonsense – but which was common knowledge to the educated. It was available in books dealing with astronomy or astrology indifferently (the modern distinction does not appear in antiquity).[17] Appeal to such knowledge enabled the Mysteries to use 'facts' of an empirical, objective order as grounds for non-empirical claims. The heavens were presented as a sort of map inscribed with coded meanings, a visible mediation between this world of changeability and death and another world, of purity and immortality. The heavenly bodies were turned, as in several ancient religions, into metaphors of salvation.[18] But the inherent complexity of the world understood by astronomy also made it suitable as a source of paradoxical, alluring, mysterious truths which, being legitimated by Nature herself, could not be accused of being the product merely of fantasy. By appealing to 'scientific' knowledge, the Mysteries sought both to gain authority not based upon tradition and a source of complex, even paradoxical, meanings – in a word, 'mystery'.

The second structural element is the use of the imagery of heroic achievement established within the Graeco-Roman world. The language

IV

THE MYSTERIES OF MITHRAS 49

of 'invincibility', of 'physical' strength, of struggle and victory was taken over from pre-existing narrative and iconographical patterns, which served to familiarize the unfamiliar 'Persian' god, to assimilate him to the pattern of classical heroes. This assimilation in turn helped to legitimate a much more central claim of the religion, that the gulf between this world and the Other World could indeed be bridged, just as individual heroes in the past had bridged it, not merely Herakles, whose shadow falls dark over this upstart god, but real human beings, athletes above all. The idiom of heroic action was adopted in order to implement the project of salvation.

Finally, in common with several other innovatory religions of antiquity, the Mysteries expressed their ambiguous relationship to the world of civic religion through a commentary upon civic sacrifice, the ordinary means of symbolic connection between the two worlds.[19] The bull that is killed by Mithras in the central icon of the cult differs in important respects from the ordinary domestic but unbroken animals sacrificed in civic contexts; the means by which it is brought to the killing-place; the place itself; the manner of its death – all of these constitute a structured system of differences from the rules of civic sacrifice in the Graeco-Roman world (to stress the similarities, and not the differences, between Greek and Roman civic sacrifice for the moment). The meanings generated by the act differ likewise from those of civic ritual. Moreover, whereas these latter meanings were implicit, such that it was virtually impossible for an ordinary person in the ancient world to reflect upon the 'meaning' of sacrifice, the non-traditional goals of Mithraic cult were made explicit in this 'deviant' form of sacrifice. Finally, whereas the 'political' imagery of public sacrifice referred itself constantly to pseudo-historical events, the universal claims of the Mysteries were inscribed in the cult icon itself.

We may perhaps unite these three elements of the eclectic programme of the Mysteries by observing that three terms are implicitly under discussion: divinity, nature and the social order. These same three terms are the implicit concern also of the traditional civic cults of the Graeco-Roman world. But whereas civic cult, and the imperial regime which was its parasite, tended constantly to politicize religious discourse, subordinating the gods to a theodicy of good fortune, non-traditional religions expressed their independence of that pressure by contrasting the social world against the Other World. They offered to make purity or separation the goal of the religious life; to break, at least in ritual contexts, the ties of social obligation; to ease the burden of deference; to rewrite the rules for maintaining personal honour. These social implications of 'deviant' religion were linked with new representations of nature. In traditional civic contexts, a publicly acknowledged represen-

tation of the natural world both grounded man's exploitation of nature
for his means of livelihood and provided the most important validation
of the hypothesis of an Other World. Non-traditional cults tended to
ignore such realism in favour of new, and arcane, interpretations. In
particular, nature became 'bookish', a cipher intelligible only to a few.
The aspect of nature most amenable to such reinterpretation was the
observable heavens.

The interpretation of nature offered by many new religions was thus
congruent with their marginal status. But it also was intended to provide
a novel sort of legitimation. Innovatory or 'deviant' religions must offer
relatively explicit answers, be sure of their claims, to a degree not
demanded of religious systems legitimated by tradition.[20] Consequently,
they are much more open to objections than such systems – and to
ridicule and experiential disconfirmation. They purchase high commitment at high risk. The nature of the authority claimed becomes crucial –
and Nature might be claimed a superior authority even than *ta patria*, the
customs of our ancestors. This entire essay is indeed concerned with the
invention of authority, the establishment of the right to be heard, offered
by one of the most successful of the non-traditional religions of the
Roman Empire.

I

For two reasons, our initial concern will be with astronomy.[21] It is first
of all quite evident from the iconography of the Mysteries that an
astronomical idiom was employed to make theological statements.[22]
Moreover, good progress has recently been made, above all by Roger
Beck of the University of Toronto (Erindale), in elucidating the familiar
bull-killing scene as at one level a 'map' of the ecliptic between Taurus
and Scorpius. He has also fruitfully pursued the implications of the
several different planetary orders found in Mithraic monuments.[23] The
bull-killing scene is however only one element of cult-furniture in a
temple which was itself conceived as a symbolic space. Indeed, in many
respects, icon and temple complement each other's symbolism. This
complementarity may be illustrated in two ways.

Several Mithraic bull-killing scenes (hereafter 'icons') enclose the
action within a zodiac.[24] But in the temple on the island of Ponza near
Naples, the zodiac has been shifted from the icon to the vault of the
ceiling (Fig. 1).[25]

The very fact of such a transposition at once recalls the statement of
Euboulus, quoted by Porphyry, that Zoroaster was the first to dedicate in
Persia a natural cave in honour of Mithras, which 'bore for him the
likeness of the cosmos which Mithras had created' (Εἰκόνα φέροντος αὐτῷ

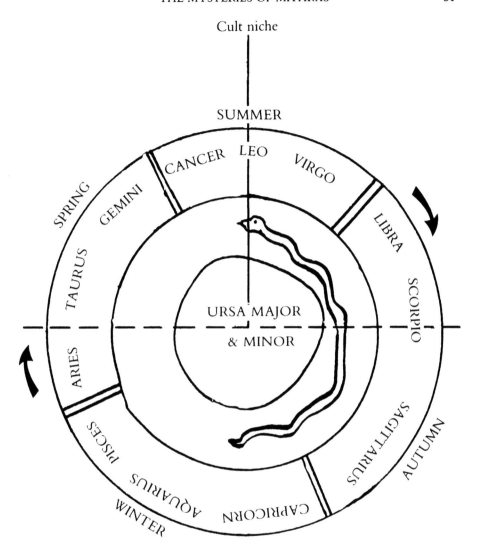

Fig. 1. The ring-zodiac on the ceiling of the temple at Ponza, enclosing the two Bears and Draco.

τοῦ σπηλαίου τοῦ κόσμου, ὅν ὁ Μίθρας ἐδημιούργησε).[26] Zoroaster, the reputed founder of the Mysteries, chose a cave because Mithras killed a bull in a cave; but the cave was actually a 'cave' – a sign for the cosmos. All Mithraic temples imitated that dedication, some literally, inasmuch as they were natural caves, and some (most) by artifice. Correlatively, the caves represented on the icon range from a natural cave, as at Capua Vetere [Cover plate], rocky and dark, through the overtly 'symbolic' cave of the relief from S. Lucia in Selce [Plate 1] or Neuenheim [Plate 2] to complete indifference, which no doubt functions as a sign of the abstractly cosmic significance of the event rather than of its historicity (for example the Alba Iulia relief [Plate 4]). One can hardly hope for a better example of rewriting the book of nature in an allegorical sense. The Mysteries took advantage of the ambiguity inherent in the notion eikōn, 'likeness', playing with a deliberately engineered uncertainty, between Mithras' mythical act, Zoroaster's 'historical' act and their own temple-building. The zodiac on the ceiling at Ponza evokes all three levels.

We can certainly go further. The zodiac is slewed in a curious way, which sets the solar and lunar houses to Right and Left respectively, and the sign of Leo closest to the end of the temple where the icon was set. The allusion to 'houses' implies astrological knowledge; the association between Leo and Mithras fits perfectly with Professor Beck's theory of the cryptic significance of the icon as a 'map' of the ecliptic. But the most important and unusual feature of the Ponza zodiac is the representation of the two Bears, Ursa Major and Minor, together with a snake, which is probably to be identified as Draco.[27]

In general terms, such a zodiac should probably be understood as a diagrammatic representation of the orderliness of the cosmos, thus highlighting one meaning of the temple. The presence of the Bears, that is, the North Pole, in relation to the ecliptic (the sequence of zodiacal signs), is however quite remarkable: there must be some further arcane significance. It seems probable that the Mysteries were familiar with an apparent paradox to which Julian refers in his usual enigmatic manner in the Hymn to King Helios (147d). He says that the Sun, the father of the seasons, who "works at the tropical points" (τὰς τροπὰς ἐργαζόμενος), nevertheless never leaves the Poles (οὐκ ἀπολείπων τοὺς πόλους). His explanation of this truth involves a reference to the "hypotheses of the mysteries" (148ab), perhaps the Chaldaean oracles, or even the Mysteries of Mithras. He says that the sun's course lies not midmost among the planets (the ordinary 'Pythagorean' or 'Chaldaean' view) but above the fixed stars (148a) – the sun is thus placed in the middle of the three kosmoi. Such a theory is stated by Johannes Lydus, de mensibus 2.6 (Wünsch) to have been taught by 'Zoroaster'. In other words, the reconciliation of the paradox "Tropic and Pole" seems to involve recourse to a cosmological theory to be found in the Zoroastrian pseudepigrapha – a likely source for some at least of the arcane learning of the Mysteries. Paradox is a favourite tool of religions which wish to appear interesting.[28]

Whether the Ponza zodiac is the learned creation of a single dedicator or a unique illustration of a doctrine widely disseminated among the cult's 'theologians', the monument provides a neat bridge between icon, temple and theology. But there were other means of achieving the same end which certainly were fundamental to the belief system, and for which the evidence is widely distributed in space and time.

We have seen that, according to Euboulus, Zoroaster dedicated the first temple to Mithras. This natural cave he deliberately turned into a metaphor of the cosmos by arranging its interior "at corresponding intervals with symbols of the heavenly bodies and latitudes", κατὰ συμμέτρους ἀποστάσεις σύμβολα φερόντων τῶν κοσμικῶν στοιχείων καὶ κλιμάτων (de antro 6). Such a charter permitted the Mysteries considerable freedom, which was differently exercised in different temples. In each case, however, a statement of belief is constructed in material form: 'We say this building "is" the cosmos'.

Sometimes, the metaphor is transparent. Representations of the planets in Mithraic temples have been shown to correspond in schematic fashion with their actual relationship on two highly unusual occasions, 21 March 172 A.D. and 25 March 173 A.D., dates which correspond roughly to the archaeologically attested dates for the temples' foundation.[29] At Ponza, it is possible that the ceiling zodiac commemorates the total solar eclipse of 14 August 212 A.D.[30] The floor of one of the Ostian temples, degli Animali, is laid out as though it were an icon, stretched between the bull (Taurus) at the cult-niche end and the scorpion (Scorpius) at the other end of the 'podia' or 'benches', with the snake between (279).

Elsewhere, the metaphor is built into the 'benches', which typically extend on each side down the length of the temple [see Cover plate]. There is an excellent example of this in the newly-discovered temple at Vulci in Etruria (Fig. 2): The 'benches' contain six main niches on each side, corresponding to the signs of the zodiac. In the centre of each 'bench' is a smaller niche, rectangular on the SW side, vaulted on the NE, whose significance I will discuss shortly. The remaining niches probably correspond to the location of statues or altars to the torchbearers, as commonly elsewhere.[31]

The most interesting example of the Mithraic interpretation of the temple as cosmos is however the Antonine temple in Ostia named by its excavator Lanciani 'Sette Sfere' after the seven semicircles set into the mosaic floor.[32] Here the signs of the zodiac have been arranged in two

54

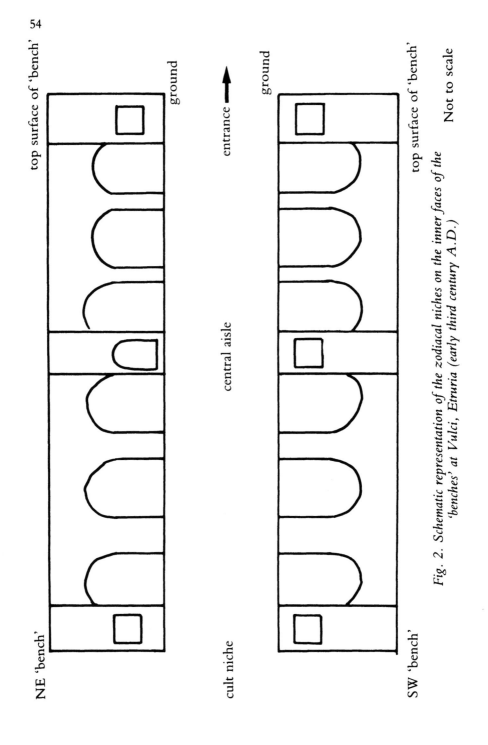

Fig. 2. Schematic representation of the zodiacal niches on the inner faces of the 'benches' at Vulci, Etruria (early third century A.D.)

Not to scale

parallel groups in mosaic along the upper edges of the 'benches'. The order of the signs is as follows:

cult-niche

Aries	Pisces
Taurus	Aquarius
Gemini	Capricorn
Cancer	sagittarius
Leo	Scorpius
Virgo	Libra

entrance

The order is thus anti-clockwise, as on most ancient zodiacs (though perhaps such a notion hardly applies to this representation). Now the usual astronomical associations of the left-hand group are with day, Spring and Summer; of those on the right, with night, Autumn and Winter. But at the end of each 'bench' is a mosaic representation of the torchbearers, Cautes, with his torch upwards, on the right and Cautopates, with his torch reversed, on the left. If Cautes, as seems obvious, is associated with dawn, day and Spring and Cautopates with evening, night and Autumn, the symbolism seems hopelessly muddled. But perhaps the muddle is really just an enigma, requiring elucidation and not despair.

The first point is that this location of Cautes and Cautopates is not casual: in all the roughly two dozen cases in which the torch-bearers appear at the ends of the 'benches' they appear in this same configuration.[33] That said, we should again turn to Porphyry, to another passage of the *de antro nympharum*, to which sense has at last been restored by the inspired guesswork of the most recent (anonymous) editors:

τεταγμένου αὐτοῖς κατὰ μὲν τὸν νότον τοῦ Καύτου διὰ τὸ εἶναι θερμόν, κατὰ δε τὸν βορρᾶν τοῦ (Καυτοπάτου) διὰ τὸ ψυχρὸν του ἀνέμον

(Mithras is placed on the equinoctial circle) while Cautes they (i.e. Numenius and Kronios) set to the South because of the heat (of the South wind), and [Cautopates] they set to the North because of the coldness of the (North) wind.[34]

Now it so happens that another of the associations of the two sets of zodiacal signs at Sette Sfere is cardinal: the signs to the left are associated with North, those to the right with South. This fact suggests at once that

56

Porphyry (or rather his sources, and ultimately the Mithraic "theologian" they learned from) is talking both about the cosmos in 'reality' and about the cosmos as represented in the temple: Cautopates is set on the left hand 'bench' because it is conceptually – we are certainly not talking about the real-world orientations of Mithraic temples, which have no clear rationale – 'to the North'; and Cautes is set on the right hand 'bench' because it is 'to the South'. But what is the significance of these cardinal associations?

Porphyry continues:

ψυχαῖς δ'εἰς γένεσιν ἰούσαις καὶ ἀπὸ γενέσεως χωριζομέναις εἰκότως ἔταξαν ἀνέμους διὰ τὸ ἐφέλκεσθαι καὶ αὐτὰς πνεῦμα, ὥς τινες ᾠήθησαν, καὶ τὴν οὐσίαν ἔχειν τοιαύτην. ἀλλὰ βορέας μὲν οἰκεῖος εἰς ταῖς εἰς γένεσιν ἰούσαις. διὸ καὶ τοὺς θνῄσκειν μέλλοντας ἡ βορέου πνοὴ ζωγρεῖ, ἡ δὲ τοῦ νότου διαλύει...

They (Numenius and Kronios) rightly assigned winds to souls coming into and out of genesis because, as some have thought, they also draw *pneuma* along with them, and have the same nature. Now the North wind is proper to souls coming into being, and therefore the breath of the North wind revives those who are about to die, while the breath of the South wind dissolves their souls (*de antro* 25, p. 24 lines 15–21 Arethusa).

'North' in the symbolism of the Mysteries was thus apparently associated with the descent of souls from heaven into the world of genesis, of becoming. There could be no better image of that descent than the down-turned torch of Cautopates, whose 'bench' is correspondingly set 'to the North' of the cosmos-temple, the left-hand side as one looks towards the cult-niche. By contrast, the up-turned torch of Cautes, associated with South, is an image of the release of souls out of genesis into blessedness. The 'heat' obviously suggested by the raised torch turns out to have an enigmatic significance, not day and Spring, but the dissolution of the soul – that is, death and release from the cycle of generation. The evening/Autumn associations of Cautopates have also an enigmatic meaning – they spell 'coming into being' – life in the ordinary sense. In effect, we can find in these placings of the two torchbearers an allusion to the central paradox with which the Mysteries were concerned, the redefinition of 'life' to mean 'real death' and the claim that what ordinarily seemed like death was in fact the opportunity for persuasively redefined 'life'.

The order of the signs at Sette Sfere has a further enigmatic significance which is worth exploring in the context of this theme of salvation.

The solstices occur in Cancer and Capricorn, an astronomical fact which at Sette Sfere could be represented by a line running North–South across the temple:

Aries	Pisces
Taurus	Aquarius
Gemini	Capricorn
N ——	—— S
Cancer	Sagittarius
Leo	Scorpius
Virgo	Libra

If the temple indeed represents the cosmos, there ought to be some significant marker of these points in Mithraic temples.

It so happens that almost all excavated temples have small niches more or less in the centre of each 'bench' – we may recall the case at Vulci (Fig. 2, p. 54), where the central niches – the only pair designed differently from each other – break the sequence of zodiacal niches just here. It is surely a reasonable guess that these 'bench'-niches, whose significance has never been explained (scarcely even discussed), stand for the solstices.

What was the significance of the solstices in the Mysteries? They were the points at which souls entered and left the cosmos, as Porphyry explains in *de antro* 22:

καρκίνον μὲν εἶναι δι' οὗ κατίασιν αἱ ψυχαί, αἰγοκέρων δὲ δι' οὗ ἀνίασι ἀλλὰ καρκίνος μὲν βόρειος καὶ καταβατικός, αἰγοκέρως δὲ νότιος καὶ ἀναβατικός

(There are two gates: of these) it is Cancer through which the souls descend and Capricorn through which they ascend: Cancer is to the North and the means of descent, Capricorn is to the South and the means of ascent (cf. also section 26).[35]

Although this is not stated explicitly by Porphyry to have been a doctrine of the Mysteries (it was after all a widely shared esoteric doctrine), the archaeology strongly suggests that it was. In this connection it is of some interest that at Capua Vetere a small relief showing Psyche and Amor (186), which is without parallel in the iconography of the Mysteries, was found fixed into the front wall of the *left hand* 'bench', directly above the niche which is, on the present hypothesis, the appropriate one for souls entering genesis. There has been no convincing explanation of its presence there.[36] In *de antro* 26, indeed, Porphyry states that it is because

58

the souls enter genesis through the Northern gate that the North wind is *erōtikos*, connected with love. We should surely conclude that the Mysteries took advantage of the metaphor of the temple as cosmos to represent the stages of the Mithraic journey of the soul inside the temple. The stages of the journey are presumably the initiatory grades – hence the paintings on the front walls of the 'benches' in the same temple at Capua Vetere [Cover plate] – but the beginning and end are represented by the niches on either side at Cancer and Capricorn, the solstitial points, the 'gates' into and out of genesis.

In some Mithraic temples, but not at Sette Sfere, a circular bowl has been let into the floor of the central aisle. In two cases, this bowl is set directly between the two solstitial niches. Elsewhere, it is set, still equidistant from either 'bench', further towards the cult-niche.[37] Why should the centre line of the temple have been appropriate?

If we go back to the scheme of the zodiacal signs at Sette Sfere, it is clear that if the solstitial line falls horizontally across the mid-point of the temple, the equinoctial line must fall at right angles to it, directly down the centre of the aisle. In that case, conceptual East must lie at the cult-niche end, and the opposite end, where almost invariably the entrance is to be found, must be conceptual West. These cardinal directions correspond exactly to Porphyry's account of the 'proper seat' of Mithras, on the 'line of the equinoxes':

ψυχαῖς δὲ γενέσεως καὶ ἀπογενέσεως οἰκεῖοι οἱ τόποι. τῷ μὲν οὖν Μίθρᾳ οἰκείαν καθέδραν τὴν κατὰ τὰς ἰσημερίας ὑπέταξαν . . . δημιουργὸς δὲ ὢν ὁ Μίθρας καὶ γενέσεως δεσπότης κατὰ τὸν ἰσημερινὸν δὲ τέτακται κύκλον ἐν δεξιᾷ μὲν (ἔχων) τὰ βόρεια, ἐν ἀριστερᾷ δὲ νότια, τεταγμένου αὐτοῖς κατὰ μὲν τὸν νότον τοῦ Καύτου

. . . and these points (North and South) are proper to genesis and apogenesis in relation to souls. They (Numenius and Kronios) assigned to Mithras as his proper seat that at the equinoxes . . . and as demiurge and lord of genesis Mithras is set on the circle of the equinoxes, with North on his right and South on the left, while Cautes they set to the South. . . (*de antro* 24).

The arrangement of the zodiacal signs at Sette Sfere thus refers cryptically both to the location of the solstices in the temple/cosmos, and so to the theme of the soul's journey, and to the location of the equinoxes and so to Mithras's function as lord of genesis. The bowls set in the centre of the aisle, and especially those placed at the crossing of solstitial and equinoctial lines, surely also have some symbolic significance.

The relation between bowl or 'krater' and Mithras apparently thus expressed spatially in the organisation of the temple seems to recur on those icons which, most commonly in Germany and the Danubian area, represent a krater with a lion (and normally a snake too) – for example, Neuenheim [Plate 2] and Alba Iulia [Plate 4]. Moreover, actual bowls, surrounded by snakes – and one recent example from Cologne has a lion on one handle, a snake on the other – are well known from Mithraic sites.[38] Snake and krater recur in association with the lion in several representations of the lionheaded god – whatever its exact Mithraic interpretation. An excellent example is one of the two monuments from the 'Fagan' temple in Ostia now in the Vatican Museo Profano [Plate 5]. Here the lionhead stands over a krater from which emerges a snake, whose head finally returns whence it came. A relief from Oxyrhynchus shows two snakes emerging from the lionhead's hands (?), that on the right extending down towards a krater (103).[39] At Strasbourg there was found a monument showing a human-headed four-winged figure holding staff and key; behind him stands a lion with its head over a krater encircled by a snake (1326).[40]

The most obvious association between snakes, lions and kraters occurs in the 'real' world in heaven: the constellation Crater is the *paranatellōn* (a constellation which rises or sets at the same time as another) of Leo, a constellation which as we saw at Ponza (p. 51) is apparently associated in the Mysteries with Mithras himself, being midway between the constellations Taurus, associated with Cautes, and Scorpius, associated with Cautopates. Heavenly Crater is immediately adjacent to Hydra – and to Corvus; and it is worth remarking that on either side of the mosaic bowl in the floor of the Sette Porte temple at Ostia is a raven and a snake.[41] Although the precise Mithraic account of these relationships cannot be reconstructed it is plausible to suppose that the matrix of the evocations was the observable relationships between constellations on or near the ecliptic at a point of special interest to the theology of the Mysteries.[42]

So little is known of this theology that an honest account of the complexity of the iconographic evidence easily turns into an incomprehensible list of apparently insignificant details. Such a specialist enquiry is inappropriate here. But the main point is by now clear: notwithstanding the wreck of Mithraic theology, we can glimpse something of the techniques employed to satisfy the cognitive demands of seven initiatory grades.[43] We can also glimpse something of the value of certain logical procedures – mild paradox, analogy and metonymy – applied to an inherently complex aspect of the natural world, the heavenly bodies. It was the products of these techniques which effectively created "mystery". Protected by the rule of secrecy, these were the procedures necessary for the development of a body of speculation, of "theology", always open to individual evocation and interpretation, which was sufficiently complex – but also sufficiently interesting – to permit such a religion to pass from the narrow confines of a particular family, place or historical moment (where most such enterprises are born and die) to become an impersonal project of a collective imagination.

II

There are however numerous aspects of the Mysteries which do not seem to have had astronomical reference, or which, at least, raise problems which have no obvious solution at that level. One of the most important of these is the issue of the representation of Mithras' status. It is notoriously undecidable whether he 'is', in the narrative commonly assumed to underlie the scenes on the complex reliefs such as those from Neuenheim [Plate 2], Kurtowo-Konare [Plate 3] and Alba Iulia [Plate 4], a god or a hero. It seems sensible to begin with the assumptions that this uncertainty is intentional, and that it bears on the central overt preoccupation of the religion, the achievement of an ordinarily impossible status, the acquisition of immortality by mortals.

One immediate question concerns the cult-title *anikeitos* or *invictus*. Some of the earliest evidence for the worship of Mithras in the western part of the empire, and in Anatolia, does not seem to include this motif.[44] The Syrian cult of Sol Invictus, which might seem relevant, in fact provides no help. But comparative evidence from the Graeco-Roman world, particularly in relation to Herakles, offers some clues.[45]

Mithras' act of killing the bull is the most concrete aspect of his 'invincibility'. The act itself evokes superhuman strength. Iconographically, it is linked to a series of heroic acts of animal domination stretching back into the Archaic period.[46] In ordinary Graeco-Roman contexts, such acts connote primarily the culture-hero status of Herakles, Theseus and their analogues. But they also find an echo in the reported exploits of another interesting group of anomalies, triumphant athletes. A number of stories about such men are at least suggestive in relation to the connotations of the title *anikeitos/invictus*. Moreover, they converge upon my third and later topic, the 'personal sacrifice' of a bull.

Lucian on several occasions, when imagining heroic achievement, lists famous athletes, Po(u)lydamas of Scotussa, Milo of Croton, Glaucus of Carystus, Theugenes of Thasos.[47] Perhaps the most famous of these, Milo, is supposed, during the festival of Zeus at Olympia, to have seized a four-year-old bull, never tamed to the yoke, and carried it over his shoulders.[48] By Quintilian's day, the deed had become so well-known that it had entered the realm of grammatical example: *Milo quem vitulum*

IV

adsueverat ferre, taurum ferebat (Inst. orat. 1.9.5). A similar story is told of the famous Biton, brother of Cleobis, who is said to have seized 'thanks to his vigour and strength', ὑπὸ ῥώμης τε καὶ ἰσχύος, one of the bulls that was being driven by the Argives to Nemea for sacrifice to Zeus, and to have carried it by himself. A statue commemorated this event (Pausanias 2.19.3).[49] These athletic exploits, which involved carrying the bull draped like a fox-fur over the shoulders, have no proper heroic analogues, though Herakles is said to have carried the Kerynitian hind over his shoulders as he walked through Arcadia (Apollodorus, *Bibl.* 2.5.3). (The motifs of carrying the Erymanthian boar and (rare) the Cretan bull are quite differently represented; the animal is slung over one shoulder only, as coal-men used to carry coal sacks.) They appear rather as adaptations of an act which, whatever its 'real-world' occurrences, is iconographically a sacral one, the motif of the *moschophoros* or the *kriophoros*. In those instances, the animal is of course small.[50]

The context of these stories about athletes – religious processions which are interrupted, but made memorable, worthy of art, by the heroic gesture, gives special interest to an uncommon scene in the so-called 'Mithras-myth', that is the sequence of bye-scenes on complex Mithraic reliefs. For among these there is one in which Mithras performs precisely this athletic-heroic gesture. The clearest example occurs on the Neuenheim monument [Plate 2, right pilaster, second scene down]. Here the bull's fore- and hind-legs are apparently tied together around Mithras' neck as he walks to the left, his head turned back.[51] Some fragmentary Mithraic commentary on this scene seems to be provided by lines 7 and 9 of the *dipinte* from the Santa Prisca temple in Rome. One of them emphasizes the dutifulness of Mithras' action: *hunc quem aur<ei>s humeris portavit more iuvencum*; the other, though the reading is doubtful, seems to shift the physical burden into a moral one: *atque perlata umeris t<u>li m(a)xima divum.*[52]

There is also a much more common scene, whose Mithraic name was *Transitus*, depicting Mithras pulling the bull along, the hind-legs over his shoulders, the fore-legs dragging over the ground [see Plates 2, 4, 6]. This has been compared with the ruse known from the myths of Hermes and the cattle of Apollo and Hercules' encounter with Cacus after the capture of the cattle of Geryon.[53] But the analogy is careless. Although the *Hymn to Hermes* 74–78 does not specify how the ruse of reversing the cattle's hoofprints was performed – probably advisedly, since there were fifty of them – all the versions of the Cacus story say that Cacus pulled the cattle he tried to steal *by their tails* as he himself apparently walked in the opposite direction.[54] Mithras does nothing of the sort: he is compelling the bull to go in a direction it is unwilling to take; he is subduing it to his will by main force by lifting both its hind-legs off the ground.

The immediate inference is that this peculiar action is a transposition of a method familiar from the farmyard for controlling smaller domestic animals, especially pigs, sheep and goats – analogous, but of course not precisely similar, actions occur in representations on gems of 'rustic sacrifices', where the sacrificer holds the victim, piglet or kid, helpless by one hind leg.[55] There is at least one reasonably close iconographical parallel to this exploit by Mithras: one of the types for Theseus mastering the sow of Krommyon shows the Athenian hero overpowering the monster by lifting her hind-legs off the ground. Not being a god, however, he has need of a rope and Hermes to perform the task.[56]

There are, however, two analogous exploits by athletes which may be relevant here. One concerns Milo, once again, and is explicitly said by Pausanias (6.5.6) to have been prompted by a desire for renown. Entering a herd of cattle, the athlete deliberately sought out the largest and wildest bull. Seizing it by one of its hind legs, he held on grimly to the hoof though the bull bucked and struggled. Finally it escaped, but only at the price of leaving the hoof in Milo's hands. The second story concerns one of Milo's most dangerous opponents, a shepherd from Aetolia named Titormus, who is said to have held a wild bull fast in each hand (Athenaeus, *Deipn.* 10. 412f, quoting Alexander of Aetolia, the third-century epigrammatist). There is some evidence, then, that controlling bulls by catching hold of their hind legs was a registered athletic-heroic achievement. I am inclined to think that the Mithraic motif refers to the same type of action rather than to the world of ruse to which it is normally assigned.[57]

This passage of Athenaeus (412f) mentions another of Milo's famous exploits performed in competition with the same Titormus. Each of them individually killed an ox or bull and ate it during the course of a single day (a history which Athenaeus not unreasonably catalogues under 'Gluttony of Athletes'). The same feat is ascribed to Theugenes of Thasos (*ibid.* 412de: ταῦρον μόνος κατέφαγεν).[58] Moreover, after carrying the four-year-old bull in procession at Olympia, Milo is said to have killed and eaten it in a single day 'reclining in front of the altar of Zeus' (Phylarchus ap. Athenaeus, *Deipn.* 10.412f). It may have been the case that victors at Olympia were expected to make a thank-offering to Zeus and that this was probably Milo's contribution. But it remains the case that he did not share the animal as normal in sacrificial contexts – he kept the whole carcass to himself.[59]

Now one of Milo's rôle-models, if we may use such an expression, was Herakles: he dressed up in a lion-skin and club to go to war with Sybaris (Diodorus Siculus, 12.9.6). Others of this group of super-athletes also looked to Herakles: Po(u)lydamas actually killed a lion barehanded on Mt. Olympus in rivalry with his exploits (φιλοτιμία πρὸς τὰ 'Ηρακλέους ἔργα :Pausanias, 6.5.6). And Herakles too indulged in heroic eating matches of a similar kind. In the competition with Lepreos, each of them slaughtered a bull simultaneously without assistance and then prepared it for eating (Pausanias, 5.5.4).[60] The motif of Herakles singlehandedly killing and eating an ox or bull occurs in two other myths: his meeting with the Lapiths, and with the Dryopian King, Theiodamas.[61] There is also a considerable iconography of Herakles as sole or non-communal sacrificant.[62] The gesture obtains its value from the negation of normal civic rules for sacrifice and meat-eating: the hero's anomalous status is registered by such violations of rule.[63]

These feats of strength, whose collective similarity to elements of Mithraic iconography is striking, are concrete signs for the notion of invincibility. They serve to set apart the person who performs them: they are boundary-markers. Once he is in that solitary state, more dramatic evocations easily follow. The same or similar signs may serve to denote ambiguity of status in 'mere' mortals or accepted heroes. There was an Eleusinian ritual, recently documented by a black-figure amphora at Viterbo, involving an allusion to the ordinary rule of civic sacrifice, that the head and neck of a large victim had to be raised after it was stunned, to allow the jugular vein or one of the carotid arteries to be cut. The Eleusinian ritual, performed by selected Athenian ephebes, went by the name of 'raising the bull' and applied to the whole animal while fully conscious what normally applied only to its head after it had been stunned. In the vase-painting, a number of tough naked young men lift a large bull/bullock high above their heads, while a 'priest' (at least a man with clothes on) thrusts a knife into its neck; another man stands by with a metal bowl to catch the blood.[64] In myth, 'raising the bull' is transposed into the story in which Theseus, whose dress and appearance are sufficiently ambiguous to cause some men working on the temple of Apollo Delphinios to give him a wolf-whistle, grabs a draught-bullock from a cart and hurls it over the roof-gable of the temple (Pausanias, 1.19.1). In each case those who perform the deed of strength are ephebes (or 'ephebes'), whose ambiguity between two statuses does not need to be further stressed.[65] But the hero performs alone a feat which even strong young mortals have to do in a group. The shift in his status, from 'real human' to 'source of magical power', which the narrative undertakes is correspondingly great.

The function of these stories about athletes is also to set them apart from ordinary men, to play a part in shifting them from normality to the status of hero. The athlete's invincibility, expressed in the concrete form of exploits with animals, is converted into the miraculous power of healing possessed by his statue. The type case is the story of the 'living' statue of Theugenes of Thasos memorably told by Pausanias (6.11.5–

9).[66] The grander exploits of Herakles permit his power not to be confined to a particular point in space: it becomes a general power of averting evil, as in the well-known distich invoking him to protect the house. His title here is *kallinikos*, "fair-victorious".[67] Varro claimed that Hercules was called Victor at Rome *quod omne genus animalium deinceps vicerit*, because of his exploits with animals.[68] Dio Chrysostom, in one of his encomia of Herakles, moralises the tradition in saying that he is *sōtēr*, saviour, not because he killed animals – by implication the usual view – but because he punished the wicked, and tyrants in particular (1.66–84; cf.8.27–35). Herakles' final triumph is over death. An interesting monument from a second-century AD tomb at Bierbach near Speyer shows four mythical scenes. Two represent death as divine punishment: Apollo and Marsyas, Artemis and Actaeon. The remaining two show Hercules killing the Nemean lion – to judge from 'hunting'-sarcophagi, lions on tombs are a figure for death – and saving Hesione from a monster. It has been plausibly suggested that Hercules should here be understood as saving a human being from the jaws of death – as it were a routinisation of the theme of Alcestis.[69]

The invincibility of human athletes is an element in a narrative process which effects an 'impossible' transition, between the status of ordinary mortal and that of hero, whose power is effectively available to others long after his death. Herakles' greater invincibility serves to make him ambiguous between two higher statuses, hero and god (in Pindar, *Nemean* 3.22 he is both together), which is ordinarily impossible. It seems to me that the iconography suggests that something similar is true of 'ephebic' Mithras, that he is both hero and god, capable both of being a servant and of being demiurge of the world – statuses which are normally, and to a sensible person, quite incompatible. The key to the transition between statuses is the notion of 'invincibility' concretely conveyed by the exploits with the bull set in the context of parallel stories about humans who became heroes and heroes who became gods. And if there is a temptation to look among such stories for the raw materials from which the Mithras figure was created, I do not think it should be resisted, even if no precise historical connections can be made.

III

There is yet another ambiguity in the Mithraic iconography relating to the capture and killing of a bull which may also be related to the 'ephebic' status of the god. This is the question of whether the death of the bull should be understood as a hunting death or as a sacrifice – granted that these are merely two aspects of a wider domination of the natural world by man, hero or god.[70] We have already seen how, in the case of the

Greek athletes of the archaic and classical periods, the heroic gesture with the bull in procession sometimes led to a feast upon the meat which was, if not a parody of civic sacrifice, at least deliberately paronomastic: the great athlete, or Herakles, shows his superiority of status by killing the victim without aid and eating it whole. Once again, it seems to me, the Mithraic case is interesting because it generates a deliberate ambiguity.

There can, first, be no doubt that the Mithraic bull was understood to have been hunted – and hunting is of course an activity perfectly appropriate for ephebes, for young men of anomalous status.[71] There is at Dura-Europos a unique bye-scene in which the bull, having been overcome by Mithras, is shown trussed to a pole carried by the two torchbearers (or at least by two figures dressed in 'Persian' attire) (42.12).[72] This is one of the less common conventions on 'hunting'-sarcophagi and elsewhere of denoting 'successful completion of the hunt'.[73] The motif serves at once to contrast this bull with those ordinarily used in civic sacrifice, which, though never yoked, were not wild either and could not be hunted in such a manner (the Arch of the Argentarii in the Forum Boarium at Rome shows them grazing peacefully in fields before being transported to the city).[74]

It is virtually certain that the iconography of Mithras' act of killing the bull is derived from that of the goddess Nike.[75] The earliest datable image, which is also typologically unique, comes from Rome and is Trajanic (593) – by contrast, the earliest archaeologically datable temples are all from around 150 A.D. Attempts to derive the Mithraic image from hellenistic originals are therefore groundless: the reasonable inference is that the new popularity of the Nike motif on public monuments of the Trajanic period made it an appropriate means for the Mysteries, as they began to spread at the same time, to represent Mithras' act.[76] It is relevant to ask in what sense this image of Nike killing a bull represents a sacrifice. The image summarizes the payment of vows undertaken by the state especially in time of war. The actual processions and slaughter of civic sacrifice undertaken in thanksgiving for victory are however neatly abstracted or transcended. The violence of actual sacrifice, alluded to in one type of representation, known mainly from Rome but originally Greek, the *immolatio boum*, is here elided. In that image, while the human sacrificant pours libation on one side (or in the centre), one of the *popae* twists the bull's head down and round by main force – as slaves, the *popae* are always shown naked to the waist, so that their muscles may bulge – while another raises the axe or hammer for stunning the animal.[77] In the Nike image even this allusion is suppressed: with the lightest of feet – sometimes not even touching the victim – she crushes it to the ground, pulling the head back with one hand. The other hand holds a dagger, though she is but rarely shown actually delivering a blow.

The Nike-type of course makes reference to an ideal model of civic sacrifice. The animal is the 'paraded limit' victim, an adult bull. It has collapsed to the ground, immobile. The head is raised to expose a vein or artery to the knife. Sometimes an altar, *thumiaterion* or some other object of cult-use stands as a sign denoting 'sacrifice'. But it is equally clearly not just a sacrifice: above all, the notion of ritual procedure is lacking. There is no procession, no basket, no ceremonial trays or buckets; no turning around the altar, no libation, no cutting of the hair, no scattering of barley. The bull's refusal to be done to death is evident: there is no figurative assent. There is no division of labour between superior sacrificant and socially inferior butchers. In the case of Nike, these absences connote primarily the overwhelming might of the divine agent, and metaphorically the splendour of victory. Those connotations are surely also present in the case of the Mithraic monument. But in this case much more besides.

The different implications of the Mithraic image of the bull-killing will perhaps be most easily understood if I list the apparent references to, and refusals of, civic sacrifice.[78] As Jean Rudhardt long ago remarked, such a notion as 'civic sacrifice' is a mere abstraction, perhaps even a chimera.[79] But some such device is necessary if we are to establish the general point that the Mysteries constructed a paronomastic version of sacrifice in keeping with their wider commentary upon, or transformations of, the functions of civic religion.

Two minor details first. The point about the absence of barley-corns is not trivial. Barley-corns in civic sacrifice signified the relationship between agricultural labour and the obligation to make sacrifice to the gods; in the case of Mithras, there could be no such gesture, since the killing of the bull itself in some sense gives rise to the existence of corn – supposing that to be one – the most elementary – significance of the ears of wheat which emerge from the animal's tail.[80] Moreover, in civic sacrifice the blood from the animal was generally collected in a bowl before being thrown over the altar; in the Mithraic image, it is apparently consumed by the snake and the dog (clear on 615, 650 etc.). We must assume that these choices were conscious variations from the rules of civic sacrifice, and were part of one or more theological interpretations of the significance of the bull's death. We perhaps glimpse one such interpretation on an altar now in the Rheinisches Landesmuseum, Bonn, which is not known to have come from a Mithraic context and which is unique in the corpus [Plate 7]. A bull grazes beside a large vine (?) which arches over it and in which a snake can be seen. A *patera* apparently lies beneath the bull's testicles. A crescent moon (not shown in my photograph), which could be illuminated from behind, has been hollowed out at the top of the altar.[81] The Mithraic connection between the moon,

Cautopates and the fertility of the natural world is well-known from other monuments.[82] On the Bonn altar, this complex of associations seems to be focussed upon the bull itself (which is elsewhere, as at Neuenheim [Plate 2, top scene, right pilaster], shown grazing). The libation bowl would refer proleptically to its death, connoting a form of sacrifice. The vine would refer to natural growth, but perhaps also to genesis, the entry of souls into the world.[83] In effect, whereas civic sacrifice reproduced ancestral ritual, which in turn grounded a political community, 'sacrifice' in the Mysteries generated enigmatic truth – mystery – at odds with the implicit commonsense of civic ritual, and requiring special commentary and exegesis. That knowledge in turn delimited a special community, that of the *syndexioi* or *consacranei*, the worshippers of Mithras in a given temple.

There are three further peculiarities of Mithras's act worth noticing here.

In 'normal' sacrifice, at any rate in Greece, the victim's thigh bones were extracted and burned on the altar in honour of the gods, thus giving rise to one periphrasis for 'sacrifice'. Representations of the thighs after this operation give them the appropriate appearance of being flaccid.[84] In the Mithraic context, this ritual is apparently referred to but distorted. First, the thigh-bone does not seem to have been extracted; and therefore it cannot have been burned on an altar. Rather, the whole haunch of the bull seems to be used in an encounter between Sol and Mithras which is frequently, if summarily, represented among the bye-scenes.[85] The clearest examples, the scenes on the reliefs from Nersae (Nesce in Lazio) (650) and Virunum (1430, C5) [Plate 8], and on the Marino fresco, all show Mithras grasping the entire hind leg and holding it over Sol, who kneels before him. Whatever the significance of the action, the very choice of the haunch suggests a conscious adaptation of the normal sacrificial rule. The motivation for the adaptation may be related to the fact that in public contexts the *skelos* and *kōlē* together were often the perquisite of the officiating priest or official.[86]

These parts of the dead bull are plainly visible in another bye-scene related to this, represented only once, on the face of a mid-third century altar from Poetovio III (1584) [Plate 9]. The bull's entire hind leg lies on the ground in front of the altar. On either side stand Sol (L) and Mithras (R) jointly holding a spit (or possibly a dagger) vertically over the flames of the altar. A raven in the air above apparently grabs some of the meat. A spit appears clearly in a parallel, but less detailed, scene on the Barberini fresco (390 R3), where Mithras and Sol each hold one vertically. Such menial tasks are in civic sacrificial contexts generally performed by boys or young men (a Raven-assistant does offer a spit with meat on it to Mithras at Dura-Europos [42, 13], cf. also 1510 bottom scene). Some at least of these details must remind us of the solitary 'sacrificial' cooking of Herakles, and the contribution of that rule-breakage to his major shift of status from heroism to divinity.

Second, the animal's hide in 'normal' sacrifice was generally allocated as a perquisite to the officiating priest, though it was sometimes sold for temple funds.[87] In the Mysteries, the bull's hide serves as the covering on which Sol and Mithras sit for their feast. The clearest example of this motif is the recent find from Ladenburg (Nordbaden) [Plate 11], on which the skinned hide retains face and horns.[88] This motif can be evoked in several divergent directions. The hide of a hunter's trophy might be dedicated before a god's statue (Longus, *Daphnis and Chloe* 2. 31.3), or on the walls of a temple – this last a gesture worthy of a Roman Emperor or the heroes who hunted the Calydonian boar.[89] The pelt of a hunted victim might itself be considered a *geras* just as the hide of a sacrificial victim was, the distinction between sacrifice and hunting being here elided: the death of the sons of Thestius was due directly to their refusal to allow the pelt of the Calydonian boar to be allocated to Atalante.[90] A different direction of association leads us to the practice of using the skin of a freshly-sacrificed ram as mediator in consultations of oracles or incubation, as in the case of the oracles of Amphiaraus and of Menelaus.[91] The implication here is that the hide of an animal already sacrificed constitutes a metonymic – and so perhaps more decisive – link with the Other World which the incubation or consultation seeks to build upon.[92] In other words the hide is a sort of magic carpet for taking extraordinary (spiritual) journeys. A third possible evocation is suggested by an Alexandrian coin-type from the reign of Antoninus Pius. Herakles sits in comradely fashion with the centaur Pholus on a rock, which is covered by his lionskin. The hero grasps in one hand a lyre, his friend with the other; while a servant draws wine from a krater standing on a rock.[93] Here the pelt is a sign for heroic courtliness, for a sort of 'wild civilization'.

In none of these evocations is the hide simply that of an animal sacrificed under normal civic rules. The anomalous status of the death of the Mithraic bull is reaffirmed in the oddity of the use to which the hide is put, whichever the direction in which the theologians of the Mysteries chose to evoke its significance. My preference is for the notion of a magic carpet – more formally: the establishment of a specially interesting transit-point between the two worlds, between Here and There. In mythical terms, that point of transition is created by the death of the bull; in ritual terms it is reconstructed in the Mithraic feast.[94]

We may notice finally the Mithraic treatment of the dagger with which Mithras kills the bull. In Greek sacrificial iconography, the butchers' instruments have no special place. At Rome, although there was of course an extensive iconography of ritual utensils, apparently first deployed in full on the frieze of the temple of Vespasian in the Forum Romanum, the characteristic sacrificial knife has no special place in it.[95] On dedicatory and sacrificial altars, it appears frequently, often with the *securis* (axe), on one side, contrasting with the 'decent' instruments, the *patera* and *urceus*, on the other. But the knife is marked indelibly by its association with the social status of the public slaves who performed the actual killing in public sacrifice. In the Mysteries, by contrast, the dagger – quite apart from sometimes being made to resemble a sword[96] – is elevated to peculiar prominence in a number of monuments. It is, first, already in the hand of Mithras when he is 'born' from the rock, and may have been transmitted to him by 'Saturnus', one of the enigmatic figures of the early phases of the bye-scenes.[97] Moreover, it serves as a sign that Mithras never stoops to ruse when mastering the bull, never employs the apparatus of nets, snares, dogs, callers so familiar from the hunting sarcophagi. But the strangest role of the Mithraic dagger is at the feast, where on a number of representations it receives special prominence. A good example is on the reverse of the Heddernheim I relief (1083) [Plate 10]. Here the dagger is set vertically between Mithras and Sol, crowned with a 'phrygian cap' and emitting rays like an imitation sun. On the reverse of the Rückingen monument (1183), the dagger wears a crown with nine rays. On another monument, it is carried by Mithras into the chariot of the Sun (1579). Some altars also bear multiple images of daggers, evidently recalling its place of honour at the feast.[98] By contrast to the reticence of civic sacrifice, the Mysteries gloried in the instrument of the bull's death.[99]

Whatever the case with actual Mithraic ritual sacrifice, about which we know extremely little,[100] Mithras' bull-killing as represented on the cult-icon and the bye-scenes was deliberately anomalous, just as the imagery which it shares with Nike is anomalous. Discreetly or blatantly, the act is distanced from the norms of Graeco-Roman civic sacrifice. It seems clear that such deliberate deviation from several implied norms signals criticism. And criticism in turn implies the assertion, through the icon, of goals and meanings quite different from those of civic sacrifice. But to what end?

In a word, I think, purity. We know that during one of the important initiatory rituals of the modal grade Lion initiates were expressly bidden to keep their hands 'pure from everything painful, harmful and filthy (or sinful)', καθαρὰς . . . ἀπὸ παντὸς λυπηροῦ καὶ βλαπτικοῦ καὶ μυσαροῦ and as they were told this, honey was poured on their hands – instead of water – to purify them (Porphyry, *de antro* 15).[101] The object of symbolic boundaries of this type is to create and reinforce commitment to sharp categorical oppositions, between past and present, good and evil, Here and There. We have good reason to believe that within the Mysteries the most dramatic and horrible image of Here was Woman, represented symbolically as a hyena, which in the Graeco-Roman bestiary was the type-inversion of proper rules and boundaries, the very opposite of the behaviour deemed typical of the lion.[102] So far from being a curious fact about the Mysteries of Mithras, the exclusion of women was quite fundamental to its conception of the world and of the religious project. The 'curious' birth of Mithras from a rock can be seen as (among other things) a deliberate denial of a more normal type of birth; the names for the grades as motivated by a specific rejection of feminine categories; the choice of Lion as modal grade as related to the supposed distaste of real (male) lions for sexual intercourse; and so on. Women represented the world that the Mysteries enabled initiates to escape from; as such, the Mysteries can be seen as merely reproducing one of the oldest dreams of patriarchal society, the abolition of women in order to create a fair, just, untroubled existence. Not in reality, of course – several Mithraists are known to have had sons – but in the 'reality' of the religious life and certainly in the 'reality' of the salvation anticipated.[103]

When Phaedra in Euripides' *Hippolytus* dreams of joining Hippolytus in the hunt on the mountainside, we are aware that something is dreadfully wrong. Hunting, like war, was one place where women – the exception of Atalanta proves the rule – could be forgotten. The virginal ephebe Hippolytus has thus an elective affinity with his pastime, even were he not a devotee of Artemis. Mithras' hunting of the bull is no less appropriate to his rejection of women, and no less appropriate to his age-status. But the motifs which in the Greek myth spell doom for the hunter are converted in the Mysteries, in an entirely different religious context, into the means of salvation and immortality. Freedom from women was merely an image: the real aim was to be free from this world, the world of genesis, of becoming, of change.

So radical an aim involved the unravelling of a good deal of knitting, indeed nothing less than the rejection of the entire set of implicit associations between agriculture, sexual reproduction, sacrifice and divinity which passed for the anthropology of the Graeco-Roman world.

We have seen already how the Mysteries provided an account of the origin of corn, from the body of the bull. We may add that when Mithras springs from the rock he generally holds not only the dagger but also a torch: which looks like a Mithraic counter to the myth of Prometheus (Mithras is indeed said to be the Persian Prometheus in a papyrus glossary, *POxy.* 15, 1802 line 64). Now that myth, in Hesiod's version at least, understood sacrifice as a necessity deriving from the trick at Mekone when Prometheus deceived Zeus, after which men no longer sat at the tables of the gods; and agricultural labour, women and death as further consequences.[104] But the Mysteries sought to reverse the values of 'life' and 'death', to reject this world by providing a re-reading of the true significance of the notion 'life'. One fundamental move was easy: to make the dominantly negative patriarchal view of women still worse, identifying Woman as a figure for impurity. One of the basic props of the Hesiod view – the inevitability of marriage – could thus be converted into the starting-point of the religious quest. Both corn and fire could be removed from the chain of Promethean theft and guile by being given an alternative origin, as gifts of Mithras. This did away with the metonymic relation between 'hiding the seed' in agricultural labour and sexual reproduction; and turned civilization (fire) into a magical good, related further to the essence of the lion/Lion at the core of the symbolism constructed by the religion. On the basis of these shifts, sacrifice, which traditionally marked the gap between heaven and earth as much as it marked the possibility of communication, could be reconstructed so as to restore commensality between gods and men (which is perhaps what is signified by those monuments on which a group appears at the feast, not simply Mithras and Sol).[105] 'Commensality' was one of the connotations of immortality; purity its indispensable precondition. But the rigours of this reversal of traditional assumptions were such that the walls around the fantasy world had to be made as impervious as possible – it is not an accident that the Mysteries tended to spread within groups already closed in the 'real' world, that they had none of the marks of a 'normal' ancient religion, such as processions, public iconography, public sacrifice, that the groups remained small, preferring to split rather than to increase in size. Even so, in the context of the Roman Empire, the offer of a practical road to radical purity served this upstart religion well.

★

It is easy to suppose that the proper way to enquire into an ancient religion of this kind, about which very little can be known, is to investigate specifically religious beliefs, to pursue similarities and contrasts with other contemporary religions, to construct morphologies and typologies – in other words to be a historian of religion. That certainly may be one way of making an enquiry. But it takes the religious enterprise as a finished whole, as a given, instead of as a project of the imagination, which, because it is a fantasy, must be constantly worked at if it is to remain credible and, still more, effective. The more ambitious the fantasy, the more ideological work it demands of its believers. What procedures do they adopt? What logical methods? How are meanings established, rejected, refined, evoked? What is the role of appeal to commonsense, empirical evidence? The Mysteries of Mithras is a long-dead religion. The effort of reviving it as an object of knowledge is considerable; and the game is only worth the candle if the questions asked can be truly historical, not antiquarian. We need to remember that the Mysteries were in principle as human and frail an enterprise as that revealed by Leon Festinger in his small masterpiece, *When Prophecy Fails*.[106] Herself sincerely religious, Jocelyn Toynbee had always that generous and lively perception.

NOTES

[1] Unless otherwise stated, the numbers placed after monuments or inscriptions mentioned in the text refer to M.J. Vermaseren, *Corpus inscriptionum et monumentorum religionis mithriacae* (2 vols., The Hague, 1956–60). We have learned with regret of the death of Professor Vermaseren, in whose debt all students of the Mysteries stand.

It will be noted that I do not refer to this religion as 'Mithraism', which is a pseudo-scientific neologism, but by a term which is at least evidenced in antiquity, the Mysteries of Mithras.

[2] See also Chaeremon's account [Neronian] of the exclusive life and learning of the Egyptian priests, edited with commentary by P.W. Van der Horst, *Chaeremon: the fragments*, EPROER 101 (Leiden, 1984), frg. 10. Our best source for the type of speculation to which Origen is referring is Plutarch's *De Iside et Osiride*, with commentary by J. Gwyn Griffiths (Cardiff, 1970). Garth Fowden has now provided an exemplary account of one type of such theosophy in the later Principate: *The Egyptian Hermes* (Cambridge, 1986).

[3] This surely refers to the religion we know as the Mysteries of Mithras, which claimed to have been founded by Zoroaster; but the distinct learning and wisdom of the *magoi* caused Plutarch, for example, to quote them as a possible source for the doctrine of *daemones* :*De def. orac.* 10 (415a–b).

[4] Lists of the wise nations are given by Origen, *Contra Celsum* 1, 14 and 16, deriving from Celsus. A similar list is offered by both Diogenes Laertius, *Vit. phil.* 1, 1–11 (Proem.) and Augustine, *Civ. Dei*, 8, 9. The earliest, rudimentary, list seems to be Philo, *Quod omnis probus*, 74–5, 92–6: he ascribes to Alexander a concern to reveal the wisdom of the barbarians to the Greeks. On the Christian versions of the trope, J.H. Waszink, 'Some observations on the appreciation of the "Philosophy of the Barbarians" in early Christian literature', *Mélanges Chr. Mohrmann* (Utrecht, 1963), 41–56.

[5] An interesting example of 'lies' mixed with (half-) truths in an initiatory context may be found in F. Barth, *Ritual and knowledge among the Baktaman of New Guinea* (New Haven, 1975), though it must be admitted that Barth was among the Baktaman for less than a year, and for most of that time could hardly speak the language: M. Crick, 'Anthropological field research, meaning creation and knowledge construction', *Semantic Anthropology* (ed. D. Parkin), ASA Monographs, 22 (London, 1982), 15–37, 19.

[6] In objecting to an astronomical reading of the temple of Sette Sfere in Ostia, Vermaseren takes it as a fixed principle that the Mysteries had a very simple message. The simplicity of this message is supposed to be guaranteed by the monumental evidence (*The Mithraeum at Marino*, EPROER 16.3 [Leiden 1982], 56–9). Since this is far from simple (as well as far from transparent), the argument is evidently a priori and not empirical. The hidden premise is that the initiates were merely bluff soldiers – which is of course not true in any exclusive or simple sense, and anyway neglects the obvious point that there can be many levels of understanding. Moreover, when it suited Vermaseren's purpose, he was

quite ready to use information provided by the very sources – Euboulos, Pallas, Kronios and Numenius – he believed to be tainted with neo-platonist fancy (e.g. *ibid.* p. 75).

[7] Cumont never altered his view of the Iranian basis of the Mysteries, despite the increase in disconfirming evidence in his lifetime, particularly the excavations at Dura-Europos and Ostia: see especially, 'La Fin du monde selon les mages occidentaux', *RHR* 103 (1931), 19–96; 'L'iniziazione di Nerone da parte di Tiridate d'Armenia', *RivFil* n.s.11 (1933), 145–54; 'Mithra en Asie Mineure', *Anatolian Studies in honour of W.H. Buckler* (Manchester, 1939), 67–76; 'The Dura Mithraeum' (ed. E.D. Francis), *Mithraic Studies*, ed. J.R. Hinnells (Manchester, 1975), I, 151–207. Yet his own work on the Zoroastrian pseudepigrapha (with J. Bidez, *Les Mages hellénisés: Zoroastre, Ostanès et Hystaspe d'après la tradition grecque* [Bruxelles, 1938]) should have made him more aware of the degree to which 'Zoroaster' was a figment of the Greek imagination. For a full discussion of the issue of the survival of authentic Iranian religion in Anatolia during the hellenistic and Roman periods, M. Boyce, *A History of Zoroastrianism*, vol. 3, Handbuch der Orientalistik, ed. B. Spüler, 1,8,1,2: 2c (Leiden/Köln, forthcoming).

[8] See S. Wikander, 'Études sur les mystères de Mithras', *Arsbok Vetenskaps-societeten i Lund* (1951), 5–46; R.L. Gordon, 'Franz Cumont and the doctrines of Mithraism', *Mithraic Studies*, I, 215–47.

[9] The very excesses of the extreme Iranian thesis of L.A. Campbell, *Mithraic iconography and ideology*, EPROER 9 (Leiden, 1968) have hurried the process of rejection, so that it is now generally agreed that,'si Mithra est iranien, le mithriacisme est gréco-romain': Robert Turcan, *Mithra et le mithriacisme* (Paris, 1981), 96.

[10] We are fortunate now to be able to refer to the judicious and exhaustive account of modern developments by R.L. Beck, 'Mithraism since Franz Cumont', *Aufstieg und Niedergang der römischen Welt*, eds. H. Temporini, W. Haase (Berlin-New York, 1984), II, 16, 4, 2003–2115.

[11] When already long retired, she examined my own dissertation with a critical but kindly eye. (The bookplate is reproduced at the front of this book.)

[12] See 'Still more about Mithras', *Hibbert Journal* 54 (1955–6), 107–14 (a reply to earlier articles in the same journal by S.G.F. Brandon and J. Ferguson); *A silver casket and strainer from the Walbrook Mithraeum*, EPROER 4 (Leiden, 1963); *Art in Roman Britain* (Oxford, 1964), 97–101, 168–71; *The Roman Art Treasures from the Temple of Mithras* (London, 1986).

[13] The arguments by which Robert Turcan sought to discredit the information provided by Euboulos and Pallas (and also Numenius and Kronios) leave me entirely unconvinced, based as they were upon the premise of a genuinely Zoroastrian basis for the Mysteries, a view he has now modified. On the contrary, their evidence is among the most important available to us: *Mithras Platonicus*, EPROER 47 (Leiden, 1975), 23–43.

An Ostian inscription neatly emphasizes the antiquity of the Mysteries in the eyes of their initiates, as expressed in iconography: *Deum vetusta religione in velo formatum et umore obnubilatum marmoreum . . . fecit Sex. Pompeius Maximus pater* (233; correct reading in CIL XIV 4314).

[14] Although the term *mithraeum* is usual, and convenient, it has no ancient authority. Temples of Mithras are usually termed in inscriptions *templum, aedes, spelaeum* (none of them specific terms). At S. Gemini in Umbria a recently published inscription with numerous peculiarities (cf. CIMRM 688 = CIL XI 5737, from Sentinum/Sentino), from the late third century, names the temple *leonteum* : U. Ciotti, 'Due iscrizione mitriache inedite', *Hommages à M. J. Vermaseren*, eds. M.B. de Boer and T.A. Edridge, EPROER 68 (Leiden, 1978), I, 233–46, 234 (not recorded in *L'Année épigraphique*). This cannot be taken to be the normal Mithraic term.

[15] More difficult to assess are (1) the name *Arimanius*, which occurs on five inscriptions as the recipient of votive offerings, and which obviously recalls the Iranian opponent of Ahura Mazda/Ohrmazd, on which see most recently, H. Jackson, 'The meaning and function of

the Leontocephaline in Roman Mithraism', *Numen* 32 (1985), 117–45, 18–19; (2) the names of the torchbearers, Cautes and Cautopates, which may well be Iranian: see M. Schwartz, 'Cautes and Cautopates: the Mithraic torchbearers', *Mithraic Studies*, II, 406–23, though no two Iranists agree on the etymology – Schwartz's most important point is that Avestan *pati* standing after (or before) a noun in the accusative or locative connotes 'opposing, against, towards' (p. 421).

[16] I have attempted a neutral report in 'The date and significance of CIMRM 593 (British Museum, Townley Collection)', *Journal of Mithraic Studies* (hereafter *JMS*) 2 (1978), 148–74. It seems likely that the Zoroastrian pseudepigrapha were the means whereby a small local cult, presumably mainly the work of a single individual, grounded in one of several post-Iranian cults of Mithra(s), might have come to the notice of learned exegetes such as Euboulos and Pallas, and so of Numenius and Kronios in the latter part of the second century A.D. For a survey of other views, see Beck, 'Mithraism', 2071–78.

[17] In connection with the use of astronomical-astrological lore on public monuments, see R. Turcan, 'Le Piédestal de la colonne antonine à propos d'un livre récent', *RA* (1975), 305–18, 308–14; R. Hannah, 'The Emperor's stars. . .', *AJA* 90 (1986), 337–42. In the case of the Mysteries, it is not necessary to suppose any profound understanding of principles on the part of ordinary initiates, or even Fathers (the highest grade). The construction of icon and temple was normally a matter no doubt of applying a prepared scheme – it did not have to be based upon personal knowledge.

[18] See recently I.P. Culianu, *Psychanodia, I*, EPROER 99 (Leiden, 1983), though his discussion of the issue in relation to the Mysteries is superficial, confined as it is to the unreliable and problematical account by Celsus of the planetary ladder (Origen, *Contra Celsum*, 6.22) on which see now the discussion of R.L. Beck, *The Planetary Gods and Planetary Orders in the Mysteries of Mithras*, EPROER 109 (Leiden, 1988).

[19] One of several obvious points missed by R. MacMullen, *Paganism in the Roman Empire* (New Haven, 1981), 122–26, who dismisses the Mysteries as an uninteresting blend of quackery and good fellowship. See also the apt comments of S.R.F. Price, *JRS* 72 (1982), 194–96.

[20] From this perspective, the cults of the Magna Mater and of Isis and the Egyptian gods count as traditional religions, though not the mysteries developed in the Graeco-Roman world within them. As so often, the notion 'Oriental Religion' is hopelessly inappropriate to the problems.

[21] In what follows, I denote 'astronomy-astrology' by the term 'astronomy'.

[22] See Beck, 'Mithraism' [n. 10], 2081–3.

[23] 'Cautes and Cautopates: some astronomical considerations', *JMS* 2, 1 (1977), 1–17; 'The Mithraic torchbearers and "absence of opposition" ', *Classical Views* n.s. 1 (1982), 126–40; *Planetary Gods* [n. 18].

[24] Bull-killing scenes: Sidon (75); London (810); Siscia (1472); feast-scenes: Banjevac (Zotović in *JMS* 2,2 (1978), 189–91; perhaps the Stockstadt fragment (1161); rock-birth: Housesteads (860), Trier, Altbachtal (Spring-Summer quadrants only) (985).

[25] R.L. Beck, 'Interpreting the Ponza zodiac, 1', *JMS* 1, 1 (1976), 1–19; II, *JMS* 2, 1 (1977), 87–147; the original publication was by M.J. Vermaseren, *The Mithraeum at Ponza*, EPROER 16.2 (Leiden, 1974).

[26] Porphyry, *de antro nympharum* 6 = Arethusa edition, p.8, lines 15–19.

[27] This was Vermaseren's conclusion, supported by H.G. Gundel, '*Imagines zodiaci*. Zu neueren Funden und Forschungen', *Hommages Vermaseren* [n. 14], I, 438–54, 449–53. Beck, 'Ponza, I' argued that it was rather a unique representation of an arcane astral entity, the dragon of the lunar nodes, which was supposed to cause eclipses. Gundel objected that this was over-interpretation (p. 452). The question is undecidable since no other representation of the dragon is known; and in the second part of his article Beck tacitly allowed that the snake was an allusion to the Pole.

[28] This same passage of Julian's *Hymn* also states implicitly another paradox which certainly seems to have featured in the Mysteries of Mithras, the identity of Helios (-Mithras?) and Oceanus. As such, Helios is "Lord of a double essence", διπλῆς ἡγεμὼν οὐσίας (147d); cf. Vermaseren, 'The miraculous birth of Mithras', *Mnemosyne* [Ser.4] 4 (1951), 285–301.

[29] Beck, 'Sette Sfere, Sette Porte and the spring equinoxes of A.D. 172 and 173', *Mysteria Mithrae*, ed. U. Bianchi, EPROER 80 (Leiden, 1979), 515–29.

[30] This was suggested by Dr. W. Schlosser in a letter to Professor Beck (Beck, 'Ponza, II', 135–6): it is a certain inference only if, as seems unlikely, the snake does represent the dragon of the lunar nodes.

[31] On Vulci, dated early third century, see A.M. Sgubini Moretti, 'Nota preliminare su un mitreo scoperto a Vulci', *Mysteria Mithrae*, [n.29] 259–77. with figs. 3, 4, 5.

[32] I have discussed the zodiacal symbolism of this temple in 'The sacred geography of the *mithraeum*: the case of Sette Sfere', *JMS* 1, 2 (1976), 119–65, 126–38, though I now agree with Beck that some interpretations offered there are far-fetched or plain wrong ('Mithraism' [n. 10], 2025 n.32).

[33] See Campbell, *Iconography* [n. 9], 42 with n. 47. This statement applies to those cases only in which the torchbearers, or substitute signs such as the cock and owl at Mitreo degli Animali in Ostia (279 with G. Becatti, *Scavi di Ostia*, II: *I Mitrei* (Rome, 1954), 89 and fig. 19), were found *at the ends of the 'benches'* and not, for example, on the side-walls, as at Pareti dipinte (268.2).

[34] *De antro* 24. The reading adopted is that of the Arethusa editors, p. 24 lines 11–15. By realising that †κατ'αὐτοῦ V, κατὰ τοῦ M must conceal the unfamiliar proper name τοῦ Καύτου – which demands the supplement of the other torchbearer Cautopates, these editors have provided a signal service to the study of the Mysteries. If they had known more of the conventional scholarship on this matter, the suggestion would probably never have occurred to them.

[35] Macrobius, *Comm. in Somn. Scipionis* 1.12.1–2 presents a slightly more elaborate version of the same claim, derived either from Porphyry here or from his source, Numenius of Apamea: see Regali, *ad loc.*, pp. 319–22. The entire chapter 12 is an elaborate account of the soul's astral journey into genesis, part of which [=Numenius frg.34 des Places] has recently been used to argue that in the Mysteries Leo was the point, after Cancer, in which souls took their first step towards birth: Jackson, 'Leontocephaline' [n. 15], 25–6.

[36] Vermaseren, *The Mithraeum at S. Maria Capua Vetere*, EPROER 16.1 (Leiden, 1971) 22–3 with pl.XX does not even discuss the issue; but cf. the remarks of H. Sichtermann, 'Die Flügel der Psyche', *Studies in Classical Archaeology* (Festschrift K. Kerenyi), Acta Univ. Stockholm. 5 (Stockholm, 1968), 49–58.

[37] The two cases of bowls set midway between the central niches: the temple near the Circus Maximus: C. Pietrangeli, 'Il Mitreo del Palazzo dei Musei di Roma', *BCAR* 68 (1940), 143–73, 156–7 with fig. 10; Dura-Europos, second and third phases: M.I. Rostovtzeff, *et. al.*, *The Excavations at Dura-Europos: Preliminary Report of the Seventh and Eighth Seasons (1933–4, 1934–5)* (New Haven, 1939), 73, 74 with fig. 35.
  The niches themselves usually contain small altars (which may be related to the sequences of altars found on the icon). In the Palazzo Imperiale temple at Ostia, the niches contained double images of Cautopates (L) and Cautes (R): Becatti, *Mitrei* [n.33], p. 54 and fig. 11. This certainly suggests that the torchbearers were considered to be in some sense the guardians of the gates.

[38] W. Ristow, *Mithras im römischen Köln*, EPROER 42 (Leiden, 1974), 22 no. 14 and pl. 19, from the supposed third temple outside the walls.

[39] There are in fact three snakes; the third emerges from the lionhead's mouth and descends towards an altar on the left.

[40] Note also 1141 (Rückingen) and 1298 (Wahlheim).

[41] The bird is mistakenly identified by Becatti, *Mitrei*, 98 with pl.XX.3, as an eagle. Although Cumont himself noted that Hydra, Crater and Corvus are all neighbouring constellations, he dismissed the fact as mere decoration upon an essentially Iranian theology. But he did call attention to an important monument from Apulum (1974: unfortunately not illustrated in CIMRM) on which a krater appears in the field immediately beneath the raven (Vermaseren: "on the border of which a raven is perched"): *Textes et monuments figurés relatifs aux mystères de Mithra* (Brussels, 1896–99), 1, 202.

[42] Macrobius, *Comm. in Somn. Scipionis* 1.12.8 knows of a theory that Crater is the point at which souls on their descent become drunk with the influx of matter and forget heavenly things: the Mithraic doctrine was undoubtedly more complicated.

[43] The claim by MacMullen, *Paganism* [n. 19], 124 that other cults had equally, or more, numerous initiatory grades is based on an elementary confusion between initiatory grades and posts or functions.

[44] For details, see Gordon, 'CIMRM 593' [n. 16], 259–60.

[45] The standard collection of evidence is still St. Weinstock, 'Victor and invictus', *HTR* 50 (1957), 211–47; *id.*, s.v. Victor and Victoria, *RE* VIII A2 (1958), 2485–500; 2501–42, esp. 2494–6 on Hercules Victor and Invictus; also M. Guarducci, 'Sol Invictus Augustus', *MPAA* 30–1 (1957–9), 161–9.

[46] F. Saxl, *Mithras: Typengeschichtliche Untersuchungen* (Berlin, 1931), 54–7 makes this point more clearly than Cumont.

[47] Lucian, *Imag.* 19; *Herod.* 8; *Hist.* 35; such lists were apparently standard rhetorical fare: Galen IV 751 Kühn (Dion, Milo, Herakles, Achilles).

[48] This exploit was the subject of an epigram by Dorieus which tellingly comments that he made the monster (τὸ πελώριον) seem like a young lamb (quoted by Athenaeus, *Deipn.*10. 412f–413a from Phylarchus, *FGrH* 81 F 3). That the motif retained its suggestiveness in the early Empire seems probable from Petronius's invention of a gigantic Cappadocian *qui valebat: poterat (b)ovem iratum tollere* (accepting Reiske's emendation of IOVEM in H, which Pellegrino, for example, capitalizes into *Iovem*, which is surely nonsense): *Satyricon* 63.

[49] The source of this story is an Argive poet, Lykeas, known only because Pausanias quotes him several times; date unknown, but presumably hellenistic.

[50] The gem-cutter Anteros devised a type which occurs on hellenistic and Roman gems, pastes, cameos, reliefs and even glassware: a crowned youth carries a calf over one shoulder – the animal is upsidedown and its forelegs wave in the air. This type might refer to such exploits as those of Milo, given the wreath, though this is not suggested by J. Boardman, *The Ionides Collection* (London, 1969), 98 no. 48 with fig. (cf. 103, no. 81).

[51] It occurs also at Rückingen (1137, face, scene 2e) [Vermaseren wrongly suggests that it occurred also in his scene 2d]; and probably at Königshoffen (1359, right pilaster, scene 7) – enough remains at the top of the fragment to make Ernest Will's identification plausible: 'Le Bas-relief mithriaque de Strasbourg, Königshoffen', *RA* (1950), 67–85, 74 no. 5; 81.

[52] The readings in C.C. Van Essen and M.J. Vermaseren, *The Excavations in the Mithraeum of the Church of Sta Prisca in Rome* (Leiden, 1965), 200–5, are now open to considerable doubt.

[53] See Cumont, *Textes*, I, 171–2; Saxl, *Mithras*, 56–7; H. Gressmann, 'Mithras, der Rinderdieb', *DLZ* 44 (1923), 79–92, 91–2; C. Clemen, 'Der Mithrasmythus', *BJ* 142 (1937), 217–26, 25. The best evidence for the motif of 'bull-theft by Mithras' in the Mysteries is Porphyry, *de antro* 19, *bouklopos theos*, whose reference to the Mysteries of Mithras is confirmed by Firmicus Maternus, *De errore* 5.2 [acclamation] *Musta boöklopiēs*, which must mean "initiate of the theft of the bull". Cf. Cumont, *Textes*, I, 171 and Bidez-Cumont, *Mages hellénisés* [n. 7], II, 153–4 on frg.09a.

[54] Vergil, *Aen.* 8.209–11; Livy, 1.7.5; Dionysius of Halicarnassus, *AR* 1.39.2.

⁵⁵ See for example G.M.A. Richter, *Catalogue of Engraved Gems, Metropolitan Museum* (Rome, 1956), 82 no.356 pl.XLVI (Nike sacrificing a piglet held by a hind leg – apparently modelled on a fourth-century statue or relief); U. Pannuti, *Museo arch. naz. di Napoli: catalogo delle collezione glittice* (Rome, 1983), no. 57 (old man pouring from an oenochoe over a piglet held by its hindleg; from Pompeii). A gem in the Kunsthistorisches Museum, Vienna with a similar scene of 'rustic sacrifice' seems to show a young man at the rear holding a kid by the foreleg: E. Zweierlein-Diehl, *Die antiken Gemmen* (Munich, 1973–9), I, 154, no. 498 pl.83.

⁵⁶ See for example a red-figure *kylix* in the British Museum, c. 500 B.C., BM Cat. E36: F. Smith, *Catalogue of Vases*, III (1896), pl. II; K. Schefold, *Götter – und Heldensagen der Griechen in der spätarchaischen Kunst* (Munich, 1978), 163 fig. 219. This cup also represents the capture of the Bull of Marathon. There is no reason to suppose that an iconographic tradition of such an exploit survived into the period of the formation of Mithraic theology or art. But I am not here concerned with 'survival'.

⁵⁷ It refers in fact to the entire process of removing the bull from its original home, wherever that was, and the circumstances under which that process took place, whatever they were: we have, bluntly, virtually no idea at all. But I am struck by the heroic, violent representation of the process in Mithraic art.

⁵⁸ The feat was celebrated in an epigram by Posidippus: Gow-Page, *Hellenistic Epigrams*, I, 170 Posidippus no. XIV (mid-third century B.C.); see also Pausanias, 6.11.6.

⁵⁹ D.L. Page, *Further Greek Epigrams* (Cambridge, 1981), 45–6 makes the first point but does not comment on the obvious infringement of a rule.

⁶⁰ See also Aelian, *VH* 1.24. There is no iconographical tradition: F. Brommer, *Herakles II: Die unkanonischen Taten* (Darmstadt, 1984), 13.

⁶¹ Lapiths: Pindar frg. 168 Snell; Theiodamas: Apollodorus, *Bibl.* 2.7.7 (with Frazer's note); cf. Philostratus, *Imag.* 2.21 (no other known iconography). For Herakles *bouthoinos* at Lindos, see M.P. Nilsson, *Geschichte der griechischen Religion*, ed. 3 (Munich, 1967), I, 153–4; W. Burkert, 'Bouzyge und Palladion: Gewalt und Gericht im altgriechischen Ritual', *ZRGG* 22 (1970), 356–68, 364–5.

⁶² For example, K. Schefold, *Götter- und Heldensagen*, [n. 56] 104 fig. 127 [red-figure amphora, Boston]. The *splangkhnoptēs* motif, which depicts the cooking of the noble innards on spits, is especially noteworthy in this connection: S. Rizza, 'Una nuova pelike a figure rosse e lo "Splanchnoptes" di Styppax', *ASAA* 37–8 (1959–60), 312–45.

⁶³ J-L. Durand, 'Sacrifier, partager, repartir', *L'Uomo* (Rome), 9 (1985), 53–63, 59–61.

⁶⁴ C. Bérard, J.-P. Vernant *et al.*, *La Cité des images* (Lausanne-Paris 1984), 55 fig. 83: also J. Rudhardt, *Notions fondamentales de la pensée religieuse et actes constitutifs du culte dans la Grèce classique* (Geneva, 1958), 261, presciently rejecting Stengel's view of the meaning of the expression *ton boun anairein*.

⁶⁵ See recently F. Graf, *Griechische Mythologie* (Munich–Zurich, 1985), 109.

⁶⁶ The statue of Po(u)lydamas was also capable of healing illness: Lucian, *Deorum concil.* 12; cf. also the material collected by S. Eitrem, s.v. Heros, *RE* VIII.15 (1912), 1111–45, 114–5.

⁶⁷ Several versions are known, the earliest ascribed to Diogenes the Cynic (Diogenes Laertius, *Vit. phil.* 6.50). It has been found in Greek on a Pompeian wall (*CIL* IV 733) and in Latin (*CIL* VI 30, 738): O. Weinreich, 'De dis ignotis quaestiones selectae', *ARW* 18 (1915), 8–15.

⁶⁸ Varro, *Inst. div.* frg. 61 Cardauns (Servius, *ad Aen.* 8.363; Macrobius, *Sat.* 3.6.10).

⁶⁹ C. Schneider, 'Herakles der Todüberwinder', *Wiss. Zeitschr. Univ. Leipzig, Gesellsch.-Sprachwissen. Reihe* (Heft 5), 7 (1957–8), 661–66. A statue of Hercules with Cerberus was found in temple I at Stockstadt, apparently part of the cult furniture (1180).

⁷⁰ Cumont always understood the act as mere putting to death: *Textes*, I, 185–6). The issue has been raised once again by Robert Turcan's important discussion, 'Le Sacrifice

mithriaque: innovations de sens et de modalités', *Entretiens Fondation Hardt* 27 (1981), 341–73, who rightly sees the issue as one of 'refusal' or 'rejection' of normal Graeco-Roman rules for sacrifice. This is a rewarding article, though I differ from him in a number of emphases.

71 I pass over the frequent representations of Mithras as hunter on horseback.

72 Oddly enough, Cumont omits this scene in his lengthy description in 'The Dura Mithraeum' [n. 7], 174–5. It is best seen in the photograph in R. Merkelbach, *Mithras* (Königstein, 1984), 274 fig. 15, though as usual his interpretation is eccentric. The painting dates from the third phase, mid-third century AD.

73 The earliest example seems to be on the lid of a Hadrianic sarcophagus now in the Merseyside County Museum: B. Ashmole, *Ancient Marbles at Ince Blundell Hall* (Oxford, 1929), no. 307 pl.48. For the motif in general, B. Andreae, *Die römischen Jagdsarkophage* (Berlin, 1980), 79–80. The stag on the fragmentary lid of a sarcophagus from the catacomb of S. Callisto is very similar to the Duran image (Andreae, cat. 99, pl. 107.6). These images resume an archaic iconongraphy, for example of Herakles carrying the Kerkopes (F. Brommer, *Vasenlisten zur gr. Heldensage*, ed.3 [Marburg, 1973], 98–9 lists nine certain examples), or the figure (?Orion) on a late seventh-century metope from the Temple of Apollo at Thermos trudging home with his booty on a pole: K. Schefold, *Frühgriechische Sagenbilder* (Munich, 1964), 34 with pl.21.

74 D.E.L. Haynes and P.E.D. Hirst, *Porta Argentariorum*, Supplement to PBSR (London, 1939), 31–2, relief I, fig. 17.

75 Saxl, *Mithras* [n. 46], 12–13 rightly objected to Cumont's idea that the motif was based directly upon the Nike of the balustrade of the fifth-century B.C. temple of Nike on the Athenian Acropolis: the image had become banalised in the hellenistic period.

76 A.H. Borbein, *Campanareliefs*, MDAI[RA] Ergänzungsheft 14 (Heidelberg. 1968), 60–2, develops a totally misconceived argument to prove that the original of the Mithras-type must be the Myrrhina terracottas. He does not however explain why the earliest datable Mithraic icon should occur 250 years later.

For the chronological framework of the Nike-representations, I rely upon the sound study by N. Kunisch, *Die stiertötende Nike: typengeschichtliche und mythologische Untersuchungen* (Diss. Munich, 1964). It is of course at this period that the title *invictus* comes to be attached informally to the emperor: Pliny, *Panegyr.* 9.2.

77 The most convenient collection of material is that by O. Brendel, 'Immolatio boum', *MDAI(RA)* 45 (1930), 196–226, catalogue pp. 204–7.

78 Turcan, 'Sacrifice' [n. 70] takes Roman sacrifice without explicit argument to be the point of departure: I suppose his reasons are related to the appearance on some Mithraic monuments of a *dorsuale* round the bull's girth (e.g. 374, 556, 1721, 1916, 2223). I assume that Greek, or more vaguely 'hellenistic conflate' sacrificial rules are those being referred to. The significance of the victim's thighs is the principal justification for this choice, apart from the general grounds, which seem to me to be very strong, for thinking that the Mysteries were founded in hellenised Anatolia and are likely therefore to have based their fundamental imagery on materials known there rather than in Rome. I understand the *dorsuale* not as a sign for 'Roman sacrificial rules' but as a further reference, influenced by Roman sacrificial practice, to the ambiguity of the fate of the bull; cf. also Saxl, *Mithras* [n. 46], 13.

79 "A l'intérieur de chaque type sacrificiel (dans la mesure ou il est possible de définir des types), les rites varient indéfiniment au gré des traditions locales ou gentilices" (*Notions fondamentales* [n. 64], 257) – a point even more true of the hellenistic and Roman worlds than of the archaic and classical one.

80 On the earliest datable bull-killing monument, 593 (Townley Collection, British Museum) (p. 65 above), the ears of wheat emerge from the wound itself (the tail is lost, so we cannot know whether they emerged also from it). This detail is unique. On 1599 (Poetovio III), the snake at the wound has a triple head, which gives a rather similar

impression to the ears of wheat emerging from the tail. The resemblance is presumably intentional.

[81] Taken to be Mithraic mainly because of the crescent moon by Dirk Wortmann, who first published the altar: 'Ein Mithrasstein aus Bonn', *BJ* 169 (1969), 410–23. E. Schwertheim, *Die Denkmäler orientalischer Gottheiten im römischen Deutschland*, EPROER 40 (Leiden, 1974), 35–6 no. 36 fig. 7, expresses doubts about the the sex of the animal and the *patera* in particular, without being conclusive. My own study of the stone seemed to confirm Wortmann's view that a *patera* lies on the ground beneath the bull's testicles. All are agreed that the image is highly original.

[82] See Gordon, 'Sette Sfere' [n. 32], 123 on CIMRM 694 (Bologna) and 1127 (Heddernheim).

[83] Bunches of grapes and other apparently Dionysiac images do sometimes occur in Mithraic contexts, especially in the feast scene. On the reverse of the Heddernheim I monument (1083), Mithras holds a bunch of grapes in his right hand [Plate 10]. On the Ladenburg feast-scene [Plate 11], a bunch of grapes lies on the *trapeza*, as on funerary monuments. On the Königshoffen complex relief (1359. 14), in the feast-scene on the frieze, Sol holds a bunch. Unfortunately, the two columns at Poetovio II which show a kantharus and vines were found outside the temple. The dedication is lost and they may have been re-used as statue-bases (1529; M. Abramić, *Führer durch Poetovio*, ed. 3 [Vienna, 1925], 69 mentions the second one, omitted by Vermaseren). Grapes also appear on one of the wings of the lionhead dedicated by C. Valerius Heracles from the 'Fagan' temple in Ostia (312), together with other 'mystical' signs. Wortman (p. 421) was right to claim that there is no a priori reason for rejecting the Bonn altar merely because it shows a vine (though some of his evidence is imaginary).

[84] For such representations, G. Berthiaume, *Les Rôles du mageiros*, Mnemosyne suppl. 70 (Leiden, 1982), 49. Roman rules were rather different: C. Santini, 'Il lessico della spartizione nel sacrificio romano', *L'Uomo* 9 (1985), 63–73.

[85] In J.R. Hinnells and R.L. Gordon, 'Some new photographs of well-known Mithraic monuments', *JMS* 2 (1977–8), 198–223, 213–23, I have listed 58 monuments on which the scene or its analogues appear.

[86] F. Puttkammer, *Quomodo Graeci victimarum carnes distribuerunt* (Diss. Königsberg, 1912), 7–8, 10–11; for a possible significance of the practice, J-L. Durand, 'Bêtes grecques', in *La Cuisine du sacrifice en pays grec*, eds. M. Detienne and J-P. Vernant (Paris, 1979), 133–65, 157.

[87] Puttkammer, 5, 7–8; P. Stengel, *Die griechische Kultusalterthümer*, ed. 3 (Munich, 1920), 116–7.

[88] Schwertheim, *Denkmäler* [n. 81], 188–9 no. 144, pl. 42. Other examples: CIMRM 42. 12 with Cumont, 'Dura Mithraeum' [n. 7], 176–7; 397 rev. (head retained); 641 rev. (head and horns retained); 1083 rev.; 1137 rev.; 1161 rev., but fragmentary and doubtful; 1292. 5g (head retained); 1896 rev. (head retained).

[89] Hadrian dedicated in the temple of Eros at Thespiae the hide of a bear (*akrotheinion . . . arktou*) he had killed from horseback in Mysia (probably): *IG* VII, 1828 = Kaibel *Epigr. gr.* 811 with W. Weber, *Untersuchungen zur Geschichte des Kaisers Hadrianus* (Leipzig, 1907), 157. Augustus took, as the spoils of war after Actium, the splendid tusks of the Calydonian boar and set them up in a shrine of Dionysus in the Palatine gardens (Pausanias 8.46.1; 4–5), but the moth-eaten hide remained to grace the walls of the temple of Athena Alea in Tegea (*ibid.* 47.2). On such dedications, see also Fr. Pfister, *Die Reliquienkult im Altertum*, RGVV 5, 1–2 (Giessen, 1909–12), I, 324–5.

[90] Callimachus, *Hymn to Artemis* 219–20; Apollodorus, *Bibl.* 1.8.2–3. For the iconography, see G. Koch, *Die mythologischen Sarkophage: Meleager* (Berlin, 1975), no. 116 pl. 103b and 107b (Louvre sarcophagus); his nos. 112, 115, 117, 120–22 show the same scene but less well.

[91] See J. Pley, *De lanae in antiquorum ritibus usu*, RGVV 11.2 (Giessen, 1911), 3–16 for relevant examples. Some other material in L. Gernet, 'La notion mythique de la valeur en Grèce', in *Anthropologie de la Grèce antique* (Paris, 1968), 93–137, 125–6.

[92] Although the well-known story in Lucian, *Toxar.* 48 concerning Scythian rules for administering oaths of loyalty on a bull's hide, is not relevant here, Robertson Smith's commentary surely is: W. Kroll, 'Alte Taufgebräuche', *ARW* 8 (1905), Beiheft (at end of volume), 27–53, 39.

[93] *BMC Alexandria*, 124 no. 1057, pl. VI (not in Milne, *Catalogue*). This imagery is not, so far as I can discover, classical: see Brommer, *Herakles*, II [n. 60], 54–8.

[94] See J.P. Kane, 'The Mithraic cult meal in its Greek and Roman environment', *Mithraic Studies* [n. 7], II, 313–51, with the remarks of Beck, 'Mithraism' [n. 10], 2083–4. On the wider implications of collective eating in the Roman world, J.H. D'Arms, 'Control, companionship and *clientela*: some social implications of the Roman communal meal', *CV* 3 (1984), 327–48.

[95] R. von Schaewen, *Römische Opfergeräte*, Archäologische Studien, 1 (Berlin, 1940), 53–6.

[96] As on the relief probably from Rome and now in the Cincinnati Art Museum: Gordon, 'A new Mithraic relief from Rome', *JMS* 1,2 (1976) 166–86, pl. I; cf. G. Ulbert, 'Gladii aus Pompeii', *Germania* 47 (1969), 97–128, pl.17 nos. 1, 2; pl.18 nos. 1a,b; pl. 29.

[97] The fact is well known, but not discussed, e.g. Cumont, *Textes*, I, 161; Vermaseren, 'Miraculous birth' [n. 28], 291; see further, Gordon, 'Sette Sfere', 125.

[98] Sequences of daggers: 335 (Ottaviano Zeno, Rome: six daggers alternating with altars on frieze); 839 (Rudchester, Hadrian's Wall: three daggers on LHS of altar); 1727 (Brigetio:) two on the garland forming the cave); 1973 (Alba Iulia, seven alternating with other signs over the cave).

[99] Note also a dagger with the raven, 1496 and 1508 (Poetovio I); and with bow and arrows, 1584, left side (Poetovio III).
A normal Roman *culter*, as used by *popae*, appears on the mosiac floor of the degli Animali temple at Ostia, beside the bull's head and tail (290 but wrongly: see Becatti, *Mitrei*, 89 fig. 19 and plate XVIII.6). This certainly suggests that in some sense the death of the bull was understood as a sacrifice.

[100] See Turcan, 'Sacrifice mithriaque' [n. 70], 346–51 for a survey, though I am surprised that he seems to accept late nineteenth-century archaeologists' claims to be able to identify the bones of 'wolves' and 'foxes' at Saarburg (980).

[101] Since lions were considered to be fiery, Mithraic Lions were also symbolically associated with fire, as Tertullian, *adv. Marcion.* 1.13.4 remarks. Consequently, water was considered to be inimical to them; honey is a liquid which is pure but not watery. Honey was therefore the means of purifying the hands of Lions.

[102] The key text is Porphyry, *de abstin.* 4.16. I have discussed the association between hyenas and women at some length in 'Reality, evocation and boundary in the Mysteries of Mithras', *JMS* 3 (1980), 19–99, 57–9, 65. On the rejection of women by the Mysteries, Cumont, *Textes*, I, 330 and Jocelyn Toynbee, 'Still more' [n. 12], 108–9.

[103] There are at least 11 cases of sons associated with their fathers on Mithraic dedications: 473–4; 510; 526; 563; 732; 863; 911; 1434; 1524; 1728; 1766; doubtful cases: 313, 518, 687, 730, 1717. In 1165 a *nepos* is associated in a dedication. 511 and 708 include a wife in a funerary list. 2007 is offered as a votive for a son and a wife.

[104] See J-P. Vernant, 'A la table des hommes', in Detienne and Vernant, *Cuisine* [n. 86], 63–71.

[105] CIMRM 390, R5 (Barberini) (at least three people); 782 (Emerita) (three people with servants: best photo in A. Schütze, *Mithrasmysterien und Urchristentum* [Stuttgart, 1972], pl. 98); 1175 (Stockstadt) (fragment – six bearded men reclining: photo in Schütze, pl. 12). These monuments are noted by Kane, 'Mithraic cult meal', 350, though he believes that they denote a genuine cult meal. Turcan, 'Sacrifice mithriaque', 355–7 rightly stresses the point about commensality.

[106] Turned into a witty novel by Alison Lurie, *Absent Friends*.

Plate 1. Relief from near S. Lucia in Selce, Esquiline, now in the Vatican [CIMRM 368]. The lefthand torchbearer, Cautes, is a false modern restoration; two of the stars above the bull's head are also restored.

Plate 2. Complex panelled relief from Neuenheim, Heidelberg, now in the Schloß museum, Karlsruhe [CIMRM 1283]. Mithras's heroic acts appear on the right pilaster.

IV

Plate 3. Openwork 'Danubian' relief from near Kurtowo-Konare, Bulgaria, now in Plovdiv [CIMRM 2338]. The transitus motif appears on the left, above Mithras riding the bull (another heroic gesture).

Plate 4. Relief, probably from Apulum, now Alba Iulia, Romania [CIMRM 1972].

Plate 5. One of the 'Fagan' lionheads found at Ostia in the 1790s and now in the Vatican [CIMRM 314].

Plate 6. Detail of the transitus scene from the complex panelled relief from Dieburg [CIMRM 1247]. Note the ears of grain emanating from the bull's tail even before its death.

Plate 7. Detail of a probably Mithraic altar from Bonn, now in the Landesmuseum, inv. no. 62. 1107. Above this scene, the altar is pierced by a hole in the shape of a crescent moon.

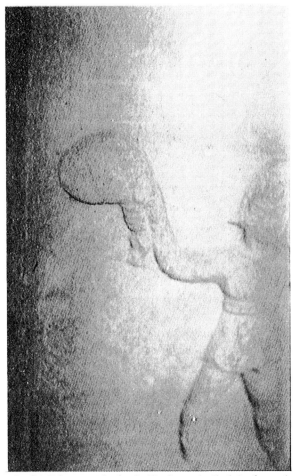

Plate 8. Detail of Mithras with the bull's haunch (kole), from the right-hand pilaster of the fragmentary relief from Virunum, now in the Landesmuseum, Klagenfurt [CIMRM 1430].

Plate 9. Detail of front face of the altar of Flavius Aper, from Poetovio (Ptuj), temple III, 260–68 A.D. [CIMRM 1584]. Note the bull's kōlē on the ground by Mithras' right foot.

Plate 10. Detail from the reverse of the complex panelled relief from Heddernheim, temple I, now in Wiesbaden [CIMRM 1083]. The merit of Mithras' dagger is clearly depicted.

Plate 11. Freestanding relief of the feast-scene with Mithras (R) and Sol (L) from Ladenburg (Lopodunum), Nordbaden. Note the trapeza legs made from the bull's hocks and hooves.

Reality, evocation and boundary in the Mysteries of Mithras

> Alice was too much puzzled to say anything, so after a minute
> Humpty Dumpty began again. 'They've a temper, some of them -
> particularly verbs, they're the proudest — adjectives you can
> do anything with, but not verbs — however *I* can manage the
> whole lot! Impenetrability! That's what *I* say!'
> 'Would you tell me, please,' said Alice, 'what that means?'
> 'Now you talk like a reasonable child,' said Humpty Dumpty,
> looking very much pleased. 'I meant by "impenetrability" that
> we've had enough of that subject, and it would be just as well
> if you'd mention what you meant to do next, as I suppose you
> don't intend to stop here all the rest of your life.'
> 'That's a great deal to make one word mean,' Alice said in a
> thoughtful tone.
> 'When I make a word do a lot of work like that,' said Humpty
> Dumpty, 'I always pay it extra.'
> 'Oh!' said Alice. She was much too puzzled to make any other
> remark.
>
> Lewis Carroll, *Through the Looking Glass*.

Other worlds have other words; and other words help make other
worlds. Had Alice had the benefit of an interview with Tzvetan
Todorov, she would not have been so rapidly reduced to a
monosyllable: she would have seen that once on the other side
of the looking-glass, everything had to be different, and not
casually so. She would have understood at once why she should
have to cut the cake *after* handing it round to the Lion, the
Unicorn and the White King and they had taken their slices;
and why, when she is looking for Tweedledum and Tweedledee,
the signs at every crossroads mark her destination in opposite
directions. And she might equally have expected that words
in that world, instead of lying down inertly in their lexical
places, should have had to queue for their wages on Saturday
nights. For fantasy worlds are not the pointless products of
'wild' imagination: they are necessarily better structured

than the 'real' human world.   And if we cannot predict
fantasy worlds, we can always in principle reconstruct
their logic.
     Now it is obvious that no great gulf separates fantasy
worlds from real worlds, for the good reason that we order
and give significance to the real world by virtue of the same
mental principles which allow any man to construct a fantasy.
'Condensation' and 'displacement'are functions of consciousness as much as of the unconscious, making possible imagination, sudden 'intuitive' comprehension, insight; and the same
small stock of logical possibilities — inversion, negation,
analogy, substitution — governs the process of thinking the
'unthought' as of thinking that which has already been
thought.   And if analytically we may oppose the prosaic to
the fantastic, as the two poles of a continuum of cognitive
possibilities, that does not mean that the prosaic is not
fantastical, or the fantastic not prosaic.   To grant significance to some element of the real world is to appropriate it
into a pre-existing network of other significations (a human
process which has no thinkable end as it has no imaginable
beginning), a network which is not 'factual' but precisely
'theoretical', and which, as Lévi-Strauss rightly contends,
has no empirical existence, merely a capacity to reproduce
its structure.   Inversely, the non-existent, the fantastical,
can be thought only in relation to that which has already
been granted a place in the network of significations — in a
word by denying elements of the world already 'known' and
substituting for them others, whose relation to what is
retained in the relevant meaning-set produces the effect of
'strangeness'.   The true inhabitants of the planets of Alpha
Centauri are simply unthinkable; but we all know about
Cyclopes, Centaurs and little green men.
     No doubt religion is all bunkum; but if it is, then so is
every other human enterprise (conscious enterprise that is —
DNA may do as it pleases).   I speak not, of course, of such
formal propositions about reality that any religion may make,
but of the manner in which it makes them, and of its cognitive procedure.   But the peculiar interest of religion is
that it constitutes the point at which recognised (and often
admitted) fantasy is brought most sharply against the prosaic
and compelled to co-exist with it.   To put the point slightly
differently, the fantastic is made real, and the real fantastic.   In religion, everything is, as it were, in quotation-
marks.   Eskimo shamans 'visit' the bottom of the sea (they
really do); spirits 'eat' offerings (they really do); Inannuk
'waits' for Dumuzid at the 'door of the storehouse' (her
temple at Eannak); the gods of Olympus 'live' on the savour
of sacrifice and the pungency of aromatics; the wine 'is' the
blood of Christ (it really is).   Now all of these are indistinguishable from ordinary propositions, not only in syntax
and grammar, but in their intended referentiality: they are

taken neither as figures of speech nor as allegories by those
who believe them. Yet they are different from boring propositions such as 'This is a black beetle' (spoken when one is
looking at a member of the species *Blatta orientalis*)
precisely in their illocutionary force: they are taken as
'interesting', as non-evident (though true). And they are
interesting precisely because they offer wide scope for
interpretation, not at the level of immediate deduction
('How long does it take the shaman's spirit to get down
there?'), but at a secondary level, the level of implication,
or, to use Dan Sperber's term, 'evocation' (1974). All
utterance, verbal or non-verbal, is naturally subject to
interpretation at this level; but some utterances matter more
than others. The more they matter, as with religious utterances, the more they receive interpretation; and although in
some societies and in some contexts a deliberate effort is
made to foreclose the majority of conceivable evocations in
favour of authoritative ones, there is no theoretical limit
to the interpretability of utterances. The only practical
limit is whether people think that a given utterance is worth
understanding.
     The fantastic element in religion is not in itself
particularly interesting, inasmuch as it is merely a sub-set
of the entire human capacity for thinking and speaking about
the non-actual, which has existed at least since the first
lie and the development of the future tense (Steiner, 1975:
110-235), and presumably long before, in that higher mammals
are capable of learning to understand and respond to symbolic
information. But what it is interesting to examine is the
nature of the frontier, constantly renegotiated, which any
particular religion defines between the actual and the fantastic, between what everyone in that social formation knows
and what no one *knows*. The history of religion is the history
of taller and taller stories being claimed more and more true,
until no one can be bothered to understand or to interpret:
the symbols and the discourse lose their evocative power; the
institution which tells the stories becomes just one of
several, with no outstanding claim upon attention, upon the
desire to interpret afresh. Its claims are just ideology,
merely mad, an affront to good sense, or irrelevant to 'real'
problems. And the viability of a religious structure is
governed by its capacity to weave the fantastic with the
actual, to link its lies to truth: more than any other kind
of human fantasy, religion is doomed to be parasitical upon
social reality, precisely inasmuch as it claims to be true.
     The specific beliefs of any religious system have little
more than curiosity value, though as 'facts' they naturally
delight positive minds; and they are an appropriate subject
of enquiry within a carefully defined context or contexts.
But far more interesting must always be the problem of how
they come to be believed, the sense in which they are

'believed', and the relation between religious beliefs and other concurrently held beliefs and practices.

Let us now turn to the Mysteries of Mithras. Part of my point can be made by saying that the Mysteries attempted — and evidently succeeded — to validate the existence of a purely imaginary world. If we do not find their version of such a world particularly odd, it is mostly because our familiarity with Christianity, which attempts something very similar, allows us to believe that religious projects of this type are normal. 'Translation flourishes where experience overlaps' (Douglas, 1975: 277). The establishment of parallels, and the work of classification and comparison, serve to elide our surprise still further: such projects were normal. Conventionally, and ethnocentrically, of course, it might appear sillier for the Karam of the New Guinea Highlands to say, when they see a group of cassowaries in the forest: 'There are (our) sisters and cross-cousins over there' (Bulmer, 1967: 18), than for a Mithraist to say: 'Mithras is the creator and father of all'. But inasmuch as the Karam's belief is not a religious one, it is fully possible for the anthropologist to piece together the rules which set the cassowary apart, and relate those rules to other rules which define relations between human beings. The apparently absurd thus turns out to be intelligibly motivated, and so comprehensible. But the Mithraic belief is not so motivated; indeed, I would argue that it is deliberately absurd — that it is one of the 'taller stories' to which I referred earlier, which all religions, but particularly non-traditional ones, find themselves forced to tell. The deliberate non-intelligibility of the Mithraic belief is confirmed by the Mysteries' attempt to deny the ultimate reality of the real world, by classifying it out: formally, the real world, of actual relationships, worries and contingency, is simply the world of genesis, alterity, illusion and death. Another truer world 'exists', a world of being, sameness, truth and life. But that world is utterly fantastic; and it is as though the Mysteries deliberately called attention to its fantastic quality by the simplicity of the selective inversions which help to construct it. And most absurd of all is the crowning paradox, that Life is Death, and Death Life.

Now I wish to argue that new religions and minority cults especially are compelled to elaborate the absurdity of their claims because this is the best way of attracting interest — such propositions are excellent opportunities for the process of dense evocation. But that very pressure means that they have a particular problem of validation, which involves reference to an already existing cultural agreement about what is real and how it is to be understood, granted significance (an agreement which is never total, and perhaps never real, just to be found in ethnological descriptions). In effect, the

more absurd the propositions of a cult, the more it is forced
to refer to the 'real' world in order to persuade would-be
adherents, and adherents, of their truth. New cults have
to cannibalize upon a whole range of banal and customary
beliefs within the society in which they exist if they are
to be more than minute evanescent, usually kin-based, groups.
But I would also argue that the process of routinisation
involves the displacement of interest away from formal propositions, and their truth, towards the elaboration of a
relatively self-sufficient network of symbolic meanings, each
of which is 'explained' by reference to another of the same
set — a process which we find well-advanced in most traditional religions studied by anthropologists and historians.
Routinisation involves the complex elaboration through evocation of the original meeting-ground of the fantastic and the
prosaic.
    The behavioural correlate of religious belief understood
in this way is predictable enough: it is pretence. Uttered
lies that have the shape of truths are mirrored by paronomastic actions, deliberate parodies of effective actions by means
of which man 'makes himself'. A pretended action is not
merely playful nor is it no-action: it is action 'in
quotation-marks', just as I observed earlier that religious
propositions are to be understood 'in quotation-marks'. But
such mimesis (which is evidently the foundation of the capacity of human cultures to reproduce themselves in a non-
biological sense), though it may receive authoritative
exegesis, itself demands evocation precisely because it does
not itself constitute real action, which necessarily is
intended to alter the real world directly. And likewise,
the products of real actions-in-the world, once placed in a
religious context, become subject to the same process of
resignification, particularly those which are specially made
for such a context (Gordon, 1979: 5-34). That process affects
all human products, of course, but is especially important in
the context of an activity so largely the realm of pretence
as religion.
    Now although it is impossible to explore these themes more
than cursorily in the space of an article, it seems to me that
any adequate discussion of the character of the Mysteries of
Mithras must refer to them. For the Mysteries' use of 'make-
believe' is transparent. If it is true that some initiates
wore masks in some contexts at least (which I am not inclined
to believe, though it is generally assumed to be true), then
that is pretence (1). If the *Pater* seated on a throne on the
upper layer of paintings on Wall I_2 at Santa Prisca wears a
'phrygian' cap and a red cloak so as to associate him with
Mithras, that is pretence (2). 'A sort of parody of martyrdom', *quasi mimum martyrii*, is Tertullian's comment on the
significance of one episode in the initiation of the *Miles*
(*de corona* 15.3 Fontaine): an observation which refers not

only to the relation between this ritual and Christian
martyrdom, but also to the literal gesture of rejecting the
crown for the sake of the 'true crown', Mithras (3).
Pretending that they were fiery, initiates into the grade
Leo washed themselves in their 'proper lustration' (οἰκεῖα
νίπτρα), honey, instead of water (Porphyry, *De antro*, 15-16
[Nauck², p. 67, 6-15 = Arethusa, p. 16 lines 25-32]). We
may plausibly argue that the Mysteries' use of pretence in
ritual was sufficiently familiar in the outside world to
inspire this parody by Ambrosiaster: *Ne enim horreant tur-
piter dehonestari se oculi illis velantur, alii autem sicut
aves alas percutiunt vocem coracis imitantes; alii vero leo-
num more fremunt; alii autem ligatis manibus intestinis
pullinis proiciuntur super foveas aqua plenas, accedente
quodam cum gladio et inrumpente intestina supra dicta qui
se liberatorem appellet* ('Their eyes are blindfolded that
they may not refuse to be foully abused; some moreover beat
their wings together as birds do, and croak like ravens, and
others roar like lions; and yet others are pushed across
ditches filled with water: their hands have previously been
tied with the intestines of a chicken, and then somebody
comes up and cuts these intestines (he calls himself their
"liberator")') (4). And beyond ritual, the very status of
the *mithraeum* as an 'image of the cosmos' (εἰκόνα ... τοῦ
κόσμου) is a deliberate fiction, a fact highlighted by its
decoration with stars on the ceiling or within the cult-
niche. For such decoration does not signify that the
mithraeum is the cosmos, but is a sign for a statement of
belief: 'We say this "is" the cosmos' (5). The point may
also be put slightly differently. If we turn these pretended
actions into statements — for example, 'I am Mithras', 'I am
a Raven', 'Mithras is my crown', they are all clearly utterances which demand evocation: they are deliberately non-usual
utterances. Such claims are wholly appropriate among 'those
who pass beyond the bounds of reason and society and give
glimpses of a truth which escapes through the mesh of structured concepts' (Douglas, 1975: 108) — which is Mary
Douglas's account of the joker, 'a kind of minor mystic'.
Moreover, what may lie between the cracks in the structure
of the 'given world' cannot be simply or permanently apprehended: behaving 'as if' is the only appropriate mode. From
that point of view, pretence is the behavioural correlate of
the Mysteries' assertion that the true purpose and goal of
life is not given in society.
    I have referred already to the iconographic evidence that
initiates into the grades *Leo* and *Corax* could be represented
as men with the heads (or maybe masks) of lions and of ravens
respectively (note 1). Now that point allows the inference
that the pretence that the initiates into these grades 'were'
Lions and Ravens was insisted upon in the Mysteries; which
inference can itself be supported by the use of honey in the

initiation ceremonies for *Leones*. But why name grades after
animals? And why these animals? Now one might have thought
that such questions would have been of some concern to students of the Mysteries; but it is not so. The one answer
offered (by Cumont) is that the use of such names taken from
animals is 'primitive', part of the oldest stratum of the
Mysteries' history, and derives directly from traditional
rites of passage (6). Pseudohistory thus surreptitiously
legitimates the belief that the Mysteries in their western
form are immensely old. No doubt the Magi were too lazy to
change these odd names when they invented the grades, and
thought them suitably quaint. But of course to have taken
no interest in the significance and intentions of the grade-
names is simply part of a much wider miscognition of the
Mysteries which turned them (and still turns them) into a
lunatic mumbo-jumbo of meaningless and pointless beliefs:
and no attempt is made to ask how people in the ancient world
could have believed such stuff, or why they should have done
so. It has proved fatally easy for historians of religion
to be quite as ideological about their objects of study as
the Creuzers and Pan-Babylonists in their day ever were; and
to be just as little informative. For the quite simple reason
that a narrative-historical perspective is not the most
appropriate one for an understanding of symbolic sets as
modes of constructing meanings.

                              I

I propose to consider first the name *Corax*, Raven, the name
of the lowest — that is, first — of the seven Mithraic
initiatory grades. The objects connected with this grade
in the floor-mosaic of the mid-third century Mitreo di
Felicissimo in Ostia are these:

        raven   small one-   caduceus
                        handled cup

The object on the extreme right, the caduceus, is generally,
and rightly, understood as a sign for the planet Mercury, the
tutelary planet of the grade (Becatti, 1954: 108-10) (7).
But there is no such obvious rationale within the Mysteries
for the two other objects: above all, what is an ordinary
raven doing on the left? Higher up in the sequence, we find
objects that at least seem to be 'sensible', such as the
(military?) bag in the *Miles* frame, or the fire-shovel in
the *Leo* frame. Of course it might be that this was just a
reminder to the ignorant initiates who could not remember
what the grade was called.... (see Gordon, p. 220 below, for
just such an argument). But there may be a less derisive,
and desperate, hypothesis. Perhaps we should turn to the

prosaic world, and leave behind the world of fantasy for a
moment? Perhaps we should consider what the Graeco-Roman
world thought about real ravens? Especially if the Mysteries
pretended that initiates into the grade *Corax* 'were'
ravens....

The raven was not just any old bird in the kept knowledge
of antiquity (8). The first important point is that it was
believed to be able to talk, just like the parrot - though,
Apuleius hastily explains, the latter could not really do more
than imitate (*Florida* 12 [p. 17.5-25 Helm]). But there were
plenty to disagree with him. For years in the first century
AD there was in Rome a famous talking raven, who used to come
to the Forum every day to say 'Good Morning' to Tiberius the
Emperor, and to Germanicus and Drusus. When the bird was
killed by a man jealous of its owner, an immense funeral was
held in its honour, and the murderer was driven out of Rome
by the crowd — indeed, some said he was actually killed
(Pliny, *HN* 10, 121-23). And while we might be tempted to
write such a story off by invoking the British love of dogs,
such a notion is quite out of place among the Romans, not
noted for their sentimentality to animals. Indeed, Pliny
himself provides the key: for he notes in passing that one of
the raven's owner's motives in encouraging it to hang around
his work-place was a religious scruple (121). Birds are not
supposed to be able to talk, which is one of the defining
characteristics of man; animals which can talk are therefore
ambiguous, 'sort-crossers', potentially dangerous. We are
reminded of the way in which Alexander the False Prophet made
his fortune — with a talking snake (Lucian, *Alexander/Pseudo-
mantis*); and of innumerable prodigies involving utterances by
animals. But while odd occurrences can be disposed of by *ad
hoc* rules, the existence of anomalous *species* cannot. The
raven became a bird of omen, its blurring of the boundary
between man and bird making it an ideal mediator between god
and man. The raven became the bird of Apollo, god of oracles.

But there were of course other such birds of omen. What
was unique about the raven was its extraordinary ability to
understand the messages it conveyed between god/nature and
man: *corvi in auspiciis soli videntur intellectum habere
significationum suarum*, 'ravens are apparently the only
creatures which have a conscious understanding of the meaning
of their signs in auspicy' (Pliny, *HN* 10, 33; cf. Aelian,
NA 2, 51). That 'fact' suggests that the raven was believed
to be doubly ambiguous: not only could it mediate between
Nature (understood here as a set of signs proposed by divinity) and Culture (human beings in society), but it shared
with men a rational faculty (cf. Aelian, *NA* 2, 48).

It was that rationality which got the most famous raven
in the Graeco-Roman world into trouble — and immortality.
For there were two sorts of raven (at least): feathered
friends and a constellation in the sky. One of the most

famous of all catasterismic stories was told about how it
got there (9).   One day Apollo wanted to sacrifice, but
lacked the necessary water.   So he sent the bird under his
special protection, the raven, to fetch some.   When the bird
arrived at the pool, he saw some unripe figs on a nearby
tree, and decided to wait until they were ripe.   Eventually
he was able to eat them up, and then suddenly realised how
long he had been away — so he scooped up a water-snake
(*hydros*) into his water-jar (*hydria*) together with some
water, and hurried back to Apollo.   Apollo refused to believe
his story that the snake had prevented him from getting the
water, and decided to punish him by putting him into heaven
with his back to the *hydria* and the *hydros*.   That meant that
he could never drink, a point stressed constantly in the
sources.   And it is crucial to understand that this catasterismic story is not a random invention: it is motivated by
another aspect of the kept knowledge of antiquity about
ravens — that they could not drink for part of the year.
Pliny (*HN* 10, 32) reports as one of the differences between
the crow and the raven: *corvi ante solstitium generant, idem
aegrescunt sexagenis diebus, siti maxime, antequam fici
coquantur autumno; cornix ab eo tempore corripitur morbo*
('ravens have their chicks before the [summer] solstice,
and they sicken for sixty days — mostly on account of their
inability to drink then — until the figs ripen in autumn;
the crow only becomes sick at that time').   Crows and ravens
may look very much alike, but one of the ways of telling them
apart is their respective timetable of disease.   This feature
of the life of real ravens is reproduced in the catasterismic story, for the Scholiast on Aratus, *Phaenomena* 449
(p. 425 Maass) specifies a period of time during which the
earthly raven, Apollo's servant, was unable to drink, *before*
being turned into a constellation: Ἀπόλλωνα δὲ γνόντα
τάληθὲς τὸν μὲν [the 'real' bird] ποιῆσαι διψῆν περὶ τὴν
ἀκμὴν τῆς ὀπώρας.... ('but Apollo knew what had really
happened, and caused him to go thirsty during the height of
of summer...') (10).
    This complex of associations which 'placed' ravens in the
kept knowledge of the Graeco-Roman world seems to me extremely
suggestive in the context of the Mysteries.   The raven is an
ambiguous bird, belonging of course to the animal kingdom, but
in certain ways assimilated into humanity — by its capacity to
talk and by its ability to understand signs.   Its mediatory
position between beasts and men allows it to mediate between
gods and men too.   The catasterismic story pursues this mediatory theme in a slightly different direction by connecting
real ravens on earth in a more than casual fashion with the
raven in the sky — the story reproduces the structure of the
account of the raven in the 'encyclopaedic' knowledge of the
Graeco-Roman world.   I suggest that there are at least the
following links between real ravens and the Mysteries:

V

(1) a foundation-myth about a constellation whose three
constituent elements have been claimed by both Roger Beck
and Stanley Insler (on slightly different grounds) to appear,
at one level of interpretation at least, in the bull-killing
relief (Insler, 1978: 519-38; Beck 1977a: 9-11; 1977b);
(2) a theory about the relation between things-in-the-world
and things-in-the-sky perfectly in keeping with the major
concerns of the Mysteries, and which may well have been
understood as a preliminary version of a (naturally) hidden
'truth' whose full implications could only be revealed later
in the hierarchy of initiations; (3) a story which gives
significance to a particular part of the year, the two months
before the autumnal rising of Arcturus (September 20th in
Rome during the first century AD), which was extremely hot,
and which seems also to have been of some interest in the
Mysteries (11); (4) an explanation of ravens' inability to
drink, which might allow us to give slightly greater credence
to the Scholiast tradition on Gregory Nazianzen *Oratio I
Contra Iulianum* (6) (=Migne *PG* 36, col. 989d): αἱ δὲ
κολάσεις εἰσὶ τὸ ... διὰ πείνης καὶ δίψης ('the endurance-
tests [include] hardship and thirst') - at least in relation
to the initiation rituals for the first grade (12).

I wish then to suggest that factual knowledge of a selected
kind about real ravens may help us to glimpse connections between a number of disparate items of Mithraic evidence which
cannot be linked without an appeal to such knowledge. On the
other hand, it does not seem to me necessary to suppose that
such ideas about real ravens were the major overt focus of the
Mithraic understanding of the grade *Corax* — knowledge about
real ravens was surely overlaid by specifically Mithraic
interpretations and evocations, as part of the process of
routinisation to which I referred earlier. Nevertheless,
I think that there may be references to 'encyclopaedic' knowledge about ravens at some level in the iconography of the
Mysteries. That iconography of the raven is extremely
diverse, and largely no doubt unintelligible to us (as is the
case with the iconographical material on Mithraic lions
collected by John Hinnells, 1975: 333-69), given that we
possess no discursive texts of a specifically Mithraic
character. But the following evidence is at least suggestive:

1. The raven as Apollo's bird. The small amount of iconographical evidence in relation to the raven in the bull-
killing scene is collected elsewhere in this issue by Malcolm
Davidson and Roger Beck (p.187 below). But there are one or
two indications that the idea that the raven was Apollo's
servant led to the raven being used as a sign 'for' Cautopates. On a *terra sigillata* bowl at Trier with a moulded
representation of the feast-scene, we find, in addition to
two 'servants' in Persian dress, a cock (L) and a raven (R)
on either side of a crater entwined by a snake, and a large
lion immediately above (*CIMRM* 988). In view of other

evidence that the cock is associated with Cautes (Vermaseren
1950: 147; Gordon, 1976: 153 n. 50), it seems reasonable to
suppose that this raven is associated with Cautopates. On
318, a brooch or mounted medallion from Ostia, now in the
Ashmolean, which shows Mithras killing the bull, there occurs
not only the raven in the usual place, but also a cock (R) and
a bird which appears identical to the raven above (L) where
the torchbearers are usually to be found. We must surely
allow that the raven might be used as a sign for Cautopates,
just as elsewhere (for example, the end of one of the benches
in the Mitreo degli Animali in Ostia) an owl is used (Gordon,
1976: 150 n. 28; 153 n. 50). I suggest that we should appeal
here to Professor Beck's theory that the location of the
torchbearers on the relief is to be explained, at least at one
level, by their association with Aldebaran and Antares, which
allowed them to be both signs for morning and evening *and* for
spring and autumn (Beck, 1977a: 1-17). If the owl is clearly
a night-bird (13), the raven is associated with the change
from summer to autumn, for it is almost at the beginning of
autumn that it regains its health (14). Cock (R) and raven
(L) reappear, this time with the torchbearers in their usual
Italian positions (Cautes on L, Cautopates on R) on *CIMRM* 334
(Rome), which may consequently be understood as registering
both the diurnal and the seasonal aspects of the torchbearers
on the same monument (15). But I would suggest that all
three of these monuments use the raven as a sign for Cautopates at least partly because in the 'encyclopaedia' the raven
was Apollo's servant, just as the cock was the male herald of
sunrise (16).
     A denser opposition between raven and cock seems to be
implicit in their appearance on opposite sides of an altar
from Ptuj I dedicated by a member of the local office of the
publicum portorii Illyrici (1946). On the left side, from
top to bottom, we find a star, a raven, a bow, a 'phrygian
cap' and a dagger; on the right, a cock standing on a tor-
toise (?) — animals otherwise connected with Mercury. The
raven is also associated with the dagger on 1508 (from the
same Mithraeum) and on 1765 (Aquincum, ?Mithraeum III), where
it is shown on the left face of an altar holding in its beak
a long wedge-shaped object. On the right face is a lion,
which is elsewhere found in association with Cautes (Gordon,
1976: 154 n. 51). 1706 (Carnuntum) presents the same opposition of the two creatures, though the raven (again on the L)
is here represented with an ear of corn and a snake. Whatever
the precise significance of such images (see note 17 below),
they seem to represent in figurative terms a process of dense
evocation which takes different aspects of the raven in the
'encyclopaedia' and sets them in relation to a series of
specifically Mithraic themes, in layer upon layer of sense.
For it must be obvious that there are several different
'kinds' of ravens in the Mysteries — the raven who attends

the bull-killing, the raven/Cautopates, the raven opposed
to the lion (which might of course be the grade in some
sense), raven-headed men, and doubtless others still.
    2. The catasterismic story. In the 'encyclopaedia' this
theme is intimately related to the first, and is just one of
several stories which tell how the raven failed Apollo in
some service (cf. the story of Coronis, which explains how
the raven, which used to be white, became black through
neglecting his charge). In the catasterismic story, the
raven sat in a tree to wait until the figs were ripe (Ovid,
Fasti 2, 255-56); and, strangely enough, on the Quadraro
monument (321 L2) there is a raven in one of the side-scenes
sitting in a tree — a unique case (and it may be that the
scene also doubles as a representation of the raven in the
bull-killing: for some parallel 'doubles', see Gordon, p. 218
below). But there may be a much clearer allusion to the
catasterismic story on the floor-mosaic of Sette Porte, also
in Ostia (Becatti, 1954: 98; cf. 108 = *CIMRM* 287²). Here a
crater or *hydria* is shown in the middle of the floor, with a
snake emerging from a rock to the right (as one looks towards
the 'east' end of the Mithraeum). On the left is a bird
facing the crater and standing on a long thin rod. This bird
was hesitantly identified by Becatti as an eagle, because of
its small head, its curved beak and its elongated wings. But
neither the first nor the last of these criteria is in the
slightest telling; and with the best will in the world it
is impossible to agree with him that the beak is curved (see
his Pl. XX.3). But the real reason that he wished the bird
to be an eagle was his prior theory that these were symbols
of the four elements (snake = earth, crater = water, eagle =
air ...). Fire had to come in somewhere then; and it had to
be the rod, which was duly identified as a thunderbolt, even
though it bears no resemblance whatever to a true thunderbolt
a couple of feet away, in the hand of Jupiter (for the same
argument, cf. Cumont, 1945: 415; Vermaseren, 1950: 148 n. 28).
If one must hazard a guess, I suggest it might be an ard
(plough) of the kind represented in the Perses-frame at di
Felicissimo (see n. 88 below): there is a curious curved shaft
which turns off the rod beneath the bird's feet. If so, I
think that might plausibly be linked to Raven/Cautopates/
autumn/ploughing; which suggests in turn that the Mysteries
understood the catasterismic story, at least at one level,
as an account of the relation between *genesis* (cold) and
apogenesis (heat); for, as we shall see later, the 'encyclopaedia' was extremely interested in the raven's internal
shifts between wetness and dryness, cold and heat (p. 45
below). But I think we might also link this representation
at Sette Porte, if indeed it does represent snake, crater
and raven and thus refer to the catasterismic story, with
CIMRM 988, which I mentioned earlier, and where raven/Cauto-
pates stands by the crater entwined by a snake with the lion

above — the feast-scene: yet another Mithraic understanding
of the catasterismic story may have been in relation to the
bull-killing and the subsequent feast. But then that is
merely another way of referring to the relation between
genesis and *apogenesis*: perhaps there is really just one
dense Mithraic interpretation which could be represented
in several different ways? (17)

Each of the elements of the catasterismic story, Apollo,
raven, snake, *hydria*, water, a period of the year between
the rising of Sirius and that of Arcturus, seems to have
played some part in the Mysteries. We can obviously not
be sure that they were all linked; but it is a reasonable
guess given the evocative possibilities provided by a 'true'
connection between real ravens and the constellation Corvus.
But even if the catasterismic story was used in the Mysteries, it is evident that each of the elements has been densely
reinterpreted and made to serve new and complex purposes, so
that it is impossible to unravel the consequent shifts of
meaning. All I would claim is that the catasterismic story
may have provided the basis for these Mithraic evocations,
and have helped the initiates believe that the Mysteries'
higher claims were not mere fantasies but were based upon
truths, upon ordinary, well-known facts about the world and
their commonly-accepted significations.

3. The raven as a thieving creature. This aspect of
beliefs about real ravens is to be found in several texts
(18), and is duly applied to people in the physiognomic
tradition. For example, the person who 'is' a raven is
said by Polemon, *de physiogn.* 2 s.v. *corvus* to be: *prudens,
pavidus, rapax, fugax, imitator morum agrestium, solitudinis
amans*, 'canny, fearful, greedy, cowardly, inclined to pretend
to be boorish, fond of being alone' (ed. Hoffmann ap. Förster,
I p. 184, 6-7). And there seems to be a reference to this
aspect of the 'encyclopaedia' (whatever its immediate Mithraic interpretation) in an important scene on a mid third-
century altar from Ptuj III, where the raven flies down
towards the meat held on a spit over the altar-flames by
Mithras and Sol after the killing of the bull (1584) (and
see further, p. 62 below). Again I would argue that factual
knowledge about ravens motivates a specific Mithraic motif.

The implication of all this, I think, is that the raven
which appears on the floor-mosaic in the di Felicissimo
Mithraeum evokes simultaneously real ravens in the world
(it looks like one), the constellation Corvus in the sky
and the grade *Corax* in the Mysteries. The utterance 'I
am a Raven' did not have simply an 'allegorical' or 'metaphorical' sense, but a literal one, which could be pursued,
interpreted, in a number of different ways in keeping with
the place of the Raven in the initiatory structure of the
cult. The human Raven was fully as ambiguous between the
world of non-initiates and full initiates as the real bird

was between the animal world, the world of men, and heaven.
And inasmuch as the catasterismic story puts that ambiguity
in the sharpest focus it seems to me likely to have had a
place in Mithraic raven-lore. But we may perhaps go further.
With these points in mind, we may be able to identify the
small 'cup' represented at di Felicissimo next to the raven
in the *Corax*-frame. Becatti, 1954: 109, observes of this
'cup': 'un piccolo vasetto semi-ovoidale con un ansa ad
occhio orizzontale di una forma ridotta ma simile a quella
del cratere tenuto in mano da uno dei *leones* che recano
offerte nel mitreo di S. Prisca. Vaso quindi rituale ... ';
indeed, just as the *hydria* in the catasterismic story was a
ritual jug for sacrificial purposes. Perhaps this insignificant object itself has a double history, both on earth and,
like the raven/Raven, in heaven?

With the example of ravens in mind, let us turn now to the
fourth grade, *Leo*, Lion. The objects associated with this
grade on the mosaic floor of the Mitreo di Felicissimo at
Ostia are these:

> fire-shovel   sistrum   thunderbolt

If it easy enough to appreciate that it may have been appropriate for the Mysteries to name the lowest grade after an
ambiguous bird, which crosses the boundary between the animal
world and the human world as well as that between this world
and heaven, the appearance of an animal grade as the fourth
in the sequence, after *Nymphus* and *Miles*, two grades which at
least seem to refer to ordinary human rôles, must appear very
surprising. What could have motivated recourse at this stage
of the initiate's spiritual progress to the animal kingdom?

It is generally granted, even by those who find parts of
the passage suspect, that Pallas's observation that while the
members of the grade *Corax* were called ὑπηρετοῦντες ('servants'), the members of the grade *Leo* were called μετέχοντες
('participants'), is to be trusted (20). This point seems to
me, as to others, to allow the implication — indeed to necessitate it — that the grade *Leo* marked a very important moment
in the initiate's progress; an implication confirmed by the
fact that there are many more references in the epigraphic
evidence to this grade than to all others put together (except
Pater of course, Gordon, 1975a: 242 n. 108). But if we look
at the problem as one of structure it becomes plausible to
suppose that *Leo* is to the higher grades what *Corax* is to the
grades *Nymphus* and *Miles*: they are both crucial points of
transition from one state to another. The grade *Corax*
effects the transition from the outside world, of complete
ignorance, to some preliminary state of knowledge: as it were,
a transition from the utterly 'wild' to some sort of 'domestication'. The grade *Leo* effects a similarly large shift in
status, from some stage of preparation to 'membership'. In

other words, the grade *Leo* is the counterpart of the grade
Corax at a higher level. And if the first grade has the
name of an animal, so must the higher one — but it must be
an altogether 'higher' animal which nevertheless possesses
the same kind of ambiguity as the raven. And, of course,
that is just what the lion is.

If the raven possessed one or two human qualities, the
lion in the Graeco-Roman world was one of the most fully
anthropomorphised creatures in the 'encyclopaedia'. It
was believed to be capable of discerning moral faults in
human beings, and to have an uncanny capacity to remember
those who had harmed it or helped it (21). Man-eating lions
in Libya were crucified as though they were human malefactors
(22). It was thought a sign of *megalopsychia* and *eleutheria*
to look 'leonine' — not only by Alexander but by the entire
tradition of physiognomic 'science' in the Graeco-Roman world
(23). But the most startling traditions about lions to be
found in our first- and second-century AD sources come from
Egypt. In Egypt, it seems clear that the lion had a particularly important rôle as a mediator between gods and men
(Hopfner, 1913: 40-44; de Wit, 1951; Griffiths, 1970: 444-45).
For my purposes, it scarcely matters whether our Graeco-
Roman sources, but above all Aelian *NA* 12, 7, are 'correct'
or not; but for what it is worth, the most exhaustive discussion of the rôle of lions in Egyptian religion concluded
that the Graeco-Roman sources were well-informed (de Wit,
1951: 138-47).

It will be recalled that the Graeco-Roman 'encyclopaedia'
attributed human qualities to the raven, and so made it a
mediator between man and god; the catasterismic story reproduced this structure. The same is true of Graeco-Roman-
Egyptian accounts of lions. The catasterismic tradition held
that because the lion was the king of the quadrupeds (another
aspect of the blurring of the boundary between animal and man,
this time at the level of political system), it was specially
favoured by the king of the gods; and it was for that reason
assigned a constellation, *Leo*, containing one of the brightest
stars— Regulus (24). Because the sun entered Leo in the
hottest part of the year, it was deemed appropriate to make
Leo the 'domicile' of the sun, which had one domicile only;
and, equally naturally, that was 'on the sun side', ἡλιακός.
Leo was also considered one of the male signs (25). And
although it may seem surprising to us, this association
between sun and Leo was reproduced as an aspect of the nature
of real lions on earth. Fiery Leo became fiery lion: if one
cuts through a lion's bone, fire comes out (Aelian *NA* 4, 34).
Arabia was said to be the 'mother and nurse' of lions (*NA* 17,
36). Lions avoided drinking, just as the sun 'hates' water
— because it dries up moisture which is female (Pliny *HN* 2,
222; Aelian *NA* 4, 34; cf. Aristotle *HA* 8, 5: 594b 21-26).
Without perceptible embarrassment, Aelian shifts from earthly

lions to heavenly Lion: διάπυρον δέ ἐστι τὸ ζῷον ἰσχυρῶς ...
τὸ δὲ ἔξωθεν πῦρ δυσωπεῖται καὶ φεύγει πλήθει τοῦ ἐνδοθέν
φασιν. ἐπειδὴ δὲ ἄγαν πυρῶδές ἐστι, οἶκον Ἡλίου φασὶν εἶναι ·
καὶ ὅταν γε ᾖ ἑαυτοῦ θερμότατος καὶ θερεΐοτατος ὁ ἥλιος,
λέοντι αὐτὸν πελάζειν [τῷ οὐρανίῳ] φασί (NA 12,7 Hercher)
('The animal is extremely fiery ... they say that it is
afraid of external fire, and runs away from it, on account
of its excess of internal fire. And because of its excessively fiery nature, they say that it is the 'domicile' of
the sun; and when the sun is at its hottest in the height
of summer, they say it is approaching the Lion') (26).
     At Heliopolis in Egypt lions were kept outside the temples
of the gods, according to Aelian, because 'they share, the
Egyptians say, in some degree the nature of the gods'
(θειοτέρας τινὸς μοίρας ὡς Αἰγύπτιοί φασι μετειληχότας:
NA 12, 7). In support of the same theme, he quotes Empedocles' *Katharmoi* on the fate of the soul: if it falls to the
soul's lot to become an animal in some incarnation, it is
best for it to enter into a lion:

    ἐν θήρεσσι λέοντες ὀρειλεχέες χαμαιεῦναι
    γίνονται, δάφναι δ'ἐνὶ δένδρεσιν ἠυκόμοισιν,

    'Among wild animals (they) become lions that bed on the mountains
        and sleep
     on the ground; and among head-dressed trees, bay-trees' (27).

Aelian then describes in elaborate detail the anomalous
treatment of lions somewhere in Egypt as 'human beings':
they eat to the accompaniment of song, live in halls of
residence fitted out with gymnasia and a palaestra, are
encouraged to keep fit by wrestling. One could hardly wish
for a more perfect illustration of structuralist principles:
the reclassification of lions as anomalous animals turns them
into living deities (or perhaps rather visible manifestations of deity, in this case 'Hephaestus' (28).), a category
of beings itself ambiguous. The initial ambiguity of humanoid
lions is stressed in order to evoke a reference to the
claim that gods 'live' — a claim that Egyptian religion wished
to legitimate. One 'true absurdity' (lions treated as human
beings) reproduces the structure of another true absurdity
(ordinary lions out in the bush are like human beings/the lion
in heaven is like them too) in order to 'prove' a third true
absurdity, that gods are alive in the world.
     The anomalous status of these lions is made quite clear by
a small detail which Aelian inserts: while they ate, they were
entreated not to lay the evil eye on any of those who saw them
('μὴ βασκήνητέ τινα τῶν ὁρώντων') (29). Readers of Mary
Douglas will have no difficulty in seeing why: classification
as anomalous grants power to the being so classified, power
either for good or for evil — precisely how the power turns

out depends upon context and the relevant set of rules
(Douglas, 1966; see also 1975: 276-318). This 'direct'
capacity of the anomalous lions is reproduced at another
level: lions in Egypt were believed to appear in dreams
to those favoured by the gods, but also to those who had
perjured themselves: καὶ τοὺς ἐπίορκον ὀμόσαντας οὐκ ἐς
ἀναβολὰς ἀλλὰ ἤδη δικαιοῦσι, τοῦ θεοῦ τὴν ὀργὴν τὴν δικαίαν
αὐτοῖς καταπνέοντος ('and those who have perjured themselves
they punish at once, brooking no delay, for the god breathes
into them just anger'). Now this notion that a god 'breathes
anger' into lions may be more than a figure of speech. For
the theme of the power of real lions' breath was a commonplace in the 'encyclopaedia' of the Graeco-Roman world (and
presumably also in Egypt). Pliny observes that the 'power/
stench of the lion's breath is formidable' (animae leonis
virus grave: HN 11, 277; cf. 8, 46 [from Aristotle]) (30).
Aelian puts the belief into a 'naturalistic' context which
simply confirms the classification of the lion as king of
the quadrupeds and so as part-human: if a lion wants to
protect a kill from other animals while he goes away, 'he
opens his mouth and breathes over the kill, making his breath
sentry over it while he himself goes away; when any other
animal comes along and notices the kill lying there abandoned,
it dares not approach but clears off ... ' (περοχανὼν ἐμπνεῖ
μὲν τοῦ καθ' ἑαυτὸν ἄσθματος, καὶ τούτῳ τὴν φυλακὴν ἐπιτρέπει,
ἀπαλλάττεταί γε μὴν αὐτός · τὰ δὲ ἄλλα ζῷα ἥκοντα καὶ
αἰσθανόμενα ὅτου λείψανόν ἐστι τὸ κείμενον, οὐ τολμᾷ
προσάψασθαι ἀλλὰ ἀπαλλάττεται...: NA 5, 39). I would argue
that the Egyptian motif quoted by Aelian in NA 12, 7 is a
transposition of this general belief about lions into the
specialized context of lions understood as privileged mediators between heaven and earth: lions' potent breath has been
turned into a means of divine punishment upon those who commit
perjury. God breathes 'just anger' into them, and they
breathe it out upon their victims (31).

    This discussion of the Graeco-Roman-Egyptian 'encyclopae-
dic' lore about lions and 'lions' may appear to be quite
irrelevant to the Mysteries of Mithras, which were, as we
have it on the very best authority, 'Persian'. But perhaps
it is not. For it will be remembered that the object in the
central column of the Leo-frame at di Felicissimo in Ostia
is a sistrum. Now the sistrum was known in the Graeco-Roman
as a specifically Egyptian instrument (a sacred rattle); it
seems to have been imported as part of the sacred cult-
equipment of the cult of Isis. The general agreement is that
it was used in Egypt, and presumably also in the hellenistic-
Roman cult of Isis, to ward off evil powers; and as a sign of
power derived from a particular divinity (32). But what is
it doing in a mithraeum; and in particular what has it to do
with the grade Leo? There has never been an adequate explanation; indeed, scarcely anyone has even considered the matter

worth a moment's consideration (33).

I would argue that the *sistrum* in the Mitreo di Felicissimo must be understood in the context of the lore I have
just discussed about real lions in the Graeco-Roman world,
and especially Egyptian lions. As I have shown, the Egyptians were believed by the Greeks and Romans of the early
Empire (and doubtless earlier) to have partially reclassified
lions into two other categories of living beings, humans and
gods; to think of them as fire-filled and as intimately
associated with the sun; and to have used the traditional
theme of the power of lions' breath in the context of divine
punishment: they were believed to have viewed lions as powerful god-beloved creatures which were especially moral and
punitive. Although many of these themes appear *in nuce* in
the rest of the Graeco-Roman tradition, they appear together
only in Egypt (or perhaps 'Egypt').

The relation between these 'Egyptian' beliefs and those
of the Mysteries is immediately evident. The association in
the Mysteries between Lions (the grade) and fire is amply
demonstrated and well known. But this new context must
surely help us to see the obscure Duran phrase

πυρωπὸν ἄσθμα / τὸ καὶ μάγοις ᾗ ν[ί]πτρον ὁσ⟨σ⟩ίω[ν],

'fiery breath, which is for the Magi too the baptism/lustra-
tion of holy (men)', in a new light (34). The role of 'fiery
breath' here is evidently compatible with Aelian's point about
Egyptian lions, to say no more; but my point is that an association with the grade *Leo* here would enable us to see a
thematic link between this Duran phrase and two of the most
important lines from Santa Prisca (16-17 on Wall K_2, lower
layer):

Accipe thuricremos Pater, accipe Sancte Leones
Per quos thuradam[u]s, per quos consumimur ipsi,

'Father, receive those who burn incense, Holy One, receive
the Lions, through whom we offer (the) incense, through/by
whom we are ourselves consumed'. Some years ago, I noted
the significance of the mention of incense here (1975a: 241
[written in 1971]), but stressed only the fact that incense
has to be burned in order to obtain its benefits. Marcel
Detienne has now shown that the Graeco-Roman 'encyclopaedia'
concerning aromatics, and especially incense, is even more
appropriate to the grade *Leo* in the Mysteries than I had
thought (1972: 19-68). Collected in Arabia (the nurse of
lions, as noted earlier), aromatics were intimately associated
with the sun; those who gathered them were subject to rules of
purity, and in particular to seclusion from women (a theme to
which I shall return). The substances themselves had to be
gathered at the time of the rising of Sirius, the Dog-Star, at

the hottest time of the year (35); they were conceived in
the (learned) botanical tradition, but probably also at the
level of popular culture, as doubly 'cooked' by the sun, and,
therefore peculiarly appropriate as sacrificial substances
— 'naturally civilized' plants, perfect mediators.

The lines from Santa Prisca have generated some heat but
little light (36). I would urge that they can only be understood by realising that the key links between the words
thuricremos, *Leones*, *thuradamus* and *consumimur* are generated
by the Graeco-Roman-Egyptian encyclopaedic knowledge about
lions, and are not stated (neither could nor needed to be
stated: we have to do with a Graeco-Roman Mystery). The most
important are the links between lions and fire, and lions as
moral agents. The members of the grade *Leo* are the appropriate burners of incense in the cult, precisely because real
lions are so intimately connected with the same things with
which aromatics, and especially incense, are connected: fire,
sun, purity, mediation; other members of the cult (but
which?: we need very badly to know what we never can know in
the absence of further evidence, the identity of those who
uttered this formula in the ritual) have to offer incense
through the lions/Lions. And another aspect of this cluster
of associations motivates the idea of *being consumed*: first,
at the literal level of what lions do to their prey; but also
at the level of the power of lions' breath to destroy the
wicked; and then at the level of what fire does to fuel —
which takes us back to the phrase at Dura, where 'breath' is
explicitly 'fiery' and also a *niptron*, a means of washing
clean. Literal fire generates the evocation 'purity'. And
if we need further corroboration, we can go back to the
familiar lustration (also *niptron*) of the Lions with honey
(p. 24 above), another 'naturally civilized' substance, made
this time by sexually-pure male bees (cf. the ritual purity
of the collectors of incense) and implicitly conceived in the
'encyclopaedia' as a fiery liquid (37). The *sistrum* on the
floor of the Mitreo di Felicissimo may be read as a condensed
sign for all these interrelated implications, explicit teachings and relevant evocations from the 'encyclopaedia'. There
is, I would urge, nothing accidental, or even odd, about its
presence: the Egyptian sacred rattle is a sign for 'Egyptian'
lore concerning the meaning of lions (and so Lions) in the
Mysteries (38).

My thesis then is that the 'absurdity' of the Mysteries'
treatment of two of its grades, *Corax* and *Leo*, can be understood only by an examination of the structural homology
between the generalised 'encyclopaedic' knowledge of the
Graeco-Roman world concerning real ravens and real lions on
the one hand, and the rôle played by these grades in the eco-
mony of the cult on the other. The possibility of interplay
between the two levels is guaranteed by the names of the
grades, so that for example Lion/*Leo* 'is' lion/*leo*, the

literalness of the consequent evocations providing a structure
of meanings in which it is not possible to distinguish 'truth'
from 'lie', 'fact' from 'fiction' — the positive content of
the Mysteries' meanings is itself patterned upon, as well as
expressive of, the Mysteries' epistemological and cognitive
assumptions. Because the Mysteries as a whole are dedicated
to the 'proof' of an absurd proposition, that Life is Death,
and Death Life, every aspect of them must share in the pattern
of subsequent subversions of good sense made necessary by that
primary claim. The cult's central claim was in effect that
+ is - and - is + (an absurd claim); and the problem was the
validation of that claim. A technique had to be found which
might legitimate some preliminary absurdities, whose structural homology with, and logical relationship to, the central
proposition might reasonably persuade adherents of its validity. Among these preliminary absurdities are the propositions that men 'are' ravens and lions; and these propositions
were legitimated by appeal to aspects of the Graeco-Roman
'encyclopaedia' about these animals, which turned obviously
mad ideas ('You are a raven') into relative sense ('You are
a raven in that you are between two worlds, earth and
heaven'). For no one would be likely to say, on hearing this
utterance, or on receiving a similar message through the play
of symbols, 'But all these ideas about ravens are nonsense';
for the initial theses about ravens were not invented by the
Mysteries at all — they were part of accepted, ordinary knowledge about the animal world current in the first two centuries AD and doubtless long before. The Mysteries had to
validate their absurd claims by appeal to true knowledge in
'the world outside'. But of course they selected, from among
all the things in the world outside, only carefully chosen
facts, not random ones. It was the *structure* of the selected
aspects of the 'real world outside' which effected the crucial
link between 'truth' and 'lie', between the fantastic and the
prosaic. And a carefully controlled process of selective evocation then led step by step to the validation, or at least
the intelligibility, of the absurd claims which the Mysteries
were really interested in making.
  But it must be evident that this is only part of the story.
If we understand them as a form of pretended action, the Mysteries effected, or claimed to effect, a shift in status for
their adherents, not in the real world but in the 'real' world.
That shift was conceived as a journey which took place at a
specific time (the lifetime of the believer) and in a specific
location (in the space between earth, the starting-point, and
heaven, the goal). But of course this too was not a journey
but a 'journey', a movement conceived in deliberate contrast
to real journeys: they take place more or less horizontally
over land or sea, the Mithraic one vertically. Now vertical
journeys in the ancient world were obviously fantastic, as we
can see from Aristophanes' *Birds*; and the Mithraic one is no

exception. For it purported to carry one from our fully
human world to one which was conceived as more or less its
inversion, characterised by such properties as essence,
stability, truth, life and so on. The absurdity of the
project is fully confirmed by the absurdity of the goal;
to put it the other way round, if one wants to go to mad
places, one has to do mad things (like slipping through
mirrors, for example). Now one way of understanding that
is Tzvetan Todorov's, who argues that a typical entry into
the world of (literary) fantasy is to take metaphors literally; when children do this, we call it a mistake, but
consciously used it is clearly a technique, a sign of altered
rules (1970: 29-32). But such a formulation raises as many
difficulties as it resolves, particularly in connection with
the status of metaphor; and I think it is preferable to use
here the notion of evocation once again. For whereas the
metaphor of the heavenly journey had become almost completely
clichéd by the time the Mysteries developed their classic
western form (presumably in the first century BC — first century AD), the Mysteries offered an original variant: this
journey was a 'real' journey through the planets, a journey
whose steps were marked by the planetary structure of the
space between earth and the fixed stars, and reproduced in
the grade-structure. And if one's body could not take that
path, one's soul could. But one's soul is forced to be with
the body (until it has to leave); and therefore the body could
itself enact the spiritual journey while still on earth — no,
in the 'cosmos', in the *mithraeum*, a sacred space marked out
so as to imitate the path of the journey. A perfectly liminal
space for perfectly absurd journeys for perfectly absurd ends.

The journey is thus (1) a 'journey' which one can in truth
only perform in spirit (2) a 'journey' which purports to be
vertical but which is in fact horizontal (3) a 'journey' which
takes place entirely within a room which is called the 'cosmos'
(4) a 'journey' which can be known only by its external markings in the cult, the grades, through which one climbs simply
by fulfilling the overt ritual and moral requirements.
Pretended (if actual) acts-in-the-world take one along an
improbable path to an absurd goal — and all without one's
having to move at all. Real acts, that only change the real
world, could never achieve such things; but, by pretended acts,
you can 'do' anything.

                                II

My stress upon the importance of the space between 'here' and
'there' in the Mysteries should serve to remind us of a potentially interesting analogy. For we can aptly schematize the
Mysteries' project in terms of Arnold van Gennep's threefold

pattern of 'primitive' *rites de passage*: separation, exclusion, consciously novel reincorporation (39). Many scholars since then have observed that normal rules are frequently inverted in order to effect the initiate's transition from one status to another, particularly at the point of 'exclusion', and that it is here that we tend to find masquerades and deliberate redefinition of perfectly ordinary spaces and times (40). What is peculiar about the Mysteries of Mithras is their neat inversion of traditional Graeco-Roman *rites de passage*. Whereas these divided locations on the ground into 'human' space and 'marginal' space, the Mysteries pretended that their marginal space, the *mithraeum*, a sacred space opposed to the profane world, was actually the path of the vertical journey through the planets, and so the only truly human space, in spite of the fact that ordinary human beings could not live there — a project perfectly in keeping with the Mysteries' prior rejection of ordinary assumptions, in the ordinary world, about the nature of human life. Whereas ordinary *rites de passage* effected a shift in real-world status, the Mysteries used an identical pattern of ritual action to effect a shift in ontological status. But while that project was appropriately absurd, one of the taller and taller stories of new cults in the Graeco-Roman world, I believe that beneath the overt discourse there is another much more in keeping with the traditional pattern of ritual action which the Mysteries used to further the pretence that radical escape was possible. For if *rites de passage* effect shifts of status, they also define boundaries.

If the Mithraic journey through the grades corresponds to van Gennep's period of 'exclusion' (which may have taken many years to complete), it will be evident that the motivation for 'separation' must have been in keeping with the overt teachings of the Mysteries on the one hand, and intelligible to would-be initiates on the other. And it might seem obvious that we should relate the motive for 'separation' to the Mithraic teaching concerning the soul, and in particular its *kathodos* through the Gate of Cancer to earth, and to the Mysteries' promise of *apogenesis*, of a form of immortality. That is the usual answer: religion has its own discourse, and it must be discussed in terms only of that discourse. I wish to argue that this is an inadequate view, because it grants the religious discourse its claimed privilege of being taken on its own terms; and because it presupposes that choice of belief in such stories is itself unamenable to discussion. And there seems to me some evidence that the rationale for the Mithraic journey was far more complex, and interesting, than is generally supposed; evidence, indeed, which permits us to understand their social rôle in the Roman Empire in a new way.

We may begin with danger-beliefs. The initiatory ritual for Lions to which I have already referred (p. 24 above), metonymically equates honey with moral purity. The person(s) who

poured the honey on to the initiates' hands urged them 'to keep
their hands pure ... from all that is wicked, harmful and sinful':
καθαρὰς ἔχειν τὰς χεῖρας ... ἀπὸ παντὸς λυπηροῦ καὶ βλαπτικοῦ
καὶ μυσαροῦ (Porphyry, *De antro* 15).   Now although the
choice of these three words (supposing this to be an accurate
quotation), (*to*) *lupēron*, *blaptikon*, *musaron*, may have had a
direct inverse relation to specific properties ascribed to
honey in the Graeco-Roman 'encyclopaedia' (41), in *koinè* they
all three often had moral connotations (42).   This ritual
for the initiation of Lions reveals an institutional remedy
against one form of pollution, by sin; and that we have to do
with pollution is clear not only from the word *musaron* but
from the remedy, lustration.   Now Mary Douglas has argued
that danger beliefs may be used to underline rôles and obligations expected of one, and to maintain (and refuse) status-
claims (43).   Accepting that idea, we can say that from one
point of view such pollution-fears or danger-beliefs served
to define the rôle of Lions against the rôles of other grades
in the Mysteries, of whom such demands were not made; and no
less obviously, that such beliefs served to characterise the
'world outside' in morally negative terms, and therefore to
give a particular character to the general project of escape
from the world.   The implication of the grade-structure is
that the world outside was understood to be characterised by
certain kinds of pollution which it was the rôle of each grade
to oppose in their different ways.   The rationale of Mithraic
'separation' from the world gradually became clearer to
initiates — it was not revealed all at once.   From this point
of view, the complexity of the Mysteries' understanding of
'separation' is reflected in the unusually complex initiatory
structure of the seven grades.
   Rituals against pollution can be seen then as ways of constructing boundaries, and thus of constructing meanings.   The
Mysteries defined themselves in terms of positive, overt,
goals, but also in terms of what they were not, what they
helped one escape from.   The relation between the two can be
illustrated by constructing a table of adjectives and nouns
used to qualify status within the cult:

Pater	*dignissimus* [423]; *pientissimus* [1821]
Heliodromus	στερεωτής (44); σοφιστής; ἀγαθός; ?εὐσεβής (all at Dura-Europos)
Perses	?[θ]ελεμνος (45) (Dura-Europos)
Leo	?ἁβρος (46) (Dura-Europos)
Miles	ἀκέραιος (Dura-Europos)
Nymphus	ἀγαθός (Dura); ?*cryphius* (4th cent.; ? Rome only) (47)
Corax	ἱερός (Dura; Rome cf. *hierocoracica* in *CIMRM* 403³)

Each of these adjectives and nouns makes a positive claim to

V

a moral virtue of some kind, purity, goodness, holiness,
piety or wisdom, or to a special theme in a particular grade
— dignity in the case of the Father, cosmic freedom in the
case of Heliodromus, firm-rootedness for Perses or brightness
for Lions (48). But each of these positives implies a
correlative negative, not by contrast with other members of
the cult, but with the world outside; and from that point of
view the word *hieros*, 'holy', as the proper adjective for the
lowest grade *Corax*, is particularly significant: even the
lowest grade is sharply marked off from the profane world
(49). The general point can be made by considering one of
the Duran graffiti first published by Professor Francis (*ap.*
Cumont, 1975: 204 n. 296), which contains two separate items
(1) a red dipinto: τ]οῖς δικαίοι[ς (2) a graffito probably
in a different hand:

τοῖς δὲ ἀδίκοις ν[
....]αβλη ἀπὸ τῶν ἱεραίων.

Although we cannot accept Cumont's statement (1975: 204) that
'in one graffito the *dikaioi* are opposed to the *adikoi*', the
very appearance of these contrasting words, the 'just' against
the 'unjust', with quite generalised (non-grade) referents,
suggests that the Mysteries had developed explicit boundary
terms structured as simple opposites: these Duran graffiti
support my contention that the adjectives and nouns which
qualify the grades served simultaneously to exclude and to
include.
    Now the most obvious exclusion practised by the Mysteries
of Mithras was that of women. That exclusion is usually
treated merely as a 'fact' about the cult, and quickly dismissed. But it seems to me of central importance in any
attempt to define the nature of the 'separation' which motivated the pursuit of salvation in the cult. I grant, of course,
that the exclusion of women might have been casual, on some
such argument as this: in attempting to define themselves as
a new cult in the Roman world, the Mysteries were faced with
a choice of possible models at an institutional level. On the
one hand, one obvious model for a specialized non-familial
institution was the *collegium tenuiorum*, private associations
for social, religious and business purposes. These *collegia*
regularly excluded women, and in that respect simply reproduced traditional rules about relations between the sexes in
spite of being non-traditional institutions (50). By contrast,
mysteries and new cults often admitted both sexes, though we
do not know very much about the rules and conditions of entry
and membership; at any rate it is clear that to admit both
sexes, on whatever terms, was to highlight the marginal status
of the cult which did so. Breaking rules for relations between the sexes, especially on a long-term basis, was to make
a statement about the cult's relation to traditional religious

goals, and therefore to make a comment upon the whole
structure of meanings, and in particular the distribution
of power, both expressed in and validated by the traditional
religious structure (51). In choosing to exclude women, the
Mysteries might be understood as attempting to define themselves by a play of differences: as a marginal cult which
nevertheless rejected the usual means of announcing marginality and based itself unambiguously upon the 'traditional'
sexual model of the *collegia tenuiorum*. Although I have some
sympathy with such an argument, it seems to me that the exclusion of women was much more important in the Mysteries' self-
definition than it would allow; and indeed, that women provided the central justification for the whole mad enterprise
of separation in its extreme Mithraic form, the vertical
'journey' to heaven.
     A questionnaire sent to all Mithraic scholars on the sub-
ject of women in the Mysteries would undoubtedly reveal a
consensus that we know nothing whatever about the way in which
women were presented by the cult. But nothing could be further from the truth: it is merely that no one has yet thought
of appropriate ways of asking the question. We may start with
the names of the seven grades themselves. The highest grade
Pater, Father, explicitly denotes only the male aspect of par-
entage, and by connotation, sexual and authority roles. Again,
Pierre Vidal-Naquet has remarked on the association between
'running' and male membership of Greek, and especially Cretan
cities; and the point can be confirmed by the mythical treatment of Atalanta, an anomalous female runner (52). 'The runner
of the sun' (or perhaps the 'runner along the course of the
sun'), *Heliodromus*, may well therefore have a deliberate
sexual implication, one moreover related to traditional rites
of passage in the Graeco-Roman world (53). The name *Perses*,
Persian, has no corresponding female form, and was anyway a
common man's name; and we may remember that it was declined
in such a way as to recall the Greek mythical hero Perseus.
Both in Latin and in Greek the word for lion is differentiated
from the word for lioness, so that Lion explicitly excludes
Lioness. Of the masculine connotations of the soldier there
can of course be no question. I shall discuss *Nymphus*, the
sixth grade, more fully in a moment. Finally, there is *Corax*,
Raven. The fact that neither Greek nor Latin has a separate
word for the female raven is remarked upon, curiously enough,
by Varro, who evidently thought it rather peculiar: *dici
corvum, turdum, non dici corvam, turdam* ('we say *corvus* and
turdus ('dove'), not *corva* and *turda*') he says, and then
explains that it is because we have no interest in making such
distinctions in these cases, although they exist in nature,
for they are of no use to us: *corvus et corva non, quod sine
usu id, quod dissimilis naturae* (*Ling. Lat.* 9, 55-56). I
observe simply that in this case we find a masculine substan-
tive ending which was clearly felt by Varro to raise a

difficulty about where to place the female, which ought to be 'noted' separately but is not. Given the acute sensibility of the ancient world to matters of gender and correlative status, and the frequent reluctance to make (and consistently maintain) what is to us the obvious point, that grammatical gender has nothing to do with the real world, it would be unwise to assume that those who invented the term *Corax* as the name of the lowest grade in the Mysteries were uninterested in the query raised by Varro (54).

I would argue then that all the names of the grades in the Mysteries are interesting precisely because they all, in different ways, seem to stress the exclusion or suppression of the female or the feminine, either liguistically or socially. But let us look more closely at the first four grades (I omit *Perses*, *Heliodromus* and *Pater* partly for reasons of space and partly because we know practically nothing of the first two, and I have dealt with *Pater* extensively elsewhere). Since I have already suggested that *Corax* and *Leo* are structurally homologous grades, it will be simplest to deal with them first.

In my earlier discussion of the Graeco-Roman ideas about ravens and lions in the real world, I deliberately omitted some very important information concerned with sexual matters which is highly instructive in the present context. Ravens were popularly believed not to have sexual intercourse in the ordinary way of birds, but *through the beak: ore eos parere aut coire vulgus arbitratur* ('ordinary people believe that they lay eggs or have intercourse through the beak') observes Pliny (*NH* 10, 32; cf. André, 1967: 62). And he instructively proceeds to associate that belief with a number of others which directly relate human behaviour and ravens' behaviour. If a pregnant woman eats a raven's egg, she gives birth to her baby not through the vagina but *through her mouth* (the Latin *os* means both 'beak' and 'mouth'); and more generally, the presence of a raven in the house will make the birth difficult: *gravidas, si ederint corvinum ovum, per os partum reddere, atque in totum difficulter parere si tecto inferantur* (cf. Aelian, *NA* 3, 43). In other words, the raven was for some reason conceived to be hostile to the process of birth, and the belief was clearly in the popular mind (we cannot of course tell how generalised the belief was in the Graeco-Roman world) related to the raven's sexual habits. Now as an orifice in the face the mouth is often opposed, for reasons that will be obvious to those habituated to structural analysis, to other orifices. A good example is the institutionalised kissing of the Devil's anus in Continental fantasies about witches' sabbats in the early modern period. In this inversion of the norms of the Catholic Mass, a symbol of proper relations between certain persons, the kiss (two mouths brought together), is appropriately inverted: one mouth (a human mouth) is brought into contact with the opposite of a mouth, in this case an anus, of a non-human creature, either

the Devil in person, as in the fully-developed fantasy, or
that of a monstrous animal, cat, dog, or toad. But we know
from the analyses of Hesiod by Jean-Pierre Vernant that in
Archaic Greece the woman's mouth was conceived in direct
relation to another orifice, the vagina. The male laboured
in the fields to produce food, which was consumed by the
idle drone, the woman; and just as the man ploughed the
fields and hid in them the seed which would grow into food,
so he ploughed the woman and hid in her the seed that would
grow into a child. But he could not 'fill her belly' in
sexual intercourse without 'filling her belly' (the terms
are not differentiated: there is no distinction between
'stomach' and 'uterus' here) by giving her food. The two
sorts of 'ploughing' are exactly parallel, and equally
necessary; and of course both of them are the result of
Prometheus's trick at Mekone (55). In structural terms
then, the vagina is the opposite of the mouth, an opposition
mediated in Hesiod's account physically by the 'belly' and
institutionally by male sexual and agricultural labour. In
this connection, the raven is the direct opposite of humans:
its beak performs both functions, alimentary and sexual, and
it thus denies the central human meaning provided by the
opposition between mouth and vagina in the human female.
And that structural point seems to me to provide the reason
for the danger represented by the raven to human parturition,
which was a special danger because of the raven's much wider
ambiguity between the animal and the human worlds. But I
think we must go further.
    It will be recalled that the raven experienced thirst be-
tween the rising of Sirius at the height of summer and the
autumnal rising of Arcturus, around 20th September in the
first century AD. Now that obviously implies that the raven
became progressively *drier* during that period (the point is
made explicit by Aelian *NA* 2, 51 [end] (56)), and *weaker*.
And we do not have to search hard to see why that was interesting to the Graeco-Roman world. For precisely the same was
believed to happen, during the very same period of time, to
the human male: at this level, the raven is an exact parallel
to the human male in the animal kingdom (57). Moreover, as
the creature composed of dry and hot elements goes off the
top of the thermometer, as it were, the creature composed of
the wet and the cold rises on the same scale, to the point
previously occupied by the now exhausted male: this period of
the year was the one in which the human female was at her most
sexually dangerous and aggressive, most like the human male.
Marcel Detienne has suggested with some plausibility that
this pattern of sexual relationships was reproduced in Greek
religion (or at least in classical Athenian religion) in the
cult of Adonis, with its rapidly-withering gardens planted by
non-wives, and its association between licentiousness on the
part of women and sexual exhaustion on the part of the

male (58). I would argue that Graeco-Roman beliefs about
ravens are, at this level, genuine boundary fantasies:
ravens' weakness at this crucial point of the year means that
they are 'just like' human males; another fact about ravens,
their peculiar method of reproduction, thus becomes important,
and applicable to humans. At that level, ravens are agents of
pollution, since they cause human females to imitate raven
females' method of producing young, through the mouth. But
imitation of ravens here on the part of human females is
inevitably related to imitation of ravens in summer; the
classification of ravens as pollutants at the time of parturition is also an interdiction at the time of greatest heat. In
a word, women must not be sexually aggressive when men are
weak. The concrete threat to normal birth which the raven was
thought to offer is also a reference to the threat offered to
male predominance by human females at the hottest time of the
year. Pollutant ravens are a way of talking about the familiar, and unresolvable, conflicts between the sexes to be
found in patrilineal virilocal societies like the Graeco-
Roman world. If so, the Mysteries' choice of the raven as a
name for the first grade may have been motivated by this
aspect of the Graeco-Roman 'encyclopaedia' too: both ravens
and Ravens are connected with the relations between the sexes,
just as they are connected with other boundaries and margins.
And if one grants that it was precisely the raven's crossing
of the boundaries between animal and human, heaven and earth,
that prompted its choice as a grade-name in the Mysteries, it
is only a small step also to grant that they were seen to be
further appropriate because of their popular connection with
the male/female boundary (59).

If ravens merely refer to the problem of male/female relations, and suggest the necessary predominance of the male in
human society, lions were believed to tackle the problem in a
much less oblique way. As everyone knows, Atalanta and her
husband Melanion were turned into lions after having had
sexual intercourse in the temple of the Magna Mater; and the
scholiast tradition tells us explicitly that this was because
lions were unable to have intercourse (60). And although the
learned 'encyclopaedia' at any rate certainly discussed the
offspring of lions, and Aristotle knew of their mating
habits (61), the tradition about lions' sexual purity turns
up in a slightly different form in popular beliefs. Lionesses were supposed to be singularly lustful, and to have
indiscriminate intercourse with similar animals, leopards,
panthers, and other large felines, so that they produced
'variegated' offspring which were not true lions (62). But,
as I have observed earlier, lions were among the most anthro-
pomorphic of beasts, and the effect of that reclassification
is nowhere more evident than here. For lions became a means
of projecting the sexual ethics (or at least an aspect of
them) of a patrilineal society into Nature, and thus 'proving'

that such ethics were not just invented by men (as opposed to
women). *'Magna his* [i.e. the lionesses] *libido coitus et ob
hoc maribus ira'* observes Pliny (*HN* 8, 42): 'The lionesses
are very eager for sexual intercourse, and this makes the
males angry'. But lions were not merely angry: they punished
lionesses guilty of adultery with another feline: *'Odori
pardi coitum sentit in adultera leo totaque vi consurgit in
poenam; idcirco culpa flumine abluitur, aut longius comitatur'*,
'The lion discovers the sexual intercourse by the smell of the
leopard clinging to the adulterous lioness, and summons up his
whole mighty strength to punish her: and to that end her moral
iniquity is washed off in a river, or else the lion keeps a
great distance between himself and her' (Pliny, *HN* 8, 43).
The small detail about washing off the pollution makes my
point perfectly: the king of the beasts proves that human
males' wrath at their wives' adultery was 'natural'. And
although I know of no other text which makes this point, the
theme of the lion staying away from the lioness occurs elsewhere: they were, for example, supposed to eat and drink
alone (63).
    But what is the connection between solitary lions, lions
unable to have intercourse, and sex-mad lionesses who have to
commit adultery? The key must surely lie in the connection
between real lions and Leo the constellation, which the sun
entered at the hottest time of the year. Lions must have been
thought to be so hot 'inside' that they were sexually impotent,
not just in the height of summer as with human males, but all
the time; the females therefore must have been thought to have
been *permanently* like human women in summer — oversexed, and
a threat to the moral order. In other words, the lion is *all
the time* what the raven is for sixty days in the summer — a
further confirmation of my earlier point about the parallelism
between the two species; and there could scarcely be a better
image of the relation within the cult between *Corax* and *Leo*.
Moreover, this link can be arrived at only through the notion
of *internal heat*, as it were 'cooking'. That reminds us of
what Porphyry says (*De Antro* 24), that heat in the theology
of the Mysteries was correlated with the South, with the Tropic
of Capricorn and with immortality, *apogenesis*. Here surely we
have a central reason for naming two of the crucial grades in
the Mysteries after animals: because they were both believed to
be specially hot, but in different time-spans, and the sacred
geography-cum-physics of the Mysteries demanded the inclusion
of the opposition between cold (North, coming-into-being) and
hot (South, *apogenesis*). Moreover, both raven and lion are
connected in the 'encyclopaedia' with what one might call
'physiological purity', an hostility to the female on account
of this same motif of heat — a connection explicit in the case
of lions, merely implicit in the case of the raven. The contrast seems to me to be linked with the nature of revelation
in the Mysteries, the slow unfolding of a central secret,

which keeps being 'referred to' in different ways.

Once again we can see the process of evocation at work.
We may think it absurdly childish to transfer the idea of
'heat' from animals to men, and then to link that literal
heat to another form of literal heat (which Mithraic scholars
have always taken allegorically, if they have noticed the
point at all), the heat of the Tropic of Capricorn in the
South, of heaven and of the world, which releases the soul
from its worldly state of *genesis*. But as I have stressed
before, new cults are condemned to stranger and stranger
stories, which they must link to 'true' facts. The Mysteries
were simply working out the implications of commonly accepted
true facts about the world, innocently proving their really
important and really absurd lie (Life is Death, and Death
Life) 'true'. And is seems to me clear that among the facts
here selected so as to be 'interesting' occurs the motif of
the female as a lower margin, as a point of separation. But
we must go further: for if that is plausible in the case of
Lions and Ravens, it is evident in the case of the second
grade, *Nymphus*.

The most obvious point about the grade *Nymphus* is its very
name. For it seems that until the Mysteries invented it, the
word νύμφος/*Nymphus* did not exist. Now what could have been
the purpose of such a coinage? Precisely, I suggest, to dif-
ferentiate the Mithraic initiate from two opposite sorts of
people, from *brides* on the one hand, and *grooms* on the other.
When Firmicus Maternus glossed (*De errore* 19, 1 Ziegler)
νύμφος/*Nymphus* as *sponsus*, 'bride-groom', he simply revealed
how little he knew about the Mysteries — as Cumont observed
before passing on to propose something equally implausible (64).
I would argue that the Mithraic word νύμφος/*nymphus* occupies a
deliberately impossible semantic space, that it mediates between the two mutually exclusive terms of the binary opposition
bride vs *groom*. Now no one in their right mind would *want* a
mediator here: on the very good principle that two is company
but three's none (65). But my point seems actually forced
upon our attention by the form of the word νύμφος itself (I
take this to be prior to the Latin *Nymphus*, which is simply a
transliteration). The pitch-stress of the two words which com-
pose the original pair of opposites clearly marks them as related yet different: νυμφίος against νύμφη (*numphĩos/nŭmphe*).
The contrast at the phonetic level is exactly parallel to the
opposition-in-identity of their semantic meaning. In that
connection, the accentuation of Mithraic νύμφος is instructive
(granted that we do not actually *know* what its accentuation
was and simply apply the 'rules'): νύμφος. That accentuation
produces a sound/stress in the first syllable which is exactly
that of one of the original words, νύμφη, 'bride', but no less
obviously, the ending is masculine. Female first syllable is
countered by male second syllable: phonetic expectation is be-
lied by grammatical form. The word νύμφος is a deliberate

paradox, and deliberately constructed to be like two other
words which form a binary set. And semantically I would argue,
the νύμφος must be a sort of marital androgyne, a fusion of
male and female at the point of marriage. No wonder it is
untranslatable: it is only conceivable within the world of
the Mysteries (66).

If we refer now to the objects associated with the grade
Nymphus in the Mitreo di Felicissimo at Ostia we find the
following:

		diadem
(lost)		lamp

The top right-hand object is generally agreed to be a sign
for the planet Venus, in keeping with the general pattern of
the mosaic (all the right-hand objects seem to refer in the
first instance to the tutelary planets of the grades). We
have already seen that the objects in the central column
(assuming the lamp to have been 'displaced' by some large
symbol now lost) in at least the two cases we have discussed,
Corax and *Leo*, seem to refer to relevant knowledge from the
'encyclopaedia' of shared ideas in the Graeco-Roman world.
What, then, might be the significance of the lamp in relation
to the grade *Nymphus*? I believe that we must begin (granted
that the left-hand object is lost) with Graeco-Roman ideas
about the planet Venus.

Although all the planets were understood to have regularly
irregular courses, the planet Aphrodite/Venus had a special
peculiarity: although it was known to be 'one', it had two
names. As Cicero puts it: '...*stella Veneris, quae* φωσφόρος
*Graece, Lucifer Latine dicitur, cum antegreditur solem, cum
subsequitur autem* Ἕσπερος' ('Venus's star, which is called
in Greek *Phōsphoros*, and in Latin *Lucifer* [i.e. 'Bringer of
light'] when it precedes the sun, but when it comes after it,
Hesperos [i.e. 'Evening']': *ND* 2, 53 = Pease II, pp. 676-77)
(67). Although the denominated interval was sometimes thought
of as the period morning→evening, those who 'knew' claimed
that Venus really linked *evening* to *morning* (68). This made it
appropriate to invoke Venus to restore light, in an evident
play upon the double sense of *Phōsphoros* (69). Perhaps the
most relevant example for my purpose is a brief epigram by
Meleager (*Anth. Pal.* 12, 114 = Gow-Page, *The Greek Anthology:
Hellenistic Epigrams*, I no. 75, p. 237):

> Ἠοῦς ἄγγελε χαῖρε φαεσφόρε, καὶ ταχὺς ἔλθοις
> Ἕσπερος, ἣν ἀπάγεις λάθριος αὖθις ἄγων

'Hail Lightbringer (*Phōsphoros*), messenger of dawn; come
quickly Hesperos, and bring back my girl whom you (now) take
from me once again under the cover of darkness'. The epigram
depends utterly for such point as it has upon the fact that

it is the same star, Venus, which both forces the girl to
leave in the morning (Phōsphoros) and brings her back at
night (Hesperos).

This first point about the planet Venus seems to have
direct relevance to the Mysteries. For we cannot but be
reminded of a familiar Mithraic *logion* which Cumont correctly
identified on the basis of the finds at Dura (70). It is
quoted by Firmicus Maternus, *De errore* 19, 1:

]δε Νύμφε, χαῖρε Νύμφε, χαῖρε νέον φῶς.

But if Cumont was correct about the Mithraic provenance of
these words, his translation was curiously prejudicial,
involving the claim that χαῖρε means here 'rejoice' rather
than what we would expect, 'Hail'. The *logion* became a command, not an acclamation:

'(Sing) Nymph, rejoice Nymph, rejoice at the new light'.

But as Professor Vermaseren rightly saw (1963: 142) this is
to impose an unnatural translation because of a preconceived
notion about the meaning of 'new light' - understood to be
Mithras (71). Without that assumption, the *logion* makes
perfect sense taking χαῖρε in its usual meaning (and adopting
Friedrich's conjecture ἰδέ, as against ἴδε or αἴδε):

'Behold Nymphos! Hail Nymphos! Hail New Light!'

Just as the planet Venus in one of its manifestations was
Bringer of Light, so was the grade in the Mysteries which
came under its tutelage: the *Nymphus was* 'new light'. The
lamp at di Felicissimo refers both to Venus as Phōsphoros
and to the correlative, and appropriate, value of the grade
(72).

But the Mysteries of Mithras seem to have taken the idea
of 'new light' quite literally: before there can be new light
there must be a period of darkness, just as in the relationship between the two aspects of Venus as morning star and
evening star. On the top layer of paintings on wall I_2
at Santa Prisca occurs a representation of the *Nymphus* with
his face covered by a veil; on the lower layer of paintings
on the same wall, the *Nymphus* hold a *flammeum* (a red veil)
in his hands (73). One could hardly wish for a clearer reference to the motif of 'hiding' and 'revealing': the act of
removing the veil is the act of revelation of the *Nymphus*
as 'new light'. Just like the tutelary planet Venus, the
grade *Nymphus* is characterised by a play between light and
darkness.

Let us go back to the planet Venus. The planet's
association with both light and darkness gave rise inevitably to a belief that it was itself ambiguous. Its colour

might be said to be *poikilē*, a blend of colours, not a pure
colour (74). It was the brightest of all the planets (apart
of course from the sun and the moon) — so bright that it
alone could be seen by day (Martianus Capella, 8, 883); so
bright that it threw shadows (Pliny *HN* 2, 37; Martianus
Capella, *ibid*.). At the same time it was believed to be
'dark', 'gloomy' (75). This ambiguity is expressed formally in the astrological tradition, where we find the epi-
thet 'two-faced' (διπρόσωπος) for Venus (76). We seem
already to be close to my claim about Mithraic νύμφος/
Nymphos, the 'marital androgyne'. Yet not quite close
enough. But there is one passage, admittedly late, of
extreme interest in connection with the planet Venus.
Johannes Lydus has a discussion of the chronocrators of
each day of the week, a theory which he explicitly refers
to the speculations of the Chaldaeans and the Egyptian
astrologers (*de mensibus* 2, 4 = p. 21.1 Wünsch), and he
deals in sixth place ('Friday') with the planet Venus (p.
31. 20-1 Wünsch): τὴν δὲ ἕκτην (ἡμέραν) ἀναφέρουσι φωσφόρῳ,
θερμαίνοντι ἅμα καὶ γονίμως ὑγραίνοντι: 'The sixth day they
assign to Phōsphoros, a planet which is both warm and wet,
suitable for generation...'. And in developing the significance of this choice, he observes: 'and, in a word, (the
planet) is both male and female, just like Aphrodite herself, who is by nature both male and female and is for that
reason called 'masculo-feminine' by the theologians' (καὶ
ἁπλῶς εἰπεῖν ἄρρην τε καὶ θῆλυς εἶναι πέφυκεν, ὡς καὶ αὐτὴ
Ἀφροδίτη, τὴν τοῦ ἄρρενος τήν τε τοῦ θήλεος ἔχουσα φύσιν
καὶ διὰ τοῦτο παρὰ τοῖς θεολόγοις ἀρρενόθηλυς καλουμένη).
Now it is evident that even in the Archaic period Aphrodite
was conceived as more than merely 'female'. She was born
asexually from the infertile sea and Ouranos's fallen testicles (Hesiod, *Theogony* 188-206 with West's commentary);
she crosses boundaries with gay abandon (mating of gods and
humans in *Homeric Hymn* 5); exercises a proverbial *mētis*
(Detienne and Vernant, 1974: 267-8; 278). In the tradition
of Homeric exegesis, from Alcman's cosmogonic poem onwards,
she (often with Ares) was seen as the fundamental cosmogenic
principle (cf. Buffière, 1956: 168-72). It is equally evident that bisexual supreme cosmogonic principles were the
stock-in-trade of any number of speculative cults in the
ancient world (77). But Johannes Lydus's specific point
here is not, so far as I know, to be found anywhere else in
the Graeco-Roman 'encyclopaedia' — learned or popular —
concerning Aphrodite/Venus, even though it might conceivably
have been fairly easy to deduce from familiar astrological
doctrines such as the 'masculinization' of the female planet
when it rises in the morning (for example Ptolemy, *Tetrab.*
1, 6 cf. 3, 14 [171]) (78). It would therefore be
reasonable to accept that this idea about both divinity and
planet was believed to be a secret Chaldaean and Egyptian

astrological doctrine; if so, it may have been known as such
in the Mysteries, since we have every reason to believe that
Johannes Lydus did not invent it (79). And it is tempting
to suppose that it was precisely some such 'Chaldaean' or
'Egyptian' doctrine about Aphrodite/Venus which prompted the
Mysteries to create the androgynous *Nymphus*, once again
exactly patterned upon the nature of the grade's tutelary
planet.

But why? I think we must go back to the question of boundaries, back to the primary issue of separation. I mentioned
a little earlier that the Mithraic iconography of the grade
Nymphus included a veil, a *flammeum*. But the *flammeum* (and
there can be little doubt that that is what the splodges of
red colour are in the paintings) was of course the Roman
marriage-veil, taken off during the marriage-ceremony as a
symbolic ritual of passage from one status to another. That
aspect of the initiation ceremony of the *Nymphus* is related
not only to the planet Venus but also to real rituals in the
ordinary world (80). One interpretation of the *flammeum*-
ritual in the mysteries takes it as the enactment of some
sort of *hieros gamos*, a sacred marriage, between initiate
and Mithras: the *Nymphus* is supposed to be the 'bride of
Mithras' (81). Cumont, in criticizing Ferrua's version of
the theory (1940: 76), objected: 'aucune femme ne partici-
pant aux mystères mithriaques, la cérémonie du dévoilement
aurait dê être transportée de l'épouse à l'époux' (1945:
403 n. 3). It does not seem to have occurred to him that
just such an absurdity may have been the point; but let that
pass, since the theory of a *hieros gamos* seems to me, at
least in the form in which it is normally held, as unsatisfactory as it seemed to Cumont.

It will be recalled that Johannes Lydus, when introducing
the subject of Venus as chronocrator, refers to its 'warmth'
and its 'fecund dampness'. This reminds us of the common
astrological association between the planet Venus and marriage (82). Venus 'governed' marriage and procreation. The
problem for the Mysteries was to relate the grade governed by
venus to the commonly accepted meanings of the planet in the
'encyclopaedia'. That could be done easily enough, as we
have seen, in relation to light and darkness, which constitute a central theme in the part that the *Nymphus* played in
the economy of the grade structure. But what about marriage
and procreation in a cult which excluded women, and which,
as I argue, did so deliberately in pursuit of a particular
and hostile classification of the female? The problem was
to be faithful to ordinary meanings and yet to exclude the
acceptance of marriage and procreation evident in ordinary
ideas about the planet Venus. The answer, I would urge,
lay in the bisexuality of Venus — a 'secret' truth. Bisexuality meant that the female principle was in a sense *expen-
dable* because it could be integrated at least partly into

the male instead of being seen as its opposite. The female
is not an independent principle, it is part of the male.
And the symbolism of ordinary marriage is of course utterly
appropriate: for in marriage the woman accepted her new
κύριος or *dominus*, she passed from one sort of ownership
into another; at the same time, the allusion to marriage,
made necessary by the ordinary significance of the planet
Venus, is surreptitiously interpreted in terms of a more
'interesting' Mithraic meaning — the motif of hiding versus
revelation, with its wide reverberations in the theology of
the Mysteries. And if we find this sort of denial of the
female strange or 'unlikely', we have only to refer to the
equally 'strange' and 'unlikely' theories the Graeco-Roman
world produced to classify out the female at the level of
her most obviously crucial function, procreation — the predictable science of a patrilineal society (83). The 'marital
androgyne', the *Nymphus*, is, at least in part, a reproduction
within the Mysteries of precisely the same attitude towards
the female.
    Since the military life so obviously excluded the female
in the Graeco-Roman world that the motif provided not only
the major transposition of values in the most perfectly
topsy-turvy society the Greek imagination produced, that of
the Amazons, but also what one might call the Locris- Tarentum syndrome (legends whose primary function is mythic, inasmuch as they are fantasies about what women get up to when
their husbands are away at war) (84), it is scarcely necessary to argue the compatibility of the grade *Miles* with my
case. In relation to the Roman Empire, it is worth simply
remarking on the fiction that serving soldiers were not
allowed to contract *matrimonia*, full civil marriages (85);
and that the Christian theme of *militia Christi* was felt
appropriate precisely because the military life involved
the cancellation of the complex of social obligations,
rights and reciprocities which make up ordinary life (86).
The marginality of the soldier in relation to civil society
is matched by the marginality of the hunter, who operates
in the 'wild', τὸ ἄγριον, pitting wits and strength against
wild animals: 'thieving' Mithras, who is also a hunter, is
surely the structural counterpart of the Mithraic grade
Miles (87). If getting to heaven is a matter of looking
for the cracks in the given world, not belonging to the given
world socially — being socially marginal — is a prerequisite
for success; Ravens, marital androgynes, Soldiers and Lions
are just such social marginals — men who are birds and beasts,
mediators of binary oppositions, excluded from civic rights
because of their profession. And starting from that proposition, I think we can properly argue another: that the structure of the three higher grades *Leo — Perses — Heliodromus*
is exactly the same as that of the three junior grades
Corax — Nymphus — Miles. Another way of making the same point

is to say that what *Corax* is to *Leo, Nymphus* is to *Perses,*
and *Miles* to *Heliodromus:*

Corax : Leo :: Nymphus : Perses :: Miles : Heliodromus.

The key is surely provided by the relation I have already
suggested between the two animal grades — *Leo* reproduces
at a higher level the ambiguity of the *Corax* between two
worlds. The tutelary planets of *Nymphus* and *Perses* are the
only female planets, and both grades have associations with
generation, the one at the level of human society, the other
at the level of plants and fruits in general (99). *Miles*
is a specifically male social marginal; *Heliodromus* is the
specifically male ('runner') cosmic marginal. A simple
triadic structure is thus reduplicated around the point of
full incorporation into the Mysteries (*Leo*), and serves to
highlight the superiority of the seventh grade, the Father;
but, as we shall see, there is an important thematic link
between that highest grade and the initial terms of the
other two triads. And I shall argue that this thematic
link, which has hitherto been thought incomprehensible, is
intelligible only if we accept the propriety of my present
argument that the grade-structure of the Mysteries consists
of a reduplicated triadic scheme in which the themes of the
lower three grades are reproduced at a higher level, are,
if one likes, 'resolved', by the next three grades, *Leo →
Heliodromus.*
  If the argument is taken to imply that at the higher
levels of initiation the issue of the female became less
explicitly important, I think that quite reasonable. But
it seems to me absolutely inescapable that the ideological
rejection of women was enforced elsewhere than in the grade-
system — in the myth about Mithras himself. It is a tedious
commonplace in the study of the Mysteries that Mithras is
represented as 'born from a rock'; but the commonplace
receives scarcely any attention. Although Cumont rightly
rejected the naturalistic explanations current in the last
century ('sun appearing over the mountains in the morning')
he did so, as so often, in favour of a pseudo-historical
explanation - that it was the hellenised Magi who borrowed
the idea of rock-birth from Anatolian cults (1899: 159-63).
The reason for the borrowing was simply not an issue for
him. And the only recent discussion which is more than
cursory, by Professor Vermaseren, attempts to read the monumental evidence 'symbolically' by arguing that 'we know'
that the rock is a symbol of heaven (1951: 93-109) — a solution indistinguishable in its principles from that of the
pre-Cumontian naturalists. But Professor Vermaseren did note
that Mithras's birth from the rock serves to contrast this
god from others born in a more usual way (p. 94); and it
seems to me that we must start from there.

Everyone knows that one *profani sacramenti signum*, one
cryptic utterance betokening a deep truth in the Mysteries,
was the phrase θεὸς ἐκ πέτρας, 'God out of rock' (Firmicus
Maternus, *de errore* 20.1; cf. 20.5). And it is the paradigmatic significance of the *signum* rather than its discursive content (about which we can know virtually nothing)
which should be of interest to us. For its implicit claim
is that Mithras was not born of a divine or human female,
but from a rock, which in itself is inanimate and sexless.
The notion of a *petra genetrix*, of a generative rock, is
interesting precisely because it is absurd; and the absurd
should always interest us, first because no one believes
absurdities without good cause, and secondly because absurd
propositions are evidently excellent material for dense evocation.

The theme of sexless generation received a good deal of
comment in Greek myth (Detienne, 1976: 75-81), and we can
see it at work in a highly ideological context in Athena's
justification for voting to acquit Orestes in Aeschylus's
Eumenides (734-53 Page; cf. Winnington-Ingram, 1948: 130-47;
Zeitlin, 1978: 149-84). But it also appears elsewhere in
the inventory of familiar Mithraic passages: pseudo-Plutarch,
de fluviis 23.4 (= Müller, *Geogr. Gr.* II p. 663). Roundly
condemned by Cumont as pure fantasy (1889: 36), that is just
what this story is. But the interest of fantasies lies in
their structure. This one explains how the mountain called
Diorphon (or Diorphos) in Armenia received its name, and it
starts with a person called Diorphos, who was presumably a
local *herōs* believed to have been generated from the earth
(γηγενής). The account of his birth is this:

> Mithras wished to have a son, but detested the race of women;
> and so he masturbated on to a rock. The stone became pregnant
> and when the proper time had come it produced a child named
> Diorphos.
>
> Μίθρας, υἱὸν ἔχειν βουλόμενος καὶ τὸ τῶν γυναικῶν γένος μισῶν
> πέτρᾳ τινὶ προσεξέθορεν · ἔγκυος δὲ ὁ λίθος γενόμενος μετὰ τοὺς
> ὡρισμένους χρόνους ἀνέδωκε νέον τοὔνομα Δίορφον.

When the child grew up, he challenged 'Ares' to a duel, lost,
and was transformed into a mountain (89). This latter part
of the myth must surely remind us of a much better-known
Greek myth, that of the Spartoi at Thebes. The two major
themes of that myth, the correlation between autochthony
(the Spartoi grew out of the ground from the 'seeds' of the
dragon killed by Cadmus) and extreme insistence upon the male
(they grew armed to the teeth) on the one hand, and the
impossibility of sustaining a human society under these conditions on the other (the Spartoi kill each other, and there
are no women), are present in the Diorphos myth also, but in
an interesting transformation (90). Like the Spartoi,

Diorphos is literally autochthonous, he is born from a piece
of local soil, and he is an outstanding warrior — so much so
that he challenges the god of war to a duel. But the theme
of the rejection of the female which is merely implicit
the myth of the Spartoi, and in parallel Athenian myths
(Loraux, 1979: 3-26), is quite explicit in the myth of Diorphos: his father Mithras detested the 'race of women'. Now
the term 'race of women' is quite standard in Greek accounts
of the relations between the sexes — it is, one might say,
the standard contemptuous classification of that patrilineal
society, as Nicole Loraux has recently shown (1978: 43-87).
And if male homosexuality was one obvious correlate of the
rejection of women, masturbation is another: both are sexual
modes of the denial of the female. And whereas in the 'real'
world both are forms of sterility, in the world of myth masturbation can be fecund — except that here (quite predictably for a Lévi-Straussian analysis) that theoretical option
is denied in working out its logical consequences: excessive
stress on the male → excessive stress upon war → destruction.
    If such a (truncated) analysis of the Diorphos myth is at
all appropriate, it suggests that in Armenia Mithras was
understood to be a fit divinity to employ in such a context;
that is, the Iranian practice of excluding women from the worship of Mithra was transformed into an Armenian myth about
the problem of autochthony. I would argue that there is no
direct relation between Mithraic 'God out of rock' and this
Armenian myth (91), that the latter is in no sense a 'borrowing' from or a 'corruption' of the former, as is usually believed. They are rather structural transformations of the
same theme, different ways of making sense of a common issue,
the opposition between male and female, in relation to a pre-
existing fact, Mithras's hatred of women. In the one case
Diorphos is autochthonous, warlike, and comes to grief (the
Armenians had to account for the reality of the presence of,
and the necessity for, women); in the other, Mithras is
autochthonous, warlike — and so not human. The birth from
the rock both guarantees his divinity, his non-subjection to
human rules, and affirms his independence of the 'race of
women'.
    The myth of Diorphos is then only a 'fantasy' in the
pejorative sense on the assumption that there was only one
'true' Mithraic tradition, that preserved by the hellenised
Magi. And although we may be sure that communities of Zoroastrians continued to exist in eastern Anatolia, and were
recognised as such by the Sasanians (92), the myth makes it
clear that Iranian ideas were assimilated into prior indi-
genous traditions, certainly in Armenia, and by analogy elsewhere in Anatolia. In fact, Cumont might have made use of
the myth as excellent evidence for the Anatolian antecedents
of the Mysteries; but could not, because for him there was
only one way in which they could have been transmitted to the

Roman Empire.   But if we abandon the hypothesis of a complete
religious tradition handed down intact by the hellenised Magi,
the myth of Diorphos becomes precious evidence of the sort of
evocations and transformations which Iranian themes underwent
in Anatolia; and from such transformations were developed the
Mysteries. We may note another interesting detail in this
connection: the stone upon which Mithras masturbated acted
just like a pregnant woman. It took nine months for it to
produce its impossible offspring. If Mithras did not like
women, he did like order. Not only does the Armenian myth
have a direct relation to 'properly' Iranian — and indeed
Vedic — beliefs about Mithras as 'looser' (Kuiper, 1961-62:
36-60; Lentz, 1970: 245-55; Boyce, 1975: 29-30); it also
suggests that the Mysteries' insistence upon Mithras's cosmic
ordering function reproduces, and transforms, an earlier
Anatolian — and ultimately Iranian — theme.

So far, though, I have shown only that among the meanings
constructed by the Mysteries for their adherents is a systematic denial of the female. The demonstration can only be convincing if one can show that the Mysteries formulated this
principle in explicit terms; and that, I would claim, is
precisely what is done by a text which everyone knows but
which has been quite generally 'refused'.   I refer to the
quotation of Pallas by Porphyry, *De abstinentia* 4, 16, which
I have already used (p. 32):

> τὴν γὰρ κοινότητα ἡμῶν τὴν πρὸς τὰ ζῷα αἰνιττόμενοι διὰ τῶν
> ζῴων ἡμᾶς μηνύειν εἰώθασιν · ὡς τοὺς μὲν μετέχοντας τῶν αὐτῶν
> ὀργίων λέοντας καλεῖν, τὰς δὲ γυναῖκας ὑαίνας, τοὺς δὲ
> ὑπηρετοῦντας κόρακας.
>
> (Those responsible for initiations in the Mysteries) typically
> allegorised our common nature with the animals by imaging us in
> the form of animals; thus they called the initiates who had been
> fully admitted into their Mysteries 'lions', women 'hyenas', and
> the underlings 'ravens'.

It was Franz Cumont who set the tone of fastidious incompre-
hension of this passage in his note on the text (1896: 42 n.2):
'Voilà un détail bien étrange. Nulle part ailleurs il n'est
question d'un grade de l'hyène dans les mystères mithriaques.... Cette partie du texte de Porphyre est si corrompue
qu'il vaut mieux renoncer à l'expliquer'. And seventy-nine
years later Robert Turcan writes: 'la participation de
femmes aux mystères n'est directement confirmée par aucun
document. Dans la citation de Porphyre, s'agit-il d'"hyènes"
(si l'on conserve le texte des manuscrits) ou de "lionnes"
(si l'on retient avec A. Nauck la conjecture de Felicianus)?'
(1975: 36) (93). But perhaps we ought to read the text without quite so many preconceptions. Nowhere does Pallas say
that women were initiates into the Mysteries: indeed, he
explicitly states that they were not, by opposing his first

category τοὺς μὲν μετέχοντας ... μύστας ('the initiates who
are full members') from his second τὰς δὲ γυναῖκας, and from
his third, τοὺς δὲ ὑπηρετοῦντας ('the underlings'). If he
had wanted to talk about what we might want him to talk about
('were women initiated into the Mysteries?'), he would have
put his point differently. But of course he knew that they
were not, and could not imagine anyone asking the question;
and anyway this is a contextless quotation from a book in
several volumes. Moreover, Pallas is talking about the use
of animal terms for human beings in the Mysteries, so that
the order in which he makes his points does not matter (94).
His argument is directed against the 'common opinion' that
this feature of the Mysteries had to do with the zodiacal
signs and the ecliptic, for he 'knew' that the practice was
really connected with the Mysteries' belief in metempsychosis — which is why Porphyry quotes him in the first place.
  Now it is my belief that this passage provides the only
explicit evidence we possess about the role of women in the
Mysteries. But in order to understand it we have first not
to misunderstand it by reading into it what is not there,
let alone by a desperate recourse to emendation (that sove-
reign means of foisting our own ideas on to texts we do not
understand) (95). And we have then to consult the Graeco-
Roman 'encyclopaedia' to find out what Pallas, and the
Mysteries, may have meant by calling women 'hyenas'.
  The hyena is included by Ovid, *Metamorphoses* 15, 408-10,
in a list of creatures which experience transformations of
one sort or another: the phoenix, the chameleon, lynxes'
eyes, coral. But the hyena's transformation was altogether
unusual: it repeatedly changed its sex. The female hyena
one saw one day would have turned into a male the next time
one saw it, and likewise with a male one:

> Si tamen est aliquid mirae novitatis in istis,
> alternare vices et, quae modo femina tergo
> passa marem est, nunc esse marem miremur hyaenam,

'But if these things are odd, it is really extraordinary that
the hyena changes (its sex): the animal which at one moment
is female and is mounted by the male, is next moment male.'
The theme recurs repeatedly; Tertullian, *de pallio* 3. 2 Gerlo,
reports that the transformation took place annually, a point
elaborated by Aelian, *NA* 1, 25: κοινωνοῦσί τε ἀφροδίτης
ἑκατέρας, καὶ γαμοῦσί τε καὶ γαμοῦνται, ἀνὰ ἔτος πᾶν
ἀμείβουσαι τὸ γένος: 'they have bisexual mating habits,
inasmuch as they both mount and are mounted, changing their
sex every year'. And he continues: 'So this animal proves
Kaineus and Teiresias old-hat not by fine-sounding words but
in deed' — a comment whose underlying assimilation of animal
sexuality into human sexuality will not be lost on us after
my earlier discussion of the raven and the lion. A related

popular belief is also worth remarking: the female hyena was
supposed to be able to produce offspring without the male,
parere sine mare vulgus credit (Pliny *NH* 8, 105). The antiquity of the belief, and its pervasiveness in Greece in the
fourth century BC, is suggested by Aristotle, who actually
took the trouble to get hold of specimens of hyenas from a
professional hunter in order to decide whether the popular
view was correct or not (*HA* 579b 16-28). And although he
showed that it was quite false, no one cared what science
thought, as no one now cares what natural historians think
about hyenas — because our social use of hyenas is much more
important to us than 'true' facts about them. Whether or
not we have in contemporary western Europe seen a hyena, all
of us 'know' that they are carrion-eaters, that they laugh
'like human beings', and that they take the leavings of that
noble beast, the lion. Some of us know that all of those
ideas are more or less completely false, but we still make
use of the prior social lie in finding images of the loath-
some. Hyenas, like lions, have a cultural significance
even in societies in which they are not directly known.
    If what I have argued about the significance of the *signum*
θεὸς ἐκ πέτρας in the Mysteries is correct, we can see already one Mithraic reason for calling the human female a
'hyena': if the Mysteries believed a myth which made Mithras
the ideal pattern of generation (without the female), the
hyena represents the opposite, an order in which the female
reproduces without the male, just as it provides an instance
of an order in which the distinctions between the sexes are
confused and ambiguous. But there is more. The hyena was
supposed in the Graeco-Roman 'encyclopaedia' to be able to
imitate the human voice not, as in the case of the raven,
harmlessly or as a means of permitting communication between
the divine and the human worlds, but for the sake of evil.
Hyenas could learn the name of a shepherd, call him out of
his hut and devour him (Pliny *HN* 8, 106).. A cross between
the hyena and the Ethiopian lioness (of course!) produced a
creature called the *corocotta*, which could imitate the sounds
of men and of cattle (*HN* 8, 107) (96). But the hyena had
even more mysterious powers: according to Aelian (*NA* 6, 14),
quoting Aristotle, any creature which it touched with its
left paw fell into a torpor. It would prowl around animal-
pens or stables, touch its victim in this manner, dig out
the earth from under its head as it lay on the ground, and
expose the throat. It then suffocated the animal, by biting
the throat, and dragged it away. The hyena was also believed
to have a particular enmity against the dog (which had in the
Graeco-Roman world a special status in relation to human
beings, marked above all in its casual admittance into the
house) (97). It would imitate the sound of human vomiting
(itself a detail of unusual interest, since vomiting involves
(1) a human sound which is not speech (2) the reverse of

normal digestion — it is a perfect reversal of norms), and attract dogs to the scene — and then pounce on them and kill them. According to Pliny, *HN* 8, 106 (cf Proclus *In plat. Rempubl.* 1, 290, 17 Diehl), its shadow prevented dogs from barking — that is, hindered them from one of their domestic functions — while Aelian (*NA* 6, 14) adds that this happened when the moon was full: the baleful shadow cast on dogs was a *moon-shadow* (cf. Cassianus Bassus, *Geoponica* 15, 1, 10-11 = Bidez-Cumont, 1938: II, frg. 052, pp. 193-97). And he instructively draws an explicit parallel between this activity of the hyena and human witches or sorceresses: καταγοητεύσασα ὡς αἱ φαρμακίδες — and it is important that he compares the hyena to *female* witches (98). When we add that the hyena was believed to be the only animal which digs up graves (*sepulchra*) to get at human corpses (Pliny *HN* 8, 106), it becomes appropriate to think of the hyena as the equivalent in the animal world of the *lamia*, the 'night witch' figure of Greek folklore, a creature fascinating for the structuralist, in that it was conceived both as an arch-'sort-crosser' and as the epitome of the anti-human: hermaphroditic, capable of metamorphosis, wont to remove its eyes, in some sense human (indeed female) yet looking like a wild animal, inhabiting marginal spaces (ravines, woods, ruined towers, caves), cannibalistic, feeding especially on the flesh of babies (90). And it must be obvious that the 'uncertainty' about the sex both of the *lamia* (f.) and of the hyena (f.) conceals a fundamental determination, characteristic of the Graeco-Roman world, to make the female the ultimate repository of the anti-human — that is, of the anti-male.

If the hyena acted like the sorceress, it was the object of particular regard on the part of 'magicians' (*magi*): *Hyaenam magi ex omnibus animalibus in maxima admiratione posuerunt, utpote cui et ipsi magicas artes dederint vimque qua alliciat ad se homines mente alienatos* ('Of all animals, the magicians had the highest regard for the hyena, so much so that they have ascribed to it their own magical arts and especially the power by means of which it snares men whom it has driven out of their minds': Pliny *HN* 28, 92). That suggests that the hyena was supposed to be able to deprive men of their rational faculties, to make them non-men. Whereas ravens and lions were animals endowed with quasi-human rationality, the hyena was an animal which turned men into animals, just as the Sirens in the Odyssey deprive men of their desire to return home by destroying their memories (Todorov, 1967: 47-55). And since the Mysteries were nothing if not means to 'wisdom' (Gordon, 1972: 100), an animal hostile to reason was perfectly suited to represent the antithesis of the means to salvation; but of course the crucial point is that this animal was further identified as 'woman' in the Mysteries. This point about human rationality is closely related to another unusual feature of the hyena, its eyes.

In oculis animus habitat, observes Pliny (*HN* 11, 145),
'the mind dwells in the eyes'; and when we kiss someone's
eyes, we seem to reach the mind itself (146). *Animo autem
videmus, animo cernimus; oculi ceu vasa quaedam visibilem
eius partem accipiunt atque tramittunt*: 'Moreover, it is with
with the mind that we see, with the mind that we make things
out; the eyes are a sort of vessel — they receive and pass
on that part of the mind which can be seen'. Man alone has,
as a species, eyes of different colours; in all other species
the eyes of every individual are alike (141). All, that is,
but the hyena: *oculis mille esse varietates colorumque muta-
tiones*, 'their eyes are always changing, and altering their
colour' (*HN* 8, 106); *in mille colores transeunt subinde*,
'(their eyes) keep changing their colour all of a sudden,
in a myriad different hues' (11, 151) (100). The eyes of
the hyena were utterly unstable: its shifty character was
resumed in its ocular physiology. And with those eyes it
could paralyse any creature at which it gazed three times
quibusdam magicis artibus, 'by magic, I suppose' (Pliny *HN*
8, 106). And although we have noted earlier that in Egypt
lions were supposed to be able to 'fascinate' (p. 34), the
hyena is the only animal in the Graeco-Roman 'encyclopaedia'
proper which possessed the evil eye. And it is clear from
Pliny *HN* 7, 16-17, that in the Graeco-Roman world it was
women who were normally supposed to possess the evil eye;
indeed Cicero apparently held that the ability to 'fascinate' was due to an interesting anatomical peculiarity, the
possession by women of a double pupil: *feminas quidem omnes
unique visu nocere quae duplices pupillae habeant Cicero
quoque apud nos auctor est* ('Our own writer Cicero observes
that any woman anywhere is able to cast the evil eye if she
has a double pupil'). I would argue that the evil eye is
another of the links between the hyena and the 'race of
women', and intimately connected with the ability of both
to derange men.
  A proper structural analysis of these, and other, ideas
about hyenas in the Graeco-Roman 'encyclopaedia' would take
me too far afield. But I have surely said enough to make it
plausible to argue that the hyena was an entirely appropriate
name for women in a cult committed to the principle of the
supremacy of the male or the masculine. Capable of partheno-
genesis, a creature of the night, the producer of parodic
human utterances, eater of corpses, destroyer of the mind, a
thing that is human and not-human, the hyena is man's worst
enemy in the animal kingdom, the destroyer of the possibility
of human culture, a nightmare that is almost a 'night witch'.
It renders human meanings null; subverts all the rules; in-
carnates disorder; erases reason. It is the low point of the
world of genesis, the point at which nothing makes any sense
and all categories are jumbled together. Perhaps Pallas knew
what he was talking about after all? (101)

Acceptance of this idea that Woman was termed 'hyena' in the Mysteries of Mithras helps us to understand a little better a crucial puzzle: if the world was created or, at the very least, set in order, by Mithras, why was escape into *apogenesis* so necessary? The problem is pressing inasmuch as we can no longer easily appeal to Zoroastrian theories about a dual creation by Ahura Mazda and Ahriman and assume that they will provide an explanation for the beliefs of the Mysteries. Although it may seem at first sight surprising, I think we may find some instructive contrasts between the Mysteries of Mithras and Hesiod's view of the place of man in creation — all the more so in that the work of Pierre Vidal-Naquet and of Marcel Detienne suggests that the ideas Hesiod so elegantly related to each other (as a true 'primitive intellectual') were widely accepted throughout Graeco-Roman antiquity in the form of unselfconscious associations and patterns of behaviour (102). The Hesiodic version of the origin of Woman presents her as Zeus's counter gift to men for the theft of fire by Prometheus (*Theogony* 570; 585); and fire in turn was denied men because of Prometheus's trick at the first sacrifice at Mekone (*Theogony* 561-67). As Jean-Pierre Vernant has shown, the myth is organised in terms of a series of illusions: Prometheus concealed the good meat in something unpleasant (the ox's stomach), but made the uneatable bones look appetising by covering them with fat; later, he conceals fire in a fennel-stalk; and then Zeus hides evils — 'toil', suffering, sickness, quick old age — beneath the alluring beauty of Woman. And all this concealment reproduces the structure of concealment in relation to human labour in the fields and in human reproduction (1974: 177-94; 1977: 915-19; 927-34).

To all this, the Mysteries offer sharp contrasts. The initial sacrifice, although certainly connected in some way with Mithras's theft, was performed not at some point 'in time' when gods and men could still meet on a footing of apparent equality or at least commensality (as at Mekone), but 'cosmically'; and not by the ambiguous Titan Prometheus but by Mithras himself. That implies that the sacrifice marked not a separation between man and god but the ordering of the cosmos, from the order of the heavenly bodies to the order of plant-life and, presumably, of human society. I have argued elsewhere that one of the familiar by-scenes on complex panelled reliefs represents a Mithraic account of the human institution of sacrifice: and it is performed between Mithras and Sol (1978: 217-18). Sacrifice was not a 'second-best' institution for the Mysteries; it was the reproduction of an act originally performed by Mithras himself (103). Moreover, fire did not have to be stolen from an angry Zeus, and was not placed in direct relation to the origin of sacrifice: if the *petragenes* monuments are relevant here, fire in the Mysteries was supposed to have come with the birth of

Mithras from the rock; which implies that the human use of
fire as a means of cooking and of civilization came directly
from him. The Hesiodic relations between each of these
aspects of human life are systematically denied in the
Mysteries, and they are all referred directly to Mithras
as 'culture-hero'.
    Where does that leave Woman? In Hesiod, woman is both
a source of aesthetic delight, for men and for gods, and
an evil — there is at least compensation for the drudgery
she brings men. She also has an indispensable place as a
metonymic mediator between the man's world in the fields
and the domestic space: both bread and sperm enter her
belly; she is ploughed as the earth is ploughed; she is
fecund as the earth is fecund. But the Mysteries' account
of the origin of corn, that it came from the cosmic killing
of the Bull by Mithras, undercuts that mediating rôle of
woman: there is no theme of 'hiding the corn' by means of
which woman can be socially located. The only element of
the Hesiodic view that survives is the crude binary opposition between 'good' males and 'deceptive' females. I would
argue that the Mysteries' reorganisation of this relatively
integrated traditional view of women was an extreme attempt
to found, mythically and ritually, the age-old dream of
patriarchal societies, to do away with women and leave the
world pure and unsullied: the Mysteries of Mithras determined, as it were, to take Euripides' Hippolytus utterly
seriously (104). But they chose to effect the dream in the
context not of this world (where it was evidently impossible) but of the next, and to write off this world insofar
as it was polluted by the hyena, woman. So that if we can
never know how Mithraic woman arrived to spoil Mithras's
creation, we can certainly know what the Mysteries proposed
to do about it. A taller and taller story indeed, but one
of immediate relevance in a world where the female threat
to male honour — the ultimate source of the male fear of
women in patrilineal societies — increased precisely in
step with men's uncertainties about the true locus of honour.
    No one has ever attempted a history of honour in the
Graeco-Roman world (105). Still less has anyone tried to
relate such a history of honour to the development of novel
cults in the Graeco-Roman world. But the theme might repay
study. What, for example, is the relation between 'holiness' and honour? What is the relation between, say, Euripides' doubts about the validity of the traditional structure of male honour, with all its ramifications in relation
to the cult of the body, and Plato's radical-conservative
elaboration of a theory of the tripartite soul? Honour is
crucial, of course, not merely because by definition it can
be possessed and sought only by men in a patrilineal society,
but also because, although the élites in the Graeco-Roman
world laid claim to the possession of that specialized form

of 'political' honour which involved conspicuous consump-
tion, athletics and war, as a value it was quite general
both among peasants and among the non-agricultural inhabitants of towns. To put it crudely, honour was the means
whereby men in the Graeco-Roman world articulated the
relationship between perceived rights and obligations and
negotiated with their peers for status. And if the most
radical loss of honour came through enslavement, it seems
clear that the economic and social changes of the hellenistic period, but perhaps even more, of the Roman Empire,
involved changes also in the meanings constructed by the
system of honour — changing conditions of land tenure,
relations with tax-collectors, enforced military service,
geographical and social mobility, differential access to
legal redress and citizen rights, the re-acquisition of
social rights and new sorts of obligations by freedmen
(cf. Nouailhat, 1975: 212-32). Alterations of the rules
in all these areas involved a revaluation, slight or
intense, of the honour system, and corresponding uncertainties about social rôles and social status. And under
these circumstances in a patrilineal society, two responses
seem to me utterly predictable: on the one hand, the senti-
mentalization of the family, and on the other a growing
tendency towards the polarization of the sexes, not so much
institutionally (though that is obvious even in the historical development of Greek democracy, and perhaps also
in legal changes in the late Republic in Rome) as 'mythically'. And if the Mysteries of Mithras chose to elaborate
an extreme version of the latter tendency, they were by no
means alone among new religions in the Roman Empire, particularly among sects which pursued some form of mystical
revelation. What such sects lost in terms of mass appeal
they made up for in coherence at the level of their fantasy
version of what the world is 'really' like. For in a situation in which traditional rules for the acquisition and
retention of honour by men were becoming uncertainly relevant, it was tempting to 'analyze' the situation in a
wholly familiar way: for in traditional terms, whereas a
man could be sure of his own ability to fulfil his obligations and maintain his rights within his community, he was
always open to massive loss of honour through the sexuality
of women (his wife, his daughter or his sister). The Mysteries of Mithras offered an elaborate means of escape from that
threat — produced by the application of traditional attitudes
to a new situation (real social and economic changes which
threatened the meanings encoded in the honour system) —
whereby the world of contingency and chance was at least to
an extent identified as the world of Woman (illusory, deceit-
ful, changeable, carrier of death) and the world of non-
becoming identified as the world of Mithras born from a
rock, uncontaminated by the female. Both 'honour' and
'woman' are redefined.

III

We have here gone beyond the overt discourse of the Mysteries
to consider their 'real' discourse, the nature of their relationship to real anxieties and needs for 'meaning'. But we
must return to their claims and in particular to the third
aspect of *rites de passage*, 'reincorporation'. By definition, of course, in a mystery cult, that point is an enigma,
and such cults can be thought of as constructing ever more
elaborate lies to conceal the nature of that enigma, lies
which demand in their turn ever more elaborate evocation if
they are to be comprehensible. But I think that there were
in the Mysteries privileged, if temporary, visitors to that
enigmatic centre — precisely, those who had attained the
grade of *Pater*, Father. And once again Pallas provides us
with the crucial evidence.

The passage from Porphyry, *de abstinentia* 4, 16, which
tells us that women were called 'hyenas' in the Mysteries,
continues as follows: ἐπί τε τῶν πατέρων ... ἀετοὶ γὰρ καὶ
ἱέρακες οὗτοι προσαγορεύονται. Convinced beforehand of
Pallas's untrustworthiness, interpreters have simply refused
to understand 'these words. The most recent commentator,
Professor Turcan, translates ἐπί τε τῶν πατέρων as 'et
préposés aux pères' (1975: 33-38), which, though possible
technically, makes complete nonsense. Even in hellenistic
koine ἐπί with the genitive can mean, and often does, 'with
regard to' or 'in the case of' (Mayser, 1934:470 section 4).
Nor does the fact that a word has fallen out of the text
after πατέρων present an insoluble problem: we need only
suppose that something like ταὐτό· or ὡσαύτως· has dis-
appeared. If we adopt either reading (since the two words
mean the same), Pallas says: 'And in the case of the Fathers
the same (is true): for they are called "eagles" and
"hawks"'. Not content with misunderstanding Pallas, the
tradition of Mithraic scholarship since Cumont (who was
reacting against Lajarde of course) has refused to believe
what he says, on the extraordinary grounds that there is
no relevant archaeological (or epigraphic) evidence; unlike
poor Pallas, such evidence is supposed to be 'objective',
notwithstanding its utterly haphazard character and the fact
that every act of understanding an artefact — in all archaeology, not simply Mithraic archaeology — is itself necessarily
based upon prior theory. And the muddle is further com-
pounded by the general conviction that eagles in Graeco-
Roman iconography are always 'symbols' of something — be it
'heaven', 'the sun', the 'power of the gods', or whatever.
But instead of rewriting Pallas to make him talk of symbols, let us look at the Graeco-Roman 'encyclopaedia' one
last time in order to find out what he might have meant,
and what the Mysteries might have meant, by saying that
Fathers in the Mysteries were called 'eagles' and 'hawks'
(106).

Pliny turns to the eagle immediately after discussing that fabulous bird of the Sun, the Phoenix, and the ostrich. Neither of these birds, he says, is really a bird. The ostrich, because of its anatomical peculiarities, 'almost' belongs to the beasts (*HN* 10, 1), while the Phoenix probably never eats and it has a quite peculiar method of reproduction (10, 3-5). So the eagly is Pliny's first 'proper' bird. And for good reason: *ex his quas novimus aquilae maximus honos, maxima et vis*, 'of the birds known to us, the eagle has the greatest dignity as it has the mightiest strength' (10, 6; cf. Antoninus Liberalis, 6 [Periphas] 4). It comes therefore first in the kingdom of birds, as the lion comes first in the kingdom of quadrupeds (cf. Oppian, *Cynaegetica* 1, 68); and something of the ideological value of the eagle in Graeco-Roman antiquity will already be evident — that it was understood in terms appropriate to human 'political' honour (*honos, vis*).

As the king of the birds, it received due recognition from the king of the gods: of all birds, it is the only one never to be struck by lightning; and it was therefore taken customarily as Jupiter's 'squire' (*ideo armigeram Iovis consuetudo iudicavit: HN* 10, 15; cf. 1, 146). And while lions had a rational moral sense, eagles had an altogether more subtle rationality: they would test whether their eaglets were 'true' eagles by making them stare at the sun. If an eaglet blinked, unable to endure the sun's rays, it was cast out of the nest. And Aelian's account of this is particularly instructive: ἐὰν δὲ ἀντιβλέψῃ καὶ μάλα ἀτρέπτως, ἀμείνων ἐστὶν ὑπονοίας καὶ τοῖς γνησίοις ἐγγέγραπται, ἐπεὶ αὐτῷ πῦρ τὸ οὐράνιον ἢ τοῦ γένους ἀδέκαστός τε καὶ ἄπρατος ἀληθῶς ἐστιν ἐγγραφή ('but if it can look at the sun quite unflinchingly, it is above suspicion and is enrolled among the legitimate offspring, inasmuch as the heavenly fire is truly the unbribed and unpurchased registration of its legitimacy': *NA* 2, 26). That is to say, the eagle loves its offspring not from *pathos*, feeling, but from a rational judgement of the offspring's worthiness (cf. *NA* 9, 3) (107). And eagles were lovers of wisdom in more ways than this. According to Pliny, the kind of eagle which judged its offspring in this way did not really have any babies of its own: *haliaëti suum genus non habent; sed ex diverso aquilarum coitu nascuntur* ('the haliaetus does not engender its own offspring — they are born of the mating of other species of eagles': *HN* 10, 11) (108). Because of their *megalonoia*, their high-souled indifference to petty things, eagles were able to disdain the petty spitefulness of crows and other pests who took it upon themselves to try and annoy them (Aelian *NA* 15, 22) (109). They knew how to enter the human structure of reciprocity, for they would return kindness with kindness (*NA* 17, 37), and, in captivity, even honoured their master's death by self-destruction (*NA* 2, 40).

Whereas ravens suffered from thirst for sixty days in the
year, eagles, even more than lions, disdained water (110).
And they were indifferent to earth also: they chose to
cleave the aether-filled vault of heaven (breathing divine
air, that is), from thence gazing down upon the earth, just
like the sun: ὑπερφρονῶν δὲ καὶ τῶν ὑδάτων καὶ τῆς ἀναπαύσεως
τὸν αἰθέριον τέμνει πόλον καὶ ὀξύτατα ὁρᾷ ἐκ πολλοῦ τοῦ αἰθέρος
καὶ ὑψηλοῦ (NA 2, 26, cf. Apuleius, *Florida*, 1). Most
curious (and for my purposes, appropriate) of all, although
most eagles were of course believed to be carnivorous, one,
the 'eagle of Zeus', ate not flesh but greenstuffs (πόα): as
Aelian aptly observes, and though it has never heard of
Pythagoras of Samos, yet it rejects the flesh of creatures
that are endowed with consciousness' (καὶ Πυθαγόρου τοῦ
Σαμίου διακούσας οὐδὲ ἕν, ὅμως ἐμψύχων ἀπέχεται: NA 9, 10).
In view of the context in which Porphyry quotes these words
of Pallas with which I started — Euboulus's contention that
in Persia the highest grade of Magi were vegetarians, because they believed in metempsychosis — perhaps we should
not find this the least interesting point in the catalogue of
aquiline virtue (111).

My argument is of course quite predictable. I think we
should deduce from this account of the Graeco-Roman beliefs
about eagles the following structure in the Mysteries of
Mithras: what the raven is to the lion, the lion is to the
eagle. The threefold recourse to the animal kingdom is
wholly intelligible on that hypothesis. For each of the
animals was presented in the 'encyclopaedia' in very similar
terms, as ambiguous between the world of animals and the
world of man; but just as the lion is superior in its reclassification to the raven, the eagle is superior to the
lion — indeed, it is very evidently a dweller not on earth
but 'in heaven'. So we do not have simply a reduplicated
triadic structure in the grade-system, we have a truncated
triple triadic structure in which the point of recourse to
the animal world marks the point of significant difference
from what came before. The clearest transitions, in fact,
are the ones which involve the most masquerade, the greatest
threat to 'normal' meanings. Thus

        Pater   -   -
        :
        Leo   :: Perses :: Heliodromus
        :   :   :
        Corax   Nymphus   Miles

To have achieved the grade *Pater* was to be in the grade-
system yet also out of it, was to be so marginal to the real
world that one brushed against the enigma, just as the eagle
breathed the aether like the gods and gazed down on earth
like the sun, whose light, alone of all creatures, it had

learned to gaze into without blinking. Surely, once again,
we have every reason to believe that Pallas is telling the
truth? (112)

It will no doubt be felt, particularly by those who have
little sympathy with any form of structuralism (113), and by
those who believe Cumont's paradigm still to be appropriate, that the case I have outlined here is quite unconvincing. That may be, but I would observe that traditional
Mithraic scholarship has either ignored or actually mis-
represented the specifically Mithraic evidence from which
I have in each case begun; and I would then ask whether it
is less absurd to believe that one can get to heaven than
to believe that one 'is' a raven, lion or eagle. My argument
would be that one has to believe a small absurdity in order
to believe a larger one. But of course the crux of the
matter is this: we require to supply not only an immediate
context for the Mysteries' evocations of utterances such as
'I am a raven', but a wider context. I have argued that in
the case of the Mysteries the wider context, the content of
the Graeco-Roman 'encyclopaedia' concerning certain animals,
also supplies some of the narrower context, and that this
provides us with evidence of the frontier negotiated by the
Mysteries between the fantastic and the prosaic. By dis-
regarding that wider context, traditional Mithraic scholarship has condemned itself to a predictable miscognition of
the Mysteries, either in order to write a pseudo-history
linking Rome with Iran or so as to make of them a purely
'spiritual' cult whose ideological structure can be ignored
in favour of its manifest teaching, its 'theology' (114).
But utterances do not mean anything — very little certainly
— 'in themselves'; to have any deeper understanding of them
we need to know a good deal about their context, and indeed
the context of that context. And the more opaque the
utterance, the more we need the context to make any sense
at all (115). The problem of sense-making is most acute in
the case of a structure of knowledge founded, like the Mysteries, upon an enigma, upon a claim necessarily opaque not
merely to those who would reconstruct it but to those who
made the claim. Even so, the Mysteries had to start somewhere, and they began with the real: at the level of technique, with the familiar institutional pattern for altering
status in the real world, the pattern of *rites de passage*;
at the level of structure, with 'true' knowledge about the
order and pattern of the cosmos; at the level of meaning,
with 'true' facts about human society. And in order to found
their claim that it is possible to perform the absurd journey
upwards to heaven, they began, and ended, with animals which
have themselves performed absurd journeys, have become 'men'
and entered heaven.

'When I make a word do a lot of work like that' said
Humpty Dumpty, 'I always pay it extra.' One cannot help

thinking that a Mithraic Father would have seen Humpty
Dumpty's point, and dug deep into his pocket (116).

NOTES

1 Of course we do not 'know' that the Mithraists wore masks, as is so
   often assumed (following Cumont, 1899: 316). A simple-minded empiri-
   cism will appeal to the apparently clear use of a Raven-mask and a
   Lion-mask on the reverse of the Konjić relief (*CIMRM* 1896) and to the
   other well-known instances of human figures with raven-heads, 42[13]
   (from Dura, where the head is painted in black) and 397 (Rome).
   J. P. Kane (1975: 319) deduces from the imaginative sketch reproduced
   in Campbell, 1968: fig. 11 facing p. 176, that there was at Dura
   another raven-headed figure on the right-hand wall flanking the cult-
   niche (as one looks from the cult-niche) during the second period of
   the Mithraeum. In spite of a fairly full discussion of Mithras and
   Sol on this panel, the Report makes no mention of this detail
   (Rostovtzeff *et al.*, 1939: 103-04), and I conclude that it is a
   fantasy based on a simple analogy with 42[13] (third Mithraeum).
       I am glad to see that in his recent discussion of this evidence
   (in a different context), Robert Turcan says simply: 'Ces versions du
   banquet présentent la singularité de mêler aux dieux la représentation
   de mystes mithriaques revêtus des insignes parlants de leur grade'
   (1978: 155). All these instances of animal-headed humans occur in
   the 'feast-scene' between Mithras and *Sol*; and that scene has no
   simple significance. It is a polyvalent sign for at least the following (1) an 'historical' moment in a sacred narrative (2) a 'charter'
   for a ritual (3) part of the rationale for the existence of some
   grades, and doubtless (4) part of the 'instructions' for the rôle of
   particular grades in the cult. We can scarcely use such images for
   resolving matters of fact, when they have nothing to do with our
   narrowly conceived problem, just as the passage from Ambrosiaster
   quoted immediately below proves nothing in this connection. We may
   put the problem rather differently. If one wished to represent a
   symbolic value, say a metonymic interpretation of a human rôle, one
   might either name it explicitly or represent it, 'show' it. In this
   case, we duly find (1) named occupants of named grades without
   animal-heads, as at Santa Prisca (2) raven- and lion-headed men (3)
   representations of lions and ravens which may refer (among other
   things) to the grade-names. Nevertheless, the occurrence of raven-
   and lion-headed men is clear evidence of 'sort-crossing', of attention
   deliberately called to the oddity of calling real men 'Ravens' and
   'Lions'; and it is that which interests me here.
2 See van Essen and Vermaseren, 1965: 155; and note the similar figure
   on the lower layer of paintings on the same wall, p. 168. Vermaseren
   usefully calls attention to the theme of religious pretence in philosophical writing under the Empire, p. 159 n. 8, though he does not
   pursue it, and indeed elsewhere shows that he does not take 'pretence'

seriously as a mode of religious behaviour. This leads him into a
number of tendentious 'identifications': p. 169 'where the Father
(= Mithras) is reclining at the sacred meal'; p. 180 'we know that
the Father is the representative on earth of the divine Mithras-Sol
in the firmament'. He is on much surer, and more interesting, ground
when he argues that the seated Father receiving the initiates in
procession evokes the *patronus* greeting his clients, or the Emperor
greeting Senators. Obviously the seated Father is not *identified*
with such persons; and I would say that it is equally obvious that
the Father is not identified with Mithras: to imitate is to call
attention to the fact that one is not that which one imitates, so
that even 'representative' is to put the matter too strongly (and
to refer, however covertly, to Christian theories of the relation
between priest and god). Once again, though, the deliberate evocation
of Mithras by the Father's dress registers an ambiguity — a man pretending to be a god. And as we shall see later, there is good reason
to believe that the Mysteries registered this ambiguity of the Father
in other ways as well.

3   Imitations of death, as well as of blindness, and 'being in the dark',
may be inferred from the paintings on the benches at S. Maria Capua
Vetere (*CIMRM* 187-97).

4   Ambrosiaster, *Quaest. vet. nov. test.* 114 (CSEL). There is no doubt
a similar play in Firmicus Maternus, *de errore* 20.1 (referring to θεὸς
ἐκ πέτρας, 'God from rock'): *Quid tu ad commaculatas superstitiones*
furtiva fraude venerandi transferis nominis dignitatem? Lapidem tuum
ruina sequitur et cadentium culminum funesta collapsio (ed. Heuten),
'Do you indeed by *stealthy sleight-of-hand* convert the dignity of the
God we ought to revere into corrupted mumbo-jumbo? Ruin and the dire
collapse of falling towers (shall) attend your (foundation-)stone'.

5   I have tried to show elsewhere that Porphyry's expression 'an image
of the cosmos' is perfectly appropriate to the Mysteries' endeavour,
and that it cannot be written off as mere neo-platonist 'speculation'
without insight into or relevance to the way in which the temple was
conceived by Mithraists as *espace sacré* (1976: 119-65); and I think
that further confirmation can be found in the fact that the bull's
so-called 'house' is in reality a temple, conceived in proper Roman
fashion as 'heaven' (1978: 204-13).

6   Cumont's original text on this matter is a classic piece of counterfeit history (1899: 315): 'Ces masquerades sacrées ... étaient inter-
pretées par les theologiens païens comme une allusion aux signes du
zodiaque, ou bien à la metempsychose. De telles divergences d'interprétation prouvent simplement que le veritable sens de ces travest-
issements n'étaient plus compris. Ils sont en realité une survivance
d'usages primitifs qui ont laissé des traces dans de nombreux cultes
(listed in n.6 on the same page) ... Ils remontent jusqu'à cette
période de l'histoire ou de la préhistoire où l'on se représentait
les divinités elles-mêmes sous une forme animale, et où le fidèle,
en prenant le nom et l'aspect de son dieu, croyait s'identifier avec
lui.... Aux titres primitifs de Corbeau, de Lion, on en avait par la
suite ajouté d'autres pour arriver au chiffre sacré de sept'. And I
find it extremely instructive that this view has never been challenged,

yet it is rarely explicitly accepted: the problem of the names of the
grades has slipped silently out of the discourse. From one point of
view, the whole of this article can be seen as a commentary upon these
words of Cumont. A similar piece of counterfeit history may be found
in Widengren, 1960: 61 (on the grade *Miles*).

7 One of my more general tasks here is to attempt a more serious discussion of the logic behind the objects represented on the mosaic floor
in this Mithraeum than has hitherto been enterprised; for it would be
no exaggeration to say that they are our most important evidence for
the character of the grade-structure in the Mysteries. There are of
course several ways of avoiding the problem these objects present.
We can say they are late (that is, mid-third century); and therefore
unrepresentative: but that is an apriorism which must take second place
to an examination of the relation between them and other Mithraic evidence, widely scattered in time and space; it presupposes, moreover,
that there were no limits to the ability of believers to interpret and
alter the beliefs of the Mysteries. If we seriously believe that,
then the entire enterprise of post-Cumontian scholarship is pointless,
because there were no Mysteries to reconstruct. It is the notion of
structured evocation which allows us to steer between the absurd
assumption that the artefactual remains of the Mysteries offer no
coherence on the one hand, and the equally absurd thesis that every
Mithraist in the Roman Empire over 350 years subscribed to identical
doctrines. Another argument, no less implausible, is that none of
these objects had any specifically Mithraic meaning. So Laeuchli
(1967: 47): 'In the floor mosaic of Felicissimus practically every
symbol can be documented by other religious or non-religious parallels, as, for instance, the thunderbolt, the sistrum, the staff of
initiation or the diadem of Venus. A man did not find new symbolism
when he entered the Mithraic sanctuary...'; which is as though one
were to say that nothing new could be said because we all have to
employ words, which pre-exist us and which will continue to be used
long after any single individual is dead. A third argument will hold
that, although one or two of the representations are readily intelligible, for example the 'phrygian cap' among the objects associated
with the grade *Pater*, or the fire-shovel among those associated with
the grade *Leo*, most of them are not. One can make two observations
here: first, that nothing about a religious system is intelligible
unless one takes it as a *structure*, with its proper rules and procedures, which is how alone it makes sense to the believer; and
second, that we are too easily inclined to assume that once we can
see one plausible 'meaning', there is nothing more to be said — on the
contrary, single meanings in religion, as in language, do not exist.
And although I have not here attempted a full discussion of the
objects associated with the grades in the Mitreo di Felicissimo,
having other prior concerns, it would be as well to understand right
from the start that I proceed from the assumptions that they were
understood in a polyvalent sense by initiates; that that complex
sense was not fully apprehended by any except those initiated into
the highest grade; and that those who did have full understanding
need not have agreed entirely upon all the meanings offered — there

are no certainties about the resolution of an enigma.

8 I have in general made use only of sources from the first two centuries AD, and of the Elder Pliny and Aelian above all. In a sense,
   of course, it is absurd to talk about *the* 'encyclopaedia' (by which
   I mean factual knowledge about the 'real' world) of Graeco-Roman
   antiquity, inasmuch as that world consisted in reality of innumerable
   different communities with very different social structures and, at
   the minute level, different cognitive structures. I believe nevertheless that, at least in the cases of the animals I discuss, there is
   good reason to believe that some ideas about them were very widely
   held, and that Pliny and Aelian do indeed reproduce not esoteric
   ideas but current ones — indeed both on several occasions say that
   'ordinary people' believe such-and-such. Furthermore, inasmuch as
   the Mysteries became a universal religion, it seems to me quite
   proper to suppose that in their use of the 'real' world they drew
   not upon esoteric or geographically specific notions, but upon banal
   ones. And more generally, I would observe that the normal relation
   to 'wild' animals in the Graeco-Roman world came to be a matter not
   of acute empirical investigation (Aristotle is of course an exception,
   as are hunters) but of constructing useful social meanings on the
   basis of assumed knowledge. In simpler societies without cities, the
   situation is of course often different (see Willis, 1974 ; Bulmer,
   1967: 15-25, and more generally, Lévi-Strauss, 1962), and social
   meanings are related to empirical knowledge in a more complex manner.
       It must be stressed that I have been selective in my discussion of
   Graeco-Roman ideas about ravens, as about the other animals discussed
   below, as a glance at Thompson, 1936: 159-64; Keller, 1909-13: II, 92-
   109, and Gossen, 1920: 19-23 will amply reveal.

9 Ovid, *Fasti* 2, 243-66 [with Bömer's commentary, pp. 99-100]; Hyginus,
   Astronom. 2, 40 (p. 76 Bunte); other texts in *Eratosthenis Catasteris-
   morum reliquiae* (ed. Carl Robert), pp. 188ff. The story is also found
   in relation to Coronis, cf. Ovid, *Metam.* 2, 531-41 [with Bömer's
   commentary, p. 371]; Hyginus, Fab. 202, etc.

10 Aelian, *NA* 1, 47 (which gives a slightly different account, substituting
   wheat for figs; cf. 2, 51) confirms this: καὶ ὑπὲρ τούτων ἐν τῇ μάλιστα
   αὐχμηροτάτῃ ὥρᾳ διψῶν δίκας ἐκτίνει ('and because of this, the raven is
   punished with thirst during the hottest period of the year'). A further
   insight into the matter is provided by another passage from Aelian (2,
   51 end), where the general belief that ravens went thirsty in summer
   is explained 'scientifically' by saying that 'all through the summer
   they are troubled by a *rhusis gastros*,' which I suppose to mean something like 'an excess of water in the alimentary canal', or possibly
   diarrhoea. One can only speculate on the relation between this scientific explanation and the story about figs...; but it is clear that the
   explanation itself depends upon the popular story preserved in the
   catasterismic and mythological writers.

11 According to Pliny, the autumnal rising of Arcturus occurred fourteen
   days before the autumnal equinox (*HN* 11, 41). The period of the raven's
   thirst began two months earlier, which means that it occurred at the
   heliacal rising of Sirius, which was in the first century in Rome deemed
   to be July 17th (Pliny *HN* 2, 123). But this was also the day the sun

entered the first degree of Leo (which was followed by 30 days of
Etesian winds, related by Schol. in Arat. 152 (p. 366 Maass) to the
period of the raven's thirst). According to Professor Beck's
theory, if Cautes and Cautopates are properly to be associated with
Aldebaran and Antares respectively, the mid-point between them on
the ecliptic is Leo (see Beck, 1977a: 14 n.16; 1977b and my notes
24, 25, 38). And the first degree of Leo was probably one of Mithras's 'seats'.

12 This particular point occurs nowhere else in that Scholiast tradi-
    tion, except in the Syriac version (ed. Sebastian Brock, p. 85).
    The expression διὰ πείνης καὶ δίψης was of course, as Wüst pointed
    out (1935: 215-16), a rhetorical cliché, which naturally affects the
    issue. But I would stress that the raven's thirst was not merely
    his punishment by Apollo, whose 'servant' (θεραπών) he was, it was
    an attempt to account for his croak; and Aelian provides an interest-
    ing variant on this when he says that the raven tries to imitate the
    sound of raindrops by croaking — the fundamental relation between
    water (or no-water) and the raven appears once again, in a structural
    transformation. In confirmation, we may note that it was supposed to
    be a sign of imminent rain if a raven imitated the sound of rain fall-
    ing (Theophrastus, de signis 1, 16 Hort); this is 'referred to' in
    the proverb κόραξ ὑδρεύει (Hesychius and Suda, s.v.). The emblem of
    Krannon in Thessaly was a hydria on wheels, which was associated both
    with ravens and with rain: Antigonus of Carystus, hist. mirabilium 15
    (in Keller, Rerum naturalium scriptores, I) and BMCG (Thessaly to
    Aetolia) p. 16 with Plate II, 13.

13 I single out only those passages which refer to the glaux/noctua,
    with which these Mithraic representations are to be identified:
    Aristotle, HA 1, 1(488a 26); 8, 3 (592b 8-9), which is partly repro-
    duced by Pliny, HN 10, 34 (classification as crooked-taloned and
    night-loving); according to Antoninus Liberalis, Metam. 10 (Min-
    yades) 4, it 'shuns the light of the sun'. Cf. Thompson, 1936:
    45-6; Sauvage, 1975: 179-84.

14 In other words, the choice of owl or raven as a sign for Cautopates
    was not indifferent: each stresses a different aspect of his Mith-
    raic significance. At the same time, raven and owl were not thought
    to be totally dissimilar birds. Both ate flesh (Aristotle, HA 8, 3:
    592b 15; Pliny, HN 10, 31); both gave signs, in relation to the
    weather and in other contexts (see n. 12 above and Pliny, HN 18, 362;
    Theophrastus, de signis 4, 52 [sign of good weather if the glaux
    hoots softly in winter/in a storm by day or by night; the raven re-
    appears here]; Aelian, NA 7, 7 [both glaux and raven again]); both
    were connected with periods of sixty days (according to Nigidius
    Figulus, the noctua hibernated in winter for 60 days: Pliny, HN 10,
    39); and both were supposed to be intelligent (for the owl, note
    especially Dio Chrysostom, Or. 12, 6-8, and Aesop, Fab. 105, 106;
    cf. Keller, 1909-13: II, 39-45).
        I should of course point out that the associations of Cautopates
    and of the raven with autumn are not of the same order: the ripening
    of the figs occurred at the autumnal rising of Arcturus (two weeks
    before the autumnal equinox); the sun came into conjunction with

Antares at the mid-point of autumn (3/4 October–22/23 November in the second century AD): Beck 1977a: 7.

15 Vermaseren, 1950: 147 had this to say on this aspect of *CIMRM* 334:
'(The raven) is Sol's messenger who also has to take the message to the Persian god that he has to kill the bull. He is an *hierokeryx*, playing an important part as such in the legend. He serves as an example to the *mystai* who perform the serving function of the raven... The pendant of this corax is another *keryx* the cock announcing the dawning light and chasing the evil demons. The Persian bird ... is often represented near Cautes, the torchbearer with the raised torch who in himself is a symbol of dawn. That the chanteclair on our monument has not been put on the sun's side but between Luna and Cautopates ... is due to a symmetry which the artist has tried to carry through as rigorously as possible. This is the reason that the cock is here placed at the side of the fading light, a thing which with other representations is due sometimes to a lack of exact understanding of the symbolism to be expressed ...'.

16 Towards the end of his life, Cumont argued vigorously that the cock was thought of specifically as a Persian bird in the Graeco-Roman 'encyclopaedia' (1942: 284–300, and several other studies summarized in 1949: 230 with note complémentaire XV [pp. 409–11]; whence Vermaseren's point about chasing demons cited in the previous note). But a glance at ordinary ideas about the cock scarcely confirms him: the Greeks and Romans had plenty of ideas of their own about so familiar an animal as the farmyard cock. It was of course a cliché that they announced the dawn (Thompson, 1936: 22; Sauvage, 1975; 265). More interesting, perhaps, in the present context is Theophrastus's observation (recorded by Aelian, *NA* 3, 38) that cocks do not crow when or where it is wet, which implies that they needed the sun (Aelian goes on at once to make a similar point about the cicada). In this respect, there seems to be an opposition not only between the cock and the owl, which is obvious, but between the cock and the raven in relation to the opposition between hot/dry and wet/cold. The raven is a humanoid creature which has an intimate connection with rain/water and can become, in summer, too hot and dry; the cock has associations with the heavens (*norunt sidera et ternas distinguunt,* 'they reckon the stars and tell the watches of the day': Pliny, *HN* 10, 46)— and with the sun especially — and is hostile to water. The usual hostility between cocks and lions is undoubtedly related to their common fieriness (cf. Aelian, *NA* 3, 31; 14, 9).

17 If Roger Beck is right to argue that the ear of corn was at some level in the Mysteries understood to refer to Spica, the lucida of Virgo, which marked in the first and second centuries AD the autumn equinox (1977b), we may here be presented with one of the Mithraic interpretations of the catasterismic story: Virgo and Hydria-Corvus-Hydra 'look at each other' (are near each other) in heaven ('Hyginus', *Astron.* 3, 24; cf. Vitruvius, *de arch.* 9, 5, 1); Corvus (like real ravens) marks a period of transition from the sun's period of greatest heat in Leo and the beginning of autumn in Virgo; ravens' connection with the ripening of figs associates them with one aspect of genesis (its fulfilment); the use of the raven as a sign for

Cautopates associates it with another (coming-into-being), which is
reinforced by the intimate link between Corvus and Crater/Hydria
(cf. Macrobius, *Comment. in somn. Scipionis* 1, 12, 8) — supposing
that constellation to be the final staging-post of souls on their
way to incarnation. Whether or not this suggestion is appropriate,
it seems to me clear that the different contexts within which ravens
appear in Mithraic iconography must at some level — surely astronomical — be related to the 'encyclopaedia', precisely because the latter
supplies (in the context of other Mithraic animals) the most convincing context for the name of the lowest grade.

18 Cf. Thompson, 1936: 91; Sauvage, 1975: 189-90.
19 [Arist.] *Physiogn.* 61 (Forster, I p. 66.7-9) links the raven with
    greed or 'shamelessness'; a theme which is specialized in a sexual
    sense in 68 (p. 78.3-5).
20 Although, as we shall see, Cumont believed this text to be so corrupt
    that we should abandon any attempt to make sense of it (below, p. 57)
    he still believed that 'on peut conclure ... que la collation des
    trois premiers grades n'autorisait pas la participation aux mystères'
    on the basis of Pallas' wording in relation to the grades Lion and
    Raven (1899: 317). For similar assessments, see Francis 1975a:
    441-42; Vermaseren, 1963: 140 (who half-believes it); Becatti,
    1954: 108.
21 Cf. Aelian, *NA* 7, 23 (from King Juba of Mauretania) and 5, 39. The
    lion was also supposed to be merciful to suppliants, and when angry
    would attack men rather than women (in a very British way): Pliny,
    HN 8, 48; according to an Egyptian tradition (Horus), it was a help
    to those in trouble (Plutarch, *De Iside* 19 [358c]). On occasion, it
    might even ask humans to help it (Pliny, *HN* 8, 56-58); and it was a
    stranger to guile and suspicion (Pliny, *HN* 8, 52; Aelian, *NA* 4, 34).
    All of this suggests that the moral sense of lions was something of
    a favourite *topos* in the Graeco-Roman 'encyclopaedia'.
        It will of course be obvious that I have not mentioned (and will
    not mention) other typical qualities attributed to the lion in
    Graeco-Roman antiquity, particularly the theme of its ferocity and
    strength, because I have deliberately assumed that the Mysteries
    permitted only 'appropriate' evocations from the 'encyclopaedia'.
    But it is of course important that we should understand that the
    fundamental motive for attributing human qualities to the lion was
    its 'natural' reproduction of heroic values, as Otto Manns percep-
    tively remarked in his discussion of Greek hunting: 'Die hervor-
    ragendsten Eigenschaften des Tieres sind Mut, Kraft und stolzes
    Bewusstsein derselben, Eigenschaften, die zumeist seine Erwähnung
    in Vergleichen bei Gelegenheit des Auftretens namhafter Helden ver-
    anlassen' (1888: 25). This made it a naturally appropriate royal
    hunting quarry, for example by Alexander: Plutarch, *Vit. Alex.* 40;
    Pliny, *HN* 34, 63 (a theme also to be found, of course, in Babylonia
    and Assyria, cf. Cassin, 1965: 453-55).
22 Cf. Pliny, *HN* 8, 47 and Aelian, *NA* 17, 27.
23 Alexander: Plutarch, *De Alex. fort. aut virtute* 335b; in the physio-
    gnomic tradition (briefly noted by Steier, 1927: 978), especially:
    [Aristotle] *Physiognomonica* 4 (I p. 12.3 Förster); 9 (p. 18.11-18);

41 (p. 48.14ff-p. 50.21); 59 (p. 64.3-4); 60 (p. 63.7-10); 61
(p. 66.4-6); 63 (p. 70.6-7); 64 (p. 70.14-15); 70 (p. 82.11-12);
the same associations are to be found in Pseudo-Polemon (e.g.
Förster, I p. 376.15-17); and in the epitome of the Hadrianic
writer Polemon by Adamantius, e.g. 2.24 (Förster, I p. 372.9-
373.2); 40 (p. 400.2-4). The association was clearly popular by
Aristotle's time, *Anal. Priora* 2, 27 (70b, 7 ff) = Förster, II
p. 256.23-25; 257.10-12.

24 Eratosthenes (ed. Robert, p. 96) 12 = Schol. *Arat. Lat.* v. 148
(p. 206 Maass): (Λέων) Οὗτός ἐστι μὲν τῶν ἐπιφανῶν ἄστρων, δοκεῖ
δ'ὑπὸ Διὸς τιμηθῆναι τοῦτο τὸ ζῴδιον διὰ τὸ τῶν τετραπόδων ἡγεῖσθαι
... ('This is one of the bright constellations; this sign of the
zodiac is said to have been specially honoured by Zeus because (the
lion) is king of the four-footed beasts'); cf.'Hyginus' *Astronom.*
I, 24. According to the Greek scholiast on Aratus, *Phaen.* v. 147,
the Chaldaeans ascribed a particular power to Regulus: ὁ Λέων
ἔχει ἐπὶ τῆς καρδίας ἀστέρα Βασιλίσκον λεγόμενον, ὃν οἱ χαλδαῖοι
νομίζουσιν ἄρχειν τῶν οὐρανίων ('Leo has as its heart a star called
'Royal', which the Chaldaeans believe to be ruler of the heavenly
bodies') (p. 364 Maass): this tradition is not found in the Greek
catasterismic tradition, though the relation of Leo, and the *stella
regalis* in particular, to royal power is discussed by astrological
writers, for example Firmicus Maternus, *Math.* 6, 2, 1-3. Although
in modern terms Regulus is the least bright of the 20 stars of first
magnitude (1.3), in the ancient world it seems to have been differently evaluated, no doubt because of the special relation between
Leo and the Sun (see G. P. Goold's useful list of ancient star-
magnitude classifications, 1977: ci-cv).

25 Cf. Aratus, *Phaen.* 149-51, with Martin's note on θερείταται (p. 34);
also Bouché-Leclercq, 1899: 185; 190; 427 etc.; and the table in W.
and H. Gundel, 1950: 2133. Fire is of course a central mediator in
the Graeco-Roman world (as everywhere else!), between Nature and
Culture and between heaven and earth; and Varro tells us that it was
male because it contains semen/seed, for all its Greek and Roman
associations with female divinities and female activities and places
(*LL* 5, 61). This ambiguity of fire undoubtedly helps us to understand the ambiguous relation between Leo and fecundity/fertility
evident in the astronomical tradition: cf. Beck, 1978: 112.

26 This explanation of the contrast between the animal's internal heat
and its fear of external fire occurs elsewhere, e.g. Aelian, *NA* 4,
35; 6, 22; 7, 6; Pliny, *HN* 8, 52. Since the theme of the lion's fear
of fire is Homeric (*Iliad* 11, 548-55; 17, 657-64 etc.), it would be
reasonable to suppose that the opposition inside/outside was intended
to reconcile two incompatible items in the 'encyclopaedia', the
Homeric item and the astronomical one. At *NA* 5, 39, Aelian offers
another Egyptian explanation for the association between (real) lions
and the sun — the fact that they never sleep: καὶ γάρ τοι καὶ τὸν
ἥλιον θεῶν ὄντα φιλοπονώτατον ἢ ἄνω τῆς γῆς ὁρᾶσθαι ἢ τὴν κάτω
πορείαν ἰέναι μὴ ἡσυχάζοντα ('for indeed the sun, being the most
tireless of gods, either is visible above the earth or
else never rests upon its journey below'). This aspect of the

relation between lion and sun is curiously parallel to one of the
beliefs we shall look at later, concerning the eagle; and I suspect
that the Mithraists may have been interested in the parallel. Carnivorous animals were of course supposed to be generally 'hotter' than
plant-eating ones: Theophrastus, *de causis plantarum* 1, 22, 1.

As for the easy passage between Leo and leo, we may find the
following 'dialectical' text from Martianus Capella instructive
(4, 355, p. 164 Dick): Aequivocum *est, quando multarum rerum unum
est nomen, sed non eadem definitio, ut* leo. *nam quantum ad nomen
pertinet, verum et pictus et caelestis* leo *dicitur; quantum ad
definitionem, aliter verus definitur, aliter pictus, aliter caelestis,* 'An equivocal term is one which has a number of referents which
cannot be defined identically, such as the word 'leo'; for that word
covers real lions, painted lions and the constellation (Leo). But
when we come to define it, we define real lions as one thing, painted
lions as another, and Leo as yet another'. Where ambiguities abound,
there meanings — and especially mysteries — flourish.

27 See also Diels-Kranz, *FVS* 1[6] p. 362, frg. B 127. One may suspect
    that Empedocles was interested precisely in the 'humanity' of lions,
    as in the 'divinity' of the bay-tree: both are sort-crossing elements
    of the natural world, and especially fit to receive human souls.
28 Hopfner, 1913: 40 assumes that 'Hephaestus' here is Atum-Re, an
    aspect of the Sun-god, although we have no reason to suppose that
    Aelian is still talking about Heliopolis. 'Hephaestus' must surely,
    as usual, be Ptḥ (Ptah), and the tradition be Memphitic, though we
    know nothing, apparently, from Egyptian sources of a lion-cult of
    this kind. On lions as watchers over temples, see Plutarch, *De Iside*
    38 [365f-366a] with Griffiths, 1970: 444-45; Hopfner, 1913: 44 cols.
    1-2; de Wit, 1951: 71-82 esp. 80-1.
29 For the theme of the evil eye, see Hopfner, 1913: 43-44; de Wit,
    1951: 17-18 (where he prefers to translate m'j ḥs' loosely as 'lion
    au regard terrible'); and cf. his pp. 21ff.
30 I have prepared an article on the significance of Latin *virus*, to
    appear elsewhere. Briefly, one may say that it is an 'ugh' word,
    a marker of ambiguous substances or smells to which power is attached
    by virtue of their ambiguity.
31 Aelian does not specify how the punishment was supposed to have been
    imposed, but his context suggests that it was in dreams rather than
    in 'reality'. I freely grant that Aelian himself does not make the
    connection between god's breathing of anger into the lion and the
    zoological fact about the power of real lions' breath; but his choice
    of the word *katapnein* (cf. Aristotle, *HA* 8, 5[594b 26-28]) is more
    fully intelligible if we suppose it to be motivated in the way I have
    suggested.
32 Note especially Plutarch, *De Iside* 63 (376c-f), with Griffiths, 1970:
    525-28, and on the Egyptian evidence, Bonnet, 1952: 716-20 (the
    rattle provided magical protection from evil, and also long-life and
    well-being; in the worship of Amun, it was used as a symbol of power
    [p. 719[2]]). In view of the relation between the constellation Leo
    and the annual flooding of the Nile (de Wit, 1951: 396-99), an idea
    apparently reproduced by Aelian, *NA* 12, 7, where he says that the

Egyptians ascribed the lion's forequarters to fire, and its hindquarters to water, it is worth noting that according to Servius, *in
Vergil. Aen.* 8, 696, the *sistrum* announced the flooding of the Nile
(Bonnet, 1952: 720). I am tempted to believe that this association
between Leo and water provides a key to a minor puzzle in the scheme
of zodiacal signs at Sette Sfere, where, if we take the zodiac in
its diametral aspect (which opposes pairs of signs), Leo is both
opposed and linked to Aquarius (Gordon, 1976: 134-35).

33 Cumont, 1945: 416, remarks: 'La présence de cet instrument isiaque
reste inexpliquée'; Vermaseren says simply, '... a *sistrum* (the
sacred rattle adopted from the Isis cult)' (1963: 146), to which
Witt, 1975: 489 adds nothing. Becatti, 1954: 110, goes one better
by referring the *sistrum* without question to the cult of the Magna
Mater, appealing to the well-known 'fact' that the two cults were
closely related. Not only is that quite untrue, it resolves nothing.

34 See Rostovtzeff *et al.*, 1939: 127 no. 865 (incorrectly printed in
CIMRM 68). In my view, Cumont was right to associate the line with
the grade *Leo* (Bidez-Cumont, 1938: II, 155, frg. 09e), though shortly
afterwards he abandoned that hypothesis in favour of an eschatological one (1975: 204-5).

35 For the date, see n. 11 above.

36 I cannot accept Vermaseren's view (1963: 148; cf. van Essen and
Vermaseren, 1965: 231) that the Lions are themselves consumed and
made into new men: that is simply not what the text says.
Vollgraff's comments (1960: 780-81) on Cumont's theory that the
text refers to palingenesis are surely conclusive (though I do not
believe that his own view of the meaning of *consumimur* is any
better). For although there is plenty of comparative evidence,
in Greek myth, in hellenistic mysteries and in Egyptian lore (see
Griffiths, 1970: 328 on Plutarch, *De Iside* 16[357c]), that fire
could be used as a 'passage' to immortality, the evocations in these
lines at Santa Prisca have no direct relation to such ideas (though
the insistence upon incense, a 'vertical mediator' *par excellence*,
suggests an interest in the theme at some level). Note that these
lines are addressed to Mithras in the first instance, and not to the
Father, as Vermaseren maintains.

37 Traditional discussions, such as that by Schuster, 1931: 364-84, are
not of much assistance, since they treat ancient ideas about honey
as merely bizarre. The most suggestive modern discussions, dependent
upon Lévi-Strauss, are those of Detienne, 1974: 56-75; 1977a: 137-38.
    One of the most interesting ancient texts on honey, Pliny, *HN* 11,
31ff. characterizes it as a thorough-going 'sort-crosser', since it
descends as pure heavenly moisture (11, 36: *sive ille est caeli sudor
sive quaedam siderum saliva sive purgantis se aeris sucus*, 'it might
be the sweat of heaven, or some sort of star-spit, or the sap of the
air produced by its self-cleansing mechanism'), and is then filled
with impurities, both earthly dirt and the use made of it by bees.
These formulations concentrate on the oppositions between pure/impure,
heavenly/earthly, liquid/solid, air/liquid, all of which honey mediates. The opposition liquid/fire occurs merely implicitly, in Pliny's
statement that honey is formed only at the heliacal rising of Sirius,

or after, but never before (11, 38). But to judge from Porphyry, *de antro* 15, this became an explicit theme in the ritual use of honey in the initiation ceremony for Mithraic Lions — honey is a liquid but not 'watery', and has some evident compatibility with the nature of fiery Lions who hate water: which must be its 'fieriness', its association with the rising of Sirius.

38 It will be evident that the cluster of evocations I discuss here is not exhaustive. Even in our present state of almost complete ignorance about the meanings created by the Mysteries in relation to the grade Leo, we can see that although the cluster aromatics : sun : heat : fire : lions : closeness to god served as one link between this world and heaven, there were others. One is certainly the evocation-chain lion : constellation Leo : star Regulus : Mithras; cf. Roger Beck, 1977a: 14 n.16: 'Situated midway between Aldebaran and Antares at the point on the ecliptic reached by the sun in the season of its greatest power, [Regulus] stands to Mithras as Aldebaran and Antares to Cautes and Cautopates' (and cf. my note 24 above). The Egyptian first decan in Leo, called   hr-knm = χναχουμήν (Celsus), was a lion-headed male figure: see Gundel, 1925: 1989, and de Wit, 1951: 391. Related to, but distinct from, this chain of associations is another, also concerned with 'kingship', the chain lion : king of the beasts : king of gods : Zeus/Jupiter (god and planet) : ethical purity. This chain, of course, necessitates the Mithraic guardianship of the grade *Leo* by the planet Jupiter. It is essential to understand that 'truth' was never seen as simple, or as a mere assertion of discrete facts, in the Mysteries; by a necessary mystification, every meaning had a plural relation to others (cf. Gordon, 1978: 208-13). I would say that that technique, precisely 'mysterious', was the pedagogical consequence of the Mysteries' central enigmatic claim, that Life is Death, and Death Life. The enigma necessarily defies rational exposition; even more important, the enigma is intelligible (for us) only as a form of repression of real conflicts of value in everyday experience, as I hope to show.

39 See van Gennep, 1909: 27 (using the terms [rites] préliminaires, liminaires, postliminaires). Although, as I pointed out above (n.6), Cumont was naturally aware of such anthropological thinking, and of van Gennep in particular, he persisted in maintaining a sharp cleavage between 'primitive' practices and Graeco-Roman mystery beliefs, to be linked only by counterfeit history ('survivals'). In this, he has been followed by everyone else, so far as I can see, even those, such as Nock, Wikander and Nilsson, who first rejected the 'strong' Iranian hypothesis. In my view the link between 'primitive' initiation and 'mysteriosophical' cults in the Graeco-Roman world is one not of historical continuity but of structural homology: similar techniques are used to alter status. The crucial difference lies in the *kind* of status to be altered.

40 See especially Leach, 1966: 124-36; Vidal-Naquet, 1968: 49-64; 1974: 137-68. The anthropologist who has made fullest use of such themes recently is Victor Turner, though I think that his concept of 'liminality' has been made to work far too hard (e.g. 1969; 1974: 231-71). Van Gennep has been assimilated with equally unsatisfactory

results by Mircea Eliade and the 'Chicago School'.

41 Antiphon the Sophist, for example, in speaking of marriage, uses τὸ λυπηρόν as the opposite of τὸ ἡδύ (Diels-Kranz, FVS II⁶ p. 358 lines 5-6: n.87, frg. B 49): ἐν τῷ αὐτῷ δέ γε τούτῳ, ἔνθα τὸ ἡδύ, ἔνεστι πλησίον που καὶ τὸ λυπηρόν, 'and here certainly, where there is sweetness there is also bitterness/pain lurking somewhere'); cf. Plato, *Phaedo* 60b, and, more abstractly, the opposition between ἡδονή and λύπη in Aristotle, *EN*, 7, 11-14; 10, 1-5. The opposition was a cliché. Honey is presented as the opposite of bitter bile by Porphyry, *de antro* 18 (= Arethusa, p. 20 lines 8-9); and of innumerable passages on its sweetness, we may note Aelian, *NA* 2, 57 (speaking of the bee): ζῷον φιλεργότατον καὶ τῶν καρπῶν τὸν ἄριστόν τε· καὶ γλύκιστον ἐν ἀνθρώποις παρασκευάζον, τὸ μέλι, 'It is a creature of prodigious industry, which produces the finest and sweetest of earthly fruits that men know — honey'. It is scarcely necessary to point out that it is precisely the *cathartic* and *preservative* properties of honey that Porphyry singles out in his discussion of its ritual use in the Mysteries (*de antro* 15-17 = Arethusa, p. 16 line 21- p. 18 line 23); cf. Pliny, *HN* 11, 36-37 and Robert Turcan, 1975: 69-72: and those notions are exactly contrasted with the ideas of 'pollution' and 'doing harm or damage'.

42 *Lupēron* is (probably) used in Polybius, 31, 24, 4 to refer to a 'shame' response to a criticism of an aristocrat's honour: the criticism is 'painful'; the word is used in a similar sense in the NT (Arndt-Gingrich, 1957: s.v.). The Christian meaning of λύπη (Kittel-Friedrich, 1964-74: s.v.) — except insofar as pain/suffering came to be glorified — is evidently related to the Platonic conception of worldly pain (and pleasure) as a constituent of the world of change (*Rep.* 9, 583ff.). *Blaptikos* does not occur in the NT, but is used of animals by Strabo, 15, 1, 45 (707C: p. 984.31 Meinecke) and Philo, *De opif. mundi* 21 (64) — opposed to ὠφελητικός; and in a moral sense by Philodemus, *de pietate* 99-100. *Musaros* is used to describe moral faults in I Clement, 14, 1; 30, 1 (of adultery); cf. LXX *Lev.* 18, 23; Philodemus, *On the Stoics* p. 339.2 Crönert.

43 See Douglas, 1966: 129-39; 1975: 60-72.

44 Professor Francis, 1975a: 441 with n. 89, rightly supports Cumont's derivation from στερεός 'firm' against Campbell's from στερέω (→ 'ascetic') (1968: 314). But I see no reason to follow Cumont's further suggestion, about which he was himself properly hesitant, and associate the word with a ceremony of *anointing* (Cumont, 1975: 202); or Francis's idea that the word *stereōtēs* means 'one who ratifies, confirms [a pact]'. There seem to me to be two options: (1) we may conservatively keep close to the meaning of the word in the one context in which it appears outside the Mysteries (and indeed, outside Dura), namely the Scholiast on Oppian *Halieutika*, 4, 421, where it is used to explain the word ὑφορμιστήρ, a rope tied to an anchor, and where it must mean something like 'something which keeps something else steady'. Used of a person, this would give us a a sense 'Confirmer (of the faith?)' for the Mysteries' usage. (2) In view of the general agreement that *stereōtēs* at Dura does duty for *Heliodromus* at Rome (so Francis, 1975a: 443, following Cumont and Rostovtzeff), it may be relevant to note that one common

meaning of *stereōma* in *koinè* is 'firmament', 'sky'. A meaning
'firmament-person', 'sky-person', would be truly close to *Heliodromus*. As we shall see later, this would not be the only instance
in the Mysteries of 'absurd' terms invented in order to mark their
difference from the norms of the 'real' world; and I confess that
I find it very attractive. (I assume of course that we permit the
notion of 'semantic motivation' to operate here, and that we do not
have to suppose that words float into existence on the back of
Brugmannite 'laws'.)

45   This supplement is of course a mere guess, but perhaps one that is
worth defending. The *Report* (Rostovtzeff *et al.*, 1939: 120 no.856
with Plate L 2 = *CIMRM* 58) gives the following dipinto: [νά]μα λέουσιν/
[ἄβρο]υς καυ περσεσ-/[υν...]ελεμνους. There is no clear indication,
naturally, of how many letters are lost, nor is it readily intelligible
why Lions should be mentioned before Persians. Words in Greek ending
in -εμνος are very rare, and the only one which seems in the slightest
appropriate is itself highly problematical: for *thelemnos* is to be found
only in the Codex Marcianus's version of Hesychius's Lexicon, and is not
accented. It is glossed there as meaning ὅλον ἐκ ῥιζῶν, which is taken
by the LSJ Supplement to mean 'well-founded'. But this is surely wrong.
The mistranslation is owed to the fact that *thelemnos* only appears in
the Supplement because it was admitted by Diels-Kranz, *FVS* I⁶, p. 320,
into their reading of Empedocles' *Peri phuseōs* frg. 21.6: ’εκ δ’αἴης /
προρέουσι θελεμνά τε καὶ στερεωπά. This reading has consequently been much
disputed: D..O'Brien, after a full review of the possibilities , decides for
Sturz's traditional θέλυμνα, 'elements' (1969: 266-67); Jean Bollack
for θελημά, 'gracieux' (1969: 35, his frg. 63⁶). There can be little
doubt but that Kranz was wrong to insert the word Empedocles' text here.
But we have still to account for the Codex Marcianus and its gloss.
The most natural interpretation of ὅλον ἐκ ῥιζῶν is 'entirely whole',
'complete from the roots up'. And in view of Porphyry's statement
in *de antro* 15-16 that the grade Perses had a special relation to
the fruits of the earth in that it 'preserved' them, a grade-
description connected to plants through the notion of 'roots', but
which also could be evoked in a moral sense, has considerable attraction.

46   On balance, I do not find myself persuaded by Professor Francis's
thesis that the word αβρος at Dura should be derived from the Aramaic
habərā (1975a: 444-45; 1975b), and means something like 'companion'
(I am grateful to Sebastian Brock for pointing out to me the implausi-
bilities of such a thesis). The word must be deemed to be the usual
Greek ἅβρος. Although in *koinè* its connotations might be disparaging
(verging on 'effeminate'), that is by no means always the case (see
Stephanus, s.v., col. 88). It is surely relevant to note that one
Homeric adjective for a lion is αἴθων (*Iliad* 10, 24; 11, 548; Körner,
1930: 9), a word ambiguous between 'tawny-red', 'gleaming' and
'fiery', and it seems to me likely that we should suppose that *habros*
in this Mithraic context is also a word which defies our own semantic
distinctions. Its primary reference is to a particular quality of
surface, whether the gleam of young, healthy skin or the sheen of
healthy leaves; whence its connotations pass in two very different

directions, admirably summed up in the Suda's entry (ed. Adler, I, p. 12 no.87): λαμπρὸς, τρυφερὸς, ἁπαλός (and note its range of meanings in Nonnus, *Dionysiaka*: 1968: 1-2). We should probably interpret it here to mean both bright/gleaming/illustrious and fresh/young/?reborn (cf. the Santa Prisca line (18) *Nama Leonibus novis et multis annis* [Van Essen and Vermaseren, 1965: 232-39], where I take *novis* with *Leonibus*).

47 Professor Francis (1975: 441 n.85) has shrewdly suggested that the most appropriate interpretation of the Roman fourth-century term *cryphius* is that it is an innovation within the grade-system 'secondarily specialising the significance of the [*Nymphus*'s] veil' (on which see p. 50 below). The entire earlier debate on this matter achieved virtually nothing, riddled as it was with untenable preconceptions.

48 On *sophistēs* and *akeraios* see Cumont, 1975: 202-04 with Francis's additional notes; I should point out however, that there is no reason whatever to associate *akeraios* with 'Mazdeism' (as though that religion had a monopoly in its claim to concern itself with moral virtue). The word occurs twice in the New Testament, in each case figuratively (used with ἄμεμπτος and ἄμωμος in *Phil*. 2, 15; cf. *Rom*. 16, 19); see Kittel-Friedrich, 1964-74: I, 209-10; Arndt-Gingrich, 1957: 29, s.v. The *Patristic Greek Lexicon* (s.v.) suggests that it meant in a religious context in the High Empire 'pure', 'inviolate' and so, of people, 'innocent', 'simple'.

49 See CIMRM 473[12], 474[4]; correct texts in Moretti, *IGUR* I: nos. 106, 107 (with plate on p. 91). In this connection, it would be as well to recall that the raven was supposed in the 'encyclopaedia' to be able to speak in several different modes, one of which was prophetic: εἰ δὲ ὑποκρίνοιτο τὰ ἐκ τῶν θεῶν, ἱερὸν ἐνταῦθα καὶ μαντικὸν φθέγγεται, 'And if it is giving utterance to matters divine, its voice takes on a holy and prophetic note' (Aelian, *NA* 2, 51).

50 The only non-religious associations which regularly included members of both sexes were the so-called *collegia 'funeraticia'*, and only then if they were based upon the membership of a *familia*, with its freedmen and freedwomen. See Schiess, 1888: 72-73; Waltzing, 1895-1900: I, 348-49. The relationship between *collegia* and public norms in general is discussed by de Robertis, n.d.: II, 26-40.

51 See especially Detienne, 1974: 70-79; 1977: 135-60, and more generally, Lewis (1971). Naturally, the extent to which a novel cult was perceived as dangerous because it admitted both sexes varied: if Euripides' *Bacchae* provides us with a glimpse into the logic of the situation of the Dionysiac mysteries, both in classical and in hellenistic times no such danger was (generally) feared. But exactly the same fear could be excited when the cult was transferred to a foreign community, as the Senate's response to the 'reformed' Bacchanalian cult in 186 BC clearly reveals. Note especially the tone of Livy, 39.8.6-7; 11.7; 13.9-11; 13.14; 15.3; 15.12-13 and the whole of chapters 16 and 19-20; and the restrictions imposed precisely in the area of sexual matters by the *SC de Bacchanalibus* (*FIRA*[2] I, no.30) lines 10-12; 19-20; cf. Festugière, 1972: 99-106. A similar ambiguity is evident in the case of the cult of Isis: cf. Kelly Heyob, 1975: 111-27.

52 See Vidal-Naquet, 1968: 58-59; 62-63; Willetts, 1955: 11-14; and
    cf. Pleket, 1969: 281-98; Jan Bremmer, 1978: 34-35; Piccaluga, 1965:
    especially 131-68.

53 I do not intend to imply that this is the only connotation of the
    term *Heliodromus*, which, to judge from second-century Christian
    coinages that are apparently motivated in the same way (see Gordon,
    1975b: 131-32), also had the sense 'messenger', 'envoy'. But
    expressions about planets containing δρόμος are very common: Plato,
    Timaeus 38d; [Arist.] *de mundo* 399 a 8, etc.

54 Note especially the following passages from Varro, *Ling.Lat.*, 5.14;
    8.7; 8.46-47; 9.36; 38; 41; 55; frg. 24 (p. 196 Funaioli); frg. 245
    (p. 270 Funaioli); and the material in Neue, 1902: I, 915-30. I
    have not been able to find any modern discussion of ancient atti-
    tudes towards grammatical gender; there seems only to be a haughty
    philological insistence that such ideas are simply muddled and so
    not worthy of investigation in their own right. But since nature
    eyes culture so uneasily on this frontier between language and the
    world, such a study would be well-worthwhile.

55 See Vernant, 1974: 177-94; 1977: 904-50.

56 I have already alluded to this passage in n.10 above. The point I
    wish to stress here is that Aelian says that the raven seems to be
    conscious of the cause of its tummy-trouble in summer 'and for that
    reason make[s] sure that [it] does not touch wet food': καὶ διὰ
    ταῦτα ἑαυτοὺς ὑγρᾶς τροφῆς ἀγεύστους φυλάττουσιν. The 'encyclo-
    paedia' may have invited different views concerning the cause of
    the trouble, but it made it certain that the raven's life was marked
    by an opposition between the dry and the wet, and between summer and
    winter.

57 See Hesiod, *WD* 414-19; 582-88; cf. 704-05 and Detienne, 1972: 222-25.

58 Detienne, 1972; see Gordon, 1979b for some comments on the reception
    of this book, and especially on Giulia Piccaluga, 1974: 33-51.
    There is in England at the moment an interesting renewal of this
    earlier discussion, as a result of the appearance of the English
    translation in 1977: compare Kirk, 1978: 922-23 with Leach, 1978:
    684-85. Professional classicists think it all too far-fetched,
    structural anthropologists argue that it, or something like it, must
    be true. I find myself on both sides at once: Detienne spends too
    much time on side-issues such as the Pythagoreans, and many of Picca-
    luga's points are well-taken; but is Detienne's 'structure' simply
    invented?

59 I must stress that the expression 'were seen to be further approp-
    riate' is not intended to represent an 'historical' point (for it
    would be merely counterfeit history). We can have no historical
    knowledge of the way in which the Mysteries accumulated their inter-
    pretations of reality; we can only make analytical observations
    about what (to us) seems most important, and then attempt to reveal
    consequent links and evocations.

60 See Ovid, *Metam.* 10, 698-707; Hyginus, *Fabulae* 185.6 (Rose);
    Mythogr. Vaticani 1, 39 (p. 14 Bode) cf. 2, 46-47 (pp. 90-91 Bode);
    Servius in *Verg. Aen.* 3, 113 (Harvard edition, III p. 58); and fur-
    ther, Vidal-Naquet, 1968: 63 with n.2; Detienne, 1977a: 107-10.

61 Cf. Pliny, *HN* 8, 43-45 quoting Aristotle, *HA* 6, 31 (579a 33-579b15); Aelian, *NA* 4, 34.
62 Cf. Pliny, *HN* 8, 42: *multiformes ibi animalium partus varie feminis cuiusque generis mares aut vi voluptate miscente,'* there are (in Africa) all sorts of hybrids, because either violence or lust causes the males to couple indiscriminately with the females of other species'. This feature of lionesses is picked up in Attic comedy (Henderson, 1975: 179-80) and in astrology is applied to those born under Leo: Hippolytus, *Ref. haer.* 4, 19; but is foreign to the physiognomic tradition. Note also Strabo, 16, 4, 20 (Arabia).
63 See Lucian, τὰ πρὸς Κρόνου [Epist. Kron.] 34 (=Loeb edition, vol. 6 p. 132); Aelian, *NA* 4, 3.
64 Both earlier and in 1975: 200-1, he argued that *numphos* means 'adolescent', so that 'Initiation into this grade would ... represent a memory of those *rites de passage* which are recognised among so many cultures at the onset of puberty when the child is admitted to the society of men'. Pseudohistory saves us from thinking about the grade-structure of the Mysteries as a *structure* rather than as some sort of accidental precipitation of the ages; but Cumont was at least half-right in his perception that the model of *rites de passage* could be applied to a grade in the Mysteries.
65 Although I agree with Professor Francis that Cumont's examples in 1975: 201 n.276 do not justify the assumption of 'an underlying masculine form νύμφος', he unfortunately goes on to commit exactly the same *petitio principii*: 'One can readily understand how a masculine νύμφος could at least secondarily be derived from παρανύμφος regardless of that form's derivational source'. What theory of semantic motivation underlies that remark? Which was prior, 'derivation' according to the Brugmannite (or rather, by now, pseudo-Brugmannite) 'rules', or the ideological structure of the Mysteries?
66 If Cumont had not been so concerned with demonstrating his non-contention about the banality of the form *numphos* (which of course occurs in that form nowhere outside the Mysteries), he might have noticed that all his examples were highly instructive — of the sexual ambiguity of *numph*-words. In other words, the Mysteries made explicit a play upon the identity-in-opposition of brides and grooms which Greek culture at large left implicit, but which is quite visible in the lexical entries. Another ambiguity in the lexicon, between brides and Nymphs, receives elaborate treatment, for example, in Porphyry's *de antro* 10-18, where he constantly invokes 'the theologians' and 'the mysteries'. I think my point about the special character of Mithraic *numphoi* is well confirmed by Porphyry's 'failure' in this discussion to mention them at all. Compare Robert Turcan (1975: 68-69): 'On s'étonne aussi qu'après avoir assimilé les Nymphes "Naiades" aux âmes près de s'incarner, Porphyre rappelle la coutume grecque de nommer "nymphes" les jeunes mariés, sans citer les *Nymphi* de l'initiation mithriaque ...'. The 'failure' is only surprising if one has beforehand mistaken the character of Mithraic *Nymphi*, and supposes them to be 'Bridegrooms'. Why do we so constantly suppose that our sources knew less than we do?
67 Pliny, *HN* 2, 36, links this doubleness of Venus to her rivalry with

the sun and moon. Using the 'Pythagorean' theory of the order of the planets, he says: *praeveniens quippe et ante matutinum exoriens Luciferi nomen accipit ut sol alter diemque maturans, contra ab occasu refulgens nuncupatur Vesper ut prorogans lucem vicemque lunae reddens*, 'that is, when Venus precedes (the sun) and rises before sunrise, she receives the name Lucifer as an alternative sun, and because she brings daylight to maturity; and when on the other hand she shines after sunset, she is called Vesper, inasmuch as she prolongs the light and acts as a substitute for the moon'. Cf. Martianus Capella, 8,883 (p. 466 Dick) and W. Gundel 1941: 653; Rehm, 1912: 1250-51.

68 See in particular Manilius, *Astron.* 1, 173-78, with Goold's comments.

69 Cf. Martial, 8, 21.1-2, and other examples collected by Gundel, 1941: 653.

70 In Bidez-Cumont, 1938: II, 154 frg. 09b; and 1975: 200.

71 I think that Cumont's error must have been in part due to an unconscious debt to the hitherto 'legitimate' argument of Dieterich (1923: 122 and 214) that the phrase was an address *to a god*: 'Das der Gott als Bräutigam und neues Licht begrüsst wird ist klar erkennbar; ihm stellt Firmicus den wahren Bräutigam, das wahre Licht, seinen Gott Christus gegenüber ...'. Dieterich helped this interpretation along by repeatedly misquoting the evidence of the Palatine manuscript, printing as his text (p. 214, no.6): ... δε, νυμφύε, χαῖρε, νέον φῶς. Cumont brilliantly saw that this must relate to the new Duran evidence, but carried Dieterich's erroneous contextualization over into his own interpretation.

72 The *Nymphus* whose face is covered by a *flammeum* on the top layer of paintings on wall I$_2$ at Santa Prisca (see next paragraph) is holding a 'bright red object', which Vermaseren plausibly suggests to be a lamp or a torch (van Essen and Vermaseren, 1965: 157). This figure would then register both themes, 'light' and 'darkness', simultaneously. On the lamp at di Felicissimo, see Becatti, 1954: 109.

73 See van Essen and Vermaseren, 1965: 157 (upper layer); 169 (lower layer). One of the figures at Pareti dipinte in Ostia may also be a *Nymphus* holding a *flammeum*: compare Becatti, 1954: 67 (and Plate XIII.2), 'la mano regge un oggetto rossiccio rettangolare, che potrebbe essere una borsa' with *CIMRM* 2685[a]: 'In his hands he holds a red cloth (*flammeum*). Head and shoulders lost (*Nymphus*)'.

74 See for example, Vettius Valens, 4.2. One scarcely needs to stress the consequences of such chromatic alterity for a cult, such as the Mysteries, dedicated to a vision of apogenesis which involved complete changelessness. A similar matter of changeability will become evident later, in a different connection.

75 See Statius, *Thebais* 8, 159-60 (Klotz-Klinnert):

                                      sed Vesper opacus
                  lunares iam ducit equos;

and (though late) Musaeus, *Hero and Leander* 111, with Kost's commentary, p. 305.

76 See *CCAG* II, p. 82, and other texts cited by Gundel, 1941: 653-54.

77 For some examples, note Isis in Egypt (Plutarch, *De Iside* 43 [368c] with Griffiths' excellent comments); the Hermetic divine father in

Asclepius 20 (p. 231 Festugière and Nock), and cf. *Corp. Herm*. 1, 9 (p. 9); the Orphic tradition (Kern, *OF* nos. 21a; 56; 168; and cf. [Iamblichus] *Theolog. Arithm.* 5 pp. 3-4 de Falco); several Gnostic sects at least somewhere in the divine hierarchy (cf. Pokorný, 1975: 764-65); and the so-called Tübingen Theosophy no.29 Erbse, which Lewy, 1956: 23ff.; 340-43, claimed without general acceptance to be Chaldaean.

78　I see no reason to suppose that the Anatolian cult of Aphroditos is relevant here, though it should be remarked that the Chaldaean Oracles' conception of Hecate may be, since she was conceived as 'double' (two-faced and high/low, dark-light) as well as generative (cf. Lewy, 1956: 83-98; 353-66).

79　Kugler, 1907: 10, working from the Babylonian texts in the British Museum transcribed by Strassmaier, showed that the planet Venus was believed to be bisexual in Seleucid astronomy. Bidez-Cumont, 1938: II, 220-30 frg. 085, print only the opening section of this passage (p.31.20-1 Wünsch), and make no reference to the bisexual theme (whose origin in Seleucid astronomy casts some doubt upon the legitimacy of their assumption that 'chaldaean' astrology here means 'Zoroastrian' of course). Lydus's explicit reference to Egypt makes it clear that Seleucid notions had received extensive theological commentary from which he quotes (and cf. W. and H. G. Gundel, 1966: 257-8). In Greek astrology, it was Mercury that was believed to be bisexual (W. and H. G. Gundel, 1950: 2130-1).

80　Wheeler, 1930: 205-23 usefully discusses the Catullan *epithalamia* in relation to the norms of the rhetorical handbooks, especially Menander, Himerius and Choricius. Hesperus, the advent of light (raising the torches), and the invocation of Venus were all conventional subjects in this literary tradition; in the immediate connection, note especially Catullus 61, 114-5 (Fordyce):

　　　　　　　tollite, ⟨o⟩ pueri, faces:
　　　　　　　flammeum video venire.

It should also be noted that Hymen (who himself wore the *flammeum*) is conventionally presented as at least epicene if not actually androgynous: Menander, 13, 23 Bursian; Catullus 61, 9-10; 13 Fordyce; cf. Wheeler, 1930: 210-11.

81　See, for example, Vermaseren, 1963: 142, 'This male bride ... is joined to Mithras in a mystical marriage by the Father'. The section-heading ('Nymphus, the bride') is equally uncompromising. As so often, the specific intentions of the Mysteries are obscured by the pursuit of 'parallels'; cf. Smith, 1978: ix-xi.

82　Cf. Manilius, *Astron.* 2, 924-26 Goold; Pliny, *HN* 2, 36. The belief was both popular and 'learned' (Buffière, 1956: 304-6); for some of its astrological ramifications, see Ptolemy, *Tetrab.* 4, 5 [§§185-6; 188-89]; Firmicus Maternus, *Mathesis* 3, 6 (1, pp. 142-55 Kroll-Skutsch); and cf. Bouché-Leclercq, 1899: 447-53.

83　The fullest discussion of such theories is by Lesky (1951), though she generally limits herself to philosophical theories ascribable to particular schools.

84　See especially Pembroke, 1967: 1-35; 1970: 1240-70; Vidal-Naquet, 1970a: 63-80.

85 Cf. Sander, 1958: 152-63; also Garnsey, 1970: 45-53 and B. Campbell,
    1978: 153-66.
86 See von Harnack, 1905: 15-17; 21; 28-29; 34 (with texts in the Appen-
    dix); a similar theme became banal in later Stoicism, especially
    Epictetus: Edmonds, 1938: 43-46.
87 That hunting in Greece (and in Rome) was thought appropriate both for
    ephebes and as a training for adult warfare was pointed out long ago
    by Otto Manns (1888: 19-20) and was shown to be more generally true
    by Schumpeter (1951: 43-44); more recently Pierre Vidal-Naquet (1968:
    60-61; 1974: 137-68) has pursued the point most fruitfully. It seems
    not to have been generally appreciated in Mithraic studies that the
    themes of Mithras as hunter and as thief must be linked, not only to
    each other, but to the wider issue of Mithras *invictus*.
88 I have suggested elsewhere that in the Mysteries Luna was associated
    with, among other things, Cautopates, water and the generation of
    plant-life (1976a: 123; cf. 144). This renders even more interesting
    Porphyry's information (*de antro* 16 = Arethusa, p. 16 lines 30-32)
    that the grade Perses was conceived as 'guardian of fruits' — guard-
    ian understood to mean 'preserver', as is clear from the grade's
    proper initiation with honey, the preserver (see n.41 above) — inas-
    much as Luna was the grade's tutelary planet. But I wish to stress
    here the common belief that plants are *bisexual*, because they mingle
    the male and the female principles: note especially Aristotle, *de
    gen.anim.* 1, 23 (731 a 1ff.). The common classification of plants
    as 'male' and 'female' actually is consistent with this theory,
    since it quite evidently had nothing to do with reproduction: cf.
    Theophrastus, *Hist. Plant.* 3, 8-18. For a cult dedicated, as I would
    argue, to a stringent reaffirmation of traditional patrilineal atti-
    tudes, such as the Mysteries of Mithras, such notions must have been
    particularly necessary to 'place' in a suitably new framework, just as
    the grade *Nymphus* placed marriage in a new perspective. Though we
    cannot do more than guess, it seems to me likely that the reclassifi-
    cation was achieved by appealing to male agricultural labour, which
    mediates between ambiguous Nature and the Mithraic view of culture
    (note the sole-ard (plough) in the centre of the Perses-frame at di
    Felicissimo, which is usually interpreted as a *falx* or sickle — surely
    with insufficient evidence; cf. White, 1967: 123-145, with plates 10-
    11), and by reinterpreting the whole issue of plant-life allegori-
    cally, in relation to the soul and rebirth.
89 We know almost nothing of the cult of Mithra/Mehr in Armenia (compare
    Widengren, 1960: 62-86), apart from the existence of a large and
    important temple at Bagayarišn or Bagayarič: see Chaumont, 1965:
    167-81; we can only say, in the most general terms, that 'Armenia
    was a premominantly Zoroastrian land' (Boyce, 1979: 84) in the late
    Parthian period. But small items of evidence, direct as in the case
    of *de fluviis* 23.4, or indirect, as in the case of the folklore
    tradition centred on Mher the Younger (Widengren, 1960: 65-67; 1965:
    208-10; 239; Boyle, 1976: 107-18; 1978: 59-73), suggest that there
    was a good deal of 'Armenianisation' at the popular level, whatever
    the fidelity of the priests to the tradition of Iranian Zoroastrian-
    ism.

90 Note Vian, 1963: 158-76; 202-15; Lévi-Strauss, 1958: 236-41; cf.
Loraux, 1979: 3-26.

91 It is important to take *de fluviis* 23.4 in context. The chapter as
a whole concerns the River Araxes, and much of it is taken from
the geographer Ktesiphon (cf. Laqueur, 1922: 2079). A great deal of
it concerns issues such as menstruation, impotence, virginity, blood,
and it seems clear that the story about Mithras was just one of many
local myths about the origin of the two sexes, and their relations.
And it looks very much as if we have here another instance of the kind
of Greek 'anthropology' so well discussed in the case of Herodotus by
Rosellini and Saïd, 1978: 949-1005.

92 Cf. Boyce, 1979: 110-111; note that both Kirder (Kartir) in the mid-
third century, and Basil of Caesarea in the fourth, stress the cult
of fire above all among these communities. But I do not think that
we can share Mary Boyce's evident feeling that these illiterate
scattered Zoroastrian communities in Anatolia had preserved their
religion unchanged, particularly in relation to 'non-theoretical'
issues. On the complexity of the situation recreated by the fragments
of Persian 'lore' see particularly Bidez-Cumont, 1938: I, 56-84;
Messina, 1930: 13-38.

93 It should, of course be noted that Cumont was quite properly reacting
against Lajarde, who believed this text to be evidence of female
membership of the Mysteries — like John Ferguson, 1954-55: 310. The
main tradition of Mithraic scholarship has at least preferred to say
simply that the passage is unintelligible.

94 As a matter of fact, his order is quite intelligible: lion, hyena
(two quadrupeds opposed in every sense), then raven, eagle/hawk (two
birds somewhat similar but in most senses opposed). But in order to
make such an observation, we need to know something of animal-
classifications in the 'encyclopaedia'.

95 Let us consign Felicianus's λεαίνας once and for all to the waste-
heap from which it came.

96 Aelian, *NA* 7, 22 tells about the *korokotta* a story similar to that
which Pliny tells of the hyena here. This stealthiness of the hyena
had a physiological cause — like other cowardly creatures it has a
large heart: Pliny, *HN* 11, 183, quoting Aristotle, *de part. anim.*
3, 4 (667a 20-23), who interestingly adds καὶ τἆλλα σχεδὸν πανθ᾽
ὅσα φανερῶς δειλὰ ἢ διὰ φόβου κακοῦργα, 'and all other creatures
which are obviously cowardly, or do harm because they are afraid'.
The physiognomic tradition gave this belief a slight twist, as in
Polemon, *de physiognomonia* 2, s.v. *Hyaena: valde stolida socors
facilis deceptu gulosa valde adultera, in penetralibus domus suae
submissa, foris fortis* ('terribly stupid, feckless, easily deceived,
greedy, much given to adultery, submissive in the privacy of home,
aggressive out of doors') (ed. Hoffmann ap. Forster, I p. 172.
18-20).

97 In general, the dog tends to be well thought of in the 'encyclopaedia', particularly insofar as it could be considered as typically
male, and endowed with admirable male qualities (Pliny, *HN* 8, 106;
Aelian, *NA* 7, 22). But as in so many societies (cp. e.g. Tambiah,
1969: 424-59; Leach, 1964: 31-2; 57), its revolting habits,

especially of scavenging, seem to have caused it to be more than a
little suspect. This ambiguity is perfectly betrayed in the physiognomic tradition, and especially Polemon, *de physiog*. 2 s.v. *Canis*:
*mansuetus, fidelis, patiens, auxiliator, tutor avidus, vigil propter
familiarium studium, litigans in necessitate sua, fortis in medio
domicilio suo, foris submissus, peregrini osor | cupidus, tenax,
iurgiosus, garrulus, gulosus, immundus morum pravorum, impudens,
vilis cupidinis* (ed. Hoffmann, ap. Förster, I. p. 174).

98 So far as I am aware, nothing has been written on ancient popular
witchcraft of any sociological value, which is scarcely surprising,
because the subject demands some considerable knowledge of the
anthropological literature on modern (and especially African) witchcraft. But the parallels between the witchcraft incidents of Apuleius's *Metamorphoses* (especially the story of Socrates, 1, 2-20,
and of Thelyphron, 2, 19, 1-31, 1 [Helm]) and these stories concerning the hyena are only too evident: both sets deal in oppositions, between night and day, reality and illusion, inside and outside, flesh and not-flesh, life and death; and in transformations of
shape. There are however some sensible remarks in van Thiel, 1971-72:
I, 194-200; and on élite categorisations of magic, note Garosi, 1976:
13-97.

99 The *locus classicus* on the *lamia* is Philostratus, *Vit. Apollonii Tyan.*
4, 25, cf. 8, 7, 9; a great deal of instructive material is to be
found in Schwenn, 1924: 544-96, though without the necessary analysis.
On the notion of the 'night watch' in Africa, see Lucy Mair (1964);
Mayer, 1970: 60-64.

100 It is true that a fish called *vitulus marinus* shared this trait with
the hyena (Pliny, *HN* 11, 151). Elsewhere, Pliny remarks that a magical stone was derived from the hyena's eyes *et, si credimus, linguae
hominis subditi futura praecinere* ('and, if we credit it, utters
oracular pronouncements when placed under someone's tongue': *HN* 37,
168 Mayhoff).

101 I would argue, in effect, that the hyena is simply the Mithraic version of the familiar insulting terms from the animal world applied to
women — or said to be their dams — well analysed by Nicole Loraux,
1978: 57-62, à propos Semonides 7, 94 West: it may be a term appropriate to the Mysteries' conception of salvation and its opposite, but
the technique of metaphorisation is at least as old as the Archaic
period.

102 Detienne, 1975: 49-79; 1977: 135-60; Vidal-Naquet, 1970b: 1278-97;
Rosellini and Saïd, 1978: 949-1005. I do not of course mean to imply
more than that Hesiod presents in a particularly explicit and formal
way a series of fundamental connections between men, women, gods,
animals, sacrifice, alimentary codes, agriculture and funerary practices which, though they were undoubtedly elaborated differently, and
partially transformed by intellectuals over centuries, remained characteristic of Greek anthropology until Christianisation. It was the
achievement of Sabbatucci, 1965: 41-83, to point out that 'mysteriosophical' religions realized their differences from what we may call the
mainstream of Greek religion precisely by denying some of these normal
— even axiomatic — associations. The Hesiodic analysis itself (as

elucidated above all by J-P. Vernant) stands, as it were, as an ideal-type in relation to the actual complexity of meanings and associations in the minds of historical Greeks (and Romans).

103 It seems likely to me that *CIMRM* 1584 (discussed p. 31 above) which shows Mithras and Sol holding a spit, apparently with meat skewered on to it, over the lighted altar, and the raven flying down to eat, while the bull's haunch lies on the ground, should be be understood as a representation of 'the first sacrifice'. If that is reasonable (and it must then be linked at once with other representations of spits, which occur in feast-scenes), it seems to me perverse to insist, as does E. Will, 1978: 528-31, that the killing of the bull by Mithras cannot be understood as a 'sacrifice'. If anything is clear about Mithras, it is his rôle as culture-hero, a kind of Persian Prometheus (which is indeed what he is called in the fragmentary glossary *P.Oxy. XV*, 1802[64]); and quite typically he is both a thief and a hunter. He *hunts* the heavenly bull, which is itself anomalous (a domesticated creature which is nevertheless wild). This is quite evident from the panel at Dura which shows Cautes and Cautopates carrying the bull lashed to a pole (*CIMRM* 42): this is a conventional scene on Greek vases showing hunts (Manns, 1890: plate 1 fig. 4, facing p. 22, with pp. 6-7; 1888: 13). But the killing of the hunted bull — which is of course why the scene is modelled upon the cliché of heroic subjugation of wild animals — *turns into* a sacrifice: Nature is transformed into Culture (and salvation) in the process, with anomalous god and anomalous victim as the mediators.

104 I find it quite extraordinary that W. S. Barrett should make absolutely no comment upon the significance of the outburst by Hippolytus in his commentary on ll. 616-68: for him, the play is just a series of tropes and 'parallels'. But for some better directed remarks, see Vernant, 1971: I, 133-34, and Loraux, 1978: 43-54. The physiognomic tradition presents some of the most perfectly oppositional passages in this regard: note especially Adamantius Sophistes, *Physiogn.* 2,2 (Förster I, p. 350).

105 But for some fragmentary beginnings, see Alvin Gouldner, 1967: 3-161, and the review essay by H. W. Pleket, 1971: 349-81. There is not even much worth reading on the most obvious aspect of the subject, the 'political' honour of Graeco-Roman élites. In essaying such a history, the best place to start seems to me Bourdieu (1977).

106 Apart from Keller, 1909-13: II, 1-12 (eagles), 13-26 (hawks); Thompson, 1936: 2-16; 65-67; and Sauvage, 1975: 161-175; 175-77, there is an acute discussion of Graeco-Roman ideas about eagles — in relation to the phoenix — in Hubaux and Leroy, 1939: 132-52, who pursue the theme in the writings of the early Fathers.

107 The story is told of the *haliaëtos* (the fishing eagle) by Aristotle, *HA* 9, 34 (620 a 2-5), whence it appears in Antigonus of Carystus, *Hist. mirab.* 46; and it is to be found of eagles in general in a number of Latin poets (Hubaux-Leroy, 1939: 133). One is almost forced to suppose that the belief is based partly upon a vernacular etymology (cf. Ardener, 1971a: 222-27; Collart, 1978: 15-18), which converted 'sea-eagle' (ἅλς : ἀετός) into 'sun-eagle' (ἥλιος : ἀετός),

though I know of no text which says this explicitly. Aelian, *NA* 10,
14 (and many other texts, cf. Thompson, 1936: 8-9) tells the same
story about the hawk.

108 Cf. *HN* 10, 6: only the Black Eagle was supposed to rear its own
young — and it was odd, because it had no cry. Pliny even avers
that eagles hate their offspring (10, 13-14), but compare Aelian,
NA 2, 40.

109 In the physiognomic writers, to resemble the eagle, whether in one's
nose, or in one's keen eyes, was a sign of *megalopsychia*: see, for
exmaple, [Aristotle] *Physiogn.* 61 (Forster, I p. 66.9-10); 68
(p. 76.15-16) etc. Olympiodorus, on Plato *Alcibiades* 1, 120eff.
p. 153.12-19 (p. 98 Westerink) says that the Persians were very keen
that a boy should look like an eagle, especially as regards the nose:
among them it was a sign of royal quality and a capacity to rule. In
that connection, we should perhaps remember that Achaemenes, the
founder of the Persian royal dynasty of that name, was supposed to
have been fostered by an eagle: Herodotus, 1,209, 1 and 4; Xenophon,
Cyropaed. 7, 1, 4; Aelian, *NA* 12, 21.

110 Cf. Aelian, *NA* 4, 20: γαμψώνυχον δὲ ἄρα οὐδὲ ἕν οὔτε πίνει οὔτε
οὐρεῖ οὔτε μὴν συναγελάζεται ἑτέροις, 'no bird with talons either
drinks or makes water, nor does it keep company with others'; this
permits us to link the hawk with the eagle in two crucial respects:
hostility to water (presumably because they are all flesh-eaters)
and solitariness. We should note here that the Egyptians believed
the hawk to be a 'bird beloved of god': when a hawk died and became
disembodied, it gave prophecies and sent dreams — became a mediator
between this world and the gods (Aelian, *NA* 11, 39). And in view
of the growing evidence for 'Egyptian' ideas in the Mysteries (Gordon
1978: 218), we perhaps should not dismiss this out of hand.

111 On the symbolic importance of breaking dietary norms, see Detienne,
1977b: 152-60 and his forthcoming book *La Cuisine du sacrifice*; in
relation to Christiantiy and its Jewish background, Soler, 1973:
943-55.

112 If to believe Pallas here I have to believe that the Mysteries were
infected with 'neo-platonism', as Professor Vermaseren claims (1978:
41), then I do indeed believe it. But of course the complaint is
entirely misconceived: the question is not whether the Mysteries
were 'neo-platonist'—and I do not quite know what such a claim
would involve one in showing — but why the Platonists of the second
and third centuries AD were interested in the Mysteries. Insofar as
Robert Turcan's book (1975) was conceived as an answer to that question, it must be counted a failure, for all its elegance and clarity
of exposition. We either believe that Euboulus, Pallas, Numenius
and Porphyry simply made up their information (which is a mere
apriorism) or we attempt to explore possible relations between their
observations and other properly Mithraic evidence; which is to claim
neither that they 'knew all' nor that every Mithraic Father would
have agreed with them. For me the question is an empirical one,
which does not mean that one starts with an empty head.

113 Or rather 'structuralism': cf. Ardener, 1971b: 449-67. Subscribing to
Sperber's critique of Lévi-Straussian structuralism, I am committed
neither to 'totality' nor to 'coherence'.

114 Nowhere is the tendency to disregard context more evident than in the current fashion for rewriting the content of the Mysteries so as to 'prove' that they were really some other cult which simply appropriated the name of Mithras, or that Mithras is 'really' some constellation in the sky. Cumont may have written a pseudo-history of the Mysteries in order to reconstruct their theology, but his fundamental assumption, that they were in some sense Iranian, seems to me quite indisputable: it is merely that he over-stated the case by constructing an excessively simple narrative concerning the relation between Iran and the Graeco-Roman world. What I have tried to show here is one aspect of the process of translation of an Iranian cult, embedded in an almost entirely different religious and cultural tradition, into one which could 'save' inhabitants of the Graeco-Roman world.

115 Cf. Zaretsky, 1974: 166-219 (on Spiritualists on the West Coast of the United States).

116 I am most grateful to Jan Bremmer for his helpful comments and criticisms, and am sorry only that printer's deadlines prevented me from incorporating more of them.

BIBLIOGRAPHY

André, J. 1967. *Les noms d'oiseaux en latin*. Etudes et commentaires, 66. Paris.

Ardener, E. 1971a. Social anthropology and the historicity of historical linguistics. *Social anthropology and language* (ASA Monographs, 10), pp. 209-41 (ed. E. Ardener). London.

Ardener, E. 1971b. The new anthropology and its critics. *Man*, n.s. 6, 3, 449-67.

Arndt, W. F. and Gingrich, F. W. 1957. *A Greek-English lexicon of the New Testament...* (adapted from Bauer's *Wörterbuch*). New York.

Becatti, G. 1954. *Scavi di Ostia, II: I Mitrei*. Roma.

Beck, R. L. 1977a. Cautes and Cautopates: some astronomical considerations. *JMS*, 2, 1, 1-17.

Beck, R. L. 1977b. Mithraism and astrology. Unpublished paper presented to Dept. of Classics, University of Toronto, February 25.

Beck, R. L. 1978. Interpreting the Ponza Zodiac, II. *JMS*, 2, 2, 87-147.

Bidez, J. and Cumont, F. V. M. 1938. *Les mages hellénisés: Zoroastre, Ostanès, et Hystaspe d'après la tradition grecque*. 2 vols. Bruxelles-Paris.

Bollack, J. 1969. *Empédocle, II: Les Origines. Edition et traduction des fragments et des témoignages*. Paris.

Bonnet, H. 1952. *Reallexicon der ägyptischen Religionsgeschichte*. Berlin.

Bouché-Leclercq, A. 1899. *L'astrologie grecque*. Paris.

Bourdieu, P. 1977. *Outline of a theory of practice*. (ET, with altera-tions, of *Esquisse d'une théorie de la pratique*, Paris, 1972.) Cambridge.

Boyce, Mary. 1975. *A history of Zoroastrianism, I: The early period*. Handbuch der Orientalistik (ed. B. Spuler), I, 8, 1, ii, 2a. Leiden-Köln.

Boyce, Mary. 1979. *Zoroastrians: their religious beliefs and practices*. London, Henley and Boston.

Boyle, J. A. 1976. Mher in the carved rock. *JMS*, 1, 2, 107-18.

Boyle, J. A. 1978. Raven's rock: a Mithraic *spelaeum* in Armenian folklore? *Études mithriaques* (Proceedings of the Second Mithraic Congress, Tehran 1975), pp. 59-73 (ed. J. Duchesne-Guillemin). Acta Iranica, 17. Téhéran-Liège.

Bremmer, J. 1978. Heroes, rituals and the Trojan war. *Studi storico-religiosi*, 2, 5-38.

Buffière, F. 1956. *Les mythes d'Homère et la pensée grecque*. Paris.

Bulmer, R. 1967. Why is the cassowary not a bird? A problem of zoological taxonomy among the Karam of the New Guinea Highlands. *Man*, n.s. 2, 1, 5-25 (repr. in Douglas, 1973: 167-93).

Campbell, B. 1978. The marriage of soldiers under the Empire. *JRS*, 68, 153-66.

Campbell, L. A. 1968. *Mithraic iconography and ideology*. EPROER 9. Leiden.

Cassin, Elena. 1965. Techniche della guerra e strutture sociali in Mesopotamia nella seconda metà de II millennio. *RSI*, 77, 2, 445-455.

Chaumont, M-L. 1965. Le culte de la déesse Anāhīta dans la religion des monarques d'Iran et d'Arménie au ler siècle d.n.è. *JA*, 253, 167-81.

Collart, J. 1978. L'oeuvre grammaticale de Varron. *Varron: grammaire antique et stylistique latine*. Publications de la Sorbonne, série Études, 14: Recueil offert à J. Collart, pp. 3-21. Paris.

Cumont, F. V. M. 1899. *Textes et monuments figurés relatifs aux mystères de Mithra*. Vol. I. Bruxelles.

Cumont, F. V. M. 1942. Le coq blanc des Mazdéens et les Pythagoriciens. *CRAI*, 284-300.

Cumont, F. V. M. 1945. Rapport sur une mission à Rome. *CRAI*, 386-420.

Cumont, F. V. M. 1949. *Lux perpetua*. Paris.

Cumont, F. V. M. 1975. The Dura Mithraeum. *Mithraic Studies*, I, pp. 151-207 (ed. J. R. Hinnells). Manchester.

Detienne, M. 1972. *Les jardins d'Adonis: la mythologie des aromates en Grèce*. Paris.

Detienne, M. 1974. Orphée au miel. *Faire l'histoire*, III, pp. 56-75 (eds. J. Le Goff and P. Nora). Paris.

Detienne, M. 1975. Les chemins de la déviance: orphisme, dionysisme, pythagorisme. *Orfismo in Magna Grecia* (Atti del 14 Convegno di studi sulla Magna Grecia, Taranto, October 1974), pp. 49-79. Napoli. (Published, January 1979.)

Detienne, M. 1976. Potagerie des femmes ou comment engendrer seule. *Traverses*, 5-6, 75-81.

Detienne, M. 1977a. *Dionysos mis à mort*. Paris.

Detienne, M. 1977b. La viande et le sacrifice en Grèce ancienne. *La Recherche*, 75 (February), 152-60.

Detienne, M. and Vernant, J-P. 1974. *Les ruses de l'intelligence: la mètis des Grecs*. Paris.

Dieterich, A. 1923. *Eine Mithrasliturgie*. 3rd. ed., by O. Weinreich. Leipzig-Berlin.

Douglas, Mary. 1966. *Purity and danger: an analysis of concepts of pollution and taboo*. London.

Douglas, Mary (ed.). 1973. *Rules and meanings: the anthropology of every day knowledge. Selected Readings.* Harmondsworth.
Douglas, Mary. 1975. *Implicit meanings: essays in anthropology.* London, Henley and Boston.
Edmonds, H. 1938. Geistlicher Kriegsdienst: der topos der militia spiritualis in der antike Philosophie. *Heilige Überlieferung: Festgabe I. Herwegen, pp. 21-50.* Münster-Westfalen. (Repr. in Harnack, 1905: Darmstadt, 1963.)
van Essen, C. C. and Vermaseren, M. J. 1965. *The excavations in the Mithraeum of the Church of Sta Prisca in Rome.* Leiden.
Ferguson, J. 1954-55. More about Mithras. *Hibbert Journal,* 53, 319-26.
Ferrua, A. 1940. Il Mitreo sotto la Chiesa di S. Prisca. *BCR,* 68, 59-121.
Festugière, A-J. 1972. *Etudes de religion grecque et hellénistique.* Paris.
Francis, E. D. 1975a. Mithraic graffiti from Dura-Europos. *Mithraic Studies,* II, pp. 424-45 (ed. J. R. Hinnells). Manchester.
Francis, E. D. 1975b. Menandrian maidens and Mithraic lions. *Glotta,* 53, 43-66.
Garnsey, P. D. A. 1970. Septimius Severus and the marriage of Roman soldiers. *California Studies in Classical Antiquity,* 3, 45-53.
Garosi, Raffaela. 1976. Indagine sulla formazione del concetto di magia nella cultura romana. *Magia: studi di storia delle religioni in memoria di R. Garosi,* pp. 13-97. Roma.
van Gennep, A. 1909. *Les rites de passage: étude systématique des rites.* Paris.
Goold, G. P. 1977. Manilius, *Astronomica* (ed. and comment.: Loeb edition). Cambridge, Mass., and London.
Gordon, R. L. 1972. Mithraism and Roman society: social factors in the explanation of religious change. *Religion,* 2, 2, 92-121.
Gordon, R. L. 1975a. Franz Cumont and the doctrines of Mithraism. *Mithraic Studies,* I, pp. 215-48 (ed. J. R. Hinnells). Manchester.
Gordon, R. L. 1975b. Contributions to the First Plenary Discussion, printed in *Mithraic Studies,* I, pp. 125-34 (ed. J. R. Hinnells). Manchester.
Gordon, R. L. 1976. The sacred geography of a *mithraeum*: the example of Sette Sfere. *JMS,* 1, 2, 119-65.
Gordon, R. L. (with J. R. Hinnells). 1978. Some new photographs of well-known Mithraic monuments. *JMS,* 2, 2, 198-223.
Gordon, R. L. 1979a. The real and the imaginary: production and religion in the Graeco-Roman world. *Art History,* 2, 1, 5-34.
Gordon, R. L. 1979b. Reason and ritual in Greek tragedy. *Comparative Criticism* 1 (ed. Elinor Shaffer), pp. 279-310. Cambridge.
Gossen, H. 1914. Art. 'Rabe'. *RE,* cols. 19-23.
Gouldner, A. W. 1967. *Enter Plato: classical Greece and the origins of social theory.* London. (New York, 1965).
Griffiths, J. G. 1970. *Plutarch's De Iside et Osiride: edited with an introduction, translation and commentary.* University of Wales Press.
Gundel, W. 1925. Art. 'Leo' 9. *RE,* cols 1973-92.
Gundel, W. 1941. Art. 'Phosphoros'. *RE,* cols. 652-54.
Gundel, W. and H. G. 1950. Art. 'Planeten'. *RE,* cols. 2017-2185.

Gundel, W. and H. G. 1966. *Astrologumena: die astrologische Literatur in der Antike und ihre Geschichte*. Sudhoffs Archiv, Beiheft 6. Wiesbaden.

Harnack, A. von. 1905. *Militia Christi: die christliche Religion und der Soldatenstand in den ersten drei Jahrhunderten*. Tübingen. (Repr. Darmstadt, 1963.)

Henderson, J. 1975. *The maculate muse: obscene language in Attic comedy*. New Haven and London.

Hinnells, J. R. 1975. Reflections on the lion-headed figure in Mithraism. *Monumentum H. S. Nyberg*, I, pp. 333-69 (ed. J. Duchesne-Guillemin). Acta Iranica. Téhéran-Liège.

Hopfner, Th. 1913. *Der Tierkult der alten Ägypter*. Denkschriften der kaiserl. Akademie der Wissenschaften in Wien, Phil.-hist. Klasse, 57. Abh. 2. Wien.

Hubaux, J. and Leroy, M. 1939. *Ly mythe du Phénix dans les littératures grecque et latine*. Bibliothèque de la Faculté de Philosophie et Lettres de l'Université de Liège, 82. Liège-Paris.

Insler, S. 1978. A new interpretation of the bull-slaying motif. *Hommages à M. J. Vermaseren*, II, pp. 519-38 (eds. M. de Boer and T. A. Edridge). EPROER 78. Leiden.

Kane, J. P. 1975. The Mithraic cult-meal in its Greek and Roman environment. *Mithraic Studies*, II, pp. 313-51 (ed. J. R. Hinnells). Manchester.

Keller, O. 1909-13. *Die antike Tierwelt*. 2 vols. Leipzig. (Repr. Hildesheim, 1963.)

Kelly Heyeb, S. 1975. *The cult of Isis among women in the Graeco-Roman world*. EPROER 51. Leiden.

Kirk, G. S. 1978. Review of Detienne, *The Gardens of Adonis* (1977). *Times Literary Supplement*, 18 August, pp. 922-23.

Kittel, G. and Friedrich, G. 1964-74. *Theological Dictionary of the New Testament*. 10 vols. (Edited and translated by G. W. Bromiley: compare Kittel-Friedrich, *Theologisches Wörterbuch*, 8 vols., 1930-73.) Grand Rapids, Michigan.

Körner, S. 1930. *Die homerische Tierwelt*. 2nd. ed. München.

Kugler, F. X. 1907. *Entwicklung der babylonischen Planetenkunde von ihren Anfänge bis auf Christus: Sternkunde und Sterndienst in Babel, I*. Münster Westf.

Kuiper, F. B. J. 1961-62. Remarks on the Avestan hymn to Mithra. *IIJ*, 5, 36-60.

Laeuchli, S. 1967. Mithraic dualism. *Mithraism in Ostia: mystery religion and Christianity in the ancient port of Rome*, pp. 46-66 (ed. S. Laeuchli). Evanston, Ill.

Laqueur, R. 1922. Art. 'Ktesiphon' 3. *RE*, col. 2079.

Leach, E. R. 1964. Anthropological aspects of language: animal categories and verbal abuse. *New directions in the study of language*, pp. 23-63 (ed. E. H. Lenneberg). Cambridge, Mass.

Leach, E. R. 1966. *Rethinking anthropology*. LSE Monographs on Social Anthropology, 22. 2nd ed. London.

Leach, E. R, 1978. Review of Detienne, *The Gardens of Adonis*. Man, n.s. 13, 4, 684-85.

Lentz, W. 1970. The social functions of the Old Iranian Mithra.

W.B. Henning Memorial Volume, pp. 245-55. London.

Lesky, E. 1951. *Die Zeugungs- und Vererbungslehren der Antike und ihr Nachwirken*. Akademie der Wissenschaften zu Mainz, Abh. der Geistes- und Sozialwissenschaftlichen Klasse (1950), 19. Wiesbaden.

Lévi-Strauss, C. 1958. *Anthropologie structurale*, 1. Paris.

Lévi-Strauss, C. 1962. *La pensée sauvage*. Paris.

Lewis, I. M. 1971. *Ecstatic religion: an anthropological study of spirit possession and shamanism*. Harmondsworth.

Lewy, H. 1956. *Chaldaean oracles and theurgy: mysticism, magic and platonism in the Later Roman Empire*. Recherches d'archéologie, de philologie et d'histoire, 13. Le Caire/Cairo. (Repr. Paris, 1978.)

Loraux, N. 1978. La race des femmes et quelques unes de ses tribus. *Arethusa*, 11,43-87.

Loraux, N. 1979. L'autochthonie: une topique athénienne. Le mythe dans l'espace civique. *Annales ESC*, 34, 1, 3-26.

Mair, Lucy. 1969. *Witchcraft*. London.

Manns, O. 1888. 1889. 1890. *Über die Jagd bei der Griechen*. Printed in three parts in the Jahresbericht der Königl. Wilhelms-Gymnasium zu Cassel: I, Jahresbericht Ostern 1887-Ostern 1888, p. 7-38 (containing sections 1 and 2); II, Jahresbericht 1888-89, pp. 3-30 (section 3.1); III, Jahresbericht 1889-90, pp. 3-21 (section 3.2). Cassel.

Mayer, P. 1970. Witches. Inaugural lecture, Rhodes University, S.A., 1954. Repr. in *Witchcraft and Sorcery*, pp. 45-64 (ed. M. Marwick). Penguin Modern Sociology Readings. Harmondsworth.

Messina, G. 1930. *Der Ursprung der Magier und die zarathuštrische Religion*. Scripta Pontificii Instit. Biblici. Rome.

Neue, F. 1902. *Formenlehre der lateinischen Sprache*. 4 vols. 3rd ed. by C. Wagener. Leipzig. (1892-1905 in fact.)

Nouailhat, R. 1975. Remarques methodologiques à propos de la question de 'L'hellénisation du christianisme'. Syncrétisme, herméneutique et politique. *Les syncrétismes dans les religions de l'antiquité* (Colloque de Basançon, Oct, 1973), pp. 212-32 (eds. F. Dunand and P. Lévêque). EPROER 46. Leiden.

O'Brien, D. 1969. *Empedocles' Cosmic Cycle: a reconstruction from the fragments and secondary sources*. Cambridge.

Peek, W. (ed.). 1968-75. *Lexicon zu den Dionysiaka des Nonnos*. 4 vols. Hildesheim.

Pembroke, S. G. 1967. Women in charge: the function of alternatives in early Greek tradition and the ancient idea of matriarchy. *JCWI*, 30, 1-35.

Pembroke, S. G. 1970. Locres et Tarente: le rôle des femmes dans la fondation de deux colonies grecques. *Annales ESC*, 25, 1240-70.

Piccaluga, G. 1965. *Elementi spettacolari nei rituali festivi romani*. Quaderni di SMSR, 2, 5-174.

Piccaluga, G. 1974. Adonis e i profumi di un certo strutturalismo. *Maia*, 26, 33-51.

Pleket, H. W. 1969. Collegium Iuvenum Nemesiorum: a note on ancient youth organisation. *Mnemosyne*, ser. 4, 22, 281-98.

Pleket, H. W. 1971. Griekse ethiek en de 'competitive society'. *Lampas*, 3, 349-84.

Pokorný, O, 1975. Der Ursprung der Gnosis. *Gnosis und Gnostizismus*,
  pp. 749-67 (ed. K. Rudolph). Wege der Forschung, 262. Darmstadt.
  (Repr. from Kairos, 9, pp. 94-105.)
Rehm, A. Art. 'Hesperos'. *RE*, cols. 1250-57.
de Robertis, F. M. n.d. *Storia delle corporazione ... nel mondo romano*.
  2 vols. Bari.
Rosellini, M. and Saïd, S. 1978. Usages des femmes et autres *nomoi*
  chez les 'sauvages' d'Hérodote: essai d'analyse structurale. *ASNP*,
  ser. 3, 8, 3, 949-1005.
Rostovtzeff, M. I. *et al.* 1939. *The excavations at Dura-Europos:
  Preliminary report of the seventh and eighth seasons (1933-4, 1934-5)*.
  New Haven.
Sabbatucci, D. 1965. *Saggio sul misticismo greco*. Quaderni di SMSR,
  4, 7-235.
Sander, E. 1958. Das Recht der römischen Soldaten. *RhM*, 101, 152-91;
  193-234.
Sauvage, A. 1975. *Etude des thèmes animaliers dans la poésie latine*, I.
  Collection Latomus, 143. Bruxelles.
Schiess, T. 1888. *Die römischen collegia funeraticia nach den Inschrif-
  ten*. Munchen.
Schumpeter, J. A. 1951. *Imperialism and social classes* (ed. P. M.
  Sweezy). Oxford and New York.
Schuster, M. 1931. Art. 'Mel'. *RE*, cols. 364-84.
Schwenn, F. 1924. Art. 'Lamia' 1. *RE*, cols. 542-46.
Smith, J. Z. 1978. *Map is not territory: studies in the history of
  religions*. Studies in Judaism in Late Antiquity (ed. J. Neusner),
  23. Leiden.
Soler, J. 1973. Sémiotique de la nourriture dans la Bible. *Annales ESC*,
  28, 943-55.
Sperber, Dan. 1974. *Le symbolisme en géné 1*. Paris. (ET, *Rethinking
  symbolism*, 1975.)
Steier, A. 1926. Art. 'Löwe'. *RE*, cols. 968-990.
Steiner, G. 1975. *After Babel: aspects of language and translation*.
  Oxford.
Tambiah, S. J. 1969. Animals are good to think and good to prohibit.
  Ethnology, 8, 4, 424-59. (Partly repr. in Douglas, 1973: 127-66.)
van Thiel, H. 1971-2. *Der Eselsroman*. 2 vols. Zetemata 54/1, 2.
  München.
Thompson, D'Arcy W. 1936. *A glossary of Greek birds*. 2nd ed. London.
Todorov, T. 1967. Le récit primitif. *Tel Quel*, 30, 47-55.
Todorov, T. 1970. *Introduction à la littérature fantastique*. Paris.
Turcan, R. 1975. *Mithras platonicus: recherches sur l'hellénisation
  philosophique de Mithra*. EPROER 47. Leiden.
Turcan, R. 1978. Note sur la liturgie mithriaque. *RHR*, 194, 2, 148-57.
Turner, V. W. 1969. *The ritual process: structure and anti-structure*.
  L. H. Morgan Lecture, 1966. London.
Turner, V. W. 1974. *Dramas, fields and metaphors: symbolic action in
  human society*. Ithaca and London.
Vermaseren, M. J. 1950. A unique representation of Mithras. *VChr.*,
  4, 142-56.
Vermaseren, M. J. 1951. The miraculous birth of Mithras. *Studia*

archaeologia G. van Hoorn, pp. 93-109. Amsterdam.

Vermaseren, M. J. 1963. *Mithras, the secret god.* London.

Vermaseren, M. J. 1978. *Le monument d'Ottavio Zeno et le culte de Mithra sur le Célius.* Mithriaca IV: EPROER 16.4. Leiden.

Vernant, J-P. 1971. *Mythe et pensée chez les Grecs.* 4th ed. 2 vols. Paris.

Vernant, J-P. 1974. Le mythe prométhéen chez Hésiode, in *Mythe et société en Grèce ancienne*, pp. 157-75. Paris.

Vernant, J-P. 1977. Sacrifice et alimentation humaine à propos du Prométhée d'Hésiode. *ASNP*, ser. 3, 7, 3, 905-40.

Vian, F. 1963. *Les origines de Thèbes. Cadmos et les Spartes.* Paris.

Vidal-Naquet, P. 1968. The Black Hunter and the origin of the Athenian *ephebeia.* PCPhS, 194 (n.s. 14), 49-64.

Vidal-Naquet, P. 1970a. Ésclavage et gynécocratie dans la tradition, le mythe, l'utopie. *Recherches sur les structures sociales dans l'Antiquité classique*, pp. 63-80. Besançon-Paris.

Vidal-Naquet, P. 1970b. Valeurs religieuses et mythiques de la terre et du sacrifice dans l'Odyssée. *Annales ESC*, 25, 1278-97.

Vidal-Naquet, P. 1974. Le cru, l'enfant grec et le cuit. *Faire l'histoire*, III, pp. 137-68 (eds. J. Le Goff and P. Nora). Paris.

Vollgraff, W. 1960. Le rôle des lions dans la communauté mithriaque. *Hommages à Léon Herrmann*, pp. 777-85. Collection Latomus, 44. Bruxelles.

Waltzing, J-P. 1895-1900. *Les corporations professionelles chez les Romains* ... 4 vols. Louvain.

Wheeler, A. L. 1930. Tradition in the epithalamium. AJPh, 51, 205-23.

White, K. D. 1967. *Agricultural implements of the Roman world.* Cambridge.

Widengren, G. 1960. *Iranisch-semitische Kulturbegegnung in parthischer Zeit.* Veröffentlichungen der Arbeitsgemeinschaft für Forschung des Landes Nordrhein-Westfalen, Geisteswissenschaften, Heft 70. Köln-Opladen.

Widengren, G. *Die Religionen Irans.* Die Religionen des Menscheit, 14. Stuttgart.

Will, E. 1978. Origine et nature du Mithriacisme. *Études mithriaques* (Proceedings of the Second Mithraic Congress, Tehran 1975), pp. 527-36 (ed. J. Duchesne-Guillemin). Acta Iranica, 17. Téhéran-Liège.

Willetts, R. F. 1955. *Aristocratic society in ancient Crete.* London.

Willis, R. G. 1967. The head and the loins: Lévi-Strauss and beyond. *Man*, n.s. 2, 4, 519-34.

Willis, R. G. 1974. *Man and beast. Approaches to anthropology.* London.

Winnington-Ingram, R. P. 1948. Clytaemnestra and the vote of Athena. *JHS*, 68, 130-47.

de Wit, C. 1951. *Le rôle et le sens du lion dans l'Égypte ancienne.* Leiden.

Witt, R. E. 1975. Some thoughts on Isis in relation to Mithras. *Mithraic Studies*, II, pp. 479-93 (ed. J. R. Hinnells). Manchester.

Wüst, E. 1935. Über einige Probleme der Mithrasmysterien. *ARW*, 32, 211-227.

Zaretsky, I. I. 1974. In the beginning was the word: the relationship of language to social organisation in Spiritualist Churches. *Religious Movements in Contemporary America*, pp. 166-219 (eds.

  I. I. Zaretsky and M. P. Leone). Princeton.
Zeitlin, Froma. 1978. The dynamics of misogyny; myth and mythmaking in
  the Oresteia. *Arethusa*, 11, 149-84.

VI

The sacred geography of a *mithraeum*: the example of Sette Sfere

The recent publication of the Ponza *mithraeum* with its ceiling zodiac, now more fully interpreted by R. L. Beck,[1] has served to remind us of one of the central problems of the mysteries of Mithras: the nature of the cult's use of astronomical symbolism. One of the most familiar Mithraic temples is Sette Sfere in Ostia (Reg. II, Ins. VIII. 6), perhaps discovered by Petrini early in the nineteenth century, and excavated by Lanciani in 1886.[2] It has been exhaustively described by Franz Cumont (1891: 5–23; 1896: 243–245, no. 84) and by Becatti (1954: 47–51). Yet its potential interest has not been fully explored. To a degree, that has been because of errors;[3] perhaps still more through a readiness to adopt *ad hoc* explanations for some of its features rather than attempt a systematic enquiry. Yet beyond those factors is a more important one: the sheer banality of the zodiacal sequence on reliefs persuades us that we comprehend their significance – their familiarity reassures us. Cumont's general notion that the zodiac and the planets were the object of worship in the mysteries passes for our solution. And it is precisely this general assumption of Cumont's that caused him to neglect the detailed exploration of the astronomical-astrological implications of the Mithraic monuments known already in the late nineteenth century; and even after the discovery of Santa Prisca and the Mitreo di Felicissimo.[4] The mysteries were not conceived as capable of selection and manipulation of generally available beliefs: they had to be dominated by genethliacal astrology. This interpretation was of a piece with his understanding of the relation between grades and planets. He held that the souls disembarrassed themselves of accumulated earthly evils as they passed through the planetary spheres after death.[5] This view of the matter, based on extra-Mithraic evidence inevitably, has been rendered unconvincing by more recent discoveries.[6] And new work has suggested the attractive possibility that the mysteries were perfectly capable of distinguishing astronomical concerns from astrological ones.[7]

I take it for granted, unlike Cumont, that religion is a rational enterprise: it seeks to impose specific cognitive 'grids' upon the experience of the believer, and employs specific means to reinforce its categories in so far as these are not already shared much more widely within the society in which it exists. It is at the same time constantly generative of new meanings, just as language permits us to generate ever new fictive worlds: religion one might say is *deliberately* polysemous in its search for particularity and in-clusiveness.[8] Symbols do not 'mean' one thing, as Cumont's language of 'personification' so clearly implies: they are terms in a semantic code which are as open-ended as the terms in the linguistic code; and every transposition to another semiotic mode simply enlarges their self-generative capacity. At most one can attempt to describe some rules within which new symbols are generated. And that is my task here.

I

We may begin with Euboulus' familiar point that the first *mithraeum* was conceived by Zoroaster specifically as an image or likeness of the cosmos, whose demiurge Mithras is: πρῶτον μὲν . . . Ζωροάcτρου αὐτοφυὲc cπήλαιον . . . ἀνιερώcαντοc εἰc τιμὴν τοῦ . . . Μίθρου, εἰκόνα φέροντοc αὐτῷ τοῦ cπηλαίου τοῦ κόcμου, ὅν ὁ Μίθραc ἐδημιούργηcε (ap. Porphyry, *De Antro* 6 [=Nauck², 60, lines 4–9]=Arethusa, 8, lines 15–19).[9] Now evidently the notion of the 'cosmos' need not be taken in a merely ideal sense: a *map* would be static of course but a *likeness* would have to move, just as the elements of the heavens 'move'. We have three terms: the actuality of the cosmos; a likeness of it; an inert map of it, like a star chart. The likeness mediates between the extremes of actuality and of human map-making: part human, part divine. The *mithraeum* is like a statue of a god in that respect. Now there can be two ways of representing such movement symbolically: by opening the temple to actuality, by admitting evidence of cosmic change from the cosmos itself, as Professor Lentz has forced us to recognize; or by means of the implications of static internal symbols, whose semantic 'charge' would be virtually the same.[10] And of course *temps religieux* can be transposed to quite a different semiotic mode by means of the calendar of ritual acts, which makes some time 'inert' and other time 'alive'.

A 'moving' *mithraeum* is a characteristic religious fiction; and it is the essential seedbed for the dependent symbols which organized for the adherents of the mysteries their sacred space, which in turn is the essential preliminary to the validation of those symbols in ritual. The speaker of a language does not question either the lexical items available to him or the rules of his language: he uses them, but is their creature. So the believer enters into a set of symbols which he did not make, but which he can use on their own terms. That is the justification for the following indicatives.

Sette Sfere is the only excavated *mithraeum* which tells us much about Mithraic beliefs about sacred space: for the most part a few isolated symbols were deemed adequate – which functioned as signs of the full range of possibilities. Benches, niches, odd statues, all are part of a language largely non-intelligible to us. But Sette Sfere provides something like a code-key.

As one enters Sette Sfere,[11] two symbols catch the eye (Becatti, 1954: pl. VI. 1; *CIMRM* fig. 72). On the floor by the south wall (the wall immediately to the left of the entrance), slightly off-centre, is a U-shaped basin, 0·45 m. across, set in the floor, as in many excavated *mithraea*. Near the corner of the right-hand bench is a dagger in mosaic. Cumont suggested that they were linked: the basin might have been for the blood of victims (1891: 9–10). Yet the very frequency of such basins in the same liminal spot suggests a different symbolism, concerned with beginnings. Now we may argue from the existence of pipes in some other such basins that they were for water. In that first *mithraeum* of Zoroaster's the water came from a stream; τῶν μὲν κρατήρων cύμβολον τῶν πηγῶν φερόντων καθὼc παρὰ τῷ Μίθρᾳ ὁ κρατὴρ ἀντὶ τῆc πηγῆc τέτακται ([Nauck², 69 lines 1–3]=Arethusa, 18,

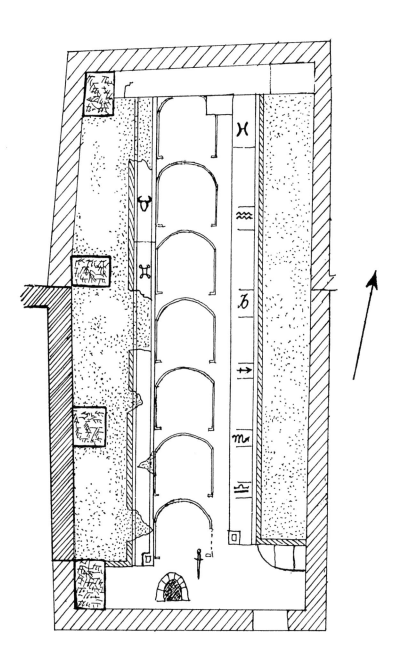

Figure 1 Plan of Sette Sfere (the representation of the zodiacal signs has been conventionalized)

lines 24–26) adds Porphyry in a later passage (*De Antro* 17). We may conclude that this basin was conceived as a symbol of that original spring in the mountains of Persia, of which every *mithraeum* at one level is a reproduction. At this level every *mithraeum* reproduces those actions of Zoroaster: it makes a historical reference to the beginning. At the same time, by being a *reproduction* it negates history: it pretends that the present can be just like the past.

But this 'stream' is also a liminal symbol. From that point of view it serves to set the *mithraeum* apart as *espace sacré*, a statement of its otherness, of its being not *earth*, but the passage between earth and heaven. At this point two notions of movement come together: the *mithraeum* reproduces the movement of the heavens, as I have just suggested, but it is also the locus of the spiritual journey between earth and heaven. It 'moves' in a double sense. Further, the cosmos, which the *mithraeum* reproduces, is evidently the space between earth, taken as first term (it is not conceived as a planet for example), and the fixed heaven, which is beyond it: it is a kind of passage between them.

The water is, as it were, the barrier of purity. We may infer from *De Antro* 15: ὅταν μὲν οὖν τοῖς τὰ λεοντικὰ μυουμένοις εἰς τὰς χεῖρας ἀνθ' ὕδατος μέλι νίψασθαι ἐγχέωσι ... οἰκεῖα νίπτρα προσάγουσι, παραιτησάμενοι τὸ ὕδωρ ὡς πολεμοῦν τῷ πυρί ([Nauck², 67, lines 6–15] = Arethusa, 16, lines 25–30) that water was the normal means of purification in the mysteries, unless some special reason caused it to be inappropriate, as in the case of the grades Leo and Perses. Touching water is part of the ritual of escape from the world; and the appearance of this 'spring' at the entrance suggests that ritual contact with it upon one's entering was a means of reintegration with the sacred, as well as a recapitulation of one's initiation ritual into each grade.

The meaning of a word, in a full sense, is not given by the relevant entry in a lexicon: it is rather constituted by the sum total of its uses by all speakers of that language both past and present.[12] In the same way the meaning of this liminal basin is not exhausted by the fact of its liminality. For it refers also to the role of water not only in the rituals (about which we know little) but in the verbal representations of belief, in the myths. We may say it is a *sign* of such beliefs and actions.

Porphyry (*De Antro* 17–18), in the passage from which my earlier quotation is taken, discusses the connection between water and generation. He explains that honey is used as protection against physical decay (purity: pollution), and provides the Nymphs with a useful symbol of the purifying power of water: εἰς τὸ ἄσηπτον τῶν ὑδάτων ὧν ἐπιστατοῦσι καὶ τὴν κάθαρσιν αὐτῶν καὶ τὴν <εἰς> γένεσιν συνεργίαν, συνέργει γὰρ γενέσει τὸ ὕδωρ ... (there follows the passage quoted above after a clause about bees storing their honey in craters and amphorae) ([Nauck², 68, lines 20–22] = Arethusa, 18, lines 21–23). We may tentatively suggest that it was partly a Mithraic connection between water and generation which prompted Porphyry to give the example he actually gives. Now such a connection may be referred to in those monuments in which Oceanus with crater or a water symbol is associated with generation, as in *CIMRM* 778 (Merida: Oceanus leaning on a dolphin and holding the remains of a cornucopia) or 2334³ (Sinitovo: Oceanus with crater and holding a tree with five branches); but also by the monuments in which Oceanus with crater appears in the bull-killing scene, whose association with generation is fundamental, whatever the complexity of its 'full' meaning.[13] And it may be that *CIMRM* 666 (Firenze: Mithras *petragenes* with Oceanus below, with a hole from the back to his mouth) registers some relation between Oceanus and birth – specifically the *petra genetrix*, which is also explicitly fiery, as in the third scene on the left at Marino – about which we can only speculate.[14] But a connection in the mysteries between water and generation is implied even more clearly by some other monuments.

First we may take *CIMRM* 694 (Bologna) with 1127 (Heddernheim III). On the first, against a background roughened to represent rock, is Cautopates with a bull's head at his feet, and to his left a conventional representation of growing plants. Higher up, on his right, is a crater with water flowing out, and finally a crescent moon. Face C of the monument from Heddernheim III seems to suggest a connection betweeen Cautopates and Oceanus, just as the corresponding lateral face suggests one between Cautes and Caelum. Both monuments show a crater gushing with water – streamlike – and at least on the Bologna piece, the crater is definitely associated with Cautopates and Luna (note 1347 [Strasbourg] for a repetition of this pairing). It scarcely needs to be pointed out that Luna is the tutelary planet of the grade Perses, one of whose functions was to be φύλαξ καρπῶν (*De Antro* 16 ([Nauck², 67, lines 13–15]=Arethusa, 16, lines 30–32). In this position the bull's head seems to be a reference to the effects of Mithras' act rather than Taurus:[15] now that achievement is usually taken in the iconography in its *spiritual* sense, in the feast-scene between Mithras and Sol with its explicit role as legitimator of Mithraic ritual, as on the reverse of the Konjić relief *CIMRM* 1896. But here we have a reference to the first level meaning, the generation of vegetable life. In other words the Bologna relief is a more explicit version of the symbolism of those monuments on which Cautopates is associated with the bull's sprouting tail.[16] Although it shows us no water, the Bonn altar (Wortmann, 1969: 410–23) can also be seen in this context, with its explicit association between the lunar crescent and the fertility created by the bull's death, and its reference to the sacrifice in the *patera* beneath the testicles (cf. perhaps *CIMRM* 1857b).[17]

We may take next *CIMRM* 1974 (Apulum) with 1706 (Carnuntum: not from a mithraeum), both otherwise unremarkable monuments. 1974 shows the raven in the usual place but perched on a crater; 1706 represents on the left-hand face a raven, an ear of corn and a snake in vertical sequence. The clear association here between the bird and these particular aspects of the bull-killing suggest that the raven may have been thought to have some particular link with the first level sense of generation. An association highly suitable in so far as the raven 'is' the grade Corax.[18]

One final association of the crater may also be adduced, though the problems raised by it are too complex to discuss fully here. A signal representation of a crater occurs on *CIMRM* 314 (Mitreo di 'Fagan', Ostia). The snake which entwines the lionheaded god is represented as both leaving and entering the mouth. Amid the uncertainties which surround the lion-headed figure one point at least seems clear: its association with generation (cf. 545, 879). The other lionhead found in the same *mithraeum* is of course the famous one dedicated in A.D. 190 by C. Valerius Heracles (*CIMRM* 312), whose four wings are decked with generalized symbols of fertility in the plant-world.[19] Other similar figures are also shown with a crater: the Wahlheim figure (*CIMRM* 1298) – though there are no palpable traces of a lion's mane – is surrounded by one (or two) snake(s) which emanates from and returns to a crater carved on the very torso. In *CIMRM* 103 one of the snakes descends from the god towards a crater on a small base on the right (Oxyrhynchus). In 1326 (Strasbourg) the lionhead is accompanied by a lion and a snake which entwines a crater.[20] These scraps of evidence lead in two directions. On the one hand, the association lionhead-snake-crater recalls the lion-snake-crater triad on the bull-killing reliefs, of which it is surely a representation (in other words, the lionheaded figure indeed does appear on the reliefs). And that same set of figures reappears on some of the so-called Schlangengefässe, the latest of which shows both a lion and a snake on the rim.[21] In effect, the lionhead appears in the *ritual equipment* of the mysteries in some sense, in a context in which the crater is the primary value. A 'lionhead-snake-entwined-bowl' was *used* for some purpose. I will return to this point later (p. 133). On the other hand, the motif of a lighted altar surrounded by a snake, which appears on the Oxyrhynchus monument (103), recurs in an unexpected place, the feast-scene between Mithras and Sol.[22] *CIMRM* 641b (reverse of the Fiano Romano monument) shows one of the torchbearers in an unusual activity (the other is serving). The one on the right is holding a *caduceus* towards a fire lit beside an altar entwined by a snake;[23] while on another feast-scene (798 [Troia, Lusitania]) the crater holds the same central position: both torchbearers seem to be serving, but between them is a large crater entwined by a snake, which seems to be entering the mouth.[24] Both of the Oxyrhynchus symbols associated with the lionhead appear in feast-scenes; while the caduceus on 641b cannot but remind us of the caduceus by the feet of one of the Fagan lionheads (312), itself beside the cock and pinecone, symbols otherwise associated with Cautes.[25] So in some sense the lionhead is 'present' at the feast, as well as at the bull-slaying. And a preliminary hypothesis might be that the crater is the source of souls, which ordinarily exist in time unless saved by Mithras: it is generative, but *bound to* generation; regeneration in the sense of salvation is part of the meaning of the feast-scene, which is the point at which the souls escape from generation into apogenesis. Such an hypothesis exists only to be disproved, of course: but it may provide a line of investigation so as to discover falsifying evidence. But the link between the crater and genesis is surely present in this context also.

These further meanings are then inherent in the liminal crater: it turns out to be a preliminary term quite as much as a 'barrier'. And therein lies an important ambiguity, characteristic of the mysteries: the same symbol refers in one context to separation *from* the world and in another to generation, to involvement *in* the world.[26] Yet those contexts meet in the symbol: it is a mediating term between opposites.

The second symbol to catch one's eye in the *mithraeum* floor is a dagger, its hilt towards the cult-relief end (actual NW.). Here we must be much more tentative, because Porphyry offers us little apparent guidance. For in *De Antro* 24 his explanation of the significance of the dagger, that it is the weapon of Ares (Mars), the planet whose domicile is Aries, the first equinoctial sign of the zodiac, can only be understood in the context of his argument, which is an account of why north and south in the mysteries are the points of genesis and apogenesis. To do that, he has to explain that Mithras is associated with an east–west axis, and his reference to the dagger is part of that explanation. Now I do believe that this was in some sense a Mithraic belief but it is context-specific:[27] so that although it inevitably refers to that belief, the liminal dagger cannot be fully understood in those terms.

At least though Porphyry (or rather perhaps, Numenius and Cronius, and indirectly their Mithraic informers) makes one point: that the dagger is specifically associated with Mithras. At the level of their discussion, it refers to Mithras' cosmic location on the line of the equinoxes (which is a crucially important Mithraic belief, as will appear). At another level, which is the usual explanation among modern scholars (Becatti, 1954: 48), the dagger refers to Mithras' sacrifice of the bull. Another floor mosaic in Ostia comes immediately to mind, roughly contemporary with Sette Sfere: near the cult-niche of the Mitreo degli animali (*c.* A.D. 160–170) is figured the bull's head. On the right as one looks from the cult-niche is its tail; and on the left a sacrificial knife of the common Roman type (Becatti, 1954: 89, fig. 19).[28] The greater explicitness of these symbols (which, it may be remarked are not *liminal* but intestine), though tending to confirm the usual interpretation of the Sette Sfere dagger, excludes the pregnancy of the latter. For although the dagger recalls Mithras' sacrifice, perhaps it also does much more.

Now the dagger may be said to be Mithras' natal instrument quite as much as his bull-killing weapon: almost all the representations of his birth show him holding it.[29] The dagger has a history within the narrative sequence between Mithras' birth and his ascension, as we shall see. But it seems also to have a pre-history. One of the panel-scenes on the obverse of the Dieburg relief – in fact the first – shows a figure sitting on a rock, holding a dagger; the next in sequence shows Mithras born from the rock, holding a dagger (and the next Mithras 'cutting reeds' with it) (*CIMRM* 1247A); and it is clear from two other monuments that the first figure sitting on the rock must be 'Saturnus', as Vermaseren rightly held. On the first (1656, Stix-Neusiedl) the reclining figure generally identified as 'Saturnus' (whatever such an identification means in a Mithraic context) is represented above the birth-scene: he touches Mithras as he is born.[30] On the other (1593: Ptuj III), which is mid-third century, 'Saturnus', in a similar position above the rock-birth, is being crowned by Victoria, and the dagger is set midway between him and Mithras (who is also represented as holding one).[31] The rock then 'belongs' to 'Saturnus'; and the obvious, though unconfirmable, implication is that the dagger also 'belongs' to him – that it is 'really' a *harpè*;[32] hence perhaps, Mithras 'cutting reeds' – or is it corn?

'Saturnus' then has some very important role in the myth of the origin, and therefore the meaning, of the dagger. It must be older than Mithras, and perhaps was conveyed to him because of its burden of meaning. It also receives special honour after the bull-killing: on 1137B (Rückingen), where neither Mithras nor Sol has a radiate crown, the dagger wears a crown with nine rays; while on 1083B (Heddernheim I), in the corresponding scene, the dagger supports a phrygian cap with a radiate crown (4 at least of whose rays are original): again neither god has one. It also figures once in Mithras' hand as he ascends in Sol's chariot, thus presumably finding a place in heaven.[33]

So the dagger has a specific history which is also connoted by the dagger in Sette Sfere. Analytically distinguishable is the latter's reference to the act which produces generation, and then salvation: *et nos servasti eternali sanguine fuso* (line 14, Santa Prisca). And there is another level yet of meaning, the use of swords within Mithraic ritual, in the rituals of prostration, binding and beseeching figured in the late bench-paintings at S. Maria Capua Vetere,[34] in the Miles ritual of the rejected crown proffered on a sword (Tertullian, *De Corona* 15. 3, dated A.D. 211 or earlier), in the ritual of death perhaps implied by the curious sword found by Cämmerer and Schwertheim in their recent re-excavation of the Riegel *mithraeum* (Kaiserstuhl), which has been cut in half and rejoined with a hoop of metal just large enough to fit round the waist.[35] And just as the crater is ambiguous, so surely is the sword: it is an instrument in these rituals of fear and death, as it is the means of killing the bull; yet both ritual and bull-killing are the means to life – the dagger unites, in its turn, the opposites of death and life.[36]

The two liminal symbols at Sette Sfere are then highly charged: the meaning of both is at the same time unintelligible to the uninitiated. They speak only to those who know. In their muteness to outsiders, they are expressions of the arcaneness of the mysteries. But to those who know, they resume central beliefs of the cult, expressed as narrative, as icon, as ritual and as cosmography elsewhere in the *mithraeum*.

II

I have already referred (p. 120) to Euboulus' account of Zoroaster's first *mithraeum* in the mountains of Persia 'with its interior arranged at corresponding intervals with symbols of the heavenly bodies and latitudes': τῶν δὲ ἐντὸς κατὰ cυμμέτρουc ἀποcτάcειc cύμβολα φερόντων τῶν κοcμικῶν cτοιχείων καὶ κλιμάτων (*De Antro* 6).[37] Now cτοιχεῖα is the technical term for the signs of the zodiac and the planets,[38] and of these I propose to deal first with the signs of the zodiac on the benches of Sette Sfere (see fig. 2, p. 127).

Fig. 1 (p. 121) shows that they are arranged in a sequence from top left to top right, that is starting and finishing beside the cult-relief. The order is

Aries	Pisces
Taurus	Aquarius
Gemini	Capricorn
Cancer	Sagittarius
Leo	Scorpio
Virgo	Libra

that is, an anticlockwise order, the most common order in ancient zodiacs.[39] Now normally in the astronomical/astrological writers the signs Aries-Virgo are taken as the northern signs, Libra-Pisces as the southern signs.[40] I propose to take that as an initial hypothesis here too. If we apply the hypothesis to Sette Sfere, the left hand side of the *mithraeum* will correspond to north, the right hand to south; which implies that the cult-relief end is east and the entrance-end west.[41] Now all of these directions are entirely arbitrary, in the sense that they do not correspond at all with the true 'real-world' orientation of the *mithraeum* (which is roughly SE.–NW., the cult-relief lying towards the north: see fig. 1). And surely this possibility of arbitrariness helps us to understand why *mithraea* are notoriously found facing in every conceivable direction: for what mattered was the interior organization, not necessarily some correspondence between this organization and the real world (even though that may have been true, as I have observed, of some *mithraea*).[42] Which suggests that the directions Euboulus mentions refer not to the relation *mithraeum*: 'real world' but to the relation *mithraeum*: (ideal) cosmos – which of course is what he says.

In the astrological writers this division of signs also corresponds to the seasons: Aries-Gemini = spring; Cancer-Leo = summer; Libra-Sagittarius = autumn; Capricorn-Pisces = winter.[43] Applied to Sette Sfere, this would mean that the left bench belonged to spring and summer, the right bench to autumn and winter. Each season would thus occupy a quadrant of the *mithraeum* as in fig. 2.[44] The same divisions in the astrological writers are often associated with day (Aries-Virgo) and night (Libra-Pisces).[45]

This gives us the following associations:

Left	Right
Spring	Autumn
Summer	Winter
Day	Night

Now this diurnal and seasonal symbolism immediately reminds us of one common mode of organizing the relief:

Sol	Luna
Cautes	Cautopates[46]

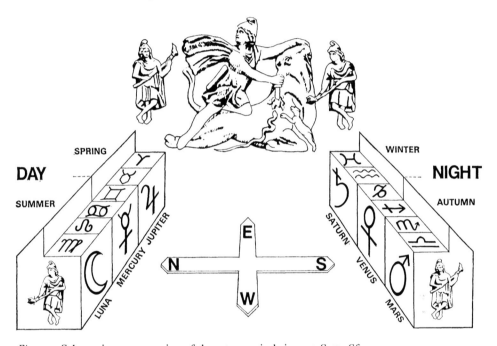

Figure 2 Schematic representation of the astronomical signs at Sette Sfere

If we accept for the moment the usual understanding of the symbolism of the torchbearers, it will be evident that on these reliefs it is the symmetry of the opposition Sol/Cautes: Luna/Cautopates which is being stressed; and this opposition corresponds precisely to the associations of the two benches, left = spring, summer, day; right = autumn, winter, night. Relief and *mithraeum* 'say' the same thing. But what of the reliefs which show the reverse association, Sol/Cautopates, Luna/Cautes?

In every *mithraeum* in which there was a pair of torchbearers at the *ends of the benches*, and whose positions are known from scientific excavation, they are placed as they occur at the ends of the benches in Sette Sfere: Cautopates on the left, Cautes on the right.[47] In other words, although the relief was deemed free to vary the positions of the torchbearers, the benches were not. Why not? Because the benches 'properly' correspond to north and south, although that cardinal significance also involves secondary associations with day and night, spring/summer, autumn/winter. And those directions in the mysteries are linked to the genesis and apogenesis of souls. It is worth looking again at *De Antro*, 24–25. Probably quoting Numenius and Cronius, Porphyry begins by saying that Mithras is set on the line of equinoxes, with north on his right and south on his left (a point I shall return to), the first of which is cold, the second hot. He proceeds (25): ψυχαῖc δ'εἰc γένεcιν ἰούcαιc καὶ ἀπὸ γενέcεωc χωριζομέναιc εἰκότωc ἔταξαν (that is, either Numenius and Cronius, or their Mithraic informants) ἀνέμουc διὰ τὸ ἐφέλκεcθαι καὶ αὐτὰc πνεῦμα, ὥc τινεc ᾠήθηcαν, καὶ τὴν οὐcίαν ἔχειν τοιαύτην. ἀλλὰ βορρᾶc μὲν οἰκεῖοc εἰc γένεcιν ἰούcαιc . . . ([Nauck², 73, lines 11–15]=Arethusa, 24, lines 15–18). The north is associated with coming-into-being and revivification;[48] the south is warm and frees souls from generation: ἡ μὲν γὰρ πήγνυcι ψυχροτέρα οὖcα καὶ ἐν τῷ ψυχρῷ τῆc χθονίου γενέcεωc διακρατοῦcα, ἡ δὲ διαλύει θερμοτέρα οὖcα καὶ πρὸc τὸ θερμὸν τοῦ θείου ἀναπέμπουcα ([Nauck², 73, lines 17–20]=Arethusa, 24, lines 21–23). Now earlier (6), quoting Euboulus specifically, Porphyry mentions a point which he wanders away from, but which in effect he now picks up, namely: οὕτω καὶ Πέρcαι τὴν εἰc κάτω κάθοδον τῶν ψυχῶν καὶ πάλιν ἔξοδον μυcταγωγοῦντεc τελοῦcι τὸν μύcτην, ἐπονομάcαντεc cπήλαιον <τὸν> τόπον . . . ([Nauck², 60, lines 1–4]=Arethusa, 8, lines 13–15).[49] But could there be any more appropriate symbol of *kathodos*, of descent, than Cautopates' downward-pointing torch; or of *exodos*, of ascent, than Cautes' upward-pointing one?[50]

The invariable association between Cautopates and the left bench, Cautes and the right bench is then explained by the cardinal symbolism of the *mithraeum*, betrayed by the organization of the zodiacal signs. It is this symbolism which is picked up by those reliefs which associate Cautopates with the left side of the relief and Cautes with the right side.[51] Here again, relief and *mithraeum* 'say' the same thing: but the statement is different from that in the first case. In effect, depending upon the 'grid' used, each side of the *mithraeum* had exactly opposite meanings, meanings which are yet thoroughly intelligible by means of the zodiacal order at Sette Sfere. Another, and highly contrived, ambiguity.

This hypothesis may also, however, be used as an unexpected confirmation of the Arethusa edition's reading of *De Antro* 24 at this point, which offers the brilliant guess that the names of Cautes and Cautopates have fallen out. I give its text: δημιουργὸc δε ὢν ὁ Μίθραc καὶ γενέcεωc δεcπότηc καὶ τὸν ἰcημερινὸν τέτακται κύκλον, ἐν δεξιᾷ μὲν <ἔχων> τὰ βόρεια, ἐν ἀριcτερᾷ δὲ τὰ νότια, τεταγμένου αὐτοῖc κατὰ μὲν τὸν νότον τοῦ καύτου διὰ τὸ εἶναι θερμόν, κατὰ δὲ τὸν βορρᾶν τοῦ <καυτοπάτου> διὰ τὸ ψυχρὸν τοῦ ἀνέμου (24, lines 11–15).[52] In his discussion of the Ponza zodiac, Professor Beck justly observes that this reverses the usually accepted symbolism of the torchbearers by associating Cautopates with genesis and Cautes with apogenesis (1976: 15 n. 10). But if we accept the argument that Sette Sfere associates the left bench (Cautopates) with north, which is also cold, the problem is resolved: that is the side of the *mithraeum* by which the souls come *into the world*, into genesis, from *above*. And the right side, that of Cautes, is south, the side of the *mithraeum* by means of which souls escape from the world, upwards, to *apogenesis*. 'Up' in the language of the mysteries means 'heat', and 'heat' means 'escape out of the world'; and 'down' means 'cold', and 'cold' means 'entry into the world'.

I think we can now correct Cumont's attribution of significance to the torchbearers so as to relate more closely to Mithraic belief. For him (1899: 211) they were simply *oppositional* terms:

Cautes	*Cautopates*
the morning sun	the evening sun
the spring sun	the winter sun
increasing heat	decreasing heat
the resulting fertility	the resulting death of vegetation
life	death

Now I do not believe that there is any adequate evidence for supposing that the torch-bearers personify, to use Cumont's improper term, the sun's aspects. They are associated rather with (1) the luminaries (Cautes with Sun, Cautopates with the moon) (2) the two seasons associated with the equinoxes, spring and autumn (3) consequently with (increasing) heat and cold (4) with the points of entry of the souls out of and into *genesis* (5) with *apogenesis* and *genesis* (6) with the southern and northern signs of the zodiac (7) with the seasons associated with these signs, autumn/winter, spring/summer (8) with the diurnal symbolism of these signs, night and day. In other words, quite logically, they end up representing the *opposite* of their initial 'meanings': a perfect Mithraic 'mystery' of ambiguity. The full complexity may be understood if we put these associations into list-form:

Cautes	*Cautopates*
Sun	Moon
Spring	Autumn
Heat	Cold
Exit from earth	Entry to earth
Apogenesis	Genesis
The southern signs	The northern signs
Autumn/winter	Spring/summer
Night	Day

The significances of the pair are tantalizingly intertwined; and perhaps that is why they are called *fratres* (*CIL* XIV 4315 = Becatti, 1954: 130 no. 7 with pl. XXXIX³ = *CIMRM* 308: probably late).[53] Now one of the properties of brothers is that they are the *same* (same father and mother) but *different*. Cumont's 'la valeur allégorique des dadophores mithriaques n'est point discutable...' (1899: 211) is profoundly untrue in the thinking of the mysteries: their associations slide ambiguously into each other. The nature of the successive oppositions is such that they keep blurring into each other's identity – in a sense they are the same, yet always opposed.[54] And perhaps the central point of their ambiguity is the nature of Mithraic genesis: the genesis associated with Cautopates is an earthly genesis, evidently good in so far as it is associated with Mithras' killing of the bull; but evil in so far as it implies also death, just as it comes from *cold*. The genesis associated with Cautes is (perhaps) a spiritual genesis, which involves escape from the world, a genesis which is therefore *sterile*.[55] No good then comes without loss: earthly fecundity spells death – but spiritual escape separates one from that desirable, and necessary, fecundity. The mysteries are not only about escape, but about life, itself a revealingly ambiguous notion in all religions dominated by an actual or potential opposition between the world and spirit.

The opposition-in-identity of the torchbearers bears some further discussion. It certainly may help us to understand why in so many monuments now one, now the other, is represented with attributes which a simpler view would be tempted to associate with one only: corn ears are a particularly good example, whether held in the hand or in the bull's tail;[56] and why sometimes they are given two *peda* or torches, one up, one pointing downwards.[57] Their ambiguity may also be conveyed by their stance with crossed legs – a fine symbol of opposition-in-unity. And perhaps some monuments may now receive a more perceptive explanation. In the later of the two Duran reliefs (*CIMRM* 42, A.D. 170/1), at least before the final alterations to the cult-niche, summer seems to have been represented on the right, winter on the left: cold to the left, heat to the right. In other words, the monument refers to the cardinal symbolism of the *mithraeum*. It is entirely consistent with this that, before erasure (perhaps simultaneous with the covering of the seasons with plaster), Luna was on the *left*, Sol on the right. It is equally consistent that the zodiacal order on the relief begins with the northern signs on the left.[58] In the last stage of the *mithraeum* (after A.D. 230), the back of the arch above the reliefs was provided with a zodiac in reverse order (Aries on the right, Pisces on the left) (Rostovtzeff *et al.*, 1939: 75, 102). And perhaps the explanation of this very unusual order is to be found precisely in a desire to represent the other associations of Cautes (on the right side of the *mithraeum*), not with *apogenesis* and heat this time, but with the sun and spring (the associations of the northern signs), and likewise for Cautopates. But this same reversal neatly puts the torchbearers' proper signs (Cautes: Taurus; Cautopates: Scorpio) in their 'proper' place, the other order remaining on the relief itself. In other words, the reversed zodiacal order has in a sense the same significance as the original representations for summer (right) and winter (left) on the relief: which is perhaps why they were covered over.

The two different orders at Dura recall the two orders in the Barberini *mithraeum* in Rome (390), though the zodiac attached to the fresco itself is the one which is reversed (*CIMRM* 390 is of course wrong about the order). The more usual order, with Aries on the left is found in the soffit of the arch of the cult-niche.[59] On the fresco Cautes is on the left, Cautopates on the right. So the fresco ingeniously recalls both the seasonal and diurnal/nocturnal associations of the benches while at the same time reminding us of the fact that Cautopates is cold (north), Cautes hot (south).

Finally, on the complex relief from Heddernheim I (1083A[11–14]) the seasons are represented in the following order:

Left panel	Right panel
Spring	Summer
Winter	Autumn[60]

Although the order here is apparent enough, its significance is not. But there may be another reference to the torchbearers' ambiguity. On the obverse of the revolving panel. Cautopates is shown on the left, so that we can see good reason to represent on his side both spring (the significance of the northern signs) and winter (cold: genesis); and likewise with Cautes on the right (summer: heat: apogenesis, but also autumn, the southern signs). But it must be noted that the formal design of the relief necessitated some decision about the order of the seasons, and the decisive factor may have been the desire to begin the sequence with spring near Aries. At the very least, however, the monument offers a happy consistency with the hypothesis.

III

Let us return to the zodiac in Sette Sfere. One of the simplest ways of relating the zodiacal signs to each other is the system of parallels, called by Firmicus Maternus the *antiscia*.[61] This form of association is by couples. Signs can be linked in two ways: by proceeding parallel to the axis which joins the equinoctial signs Aries and Libra; by proceeding parallel to the axis which joins the solstitial signs Cancer and Capricorn. Fig. 3 makes the procedure clear.

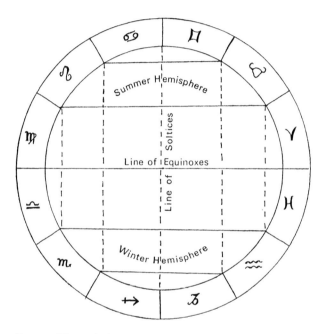

Figure 3 The antiscia

The first method links all the signs with the same latitude or zone (ὁμόζωνα, cύζυγα) in pairs. When the sun is in one or other term of these pairs, the day (and the night of course) is the same length in each – hence the astrologers' name ἰcoδυναμοῦντα (Ptolemy, *Tetrabib.* I. 16, etc.). By this method we obtain the following links between signs:

	Cancer	Gemini
	Leo	Taurus
	Virgo	Aries
Equator———	—————————————	———————————
	Libra	Pisces
	Scorpio	Aquarius
	Sagittarius	Capricorn

If we go back to Sette Sfere, we can see that each bench contains its own homozones: Aries-Virgo, Taurus-Leo, Gemini-Cancer (left bench) and Pisces-Libra, Aquarius-Scorpio, Capricorn-Sagittarius (right bench): each bench 'looks at itself' down the line of the equinoctial equator. Which implies two things: first, that the equinoctial equator lies down the *middle* of the *mithraeum*, between the two benches, which is exactly where it should be if *De Antro* 24 is correct, and the mysteries taught that as γενέσεως δεσπότης Mithras stands on, or is placed on, the line of the equinoxes with north on his right and south on his left. We can now see that Numenius and Cronius are referring to the place of Mithras in the *mithraeum*, with the left bench (north) on his right and the right bench on his left (south). In effect Mithras is imagined as looking west straight down the length of the *mithraeum*, which is the cosmos.[62] The second implication is that each bench may in itself be an ingenious series of 'equinoxes', in that each pair consists of periods when day and night are of the same length in each – imitations, as it were, of *the* equinoxes, though it is impossible to demonstrate that this was in fact how the Mithraists imagined the benches.

If we read the same diagram in the other direction, we see the connections between the signs which 'listen to each other' (ἀκούοντα). This reading gives the following relationships:

	Aries	Pisces
	Taurus	Aquarius
	Gemini	Capricorn
N—————————————————————S		
	Cancer	Sagittarius
	Leo	Scorpio
	Virgo	Libra

which of course is exactly the position of the signs in Sette Sfere. But this order is constructed in relation to the solstitial line, which comes therefore across the middle of the *mithraeum* in the place indicated in the diagram: above Cancer on the north, and below Capricorn to the south.

Now this division is also the one between the fast-rising signs (Capricorn to Gemini) and the slow-rising ones (Cancer to Sagittarius). The astronomical reason for this is that the ecliptic varies in its relation to the eastern horizon, so that it is most oblique during the winter and spring, and steepest in summer and autumn. If the Mithraists believed that Mithras occupied the east end of the *mithraeum* they may also have thought it appropriate that the signs in a sense 'nearest' the east should be placed nearer to Mithras, though I agree with Beck that it is difficult to see that this distinction can have been more than a casual additional complexity, since the desire to place north on Mithras' right (the left of the *mithraeum*) and south on his left must have been primary.[63] But the solstitial line must nevertheless have been important in the planning of the *mithraeum*, because it marked north and south 'precisely', the points of genesis and apogenesis. And, of course, it is on this line that we find the recesses in each bench which Cumont suggested were filled with water (1891: 11). Virtually all excavated *mithraea* possess them; but only one or two have yielded any interesting finds. At Sette Porte in Ostia, they were occupied by a pair of small altars, but uninscribed; fragments of a vase encircled by a snake were found in the right-hand niche in the *mithraeum* beneath the Palazzo dell'Arte in Rome (Circo Massimo), and in this *mithraeum*, as in Dura (phases II and III), a crater is set in the floor between the niches.[64] The observation that these niches are set on the solstitial line suggests at once the hypothesis that they represent the gates of heaven, through one of which, on the north, the souls descend into genesis, and through the other (south) ascend to apogenesis.[65] And if this is so, we begin to understand that otherwise puzzling shift in *De Antro* 24,[66] where Porphyry suddenly moves on to talk about Mithras' proper seat:

οὔτ᾽ οὖν ἀνατολῇ καὶ δύcει τὰc θύραc ἀνέθηκεν οὔτε ταῖc icημερίαιc, οἷον κρίῳ
καὶ ζυγῷ, ἀλλὰ νότῳ καὶ βορρᾷ · καὶ ταῖc κατὰ νότον νοτιωτάταιc πύλαιc καὶ ταῖc κατὰ
βορρᾶν βορειόταταιc, ὅτι ψυχαῖc καθιέρωτο τὸ ἄντρον καὶ νύμφαιc ὑδριάcι, ψυχαῖc
δὲ γενέcεωc καὶ ἀπογενέcεωc οἰκεῖοι οἱ τόποι. τῷ μέν οὖν Μίθρᾳ οἰκείαν καθέδραν
τὴν κατὰ τὰc icημερίαc ὑπέταξαν. . . .

The symbolism of the *mithraeum*-cosmos is utterly literal: the entrance and exit are inside the *mithraeum* itself, one on the north bench, the other on the south bench. This is the starting point of Porphyry's parallel between the Nymphs' cave and the *mithraeum*. In order to explain this, Porphyry has to go back to Mithras himself: it is because his proper seat is on the line of the equinoxes (i.e. down the middle of the *mithraeum*) that the gates of heaven are to the north and south. Porphyry and his sources are not talking about a relief surrounded by a ring-zodiac[67] but about the geography of the *mithraeum*. For it is surely only on that assumption that it becomes appropriate to introduce the mysteries at all at this point: he is, after all, glossing the Homeric description of the Nymphs' cave.

If the bench-niches are on the solstitial line, and represent the gates of genesis and apogenesis, what of the crater which, as I have remarked, is sometimes set between them? Is this crater the source of souls? A little later in *De Antro* Porphyry refers to a number of classical passages in which just such an association is explicit (31 = Nauck², 77, lines 15–21, Arethusa, 30, lines 5–10) and, as I have already suggested (p. 124 above), it would be in keeping with the appearance of the crater at the feast-scene, and with its specifically Mithraic associations with generation. The realization that the niches are the gates of heaven to a degree confirms that earlier hypothesis that the liminal crater is a condensed symbol.

We have seen that in a sense the benches 'belonged' to Cautopates (left-hand) and Cautes (right-hand). The relief was at the 'east' end. The important division on the line of the solstices implies that the 'eastern' half of the *mithraeum* may have 'belonged' to Mithras/ Sol, that is, the signs Capricorn–Gemini (the fast-rising signs). What then of the 'western' half, comprising the 'slow-rising' signs Cancer–Sagittarius? Although I do not wish to adduce too much evidence from beyond the data presented by Sette Sfere, it may be appropriate to recall here the representation of Luna in her *biga* on the 'west' wall of the Capua *mithraeum*, directly opposite the bull-killing scene.[68] The most plausible explanation of this opposition is surely that part of the *mithraeum* 'belonged' to Luna (and we have already seen how the two ends of the benches 'look at' each other, just as the two luminaries face each other at Capua). The opposition of the luminaries Sun and Moon on the relief corresponds, I think, to the opposition-in-unity of Cautes and Cautopates; and perhaps the east–west opposition of Mithras/Sol and Luna corresponds to some similar theme, conceivably the one which Beck plausibly argues lies behind the Ponza zodiac and its dragon, the interrelated course of the sun and moon which produces Time (1976a, Part II, forthcoming).[69]

But the implications of this opposition between the 'eastern' and 'western' halves of the *mithraeum* extend beyond this point. A fundamental principle in astrology opposes heat and light to cold and wet; the first pair is associated with day, the second with night. These αἱρέϲειϲ, *conditiones*, are naturally associated with the Sun and Moon. A corollary of this belief was that the stars (and especially the planets) rose in the east full of *wetness* and became progressively drier (more male) as they approached their culmination – marked by the solstitial line – and then progressively wetter (more female) as they approached the western horizon.[70] If we apply this to Sette Sfere, the stars rise at Mithras' end, progress down the *mithraeum* aisle and enter Luna's section of the temple to become progressively wetter and more female once they cross the solstitial line. Yet just as the right and the left of the *mithraeum* have ambiguous connotations through the ambiguity of the relation between the zodiac and the torchbearers, so perhaps do the 'eastern' and 'western' parts. For the astrological associations of the zodiacal quadrants represented in the *mithraeum* are as follows:[71]

Aries			Pisces
Taurus	wet	cold	Aquarius
Gemini			Capricorn
Cancer			Sagittarius
Leo	hot	dry	Scorpio
Virgo			Libra

The elemental connotations of the two sections separated by the solstitial line are exactly the reverse of those that they should have if the 'eastern' end 'belongs' to Mithras/Sol in any simple sense, and likewise with the 'western' end. Without the hypothesis that there is an opposition-in-association between eastern and western sections the association of wet and cold with Mithras/Sol is completely unintelligible. We must work on the assumption that every opposition is based upon some underlying unity or common term, as Lévi-Strauss so persuasively argues.[72] And here the unity is constituted by the relationship between the sun and the moon, aspects of whose treatment by the mysteries we can glimpse, without full understanding.[73] I will return to the relation between the two sections of the *mithraeum* later, in a context which is only superficially different.

Before we leave the zodiacal aspect of the *mithraeum* there are two further points to be noted, both of which concern Mithraic love of ambiguity or doubleness.

The astrological tradition had several ways of linking the zodiacal signs. Two of them, if not three, fit well with the preceding discussion.[74] Manilius, *Astron.* II 401–432, explains that when the zodiac is taken in its diametral aspect (διάμετρον, *diametrum*) the signs which are opposed to each other are moving in the opposite direction, and that when one is rising the other is setting.[75] Fig. 4 shows the relations established between the signs by this scheme, p. 135.

Now this aspect is one of the two perfect means of associating the signs. And it *links* signs which are *opposites*: a thoroughly ambiguous procedure. And that ambiguity resonates perfectly with the ambiguity of the relations, explored earlier, between eastern and western, northern and southern parts of the *mithraeum*, which are opposed but linked. By means of such a 'grid' we can see that the 'north-east' of the *mithraeum* is brought into ambiguous relation with the 'south-west': Aries and Libra are both male, and both equinoctial signs; but they are at opposite ends of the *mithraeum* and on opposite benches. Likewise the

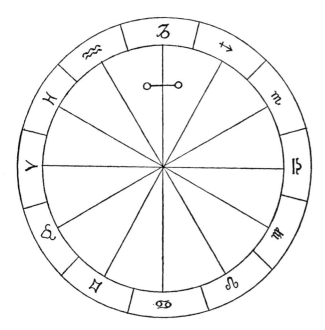

Figure 4 The diametrum

'north-west' is brought into ambiguous relation with the 'south-east' (see below, p. 142); this grid also links Taurus with Scorpio, the signs of Cautes and Cautopates, Leo with Aquarius, opposites in as much as the one is associated with fire and the other with water (as well as with cold) – though I cannot yet see any good Mithraic reason for linking them – and Cancer with Capricorn, the opposing tropics linked through the entry and exit of souls.[76]

The second relevant aspect of the zodiac is the τρίγωνον, *trigonum*. Now this is the only other perfect aspect, for by means of it, every sign is associated both left and right with its appropriate signs, as fig. 5 shows (p. 136).

The significance of this scheme is this:

1 Male: dry: fiery: Aries, Leo, Sagittarius
2 Female: cold: earthy: Taurus, Virgo, Capricorn
3 Male: hot: airy: Gemini, Libra, Aquarius
4 Female: wet: watery: Cancer, Scorpio, Pisces

If we apply this to Sette Sfere, it provides yet another link between the benches. In each case, two signs on one bench are linked to one on the opposite bench in terms of their associations with the elements which constitute the world. From the point of view of the trigonal aspect, the signs constitute four interlocking triangles. Each base lies on one bench, each point is constituted by one of the four central signs (Sagittarius, Capricorn, Gemini, Cancer). And if the *mithraeum* is a symbol of the cosmos, then surely we have here the symbols of the elements which make up the cosmos (fig. 6).

CMS

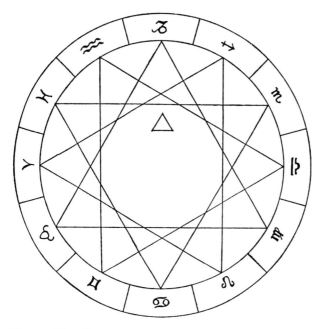

Figure 5 The trigonum

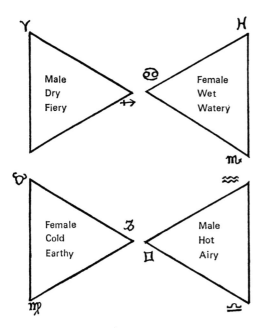

Figure 6 Scheme of triangles at Sette Sfere

The trigonal aspect may also provide us with a fresh hypothesis about the significance of Mithraic triangles whose interest has recently been commented upon by the late Dirk Wortmann and by W. Lentz.[77] A triangular monument set in the aisle of the *mithraeum* between the benches, as in the Mitreo delle Terme del Mitra at Ostia (Becatti, 1954: 31 with the fine photograph in Schütze, 1972: pl. 3), in the Palazzo dell'Arte,[78] the Terme di Caracalla (457) or at Spoleto (676; Lentz, 1975: 369), would be an appropriate reference to the trigonal aspect of the zodiac and so to the elements constituting the cosmos.[79]

A third zodiacal aspect may also be of importance: the quadrant (τετράγωνον). Although this was generally considered unfavourable by the astrologers it is relevant here because by means of it all four signs with the same function are brought into association as fig. 7 shows:

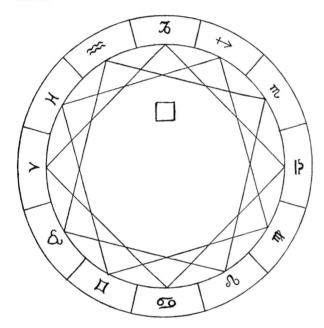

Figure 7 The tetragonon

The zodiacal aspect which associates all four τροπικά or cardinal points, Aries, Cancer, Libra, Capricorn, which are of the utmost importance in the mysteries, and which also associates the στερεά signs (see n. 47), Taurus, Leo, Scorpio, Aquarius, can hardly have failed to receive some attention.[80] On the other hand, I see no positive evidence in support of the thesis that it was an explicit theme in the mysteries, and leave the question open.

My second point about Mithraic ambiguity is this. From the preceding discussion (pp. 133 f.) it will be evident that parts of the *mithraeum* were conceived as 'belonging' to different divine *personae*, Mithras/Sol, Luna, Cautes and Cautopates. Now any group of four terms may respond to grid analysis (see overleaf).

From this, we can see that the following relationships are possible: Mithras/Sol–Luna;

Mithras/Sol	Cautes
Luna	Cautopates

Mithras/Sol–Cautes; Mithras/Sol–Cautopates; Luna–Cautopates; Luna–Cautes; Cautes–Cautopates. If we add the spatial relationships suggested by Sette Sfere, we see that in addition to the obvious oppositional relationships north–south, east–west, there are 'quadrant' relationships between the terms: Mithras/Sol–Cautopates; Luna–Cautopates; Mithras/Sol–Cautes; Luna–Cautes, as in fig. 8:

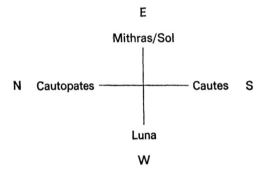

Figure 8 Oppositional relations at Sette Sfere

Such a mapping may of course have been grounds for location of certain rituals in different parts of the *mithraeum*, or for the location of statues; but we certainly have evidence for an association between Luna and Cautopates (p. 123), which we may now suggest may have had *spatial* significance too (the NW. quadrant); and probably there was a special relationship between Mithras/Sol and Cautes.[81] The relations of Mithras/Sol, Luna, Cautes and Cautopates constitute an intricately beautiful dance – each belongs now to one, now to another, each is opposed now to one, now to another. The geography of the *mithraeum* both maps a few steps in that dance (which was presumably transposed into other semiotic modes as well) and constitutes its very location.

IV

We may now turn to the representations of the planets at Sette Sfere. Their order (shown diagrammatically in fig. 2, p. 127) is this:

```
              E
    Jupiter        Saturn
N   Mercury        Venus      S
    Luna           Mars
              W
```

Now it is certain that this, if taken as a *simple sequence*, corresponds to no known order of the planets, whether Seleucid Babylonian, old or new Greek, horoscopal, days of the week or the proper Mithraic order.[82] Cumont himself considered at first that 'la disposition de ces figures à Ostie est arbitraire et due au caprice ou à l'ignorance de l'artiste' (1891 : 15), with the superb self-confidence of late-nineteenth-century classical scholarship; though later he tentatively suggested that there was a connection with the zodiac, and so with the horoscope of the foundation of the *mithraeum*.[83] Two hypotheses are open to us: first, that this order is specific to the mysteries, just as the grade/planet order is. But that would involve assuming that the order at Sette Porte was equally specific, and likewise at Spoleto:[84] and the notion that there could have been an endless set of odd planetary orders in the mysteries is lunatic, especially given our knowledge of the order associated with the grades. *One* Mithraic order is surely enough. The alternative, and much more likely, hypothesis is that the planetary orders found on the benches had some constant significance, just as we have seen that there is good reason to suppose that the significance of the Sette Sfere zodiac is generalizable.

   But what ? By taking each of the common planetary orders we can discover two possible, but hardly satisfactory, answers. If we take first the order of the planets according to their supposed dignity, Mercury, Venus, Mars, Jupiter, Saturn, Luna, [Sol],[85] we can see that there could be an attempt in Sette Sfere to oppose neighbours for some reason, as in fig. 9:

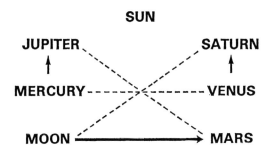

Figure 9 Possible orders of planets at Sette Sfere

   Luna is opposed to Saturn, Jupiter to Mars, Venus to Mercury. But whereas the first term of the two first pairs appears on the left bench, the first term of the last pair is on the right bench (Venus). And such an order makes no obvious sense. Again, we may take the chronocrators of the first hour of each day of the week ([Sol], Luna, Mars, Mercury, Jupiter, Venus, Saturn).[86] This is the order of Celsus' planets, though he puts them in the order Saturn→Sol. According to this scheme, we can see that the Sette Sfere order links the terms in pairs. Starting from the left and working round, we get Jupiter-Mercury, Luna-Mars, Venus-Saturn, as in fig. 9 again.

   The two pairs nearest the eastern end are linked, and there is a link between the benches at the western end. It is also true that the relation Saturn-Jupiter is the same as the relation Venus-Mercury (1 : 3 :: 2 : 4), and that the first term of the next pair is on the right (Mars), where it should be. But again, what is the purpose of such a complicated order? Until this question can be plausibly answered we will have to find a different approach to the problem.

It is a basic rule that whereas one item of evidence may generate any number of hypotheses, two immediately set limits. We must take Sette Sfere *with* Sette Porte, since these two are our only complete planetary orders on benches.[87] I give the two orders side by side for convenience:

Sette Porte	Sette Sfere	
Saturn	Jupiter	Saturn
Jupiter		
	Mercury	Venus
Mercury Luna	Luna	Mars
Venus Mars		

Now Sette Porte immediately reveals to us something that Sette Sfere conceals: that the order starts or finishes with Saturn, and then proceeds to Jupiter.[88] But what then? Surely in fact the rest of the planets are in *precisely the same order*, but set in a different direction, which one can show schematically thus:

The point becomes obvious when one realizes that in each case Mars and Luna are the *final terms* in the diagrams, as they so clearly are at Sette Sfere, being the only terms with only a single connection; or, to put it another way, that the only variable terms are Luna and Venus.[89] The order in each *mithraeum* must then start with Luna and end with Saturn: Luna, Mercury, Venus, Mars, Jupiter, Saturn.

Surely then one is looking at a Mithraic map of the order of the planets on the *night of creation*: for this is the order of the planets in the *night half* of the *thema mundi*, of which the zodiacal order on the benches is a schematic completion, with Cancer ascendant, and Aries culminating, as in fig. 10 (p. 141).

The night half of the *thema mundi* (the positions ascribed in astral lore to the signs at creation),[90] is the only grouping of the planets which necessarily excludes Sol, because that planet could not have a domicile in the night half of the circle: the Sun's unique domicile is in Leo just as Luna's is in Cancer, the point of genesis. So now we have an additional understanding of the exclusion of Sol from these bench orders: Mithras/Sol is on the wall at the east end of the *mithraeum* but he cannot be inside the *mithraeum* in the full sense, because in this context the *mithraeum* is a symbol of the darkened creation before light appears. Cumont was in a sense right: there is indeed a connection between the planetary order and the zodiac at Sette Sfere, and it is a horoscope: but it is the birth horoscope of the world. Yet the *mithraeum is* the world, and so it is a horoscope of the *mithraeum* too, but not in the way he imagined. Indeed the planetary arrangement in Sette Sfere is simply another aspect of the zodiacal order: there are not two problems, but a single polyvalent symbol of the secret teachings of the mysteries.

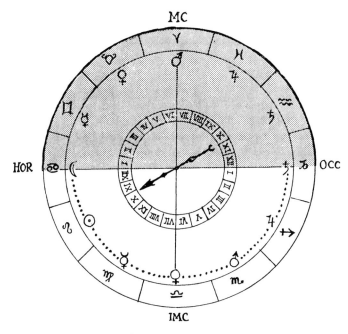

Figure 10 The *thema mundi*

Perhaps we may go further. If the order of the planets at both Sette Sfere and Sette Porte is indeed that of the *thema mundi*, we have additional evidence to support Beck's hypothesis that the Ponza zodiac is deliberately slewed so as to bring the zodiacal signs which are the solar houses of the planets into relation with the sun, and likewise with those which are the lunar houses (1976: 6), because the *thema mundi* specifically lays stress on this distinction.[91] If we add his observation that on the Walbrook and Siscia ring-zodiacs (*CIMRM* 810, 1472) Sol is set beside his domicile in Leo, we may suggest that both sections of the *thema mundi* were important in the mysteries: from one point of view the *mithraeum* is the world before the coming of light; but with the presence of Mithras/Sol – presumably as bull-killer – the world becomes the realm of light: the first night of creation becomes the first day. And perhaps this miracle is symbolized by another Mithraic paradox. From fig. 10 it is clear that the 'east' end of the *mithraeum*, taken as a map of the *thema mundi*, was the realm of night, and the 'west' end the realm of day (the ἡμικύκλιον ἡλιακόν). But this is the reverse of the Mithraic associations, just as we have seen that the elemental signifi-cance of the quadrants of the *mithraeum* reverse those associations (p. 134 above). Night becomes day in the 'eastern' end of the *mithraeum*; and day becomes night in the 'western' end. But then, so they do in the 'real' world. So the *mithraeum* is a chart of the first day and night, and of every other successive day and night, or rather, to recall my earlier phrase, a *likeness* which 'moves', a movement which is not only rectilinear, from east to west to east, but also circular, from spring to winter (east, north, west, south and back to east): and those two movements are the only perfect movements, the straight line and the circle. It begins to look as though Mithras is γενέcεωc δεcπότηc in more ways than one.

There is a final consideration. In a sense we knew that the *mithraeum* must from one point of view represent the cosmos on the night of creation all the time: for the evidence is in Porphyry, *De Antro*, 24. But no one has ever believed Numenius and Cronius to be speaking the truth. Accepting Beck's persuasive emendation of the passage (1976b: 95–98), Porphyry says: τῷ μὲν οὖν Μίθρᾳ οἰκείαν καθέδραν τὴν κατὰ ἰσημερίας ὑπέταξαν. διὸ κριοῦ μὲν φέρει Ἀρηίου ζῳδίου τὴν μάχαιραν, ἐποχεῖται δὲ ταύρῳ Ἀφροδίτης · ‹ὁ δὲ ζυγὸς Ἀφροδίτης› ὡς καὶ ὁ ταῦρος. But this is a clear reference to the planets' *lunar* houses: Aries and Taurus are only associated with Mars and Venus in the ἡμικύκλιον ϲεληνιακόν of the *thema mundi*. Numenius' and Cronius' point only becomes clear if we take fig. 10 as a map both of the *thema mundi* and of the *mithraeum*: Mithras/Sol is set at the east end *at* Aries, which is the domicile of Mars (Ares); and the next (ϲτερεόν) sign is Taurus, the domicile of Venus (Aphrodite). The Mithraic association between dagger and bull is *written* into the zodiac on the first night of creation: and that must be the *date* of the bull-killing. And just as Mithras' proper seat joins a sign which is a lunar domicile (Aries) with a sign which is a solar domicile (Libra), in a union of opposites, Cautes' sign Taurus (lunar domicile) is joined with Cautopates' sign Scorpio (solar domicile), thus confirming my earlier point about the ambiguous relations produced by a four-term series (p. 137). Cautes is now seen to be linked with Luna, and Cautopates with Sol. We have here the missing opposition-in-association between the NE. of the *mithraeum* and the SW., to balance the established opposition-in-association between NW. and SE. The Mithraists were nothing if not logical.

V

We come now to the last of the problems concerning Sette Sfere with which I want to deal: the seven spheres from which the *mithraeum* takes its modern name (see fig. 1, p. 121). For Becatti (1954: 50) these were the gates of heaven: 'simboleggiano . . . le sette porte del cielo attraversano le quali le anime dei fedeli dovevano passare nella sfere dei pianeti e delle stelle fissi, come ci dice Celso . . .'. Once again, Becatti follows Cumont's earlier view (which was actually Lanciani's, 1886: 164) without realizing that already in 1899: 485 he had suggested that the semicircles represented the 'sept sphères célestes'. Now although Cumont did not pursue this idea, and indeed in his later writings clearly takes Celsus' information as a correct presentation of Mithraic views about the fate of the soul, which I believe to be an error,[92] this seems to me more fruitful than the earlier idea. We may start with the passage from Euboulus which Cumont quoted in 1891: 12 n. 1, and from which I began my discussion of the zodiac in Sette Sfere (p. 126): ϲύμβολα φερόντων τῶν κοϲμικῶν ϲτοιχείων καὶ κλιμάτων. I have already pointed out that ϲτοιχεῖα means both zodiacal signs and planets. So what are κλίματα? They belong to the language of planetary (and zodiacal) chorography, the essential astrological assumption that the different planets and zodiacal signs governed specific parts of the earth. Astronomically and geographically, they are estimations of latitude spaced approximately according to the length of the solstitial day in summer; and they were crucial in the astrological calculation of ἀναφοραί.[93] Now although there was a good deal of disagreement among astrologers, it was commonly accepted that 'the astronomers' employed a scheme of seven (Bardesanes ap. Eusebius, *Praep. evangel.*, VI. 10. 36 ed. Mras): οἱ δὲ ἀϲτρονόμοι φαϲι τὴν γῆν ταύτην

μεμερίϲθαι εἰϲ ἑπτὰ κλίματα, καὶ ἄρχειν ἑκάϲτου κλίματοϲ ἕνα τῶν ἕπτα ἀϲτέρων.[94]
A late Christianized version of such a scheme is to be found in the *Hermippus*, II,
12–13 (pp. 52–58 Kroll), which postulates a central zone extending 13° on each side of
the equator, which is Paradise, and then successive latitudes of smaller size up to 48° of
latitude in an arithmetical regression 8, 7, 6, 5, 4, 3, 2.[95]

Now the point of the theory of κλίματα was to associate heaven and earth, to link
specific planets with specific parts of the earth. Could there be any more appropriate
symbolic scheme on the floor of a *mithraeum*? For the *mithraeum* is characterized by its
ambiguity as both a symbol of the cosmos, a map or likeness of heaven and its changes, and
as a human construction, part of earth: it *is* both heaven and earth at one and the same
time, the unique point of their meeting. The κλίματα are the astronomical/astrological
means of expressing exactly such an idea: the construction of the earth corresponds to the
construction of (part of) the cosmos.[96]

What then of the seven grades? Are they not also a means of conjoining heaven and
earth? (*Sub*) *tutela* declare the dipinti on the right wall of Santa Prisca,[97] and we should
take them seriously. For guardianship is a form of possession. As the κλίματα connect
heaven with earth, the Mithraic doctrine of guardianship connects living humans with
heaven, and with the same elements of heaven, the planets. But the planets are set
in a vertical hierarchy – in the Mithraic order, Mercury, Venus, Mars, Jupiter, Luna,
Sol, Saturn. To inhabit the grade is to inhabit the planetary sphere.[98] In effect, the
mithraeum is not only a horizontal map of the heavens on earth, it is a vertical bridge
between earth and heaven, just as the theory of κλίματα combines the principle of the
vertical sequence with the horizontal. We may represent this aspect of the *mithraeum*
diagrammatically:

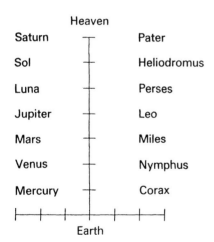

And from this we may surely identify the sequence of the κλίματα at Sette Sfere: they
correspond to the Mithraic order of the planets; they are condensed symbols of the grades
as well as of parts of the earth united by the middle term, the planets.

The theory behind astral chorography includes necessarily a belief in the character of the planets: the object was to apportion the terrestrial κλίματα according to the character of the corresponding planet. Although we possess no evidence on this point it would be entirely consistent for Mithraic chorography to have begun with Mercury as the planet dominating a latitude extending south from the Tropic of Cancer, the point of entry of souls into genesis, the grade Corax corresponding to this initial point; and to have proceeded southwards towards the Tropic of Capricorn, through the latitudes about the Equator, dominated by the planetary middle term, Jupiter (the guardian of the grade Leo, with its fiery associations).[99] The final term would be Saturn, associated with the latitude immediately to the north of the Tropic of Capricorn, the point of apogenesis – the planet which guarded the grade Pater.[100] The line drawn in some *mithraea* between what I have suggested to be the gates of heaven in either bench may support this argument for a Mithraic chorography.[101] The notion of planetary characters surely has a further importance, however, because by means of it we may begin to glimpse the Mithraic rationale for the peculiar planetary order adopted by the mysteries. The point is clearest for Saturn.

The ordinary astrological associations of Saturn are these: he was imagined to be an old man characterized by intelligence and wisdom rather than by physical vigour; by his connection with generative power and so paternity, which are linked with the god Saturnus/ Kronos, and indeed Chronos; and through his being the highest planet, with the notion of superordinate power.[102] A common physical (and mystical) theory was that the purest and most intellectual elements ascended towards the highest spheres, the domain of divinity; and consequently Saturn was the planet whose course was most rational and undeviating.[103] There were of course many other associations of Saturn: I have selected those which most clearly resonate with the character of the grade *Pater* in the mysteries.[104] It is extremely tempting to believe that it is these associations of Saturn with age and yet *pater*nity, with fruitfulness but also with wisdom, with power and majesty but also rationality, that caused the Mithraists to link the planet with the grade Pater and so upset the usual horoscopal order by placing Saturn before Sol and Luna in the hierarchy.[105]

Passing over Heliodromus whose solar associations are obvious, we come to Perses, one of the three grades about which literary sources tell us something: Porphyry, *De Antro* 16 observes that its proper initiation is with honey ὡς φύλακι καρπῶν, explaining that thereby the Mithraists τὸ φυλακτικὸν ἐν cυμβόλῳ τίθενται (see p. 123 above). The general astrological connection between the moon and fertility, and the specific Mithraic connection between Luna and the bull (through the fact that Taurus is the domicile of Luna), are too familiar to require rehearsal.[106]

Jupiter is the perfect median planet: equidistant from the coldness of Saturn and the heat of Mars. It is also pre-eminently beneficent.[107] But it seems more likely that the specific Mithraic associations of the grade Leo have more to do with the fact that Leo is the domicile of the Sun, although the location of its tutelary planet is exactly appropriate for a grade which was evidently conceived to be both the last of the 'lower' grades and the first of the 'higher' ones.[108] The last three planets in the Mithraic hierarchy, Mars, Venus and Mercury, are characterized by confusion and irrationality: Mars is 'impetuous' and 'capricious'; Venus like the Moon (cold) but heated by the Sun and heavily influenced by emanations from the earth; Mercury 'hermaphrodite', 'protean', 'unstable'.[109] Such general associations are entirely fitting for the tutelary planets of the first three grades of the mysteries, in which, we may conclude, the initiate learned to elude the temptations of fickleness and tergiversation.

This chorographic rationale for the connection between grades and planets (though it is undoubtedly partial) may also help us to understand the actual direction of the κλίματα in the floor of Sette Sfere, from west to east, up the line of the equinoxes, Mithras' proper seat.[110] Although I think it likely that from one point of view Mithraic chorography aligned the κλίματα from north (the point of genesis) to south (the point of apogenesis), from another it is wholly fitting that as symbols of the grades there should be a progression from the west (Luna) towards the east of the *mithraeum*, which belongs to Mithras/Sol, from night to day as it were, as well as from earth to heaven.[111] The symbols of the κλίματα are yet another instance of Mithraic love of doubleness, of 'mystery'.

VI

The central claim of the mysteries to authority and legitimacy rested precisely upon this complex of correspondences with the nature and the order of the cosmos. What the intellectuals of the Roman Empire knew about the constitution of the universe, the mysteries also knew. Reality legitimates belief beyond the possibility of disconfirmation. But where 'the astronomers' were merely interpreters, helpless spectators of powers they merely knew, the Mithraists had 'true' knowledge, and the true power which such knowledge affords. We may conceive of all utterance as placed somewhere upon a continuum between utter availability and utter opacity, between a pole at which nothing of the intended meaning is doubtful and a pole at which everything is obscure.[112] In the same way, the cognitive grid established by any new religion must inhabit a similar continuum between utter banality and total novelty: and the successful new cult is one which as it were plants one foot near one pole and the other near the opposite one. The mysteries do precisely that: the universe posited belonged to the public domain – it was 'real'; whereas the answer to it was new, 'private' and yet also immeasurably old, its authority guaranteed by Zoroaster, the fount of astrology.

The major problem which faces us is the formulation of an accurate characterization of the mysteries; and the problem which underlies that problem is the nature of our basic model. The legacy of Cumont (by which term I mean to refer to the generations which his life spanned, and certainly including A. D. Nock) offers one model, whose consonance with major traditions of western thought has helped to bring about its disastrous acceptance as *knowledge*, as truth inherent in reality:[113] individualist, sentimentalist, empirico-realist (by which I mean that the problems are supposed to be presented and constituted by the 'evidence'). In spite of (or perhaps because of) its adherence to a self-consciously different epistemology and problematic, the Chicago School has so far made little impression on this model in the field of the mysteries of the Graeco-Roman world.[114] Which is hardly surprising given the singular inappropriateness of its phenomenological categories to the analysis of dynamic religious forms. The explanation of religious change can be seriously undertaken only by the historical sociology of religion. In so far as religious categories are cognitive, they must respond to the wider cognitive changes which perpetually occur as a function of changing social and economic relationships. A recent theory of symbolism

(Sperber, 1975) may indeed provide the essential link between cognitive categories and symbolic constructs in the narrow sense. Of these cognitive categories, power is one of the most important, resonating as it does in every aspect of social relations. And religion is a form of discourse-and-action concerning the allocation and use of power within society.[115] Such a perception lies at the heart of the work of Peter Brown.[116] It is from this perspective that we realize that the Cumontian model is a mystification: for the proposition that the mysteries are to be understood exclusively in terms of escape from the world, of private gratification (one thinks at once of Nock's *Conversion*), contains the implication that they are, as we say, 'otherworldly'. But discourse about other worlds is inevitably a form of discourse about this one: the two are utterly complementary. Access to heaven is a form of power, power exercised and experienced according to rules: it does not matter what they are, so long as they can be legitimated. And among the endless makers of new rules in the Roman Empire are the adherents of the mysteries of Mithras. The real significance of Sette Sfere is that it enables us to chart some of those new rules more specifically, and so to achieve a more accurate characterization of the cult. The rationality of god is guaranteed by the order of heaven; his unambiguous moral character by his maintenance of that order and its changes; his involvement with earth by his concern for its fertility;[117] his power and his purity by his distance from earth. Initiation gives access to that power, in ever greater measure. The earth is punctured with 'Mithras-holes', unique meeting-points of heaven and earth, just as its physical geography is related to the order of the planets: the 'holes' are both the special points of divine penetration and the means of access to the full power of the divinity. Nothing could be more misleading than the notion that in the Roman Empire divinity was remote: the mysteries of Mithras constitute an entirely rational reformulation, in terms taken from current beliefs about the constitution of the cosmos, of the traditional theme of immanence. Only the rules for accession to power are clearer. The steps more articulate. And the recipients fewer.*

* I would like to thank Paul Bailey of the University of Manchester Audio-visual Department for figs. 2 and 9; and R. K. Britton of the University of East Anglia for figs. 1, 3–7 and 10.

Notes

1 See M. J. Vermaseren, 1974 and the discussion of R. L. Beck, 1976a: 1–19 (the second part to follow). I would like to thank Professor Beck for his trenchant and characteristically helpful comments on this article.

2 Becatti, 1954: 47, quoting Paschetto, 1912: 387–388, argues that the monuments *CIMRM* 245–249, now in the Vatican and found by Giuseppe Petrini in 1802–4, may have come from this *mithraeum*. Unfortunately the surviving records of this excavation do not support the hypothesis, though it remains possible. In fact it was Lanciani, 1886: 164, followed by Cumont, 1891: 9 n.2, who first made the suggestion. The *CIMRM* no. is 239. Date: Antonine, perhaps *c.* A.D. 160–80 (Becatti, 1954: 51).

3 Some of these are serious. The most important concerns the zodiacal signs along the top of each bench. Becatti (51) says that the zodiacal signs on the left side (as one faces the cult-relief) symbolize winter, those on the right summer. Of course the truth is the reverse. But

the error derives from Cumont, both in 1891: 14 and in 1896: 245(d), though he corrects this statement on p. 485 – not the only occasion on which Becatti wrongly follows a corrected view of Cumont. Much more puzzling, however, is Cumont's error over the order of the left-hand signs (followed by *CIMRM* 242). In 1891: 14 he gives the order from *entrance* to *cult-niche* as Aries-Taurus-Gemini-Cancer-Leo-Virgo (his *g* to *m*). This is repeated in diagrammatic form in 1899: 114 n. 7, which proves that it is not a draughtsman's error. In other words, Cumont thought that the *mithraeum* gave the zodiacal order in a double series, each beginning (looking from the entrance) with an equinoctial sign. Without remarking on the fact, Becatti (51) gives the left-hand order in reverse. This must be correct, since Taurus and part of Gemini at least survive, opposite Aquarius and Capricorn. In other words, the true order begins with Aries on the left bench at the cult-relief end, and proceeds anticlockwise to Pisces opposite on the right hand bench: see figs. 1, p. 121 and 2, p. 127.

While Lanciani, 1886: 163 wrongly identified several of the planets, Cumont, 1891: 14 first successfully placed them in the right order. It is therefore dismaying to find that Becatti's description (50) is simply unintelligible, a situation not helped by his confusion of true north and south at this point. Indeed his plan (49 fig. 10) simply omits the orientation, while *CIMRM* 239, fig. 71 puts north where south should be. Only Cumont gets it right on his map (1891: fig. A).

4 In 1891: 11–15 he allowed himself to be side-tracked away from a discussion of the significance of the zodiac and planets in the *mithraeum*; but even from 1896: 243–245 no. 84 and 1899: 109–115 it is not really clear what he thought to be the significance of the monument in more than general terms, in spite of a number of acute remarks. His report on the discovery of di Felicissimo and Santa Prisca is instructively vague, 1945: 386–420.

5 1899: 38; 309–310; 1942a: 140. Bianchi's interpretation of the York lionheaded figure (1975: 457–465) implies acceptance of this view, though the point is not argued; the reservations about this type of approach expressed by J. R. Hinnells, 1975b: 358–360, are well taken.

6 See Gordon, 1972: 97–98; 1975: 229–233.

7 For example, Wortmann, 1969: 410–423; Lentz, 1975: 358–377; Beck, 1976a: 1–19. Some of Lentz' ideas tend to be confirmed by the new *mithraeum* at Caesarea Maritima (Palestine), where there are two vault-scuttles, one of which may have acted as a simple *gnomon*: R. J. Bull, 1975 and personal information from Professor E. D. Francis.

8 I am here adapting some of the arguments of George Steiner, 1975: 229–232, directed towards the problems of 'meaning' in language with particular reference to translation.

The use of current work in literary criticism concerned especially with semiotics may indeed have much greater value than has been realized in providing a model for the specialist in ancient religion, because this study must always be limited in its reconstructive ambitions. We are not, and cannot be deemed to be, engaged in a fully 'scientific' or even historical enterprise, but in one much closer to the literary critic's. In an important sense, there are as many mysteries of Mithras as there are scholars to create responsible fictions. My ambition here is indeed primarily to stimulate further work which, by showing that there is a better way of relating items of symbolism, will serve to compel more sophisticated views of the beliefs of the mysteries than those presently current. The only delusion is to believe that we 'know' anything about the mysteries independently of our general interpretative framework.

9 'Zoroaster was the first to dedicate a natural cave in honour of Mithras. . . . This cave bore for him the image of the cosmos which Mithras had created . . .' (trans. Arethusa). It is extremely welcome that in Turcan, 1975: 23–43, we now have a modern, critical discussion of the problems connected with Euboulus and Pallas, though I cannot always follow him in his conclusions.

10 Although Professor Lentz' re-examination of the evidence concerning Mithraic temples, altars and triangles in particular is suggestive, it remains to be shown that natural light could have been admitted through the ceiling apertures of the Mitreo delle Terme del Mitra, say, or S. Clemente, given their subterranean position. But I certainly think it possible; just as it is possible that a similar end was achieved by means of artificial light.

11 I assume knowledge of the elementary features of the *mithraeum* and do not propose to describe it here. With the provisos noted in n. 3 above, Becatti's description is the most satisfactory, 1954: 47–51.

12 Steiner, 1975: 161–205 (see also 1971: 78–86).

13 As at Santa Prisca (Vermaseren and van Essen, 1965: 34–35 with fig. 9) and on Topham's water-colour of the fresco found near the Colosseum in 1668 (*CIMRM* 337).

14 Note, for example, Vermaseren, 1951: 100–102 and 1965: 35. A preliminary discussion of the Marino fresco is to be found in Lavagne, 1974: 191–201.

15 Taurus is exclusively associated with Cautes of course, Cautopates' normal sign being Scorpio, as on *CIMRM* 335 (with Cumont, 1896: fig. 63) and 693. For further complications, J. R. Hinnells, 1976: 44–45 (presumably the two instances of a scorpion with Cautes do not refer to the zodiacal sign). The most recent monument representing the feast-scene, the relief from Ladenburg now in the local museum (see Cämmerer *et al.*, 1972: pl. 14 and Hinnells, 1975a: pl. 11a), has the divine pair sat clearly upon the bull: the stool or table before them has legs made from the bull's hocks and hooves. 782 (Emerita, mysteriously omitted by Garcia y Bellido, 1967, though it appears inadvertently in the background of Pl. IV) shows a figure bringing the bull's head to the feast (see the photo in Schütze, 1972: pl. 98). In 966c 5 (Saarburg) the feast scene includes the bull's head and the raven. Luna appears in the top *left* corner of the reverse of the Fiano Romano relief 641b (feast-scene).

16 For example, *CIMRM* 1972 (Apulum), 2216 (Viminacium); Zotović, 1976: 202 no. 3; possibly also 1656, 1975 and 2062. But the interrelation between the torchbearers means that we also find Cautes in a similar connection with the bull: 415 and perhaps 593 are examples. See also Hinnells, 1976: 44–45, figs. 11–12. On the new monument from Tekija (Zotović, above), Cautes holds two corn ears, while Cautopates seems to grasp the tail. My later argument will reveal how simplistic my point in the text here actually is.

17 Some other monuments are also relevant in this connection. *CIMRM* 1765 (Aquincum) shows Cautes (R) and Cautopates (L) standing on the base, on either side of a crater. Cautes at least holds a *peltum*, Cautopates possibly a scorpion (see photo in Kuszinsky, 1937: fig. 42 a, b, c with pp. 305–306). Beneath this scene, on the lower part of the base, is a square hole with a small channel, possibly for water to run into a bowl inside. On the front cornice, a *patera*, and on either side of the base a raven (L)—perhaps with a torch in its beak; or a dagger? – and (R) a lion with an animal between its forepaws (Kuszinsky: 115 'Tier' against Vermaseren's 'ram': *CIMRM*, ad loc.). The association between the sacrifice of the bull and water seems assured, and the additional animals recall the Trier bowl mentioned below, n. 24. Compare the mosaic crater beside the torchbearers' caps in the floor of di Felicissimo, Ostia (Becatti, 1954: 107) and the torchbearers standing on handleless craters at Dieburg (1247A). The crater emanating two streams (of water?) on *CIMRM* 1891, now in the Sarajevo Museum, overwritten with a dedication to Mithras (1892 = Šašel, 1963: no. 112, though neither reading is correct) should also be mentioned (Patsch, 1904: 265–268 with figs. 139–140, clearer than *CIMRM* fig. 487), along with the isolated crater on the 1640 engraving of *CIMRM* 530 (Galleria Giustiniana, Rome, II pl. 82 = Cumont, 1896: 230, fig. 61) and possibly the odd object in a similar position on Montfaucon's engraving of *CIMRM* 204 (*Antiquité Expliquée*, 1719: pl. CCXVI. 2).

18 My silence upon the common assumption that in general the crater symbolizes the *element*

water is to be taken neither as assent nor as dissent. I fail to see any positive evidence in its favour, and the hypothesis seems to rely more upon an assumed schematism in the mysteries than upon testimony. It will also have been noticed that I have been studiously vague about the nature of the association between the crater and fertility; but there does not seem to me any evidence to make exactitude more than specious.

19 But not I think with the symbols of the four seasons, as Vermaseren suggests. The symbols are: two uncertain birds (top right wing), corn ears? (top left), leaves and a typical riverine god's 'reed' – which looks a little like an unripe maize plant (bottom right), a bunch of grapes (bottom left). My view is also that of Gsell, 1898: 48–49. Vermaseren's view is surely based on an unwarranted transposition from those lionheads which carry tropic signs or complete zodiacs arranged in triads: *CIMRM* 545 and 879.

20 Note also 1141 (Rückingen), a figure on a base clutching a crater to his breast: head lost.

The recurrence of globes and thunderbolts with lionheaded figures (*CIMRM* 665; globe only: 390, 543, 551; lightning only: 103, 321) reminds us of the tympanum above the Trier petragenes (985). Here a bird (presumably an eagle), a thunderbolt and a globe, symbols explicitly stated by 1127B (Heddernheim III) to represent Caelum, are placed alongside the lion-crater-snake triad. Such a combination recalls the mosaic floor of Sette Porte in Ostia, where we have an eagle, thunderbolt, crater and snake, and immediately in front of these, a crater set into the floor. These associations imply that the crater has some connection with heaven, at least in this context.

21 From a doubtful *mithraeum* (? Köln III), Ristow, 1974: 22 no. 14 and pl. 19 (mid-second century). This crater also has a unique vase representation of Mithras or Sol and the torch-bearers (Cautopates on L). No other monuments of this type are so explicit, however, for example *CIMRM* 1060 (Friedberg); 1020 with Ristow, 1974: 20 no. 9, fig. 14; 21 no. 13, fig. 16–17 (two snakes); 30 no. 36, fig. 24 (doubtful); 30 no. 35, fig. 22 (two snakes over a crater, also doubtful); *CIMRM* 1269 with Behn, 1929: 39; *CIMRM* 1220, 1221 with Schleiermacher, 1928: 54–55 nos. 1, 2; note also the evidence collected by Staehelin, 1948: 551–556 on similar vases in other cults. Note also Hinnells, 1975b: 355–356.

22 See most recently J. P. Kane, 1975: 313–351 who distinguishes between three different forms of representation on inadequate iconographical grounds; I also doubt the value of the comparative method he employs here.

23 The identification of the roughened area of the stone as fire seems to me fairly certain from autopsy. It might be connected with the tongs and hammer ('of Vulcan') on the left side of the base of 312. Cf. the blazing altar on 902 (Turcan, 1972: 24–25 and pl. V; also the excellent photo in Schütze, 1972: pl. 19). Mercury with caduceus probably appears in front of the quadriga of Sol accompanied by Mithras on *CIMRM* 1430 c3 (Virunum): is there a link here with the Fiano Romano feast-scene?

24 See now Garcia y Bellido, 1967: 36, no. 20 with the photo in Schütze, 1972: pl. 96. *CIMRM* 988 (Trier: bowl from Roman cemetery) is also worth noting, as Cumont pointed out in his discussion of the Fiano Romano relief (1946: 189–191). The feast, with Mithras, Sol and the torchbearers, is the background for a rare scene: a large lion occupies the centre of the field, above a crater entwined by a snake, with a raven on the right, a cock on the left (cf. 2295, feast scene with lion). Another Gallic monument, from Entrains, seems to transpose the theme of the snake-with-crater to a slightly later point in the myth: here the group stands in front of Sol's *quadriga*, with Luna on the top right, and perhaps the raven below (*CIMRM* 942 with Walters, 1974: 96–97 no. 27 and pl. XII). Crater and burning altar appear juxtaposed at di Felicissimo, Ostia, in the mosaic by the entrance, Becatti, 1954: 107; and 2243 (Radeša) shows a snake-with-crater at the feast-scene (*CIMRM* is surely misleading here).

VI

25 For example, 243[2], 532, 431a, 2306 and note 50 below. There is a similar association with a pine-cone on other lionheads: in 125 the two pine-cones have a hole in the top, possibly for offerings (Gsell, 1898: 48–49); in 544 the lionhead stands on a pine-cone, itself decorated with a lunar crescent.

26 I may quote here a passage from Roman Jakobson (1959: 238): 'In poetry verbal equations become a constructive principle of the text: syntactic and morphological categories, roots and affixes, phonemes and their components (distinctive features) – in short, any constituents of the verbal code – are confronted, juxtaposed, brought into contiguous relation according to the principle of similarity and contrast and carry their own autonomous signification. Phonemic similarity is sensed as semantic relationship. . . . Paronomasia rules over poetic art, and whether its rule is absolute or limited, poetry by definition is untranslatable.' There is indeed merely an analogical relationship between the 'meanings' of words and figurative symbols, but the point remains instructive: and the true delusion lies in the notion that even in principle there is an exhaustive verbal (i.e. theological in this case) account of the 'meanings' of these concatenated symbols. For as Jakobson continues, 'Only creative transposition is possible . . .' – into another semiotic mode.

27 I mean that Numenius and Cronius use the belief in a particular argument, and do not pretend that this significance of the dagger is its only one in the mysteries. See below p. 142.

28 Vermaseren (*CIMRM* 279) is seriously misleading here: his 'dagger sticking in the ground' is clearly an ordinary sacrificial knife as commonly found on altars along with a *patera* and *urceus*. The bull's tail is equally evident; but there seems to be something close to the bull's ear (on the right as one looks from the cult-niche) though I cannot decide what it may be. Autopsy reveals nothing which is not evident in Becatti's photograph [pl. XVIII[6]]. It may also be observed in passing that C. L. Visconti (1868: 408, compare Becatti, 1954: 89) was quite right to think that one of the birds on the floor was an owl – the identification, clear anyway on the mosaic, is confirmed by the new relief from beneath the Hungarian Church in Rome, S. Stefano Rotondo, now in the magazines of the Museo delle Terme (to be published in *ÉPROER* by Dr Lissi Caronna). See note 50 below.

29 On 1248 (Dieberg) part of the blade is still inside the rock, like the lower part of Mithras; on 1340 (Königshoffen) there seems to be a sheath alongside his body, but the monument is badly broken (Forrer, 1915: 43 with pl. XIV 1–1a). A sheath, dagger and bow and arrow lie on the rock on 590 (?Rome).

30 Cf. 1972 (Apulum) where Mithras *petragenes* is close to 'Saturnus', who holds a curved object; and 2194 (Bucarest) where a fragment of the same figure is set above the birth scene.

31 Perhaps the same idea is represented in 2042 (Studniczka, 1883: 220 no. 40 with pl. VI 1): there seems to be a dagger above Mithras *petragenes*, and next to this 'Saturnus'. 321 (Quadraro) does not have a *petragenes* but shows 'Saturnus' beside a dagger plunged into the rock, which may be a way of referring to the birth. 1161a (Stockstadt I) seems to contain side scenes of the same type as the Dieburg relief (note 29), and the figure sitting on a rock is probably 'Saturnus', but without a knife; immediately above, as at Dieburg, is Mithras *petragenes*. In view of that, might the reverse, with its mysterious zodiac, be another 'Phaethon' relief rather than a feast scene? Stockstadt is not after all far from Dieburg. Vermaseren (1951: 102; 1965: 180) concludes from some of this evidence that 'Saturnus' is the god who commanded Mithras' deed. I do not think the inference plausible. Indeed, did anyone 'command' Mithras to do anything?

32 Although 'Saturnus' clearly carries a curved *harpè* at Dura, for example, (*CIMRM* 42[1]), the object he carries is frequently represented as straight: 1083[16] (Heddernheim I), 1283[8] (Neuenheim), 1292[4f]) (Osterburken), 1400[2] (Mauls: cf. Turcan, 1976: 70), 1430[2] (Virunum).

33 *CIMRM* 1579 (Ptuj III, but not one of the dedications by the *officiales* of V Macedonica and

XIII Gemina) and probably 2018[8] (Micia). It may also be worth noting some earlier appearrances: the dagger occurs in an obscure scene on 1301[6] (Besigheim: see now the clear picture in Filtzinger, 1974: 457 fig. 13, cf. 458–459. It seems to me quite doubtful that the fragments are from the same monument, since the stone is somewhat different, as well as details of sculptural treatment: and why a double birth-scene? – unless it was rather like Heddernheim I (1083) with a separate frame and central panel), in which Mithras advances with a naked dagger towards a figure on the right holding some round object (shield?). This comes between the *petragenes* and the (?) twelve gods (from autopsy more figures are visible than Cumont allows, 1896: 342–343 no. 242), so presumably from early in the myth-narrative. It comes equally early in 1247[4] (Dieburg) – after the birth scene – where Mithras simply proceeds to the right with a dagger amid growing corn (?) (cf. 1400[4] and perhaps 1292[2]), while in the next scene (6) he seems to be holding a cloak as well in his left hand, perhaps as he approaches the 'bull's house'.

After the death of the bull, it is once used by Mithras as a skewer for meat from the bull, one of whose hindlegs lies on the ground (*CIMRM* 1584, *c.* A.D. 256: clear from autopsy).

The familiar occurrence of isolated daggers on altars and so on may be connected with the honour bestowed on the dagger at the feast-scene: sequences of daggers: 335, 839, 1973 (there are two on the garland forming the cave on the Brigetio plaque, 1727): dagger and phrygian cap: 987; with the raven: 1496, 1508. I do not believe that 1672 (Carnuntum I) shows a dagger beneath the cap, but merely a flap, as on the very 'Persian' cap in 93 (Strygowsky, 1904 no. 7260, pp. 10–11, fig. 5): the stone shows no mark in the surface of the cap to indicate a separate object beneath (autopsy). Single dagger with bow and arrows: 1584 (Ptuj III, left side. It is worth noticing that the acroteria heads are not rams but bulls [autopsy]). On 1237 (Wiesbaden, now no. 7 in the 'Mithraeum') Cautopates apparently holds a dagger, but the entire piece is crude, so the identification cannot be certain.

34 See Minto, 1924: 367–373; cf. Vermaseren, 1972: 43–48.

35 Personal communication from Dr Cämmerer (cf. the Archaeological Reports, Germany, in this issue of the Journal, p. 198). The earlier excavation at Riegel is presented by Schleiermacher, 1933: 69–78.

36 This might be seen as a special case of the common Graeco-Roman recognition of the ambiguity of sacrifice as a means of communicating with the gods, well discussed by Vernant in relation to Hesiod, *Theog.* 535–612 (1974: 177–194).

37 Compare the Arethusa translation, which is deliberately literal: 'and the things which the cave contained, by their proportionate arrangement, provided him (Zoroaster) with symbols of the elements and climates of the Cosmos' (p. 9, lines 20–24). Turcan, 1975: 60, cf. 24, translates *kata summetrous apostaseis* 'intervalles calculés en fonction d'une mesure commune' and suggests a connection with Celsus' musical theory.

38 Manilius, *Astron.* 4. 624; = planets, *P. Lond.* 1. 130. 60; = zodiacal signs, Diogenes Laert., *Vit. Phil.* 6. 102. It is of course true that *stoicheia* are also the elements of matter. I am glad to find myself in agreement here with Cumont, 1929: 298 n. 18 and Turcan, 1975: 60–61, cf. 25.

39 Beck, 1976a: 14 n. 7 calculates that more than two-thirds of those listed by Gundel, 1972: 611–694 are in this order. It is worth noting that this order presumes that one regards the map of the heavens as drawn on a sphere (i.e. one looks at it from outside as it were), while the normal order above the cave on the reliefs is clockwise, the order of the zodiac as one looks from earth. Does this imply a deliberate change of perspective on the part of the mysteries between *mithraeum* and relief?

40 See Bouché-Leclercq, 1899: 163–4. It should be noted that I have not in general referred to specific astrological texts, which would have lengthened an already lengthy article.

DMS

41 Of course the equinoctial signs are regularly associated with East (Aries) and West (Libra).

42 See Cumont, 1899: 58; Campbell, 1968: 44–90; Beck, 1976a: 16 n.3. There is no adequate evidence that such *mithraea* were necessarily oriented east–west, although Caesarea Maritima is (Bull, 1975).

43 Bouché-Leclercq, 1899: 152, fig. 15.

44 This seasonal association seems to be reproduced on at least one representation of the bull-killing, the Brigetio plaque (1727). Here the seasons are in the following order:

Spring   Winter

Summer   Autumn

which would correspond with the plan of Sette Sfere. When we add that Cautopates is on the left (see below, p. 127), it seems clear that the left side of the plaque has an association with the northern signs, the right with the southern signs. (I would add that a full investigation of the complexity of the relation between *mithraeum* and relief is one of the most important current tasks for Mithraic scholarship.)

We may perhaps adduce 1797[6] (frg.: Budapest) where only one figure survives, in the top right-hand corner. Since it is veiled, it may be Winter. Of course other representations of the seasons on reliefs do not show this simple correspondence with the zodiacal order of Sette Sfere, and I discuss them below, p. 130.

45 Bouché-Leclercq, 1899: 155–157. It should be noted that the later Duran relief (*CIMRM* 40) shows a small lunar crescent above Taurus and a small solar disc above Aries. This might indicate that the mysteries normally taught one of the other theories about the diurnal-nocturnal significance of the signs, that the male signs were diurnal, the female ones nocturnal (Manilius, *Astron.* II, 221). That would mean that both sides of the *mithraeum* contained nocturnal as well as diurnal signs. Against that, the next sign, Gemini, in 40 has a star over it (?), and Cancer and Virgo, both female signs, have the same discs as Aries, when on this theory they should be nocturnal (Leo also has one). This implies to me that the appearance of a lunar crescent over Taurus has more to do with the fact that Taurus is the exaltation of Luna, and so refers to the complex relation between Moon, bull, Cautopates and generation rather than Manilius' nocturnal association against a diurnal one. But my full view of the problem will emerge later.

46 I do not use Beck's terminology 'abnormal' (1976a: 2) for this arrangement. On my hypothesis, as will appear, the placing:

Sol   Luna
Cautes   Cautopates

is just as likely to occur as the other:

Sol   Luna
Cautopates   Cautes

It is simply that they provide different symbolic information. Beck's criticism of Vermaseren on this point does not seem to me justified, because the location of the torchbearers at the *niche-end* (whether or not on the relief: cf. Stockstadt I, 1163, 1164) is to be distinguished from their appearance on the *benches* (see the following paragraph).

47 The relevant material has been collected by Campbell, 1968: 42, though he does not make my distinction between torchbearers at the end of the *mithraeum* benches and those near the relief. The painting of Cautopates on the right wall of Pareti dipinte is, as Campbell remarks, the only exception (though of course it is not on the bench itself): but it is not the only oddity about those paintings (Becatti, 1954: 62–66), which remain a complete mystery.

I discuss below (p. 128) Cumont's conception of the significance of the torchbearers.

Here I will comment only on his notion that the association of Cautes with Taurus and Cautopates with Scorpio is connected with the precession of the equinoxes (1899: 210-211 cf. Schwartz, 1975: 406), i.e. that Taurus was once the sign of the beginning of spring. We should surely rather appeal to the fact that these are the zodiacal signs which the sun enters immediately after the equinox (Aries→Taurus [hotter]; Libra→Scorpio [colder]). Such signs are called *sterea*, *simplicia*, 'solid', because they fix the change of temperature brought about by the preceding 'tropical' sign (Bouché-Leclercq, 1899: 152) and have a specially intimate relation to the preceding sign. Now Mithras' 'proper seat' is the line of the equinoxes: could there be any more 'proper' place for his *paredroi* than the *sterea* signs attached to the equinoctial signs?

48 Cumont omitted the rest of *De Antro* 25 (after *iousais*) in his collection of the texts (1896: 41) because Porphyry continues, quoting *Iliad* 5, 968ff., with the notion that the north wind revivifies the dying. I think it is clear that for Porphyry north is associated with terrestrial life only, which is parallel to the mystery belief. For the mysteries, *genesis* in the sense of 'coming into the world' was evidently understood as a kind of dying for the soul (hence perhaps one motive for the association between *genesis* and night/Luna, though I think there are others, as will appear), and *apogenesis* as its coming to life again. Yet *genesis* also has good associations in the sense of the growth of crops – it *is* 'life'. The interpretation of Mithras' act as simultaneously one which produces fertility in the world and one which saves men's souls is a reconciliation of this dual meaning of *genesis*. And that reconciliation is perfectly expressed in his position *between* north and south, the points of *genesis* and *apogenesis*: the moment when day and night are of the same length is one when neither the 'entry'/'exit' nor 'growing crops'/'dying crops' symbolism has precedence.

49 The passage occurs in the course of his argument that the Cave of the Nymphs is in reality consecrated to the cosmos: the cosmos is created from matter, and caves are natural, surrounded by a single mass of stone and yet 'lost in earth'. So the cosmos is properly described as a cave which is pleasant in that 'it participates in form, but obscure when one examines its foundations and penetrates with the mind to the depths of it...' (trans. Arethusa).

50 A point anticipated by the Contessa E. Lovatelli, 1892: 228, though she muddled their 'proper' positions. The cock which Cautes holds at Sette Sfere (Becatti, 1954: 51) may be associated with regeneration of a spiritual kind then, as well as with Persia and day-light as Cumont suggested (1899: 209-210; 1939: II, 75 n. 11; 1942b: 289-290). It seems to be peculiarly Cautes' bird: compare 431a, 532 (Rome) cf. Cumont, 1899: 209 n. 10 and Hinnells, 1976: 44-45. (See n. 25 above.) *CIMRM* 427 (S. Lorenzo in Damaso) is very dubiously to be identified as Cautopates, as Magi thought (1948: 239-240 no. 6) – is there really a trace of the end of the torch pointing *down* on the thigh? The animal on 431b is uncertain too – Vermaseren suggests a cock or an owl (Lovatelli's photograph is unfortunately very unclear), but the Contessa Lovatelli a dog. I think it is an owl: and that lends interest to the mosaic on the floor of degli Animali at Ostia, where the owl is set beside the cock *at the entrance to the benches* (Becatti, 1954: 89 and fig. 19) evidently as symbols of the torchbearers (we may add them to Campbell's list, 1968: 42, see note 47), and to 318, where a cock occupies the usual place of Cautes, perhaps implying that the other bird, the raven, like the owl, has a special relation with Cautopates (unless it too is meant to be an owl?).

One monument, however, *may* represent Cautopates with a cock. This is *CIMRM* 2268, from Novae/Steklen, the earliest datable monument in the West (*c.* A.D. 100: see Gordon, 1975: 231). Here we find the torchbearers in their 'cardinal' position (Cautopates on L, Cautes on R) on the altar. Each holds a bird, but that of Cautopates is damaged, and Detschew's identification of it is for that reason doubtful. The reason that Cautes here holds the cock *down* may be twofold: (1) to maintain symmetry in a relationship with four variables (two torches in prescribed positions, two birds) (2) in that he holds one object up and the other down his stance suggests the ambiguity of the torchbearers I discuss later, p. 129.

All the other representations of the cock in the mysteries seem to be associated with Mercury (*CIMRM* 1210, 1237, 1317, 1496), whose regular companion it is in Gallo-Roman art (Deonna, 1958: 643–644; Benoit, 1959: 143, 147–170). Of course that does not mean that the Mithraists did not reinterpret it, just as they reinterpreted Gallic Mercury (1211; ? 1267; I ignore 1045–1046).

51 The association between Cautes: heat: south seems to be indicated by the lion (? recalling the truth expressed by Tertullian, *Adv. Marc.* I. 13. 4) beside him on a statue at Rusicade (*CIMRM* 123) which also has the scorpion (Scorpio: autumn: southern signs); and between Cautopates: cold: north by the dolphin beside him (? = water, which is the opposite of fire = heat, as in Porphyry, *De Antro* 15). Stéphane Gsell, 1898: 46, thought that the bird beside Cautopates was an eagle. Now an owl would be immediately intelligible (nn. 28, 50) but it may indeed be an eagle, though I have not seen the monument and cannot be decisive. An eagle appears behind Mithras *petragenes* on 1687 (Carnuntum III: autopsy), and an association between the *petragenes* scene and Cautopates is guaranteed by 1504 (Ptuj I) – an early monument. More evidence for the ambiguity of Mithraic genesis?

Professor Beck objects to this interpretation of *CIMRM*, 123 that 'if Cautes' scorpion symbolizes south (Scorpius as a southern sign), his lion cannot *also* symbolize south, for Leo is a northern sign'. But there is no need to suppose that the lion is a representation of the zodiacal sign: I am suggesting that the reference is to its symbolism of fire = heat. As I show below (p. 129) this may be understood as a Mithraic means of suggesting the ambiguity of Cautes, who reconciles the astrological opposition between the ideas Sun/heat and the southern signs (= autumn/winter).

52 'As a creator and lord of genesis, Mithras is placed in the region of the celestial equator with the north to his right and the south to his left; to the south, because of its heat, they assigned Cautes and to the north ⟨Cautopates⟩ because of the coldness of the north wind' (trans. Arethusa). Nauck's text reads in part (p. 73, lines 8–11): *tetagmenou autōi kata men noton tou kat'auton hēmisphairiou. . . . kata de ton borran tou kat' ekeinon dia to psuchron tou anemou.*

53 One must suppose that the Santa Prisca line 4, '*Fons conclase petris qui geminos aluisti nectare fratres* (Vermaseren, 1965: 193–200) also refers to the identity-in-opposition of the torchbearers, cf. Vermaseren, 1975: 14–15.

54 Hence perhaps those monuments in which they each have their torches in the same position, up or down, though they stand at opposite edges of the relief.

I should, however, remark that Cumont's suggestion (1899: 208), recently elaborated with considerable ingenuity by Schwartz, 1975: 420–422, that the torchbearers' *names* are oppositional in a simple sense seems highly plausible. Although I cannot judge the persuasiveness of Schwartz' etymology of *Caut-*, his account of the significance of *pat-* (from Av. *pati* 'opposing', etc.) is more satisfactory than Schmeja's (1975: 22) from Gr. *pateo* 'tread underfoot'. The old Iranian forms *Nama* and *Nabarze* (but not necessarily *Areimanius*, though it *is* derived from the old Iranian form: it had penetrated the Greek world by the fourth century B.C.) in the mysteries surely provide some support for the general proposition that some elements of the cult are of extreme antiquity, however they arrived in it.

55 I do not understand how Turcan can argue (1975: 87) '. . . la fonction du Tauroctone est de mettre au monde les âmes des justes, de les incorporer au sens étymologique et militaire du terme . . . Mithra fait naître les guerriers d'Oromazdes . . .'. Not only does this introduce, without evidence, 'Zoroastrian' beliefs, but it assumes that Mithraic anthropology accounted only for the existence of initiates: an odd assumption, given the evidence of Porphyry. Surely

the latter is talking about the entry of *all* souls into generation; we cannot know what the mysteries taught about their exit, but no doubt non-initiates were doomed to be bound to *genesis* (perhaps in the form of metempsychosis) for ever, while those who were initiated at least began the long journey of escape to the fixed heavens. The bull's death saves only those who believe, surely. See further, n. 92 below.

56 See Hinnells, 1976: 44–46 on the interchange of symbols between them.

57 This symbolism is presumably an analogical extension of the basic symbolism relating to *kathodos* and *exodos*, based on the premise of identity-in-opposition. Cf. n. 50 above. It may be worth remarking that Porphyry makes a curious allusion to the principle of opposition-in-unity in *De Antro*, 29, where he is still discussing the idea that north is associated with cold and genesis, south with heat and immortality, and where he makes what must be an allusion (never realized as such) to the mysteries: 'Accordingly, the northern regions are proper to the race of mortals which is subject to *genesis*, the more southern regions to the more divine (race of mortals), just as the eastern regions are proper to the gods, and the west to *daimones*' (trans. Arethusa). (If we could be sure of that, we would have our first genuine evidence of Mithraic belief in *daimones*, associated with the *west* of the *mithraeum* – see below, p. 133. Numenius is certainly quoted in a similar connection by Proclus, *In Tim.* 20D : I. 76. 30 ed. Diehl.) Porphyry then proceeds to discuss the question of intellectual versus sensible progress, the latter of which must be either through the sphere of the fixed stars or through the sphere of the planets: 'There is a cardinal point above the earth, and another below it, one to the east, and one to the west. There are regions to the left and right, there is night and day. And so there is a *harmony of tension in opposition* (*palintonos hē harmonia*) and it shoots from the bowstring through opposites (*toxeuei dia tōn enantiōn*)'. I suspect that this language itself may even be Mithraic, even if also Presocratic.

58 See Rostovtzeff *et al.*, 1939: 64–80 on the various stages of the *mithraeum*. The earlier relief (*CIMRM* 37) also shows Luna on the left, Sol on the right. I would compare the roughly contemporary monument of Cn. Arrius Claudianus in S. Clemente (339), which has Cautopates on L, Cautes on R, and as akroteria, winter on L, summer on R (*CIMRM* is quite wrong here, for the face on the right base is a frontal lion [autopsy], which is doubtless a formalized version of the lion-snake-crater motif – the snake is creeping up the back of the altar. There never was a fourth figure, as *CIMRM* suggests).

59 This should be in the past tense, for the right-hand pier has long been demolished which gives the *mithraeum* now a rather different appearance from that described by Annibaldi, 1943–5 : 97–108.

60 I remain slightly sceptical of the order of seasons proposed by Cumont, 1896: 365, nos. 11–14 (no. 251) and by *CIMRM*. *CIMRM* 1685 (Carnuntum III) seems to have no relationship with the Heddernheim representation of seasons and windgods. If we take the seasons in isolation they are in an order different from that at Heddernheim:

	Summer	Spring	
Winter			Autumn

This is not a continuous order, evidently. But if we take front and sides separately, the front can be associated with the northern signs (moving right to left), the sides with the southern signs. I doubt that we can hope to identify the winds successfully.

61 See Bouché-Leclercq, 1899: 159–164; Gundel, 1972: 554–555 (who gives two separate figures). The later form found at Sette Sfere is due to Hipparchus (second half of second cent. B.C.), though we still find the older form employed by Manilius.

62 With the convincing emendations of this passage by the Arethusa edition (p. 128) and by Beck, 1976b: 95–98 (which I prefer to Turcan, 1975: 77–78, but note his p. 144), we now

have a satisfactory idea of what Porphyry (and his sources) were trying to say. I also believe that the Arethusa edition is correct to keep *echōn* in line 13 which was supplied by Lascaris (V and M omit it), and that Mithras is rightly described as *having* (from his *own* point of view, looking down the *mithraeum* from the east) north on his right and south on his left, against Beck's considerations in 1976a: 15 n. 11. For if we take Sette Sfere seriously, north is always on the *left* of *mithraea* as one looks towards the cult-niche, not on the right, and it seems to me quite as plausible to assume that Numenius and Cronius were talking about what Mithraists believed about the *mithraeum*/cosmos as that Porphyry is describing from autopsy a bull-slaying scene surrounded by a ring-zodiac with the northern signs on the *right* (see further, n. 67). But I agree entirely with Beck (4) that Porphyry cannot be reconciled with the Ponza zodiac at all: indeed, its location on the *roof* makes it certain that it is not directly concerned with the symbolism of the benches as I have outlined it so far (though I believe there is a connection). The origin of Vermaseren's difficulty is that he thinks the *actual* cardinal orientation of the *mithraeum* must be significant, which is both unnecessary and utterly ruinous to any attempt to make sense of the Ponza zodiac.

63 Beck, 1976a: 5–6. Although the distinction is important in astrology, it does here seem to be primarily astronomical.

64 Respectively: Becatti, 1954: 93 (in the south niche was buried a clay pot containing chicken bones and perhaps those of rabbits, and fragments of three cups); Pietrangeli, 1940: 156–157 with fig. 10; Rostovtzeff *et al.*, 1939: 73 and 74 with fig. 34 (middle temple); 77, fig. 35 (late temple).

65 Cumont, though not in this connection, properly adduces De Antro, 22 (= Arethusa, 22, lines 10–18). Cf. Beck, 1976a: 4 and 1976b: 96.

66 Noted by Beck, 1976b: 96. 'It is at this point that Porphyry rather abruptly switches his discussion . . .'.

67 As suggested by Beck, 1976a: 16 n. 14 and in personal letters. Turcan's discussion of this subject (1975: 84–86) is rather unsatisfactory. Not only does he suppose that Mithras *faces* East (which is exactly the reverse of what Porphyry says), he sets Mithras only in association with Aries, whereas Porphyry deliberately uses the plural *equinoxes*. His presentation of the argument for a relation between Porphyry's description of Mithras' place and the *thema mundi* (the positions of the signs at the creation of the world) also leaves something to be desired. It is easier to argue with Beck (personal letter) that Porphyry's description is a *horoscope* with Cancer in the ascendant and Aries culminating, which is exactly the position in the *thema mundi*; this configuration is found on one relief, that from Sidon (*CIMRM* 75). (See p. 140 below for another argument concerning the *thema mundi* in the mysteries which is not dependent upon that one relief [since the other ring-zodiacs do not show the same pattern], but starts from the *mithraeum* itself, which is what Porphyry demands.)

68 See Minto, 1924: 363–364 and Vermaseren, 1972: 14–16, who remark on the polarity but make nothing of it.

69 Once again the lionhead may be relevant, in so far as it also has a connection with Time, as *CIMRM* 545 (tropic signs), 879 (formerly four groups of zodiacal signs) at least clearly suggest. I do not, however, share Hinnells' readiness to assume that we can understand the significance of Time in the mysteries (1975b: 357 'The snake on some monuments passes through the zodiacal signs expressing the idea that with the passage of time the soul surmounts the cosmic forces they represent, an idea expressed differently on the Barberini painting, where the lion-headed figure stands above the zodiacal arch, and on other monuments where the figure stands on the cosmic globe' – an entirely gratuitous idea).

70 Bouché-Leclercq, 1899: 103–104, 155.

71 For these associations, see Bouché-Leclercq, 1899: 152 fig. 15.

72 For example in 1969: 155–164 commenting on Radcliffe-Brown's 'The Comparative Method in Social Anthropology' (Huxley Memorial Lecture, 1951). I was reminded of this passage by Frances Oxford.

73 In addition to Beck's forthcoming completion of his article on the Ponza *mithraeum*, and the interesting evidence he has collected (1976a: 6–7) for Mithraic belief in the planetary houses (which theory assigns half of the zodiacal signs to the Sun and the other half to the Moon, on the assumption of their *complementarity*), we may recall the familiar, though in detail doubtless highly suspect, evidence concerning the moon's inferiority to the sun to be found in the scholiast tradition on Statius *Thebaid* I, 719–720 (Lactantius Placidus, ed. Jahnke, 717, 719b), specifically referred to eclipses by 720 and *Vat. Mythogr.* II, 19 (ed. Bode, p. 80) [which are closely related texts]. The implications of *De Antro* 18 (= Arethusa, 20, lines 5–6), *kai psuchai d'eis genesin iousai bougeneis, kai bouklopos theos ho tēn genesin lelēthotōs †akouōn†* (supposing it to be Mithraic indeed) are also relevant, especially if we accept Turcan's recent emendation *apagōn* for the corrupt *akouōn* (1975: 75–77). We may take it that it was the parallel Mithraic belief about a relation between bull and Moon which causes Porphyry here to recall the mysteries after speaking about Demeter (cf. Beck, 1976c: 208–9). Souls, like plants, were then perhaps 'stolen' from the Moon by Mithras/Sol's theft of the bull (which is perhaps where eclipses entered Mithraic theology). Such a doctrine seems to me significantly different still from Cumont's theory that the Iranian belief in the moon as the home of souls was also in that form Mithraic (1899: 198 n. 1), so that Turcan's Zoroastrian language (1975: 73–77), with its reference to Ahriman, is quite inappropriate in the present state of knowledge – he does not after all make use of *De Antro* 29, which I have already suggested might be Mithraic (above, n. 57). See also Buffière, 1956: 432–437.

74 See Bouché-Leclercq, 1899: 165–179 on *schemata*, where he lists *diametron, trigōnon, tetragōnon, hexagōnon*; also Gundel, 1972: 554–559. It should be noted that what follows in this section is deliberately speculative.

75 The *diametron* can be thought of as a 'transitional' scheme between the *antiscia* discussed above (p. 131) and the properly polygonal *schemata*. The Chaldaean tradition thought of the signs linked by means of the *diametron* scheme as sympathetic: they 'look at' each other, and so act in concert; the 'Greek' tradition on the other hand thought of them as 'opposed': Bouché-Leclercq, 1899: 166–169.

76 See also below, p. 141, on the position of Pisces and Virgo in the *thema mundi*. It is also worth noting that the *diametron* associates every *seventh* sign (Aries – Libra, Taurus – Scorpio, etc.): Firmicus Maternus, *Astron.*, II. 22. 2 Kroll: *A signo ad aliud signum septimum quod fuerit, hoc est diametrum*; cf. Macrobius, *Somn. Scip.* I. 6. 57 ff. and *Hermippus*, I. 19. § 138. The *diametron* may have been the means of linking the *zodiac* with the *grades* in the mysteries.

77 Wortmann, 1976: 418; Lentz, 1975: 369–370; see also Campbell, 1968: 277–278 with the suggestion that such triangles are to be associated with the *petra genetrix*.

78 See Pietrangeli, 1940: 156, 160 with fig. 11. This triangular base is on the left of the cult-niche as one looks towards it; upon it was another smaller triangular stone fitted with a terracotta tube.

79 I do not think that the triangular monuments specifically associated with Sol or Luna should be included here; nor triangular bases such as *CIMRM* 369 or 501 (*CIMRM* 508 is surely not Mithraic, being too consistent with other Syrian monuments [Seyrig, 1971: 359]). On the other hand the triangle from Santa Prisca (Room W) with its central globe (Vermaseren, 1965: 344–361 no. 41), which was either attached to the west wall or set in the cult-niche, may be relevant.

80 The *tetragōnon* was normally regarded in the Chaldaean tradition as an unfavourable aspect, because of its association of signs of the opposite sex in equal numbers. But the association

between 'tropic', 'solid' and 'bicorporeal' signs in a square figure caused a certain doubt in the 'Greek' tradition, cf. Manilius, *Astron.*, II 653, 668–670, 674–675 with Bouché-Leclercq, 1899: 170 n. 4.

81 Implied by his peculiar association with the south bench and so *apogenesis*, so that the SE. quadrant may have been particularly sacred (and it is of course in that quadrant that so many *mithraea*, as I intend to show elsewhere, have spaces in some way cut off from the bench, as at S. Clemente [see the plan in Cumont, 1896: 204 fig. 31]). See below, p. 142, for the two missing quadrants NE. and SW.

82 Noted by Cumont, 1899: 114; I am grateful to Professor Beck for confirmation of his conclusion.

83 114: 'Je serais donc tenté de croire qu'elles sont rapprochées des constellations où elles se trouvaient au moment de la construction du temple, en d'autres termes, que le decoration de la crypte rappelait la *genitura* du sanctuaire, si la symétrie de l'ensemble ne rendait cette hypothèse difficilement acceptable.' I quote a comment made to me in a letter by Professor Beck: 'Such a disposition of the planets cannot occur in the heavens, and therefore cannot represent a genuine horoscope. Venus is put by Capricorn, Mercury by Gemini. There are thus four intervening signs, i.e., at least 120°, between the two. But the maximum elongation from the sun for Mercury in 28° and for Venus 48°. Therefore Mercury and Venus are never more than 76° from each other. And so, if Venus was in Capricorn when the Mithraeum was consecrated Mercury cannot have been in Gemini, and if Mercury was in Gemini Venus cannot have been in Capricorn.'

84 For Sette Porte, see below, p. 140. *CIMRM* 677 is slightly vague about the precise disposition of the two surviving planets at Spoleto. From Cumont, 1896: 256 no. 97 (cf. 1899: 113) and Gori, 1878/9: 59, who both saw the *mithraeum*, it is, however, clear that Saturn was first (nearest the cult-niche) on the 'north' bench (L), and Mercury next on the same side; two others were faintly visible, but unidentifiable. At any rate, it is evident that this order differs both from Sette Sfere and Sette Porte.

85 This is the regular order used by Graeco-Roman horoscopes dating before *c.* A.D. 150; almost all the literary horoscopes also use it; between *c.* 170 and 280 the order on non-literary horoscopes tends to be Saturn, Jupiter, Mars, Venus, Mercury, Sun, Moon (Neugebauer and van Hoesen, 1959: 164). For the controversies about the 'right' order, see Bouché-Leclercq, 1899: 104–123. Geminus, *Eisagōgē* I. 23–30 (ed. Aujac), though he employs the same order for the five planets, places Sol above Saturn and Luna below Mercury.

86 See fig. 42 in Bouché-Leclercq, 1899: 480 with 476–82.

87 For Sette Porte, see Becatti, 1954: 97–98. It is roughly contemporary with Sette Sfere (*c.* A.D. 170–180).

88 It is possible that a motive for not ordering the planets in a simple sequence was a desire to emphasize both Saturn and Jupiter by placing them closest to the cult-niche. And the reason for that may be their tutelary roles as guardians of the grades Pater and Leo, the first for obvious reasons, the latter because it seems to have had some special significance in spite of being lower than Heliodromus or Perses (Gordon, 1975: 241 cf. Hinnells, 1975b: 361–364; Francis, 1975: 443–445, neither of which I find especially plausible, however).

89 This makes it possible I think to reconstruct the Spoleto order with some certainty as:

Saturn	[Jupiter]
Mercury	[Luna or Venus]
[Venus or Luna]	[Mars]

Presciently, Cumont observed in 1899: 114 n. 4 'L'ensemble de la composition, si elle était conservée, s'expliquerait sans doute comme à Ostie' – though he did not mean by this quite what I mean. We thus have three different ways of representing the same symbolism in the three extant *mithraea* with planetary symbols on the benches, though in each Saturn and Jupiter, perhaps for the reasons I have just given in n. 88, appear nearest the cult-niche.

90 See Bouché-Leclercq, 1899: 185–192 with fig. 23 (187); cf. n. 67 above. Professor Beck observes that the order Saturn, Jupiter, Mars, Venus, Mercury, Luna is in fact merely a standard ancient planetary order minus the Sun (see note 85 above), and does not demonstrate conclusively that the bench-order at Sette Sfere refers to the *thema mundi*. Of course that is so, but it seems to me that the compatibility between this special hypothesis and more general knowledge about the mysteries' concerns and characteristic symbolism is a strong argument in its favour.

91 In effect, this means that the Ponza zodiac refers only to one or two of the cluster of meanings of the Sette Sfere arrangement of zodiac and planets, to the *thema mundi* and to the relation between Sun and Moon. We might of course argue that these were primary ideas in the mysteries which is the reason for their abstraction in that *mithraeum*. At the same time it implies an impoverishment of the complexity of interlocking meanings offered by the bench zodiac.

92 Celsus' order of the planets (ap. Origen, *C. Cels.* VI 22) cannot be reconciled with the grade/ planetary order evidenced by Santa Prisca and di Felicissimo. His order is in the reverse order of the days of the week, Saturn – Venus – Jupiter – Mercury – Mars – Luna – Sol, and he says that this is the Mithraic *klimax heptapulos*, explicitly referring to the *diexodos* of the soul (well discussed by Turcan, 1975: 48–50). Now it is certain that the chronocrators (the planets which rule over the first hour of each day of the week) played some part in the mysteries, since they appear in a variant of Celsus' order on the Bologna relief (693) (L to R: Sol – Saturn – Venus – Jupiter – Mercury – Mars – Luna) and on the Brigetio plaque (1727) (L to R: Saturn – Sol – Luna – Mars – Mercury – Jupiter – Venus; see Cumont, 1946–8: 156). Cumont, 1931: 31–64, referred Mithraic evidence for the chronocrators to a Magian theory of seven ages with a last Mithraic age, which I have suggested (1975: 233–240) to be inadequately supported by other evidence which he relied upon; Turcan, equally dissatisfied (1975: 50–54), has now suggested that Celsus is using a Platonic theory which integrated the fate of the soul with the revolutions of the two *periodoi* (planetary and fixed): 'le *klimax* symbolise, non pas l'ordre spatial des sphères planétaires, mais l'ordre des temps, le cycle des influences successives par lesquelles toute âme doit passer avant sa réintégration finale dans l'empyrée. Or ce processus est commandé par les revolutions célestes' (51). This seems to me convincing as an account of Celsus. But it is extremely difficult to reconcile this theory with the Mithraic theory of the grade/planet order – one cannot derive the order of the chronocrators from the Mithraic planetary order even by a Celsian musical theory. Yet Celsus says that his order is connected with Mithraic beliefs about the *diexodos* of the soul, which is certainly also true of the grade/planetary order. We may then have evidence of different Mithraic teachings (Turcan, 1975: 46, suggests that Celsus derived his information from some Syrian Mithraists) – which is possible though on such a central point perhaps difficult to accept – or we may suggest that Celsus misunderstood the precise teachings of the Mysteries about the chronocrators and confused it with the beliefs about the planetary/ grade order: did one of the Mithraic teachings about chronocrators link them with the fate of non-initiated souls, who are doomed to wander endlessly in time, a fate which those initiated escaped by proceeding through the planetary/grade order? It is of course clear from the Bologna and Brigetio monuments that the mysteries also had other beliefs about the chronocrators, perhaps linking them with the ritual calendar.

93 There is a simple technical discussion in Neugebauer and van Hoesen, 1959: 3–5. See also Bouché-Leclercq, 1899: 334–336.

94 H. J. W. Drijvers' edition of Bardaisan's *Book of the Laws of Countries* (1965: 55) translates

from the Syriac Philippus' objection thus: 'Then I said to him, "Oh Father Bardaisan, of this you have convinced us and we know that it is true. Yet you are also aware that the Chaldaeans maintain that the earth is divided into seven parts named climates, and that one of the seven rules over each of these parts, and that in each of these regions the will of his government rules and is called law?"' The theory of seven *klimata* appears in the horoscopes for the first time about the end of the first century A.D. (Neugebauer and van Hoesen, 1959: 4).

95 Other late seven-fold *klimata* are enumerated by Neugebauer and van Hoesen, 1959: 4 n. 5. It may be worth remarking that the Hermippus begins its discussion of this sevenfold scheme with the following observation (II 12 § 95 p. 52 Kroll): 'For when the sun in Aries begins to produce living things and to nourish animals and plants in the Northern hemisphere, this might be called a beginning from the first *klima*, the one at the equinox, inasmuch as this is the first point, and the best of all . . .'. See further Kroll, 1913: 856–857.

96 'Il s'agit de répartir les influences sidérales non pas tant sur la Terre considerée dans sa structure physique que sur la "terre habitée" (*oikoumenē*), c'est à dire sur le support des groupes humains appelés cités ou États, peuples, nations, races. C'est donc l'homme encore que visent surtout, pour ne pas dire uniquement, les divisions et subdivisions que j'appellerai "chorographie astrologique"' (Bouché-Leclercq, 1899: 327). I would suggest that here again the Mithraists adapted for their own purposes current astrological theories.

97 Vermaseren and van Essen, 1965: 168–169 (lower layer); cf. 179 (second layer, Pater only).

98 As I have suggested in 1972: 97–98. Of course I accept that this is merely a hypothesis, to be tested. But at least it questions the Cumontian orthodoxy which has become truth by empty repetition: we emphatically do *not* 'know' the Mysteries' teachings about the fate of the initiated. To suppose that we do involves a misapprehension of the limits of the comparative method.

99 See Gordon 1975: 241; and below on Jupiter as the median planet, p. 144.

100 We may refer at this point to a passage of *De Antro* (21). I give the Arethusa translation: 'Taking the cave as an image and symbol of the Cosmos, Numenius and his pupil Cronius assert that there are two extremities in the heavens: the winter tropic than which nothing is more southern, and the summer tropic than which nothing is more northern. The summer tropic is in Cancer, the winter tropic is in Capricorn. Since Cancer happens to be closest to us upon earth (*prosgeiotatos men ōn hēmin ho karkinos*), it has, with good reason, been assigned to the Moon, which is nearest to the earth; since the southern pole is as yet invisible to us, Capricorn has been assigned to Saturn, the most remote and highest of the planets' (p. 23, lines 1–10). This theory is based upon the domiciles of the planets (and so the *thema mundi*), though it employs the horoscopal planetary order common between *c.* 170 and *c.* 280 (see n. 85) [which perhaps implies that it is not properly Mithraic] – and it does suggest how the Mithraists may have integrated chorography with the *thema mundi*, and thus the two sets of symbols, zodiac and *klimata*, in the *mithraeum*. The course of the ecliptic is conceived as being from near us (Tropic of Cancer) to furthest away from us (Tropic of Capricorn); the fact that Cancer is the domicile of Luna reminds us that the left bench belongs to Cautopates; and Cautes enters on the other bench because Capricorn is the domicile of Saturn, the most remote of the planets, the nearest to apogenesis. But Saturn reminds us of the grade Pater and so the rest of the grades, which, as I have suggested, stretch back to the Tropic of Cancer across the *mithraeum*.

101 There is a black mosaic line at Planta Pedis, Ostia, with a snake beside it, across the *mithraeum* at the mid-point (Becatti, 1954: 78–80 with fig. 18 p. 79). At Palazzo dell'Arte, Rome (*CIMRM* 434) there is a kind of marble-paved threshold between d' and d" into which a crater is set (Pietrangeli, 1940: 155). At degli Animali, Ostia, two marble slabs look rather similar (being associated with a snake, again), but they are set at the cult-niche end of the

benches (which however are preternaturally short here): Becatti, 1954: 89 fig. 19 with p. 88 'come una soglia'. It is not clear whether the jutting walls two-thirds of the way down the benches at Ptuj II are remains of an old outside wall knocked through in an enlargement or a meaningful division of the sacred space as at Pareti Dipinte (Abramić, 1925: 67).

102 Bouché-Leclercq, 1899: 93–97.

103 Bouché-Leclercq, 1899: 95. Note also the disagreements about whether Saturn was dry or wet: such problems may well have exercised Mithraists too. But it is plain that they selected, here as elsewhere, from among current speculations rather than taking over theories wholesale.

104 Some of Vermaseren's remarks on Saturn in 1965: 180–181 anticipate my discussion. But he takes the association between planet and grade in a rather different direction, that of the *aurea aetas*, which does not seem to me legitimate given our ignorance of Mithraic eschatology.

105 See Gordon, 1975: 229–30. Professor Beck has observed to me that a misunderstanding of Neugebauer's point led me erroneously to assert there that the 'only difference' between the order of 'sidereal rotation' and the Mithraic order was the placing of Saturn above Sol and Luna. Of course this is not true. I should have said that the Mithraic order is identical with that used in earlier horoscopes (and the literary horoscopes), as given in n. 85 above, with the exception of the place of Saturn. Professor Beck argued in the same letter that we should suppose that the Mithraists adapted the order of sidereal revolution in common use from the second century B.C. (Moon, Mercury, Venus, Sun, Mars, Jupiter, Saturn) just as the astrologers did to obtain their horoscopal order. My only reservation would be that the horoscopal order already sets Luna and Sol *together* so that the Mithraic alteration would have involved only a single change, in the position of Saturn. But Beck's argument is perfectly plausible.

It may also be that the curious association between Saturn and Helios (Boll, 1919: 342–346; Cumont, 1935: 14) was an element in the formulation of the Mithraic order.

106 Bouché-Leclercq, 1899: 90–92. Note also the theory which claimed that the four phases of the moon correspond exactly to the seasons, causing the wet to predominate in spring, the hot in summer, the dry in autumn and the cold in winter (92 n. 4), a theory which integrates Moon with Sun in the same natural processes.

107 Bouché-Leclercq, 1899: 97–98.

108 Gordon, 1972: 99–100 and 1975: 241. See n. 88 above.

109 Bouché-Leclercq, 1899: 98–101.

110 It should be noted that the spheres are set slightly off-centre (fig. 1, p. 121), so that the left side actually touches the 'north' bench and a small gap is left on the right side. I do not know whether this is a consequence of some alteration of the left bench (which is slightly narrower than the right) or of design, though I doubt Becatti's suggestion that 'avendo questo passagio un significato rituale, si fossero spostate le porte, lasciando uno spazio neutro laterale dove il fedeli potesse camminare liberamente' (1954: 50). Not only is the space between spheres and the right-hand bench too small, it is unnecessary to imagine that *rituals* took place at each *klima* as Becatti suggests. But it would be fitting for the symbols of the *klimata* to be set closer to the north, which is nearer to earth than the south, insofar as they represent earthly climates.

111 If *De Antro* 29 is indeed a reflection of Mithraic belief (note 57 above), at least in part, the 'darkness' would be both of night and of the world.

112 Steiner, 1975: 170–173.

113 Of course I do not accept such an assumption, preferring a Popperian view of the nature of knowledge, with all that it implies for the role of the disconfirming critic (for example Popper, 1972), though I would not defend Popper to the last against critical theory.

114 The related 'Rome School' has more to offer with its distinction between 'mystery' and 'mysteriosophical' cults. But Weckman, 1970: 62–79 and perhaps Smith, 1971–2: 236–249, should be noted as a possible presage of more interesting ideas from 'Chicago' in this field.
115 K. O. L. Burridge, 1960 and 1969, is especially persuasive here.
116 Note particularly 1971: 80–101, and his recent Harvard lectures (forthcoming). The forthcoming dissertation of R. Van Dam (Cambridge) on relationships in late fourth-century Gaul and Spain between social and religious structure confirms the fruitfulness of Brown's perceptions.
117 I have remarked elsewhere on the involvement of Mithras in the world, on his nature as an accessible god (1972: 98–99). The new reading of the first line of the Bourg-St-Andéol inscription (*CIMRM* 897; Turcan, 1972: 32) by A. Blanc (1975: 245–246), *Num* [*ini*] *praesentis(si)mo*, if right, constitutes further evidence of this aspect of Mithraic belief. [See H. Lavagne, in this issue of the Journal, p. 223, but also R. Turcan, p. 194].

Bibliography

Abramić, M. 1925. *Führer durch Poetovio*. Ed. 1. Wien.
Annibaldi, G. with Gatti, G. 1943–5. Il Mitreo Barberini. *BCAR* 71, 97–108.
Becatti, G. 1954. *Scavi di Ostia, II: I Mitrei*. Roma.
Beck, R. L. 1976a. Interpreting the Ponza Mithraeum, I. *Journal of Mithraic Studies*, I. 1, 1–19. (Part II to appear in 1977.)
Beck, R. L. 1976b. The seat of Mithras at the equinoxes: Porphyry, *De Antro Nympharum* 24. *Journal of Mithraic Studies*, I. 1, 95–98.
Beck, R. L. 1976c. A note on the scorpion in the tauroctony. *Journal of Mithraic Studies*, I. 2, 208–9.
Behn, L. 1929. *Das Mithrasheiligtum zu Dieberg*. Leipzig-Berlin.
Benoit, F. 1959. *Mars et Mercure: nouvelles recherches sur l'interprétation gauloise des divinités romaines*. Annales de la Faculté des Lettres, Aix-en-Provence, NS 25. Aix.
Bianchi, U. 1975. Mithraism and Gnosticism. *Mithraic Studies* II, pp. 457–465 (ed. J. R. Hinnells). Manchester.
Blanc, A. and Desaye, H. 1975. Inscriptions nouvelles de la Drôme et de l'Ardèche. *Gallia*, 33, 229–256.
Boll, F. 1919. Kronos Helios. *ARW*, 19, 342–6.
Bouché-Leclercq, A. 1899. *L'astrologie grecque*. Paris.
Brown, P. R. L. 1971. The rise and function of the Holy Man in Late Antiquity. *JRS* 61, 80–101.
Buffière, F. 1956. *Les mythes d'Homère*. Paris.
Bull, R. J. 1975. The Mithraeum at Caesarea Maritima. Paper read at the Second International Congress of Mithraic Studies, Tehran, September 1–8 (to appear in the *Proceedings*).
Burridge, K. O. L. 1960. *Mambu: a Melanesian Millennium*. London.
Burridge, K. O. L. 1969. *New Heaven, New Earth*. Oxford.
Cämmerer, B., Filtzinger, Ph., Petrasch, E. 1972. *Neue Römische Ausgrabungen in Baden-Württemberg* (Ausstellung Dez. 1972–Marz 1973). Badisches Landesmuseum, Karlsruhe. Karlsruhe.
Campbell, L. A. 1968. *Mithraic Iconography and Ideology*. EPROER, IX. Leiden.
Cumont, F. 1891. *Notes sur un temple mithriaque découvert à Ostie*. Université de Gand: Recueil de Travaux, Faculté de Philosophie et Lettres, Fasc. 4, 5–23. Gand.
Cumont, F. 1896. *Textes et Monuments figurés relatifs aux mystères de Mithra*. Vol. II. Bruxelles.
Cumont, F. 1899. The same, Vol. I. Bruxelles.

Cumont, F. 1929. *Les religions orientaux dans le paganisme romain.* Ed. 4. Paris.

Cumont, F. 1931. La fin du monde selon les Mages. *RHR* 103, 29–96.

Cumont, F. 1935. Les noms des planètes chez les Grecs. *AC* 4, 5–43.

Cumont, F. 1942a. *Symbolisme funéraire chez les Romains.* Paris.

Cumont, F. 1942b. Le coq blanc des Mazdéens et les Pythagoriciens. *CRAI* 284–300.

Cumont, F. 1945. Rapport sur une mission à Rome. *CRAI* 386–420.

Cumont, F. 1946. Un bas-relief mithriaque du Louvre. *RA* (Ser. 6), 25–26, 183–195.

Cumont, F. 1946–48. Additional note to Radnóti, A., Le bas-relief de bronze de Brigetio. *AErt.* (Ser. 3), 7–9, 156–7.

Cumont, F. 1975. The Dura Mithraeum. *Mithraic Studies*, I, pp. 151–207 (ed. J. R. Hinnells). Manchester.

Cumont, F. and Bidez, J. 1939. *Les mages héllenisés.* 2 vols. Bruxelles.

Deonna, W. 1958. Mercure et le scorpion, I. *Latomus*, 17, 641–58.

Drijvers, H. J. W. 1966. *Bardaisan of Edessa.* Studia Semitica Neerlandica, 6. Assen.

Filtzinger, Ph. 1974. Die Jupitergigantensäule von Wahlheim. *Fundberichte aus Baden-Württemberg*, 1, 437–482.

Forrer, R. 1915. *Das Mithras-Heiligtum von Königshofen bei Strassburg.* Stuttgart.

Francis, E. D. 1975. Mithraic graffiti from Dura-Europos. *Mithraic Studies*, II, pp. 424–445 (ed. J. R. Hinnells). Manchester.

Garcia y Bellido, A. 1967. *Les religions orientales dans l'Espagne romaine.* EPROER 5. Leiden.

Gordon, R. L. 1972. Mithraism and Roman Society: social factors in the explanation of religious change in the Roman Empire. *Religion*, 2, 92–121.

Gordon, R. L. 1975. Franz Cumont and the doctrines of Mithraism. *Mithraic Studies*, I, pp. 215–248 (ed. J. R. Hinnells). Manchester.

Gori, F. 1878–79. Relazione della scoperta del Mitreo di Spoleto. *Archivio storico ... della Città e Provincia di Roma*, 3, 55–62.

Gsell, St. 1898. *Musée de Philippeville.* Musée et Collections archéologiques de l'Algérie et de la Tunisie. Vol. II. Paris.

Gundel, H. G. 1972. s.v. *Zodiakos. RE* Band XA, cols. 462–709.

Hinnells, J. R. 1975a. Reflections on the Bull-slaying scene. *Mithraic Studies*, II, pp. 290–312 (ed. J. R. Hinnells). Manchester.

Hinnells, J. R. 1975b. Reflections on the Lion-headed figure in Mithraism. *Monumentum H. S. Nyberg*, I, pp. 333–369 (ed. J. Duchesne-Guillemin). Acta Iranica. Téhéran-Liège.

Hinnells, J. R. 1976. The iconography of Cautes and Cautopates, I. *Journal of Mithraic Studies* I, 1, 36–67.

Jakobson, R. 1959. On linguistic aspects of translation. *On Translation*, pp. 232–239 (ed. R. A. Brower). Harvard Studies in Comparative Literature, 23. Cambridge, Mass.

Kane, J. P. 1975. The Mithraic cult-meal in its Greek and Roman environment. *Mithraic Studies*, II, pp. 313–351 (ed. J. R. Hinnells). Manchester.

Kroll, W. 1913. s.v. *Hermippus* no. 9. *RE* VIII, cols. 854–857.

Kuszinsky, B. 1937. Az Aquincumi Múzeum Római köemlékeinek ötödik sorozata. *Budapest Regísei*, 12, 61–152.

Lanciani, R. 1886. Note sulle scoperte urbane e sugli scavi del suburbio e di Ostia. *NS*, 162–64.

Lavagne, H. 1974. Le Mithréum de Marino (Italie). *CRAI* 191–201.

LeGlay, M. 1954. Le Mithréum de Lambèse. *CRAI* 269–78.

Lentz, W. 1975. Some peculiarities ... of 'Roman' Mithraic sanctuaries and representations. *Mithraic Studies*, I. 1, pp. 358–377 (ed. J. R. Hinnells). Manchester.

Lévi-Strauss, C. 1969. *Totemism* (E. T. of *Le Totémisme aujourd'hui*, 1962). Harmondsworth.

Lovatelli, Contessa E. 1892. Due statuette di ministri mitriaci. *BCAR* (Ser. 4), 226–234.

Magi, F. and Nogara, B. 1948. Mitreo della Cancellaria Apostolica. *Hommages à J. Bidez et F. Cumont*, Collection Latomus II pp. 220–238. Bruxelles.

Minto, A. 1924. Sta Maria Capua Vetere, scoperta di una cripta mitriaca. *NS* (Ser. 5) 21, 353–375.

Neugebauer, O. and van Hoesen, H. B. 1959. *Greek Horoscopes*. Memoirs of the American Philosophical Society, 48. Philadelphia.

Paschetto, L. 1912. *Ostia, Colonia Romana, Storia e Monumenti*. Roma.

Patsch, C. 1904. Archäologisch-epigraphische Untersuchungen zur Geschichte der römischen Provinz Dalmatien, VI. *WMBH* 9, 265–68 (part of a larger article.)

Pietrangeli, C. 1940. Il Mitreo del Palazzo dei Musei di Roma. *BCAR* 68, 143–173.

Popper, K. 1972. *Conjectures and Refutations: the growth of scientific knowledge*. Ed. 4. London.

Reichel, W. and Bormann, E. 1895. Funde von Carnuntum: das dritte Mithräum. *AEMÖ* 18, 169–201.

Ristow, G. 1974. *Mithras im römischen Köln*. EPROER 42. Leiden.

Rostovtzeff, M. I. *et al.* 1939. *The Excavations at Dura-Europos: Preliminary Report of the Seventh and Eighth Seasons (1933–4, 1934–5)*. New Haven.

Šašel, A. and J. 1963. *Inscriptiones latinae ... in Iugoslavia*. Situla 5. Ljubljana.

Schleiermacher, L. 1928. Das zweite Mithreum in Stockstadt. *Germania*, 12, 46–56.

Schleiermacher, W. 1933. Ein Mithräum in Riegel. *Badisches Fundberichte*, 3, Heft 3, 69–78.

Schmeja, H. 1975. *Iranisches und griechisches in den Mithrasmysterien*. Innsbrucker Beiträge zur Sprachwissenschaft, Vorträge 13. Innsbruck.

Schütze, A. 1972. *Die Mithrasmysterien und Urchristentum*. Ed. 3. Stuttgart.

Schwartz, M. 1975. Cautes and Cautopates the Mithraic torchbearers. *Mithraic Studies* II, pp. 406–423 (ed. J. R. Hinnells). Manchester.

Seyrig, H. 1971. Le culte du soleil en Syrie à l'époque romaine. (Antiquités syriennes, 95.) *Syria* 48, 337–373.

Smith, J. Z. 1971–72. Native cults in the hellenistic period. *History of Religions*, 11, 236–249.

Sperber, D. 1975. *Rethinking Symbolism* (E.T. of Du Symbolisme en général 1974 revised) Cambridge Studies in Social Anthropology. Cambridge.

Staehelin, F. 1949. *Die Schweiz in römischer Zeit*. Ed. 3. Basel.

Steiner, G. 1971. *In Bluebeard's Castle*. London.

Steiner, G. 1975. *After Babel*. Oxford.

Strygowsky, J. 1904. *Catalogue général du Musée de Caïre*. Wien.

Studniczka, F. 1883. Mithräen und andere Denkmäler aus Dacien. *AEMÖ* 7, 200–225.

Turcan, R. 1972. *Les religions orientales de l'Asie dans la Vallée du Rhône*. EPROER 30. Leiden.

Turcan, R. 1975. *Mithras Platonicus*. EPROER 47. Leiden.

Turcan, R. 1976, The date of the Mauls relief. *Journal of Mithraic Studies*, I, 1, 68–76.

Vermaseren, M. J. 1951. The miraculous birth of Mithras. *Studia archaeologia E. van Hoorn*, pp. 93–109. Amsterdam.

Vermaseren, M. J. 1972. *The Mithraeum at S. Maria Capua Vetere*: Mithriaca I. EPROER 16. Leiden.

Vermaseren, M. J. 1974. *The Mithraeum at Ponza*: Mithriaca II. EPROER 16. Leiden.

Vermaseren, M. J. and van Essen, C. C. 1965. *The Excavations in the Mithraeum of the Church of Sta Prisca in Rome*. Leiden.

Vernant, J.-P. 1974. *Mythe et Société*. Paris.

Visconti, C. L. 1868. I monumenti del Metröon Ostiense e degli annessi collegi dei Dendroforie dei Cannonfori. *Annali dell'Instituto di Corrispondenza archaeologica*, 40, 362–413.

Walters, V. J. 1974. *The Cult of Mithras in the Roman Provinces of Gaul*. EPROER, 41. Leiden.

Will, E. 1975. Origines et nature du mithriacisme. (Paper given to the Second International Congress of Mithraic Studies, to appear in the Proceedings.)

Weckman, G. 1970. Understanding initiation. *HR* 10, 62–79.

Wortmann, D. 1969. Ein Mithrasstein aus Bonn. *BJ*, 169, 410–423.

Zotović, L. 1976. New Mithraic reliefs from Yugoslavia. *Journal of Mithraic Studies*, I, 2, 201–203. (Archaeological Reports.)

VII

The date and significance of CIMRM 593 (British Museum, Townley Collection)

So long as everyone knew that the mysteries of Mithras were
the legitimate descendant of a popular Iranian religion elaborated and transmitted to the west by the hellenised magi it
was not hard to believe that the small amount of Anatolian
evidence for the god Mithras was simply part of a continuous
chain extending from Iran to Rome. But it had only to be
noticed that there was very little evidence indeed in Anatolia (the achievement of Wikander, 1950: 5-46), to set up a
debate about its significance: conservative scholars re-
worked Cumont's Iranian hypothesis (Widengren, 1955; 1966;
Campbell, 1968) without general acceptance; radical ones
rejected Anatolia altogether (Wikander, 1950: 41-46; Beskow,
forthcoming); moderates sought to make Anatolia a creative
centre for the mysteries, relying especially upon Plutarch,
Vit. Pomp. 24 (Nock, 1937; Will, 1955: 147-169; Nilsson, 1961:
675) (1). We can see clearly how Wikander's denial of
Cumont's 'strong' Iranian hypothesis (partly anticipated by
Nock, 1937) has provoked a debate about the origins of the
mysteries. But although everyone has to use the same
(shrinking) dossier of 'the evidence', utterly different conclusions are drawn (2). And the real trouble is not that
there is so little evidence but that everyone seems to assume
that the relation between Anatolia and the west must be obvious and straightforward; everyone assumes that we *know* the

form taken by the mysteries in the west and that the task is
merely to look for similar evidence in Anatolia: the one
exception is Will, who tried to find necessarily Anatolian
elements in the western iconography (1955: 186-208). But of
course these are mere presumptions. What indeed *is* essential
in the western mysteries? If there is no, or virtually no,
Mithraic iconography in Anatolia, must that mean that the mysteries did not already exist in a closely similar form there?
Is the iconography *essential* to the mysteries? How did the mysteries develop? Was there some original (Iranian?) 'core'
which slowly but coherently developed as a plant grows, predictably and systematically? Or are we faced with a creative
act of *bricolage* from disparate pre-existing elements and original invention? The problems are endless, and hardly any can
be resolved by some 'value-free' empirical search founded upon
common-sense. We must be as clear as possible about our
underlying assumptions and preconceptions.

Perhaps the most interesting aspect of a standard dossier
of evidence in ancient history is its standard mode of presentation; and the interesting point about the Anatolian dossier
is that it is usually presented geographically. But on
inspection that mode of presentation looks decidedly odd: what
could it tell one? I conclude that this categorisation is inappropriate to the explicit task of determining the relationship between Anatolia and the west (3). And it seems to me
that we would do better to look at the earliest *western* evidence for the mysteries, treating it not as part of a chain of
evidence for the 'history' of an expansion between Anatolia
(or the Crimea, or Iran, or whatever) and the west, but as a
problem in its own right: are there significant differences
between the earliest evidence in the west and later evidence?
Is the iconography different - is there evidence of hesitancy
in finding a stereotyped 'just' iconography; are there failed
experiments? Do some elements of the cult appear later than

others; if so, why? Having formulated these questions (and I do not propose to discuss them in great detail here), we may then turn back to Anatolia and see whether there are significant continuities, more significant than the iconographical similarities pointed out by Will (4).

Even if Euboulus and Pallas had survived, their account of the origins of the mysteries would presumably have been as satisfying, and inconsequential, as the accounts of the origins of the cult of Sarapis (5). Certainly Zoroaster would have figured largely; and so would the Persians and the magi. But however interesting, all that would have given us only a legitimating history, not a narrative-analytical one. To approximate to that we must use second-best strategies, and especially iconography and buildings; epigraphic evidence by itself is not sufficient. For it seems certain that there were many different forms of worship of the god Mithra/Mithras/Mithres in Asia Minor in the hellenistic and early Roman periods, and it would be plausible to suppose that we might have evidence of at least some of them beyond its boundaries: not all Anatolian cults of Mithras were mystery cults (6). We must therefore at first place on one side some of the earliest epigraphical evidence in the west: the Sidon cippus dedicated by Theodotus priest of Mithras to Asclepius (Dunand, 1967: 29; 1973: pl. XIIIa, dated 140/1 AD); the Greek inscription from Venosia by Sagaris *actor* (cf. *CIL* IX 425) of one of the Bruttii Praesentes (*IG* XIV 688 = *CIMRM* 171, probably first half of second century (7)); and the earliest military inscription, by C. Sacidius Barbarus, centurion of XV Apollinaris, from the bank of the Danube at Carnuntum (*CIMRM* 1718 cf. *JOAI* 29, 1935, col. 308 no. 248, probably to be dated before c. 114 AD (8)). I return to these inscriptions later.

The first important expansion of the mysteries in the Empire seems to have occurred relatively rapidly late in the reign of Antoninus Pius and under Marcus Aurelius (9). By

that date, it is clear, the mysteries were fully institutionalised and capable of relatively stereotyped self-reproduction
through the medium of an agreed, and highly complex, symbolic
system reduced in iconography and architecture to a readable
set of 'signs'. Yet we have good reason to believe that the
establishment of at least some of those signs is to be dated
at least as early as the Flavian period or in the very earliest years of the second century. Beyond that we cannot go,
in the total absence of relevant iconographical evidence from
Anatolia (even if the iconography were invented in the west,
we can hardly proceed to the conclusion that the mysteries
did not exist in some form in Anatolia). But, as I hope to
show, there is some positive evidence linking the earliest
western evidence with Anatolia.

On general grounds we may reasonably select as fundamental
to the religious system of the mysteries three characteristics: the saving act of Mithras as bull-slayer; the tendency
to employ oppositional symbols and ideas; the grade-structure
with its relation to the planetary-system and so to Mithraic
cosmology tout court. And each of these fundamental ideas
is, I would suggest, evidenced by the earliest datable western monuments.

Let us begin with the last. An altar or block from near
SS. Pietro e Marcellino on the Esquiline in Rome was inscribed (it is now probably lost) with a bilingual inscription
by an Imperial freedman:

Soli	Ἡλίωι Μίθραι
Invicto Mithrae	Τ· φλάουιος· Ὑγεῖνος
T. Flavius Aug. lib. Hyginus	διὰ Λολλίου· Ροὐφου
Ephebianus	πατρὸς ἰδίου
d.d.	

(*CIMRM* 362 a,b = *CIL* VI 732 = Moretti, *IGUR* I 179)
For the present purpose it is important only to establish a
probable *terminus ante* since the inscription must date from

after 70 AD. Now although in general we have to allow around
forty years after the death of the last possible manumitting
emperor in such cases, which would mean that it could date
from any time between 70 and c. 136 AD (10), there is one
piece of evidence to suggest an earlier date rather than a
later one in this case. For it is clear from his *agnomen* Ephebianus that T. Flavius Hyginus was a 'vicarianus', a man who
had entered the *familia Caesaris* by bequest or gift of a previous owner. From this name we may conclude that he had been
the slave of an imperial slave or freedman named Ephebus.
This class of slaves becomes progressively more important
within the *familia* from the reign of Claudius, but is especially characteristic of the Flavians and the reign of Trajan
(11). Such men seem to have been selected to become imperial
slaves either because of special merit or thanks to special
patronage (12). In Rome, they seem mostly to have held positions in the financial administration, like the one other
former member of Ephebus' *familia* whom we know to have entered
the imperial *familia*: T. Flavius Epaphroditus Ephebianus, *a
rationibus* (*CIL* VI 33468). Now it so happens that the only
two 'vicariani' named Hyginianus of whom we know are both
attested at Rome and both can be fairly confidently assigned
to the reign of Trajan (13). And though it is no more than a
possibility, both may have belonged to the *familia* of our Hyginus, entering the *familia Caesaris* on his death (at the time of
our dedication, he is likely to have been over forty as an
Aug. lib. and a 'vicarianus': Weaver, 1972: 219) (14). And
since *CIL* VI 8865 probably dates from between 103 and 115 (15),
we would have to place Hyginus' death earlier - perhaps by
some years.

There is then a (tenuous) argument that Hyginus is more
satisfactorily to be dated c. 80-c. 100 than in the later
period up to c. 136 (16). But the crucial importance of this
monument is its reference in the Greek section to the fact

that the dedication was set up through the mediation of Hyginus' πατήρ, Lollius Rufus. For some strange reason Vermaseren (*ad CIMRM* 362) states 'ἰδίου added in order to preclude
confusion with the grade of *pater*', though how he thought an
Imperial libertus 'vicarianus' from the *familia* of Ephebus
could have had a Roman citizen as a father, I do not understand. Moretti (*IGUR* I 179) is clearly right in observing that
πατρός here means the grade: ἰδίος is of course a common means
of denoting the possessive in *koine* (17). Lollius Rufus is
therefore the earliest of the extensive group of *patres* in the
mysteries who are mentioned as presiding over dedications
(18), so that we may reasonably conclude that our inscription
provides evidence not only for the pre-eminence of the grade
of *pater*, now as later, but also for the existence of the grade-
structure whose highest point it was. And the existence of
the grade-structure at this early date implies also the cosmological rationale which sustains it in the mysteries.

   The second characteristic of the mysteries was its use of
oppositional symbols and ideas. For this, we have a rather
more firmly dated monument: *CIMRM* 2268, a casual find from
Novae/Steklen in Moesia Inferior. It is a broken base or
altar, whose inscription reads:

[?   ] (unknown number of lost
                                                     lines)
Ḍeo

Melichrisus

P. Caragoni

Philopalaestri ... (19)

The last lines can be confidently restored: [*cond. publ. port./
Ripae Thraciae / serv(us) vil(icus) posuit*] (*vel sim.*), since Philopalaestrus is known from *AE* 1919 no. 10 line 67 (Histria) to have
been one of the earliest (if not the earliest) *conductores* of
the *publicum portorium Illyrici* in c. 100 AD (de Laet, 1949: 204
n. 4). Now the interest of this monument is that it shows
Cautopates on the left lateral face and Cautes on the right

(see photo [Fig. 52] in Detschew, 1939: B. 131-32); each holds
a torch in the usual position, and each a bird (Cautes at
least holds a cock) in the remaining hand. Although this
association between Cautes and the cock is characteristic of
later Mithraic representations, and may thus serve as an
additional argument for the relevance of this monument to the
mysteries even though it was not found in a *mithraeum*, I am more
concerned to stress the oppositional relation between the
torchbearers, forced upon our attention by the unusual (that
is, unique) motif of Cautes holding a cock upsidedown by its
feet in his left hand, while Cautopates holds a bird in the
same hand the other way up (20). The positions of the torchbearers' arms are identical, and they hold in either hand similar objects, but in reverse position. And we may reasonably
argue that this opposition is an image of that theme of opposition-in-unity which I have tried to show elsewhere to be
central to the mysteries' conception not only of the torchbearers but of the cosmos, and the *mithraeum*, as well (Gordon,
1976a: 119-165).

What then finally of Mithras as bull-slayer, the act which
not only, as I would argue, created light and set the universe
in motion but which also saved (at least some of) the souls
which had entered genesis through the gate of Cancer? The
very centrality of the act in the mysteries must have meant
that the adherents would have been forced to create an iconography very early given the representational character of
religious practice in traditional Graeco-Roman observance,
even in none existed before (which is theoretically quite possible, whether or not we assume the existence of an innova-
tive prophet who referred his ideas to the authority of Zoroaster). And it is in the absence of firmly-dated early
representations of Mithras as bull-slayer that the date of
CIMRM 593 is so crucial. Evidence for the existence of the
iconographical schema that (later at least) became standard,

roughly contemporary with the other monuments I have cited,
would establish beyond reasonable doubt the existence of the
fully-developed mysteries around 100 AD, at least in Rome
(and surely in Moesia Inferior too) so that we may be able to
reconsider the early purely epigraphical evidence.

The date of *CIMRM* 593 has not generally appeared to pose a
problem because Cumont's version of the early history of the
mysteries has for so long been dominant; and because it is
not generally appreciated how little monumental evidence
there is for the mysteries before the middle of the second
century AD. But once the traditional account has been abandoned (Gordon, 1975: 215-248) it becomes necessary to reconsider what was once taken for granted. For the traditional
date of this monument rests upon nothing stronger than the
identification by Hülsen of the *dominus* of the dedicator with
Ti. Claudius Livianus, praetorian prefect in the reign of
Trajan, though the inscription makes no reference to his
rank (21). With this frail support the date then passes
into the tradition: *CIMRM ad loc.* observes, 'The monument is the
earliest known from Rome' (22). We surely require some cor-
roborative evidence.

Now before Cumont read Hülsen's note he judged 593 to date
from the third century, on stylistic grounds. Since the present appearance of the monument (see, for example the photograph in *CIMRM*, fig. 168) is so misleading I have attempted in
Pl. I to give an impression of its original state before restoration, although it has not been possible to excise all
the additions (23). It is certain that the restorations
are modern, since there exists a note by Fr. Bianchini (1662-
1729), dated between 1702 and 1707, that it was fragmentary
when he saw it (24). It must be clear that such a 'plebeian'
monument offers no stylistic clues to its date given its im-
perfect state (25). We are left with the inscriptions. That
on the front edge of the base reads: *Alcimus Ti. Cl. Liviani ser.*

vil(i)c. Sol(i) M(ithrae) v.s.d.d.; that on the back of the bull:

        Alcimus T. Cl.

        Liviani ser. vil(i)c

        S(oli). M(ithrae). v.s.d.d. (26)

(*CIL* VI 718; 30818; *ILS* 4199; Smith, 1094: 88 and fig. 11)

Now Hülsen's sole argument that Livianus was indeed Trajan's praetorian prefect is merely implicit in his note - that epigraphy provides no evidence of any other member of the imperial élite called Ti. Claudius Livianus. But there may be a slightly better argument. Curiously enough, among all the dated cursives photographed by A.E. and J.S. Gordon (1958-65) the example closest to the cursive in our inscription is dated 101 AD (Gordon, 1958-65, II no. 161, pl. 69a [=*CIL* VI.1 2074 (part)] Arval list). There are slight differences between their respective A, M and V, but the overall impression (and especially the form of the C) is extremely similar. We may also compare nos. 175 (115 AD) and 177 (120); neither the earlier nor the mid-century cursives are close (27). And because the forms of cursive show greater diversity over time than those of monumental lettering, this similarity provides quite a strong argument in favour of Hülsen's thesis, and I think that we can now have some confidence that this Livianus is indeed to be identified with *PIR* II² no. 913, Ti. Iulius Aquilinus Castricius Saturninus Claudius Livianus, the former equestrian who became *Praefectus praetorio* in c. 101. Consequently we may probably set Alcimus alongside that Livianus' more famous *servi vilici*, Asylus and Hierus, praised by Martial (9.104) and at least twice the authors of dedications to Hercules *Invictus* (*CIL* VI 280; *AE* 1924, 15 with Marucchi, 1924: 67-69; cf. *CIL* VI 322 and Beaujeu, 1955: 80-87).

    If we may be reasonably confident that 593 is the earliest extant Roman version of Mithras as bull-slayer (and indeed the earliest such representation anywhere in the west) it may be worth examining its possible relationship to other later

Roman monuments. Now it is at once clear that it is quite
different from the early series from Rome I have examined
elsewhere, characterised by a distinctive treatment of Mithras' tunic and the placing of his left hand under the muzzle
(Gordon, 1976b: 166-186), and that the convention adopted
here for these two items (long overgarment with a belt;
longer under-garment; left arm laid along the bull's muzzle)
became stereotyped in the area of Rome. If we take a number
of minor peculiarities of this statue, the position of the
snake as it comes round the foreleg; the bull's exaggerated
dewlap; the angle of the scorpion; the treatment of the tunic;
Mithras' left leg; the bull's short offside hindleg, we can
find a number of Roman monuments, all considerably later,
which are close (28). This may be shown by the following
table:

	snake	bull's dewlap	scorpion	tunic	M's left leg	bull's hindleg
181	✓	×	✓	✓	×	✓
350	✓	×	×	✓	close	✓
366	×	✓	✓	✓	✓	✓
368	✓	✓	×	✓	close	✓
390	✓	×	×	✓	close	✓
417	×	✓	×	✓	close	✓
588	×	✓	✓	✓	close	✓

Overall, the closest in general scheme is 588 (a relief),
although the snake is not in the same position; 366 has the
largest number of identical motifs but again the snake is in a

different position; three of the four cases of identical
snakes have the scorpion at a different angle. We have then
a very clear example of that characteristic process of minor
differentiation in the sequence of the Mithraic reliefs which
I have pointed out elsewhere (1976b: 170): the relief, sculpture or painting is treated as consisting of a number of
standard elements for each of which there is a stock of traditional stereotypes. And it is the possibility of combining
these 'synonyms' in different ways which makes it so difficult to determine clear lines of filiation even within a restricted area like Rome. On the one hand it is not possible
to define a group clearly descended from this scheme; on the
other, many of its conventions are found in later Roman and
central Italian monuments (29). But 593 does provide some
evidence relevant to the question of hesitancy in finding a
stereotyped iconography (p.149 above): it offers two unique
details. The relation between the bull-killing and the production of corn (and presumably human life) is here indicated
not by the usual means (corn ears emerging from the bull's
tail) but by showing the ears emerging from the wound itself -
which clearly implies that no stereotype for that idea yet
existed. Secondly, the torchbearers not only appear on a
statue (the standard later convention was that the torchbearers were excluded from statues), they are placed together
behind the bull's hindquarters, though we cannot tell whether
they held torches (only that one hand was placed on the bull's
rump). Such a placing is at odds with the oppositional convention relating to the torchbearers; and perhaps should be
linked with the curious appearance of one inscription on the
rather roughly finished back of the bull. Might not these
details be linked with the absence of Mithraic temples until
the middle of the second century - when they are found in a
sudden rash in a number of widely separated sites? For presumably the conventions relating to the placing of Cautes and

Cautopates were established in relation to the *mithraeum* with
its characteristic equipment and benches; without the *mithraeum*
the iconography of the bull-killing serves a different purpose: the relief or statue is not an element in a complex
symbolic geography, merely a registration of Mithras' act.
While we must conclude from Melichrisus' monument at Novae
that even c. 100 the torchbearers were understood in opposition to each other (as well as in unity), it is apparent from
593 that such an understanding was not yet stereotypical of
representations of the bull-killing.

   We may now return to the earliest inscriptions, and perhaps to Anatolia. Although the Latin inscription of T. Flavius Hyginus Ephebianus (362a) gives Mithras the title *Sol
Invictus Mithras*, the Greek one offers simply ἥλιος Μίθρα(ς).
And Alcimus' name for the god, *Sol Mithras*, is a direct translation of that Greek formula (593). And it is this name
which Sagaris, *actor* of one of the Bruttii Praesentes (171)
adopts (see above, p.150): ἥλιος Μίθρα(ς). Now the name
Sagaris happens to be Anatolian - it is indeed mainly attested
from central and NW Asia Minor (30). In itself, that might
be insignificant, since Sagaris might obviously have learned
of the god after his enslavement. But it is from Phrygia
that we have evidence of a cult of solar Mithras from the
second century BC (*CIMRM* 23): Ἡλίω Μίθρα Μιδῶν [or Μίλων]
/Σώλονος/ἀνέθηκεν/εὐχην. The same emphasis upon Mithras'
solar character can be discerned in an inscription from Caesarea in Cappadocia which is undoubtedly relevant to the mysteries: *Solem / Soli invicto / Mythrae / pro salute et incolu / mitate
Chresimi Augg. / NN. dispensatoris / Callimorphus arka / rius eiusdem /
votum solvi / libens animo* (*CIMRM* 17 = *CIL* III 6772 + 12135). Though
there is a small scatter of later examples, this cluster of
titles emphasising Mithras as a solar deity rather than as
Invictus, occurring as it does in some of the earliest evidence
for the mysteries, provides at least a tentative link with

Anatolia, and Phrygia/Cappadocia in particular (31).

This tentative link may perhaps be strengthened. C. Sacidius Barbarus, as we saw (p.165 n. 8), probably dedicated his monument before 114 AD. The title of Mithras is *Invicto Mitrhe*, Now quite apart from the evidence that form provides about the pronunciation of the name (aspirated -t-), the final -e suggests that the name Barbarus knew did not end in a-pure but in -ēs: *Mithrēs* (32). And curiously enough this form is evidenced certainly only in the well-known Faraşa inscription in Phrygia (*CIMRM* 19: Σαγάριος / Μαγ[αφέ]ρνου / στρατηγὸς / ᾽Αριαραμνεί(ας) / ἐμάγευσε Μίθρῃ) and in a literary tradition represented by Strabo, Plutarch and Lucian (33), which seems to be Anatolian. On the other hand the title *Invictus Mithr(a)s* was to become one of the most frequent on the Danube, and from Hyginus' Latin inscription we have evidence that *invictus* was already a cult-title of Mithras around 100 AD in Rome; both items of evidence suggest that Barbarus may indeed have known of a mystery cult of Mithras. And his form of the name suggests also an Anatolian connection.

The usual western nominative form of Mithras' name in the mysteries ended in -s, as we can see from the one authentic dedication in the nominative, recut over a dedication to Sarapis (463, Terme de Caracalla), and from occasional grammatical errors such as *deo invicto Metras* (1443). But it is probable that Euboulus and Pallas at least used the name *Mithra* as an indeclinable (ap. Porphyry, *De abst.* II. 56, IV. 16). And curiously enough this same indeclinable form is found in the one Cilician text which refers to the mysteries (*CIMRM* 27bis): [Μ. Αὐρή] / λιος Σέλευκος ἱε[ρεὺς καὶ] / πατὴρ διὰ βίου Διὸς [᾽Ηλί]ου / ἀνεικήτου Μίθρα ...: the cult-title here was clearly Zeus Helios Aneikētos Mithra (34). And though the inscription is probably third-century AD, this item of evidence may provide a clue as to the source of Euboulus' and Pallas' knowledge of the mysteries (35).

We can then be reasonably confident that the mysteries, in
at least something approaching their typical later form in
the west, were present there about 100 AD even though there
is as yet no evidence that the *mithraeum* had been invented as
a symbolic architectural form by that date. It is also tempting to believe that there are direct links between that
early evidence and Anatolia. But this Anatolian evidence
does not all derive from the same area, which implies that
the mysteries were not simply a localised minor cult by the
date of the earliest western evidence. And this implication
lends renewed interest to that other prop (with Plutarch,
Vit. Pomp. 24) of the traditional Cumontian history, Statius'
Thebais 1.719-720:

(716: *Adsis, o memor hospitii.../....seu te....vocari/....praestat..../*)
       ... *Persaei sub rupibus antri*
indignata sequi torquentem cornua Mithram (ed. Garrod)

Now we may at once dismiss the usual assumption that Statius
is here *describing* a typical bull-slaying relief or image (36),
since the motif of holding the bull's *horns* (which seems to be
implicit in the words) failed to establish itself in the western iconography, where the convention stresses the bending
of the entire head by means of pressure applied to the nostrils or muzzle. The adoption of that convention may of
course have had something to do with the range of options
already established within the Nike/hero convention (37), but
it seems unlikely that this would have happened if the ritual
had demanded a clearly different position. (It is certainly
odd that the Kertch terracottas (c. 50 BC - 50 AD) show the
god holding the bull's horn not its muzzle however) (38).

    David Vessey has recently stressed the significance of
this passage in the thematic structure of the *Thebais* as a
whole (1973: 313) - there seem to be deliberate echoes in
12.668-671, so that Mithras here adumbrates the beneficent
activity of Hercules and Theseus at the end of the poem. He

also stresses the movement of Adrastus' speech, in which the
lines occur, from disorder to order, which again prefigures
the logic of the entire poem, 'from the symbols of madness
and grief to those of regeneration and hope' (136). But perhaps there are further implications (39). The invocation of
Apollo here (lines 696-720) is almost a literary aretalogy
by Adrastus, comparable to Apuleius' or Isis in *Met.* XI.5
(though of course this is a self-predication: Griffiths,
1975: 137-158 [an excellent commentary]). The list mentions
some of Apollo's cults in Asia Minor (*Lyciae Patarea...dumeta*
[696-97]; *Troiam...habes* [699]) and in Greece (*rore pudica /
Castaliae* [698]; *Cynthus; assiduam...Delon* [702]); moves to some of
his traditional capacities and attributes (oracles; lyre-
playing) and exploits (the myths of Tityos, Python and Niobe);
and then to an *interpretatio romana* of three foreign gods
(lines 716-720) 'with a syncretism typical of the first century' (Vessey, 1973: 135). First there comes a reference to
the Persian cult of the sun reported for example in the
Alexander-histories: *seu (praestat) te roseum Titana vocari/gentis
Achaemeniae ritu* (40). Curtius Rufus (writing some time in the
first century) describes a procession of Darius' army in
some detail, emphasising the role of the image of the Sun at
the head of the army (41). The point I wish to stress is
that this reference seems clearly to be *literary*.

No less literary, I would maintain, is the next reference,
curiously enough not to anything Persian, but to Osiris:
Osirin / frugiferum (718-19). Now this is the sole reference to
the god in Statius: that in itself suggests that it owes
nothing, say, to Domitian's building of an Iseum outside the
poemerium. It was only in myth and among the learned, to
judge from Plutarch, that Osiris was a significant figure in
'Egyptian' mysteries: indeed Plutarch has a passage on the
identification of Osiris and the sun, although he treats it
as a contentious theory (*De Iside et Osir.* 52 372D-E) (42). At

any rate, it would hardly be excessive to claim that Statius
is here again making a literary reference and not one to a
cult of which he has personal or direct experience. Then
what of Mithras? Our phrase is unintelligible until we reach
his name, the last word of the book. From the progression of
the list we may conclude that this name was most arcane of
all. One can hear the rustle of obscure texts. But which
ones? Both Strabo (15.3.13 [732C]) and Curtius Rufus (*HA*
4.13.48 [12]) tell us that the Persians worshipped the sun as
Mithrēs/Mithras, and Statius could have known both texts.
Yet neither betrays any knowledge of the act of killing
inside a Persian cave, any more than Plutarch - or Poseidonius - does in *Vit. Pomp.* 24. Statius' language almost forces
us to think of Euboulus' account of the foundation of the
mysteries of Mithras as demiurge by Zoroaster in a cave in
the mountains of Persia (ap. Porphyry, *De antro* 6). At the
least, it looks as though Statius had found a reference to,
or an account of, a myth about Zoroaster which the mysteries
had either used, or invented, as part of their legitimation
as a cult of true wisdom. And the only plausible candidate
is the Zoroastrian pseudepigrapha. Whatever the historical
origins of the mystery cult of Mithras, and wherever it began
in Anatolia, and however much versions of it had spread within Anatolia before its appearance in the west (43), I see no
alternative to the conclusion that at some point an account
of the foundation of a cult of Mithras by Zoroaster was circulated among that bizarre collection of disparate texts
(perhaps in a process similar to the creation of the Hermetic
texts in Egypt). Nor do I see any alternative to the conclusion that it was this legitimation of the mysteries which was
crucial not only to Statius' knowledge of the myth, which is
relatively trivial, but to the transformation of an Anatolian
secret cult into an elaborate and learned mystery cult incorporating current views of the nature of the cosmos, a complex

theory of the relation between cosmos and human beings, and
an intricate account of the uneasy relations between spirit
and matter, life and death. At some point a local syncretism
had to abandon its implication in local meanings and become
universal: its entry into the writings of 'Zoroaster' was, I
would urge, a necessary preliminary to the explosion of the
mysteries beyond Anatolia in the years after 100 AD (44).
In view of the Kertch terracottas one must admit that this
process of universalisation had begun by the mid-first century BC, even if the standard form of the cult in the west
was at least somewhat different. And the differences between
the Kertch version and the standard later western one for me
implies the activity of a reforming prophet or leader claiming to interpret and expound the pseudepigrapha. I do not
think we can know where that activity took place; but it must
have been during the first century AD.

Such an account of the early development of the mysteries
is frankly mythical: it does not claim to be anything but
plausible, and it serves merely to satisfy - like all mythical history - our desire to be told a story about what is unknown or unknowable. However much one protests against the
desire (Gordon, 1975: 247), the tug of aetiology, of the
Just-So Story, is evidently irresistible. In a sense of
course, that may not be improper, so long as the theory is
explicit about what it is trying to explain, and content to
remain unverifiable. Yet the task of understanding the evidence for the developed mysteries in the west has still
scarcely begun; and it remains a priority.[*]

NOTES

1 I have made no use of this overworked item (cf. Francis, 1975) here
  for reasons stated in 1975: 245 n. 119. The present note is a recon-
  sideration and amplification of the suggestions made there. I have
  changed my mind considerably since that article was written in 1971.

2 Since Cumont, 1939: 67-76 first performed the exercise, apparently in
  response to Nock, 1937, it has been repeated by Wikander, 1950: 23-28;
  Will, 1955: 154-168; Nilsson, 1961: 670-672 and most recently by Roll,
  1977: 53-68. Each time it is done, objections are found against some
  item, the Isparta relief, the Trapezus coins, the Tarsus local bronze,
  or whatever.

3 Nilsson (1961: 675) approached the problem more satisfactorily by discussing the evidence in relation to Persian culture in Anatolia (cf.
  Wikander, 1946), though he mistakenly tries to show that Persian religion in Anatolia was 'unorthodox' - a concept which has hardly any
  meaning in pre-Sasanian Zoroastrianism (Boyce, 1970). My own assumption is that we should treat the Anatolian evidence for cults of
  Mithra/Mithres/Mithras as an aspect of an Iranian *koine* in that area,
  the legacy of an imposed culture which, detached from its traditional
  source of legitimacy and authority, was gradually absorbed into
  heterogeneous patterns of social and religious development. M. Louis
  Robert has over many years drawn attention to the manifold problems
  raised by this evidence in Anatolia, but there exists no history of
  the transition from Persian dominance to hellenism. It is surely in
  the context of the fate of important Persian families, of temples,
  of festivals in scattered localities in Anatolia that we should look
  for an explanation in general terms of how the mysteries of Mithras
  became possible. I doubt whether we shall ever be able to be more
  specific.

4 In an unpublished lecture at the First Mithraic Congress (Manchester
  1971), B. Shefton argued that the typical iconography is a mélange
  of clichés, and that we have no compelling reason to date its invention much before the earliest extant examples of bull-killing
  reliefs in the first half of the second century AD. It is at any rate
  clear that talk of a 'hellenistic' iconography is simply loose and
  misleading. I have tried to show elsewhere that none of Will's Anatolian motifs demonstrates his case conclusively (1972: 41-43).

5 See most recently Fraser, 1960; 1967; 1972: 116-117; 246-259; 267-268;
  Stambaugh, 1972: 1-13; Hornbostel, 1973: 48-73.

6 Perhaps this is obvious, if not always explicitly stated. At any rate
  it seems now to be generally granted: Will, 1955: 147-169; Turcan,
  1975: 1-13; Roll, 1977: 53-54.

7 *PIR* I^2 no. 162 dates the inscription to the late Antonine period,
  assigning it to no. 165, or to his descendants, simply on the grounds
  that it contains a reference to Mithras. That would have been reasonable if there were not grounds (see p.159 below) for thinking that
  this is an early inscription: Sagaris' master may have been the
  addressee of Pliny's *Ep.* VII. 3 (*PIR* I^2 no. 161) or his son, cos. II
  139 AD (no. 164).

8 XV Apollinaris seems to have left Carnuntum in 114, and eventually

became the garrison of Satala (Ritterling, 1925: 1753-54); with extensive gaps, the legion had been based in Carnuntum since Julio-Claudian
times (Daniels, 1975: 250-251). Cumont, 1899: 252-253, assumed that
Barbarus was 'un oriental à demi hellénisé', and dated the inscription
towards 71, when XV Apollinaris returned from Jerusalem. This was consistent with his general attempt to push the western evidence as early
as possible. On the other hand we may observe that, though there is
no firm epigraphic evidence (Saxer, 1967), Domaszewski, 1896: I, 113,
argued that vexillations from this legion fought in the Marcomannic
wars. A Cappadocian vexillation as a source of the spread of knowledge
of the mysteries in the 160's *in the army* has some attractions, given
that the earliest adherents in the west seem to have been civilians,
and slaves in particular. Obviously, this is the merest speculation.

9 Apart from the four early Ostian *mithraea* between c. 140 and 160, at
least six probably date from around 150 (Emerita, Riegel [Kaiserstuhl],
Stockstadt II, Ptuj I, Aquincum I, Vratnik) - and perhaps the first
temple at Nersae in Italy (648). A rash of inscriptions at this date
confirms the conclusion: *CIMRM* 528 (Antoninus Pius?); 214 (mid-second
cent., cf. Weaver, 1972: 53 but note Chantraine, 1967: 204); 1295
(Böckingen, c. 148); 563b (reused by his sons in 183 AD; a M. Ulpius +
function); ?2286 (Troesmis: before 162). The absence of datable
mithraea in Rome itself earlier than Barberini (late Antonine) is presumably an archaeological accident in view of the Ostian evidence.

10 Weaver, 1963: 272; 1972: 30-34 (it must be later than 70 because of
the *nomen* Flavius). Manumissions for the purposes of the administration took place throughout an emperor's reign of course, not simply at
his death.

11 Weaver, 1964b: 117-128; 1972: 212-223. 'Vicarianus' is a term invented
by Weaver for such men, who were apparently deliberately adlected into
the admininstrative part of the *familia* because, as the *vicarius* of
their former master (himself or herself either an Imperial freedman or
slave), they knew his job. See also Chantraine's useful collection of
material, 1967: 293-388, and Weaver's comments, 1972: 212 n. 2.

12 Weaver, perhaps influenced by Pflaum (esp. 1958: 1-17), has tended to
insist upon the rational-legal aspects of the imperial *familia* (e.g.,
1964a: 74, 'No bureaucracy can function efficiently without order and
opportunity in its lower as well as its higher ranks. If a *cursus* did
not exist it would have been necessary to invent one...'). More
recently, he seems to allow for patronage 'on special issues or for
particular appointments' (1972: 17). Indeed he observes: 'We are considering a service where opportunities for promotion were dependent on
influence, patronage, merit and service - no doubt in that order' (219)
- but adds extraordinarily 'and where the element of competition for
available places was not unduly wasteful of talent and was stimulating
for the ambitious'. There is not even an entire section in the book on
the evidence for patronage. The forthcoming dissertation of Richard
Saller (Cambridge: Jesus College) shows how difficult it is to sustain
Pflaum's thesis of legal-rationality in the equestrian service; and his
critical questions might beneficially be turned, in systematic fashion, on the *familia Caesaris*. (Chantraine uses 'patronat' of course
only in the narrow legal sense: 1967: 281-292.)

13 Chantraine, 1967: 317 nos. 177, 178 (with a reference to our Ephebianus). 178=*CIL* VI 8865 is certainly Trajanic (see n. 15 below). Of
   the dedicator of 177 = VI 18358 (*Callistus Aug. lib. Hyginianus*) he
   notes that he was married to *Flavia Aug. lib. Helpis Caenidiana* (his
   no. 79, p. 305), who may have been a former slave of Caenis, the con-
   cubine of Vespasian (cf. *PIR* I² 174 no. 888: '*ex eius familia Caeni-
   diani*, VI 15110, 18358'; Weaver, 1972: 216, 222 also takes it for
   granted). This would imply a Domitianic or Trajanic date for Callistus.
14 It is not strictly necessary to assume the death of the master before
   entry into the *familia*, since there are some cases in which it was
   certainly earlier, Weaver, 1972: 222 n. 3.
15 Cf. Weaver, 1972: 304 s.v. Trajan D and 220 n. 1 (Ulpia Bassa).
   The relevant part of the inscription reads *Epaphorditus Imp. Caesaris
   Nervae Troiani Aug. Germa. Dacici ser. Yginianus arcar. a iuvencis*.
   This seems to be standard nomenclature in the middle period before
   116 (*CIL* VIII.5, p. 127 cf. Beaujeu, 1955: 85 on the *Herakleia epini-
   kia*).
16 This argument is intended to permit greater precision than that permitted by Moretti's arguments for a date between 70 and 150 (*IGUR* I
   no. 179, p. 162) - which is, as I have already pointed out, the immediate deduction from the name Flavius. Of course Cumont's point (1899:
   245 n. 2 cf. 1896: 468 no. 67) that the double cognomen is not found
   after the beginning of Hadrian's reign (taken from Hülsen) is wrong:
   we have to find better grounds for dating it early.
17 For some examples in a religious context, note *IOSPE* IV 207, *ton
   idion adelphon*; Frisch, 1975: 154² [*Hē*] *speira ton idion e[uergetēn
   kai hierono*] *mon tou Dionusou*.
18 Gordon, 1972: 101, and n. 50.
19 Nesselhauf, 1939: 334 (=*AE* 1940 no. 100) corrects Detschew's misread-
   ing (1939: 130 no. 7) of LEO for DEO: 'Der Herausgeber liest *leo*, die
   Photographie zeigt aber, dass das was man erwartet, auch dasteht'
   (n. 3). It is surely about time that Detschew's old error ceased to
   appear as a 'fact', as it does in Vermaseren, 1963: 147 and Turcan,
   1975: 69. *CIMRM* 2269 not only perpetuates the mistake, but gives no
   indication that the inscription is broken at the bottom as well as at
   the top, or that its date can be deduced from the name Caragonius
   Philopalaestrus. (We have of course no reason to believe that the
   name Melichrisus is a sacred pseudonym connected with the man's grade
   since there was no reference to a grade in the first place; presumably,
   with Nesselhauf, we should read [*Invicto*]|*Deo*.)
20 Detschew thought that Cautopates' bird was a cock too; but the photographs hardly confirm him. No later monuments certainly provide Cautopates with a cock (Gordon, 1976a: 153 n. 50), while at degli Animali
   in Ostia he is represented on the floor at the end of the 'north' bench
   by an owl (cf. Beck, 1977: 6-7 on Cautopates' association with
   Antares); on 318, probably by a raven (and note also 359).
21 Hülsen, 1889: 683-684; Cumont, 1896: 468 no. 69 'M. Hülsen a rendu
   très probable que le P. Claudius Livianus [*sic*], nommé dans cette inscription, est le même qui fût préfet du prétoire sous Trajan vers
   102'. The identification was at once accepted by Smith, 1904: 88-89.

22 Vermaseren's incautious indicative mistranslates Cumont's proper con-
ditional (1896: 468, no. 69): 'Ce monument mithriaque serait donc le
plus ancien de tous ce que l'on peut dater'.

23 I had the advantage of looking at the monument with Mr. Cole of the BM
staff. It is clear that (pace Vermaseren) the right arm is modern in
its entirety; also the left foreleg, most of the bull's tail and those
parts of the torchbearers excised in Pl. I. See also Smith, 1904: 89.
Mr. Cole suggests that the elaborate decoration of the scabbard may
have been intended as insets for semi-precious stone or glass. The
bull's eye was not drilled.

24 Though Vermaseren quotes *CIL* VI 30818 his bibliography is simply copied
from Cumont. 30818 notes that the monument is first recorded by Celso
Cittadini (1553-1627, cf. *CIL* VI.1, p. LVI) 'apud antiquarium Card.
Farnesii, via Iulia'; Bianchini's notes are not the first record of the
monument, as *CIL* VI 718 suggests, as Cumont consequently imagined, and
as *CIMRM* misleadingly repeats.

25 The monument gives the impression of having been conceived as a bas-
relief: the back is quite rough, and carries the marks of a coarse
chisel; and it has no 'depth'. Such impression of depth as is achieved
is obtained by drilling the point at which bull and ground meet in a
continuous line. Indeed almost all the interstices (the outline of
the bull's legs, behind its ears, the outline of the snake) are drilled, not cut. And yet it has an inscription on the *back*.

26 *CIMRM* 594 gives only the inscription on the back of the bull, but Vermaseren's failure to provide line indications (or to mention that the
inscriptions differ) gives the impression that this is the reading of
the inscription on the front. Although the *v.s.* of the inscription on
the base is abraded, it is clearly visible under proper illumination.

27 No late first century cursives are similar: Gordon, I no. 151 pl. 63
(91 and 92 AD); no. 141 pl. 59a (78 AD); the closest mid-century
cursive is II no. 223 (160 AD), but there are many differences in
detail and in overall impression. It should be noted that Livianus'
name appears on a Hadrianic *fistula* from Praeneste (*CIL* XIV 3439)
which perhaps implies that he was still alive in the 120's (cf. *PIR*
II^2 no. 913).

28 I would date them approximately as follows:

Late Antonine	368	588	
Late Antonine/Severan	181	366	417
Severan	390		
Mid 3 cent.	350		

The earliest will then be around 50-60 years later than 593. It may be
worth stressing the relationship revealed here between 'plebeian'
sculpture and the frescoes at Barberini and Capua Vetere.

29 We may take four details (excluding the monuments already compared):
(1) the left leg of Mithras with the foot showing in a curiously
'unnatural' position: *CIMRM* 172, 173, 174, 318, 321, 321bis, 350, 357,
370, 396, 435, 532, 596, 601, 607, 641, Marino, 657, ? 337. Whereas in
the Marino and Barberini frescoes, and in 596, the foot is placed in
the centre of the bull's back, in later monuments it tends to be displaced as in 593: compare 174, 321, 350, 435, 598 (but not 357). This
stance is common outside Rome and the Campagna: for example, 37, 92,

163, 1083, 1118, 1275, 1283, 1306, 1308B, 1599, 1641, 1643, 1658, 1721, 1727, 1741, 1780, 1791, 1804, 1816, *JMS* I.2, pl. VI and p. 200, 1871, 1879 etc.

(2) The snake coiled round the bull's foreleg: 530, 587, 657 cf. 357, 607. This detail occurs throughout the period from which we possess Mithraic sculpture.

(3) Exaggerated forequarters and heavy dewlap of bull: 534, 557, 650.

(4) Type of tunic (judging from what remains): 164, 172, 173, 174, 208, 318, 335, 337, 352, 370, 430, 554, 557, 584, 596, 598.

The position of the bull's legs becomes standard in Roman representations and is similar to that found in Trajanic representations of Nike killing the bull (on the frieze of the Basilica Ulpia for example: Borbein, 1968: pl. 20.1).

30 Robert, 1963: 536-68; 516 n. 2. A second century inscription from Ostia (found by Petrini; ? from Sette Sfere) calls Mithras *deum solem Mithram* (*CIMRM* 247; correct version in *CIL* XIV 61) and Pareti dipinte (late second century) has a unique *thronum solis* constructed behind the central altar (266 [cf. 223b, correct version in XIV 4312]; Becatti, 1954: 60-63 + figs. 13, 14); presumably the Mitreo Aldobrandini had something similar: 233 [correct version in XIV 4314] lines 1-4 *deum...marmoreum cum throno omnibusque ornamentis* (late second century). Ostia seems to have known a version of the mysteries which emphasised Mithras' solar character to an unusual degree.

31 *CIMRM* 17 can of course be dated between 161-180 or 197-c. 210. Both *arcarii* and the more senior *dispensatores* were slaves, opting for earlier promotion and a provincial posting, if Weaver, 1964a: 84, cf. 1972: 241, is right. *Helios Mithras* occurs on 2259, 2260 (Kreta), 2265 (Nicopolis) (both Moesia Inferior); and on 2348 = *IG* II^2 5011 (Piraeus). There are two other Latin examples, from Rome, probably late second century: 574 *Soli Mitrhae aram d.d. Ralonius Diadumenus*; and 429. Note too possible readings of DSM: 1541, 1965, 2236.

32 Wikander, 1950: 40 asserts with some force: 'Il n'existe aucune attestation selon laquelle les inscriptions que se refèrent aux mystères de Mithras auraient jamais employé la forme Mithrēs'. The question is surely more doubtful, though of course I concede that the ending -e may represent a dative in -ae which is pronounced short, as is clearly the case in the late inscription 206 (385 AD), which gives for the genitive *summi invicti Mitre* (and *pretori* for *praetori*). This identical spelling *Mitrhe* occurs on 416 (Rome: mid-Antonine); 213=348 cf. Alföldy, *Epigraphica* 28, 1966: 16-17 - an inscription associated with the cult of IOM Dolichenus; 625 (by a Roman citizen with the cognomen *Marinus*, usually associated with Syrians or men of Syrian origin). The simple -e also occurs in Italy on 149, 360 and 563; elsewhere: 1243, 1315; 1456, 1464; 1644; 1805; 1976; *Stud. Clas.* 9, 1967 p. 197 no. 4.

33 The first accurate publication of the Faraşa Greek text was by H. Grégoire, 1908: 434-447; on Lidzbarski's version of the Aramaic, see Benveniste, 1938: 28 n. 67. Probably third century BC (Benveniste). Cumont's second interpretation, 'celebrated a mazdean/magian ceremony for Mithres' (1939: 68) is probably right; I see no reason to associate *emageuse* with Av. *yastan* (to sacrifice) with Widengren (1965: 178 n. 17).

Literary form *Mithres*: Strabo 15.3.13 (732C); Plutarch, *Vit. Alex.* 30; *Vit. Pomp.* 24; *De Iside et Osir.* 46 (369E) - but contrast *Vit. Artax.* 4; Lucian, *Deor. Concil.* 9; *Jup. Tragoed.* 8. The same form occurs earlier in Xenophon, *Oec.* 4. 24; *Cyrop.* 7.5.53; Ctesias (*FGrH* 688 F50) and presumably Duris (*FGrH* 76 F5) (both quoted in the same passage by Athenaeus 10, 45 [434D]). It is this form which enters the learned tradition in the west (for example, Nonnus, *Dionys.* 21. 250; 40. 400 (ed. Keydell); Hesychius, s.v.).

34 'Which refers to the mysteries' must be true, in spite of peculiarities. The inscription was found, with the first six lines erased thanks to *damnatio memoriae* of the emperor named, at the south-west end of the stadium in Anazarbus, and seems to be a public inscription: Gough, 1952: 131-132, no. 3. In the west the only inscriptions which refer to a grade out of a ritual context are funerary: the cult of Mithras seems to have had a different status in Anazarbus from its private character in the west. Secondly, the title of Mithras is peculiar. Curiously enough however three third-century Greek inscriptions in Rome (Aventine) have a very similar title for the god: *Zeus Helios Megas Mithra(s)* (473); *Zeus Helios Mithra(s) Aneikētos* (474); *Zeus Helios Mithra(s) Phanes* (475) (=*IGUR* I 106-108); and 2007, *Io(vi) S(oli) invi(cto) deo genitori* (Doştat) - on a relief of the mid- or late-Antonine period - seems to be a Latin translation of the title. I would conclude that this form was local to Anazarbus (and perhaps elsewhere in Cilicia) and that we have evidence of its dissemination into the west, though it is theoretically possible that the movement was from the west to Cilicia (cf. Gordon, 1975: 225 n. 37).

35 Presumably Celsus' form *Mithra* (indecl.) (ap. Origen, *Contra Celsum* VI. 22) is derived from Euboulus, and perhaps Justin Martyr's (*Apol.* I 66; *Dial. cum Tryph.* 78), though he seems also to have used *tou Mithrou* (*Dial.* 70). *Mithra* could only represent the declined genitive form of a masculine *a*-stem in Doric, Lesbian or Aeolic (contraction of *-ao*) - and there is no reason to admit that here.

36 The assumption seems to have been taken over from the scholiast tradition (717 ed. Jahnke): *Quod autem dicit torquentem cornua ad illud pertinet quod simulacrum eius fingitur reluctantis tauri cornua retentare...*, endlessly repeated from Cumont, 1899: 245, 'Lorsque Stace écrivait le premier chant de la Thébaïde, vers 80 apres J.C. il avait déjà vu les représentations typiques du héros tauroctone' to Vessey, 1973: 136 n. 2, 'Statius was clearly familiar with representations of the god in his bull-slaying role'.

37 See Saxl, 1939: 4-11; Borbein, 1968: 43-97; Gordon, 1976b: 180 n. 15.

38 See Blawatsky and Kochelenko, 1966: 14-15, nos. 1-5, though their discussion (pp. 15-22) is wholly unsatisfactory. It should be observed that at least one of these figures was found in the grave of a woman (no. 1, p. 14), which indicates, quite apart from the iconographic dissimilarities, that they are not directly related to the common western form of the mysteries, though I do not agree with Will's view, expressed at the Second Mithraic Congress (see Bianchi, 1976: 85), that the figure has nothing to do with Mithra at all. We await Beskow's defence of his Crimean theory with sceptical interest.

Of course the motif of Mithras holding one of the bull's *horns* does

occur, twice on complex panelled reliefs (1301a [Besigheim: after the
'water miracle'] and 1137 [Rückingen: right hand end of second regis-
ter]); once alone on an altar (839: Rudchester); and once, if it is
not wrongly restored, on a statue (352: Rome). This motif also occurs
on Nike-monuments.

39 Turcan, 1975: 1 n. 1, picking up an implication of Bidez-Cumont, 1938:
I, 226-229, suggests that Statius may have been influenced by early
ideas about Mithras as demiurge, which presupposes the fusion 'de
Mithra avec Helios-Apollon, à qui les Stoiciens conféraient un rôle
géniteur'. I am doubtful of that on two grounds: I do not follow
Turcan in his estimate of the role of Poseidonius in this proto-
history of philosophical speculation about Mithras (cf. my comments on
Nigidius Figulus, 1975: 238 n. 95); and we have to concentrate on
Statius' knowledge of the Mithraic cave, as I stress below.

40 'Achaemenius' occurs elsewhere in Statius as a synonym for 'Persian':
Theb. 8.286; *Silv.* 5.3.187.

41 *HA* 3.3.7 (8-13). The passage clearly distinguishes 'Sol' from
'Jupiter': the first comes at the head of the army, *imago solis crys-
tallo inclusa fulgebat*, while the chariot of Jupiter follows the magi
and the 365 young men, *currum deinde Iovi sacratum albentes vehebant
equi*. Confusingly though, that chariot is followed by an *equus Solis*.
The pagan Iranian god of the sun (*Hvar* or *Hvar Khšaēta*) is familiar
from the surviving *Yašt* and from classical texts (Boyce, 1975: 68-69);
and it may be that this horse of the Sun is connected with Mithra.
The description of this military procession recalls Xenophon's (*Cyrop.*
8.3.10-13), though there are important detailed differences: the one
is not derived from the other. It is agreed that the *Thebais* was com-
pleted in 90 or 91, and begun perhaps in 79 (Vessey, 1973: 55).

42 We know from Plutarch that he obtained at least some of his information
from a certain Hermaeus (42, 368B), who wrote a book called *peri tōn
Aiguptiōn* or perhaps *peri tōn Aiguptiōn heortōn* (37, 365E), and who
probably lived in the first century AD (Griffiths, 1970: 77). Statius
may have known this text, although it is clear from Plutarch's essay
that a well-read belle-lettrist could find any number of books on
Egyptian myths and beliefs. Plutarch also dismisses those (65: 377B)
who identify literally the activities of Isis and Osiris with natural
changes (and see Griffiths, pp. 529-530) - which seems to be implicit
in Statius' identification of Osiris with the sun and his adjective
frugifer. One might conclude that Statius did not know what he was
talking about.

43 Carsten Colpe has recently (1975: 386-399) argued that the mysteries
were created deliberately with anti-Roman implications in the time of
Mithradates IV Eupator (120/112-63 BC) in Pontus. I find such a thesis
wholly unconvincing (and the more we know about the western mysteries,
the more unconvincing it appears); but he has at least reminded us of
the complexity and variety of the cults of Mithra in Anatolia. As I
have observed earlier (1975: 245 n. 119, though I no longer agree with
all my remarks there), the Mithrakana may indeed have been an important
source, though the argument that we can have any knowledge of its
ancient form depends itself upon one's opinion of Mary Boyce's general
thesis that modern evidence can properly be used to illuminate ancient

Zoroastrianism (1975: on which see the review in this issue of the Journal by J.P. Asmussen).

44 A new discussion of the relationship between the mysteries and the Zoroastrian pseudepigrapha is badly needed. Beck's interesting point (1976) about Scorpius and the planting season, quoted by Pliny, *NH* 18.55.200 from 'Zoroaster' (=Bidez-Cumont, 1938: II, 226-227), is a small addition to a convincing dossier which suggests to me that a good deal of the teachings of the mysteries circulated among the pseudepigrapha.

BIBLIOGRAPHY

Beaujeu, J. 1955. *La religion romaine à l'apogée de l'Empire, I: La politique religieuse des Antonins (96-192).* Paris.

Beck, R.L. 1976. A note on the scorpion in the tauroctony. *JMS*, 1, 2, 209-210.

Beck, R.L. 1977. Cautes and Cautopates: some astronomical considerations. *JMS*, 2, 1, 1-17.

Benveniste, E. 1938. *Les mages dans l'Iran ancien.* Paris.

Beskow, P. 1978 (forthcoming). The expansion of the mysteries of Mithras: some considerations. (To appear in the *Proceedings* of the Second Mithraic Congress, Tehran, 1975.)*

Bianchi, U. 1976. The second International Congress of Mithraic Studies, Tehran, Sept. 1976. *JMS*, 1, 1, 77-92.

Bidez, J. and Cumont, F. 1939. *Les mages hellénisés.* 2 vols. Bruxelles-Paris.

Blawatsky, W. and Kochelenko, J. 1966. *Le culte de Mithra sur la côte septentrionale de la Mer noire.* EPROER 8. Leiden.

Borbein, A.H. 1968. *Campanareliefs: typologische und stilkritische Untersuchungen.* MDAI (RA), Suppl. 14. Heidelberg.

Boyce, M. 1970. Toleranz und Intoleranz im Zoroastrismus. *Saeculum*, 21, 325-43.

Boyce, M. 1975. *A history of Zoroastrianism, I: The early period.* Handbuch der Orientalistik, ed. B. Spuler, I.8.i.2: 2a. Leiden/Köln.

Campbell, L.A. 1968. *Mithraic iconography and ideology.* EPROER 9. Leiden.

Chantraine, H. 1967. *Freigelassene und Sklaven im Dienst der römischen Kaiser.* Forschungen zur antiken Sklaverei, I. Wiesbaden.

Colpe, C. 1975. Mithra-Verehrung, Mithras-kult und die Existenz iranischer Mysterien. *Mithraic Studies*, II pp. 378-405 (ed. J.R. Jinnells). Manchester.

Cumont, F. 1896. *Textes et monuments figurés relatifs aux mystères de Mithra.* Vol. II. Bruxelles.

Cumont, F. 1899. The same, Vol. I. Bruxelles.

Cumont, F. 1939. Monuments de Mithra en Asie mineure. *Anatolian Studies in honour of W.H. Buckler*, pp. 67-76. Manchester.

Daniels, C.M. 1975. The role of the Roman army in the spread and practice of Mithraism. *Mithraic Studies*, II, pp. 249-274 (ed. J.R. Hinnells). Manchester.

Detschew, D. 1939. Antike Denkmäler aus Bulgarien. *JOAI*, 31, Beiblatt, 121-140.

Domaszewski, F. von, 1896. *Die Marcussäule auf Piazza Colonna in Rom* (with Petersen, E. and Calderini, D.). Berlin.

Dunand, M. 1967. Rapport préliminaire sur les fouilles de Sidon en 1964-1965. *BMB*, 20, 27-44.

Dunand, M. 1973. Le temple d'Echmoun à Sidon: essai de chronologie. *BMB*, 26, 7-25.

Francis, E.D. 1975. Plutarch's Mithraic pirates (Appendix 1 to Cumont's The Dura Mithraeum). *Mithraic Studies*, I, pp. 207-210 (ed. J.R. Hinnells). Manchester.

Fraser, P.M. 1960. Two studies on the cult of Sarapis in the hellenistic world. *Opusc. Athen.*, iii (Skrift. Utgiv. av. Svensk. Institut. i Athen., 4°, VII). Lund.

Fraser, P.M. 1967. Current problems concerning the early history of the cult of Sarapis. *Opusc. Athen.*, vii (Skrift. Utgiv. av. Svensk. Institut. i Athen., 4°, XII). Lund.

Fraser, P.M. 1972. *Ptolemaic Alexandria*. 3 vols. Oxford.

Frisch, P. 1975. *Die Inschriften von Ilion*. Inschriften griechischer Städte aus Kleinasien, 3. Bonn.

Gordon, A.E. and J.S. 1958-65. *Album of dated inscriptions, Rome and the neighbourhood*. 4 vols. Berkeley and Los Angeles.

Gordon, R.L. 1972. *Mithraism in the Roman Empire*. Unpublished PhD dissertation, Cambridge.

Gordon, R.L. 1975. Franz Cumont and the doctrines of Mithraism. *Mithraic Studies*, I, pp. 215-248 (ed. J.R. Hinnells). Manchester.

Gordon, R.L. 1976a. The sacred geography of a *mithraeum*: the example of Sette Sfere. *JMS*, 1, 2, 119-165.

Gordon, R.L. 1976b. A new Mithraic relief from Rome. *JMS*, 1, 2, 166-186.

Gough, M. 1952. Anazarbus. *Anatolian Studies*, 2, 85-150.

Grégoire, H. 1908. Note sur une inscription gréco-araméenne trouvée à Faraşa. *CRAI*, 434-47.

Griffiths, J.G. 1970. *Plutarch's De Iside et Osiride* (ed., trans. and comm.). University of Wales Press.

Griffiths, J.G. 1975. *Apuleius of Madaura: the Isis-Book* (Met. XI). EPROER 39. Leiden.

Hornbostel, W. 1973. *Sarapis: Studien zur Überlieferungsgeschichte, den Erscheinungsformen und Wandlungen der Gestalt eines Gottes*. EPROER 32. Leiden.

Hülsen, C. 1889. Zu Martial. *Berliner Philologische Wochenschrift*, 9 (no. 22) cols. 683-684.

de Laet, S.J. 1949. *Portorium: étude sur l'organisation douanière chez les Romains*. Rijksuniv. te Gent: Werken uitg. door de Fac. van de Wijsbegeerte en Letteren, 103. Brugge.

Marucchi, O. 1924. Frammento di una edicola sacra ad Ercole Esychiano. *NS*, 67-69.

Moretti, L. 1968. *Inscriptiones Graecae Urbis Romae*, I: nos. 1-263. Roma. [IGUR.]

Nesselhauf, H. 1939. Publicum portorium Illyrici utriusque ripae, *Epigraphica*, 1, 331-338.

Nilsson, M.P. 1961. *Geschichte der griechischen Religion*. Vol. II[2]. München.

Nock, A.D. 1937. The genius of Mithraism. *JRS*, 27, 108-113.

Pflaum, H-G. 1958. Principes de l'administration romaine impériale. *Bull. Fac. de Lettres, Strasbourg*, no. 3, 1-17.

Ritterling, E. 1925. *art.* Legio. *RE* XII, cols. 1376-1829.

Robert, L. 1963. *Les noms indigènes dans l'Asie mineure gréco-romaine*, I. Paris.

Roll, I. 1977. The mysteries of Mithras in the Roman Orient: the problem of origin. *JMS*, 2, 1, 53-68.

Saxer, R. 1967. *Untersuchungen zu den Vexillationen des römischen Kaiserheeres von Augustus bis Diokletian*. Epigraphische Studien, 1. Köln/Graz.

Saxl, F. 1931. *Mithras: typengeschichtliche Untersuchungen*. Berlin.

Smith, A.H. 1904. *A catalogue of sculpture in the Department of Greek and Roman Antiquities, British Museum*. 3 vols.[Vol. 3] London.

Stambaugh, J.E. 1972. *Sarapis under the early Ptolemies*. EPROER 25. Leiden.

Turcan, R. 1975. *Mithras platonicus: recherches sur l'hellénisation philosophique de Mithra*. EPROER 47. Leiden.

Vermaseren, M.J. 1963. *Mithras, the secret god*. London.

Vessey, D.W.T. 1973. *Statius and the Thebaid*. Cambridge.

Weaver, P.R.C. 1963. The status nomenclature of the Imperial freedmen. *CQ*, n.s. 13, 272-278.

Weaver, P.R.C. 1964a. The slave and freedmen 'cursus' in the Imperial administration. *PCPhS*, n.s.10, 74-92.

Weaver, P.R.C. 1964b. *Vicarius* and 'Vicarianus' in the Familia Caesaris. *JRS*, 54, 117-128.

Weaver, P.R.C. 1972. *Familia Caesaris: a social study of the Emperor's freedmen and slaves*. Cambridge.

Widengren, G. 1955. Stand und Aufgabe der iranischen Religionsgeschichte, II. *Numen*, 2, 47-132.

Widengren, G. 1965. *Die Religionen Irans*. Stuttgart.

Widengren, G. 1966. The Mithraic mysteries in the greco-roman world with special regard to the Iranian background. *Persia e il mondo greco-romano*, pp. 433-455. Accademia dei Lincei. Roma.

Wikander, S. 1946. *Feuerpriester in Kleinasien*. Acta Reg. Soc. hum. Litt. Lundin. 40. Lund.

Wikander, S. 1950. Études sur les mystères de Mithras: I, Introduction. *Vetenskaps-Societeten i Lund: Årsbok*. Lund.

Will, E. 1955. *Le relief cultuel gréco-romain*. BEFAR 183. Paris.

Plate I CIMRM 593 with modern restorations cut away (original photo: British Museum)

A new Mithraic relief from Rome

In 1968 the Cincinnati Art Museum acquired a Mithraic relief, the gift of Mr and Mrs Fletcher E. Nyce.[1] Although a photograph has appeared in the *Museum News*, 1969: 47 (see also *The Sculpture Collection of the Cincinnati Art Museum*, 1970: 53), the piece is of sufficient interest to merit fuller treatment (see pl. I).[2] The precise provenance is not known, but it is supposed to have been found in the Via Praeneste, Rome: there is, as we shall see, good reason to accept a Roman origin. It is in limestone, H. 0·625, W. 0·952, D. 0·178 m. Part of the right-hand side is missing, including the hindquarters of the dog and the bust of Luna except for the bottom left-hand corner of her robe. Mithras is represented in the usual attitude, and in 'Persian' dress: the left foot is naked, not booted. His left hand is placed under the bull's lower jaw, not with the fingers placed in the nostrils as usual. His head is turned towards the dagger, not towards the upper left-hand corner of the relief. The bull is relatively large, especially the forequarters,[3] and the tail ends naturalistically in ordinary hair; there are no marks representing blood around the wound. The dagger has a large pommel, which perhaps suggests that it was supposed to be a *sword*.[4] Dog, snake,[5] and scorpion (with a very long tail) are all in the usual positions; but there is no trace of the raven.

The scene itself is represented within a slightly recessed semicircle, from which Mithras himself and at least the bull's head emerge in *alto-rilievo*. The synclines created between this recess and the top border were occupied by Sol (L) and Luna (R), of whom only the first survives. This bust is carefully designed to suggest a partly-stated tondo: the head, though full-face, is slightly inclined towards the spectator. The corona has thirteen rays, the left bottom most carved in shallow relief.[6]

The work is careful, with great attention to detail: note the bull's muzzle, the hair around the horns, the shaded ribs; the nails on Mithras' toes; the curls in Sol's hair. This is itself unusual in Mithraic sculpture. There are several indications of date. Mithras' hair cascades heavily to below the nape; it has been drilled but without the raking technique common in third-century reliefs: it is mostly chiselled.[7] Sol's hair is more elaborately finished, and the drill technique different. The face is smoothed and polished in the manner associated with certain Anatolian workshops, although I do not think that there is sufficient evidence to associate this relief with one of those workshops in Rome.[8] None of the eyes is drilled, but the mouths of Sol and Mithras have a single small hole at each corner.[9] Mithras' face is intent but without that 'baroque' pathos so common in Severan and later work. These indications suggest a date in the mid-Antonine period, *c.* A.D. 160-170.

In a sense then the relief is simply an addition to the dossier for the mysteries from Rome, neither spectacular nor novel. But it does offer two potentially interesting lines of enquiry which I wish to pursue here.

I

The first concerns its relationship to other known reliefs. In 1969 Professor Vermaseren published a relief in his possession, also from Rome or the neighbourhood (called hereafter Amsterdam: Vermaseren, 1969: 643–646). [See pl. II here.] Although much smaller (H. 0·285, W. 0·455m) it shares some notable features with the Cincinnati relief. Vermaseren also called attention to some other monuments, though for various reasons I wish to introduce at this point only *CIMRM* 548 (Sala dei Animali, Vatican)[10] [pl. III here] and 662 (Asciano: now in the Accademia Belgica) [pl. IV here].[11] We may indicate the more obvious similarities by means of a table:

	Cincinnati	Amsterdam	548	662
Torchbearers absent	x	x	x	x
M's hand beneath lower jaw; bull's head pulled vertical	x	x	x	x
Bull's eye bulges	x	x	x	x
Bull's tail natural (no corn-ears)	x	x	restored	lost?
Bull flat on ground with offside hindleg fully extended	x	x	x	x
M's head pointing towards the dagger	x	x	restored but probably with good evidence	x
M's short-sleeved outer garment	x	x	partly restored	x
M's long-sleeved under-garment	x	x	restored	x
M's right foot naked	x	x	x	x
Top edge of cloak folded over	x	x	partly restored	x
Dog's paw fully extended on bull's shoulder	x	x	x	x
First coil of snake below head to left	x	x	restored but probably with good evidence	x

On these grounds alone we may surely add the Cincinnati relief to Vermaseren's series (1969: 644–645). Indeed we may go further. If we compare the new relief with 548 (Vatican), we can see that the similarities are such that one must be a copy of the other, or both be direct copies of the same original. The point is clearest if we take the manner in which the tunic-folds are treated (as I have noted, the head of 548 is modern). Above the belt, both reliefs have two major pleats, falling at the same angle, the right-hand larger than the left one; below the belt, there is in each first a large V-shaped fold and then a curious ⌒-shaped lift in the skirt between Mithras' legs. In this respect at least 662 is very close. Note also that in both 548 and Cincinnati the snake emerges from the rock itself (it is only the upper part of the snake on 548 that is restored): that the bull's ribs are in each case carefully indicated, and the inguinal pleat identically treated – likewise the hock of the off-side foreleg; that Mithras' foot meets the hindleg rather high up; that the dewlap and penis are extremely similar in each case. Cincinnati is obviously a cruder version of the original (perhaps because even free limestone is more brittle than marble) and there are slight differences: the angle of the dagger; the stance of Mithras in relation to the bull is in 548 far more naturalistically 'convincing' than in the other; the Cincinnati bull is proportionately larger.

Whether 548 and Cincinnati derive from a lost original or whether one is a direct copy of the other (and in that case I suppose that the 'high' art example need not be temporally prior), there is an obvious point to make: 548 is a statue-group, Cincinnati a relief. Now the statue-group is almost as characteristic (not peculiar) an aspect of the Roman mysteries as is the *stela*-type of the Danube or the monumental complex relief of the Southern Rhineland.[12] Yet I know of no discussion of the relation between statue and relief.[13] The establishment of a direct relationship between 548 and Cincinnati permits an initial hypothesis however: instead of dealing with the statues separately from the reliefs as though they were independent formations, we should suppose a constant oscillation between statue and relief in Rome, a constant metamorphosis of the statue into the relief, of relief into statue, and both in constant relation to painting whether on plaster or fabric. None of these modes is discrete, however much they may differ in terms of their communication of 'information'.

If we add to these two monuments Amsterdam and 662 (Asciano), a further point becomes clear: although each bears a close relationship to the first two, each is also in a number of respects divergent. Again, this may be seen best by means of a table (I leave systematic comparison with 548 and Cincinnati to the reader):

Asciano	Amsterdam
Bull's ribs shaded	Ribs unshaded
Inguinal fold same as 548 and Cinc.	Inguinal fold unemphasized
Small bull	Large bull with heavy forequarters, like Cinc.
[Tail lost]	Tail like Cinc.
Scorpion pointing half-right, with a long tail not near testicles	Scorpion like Cinc.: same direction, long tail
Snake comes from rock	Snake along ground

M.'s clothes like 548 and Cinc.	M.'s clothes folded quite differently
M.'s hair in long ringlets	M.'s hair in heavy locks, similar to Cinc.
M. set far forward	M. almost twisted backwards
Scabbard very like 548 and Cinc.	No scabbard
Peculiar treatment of cloak at brooch and shoulder	Treatment here very like 548 and Cinc.

So although each is in some ways very close to what I will for this purpose term the original, each has divergences from it, some marked. The major divergences of 662 are the size of the bull, the stance of Mithras (I am not sure what happened to the bull's offside hind-hock), and the treatment of the hair; of Amsterdam, Mithras' clothes, his hair and his stance. In effect, the latter is simply a less detailed, more casual, version, in lower relief, of the 'original', while 662 is more individualistic.[14] And it would hardly be too much to suggest that this is the true source of the bewildering variety of Mithraic representations of the bull-killing scene: not a fixed number of 'types' and 'subtypes' mysteriously found in juxtaposition (Campbell, 1954: 7–23), but endless minor alterations to a limited number of original attempts to represent the idea of the bull-slaying as imagined by the early Mithraists in the West, whether they were working from memory of earlier Anatolian attempts or not. There are, notoriously, virtually no straight Mithraic copies, in spite of the general uniformity of the overall patterning and the constituent elements, but rather infinite minor idiosyncrasy from a limited number of models. One of the most obvious features of early Roman Mithraic iconography is the variety of schemes, some of which succeed in some sense in establishing themselves as dominant, others of which are fashionable for a time but then virtually disappear (like the group we are discussing here), and yet others of which are never repeated at all so far as we know (such as Kriton's statue, *CIMRM* 230 from the Mitreo delle Terme del Mitra, Ostia,[15] or 334, with its Anatolian resonance [Vermaseren, 1950: 142–156]). And that variety is precisely what one would expect in a fluid initial situation in which a new religion was establishing itself in relation to pre-existing artistic conventions and models.

Yet the number of possible 'minor idiosyncrasies' may quickly lead even within the same type to very large apparent differences, as these four monuments show. We have two statues (548 and 662) and two reliefs. The similarity of detail between the statues does not prevent 662 from appearing very different from 548, because the bull's size and Mithras' stance are visually dominant. The differences between the reliefs are even more marked, though they are extremely close in relation to the central group itself: for Amsterdam adopts a double outer frame, and within that a roughly ogee-shaped schematic cave, above which are represented Sol and Luna quite naturalistically in fully detailed chariots (Vermaseren, 1969: 645–646), whereas in Cincinnati the luminaries, though no less 'naturalistic', are represented in tondo-form, the effect of which is to make them both more 'symbolic' and less 'natural'. In other words, the greater the information content of the item, the more variables there are. And the more variables, the more rapidly the original may become virtually unrecognizable. There is a further point here. We may surely conclude that the frame and indeed the background of reliefs were completely optional, in the sense that they could be decorated or elaborated in any way familiar to the iconographic repertoire of the sculptor. The greater range of this repertoire in Italy inevitably gave rise to the sheer diversity with which we are there presented. Frames are not then significant in the way in which Campbell imagined (1954: 10–17): one could have no frame, a linear frame, a double frame (extreme edge and cave), no specific limit, the cave as frame, and many others, all as one wished. Frames are useless as a means of organizing the range of Mithraic reliefs, except in the special cases of the Italian, Danubian and Rhine complex reliefs. In this sense, almost all Mithraic relief-art is 'original'.

We may exemplify the next point by selecting a few salient characteristics of the Cincinnati relief (which is one of the earliest datable from Rome) and trace their distribution among other and later reliefs and statues from the same area. Again, this is best shown by means of a table:

Cincinnati	Parallels from Rome, etc.
Mithras' head down	586; 662; Amsterdam; probable: 337, 530, 548; possible: 415; 556; 587
Hand beneath bull's muzzle	230; 390; 548; 662; Amsterdam
Short sleeves	181; 310; 357; 370; 546; 548; 557; 588; 598; 662; Amsterdam; probably 337, 408
Bare feet	546; 548; 557; 662; Amsterdam; possibly 245; 310; 337
Background covered with stones/rock	173, 397a, 415, 598
Luminaries in tondo	435 (Luna); 585; 641a; b (Luna); possibly 437; 588; 598
Relief without formal frame	245 (part); 321; 334; 397; 437; 554; 598; 615; 635; 654 etc. Possibly 321bis; 430
Snake from rock	See note 5 above

One has only to glance at these items to see that few of them look very close to our group. We may then argue that there is a limited number of details (the list is by no means exhaustive), details which in principle can be inventoried, just as a lexicon inventories the words in a language. And perhaps the comparison with language is worth pursuing.[16] For although the words available in a language at any one moment is limited, they can be combined according to the rules of the language in an almost unlimited number of ways. In the case of Mithraic art we have a limited number of 'words', a relatively large proportion of which are synonyms, in the sense that one can substitute for the other without radical shift of meaning. Yet the overall number of possible 'sentences' (if we include frame, proportion and 'information' too as variables) is extremely large. And of course it is this 'syntactic' possibility which generates the bewildering variety of Mithraic art. And further, this 'language', being simply a dialect of a wider and much more complex iconographical language available in the craft-community (and among their Mithraic patrons), is capable of endless innovation from that wider language.

I think it is worth pointing out a consequent analogy. The representation of divinity in the ancient world can be seen as a form of 'naming'; the wrong name is vain or even dangerous: the right one grants the namer both access and power. The just iconographical representation of divinity is a claim upon the god, with a power comparable to the 'just' name. The craftsman and his patron combine to perform the role of Plato's ὀνοματουργός in the *Cratylus* (see the brilliant treatment of this theme in Gérard Genette, 1976). Every true 'name' has to correspond with the essence of the named. And it is perhaps this obligation to the true name which is the source of the gross stereotypical quality of ancient sacred art, and Mithraic art in particular, whatever the implication of my earlier point about detailed variation. The chance of a radical departure establishing itself is immensely reduced: the new form will inevitably appear to be a 'false name'. The stereotypy of the Mithraic bull-slaying scene is not in itself, then, evidence of the coherence of Mithraic doctrines over a wide range of the Empire (though apparently minor details may be): it is evidence only of the dominance of the true form of iconographic 'naming'.

Knowing the true name, the true representation, of the god, can then be seen as an aspect of the mysteries' claim to legitimacy, a claim made in many other ways also: by means of the appeal to Zoroaster, the fount of true wisdom about the cosmos; through the ambiguities of the cave/temple; through the correspondence between planets and grades; through use of dreams and visions. There is a good parallel in the Greek name for the *Chaldaean oracles*, λόγια: for these fragments teach a θεοπαράδοτος θεολογία (Proclus, *In Tim.* I. 408. 12 Diehl), 'par contraste avec des solutions de problèmes occasionels ou personnels, ou avec des révélations de caractère privé' (des Places, 1971: 10 [in the original a cautious question]). *Logia* derive from heaven. And precisely the same need for legitimacy is expressed in the endless discussions between writer and god in the Hermetic literature.

II

We may turn now to the second line of enquiry I proposed at the beginning. It will of course have been remarked that I have hitherto remained silent about the most curious feature of the new relief, the treatment of the background. There are, I think, three normal models in the reliefs from Rome and its immediate area. First, there may be no attempt to render the cave at all in the bull-killing scene (*CIMRM* 335, 375, 408, 417, 435, 530[?], 542, 556, 585, 588, 603, 607[?]). Alternatively, the stylized representation of the cave covers the entire field (*CIMRM* 334, 339, 397a, 415, 437, 542, 598). Third, the cave may be represented either naturalistically or in a stylized manner, but the area immediately round the bull-slaying is left void and plane (*CIMRM* 245, 321, 350, 357, 366[?], 368, 530[?], 532, 534, 539, 546, 549, 552, 554, 586, 597, Tor Cervara [= Lissi Caronna, 1965: 91-94], Richmond, Virginia [Vermaseren, 1969: 646-647], Amsterdam, 641, 655). Rather different effects are achieved by each of these choices. In the first case the act itself is recalled, not the environment – one might say that the act is deliberately 'cosmicized', especially in view of the extraordinary rarity of zodiacs in Rome (390 and 635 being the only examples known to me, the first of which is a fresco). In the second, the dominance of the pressing irregularity of the surround stresses the reference to an act performed as it were in the natural world, an act *available* to men. And the third case fuses these two emphases by a deft harmonisation of void and nature: it is intermediate between them.

But in the Cincinnati relief we find a treatment of the background rather at odds with these well-defined conventions in Rome: it is carved as a wall in *opus incertum*. The representation of the stones is careful and deliberate, the interstices deeply incised, the stones flattened.[17] At the same time, as I have noted already, the recessed semicircle within which the group is set is a clear reference to the cave motif. Such a treatment is unique within the corpus of Mithraic reliefs, and provokes some discussion.

The first point is that representations of *opus incertum* on non-Mithraic Italian reliefs are preternaturally rare: I can find only one possible, though potentially interesting, example, a Dionysiac scene from Cales (Squarciapino, 1943: pl. IIb with pp. 45–46: second century A.D.). Here a Silen reclines on a construction apparently made of *opus incertum* (it differs clearly from the rocks beneath Pan, and from other more usual representations of the childhood of Dionysus, e.g. Matz, 1969, III: pl. 211 no. 202; pl. 214 no. 200 and pp. 351–352, etc.).[18] Its interest will shortly appear. It must be clear then that the Cincinnati motif is not simply stereotypical in Roman art.

A second point may be made rather more circuitously, by exploring briefly another type of construction which is much commoner in Roman art, *opus quadratum*. Representations of walls in *opus quadratum* are frequent in Roman art: apart from innumerable instances on the Columns of Trajan and Marcus Aurelius (mostly city- or fort-walls), we find the walls of mythical and real cities,[19] temples,[20] and other buildings.[21] But there is some evidence of a tendency to employ the motif more 'decoratively', in a context with only the thinnest reference to a physical location. In the Museo archeologico in Florence there is a relief with Silvanus, Pan and a satyr shown against a wall of squared stones, a development of the normal complex-aedicola,[22] and on a Dionysus-sarcophagus from Frascati a *Quaderwand* serves to highlight the central figures of Dionysus and a satyr so as to separate them from the other figures in the same complex columnar frame.[23] In each case the ambiguity of the motif is obvious: it does not precisely represent an actual building but it is not simply a decorative scheme either. There is a rather similar ambiguity in Pompeian wall-decoration. It is well-known that during the period of the so-called 'first-style' walls were commonly painted (with or without stucco addition to the plane surface) to represent *opus quadratum*, an expensive type of construction.[24] This fashion was widespread in the hellenistic east from the early third century B.C. until as late as the Antonine period.[25] Although the 'second style' introduced more ambitious architectural scenes, *opus quadratum* is still occasionally represented above these, normally in a quite straightforward fashion.[26] But on a side wall of an alcove in a *cubiculum* of the Villa dei Misteri (second style) we find this painted *opus quadratum* as the backcloth to a painted frieze showing a crater, a griffon and an Arimaspian, and a shield.[27] What had once been a simple illusionist scheme (a real wall painted to look like another kind of wall) becomes the background for another illusion, the painted frieze.

It will be clear from this discussion that representations of *opus quadratum* always retained, however ambiguously, the proper denotation of a physical, man-made construct, an artifact. I can find no instances at all of representations of *opus incertum* used merely decoratively, which suggests that it always carried a semantic 'charge' as it were, even more strongly than *opus quadratum*. What then were its connotations? Although from *c.* 210 B.C. it was a standard type of construction in Italy, becoming less usual with the development of *opus reticulatum* and other forms of brick construction, it remained into the late Empire associated with man-made constructions *in nature*, whether fountains, rustic villas, or grottoes.[28] The only *imitations* of *opus incertum* known to me confirm this association. In the western Nymphaeum at the Grotta Pertusa, cut into the hill near the Arco di Malborghetto on the Via Flaminia, the tufa surround has been sculptured to look like *opus incertum* while the lip of the artificial niche is stippled to resemble pumice (this latter a common feature of *nymphaea*).[29] Perhaps less persuasive are some of the terracotta models of *nymphaea* from Locri, where in one or two cases the clay has been shaped to represent either that mode or natural rock – though the ambiguity is itself instructive.[30] It is probably not too much to conclude that in the empire *opus incertum* tended to be used outside the city – it is often called 'rustic stonework' – perhaps especially in connection with grottoes; in the first case to emphasize the rural nature of the building, in the second to disguise the bare rock with a fitting human construction, to 'civilize'. *Opus incertum* can then be termed ambiguous between the world of the city and the world of nature, assertively human, yet associated with 'the wild'. And perhaps it is here that we may recall the *opus incertum* construction upon which the Silen reclines in the Cales relief mentioned earlier (p. 172), the education of Dionysus by the divinities of the wild presaging his inherent ambiguity as lord of nature but also of civilization (Jeanmaire, 1951; note the multiple ambiguities suggested by Detienne, 1974: 1193–1234).

At this point we may return to the mysteries. Zoroaster's first cave in the mountains of Persia was, famously, natural: αὐτοφυὲς cπήλαιον . . . ἀνθηρὸν καὶ πηγὰc ἔχον.[31] Its implication in nature was double. It was, literally, a naturally formed cave surrounded by flowers, natural growth and water; but it also symbolized what is for humans ultimately 'natural', the physical cosmos. Now all actual *mithraea* beyond the foundation myth were conscious reproductions of that natural cave, but inherently ambiguous reproductions. We may explore these ambiguities along three dimensions.[32]

The first ambiguity is suggested by Porphyry himself a little after the passage I have quoted. Having discussed some of the symbolic content of Zoroaster's cave, he continues: μετὰ δὲ τοῦτον τὸν Ζωροάcτρην κρατήcαντοc καὶ παρὰ τοῖc ἄλλοιc δὶ ἄντρων καὶ cπηλαίων εἶτ' οὖν αὐτοφυῶν εἴτε χειροποιήτων τὰc τελετὰc ἀποδιδόναι (*De Antro* 6). This implies that the Mithraists themselves were aware of an ambiguity between the ideal natural cave and the actual man-made *spelaea*. Excavated *mithraea* can be disposed along a continuum: at one pole is the 'natural' cave, such as the examples at S. Giovanni di Duino (Ianovitz, 1972: 107–8), Bourg-Saint-Andéol,[33] St Urban,[34] Zgornje Pohanca (*CIMRM* 1457) or Epidaurum I (1882),[35] in which there is a minimum of construction by human hand but in which the natural space must be organized, activated, so as to become *espace religieux* by means of cult-furniture, markings on the ground, sacred water. At the other we have the *mithraeum* built either freestanding or occupying part of a larger construction, but at any rate entirely in brick or stone, such as any of the Ostian *mithraea*[36] or that in the Terme di Caracalla (457). Midway on the continuum we may place the *mithraea* which neatly combine these aspects of 'nature' and 'culture' and which help to confirm the suggestion that the existence of this tension was apparent to Mithraists – *mithraea* such as that at Schwarzerden, where the cult-relief was cut into the living sandstone, but the actual *mithraeum* constructed of wood (*CIMRM* 1280; Wightman, 1970: 239; Schwertheim, 1974: 178–179 no. 139); or the Heidenkapelle on the Halberg at Saarbrücken, which seems to have been deliberately hollowed out of the rock (Schindler, 1963: 119–136; 1964).

The second ambiguity is a consequence of the very doubleness of the symbolism of the cave: an earthly construction that maps utter nature, the open heaven. The human construction, the earthly cave, traps the endless changes and mysteries of the cosmos: it is still, but it 'moves' (Gordon, 1976: 120). Just as the Byzantine icon is a patch of clear glass through which the bounded human may catch a glimpse of heaven so, but more arrogantly, more definitely, is the *mithraeum* a vision, not only of 'this' world but also of another.[37] Indeed it is more than a vision, as a likeness is more than a map: it is a pathway to purity through the acquisition of wisdom. But the more perfectly contrived the *mithraeum* as a construction, the more perfectly is it a metaphorical statement of the path to heaven. The best example of Euboulus' cύμβολα . . . τῶν κοcμικῶν cτοιχείων καὶ κλιμάτων are precisely the most obviously contrived *mithraea*, Sette Sfere, Sette Porte, and, in their different ways, di Felicissimo, degli Animali, Heddernheim I and II, Walbrook, Dura (especially stage III).[38] The less emphatically natural the *mithraeum* the better it served its purpose as a map of the cosmos. The Mithraists were usually forced to make a choice between the two notions Zoroaster fused into one in his first natural *mithraeum* in the mountains of Persia. And so we may suggest a second guiding continuum for the analysis of *mithraea*, between the poles 'earthly' and 'heavenly', a polarity which of course itself resonates in every aspect of the mysteries. Although every *mithraeum* was simultaneously both 'heaven' and 'earth', in practice there usually had to be a choice concerning the symbolic charge most to be emphasized in its physical construction. Ironically enough, it was the man-made *mithraeum* which best represented the 'heavenly' meaning.

The third ambiguity concerns the intelligibility of the *mithraeum* as a code. A map is a special type of symbol in which, although the set of representations is quite arbitrary (though conventional) – contour lines, massed dots for sandbanks – there is a planned resemblance between 'reality' and the symbol, perfectly represented by the fact that a map is to scale and oriented to magnetic north. For that reason it may be called an 'icon'.[39] The *mithraeum* is just such a metaphorical statement about the cosmos, as it is also a statement about certain actions in the past, present and future. But it is a highly codified and enigmatic metaphor. The intention of the *mithraeum* is to communicate a message: but both tenor and vehicle are arcane[40] – like a poem of Mallarmé it reveals its message only to those who share the communication code. I have stressed elsewhere the singularity of the Mithraic grade-structure and of the provision of multiple, and increasingly significant, initiations separated by time.[41] Each of these initiations communicated a new religious identity as it conveyed the initiate further along the ladder of the grades. Part of that process was surely a more penetrating understanding of the metaphor of the *mithraeum*. Moreover, if the metaphor communicates its message opaquely to the initiates, it is designedly mute to the non-initiate: symbols include, but they also exclude. As a code then the *mithraeum* spans a continuum between complete incomprehensibility to complete intelligibility, poles represented by would-be *corax* at one end and the *Pater patrum* at the other. The code of the temple is a representation of the secrets of the universe, finally revealed, a representation which may be likened to a palimpsest, constantly overwritten by new meanings for each item of the code as the initiate proceeds towards wisdom.[42] In the mysteries, knowledge correlates with power and purity.

The relationship between the *mithraeum* and the relief is one of obvious complexity. Not only does each constitute a map of at least two ontologically distinct kinds of unseen reality, the historical and the cosmic; not only is each a metonymic sign of the other (note the simultaneous presence in temple and relief of Cautes and Cautopates, Mithras *petragenes*, *taurophoros*, of Sol, of sevenfold patterns, of zodiacal signs, of craters, snakes and lions . . .); but ritual actions within the *mithraeum* are displayed paradigmatically in the relief, notably in the scenes in which grade-holders serve at the feast of Mithras and Sol, and in the handshake of Sol and Mithras. A close examination of these relationships is not here relevant, but it may be observed, in the present context, that they are not exhaustive: relief and temple may profitably be related in terms of the continua which I have just outlined.

Just as *mithraea* may be arranged along a continuum between the poles of 'natural cave' and 'constructed temple', I suggest that the types of background represented on reliefs may not be as arbitrary as is usually supposed. At this level, reliefs may be plotted along a continuum one of whose poles is represented by the Louvre relief from below the Capitoline (*CIMRM* 415),[43] with its naturalistic rock, trees, animals: the skills of high art have been employed to render the scene as convincingly trompiste as possible. The event takes place beyond any doubt in the 'natural' world: only Sol and Luna force an allusion to the symbolic 'meaning'.[44] The continuum proceeds through more stylized representations of the cave, such as that in the Nersae relief (650), in which the cave border has been transmuted into lateral panels so as to represent the myth-cycle;[45] to the mass of reliefs in which naturalistic background has been obliterated in favour of concentration on the stylized act of slaying itself. Yet this concentration at once calls attention to the artificiality of the convention of the relief: the absence of naturalism amplifies the convention, especially where the sacred scene is bound by a border, severe in its rectilinearity, declamatory of human artifice. The relief faces the same dilemma as that faced by the constructors of *mithraea*, the dilemma presented by the ambiguity inherent in using the natural world as an image of the cosmos. And with the relief the ambiguity is even more marked: because although the relief at the pole of 'convention' is evidently man-made, in reality it takes more *artifice* to represent the 'natural' scene.

The second polarity was between the 'earthly' and 'heavenly' aspects of the *mithraeum*. In relation to the relief, we may distinguish a parallel continuum, again beginning with the representations of the natural cave which highlight the historicity of myth, the the literalness of the bull-slaying act.[46] The other pole is best represented by the Sidon relief.[47] Here there is no possible allusion to an earthly act: it is utterly and explicitly cosmic, universal. The figure of heavenly change-in-changelessness is used deliberately to characterize Mithras' deed; and all the usual types of additional information, except a reference to the seasons (which simply amplifies the major tone), are omitted. Midway between these poles fall those reliefs in which the zodiac forms the top of a stylized cave, a reconciliation between opposites whose very self-consciousness helps to confirm the appropriateness of the analysis offered here.[48]

The third ambiguity concerned the *mithraeum* as map, as a code which both informs and conceals according to the knowledge and status of the beholder. In applying this to the iconography, we should include the statues of Mithras as bull-slayer. In this context, we may view the sacred representation as a vehicle of information, as a language; ideas have been converted into an artefact, which has in turn a reciprocal effect upon the ideas, inasmuch as the iconography suggests an *appropriate* religious style, an appropriate form of piety, to the beholder.[49] We have then two poles, the pole of 'silence' and the pole of 'garrulity'. To illustrate the former, we may take another Louvre monument from Rome, *CIMRM* 587. Though large (H. 1·25, W. 1·33 m.), it registers in a perfunctory way, uninterestedly, the act of bull-slaying. There is no 'charge' in any feature of the statue, it is a mass of clichés, an extremely narrowed metaphor. Most of the related ideas have been suppressed, retained within the area of arcane knowledge. Of course that does imply that the arcane knowledge is communicated in other ways more directly controllable than the image – presumably by means of the oral teaching of senior members of the cult, whose position may thereby have been enhanced. But the 'silent' image has its own power: the stripped metaphor concentrates the mind of the beholder upon the single idea communicated, it asserts nothing irrelevant to it. The central saving act subsumes every possible statement. And the corresponding piety is submissive.

Slightly more informative is a statue like 370 (Vatican), with its attempt to capture both the violence and the pathos of the scene: Mithras' clothes swirl, the bull contorts, its eyes roll up, pupils expressionistically drilled; Mithras' face conveys both his spiritual agony and his divine power.[50] But it also conveys something of his relationship to the sun – the hair is drilled and flared to recall the radiate crown.[51] This Vatican statue thus shifts us a little of the way towards the pole of 'garrulity', in that it conveys not only information about the physical act but about its spiritual meaning and the status of the slayer. Less is assumed, more stated. It is less of a private language, more of a public statement.[52] The other pole, that of 'garrulity', is represented by various forms of complex relief of which the Osterburken example (1292) and one of the Apulum items (1958) constitute the 'ultimate' development on Rhine and Danube respectively.[53] The relief has become a document crammed with sequences of action which are both past and somehow actual, a metaphor which expresses both narrative and credo, statement and evaluation of a very extensive kind. Its information content is enormous, which in turn implies a rather different relation between adherent and source of religious authority. At least within the confines of the initiated group, knowledge is published, made explicit. Perhaps a comment on the intention of Ignatius Loyola's *Spiritual Exercises* is not out of place: 'Essentially a work on spiritual perfection, the *Exercises* were a manual of practice rather than meditation. Ignatius did not exhort, he guided. The soul was to be subjected, bullied, trained. The *Exercises* were not directed to clergy alone; they were drawn up for both clergy and laity. They were not aimed at the spiritual direction of a monastic order, they were a weapon to enable all manner of men to reach spiritual perfection. Each man was to fulfil himself, in accordance with the teachings of the Church' (Kamen, 1976: 257). The articulation of beliefs in the iconography is an articulation to a collectivity; the language necessarily more public; the collective meaning more insistent.[54]

It may also be worth observing here that 'naturalism' (by which I mean a deliberate effort to make the sacred image conform to criteria of dignified representation generalized within Roman art)[55] is itself a form of 'garrulity', in that it conveys extensive if cryptic messages for the beholder familiar with the conventions employed. So we may discern here a subsidiary polarity between highly naturalistic representations of the bull-slaying and highly stylized ones, such as the relief from Macerata (690)[56] or that from Commagena (1423). As Robert Turcan has recently reminded us, the lack of naturalism to be found in so many provincial reliefs may have nothing to do with artistic 'incompetence', as a conventionally 'italianate' attitude might assume, but rather with a particular attitude towards religious art.[57] While naturalism brings 'near', the stylized suggests the distance of divinity. The stylization of Mithraic reliefs may be understood as another kind of 'silence': divinity becomes discreet. Such tendencies become more marked into the fourth century, as the character of religious style changes.

These three levels of analysis seem to me to be of some potential value in suggesting a means of penetrating beyond the two most common attitudes towards the iconography of the mysteries. The first of these is characteristic of early work, but current even now, as the endless references to 'cattivo stile della scultura', 'travail médiocre' indicate, namely the notion that aesthetic considerations are primary. It hardly needs to be said that there is no point whatever in applying to Mithraic artefacts criteria irrelevant to them as metaphors: if the task is to understand the art, we can never rest content with the reiteration of private judgements about style. The second attitude is that associated with the iconographical work of L. A. Campbell (1954: 24–44), but with a long pedigree among art-historians, namely the attempt to discover on purely (?) formal grounds the 'history' of the Mithraic relief. Without underestimating the iconographical work already done, I would observe that the elementary work of systematic dating indispensable to such a task has scarcely begun; and that there is a fallacy involved in the assumption that the genetic enquiry can tell us more than the underlying question it poses (or more frequently assumes) – namely, what are the origins of the motifs? In other words, the iconographical approach is too narrowly historicizing to serve as a method by means of which we may approach a characterization of the religious style of the mysteries. From inappropriate questions we can obtain only inappropriate answers. An analysis based upon the notion of continua has the advantage of being open-ended – the three possible dimensions suggested here are by no means exhaustive – and non-genetic. Moreover the device serves to point out that Mithraic art may be expressive in a hitherto unsuspected way: what might appear to be quite arbitrary modes of organizing this *espace religieux* may in fact be understood as determinate choices between options, options concerning the underlying problem, which is the relation between actuality and meaning, between this world and Mithras, between integration and escape. In principle there can never be determinate answers to these questions: the art reflects that indeterminacy, quite as much as it establishes the limits within which choices could be made.

We may return, finally, to the background of the Cincinnati relief. The unique employment of carved *opus incertum*, with its connotation of 'contrivance in nature', suggests first of all a comparison with the Fellbach relief (*CIMRM* 1306), in which is represented inside the stylized cave a lamp suspended from the 'ceiling', a dagger and an altar. The original act within the cave is assimilated into the contrived *mithraeum*: the human construction of stone, brick or wood *is* the original temple of Zoroaster, the cave in which Mithras slew the bull, and the cosmos, all simultaneously. The Cincinnati relief suggests the same condensation of meanings by a different technique: the ambiguity of *opus incertum* recalls the ambiguity of the *mithraeum*. Both are contrivances in nature, although the Mithraic use of that ambiguity is pregnant in a way the mere technique of construction is not. In this sense, the relief, which represents a historical act, sets the act in an actual *mithraeum* with its ambiguity between natural cave and human contrivance. But the background can also be related to our second continuum, since the carved wall has been recessed immediately around the bull-slaying group: the act occurs in a *mithraeum* but

178

also (indeed, by that very token) in the cosmos. It is thus localized and historicized; universalized and detemporalized. And, to relate it to the third continuum, although it is relatively inert to the uninitiated, to those who 'know' it expresses all these ambiguities integral to the doctrines of the mysteries. The three continua are distinct only for the purposes of analysis: for the adherent, each relief and each *mithraeum* speaks an immediately intelligible and unified language, even if his comprehension must have a temporal dimension. True wisdom is not gained in a day.

The use of *opus incertum* as background constitutes, of course, a failed experiment in Mithraic art. As I have tried to show, other conventions came to be adopted to express the same ambiguities. It is nevertheless an instructive failure. For it seeks to relate the ambiguity of the *mithraeum* as a man-made contrivance reproducing a natural cave to its ambiguity as an earthly construction representing heaven, and to set the saving act of Mithras within the context of those ambiguities. It attempts a double integration of opposites. It thus refers unusually explicitly to the central problem of the mysteries as a religious system, the provision of a satisfactory and legitimated way of integrating man with god, the seen with the unseen, the material with the immaterial. And I stress *integration*: for the success of the mysteries lay precisely in their not being terroristic about the separation of world and divinity. The motif of world rejection was always countered by the motif of world-involvement and world-acceptance. The search for another world is a form of the search for a meaning in this one: paradoxically enough, the Mithraists 'escaped' into *this* world. Mithras reconciles the most puzzling antinomy of all.

The point of equilibrium is Mithras' point. He represents the true meeting of heaven and earth, the point which is neither too much nor too little. Yet that point is impossible except as an ideal for humans. An oscillation between the poles of excessive spirituality and excessive worldliness was inevitable: comparison with the early Church is instructive, and with Tertullian in particular.[58] And the art, inevitably, reveals that tension, as it illuminates also the ideal.

Notes

1 Accession no. 1968: 112. I am grateful to the Museum authorities for permission to publish the relief, and in particular to Mr Daniel Walker, Associate Curator, who kindly supplied the photograph and answered some questions about details which could not be answered without autopsy. I would also like to thank Kirsten Andersen in the Department of Classical Art, Boston Fine Arts Museum.

2 It is to be shown at the forthcoming exhibition at the Metropolitan Museum, New York, *Late Antique and early Christian Art*, Nov. 1977–Feb. 1978.

3 See the comments of R. Turcan concerning the bull on the Mauls relief (*CIMRM* 1400), 1976: 71.

4 Compare G. Ulbert, 1969: 97–128, pl. 17 no. 1, 2; pl. 18 no. 1a, 1b; pl. 29 (military swords with large pommels).

5 Italian examples are instructive: *CIMRM* 245: Becatti, 1954: 98 (Sette Porte)=*CIMRM* 288[2]; ?345; ?385; ?531; 548; ?601; 615; 662; ?693; 771, since they imply that the motif was

an element of Mithraic belief; I am disinclined to add the snake which swarms up the back of
Cn. Arrius Claudianus' altar in S. Clemente (*CIMRM* 339; photo available at the church,
reproduced by Caturegli, 1966: 21, fig. 9 [a totally worthless publication otherwise]), since I
think it is to be associated with the lion on the bottom right of the face: Gordon, 1976: n. 58
(p. 155).

6 A number of divine tondi from the second century survive; though a cliché of hellenistic art,
the form perhaps deserves closer study in a Mithraic context since so many reliefs present
Sol and Luna in this manner. See Vermeule, 1965: 370–371; 1968: 55–58; 88–91; Winkes,
1969: 41 n. 5; Deonna, 1954: 5–47.
    There is a bizarre variety in the number of rays assigned to Sol in the reliefs and frescoes.
Parallels to the number 13 are 641a (Fiano Romano); ?417 (Rome) and 1314. If the precise
number is significant, which it well may not be, we may have a reference to the thirteen months
of the luni-solar calendars (Samuel, 1972: 11–12) rather than to the fact that within the
quadrant (90°) between the tropic of Cancer and the equator, a seventh part is approximately
13° – the *triskaidekamoiria tou klimatos*. But in the mysteries one never can be sure (on
Mithraic *klimata* see Gordon, 1976: 142–145).

7 The hair is similar in arrangement to, though less careful than, that of Aion on the base of
Antoninus Pius' column (Apotheosis of Antoninus and Faustina, A.D. 161): Bianchi Bandinelli,
1970: 287 fig. 321. More loosely it resembles late hellenistic Alexander types (Bieber, 1964:
66, 77 and figs. 78–85; cf. 90–91).

8 For parallels, note the portrait of Marcus Aurelius as a youth, *c.* A.D. 147 [Antiquario del
Foro]: Bianchi Bandinelli, 1970: 285 fig. 319; cf. Wegner, 1939: 191–192, pl. 15 and pl. 32
(dated *c.* A.D. 139 by Andreae, 1973: fig. 438); the portrait of Vulcacius Myropnous [Isola
Sacra, *c.* A.D. 160]: Bianchi Bandinelli, 1970: 292, fig.328; and the bust of the young Commodus
[Museo Capitolino, *c.* A.D. 176]: *ibid.* 293, fig. 329. For the hair, note the cavalcade from the
base of Antoninus Pius' column, A.D. 160–1: *ibid.* 289 fig. 323, and the left-hand figure in the
Adoption-scene on Lucius Verus' victory monument (A.D. 165–69): Andreae, 1973: fig. 507.

9 For the technique at this period, note Inan and Rosenbaum, 1966: no. 121 pl. LXXIII
1–2 (portrait of a baby, mid-second cent. Asia Minor); *CIMRM* 339 (Ostia); a little later:
Squarciapino, 1943: pl. H a–c and pp. 44–46 (Dionysiac relief from Cales); *CIMRM* 650
(Nesce near Rome); *c.* A.D. 180–210, Wegner, 1966: no. 16 pl. 23a, b; 41a (Muse sarcophagus
from Via Appia); also nos. 55 pl. 24 a, b, c; 143 pl. 4b (a Greek example); 153 pl. 13d.

10 The restorations should be noted, though enough survives to make comparison possible:
Mithras' head, part of the cloak, part of the right foot (though enough survives of the original
to make it clear that it was naked), the arms from by the shoulder, including the hands; the
bull's muzzle (part), forelegs (part), tail; the offside rear hock beyond Mithras' foot and that
part of the base; most of the dog except the paws; the snake except for its extremities and the
connections with the bull. Details such as the angle of the head are likely to be reliable in an
eighteenth-century restoration.

11 Vermaseren (1969: 644–645) cites *CIMRM* 548, 556, 415, 587, 593 and 662 as members of
his group of related statues, basing his argument on the direction of Mithras' head. He then
excludes 415, 556 and 587 on the quite proper grounds that the heads are in each case restored
(though I think that the restoration may well be right in the case of 415). But he fails to note
not only that the head of 548 is also restored but that the entire trunk of 593 (British Museum)
from the waist upwards is modern, so that no argument whatever can be drawn from it (I
have prepared a note on this monument and its problems of dating, to appear in the next issue
of the *Journal*). The group must be reduced to four, 548, 662, Amsterdam and now Cincinnati.
But of course there is one other monument in which the head is certainly pointing down,
586 (Louvre: relief), and two others in which it very probably was, 337 and 530 (both known

only from drawings). But none of them look very similar to the group I am discussing: which simply indicates that one requires more than a single criterion, however remarkable, in order to establish relationships between monuments.

12 Although statues related to the mysteries are not rare outside Italy and Sicily, and Rome especially, statues of the bull-slaying *group* certainly are. I know of only *CIMRM* 27 (Sidon); 107 (Cyrene); Paribeni, 1959: 148 no. 431 (frg.: Cyrene); 122 (Rusicade); 771 (Fuente de las Piedras); 898 (LaBâtie Montsaléon) = Turcan, 1972: 10–12; 1768 (Aquincum IV); 1947 (Apulum, *canabae*). No less than three of these are from heavily hellenized areas, which leaves five for the rest of the Empire excluding Italy. The point is well made by Ernest Will, 1955: 33, 'Dans les provinces . . . le relief est roi' (and cf. 210–211).

13 It is naturally Cumont who comes nearest to such a discussion, since most others have deliberately set out to discuss only the relief (1899: 213–219). But he is deeply influenced by irrelevant aesthetic considerations (see too below, p. 177): 'Certains petits bas-reliefs n'ont jamais été que de vraies caricatures, dont les personnages approchent du grotesque, et rappellent par leur difformité ces bonshommes de pain d'épice qu'on rend dans nos foires' (p. 215).

14 I mean of course that it selects a number of details from the iconographical 'tool-box' more widely available, and substitutes them for those chosen by the 'original'. I do not imply that 'individualism' was a good for the sculptor. There are some valuable remarks on innovation in religious art in Bickerman, 1967: 131–161.

15 The date of this is early, perhaps *c.* A.D. 150 (Becatti, 1954: 83–84; Bieber, 1956: 311). Although it differs so sharply from all other later monuments, two points are worth noting. First, Mithras' hand and the angle of the bull's head are the same as in the Cincinnati group, and the small size of the bull recalls 662. Second, the stance is close to that of other Campanian Mithraic monuments, themselves deviant from the standard Roman and Italian stances (*CIMRM* 174, 201 and cf. the terracotta plate from Lanuvium, 207). If we add the highly exceptional 200 (Cales), we may at once suspect that the source of the deviance is the Campanian terracottas with their innumerable bull-killing Nikes and heroes. *CIMRM* 200 indeed holds the bull beneath the muzzle. I know of no Mithraic instance of this outside Rome and its immediate environs. That suggests that the Campanian terracottas, which went on being produced in standard styles until the early second century A.D., may indeed have influenced the development of some Roman types, to say nothing of the possibility that they influenced directly the iconography of the bull-slaying scene *tout court*. See in general on the terracotta animal-slayer scenes, Borbein, 1968: 43–115, 172–175 (though I disagree with many of his remarks concerning their relation to Mithraic iconography).

16 I may recall some interesting comments on fashion by Alison Lurie, 1976: 17, 'A complete costume, deliberately chosen, . . . may convey many different messages at once, providing us simultaneously with "information" about the age, sex, occupation, beliefs, tastes, desires and mood of its wearer. In America, a so-called "fashion-leader" will have several hundred "words" at his or her disposal, many of them rare or specialized in other ways, and thus be able to form literally millions of "sentences" expressing a wide range and subtle variations of meaning, qualified with a great many elegant "adjectives" or accessories. The sartorial vocabulary of a migrant farm worker, by contrast, may be limited to some five or ten colloquial terms, from which it is mathematically possible to create only comparatively few "sentences", almost bare of decoration and expressing the simplest concepts.' The study of variation in Mithraic iconography might well start with some such ideas as these.

17 The deliberateness of the cutting may be seen by comparing some of the representations of natural rock on central Italian Mithraic reliefs: *CIMRM* 321, 397, 415, 426, Tor Cervara, 534, 546, 598, 650, 654, Amsterdam, Richmond, Virginia. The closest parallel I can find is

VIII

A new Mithraic relief from Rome 181

the relief perhaps from Naples and now in the Musée de Cinquantenaire (173), in which the rocks of the background are somewhat flattened, and give a rather wall-like impression. As will appear, I do not think that the Cincinnati relief simply gives us a highly-stylized *natural* cave: the question is more complicated.

18 Rather similar rock/stones are to be seen on a Dionysiac cameo, with a Maenad suckling a panther inside a cave: Boyancé, 1960–1: 109 fig. 2, though they are definitely stylized. See too below, p. 173.

19 Achilles at Troy: Robert, 1890: pl. XXI nos. 45, 46. This type seems to be derived from a hellenistic painting (Lehmann-Hartleben, 1938: 92–97 and 98–99; 104), and continues into late antique art, for example on the Capitoline *tensa* (Stuart-Jones, 1926, I no. 13 (p. 179), II pl. 68). Note also the 'urbs maritima' in the Fall of Icarus in the House of Amandus, Pompeii: Beyen, 1960, II. 2: fig. 131 cf. p. 343 (third style); and the scene between Diogenes and Alexander in Helbig, 1963–72: no. 3303.

20 For example, the temple of Jupiter Capitolinus in Stuart-Jones, 1926, II: pl. 12 and I: 22–25; temple of Pan with *peribolos*: Matz, 1969: no. 176 pl. 196 (detail, pl. 198.1) and Commentary, p. 323; an Egyptian temple (Galleria dei Candelabri, III [1] 33): Amelung, 1936, III.2 Text: 227, pl. 106.

21 Emporium: West, 1941, II: 89 pl. XXV fig. 91a; stage-buildings: Reinach, 1912, II: 290.1; and in painting, Beyen, 1938, I: 111–135 with figs. 31–33; walls behind the figures of philosophers: Cumont, 1942: 291 fig. 65 (top register); tombs: Koch, 1975: pl. 79 nos. 73, 74; tomb of Lazarus: Testini, 1966: fig. 146 (crypt A6 dei 'Sacramenti': fresco); interior walls: Koch, 1975: pl. 81 no. 96; pl. 83 no. 8; 95 no. 113; pl. 88 no. 103.

22 Inv. no. 2917. See Wissowa, 1886: 161–166 and pl. XCII. Probably from Arezzo, ? first cent. A.D. 'Il fondo è formato da un forto muro di quadrelli, dal quale si staccano tre aperture a foggia di porte . . .'.

23 Matz, 1975, IV: pl. 303 no. 278 (drawing by Eichler of a monument from Villa Taverna, Frascati, now lost); and p. 469 no. 3. Another fusion of types – a cross between a conventional *scaenae frons* and a complex *aedicola* – is to be found in Beyen, 1936, I.1: fig. 44 (fresco: Casa di Apollo), in which there is a wall in *opus quadratum* around Apollo's niche. A comparable, and very late, fusion is presented on the lintel of Al-Moâllaka on which Christ enters Jerusalem: the city walls have been broken up to serve as columns separating the figures from each other: Engermann, 1974: pl. 3, esp. nos. 2, 3, 5. It is here very difficult to draw the line between literal meaning and decorative intention.

24 Among many treatments, see Borda, 1958: 5–18; Pfuhl, 1923: section 956.

25 Dawson, 1944: 58 n. 39 against Borda: 11.

26 For example: Casa di Sallustio, wall decoration in left *ala*: von Heintze, 1969: pl. 109 (before *c.* 80 B.C.); villa di P. Fannio Sinistore (Boscoreale), alcove in *cubiculum*: Borda, 1958: figs. on 29 and 31 (mid-first cent. B.C.); Villa dei Misteri, Rizzo, 1929: pl. VI.

27 Beyen, 1938, I: pl. 20c.

28 Lugli, 1957, I: 448–449; 479 and the list of monuments, 479–483; also the good brief discussion of Ward-Perkins, 1970: 159–162. The ambiguity is formal (in the French sense) in many texts: Lugli, 1938: 155–168 esp. 156.

29 Neuerburg, 1965: no. 222 pl. 185. Note some other monuments too: marble *opus incertum* in a *nymphaeum*: no. 21 pl. 48 (Villa di Iulia Felix, Pompeii, II. 7. 1) – which perhaps recalls the Pompeian fashion of painting a rough-stonework on Lares-altars; carving to represent rough-stonework: no. 203 fig. 179 (Ingresso agli Inferi, Hadrianic villa, Tivoli).

30 Arias, 1946: 157 f., figs. 29, 31; Neuerburg, 1965: 33, 53 and figs. 8, 9.

31 Euboulus ap. Porphyry, *De Antro* 6 (Arethusa: 8, lines 16–17).

32 Cumont's discussion of the relation between the different kinds of *mithraeum* is as naively

'historical' as Euboulus' (or Porphyry's): I should say 'pseudo-historical' rather (1899: 55-65). We may surely observe that the imposition of a historical or historicizing sequence upon phenomena can no longer claim any special privilege as a mode of understanding: it is simply an option, and in this case an unhelpful one.

33 *CIMRM* 895 with Turcan, 1972: 7-9 with pl. I; Walters, 1974: 4-5; Lavagne, 1976: 222-224.

34 *CIMRM* 1442: the cave was entirely natural, and is set today amid thick woods above the lake.

35 We may probably add the cave called 'lo Perso' on the side of the Capitol in Rome (*CIMRM* 414; Vermaseren, 1951: 38-41) and the spot where the Tor Cervara relief was found (Lissi Caronna, 1965: 91).

36 Vermaseren (*CIMRM* 244) argued that Ostian *mithraea* are not below ground level because of the danger of flooding (cf. the fate of the Walbrook *mithraeum*). Whatever our judgement upon this explanation, we should observe that it assumes that for Mithraists there was a norm. For that I see no evidence: the notion of a continuum of possibilities between 'above ground' to 'below ground' would have been more appropriate to the evidence.

37 See Peter Brown (with Sabine MacCormack), 1975: 19: 'It is this translucence of the good icon that made it, as it were, a window opening on to the other world.' (I owe this reference to Ray Van Dam.)

38 Respectively: *CIMRM* 239; 287; 299; 278; 1082; 1108; 814 with Grimes, 1968: 92-117; 34-36. Perhaps we should add Sutri, which may, as Cumont suggested (1937: 96; cf. Sestieri, 1934: 33-36), have been a *mithraeum* before its conversion into a church (*CIMRM* 653): there seem originally to have been seven supporting pillars. But it must of course be added that it is cut into the rock, and is closer in that respect to the Heidenkapelle.

   We should also note those *mithraea* in which the niche has been treated so as to recall a natural cave, such as Barberini (389) and Sta Prisca (Neuerburg, 1965: 229; cat. no. 185).

39 See Leach, 1976: 9-16, who refines the terminology of Mulder and Hervey, 1972, to enable him to discuss non-verbal forms of communication. It will be observed here that I presuppose a semiological interpretation of symbols, a procedure I think defensible in the present context, notwithstanding the interesting critique of Sperber, 1975, some of which I accept.

40 For the use of these terms in the discussion of (literary) metaphor, see, e.g. Richards, 1975: 36-37.

41 Gordon, 1972: 97-98; 1975: 240-241.

42 The Proustian implication is intentional, though it must be used guardedly. I find the following passage from Gérard Genette pointedly appropriate to the ambiguities of the mysteries: '... le plus troublant paradoxe de la *Recherche* ... c'est qu'elle se présente à la fois comme œuvre et comme approche de l'œuvre, comme terme et comme genèse, comme recherche du temps perdu et comme offrande du temps retrouvé' (1966: 62). The plight of the modernist has much in common with that of the adherent of a 'moderate gnostic' cult, whatever the differences, no doubt, in their relative sophistication.

43 The extensive restorations (apparently taken from *CIMRM* 586, also in the Louvre) do not affect my point here; it is unfortunately now covered by a map of the Roman Empire in a storeroom populated only by superannuated sculpture.

44 *CIMRM* 736 (Aquileia) is a highly original variant on the theme of the natural cave: cf. Will, 1955: 420.

45 Likewise hidden away, in a storeroom of the Museo Nazionale delle Terme. On this relief and its Italian parallels, see now Lavagne, 1974: 491-493 (though his adoption of Campbell's categories is to be regretted).

46 The best examples are *CIMRM* 415; 437; 543 (top modern); 542; 736. 'Natural' forms such as these do not occur outside Italy; Lavagne, 1974: 501 n. 1 notes that the cave motif itself (not simply the natural cave) occurs more frequently in Italy than in the provinces (see also Lavagne, 1975).

47 *CIMRM* 75; the other zodiac-circles around reliefs are from Walbrook (810) and Siscia (1472), but note 1161b, which is either the sacred meal or a Phaethon (Stockstadt I). See Beck, 1976: 16 n. 14 for a discussion of their possible significance. I omit consideration of zodiacal reliefs showing Mithras *petragenes*.

48 *CIMRM* 40 (Dura); 390 (Barberini); 635a (Brontöon of Villa dei Quintili – the only Italian *relief* with a zodiac); 1083a (Heddernheim I); 1137a (Rückingen); 1149 (Gross-Krotzenburg); 1271 (Dieburg – probable); 1292 (Osterburken). All the reliefs which combine a reference to the cave with one to heaven can be considered variations upon this solution, particularly those with schematic series of trees: Will, 1955: 421–422 (though I cannot agree with his assumption of the priority of such groups). I argue below, in effect, that the Cincinnati relief is to be included among these at one level (p. 177).

49 Peter Brown, in arguing (1974: 4) that we should not ask so much what is 'meant' by a biblical episode depicted, or a rite symbolized, in early Christianity, urges that we should rather 'enter into what religious attitudes were conveyed as a total visual impression on the beholder'. To put it another way: the history of ancient religious art must adopt new strategies to escape from antiquarianism.

50 See Bianchi Bandinelli, 1970: 306, on the expression in general, and Will, 1955: 180–185, in a specifically Mithraic context.

51 See further, L'Orange, 1947: 11–38; Bieber, 1964.

52 I would date it to *c.* A.D. 170–80 rather than to the Severan period, or the third century, as the the new edition of Helbig would have it (1963–72, I: 746 no. 1036). This edition also includes the following: 'Ihre etwas grobe, summarische Marmorarbeit ist bezeichnend für die Denkmäler dieser Religion, der alle ästhetischen Momente fehlten. In dem mithraischen Dualismus zwischen Gut und Böse hatte das Schöne keinen Platz.' Also sprach der Mandarin (and see Cumont, 1899: 219 with its opposition between intelligence and aesthetic sense).

53 For some critical comments on the current view of the origins of the 'Rhine' type, see Turcan, 1976: 73–74.

54 Will, 1955: 397, sees the tendency to create more explicit types as vulgar: 'L'idée de réunir en un seul monument l'illustration essentielle de toute la doctrine, de créer une image résumant les principaux articles de la foi, n'a pu germer, en effet, que dans les âmes simples.' Quite apart from the exaggeration of 'de toute la doctrine', I think that this assumes too readily that iconographic representation is necessarily merely credal or narrative: explicitness about the myth may no less plausibly be a consequence of different assumptions about knowledge and its privileges between Rhineland, for example, and Italy: it implies a different kind of religiosity indeed, but not necessarily a more simple-minded one. I would however be prepared to suggest that the tendency towards 'garrulity' becomes less marked as the cult becomes routinized, and the icon is treated less as a form of information and more as a 'signal'.

55 Some of the meanings 'Roman art' may have in this context are pointed out by J. M. C. Toynbee, 1964: 1–11.

56 See Sadurska, 1953: 118–123, no. 53, with fig. She dates it to the early fourth century.

57 1976: 71. The problem is of course more complex, but this distinction may serve for the moment. The relative stylization of representations of I. O. M. Dolichenus is instructive.

Jean Bayet, in discussing the iconography of certain Christian sarcophagi (1962: 171–213 = 1974: 609–651), has suggested another aspect of this problem by distinguishing the sclerosis imposed by the 'just' representation on one hand, and the endless search for new formulations on the other. With refinement, I think that this could well complement my own approach based on a linguistic model: it is certainly superior to Saxl's approach, 1931: 100–107.

58 See especially A. D. Momigliano's review of T. D. Barnes' *Tertullian*, 1976: 273–276.

FMS

Bibliography

Amelung, W. (and Lippold, G.). 1903-1956. *Die Sculpturen des Vaticanischen Museums.* I, 1-2: 1903; II, 1-2: 1908; III, 1-2: 1936; III, 3-4: 1956. Berlin.

Andreae, B. 1973. *L'Art de l'ancienne Rome.* Collection: L'Art et les Grandes Civilisations, II. Paris.

Arias, P. 1946. Rosarno: scavi della necropoli in Contrada Nolio-Carozzo. *NSA,* 133-161.

Bayet, J. 1962. Idéologie et plastique, III: Les sarcophages chrétiens à grandes pastorales. *MEFR* 74, 171-213.

Bayet, J. 1974. *Idéologie et Plastique.* Collection de l'École française de Rome, 21. Rome.

Becatti, M. 1954. *Scavi di Ostia, II: I Mitrei.* Roma.

Beck, R. L. 1976. Interpreting the Ponza zodiac, I. *Journal of Mithraic Studies* I. 1, 1-19.

Beyen, H. G. 1938, 1960. *Die pompeianische Wanddekoration vom zweiten bis zum vierten Stil.* 2 vols. in 4. The Hague.

Bianchi Bandinelli, R. 1970. *Rome, the centre of power (Roman Art to 200 AD).* London.

Bickerman, E. J. 1967. Sur la théologie de l'art figuratif à propos de l'ouvrage de E. R. Goodenough. *Syria,* 44, 131-161.

Bieber, M. 1956. Review of Becatti, *I Mitrei. AJA* 40, 310-314.

Bieber, M. 1964. *Alexander the Great in Greek and Roman Art.* Chicago.

Borbein, A. H. 1968. *Campanareliefs: typologische und stilkritische Untersuchungen. MDAI (RA),* Suppl. 14. Heidelberg.

Borda, M. 1958. *La pittura romana.* Milano.

Boyancé, P. 1960-61. L'antre dans les mystères de Dionysos. *RPAA* (Ser. 3), 33, 107-127.

Brown, P. R. L. 1974. The view from the precipice. *New York Review of Books,* 21 no. 5 (Oct. 3, 1974), 3-4.

Brown, P. R. L. (with Sabine MacCormack). 1975. Artifices of Eternity. *NYRB* 22 no. 2 (Feb. 20, 1975), 19-22.

Campbell, L. A. 1954. A typology of Mithraic tauroctones. *Berytus* 11, 3-60.

Caturegli, G. 1966. *Il culto di Mithra.* Scientia veterum, 100. Pisa.

Cumont, F. 1899. *Textes et monuments figurés relatifs aux mystères de Mithra.* Vol. I. Bruxelles.

Cumont, F. 1937. Mithra en Étrurie. *Scritti in onore di B. Nogara,* pp. 95-106. Città del Vaticano.

Cumont, F. 1942. *Symbolisme funéraire chez les Romains.* Paris.

Dawson, C. M. 1944. *Romano-Campanian mythological landscape-painting. YCS* 9 (whole volume). Repr. 1965, Rome.

Deonna, W. Le Crucifix de la Vallée de Saas (Valais): histoire d'une thème iconographique. *RHR* 132, 5-47.

Detienne, M. 1974. Dionysos mis à mort ou le bouilli rôti. *ASNP* (Ser. 3), 4, 1193-1234.

Engermann, J. 1974. Zu den Apsis-tituli des Paulinus von Nola. *JbAC* 17, 21-46.

Genette, Gérard. 1966. *Figures, I.* Paris.

Genette, Gérard. 1976. *Mimologiques: voyage en Cratylie.* Paris.

Gordon, R. L. 1972. Mithraism and Roman Society. *Religion* 2, 92-121.

Gordon, R. L. 1975. Franz Cumont and the doctrines of Mithraism. *Mithraic Studies* I, pp. 215-248 (ed. J. R. Hinnells). Manchester.

Gordon, R. L. 1976. The sacred geography of a *mithraeum*: the example of Sette Sfere. *Journal of Mithraic Studies* I. 2, 119-165.

Grimes, W. F. 1968. *The Excavation of Roman and Mediaeval London.* London.

von Heintze, H. 1969. *Römische Kunst.* Stuttgart.

Helbig, W. 1963–72. *Führer durch die öffentlichen Sammlungen klassischer Altertümer in Rom.* 4 ed. by H. Speier. 4 vols. Tübingen.

Ianovitz, O. 1972. *Il culto solare nella X Regio.* Centro di Studi e Documentazione sull' Italia Romana, Monografie 2. Milano.

Inan, J. and Rosenbaum, E. 1966. *Roman and Early Byzantine portrait sculpture in Asia Minor.* London.

Jeanmaire, H. 1951. *Dionysos: histoire du culte de Bacchus.* Paris.

Kamen, H. 1976. *The Iron Century: Social change in Europe, 1550–1660.* Ed. 2. London.

Koch, G. 1975. *Die mythologischen Sarkophage, 6: Meleager.* Berlin.

Leach, E. R. 1976. *Culture and Communication.* Cambridge.

Lavagne, H. 1974. Les reliefs mithriaques à scènes multiples en Italie. *Mélanges ... à Pierre Boyancé,* Collection de l'École Française de Rome, 22, 481–504.

Lavagne, H. 1975. L'importance de la grotte dans le mithriacisme en Occident. *Paper presented to the Second Congress of Mithraic Studies,* Sept. 1975.

Lavagne, H. 1976. Éléments nouveaux au dossier iconographique du *mithraeum* de Bourg-Saint-Andéol (Ardèche). *Journal of Mithraic Studies* I. 2, 222–224.

Lehmann-Hartleben, K. 1938. Two Roman silver jugs. *AJA* 42, 82–105.

Lissi Caronna, E. 1965. Un rilievo mitriaco di marmo. *BA* 5, 91–94.

L'Orange, H. P. 1947. *Apotheosis in ancient sculpture.* Institutet for sammenlignende Kultur-forskning, Serie B: Skrifter, XIV. Oslo.

Lugli, G. 1938. Nymphaea sive musaea: osservazione sopra un gruppo di monumenti repub-blicani in Italia in rapporto con l'architettura ellenistica. *Atti IV Congresso naz. di studi romani,* I, pp. 155–168. Roma.

Lugli, G. 1957. *La technica edilizia romana.* 2 vols. Roma.

Lurie, Alison. 1976. The dress code. *NYRB* 23 no. 19. (25 Nov. 1976), 17–20.

Matz, F. 1969. *Die dionysischen Sarkophage.* Vol. III. Berlin.

Matz, F. 1975. *Die dionysischen Sarkophage.* Vol. IV. Berlin.

Momigliano, A. D. 1976. Review of T. D. Barnes, *Tertullian. JRS* 66, 273–76.

Mulder, J. W. F. and Hervey, S. G. J. 1972. *Theory of the Linguistic Sign.* Janua Linguarum: Series minor, 136. The Hague.

Neuerburg, G. 1965. *L'architettura delle fontane e dei ninfei nell' Italia antica.* Memorie dell' Accademia ... di archeologia ... di Napoli, 5 (whole volume). Napoli.

Paribeni, E. 1959. *Sculture greche e romane di Cirene: statue e rilievi di carattere religiosi.* Monografie di Archeologia Libica, 5. Roma.

Pfuhl, E. 1923. *Malerei und Zeichnung der Griechen.* München.

des Places, E. 1971. *Oracles chaldaïques* (ed. and trans.: Budé). Paris.

Reinach, S. 1909–1912. *Répertoire des reliefs grecs et romains.* Vol. I, 1909; Vol. II, 1912; Vol. III, 1912. Paris.

Richards, I. A. 1974. *Poetries: Their Media and their Ends.* The Hague.

Rizzo, G. E. 1929. *La pittura ellenistico-romana.* Milano.

Robert, C. 1890, 1904. *Die antiken Sarcophagreliefs*: Vol. II, Mythologische Cyklen; Vol. III. 2, Einzelmythen: Hippolytus bis Meleagros. Berlin.

Sadurska, A. 1953. *Inscriptions latines et monuments funéraires romaines au Musée National de Varsovie.* Warsawa.

Samuel, A. E. 1972. *Greek and Roman Chronology: Calendars and Years in Classical Antiquity.* Handbuch der Altertumswissenschaft, Abt. I. 7. München.

Saxl, F. 1931. *Mithras: typengeschichtliche Untersuchungen.* Berlin.

Schindler, H. 1963. Die Mithrashöhle von Saarbrücken. *Beiträge zur Saarländischen Archäologie und Kunstgeschichte*, 10, 119-136.

Schindler, H. 1964. *Die Mithrashöhle von Saarbrücken*. Führungsblatt 2, Staatliches Konservatoramt. Saarbrücken.

Schwertheim, E. 1974. *Die Denkmäler orientalischer Gottheiten im Römischen Deutschland*. EPROER 40. Leiden.

Sestieri, P. 1934. La Chiesa di S. Maria del Parto presso Sutri e la diffusione della religione di Mitra nell' Etruria meridionale. *BCAR* 5, 33-36.

Sperber, D. 1975. *Rethinking Symbolism* (E. T. of *Du symbolisme en général*, 1974). Cambridge.

Squarciapino, M. 1943. *La Scuola di Afrodisia : studi e materiali del Museo dell'Impero Romano*. Roma.

Stuart-Jones, H. 1926. *Catalogue of Ancient Sculpture : Palazzo dei Conservatori*. 2 vols. Oxford.

Testini, P. 1966. *Le Catacombe e gli antichi cimiteri cristiani in Roma*. Bologna.

Toynbee, J. M. C. 1964. *Art in Britain under the Romans*. Oxford.

Turcan, R. 1972. *Les Religions de l'Asie dans la vallée du Rhône*. EPROER 30. Leiden.

Turcan, R. 1976. The date of the Mauls relief. *Journal of Mithraic Studies* I. 1, 68-76.

Ulbert, G. 1969. Gladii aus Pompeii. *Germania* 47, 97-128.

Vermaseren, M. J. 1950. A unique representation of Mithras. *VChr.* 4, 142-156.

Vermaseren, M. J. 1951. *De Mithrasdienst in Rome*. Nijmegen.

Vermaseren, M. J. 1969. Two unknown Mithraic reliefs. *Hommages à Marcel Renard*, vol. III (Collection Latomus, 103), 643-647.

Vermeule, C. C. 1965. A Greek theme and its survivals: the ruler's shield (Tondo Imago) in tomb and temple. *PAPhS* 109 no. 6, 361-397.

Vermeule, C. C. 1968. *Roman Imperial Art in Greece and Asia Minor*. Cambridge, Mass.

Walters, V. J. 1974. *The cult of Mithras in the Roman provinces of Gaul*. EPROER 41. Leiden.

Ward-Perkins, J. B. (and Boethius, A.). 1970. *Etruscan and Roman Architecture*. Cambridge.

Wegner, M. 1939. *Die Herrscherbildnisse in antoninischer Zeit*. Die römische Herrscherbild, II. 4. Berlin.

Wegner, M. 1966. *Die Musensarkophage*. Die antiken Sarkophagreliefs, V. 3. Berlin.

West, R. 1941. *Römische Porträtplastik*. 2 vols. München.

Wightman, E. M. 1970. *Roman Trier and the Treveri*. London.

Will, E. 1955. *Le relief cultuel greco-romain*. Paris.

Winkes, R. 1969. *Clipeata imago : studien zu einer romischen Bildnisform*. Diss. Giessen. Bonn.

Wissowa, G. 1886. Silvano e compagni – rilievo in Firenze. *MDAI (RA)*, 1, 161-166.

Plate I Mithraic relief in the Cincinnati Art Museum. From Rome. (Photo: Cincinnati Art Museum)

Plate II Mithraic relief from Rome in the possession of M. J. Vermaseren, Amsterdam. (Photo: F. T. Kater)

Plate III CIMRM 548 (from Rome: Vatican)

Plate IV CIMRM 662 (from Asciano: Accademia Belgica)

Pannelled complications

Henry Lavagne: Les reliefs mithriaques à scenes multiples
en Italie. *Mélanges de philosophie, de littérature et
d'histoire offerts à Pierre Boyancé* (Collection de l'École
française de Rome, 22) Paris, 1974, pp. 481-504.
   The publication of this study of the Italian Mithraic
reliefs (and frescoes) with side-scenes of one sort or
another, and that, two years later, of Robert Turcan's
discussion of the Mauls relief (1976:68-76), suggest
the beginning of a long-overdue debate on the merits and
implications of Ernest Will's classic *Le relief cultuel
gréco-romain* (1955). In an effort to widen that debate,
I wish here not so much to discuss each of L.'s points as
to make a number of related observations on four major
topics: the value of the construction of formal typologies
in the discussion of the complex panelled reliefs; the
validity of the current distinction between a Rhine-type
and a Raetian-type; the sense in which the scenes are to
be understood as a form of 'narrative'; the relation between
these 'complex' monuments and other reliefs. Of course these
questions are not discrete, any more than they are exhaustive,
and their difficulty and complexity demand both a degree of
over-simplification and a rather undesirable schematisation
of presentation: but one cannot talk about everything at once.
   1. One of the more dispiriting consequences of the scien-
tistic drift in the contemporary history of ancient art is
the common concern for pigeon-holing artefacts. The desire
to escape Winckelmann's shadow and what are now seen to have
been mere prejudices on the part of earlier scholars, though
laudable in itself, produces problems of its own. First of

all, the typology becomes in itself a sort of totem: to the
historian of art, it seems to offer a value-free, objective
means of categorizing artefacts simply because it is not
based upon 'interpretation'. Yet it must be evident that
there will still be criteria of selection and relation: and
it is here that 'ideólogy' only too frequently creeps in.
How telling is a given formal criterion of difference? How
can criteria of difference be ordered in value? How does
one treat 'exceptions'? It must surely be obvious that the
task of exploring relationships between complex artefacts in
the history of art can never be 'value-free' in the sense
that is so frequently pretended: no typology is more defensible than its underlying assumptions. Second, the typology,
once established, necessarily distracts: it points to certain
relationships, and hides others. Predicated upon an opposition between form and content, it asserts the priority of
formal similarities at the expense of exploring, for example,
identities of 'meaning' (1). Perhaps in some areas of art
history such a procedure may be defensible; but surely not in
a discussion of religious art. Of course, all forms of
'understanding' demand exclusion, relation, analogy; but we
may purchase one form of understanding at too high a price.
And if our criteria of selection are too partial to bear the
weight laid upon them, the typology obscures more than it
reveals. Third, the very delineation of a formal type suggests an 'obvious' question, of origins; having created a
discrete type by a certain process of selection, we then feel
tempted to assume that it is as discrete, say, as a natural
species; the result of a deliberately partial 'way of looking' is all too often the invention of a pseudo-problem,
created by that very act of looking.
      At the moment the study of Mithraic art labours, or hovers
on the brink of labouring, under one of the most ill-
conceived of formal typologies, that of L. A. Campbell (1954:
3-60). Founded upon a tangle of indefensible assumptions and
executed in a cloud of errors, it deserves simply to be
ignored (2). And we must regret that, although he evidently
has little enthusiasm for it, and indeed argues at one point
against the identification of a North Italian group (pp. 497-
502), L. has allowed himself to repeat the categories adopted
by Campbell without question, as though they were by now the
common and legitimate coin of this discourse. There are
surely sufficiently numerous errors in the study of the Mysteries which through ignorance we cannot avoid to prevent us
from espousing the palpably foolish.
      My scepticism of the value of the formal typology in the
discussion of Mithraic art in particular must not be con-
strued as a conservative attempt to return to some older
strategy. But I would urge that instead of pretending that
we can look without value-judgements, without the visual
coding which is a historical creation of our culture, we

should design our typologies on the basis of specific hypotheses or problems, frankly accepting that the problems of
Mithraic art are too complex for any conceivable total typology to be more than an exhibit in the museum of fantastic
ideas. Further, that the criteria of association and difference should not be arbitrary but demonstrably relevant to the
rôle of the relief as an element in a complex symbolic whole
- the *mithraeum* conceived as articulated *espace religieux*;
and to its conditions of material production. There can be
no *alternative* between 'form' and 'meaning' in our discussion
of these religious artefacts. At the most general level we
may put the point with Susan Sontag: 'Of course works of art
(with the important exception of music) refer to the real
world — to our knowledge, to our experience, to our values.
They present information and evaluations. But their distinctive feature is that they give rise not to conceptual
knowledge (which *is* the distinctive feature of discursive
or scientific knowledge — e.g. philosophy, sociology, psychology, history) but to something like excitation, a phenomenon
of commitment, judgement in a state of thralldom or captiva-
tion. Which is to say that the knowledge we gain through art
is an experience of the form or style of knowing something,
rather than a knowledge of something (like a fact or a moral
judgement) in itself' (1967: 21-22). Appearance in art, as
in literature, *is* meaning. And that is true whether we
choose to discuss form as a mnemonic device or as an embodi-
ment of a complex of epistemological decisions. From that
perspective the academic determination to discuss either form
or meaning exclusively begins to look inappropriate to the
delicacy of the task of understanding. Third, I would urge
that any proposed typology should state clearly the limits of
its perceived usefulness and adequacy: what price has been
paid for *this* classification?
   2. It is a question of adequacy to which I turn next.
There seems to be a consensus, certainly shared by L., that
two types of panelled reliefs (thus distinguishing them from
the 'Danubian' types) exist: the 'Rhine' and the 'Raetian'.
This distinction is based upon two formal criteria: (1) the
Rhine type has a lintel linking the lateral pilasters or
panels (Will, 1955: 373; 388; 390-91), whereas the Raetian
type has simply lateral panels (2) the Rhine type is regularly to be read from the bottom left scene up and round to
the foot of the right panel, whereas the Raetian type begins
at the top of the left panel and proceeds downwards and then
up the right-hand panel (Will, 1955: 373-74; 389-92 [where
the Italian monuments of this type known in 1954 are stated
to belong to the Raetian group]). Now for L. these distinctions have ceased even to be hypotheses; they are part of his
presuppositions. So much so that the article is designed to
discuss the relation between the Italian reliefs with panels
or multiple scenes 'par rapport aux séries danubiennes et

réto-rhenanes' (p. 482). Now Turcan has already demonstrated
(1976: 71-74) that the late date of the Mauls relief (*CIMRM*
1400) throws considerable doubt upon Will's theses that the
panelled type came from the East and entered northern Europe
via Aquileia, and that the Raetian form is earlier than the
Rhine form (3); and he returns in a sense to Drexel's suggestion that the type emanated from Rome, though with different
arguments. Now although I am appreciative of Turcan's point
about the Mauls relief, I do not know how one would set about
proving the subsequent contention that the form spread from
Italy northwards (4). For the moment, all one can do is to
note how formal criteria and strictly historical evidence
have constantly been confused in the discussion of the origins of these types.
   Perhaps we could ask a rather different question. Is the
problem of the origin of these types a real problem or a
pseudo-problem? It can only be a genuine problem if the
typology is appropriate to the evidence. Our first question
must then be: what grounds are there for accepting a twofold
category for these complex panelled reliefs, Raetian and
Rhine?
   Let us take first the criterion that the reliefs of each
type are to be read in different directions. The first point
to make is obvious: that in many cases it is impossible to
state with any certainty that there *is* a 'direction' in which
a given panel is to be read. Now everyone knows this: Will
(p. 373) makes the point immediately before his reaffirmation
of the traditional distinction. But he does not seem to
appreciate quite how damaging it is to the thesis: the issue
is in fact evaded by the choice of words: 'irrégularités que
l'on relève dans la succession des scènes.... des variations
persistantes.... divergences d'un monument à l'autre...' —
all these phrases presuppose an order which is, for some reason he does not see fit to explain, constantly confused. But
if there is constant confusion how does one arrive at the
'proper' order? By counting the number of times a given
scene occurs in a given relation to neighbours? But how does
one then explain the exceptions? Ignorance? Oblivion? Late
date? (the strategy used by Turcan to account for the divergences from the 'canon' [his term and apostrophes], 1976: 71-
72). The real point is surely that the hypothesis of a regular reading order is itself based upon the assumption that
the scenes record a narrative sequence, and that this is
their primary rôle. I return to this question later, but
would remark here that such an assumption confuses two separate issues: our need for evidence of a supposed 'legend of
Mithras'; and the Mithraists' actual understanding of the
side-scenes. The hypothesis of a reading order also forces
us to include in the 'legend' unique or very rare scenes —
they must surely be located somewhere in a narrative
sequence. But what is to be done, for example, with the

scene in which Mithras kneels between two cypresses with one
arm raised and the other lowered (scene QQ in fig. 2, p. 217
below)? This occurs four times: on the Barberini fresco
(390) it appears on the right hand panel between Mithras
standing with the bull's haunch over Sol (below) and Mithras
and Sol with spits over an altar; on Ptuj II (1510), it also
occurs on the right panel (unfortunately broken), above a
unique scene of three cypresses with a head emerging from
each, itself above Mithras and Sol with spits over an altar;
the closest analogy with the three cypresses is a tree with
three heads emerging, which occurs at Dieburg, between a reduplicated *transitus* scene above and the feast-scene below.
On this evidence, scene QQ would be placed at some point in
what is called the 'reconciliation' between Sol and Mithras.
But the two other occurrences make this quite doubtful: on
Castello di Tueno (723) it appears at the bottom of the left
panel immediately 'after' (that is, below) a unique scene,
Sol with a veiled figure, itself below Jupiter killing the
giants; while on the Mauls relief (1400) it appears below
Mithras cutting corn and above Mithras on the bull's back,
and the stance of Mithras is reversed (left hand panel).
Is there any alternative but to conclude that the hypothesis
of a coherent narrative sequence simply will not fit this
scene?
   Rather than labour the point over the whole range of
material, let us take that supposedly typical Rhine relief,
that from Osterburken (1292), which probably dates from c.
220-230. Its scenes can be presented schematically as
follows (see Plate II):

	Transitus dei
Mithras and tree	
	Bull with lowered head
Mithras petragenes	
	'Water miracle'

'Saturnus' reclining	M. on bull's back
Jupiter and giants	M. entering Sol's chariot
Jupiter with 'Saturnus'	M. and Sol with haunch
3 figures (?Fates)	Dextrarum iunctio
'Saturnus' and 'Atlas'?	Mithras riding horse
Head in aureole	Feast-scene
(supposedly Chaos)	

Will (and Saxl, 1931: 69-74) argued that the left panel is
to be read from bottom to top, presumably on the ground that
Jupiter and the giants occur below reclining 'Saturnus' (it
will be noted that Mithras petragenes occurs outside the
panel and is not strictly part of this sequence of six
scenes). But of course this is hardly conclusive: the

surviving panel of the Castello di Tueno monument, on Will's
hypothesis a 'Raetian' relief, and therefore to be read from
top to bottom, sets 'Saturnus' reclining *above* Jupiter and
the giants. The general belief that the three lower scenes
on this Osterburken relief-panel represent events from *earlier* in the cosmogony than the scene in which Jupiter kills
the giants is of course merely a deduction from the prior
assumption of a reading order: we have no other grounds for
suggesting that they have a temporal, rather than, say, a
thematic relation to each other and the scenes higher up.
The scene between 'Saturnus' and Jupiter occurs certainly
only on one other monument, Neuenheim (1283: late Antonine),
where we find on the left panel, reading bottom to top:
'Mithras-Atlas'; 'Saturnus' reclining; 'Saturnus' and Jupiter; Mithras petragenes. Jupiter and the giants is omitted.
In other words, in its two occurrences, the scene between
'Saturnus' and Jupiter occurs in a different sequence in
relation to reclining 'Saturnus', reading both monuments in
the 'Rhine' order.
    If we turn to the right hand panel, it is clear that Mith-
ras on the bull's back is logically prior to the next scene
but one, Mithras holding the bull's haunch over Sol as he
kneels; and the '*dextrarum iunctio*' precedes the feast-scene
at Sarrebourg (966) and Mauls (1400) [where the two are
separated by Mithras entering Sol's quadriga], the only other
two monuments in which they appear (accepting the usual reading order). But the second and the fifth scenes from the top
are completely at odds with the hypothesis of a downward reading order here: what is Mithras entering Sol's quadriga doing
in second place; and Mithras as hunter in fifth? We insist
on the notion of a reading order here in blatant violation of
the evidence. And who will be found to argue that the
designer of this most complex of Rhine panelled reliefs had
forgotten his proper order? And on the arch itself, there
are similar difficulties. If the primary purpose of these
scenes was to register a narrative, why does the '*transitus
dei*' occur not in the top right-hand frame but next to Luna?
If we are to be consistent, we should have to argue that each
side of the 'lintel' is to be read *upwards*: *petragenes* → Mithras and tree → 'water miracle' → bull with head lowered →
transitus dei: a curious combination of 'Rhine' and 'Raetian'
orders.
    It must then be clear that the very notion of a reading
order is suspect — that it is not a sufficiently complex
hypothesis to account for the evidence. But let us assume
for a moment that these reliefs are indeed to be read in a
particular sequence and that it can in each case be established. Fig. 1 (pp.206-8) shows the reading orders, so far
as I can decide upon them following Will's assumptions, for
all the complete or nearly complete panel-type reliefs
including Dieburg (1247) [Plate III] and Rückingen (1137) (5).

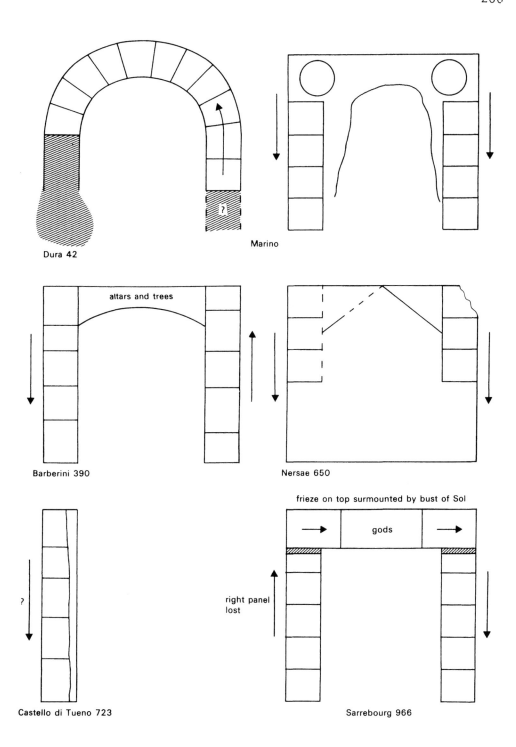

Dura 42

Marino

altars and trees

Barberini 390

Nersae 650

Castello di Tueno 723

?

frieze on top surmounted by bust of Sol

gods

right panel
lost

Sarrebourg 966

207 Panelled complications

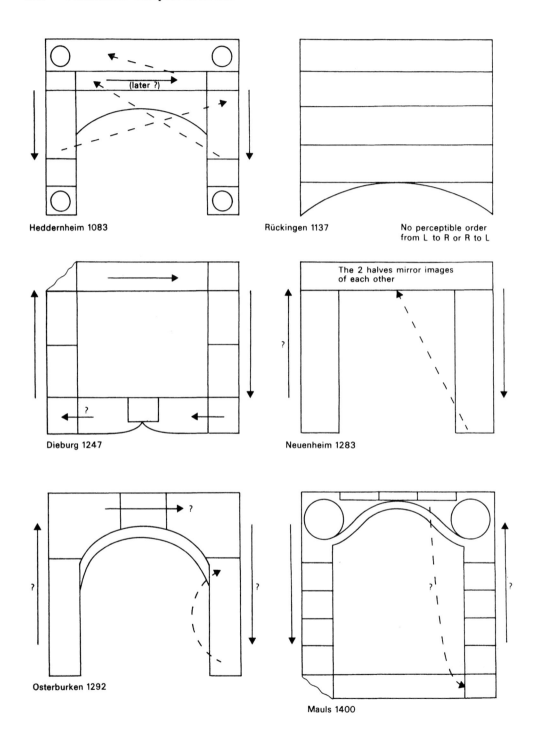

Heddernheim 1083

Rückingen 1137   No perceptible order
                   from L to R or R to L

Dieburg 1247

The 2 halves mirror images
of each other

Neuenheim 1283

Osterburken 1292

Mauls 1400

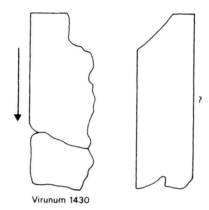

Virunum 1430

Figure 1 Apparent reading orders of complete or near-complete complex
panelled reliefs.

Now it is obvious that if we have two panels containing
sequentially ordered frames there can only be four ways of
arranging them:

From fig. 1 we can see that only the first of these logical
possibilities does not occur. Sarrebourg (966) [Plate IV],
Neuenheim (1283), possibly Osterburken (1292) can be made to
fit with the hypothesis of a 'Rhine' type; but what is the
point of singling these three out (we can surely say nothing
certain about Königshofen) and calling them members of the
'Rhine' class, when that involves one in ignoring not only
Rückingen and Dieburg, which are designed quite differently
but are no less Rhenish and no less concerned to provide
'information' in the form of discrete scenes; but also
Heddernheim (1083), both of whose side-panels must be read
downwards? And the direction in which, by the usual assumptions, we must read Heddernheim is also the direction in
which we must read two Italian reliefs, Nersae (650) and
Marino (which was unknown to Will and Saxl of course). A
new Rhenish-Italian type then? Again, Barberini (390)
[Plate V], possibly Virunum (1430) [Plate VI], Dura (42) and
Mauls (1400) must all be read from top left to top right,
but what is the sense in calling this a 'Raetian' order when
it is evidenced by 3 or 4 monuments widely scattered in time
and place, of which the earliest is probably the late-
Antonine Barberini fresco? And if next week someone finds

a complex panel relief in which both panels are to be read
upwards, are we to invent yet another type? Surely we must
conclude that the alleged reading order is not an adequate
criterion for the creation of typologies: not only is it
founded upon the unexamined, but highly questionable, assumption of a narrative sequence, but it ignores the problem of
'displacement' without even offering an explanation for the
phenomenon (which is of course simply a consequence of the
hypothesis itself); as a criterion it is at once both too
exclusive and too broad: the 'Rhine' type groups Sarrebourg,
Neuenheim and Osterburken at the cost of excluding Heddernheim, Rückingen and Dieburg for different reasons (again I
omit Königshofen), while the 'Raetian' type includes monuments as different from each other as Dura, Barberini and
Mauls (which offers marked formal similarities to both
Osterburken and Marino). Surely all we can say is that
some of the scenes seem to be logically consequent upon
others (this is especially clear in the scenes involving
the bull) and that some relative placings are more common
than others: we have no justification for arguing beyond
that to the notion of a complete narrative sequence or to
the notion that the scenes informed Mithraists of a legend
which they might otherwise not recollect.
    The second criterion, it will be recalled, concerns lin-
tels (Rhine) against parallel panels (Raetian). It is surely
no less dubious than the first. There are indeed no lintels
yet in Italy, but Mauls, classified as 'Raetian' by Will,
does include a certain amount of information in the synclines
above the cave and between Sol and Luna (?ram, ?bull, trees,
lion: Turcan, 1976: 69-70); and Dura escapes the classification altogether with its scenes arranged in the form of an
arch. Rückingen dispenses with side panels entirely in
favour of four superimposed 'lintels'; Dieburg may have a
'lintel' above, but it also has one below (of course it is
more aptly described as having a central panel surrounded by
10 smaller panels, themselves sometimes subdivided). It is
quite misleading to classify Osterburken with the four reliefs with proper lintels (Sarrebourg, Heddernheim, Neuenheim, Königshofen) (6), since the relief takes the form of a
large arch carved out of a single slab. Heddernheim adds to
its simple lintel another register on the top of the central
panel and further 'information' in the synclines between this
register and the zodiac. Again we must find a distinction
between the presence and the absence of a lintel inadequate
as a criterion for a typology: we need rather the notion of
a continuum of possibilities between, say, Barberini and
Rückingen, between the location of the panels at the side
only and their location on the top only: and I see no way
of dividing that continuum into subcategories either by location or by date.
    We must conclude from this, I think, that the current

classification of panelled reliefs into Rhine and Raetian is
both over-simple and misleading: it excludes too much relevant
evidence but also pretends to find unity where there is none.
And it should be observed that there never was any particular
rationale in the choice of criteria, reading order and lintel:
it never has been demonstrated that there were no other significant variables — the location of Sol and Luna, patterns
of inclusion and exclusion of scenes, patterns of reduplica-
tion and inversion, for example. We should begin rather from
the observation that no panelled relief can be shown to have
been directly copied from any other: the evidence forms a
group, a series, only in the sense that each surviving monument offers a variation upon a very simple idea, itself widespread within Hellenistic and especially Roman art, the addition of ancillary scenes to a relief, or more generally
around a central focus (for example, the passage through
a triumphal arch). We may distinguish two major areas of
variation in the Mithraic series: the organisation of the
frame as a whole in relation to the central relief, and the
choice of illustrative field; and the selection of scenes
and their order. We should therefore not be searching for
identities but for family resemblances. The major choice of
frame is almost identical between Neuenheim, Sarrebourg and
Königshofen, though the two last add a cornice above the lintel, and Sarrebourg a bust of Sol on top of that; but none of
them shows the slightest similarity in the choice and distribution of scenes. In that respect the two monuments closest
to each other are Nersae and Marino (see fig. 2 below,
pp.212-15),whose reading order also happens to be the same —
or perhaps it would be less prejudicial to say that if we
transcribe the scenes (arbitrarily) in one of the four logically possible ways, they appear very similar:

```
Marino:  B    C    E    P    //   R    S    W    O
Nersae:  B    C    E         //   P    S    U/W
```

But the two monuments diverge sharply in choice of frame:
Nersae abandons the panels at the midpoint of the relief
to accommodate the torchbearers below; Marino sets Sol and
Luna above the panels in a manner similar to the treatment
of the Mauls relief (1400) (see fig. 1, p. 207). Each of
the major areas of variation can be treated as a continuum
of possibilities. If we take the frame first, we can posit
two extremes: scenes only at the side of the main representation; and scenes only above it (a further possibility,
scenes only beneath, does not occur; Dieburg, Stockstadt I
and Mainz all have one panel beneath). The first extreme
occurs in Italy and Noricum but not in Germany; the second
in Germany but not in Italy. Most German reliefs occupy a
central position on this continuum; Heddernheim, however,
with only four scenes at the side, and three separate areas

of representation above, is not far removed from Rückingen's
extreme choice. And among reliefs and frescoes towards the
other end of the continuum, Mauls and Barberini in particular
add information above the side-panels. The other major area
of variation offers two rather different kinds of problem:
the ordering of the scenes in relation to each other; and
rare or uncommon scenes. These problems I discuss immediately below in the context of the intention of these reliefs.
But we are now in a position to suggest that the question of
the origins of the Raetian and Rhine types is indeed a pseudo-
problem, because the types themselves do not exist — they are
merely inadequate hypotheses. The futility of searching for
the formal origins of the panelled reliefs is no different
from the futility of searching for the origins of the bull-
slaying stereotype itself: in each case the problem is
wrongly posed. Which is not to say that there cannot be a
history of the Mithraic relief or a convincing account of
its levels of symbolic meaning.
    3. It has become an unquestioned assumption of these
studies that the scenes are primarily narrative, even if
some are allowed also to register ritual actions (7) - it
was the assumption that the scenes represented a Mithraic
narrative that led Cumont to treat Mithras as though he were
merely some kind of hero, a marginally divine figure (1899:
302, 306). There seem to me two fundamental objections to
this assumption (at least in any simple form), namely that
(1) no two complex panelled reliefs show the same selection
of scenes, and (2) no two reliefs present them in the same
order. A narrative, particularly a sacred narrative, must
have a constant sequence of events; and there must be some
agreement about the parts that are important — a demand one
would have thought all the more compelling if, as is usually
supposed, these monuments were for the instruction of the
vulgar.
    Figure 2 shows schematically the distribution of scenes
on all the complete and fragmentary monuments of this type.
The key to the letters used appears in the text, together
with the frequency of occurrence of each scene (8).

Key to Fig. 2

The first figure in the Total column refers to scenes found
on the 10 complete or virtually complete monuments: Quadraro,
Barberini, Marino, Nersae, Sarrebourg, Heddernheim, Neuenheim, Dieburg, Osterburken, Mauls. The second figure, to the
incomplete monuments: Dura, Castello di Tueno, Val di Non
(729), Rückingen, Stockstadt I (1161a), Mainz (1225), Hölzern
(1942), Besigheim *a* and *b*, Königshofen, Virunum, Ptuj II
(1510), Ptuj III (1579). I omit 1797 (Aquincum) because it
is unclear to me whether it belongs to this group or to the

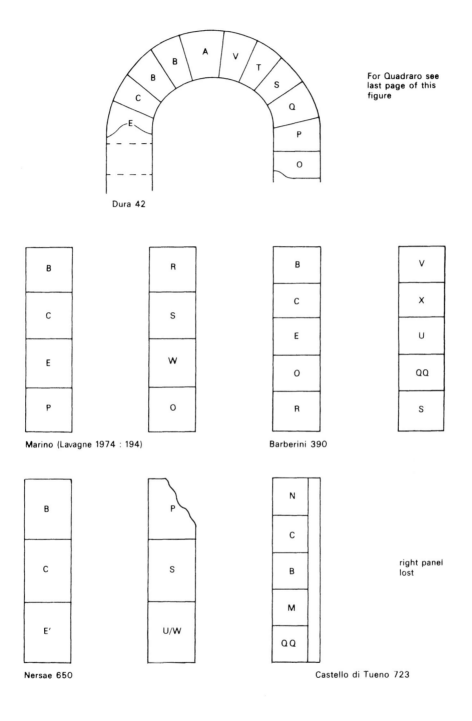

For Quadraro see
last page of this
figure

Dura 42

Marino (Lavagne 1974 : 194)

Barberini 390

Nersae 650

Castello di Tueno 723

right panel
lost

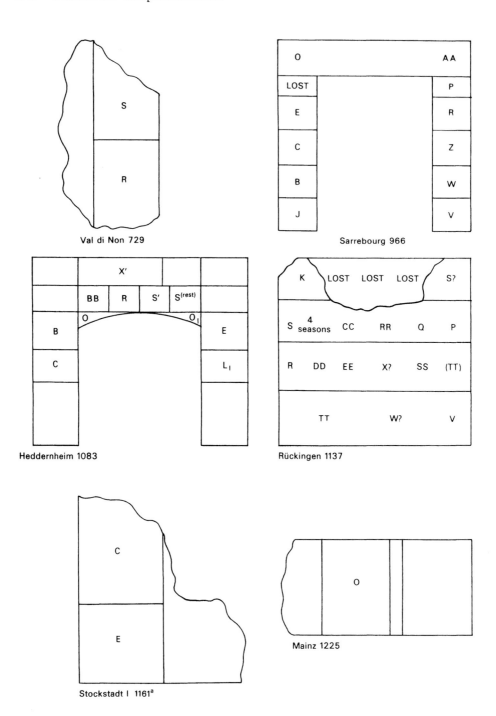

Val di Non 729

Sarrebourg 966

Heddernheim 1083

Rückingen 1137

Stockstadt I 1161ᵃ

Mainz 1225

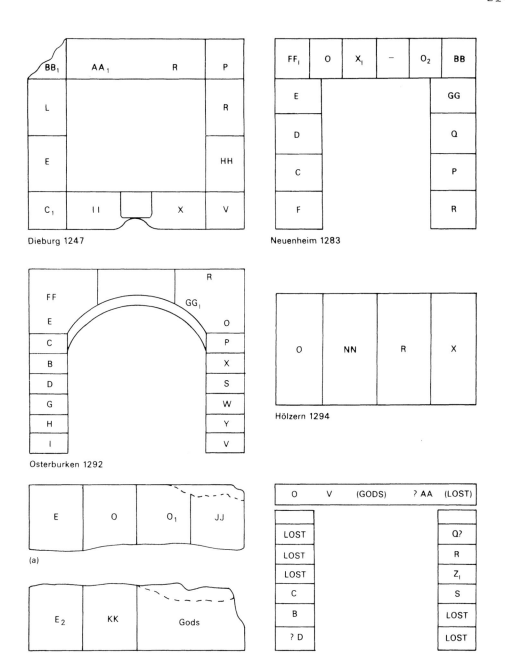

Dieburg 1247

Neuenheim 1283

Osterburken 1292

Hölzern 1294

(a)

(b)

Besigheim 1301

Königshofen 1359

215 Panelled complications

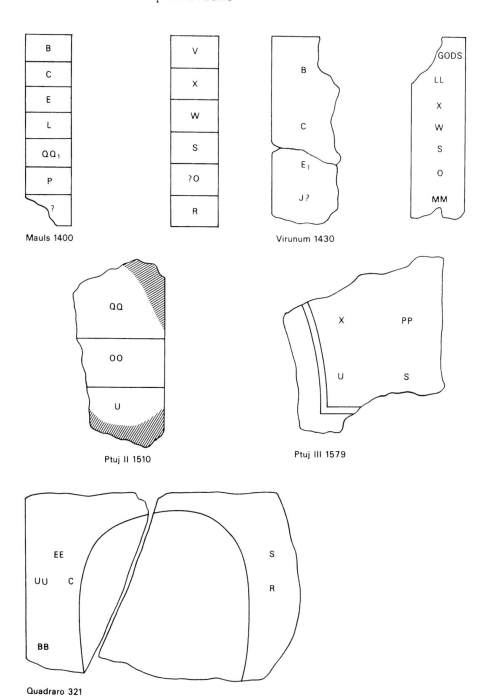

Figure 2 Schematic analysis of scenes on complex panelled reliefs
(see key on p. 211 of text).

Danubian series. Figures in brackets include doubtful
cases, which have not been used in the calculations. The
third figure in the Total column is the sum total. Doub-
lets counted as one occurrence. Assemblies of the gods,
seasons and winds omitted, as are reverse scenes and separate lateral scenes. (9)

Symbol	Reference		Total	
A	'Saturnus' with harpe	-	1	1
B	Jupiter and giant(s)	7	4	11
C	'Saturnus' reclining	10	5	15
D	Jupiter and 'Saturnus'	2	-(1)	2(3)
E	Mithras petragenes	9	5	14
F	'Mithras-Atlas'	1	-	1
G	3 figures (Fates?)	1	-	1
H	'Saturnus' and 'Atlas' (?)	1	-	1
I	Head in aureole	1	-	1
J	2 standing figures	1	-(1)	1(2)
K	Standing male figure with raised arms	-	1	1
L	Mithras cutting corn	3	-	3
M	Sol and veiled figure	-	1	1
N	Male figure with staff	-	1	1
O	'Water miracle'	6(7)	6	12(13)
P	Mithras on bull's back	7	2	9
Q	Bull on M.'s back	1	2(3)	3(4)
R	Transitus dei	9	4	13
S	M. with bull's haunch; Sol kneeling	7	6	13
T	Torchbearers carrying dead bull	-	1	1
U	M. and Sol with altar and spits (fused with W on 650)	1(2)	2	3(4)
V	Feast scene	5	3	8
W	Dextrarum iunctio	4(5)	1(2)	5(7)
X	M. entering Sol's quadriga	6	3(4)	9(1)
Y	M. riding as hunter	1	-	1
Z	Lion	1	1	2
AA	Attack on bull's house (966, 1247)	2	-(1)	2(3)
BB	M.? in tree	4	-	4
CC	Bull + figure (Rückingen)	-	1	1
DD	Figure with legs apart (Rückingen)	-	1	1
EE	Tree	1	1	2
FF	M. cutting fruit from tree etc.	2	-	2
GG	Bull grazing	2	-	2
HH	Tree with three heads emerging	1	-	1

217 Panelled complications

Symbol	Reference	Total		
II	2 inverted goats	1	-	1
JJ	M. holding bull's horns	-	1	1
KK	Figure with knife + figure with round object	-	1	1
LL	'Saturnus' with Crescent + Terra	-	1	1
MM	?Cautes and Cautopates	-	1	1
NN	M. with person? (Hölzern)	-	1	1
OO	3 cypresses with heads emerging (Ptuj II)	-	1	1
PP	Bearded figure with long staff seated on rock with approaching figure (Ptuj III)	-	1	1
QQ	M. kneeling down with R. arm raised, L. arm down	2	2	4
RR	?Female figure (Rückingen)	-	1	1
SS	?Raven (Rückingen) (Cf. 729a?)	-	1	1
TT	Seven planets (Rückingen)	-	1	1
UU	Dagger	1	-	1
		100	64	164

I distinguish 47 scenes, although the total may be reduced
slightly by the considerations advanced in n. 9 above. 10
scenes occur five or more times in all and we may call them
'common':

    B   C   E   O   P   R   S   V   W   X

But of course this does not mean that they can properly be
called 'canonical', as we can see from the pattern of inclusion and exclusion:

Monument	Common scenes omitted	Rare scenes included
Dura (2 scenes at least missing)	W X (on side wall)	T (and perhaps more)
Quadraro	B E O P V W X	BB EE
Barberini	P	U QQ
Marino	V X	-
Nersae	O V X R (fuses U/W)	-
Castello di Tueno (frg.)	at least E	N M QQ
Sarrebourg (1 scene missing)	S X	J Z AA +?
Heddernheim	P W (V on reverse)	L BB
Rückingen (frg.)	?? B C E O	K CC RR Q DD EE SS TT
Besigheim *a* (frg.)	???	JJ
Besigheim *b* (frg.)	???	KK (and note E_2)
Königshofen (frg.)	???	?AA ?D ?Q Z_1

Monument	Common scenes omitted	Rare scenes included
Neuenheim	B S V W	F D FF BB GG Q
Osterburken	-	FF D G H I GG Y
Dieburg	B O S W	L AA BB HH II
Mauls (?1 scene missing)	-	L QQ$_1$
Virunum (frg.)	P R V (probably)	at least J LL MM (includes assembly of gods on panel)
Ptuj II (frg.)	???	at least OO QQ
Ptuj III (frg.)	???	at least PP

Only two complete monuments include all the common scenes (Osterburken and Mauls) though not in the same order; and both include rare or unique scenes. Only two complete monuments, Barberini and Nersae, do not include unique or rare scenes. The obvious conclusion is that no scene (with the possible exception of 'Saturnus' reclining, which occurs on all the complete monuments) was deemed necessary to the principle or intention which lies behind these monuments. This can be shown even more clearly by another table:

Complete monuments:

No. of appearances:	1	2	3	4	5	6	7	8	9	10
No. of cases:	13	5	1	2	1	2	3	-	2	1

Fragmentary reliefs (no scene appears more than six times):

No. of appearances:	1	2	3	4	5	6
No. of cases:	20	4	2	2	2	2

Of course it is important not to underplay the extent of repetition: the eight commonest scenes on complete monuments (those which occur 6 or more times) account for 61 per cent of the total number of scenes which occur on them; unique scenes for only 13 per cent. But it must be clear from these tables and from the disparity of relative placings (so evident from fig. 2) that unless one already knew the meaning of each scene one would not be able to reconstruct a coherent narrative from any one of the surviving monuments. There is no alternative to the conclusion that the scenes were not primarily narrative in intent. And we may strengthen that conclusion by looking at redundancies. A number of monuments for some reason repeat scenes: Heddernheim repeats the 'water miracle' in the synclines above the zodiac, the one being the reverse of the other; Ruckingen seems to repeat the scene between Mithras with the bull's haunch and Sol kneeling (S); Neuenheim repeats the 'water miracle' (O) on the lintel, the

one again being the reverse of the other; and the same scene
appears in two successive frames on Besigheim *a*, the only
difference being that in one scene there are two kneeling
figures; Dieburg repeats the *transitus* scene (R). The two
cases of reversal (Heddernheim and Neuenheim) are particularly interesting, because it is clear that the two halves
of the monument are treated as mirror-images: the left is
the opposite of the right — a conclusion strengthened by the
odd point that in both cases the scene X_1 (Mithras entering
Sol's chariot) does double duty, because it also 'means' Sol
opposed to Luna, who occurs in the neighbouring frame. These
redundancies are important because they clearly suggest that
other concerns than narrative operated in these cases, just
as I argued earlier, on different grounds, for the scene QQ.
I am not of course concerned to deny that there may sometimes
be a narrative intent at some level: for example scene T at
Dura (Cautes and Cautopates carrying the bull lashed to a
pole) [but, on Will's reading, it is 'out of sequence',
because it is 'preceded' by the scene in which Mithras has
cut off the bull's haunch, whereas in T the bull is still
entire], or scenes S and S_1 at Heddernheim, which seem to be
two glimpses of the same set of actions between Mithras and
Sol. But I see no point in moving from that observation to
the conclusion that all the scenes have a narrative intention, let alone the same one, the representation of a legend
of Mithras.
     I have elsewhere suggested (1976: 175-77) that we may
relate Mithraic reliefs by distinguishing a continuum between
the poles of 'silence' and 'garrulity', that is in terms of
their 'information content'. All the panelled reliefs fall
towards the extreme of 'garrulity', just as the Danubian
series does; but the point to make here is that this idea suggests that we should think of the central scene of the bull-
slaying not as divorced from the side-scenes but as integrated with them. And then we have only to ask: what is a Mithraic relief? That question can be answered in many different
ways, depending upon the context: it represents Mithras standing on the line of the equinoxes, which divides the *mithraeum*
longitudinally; it represents the act of creation which is
also the act of salvation; if we accept Beck's brilliant
hypothesis (1977: 9-11), it represents also a *templum*, the
night sky as one looks southwards; as with the *mithraeum*,
left side is opposed to the right side (Cautes versus Cautopates; Sol versus Luna) though it is also a unity, a complex
whole; again like the *mithraeum*, the relief 'moves' from east
to west (left to right) daily and seasonally, a kind of calendar; and as we can conclude from those reliefs which possess a reverse, the relief played a crucial part in the lit-
urgy of the temple: at some moment those reliefs at least
moved *physically*. And on the reverse of all movable monuments except Dieburg is the feast scene (10), one of the
'common' side-scenes. And the clear implication is that

this scene at least appears for a *ritual* and not primarily
a narrative purpose. If so, may the same not be true of
other, perhaps most, side-scenes? 'Ritual purpose' should
not be understood in a merely paradigmatic sense (action
within the scene corresponding to ritual actions or moments)
(11), but more widely: may some scenes not represent fundamental principles of Mithraic belief — for example scene Z
(the lion) found on Sarrebourg and Königshofen; or the
curious reversed goats (scene II) on Dieburg; or Mithras
supporting the world (scene F) on Neuenheim? If so, there
would be no theological reason to dispose a given scene in
a given position, since the scenes would not necessarily be
related to each other in any immediate sense, although it
would be reasonable to suppose that some scenes which regularly appear together (if not always in the same sequence)
were thematically connected — for example 'Saturnus' reclining and Jupiter and the giants. But there must have been
some rules: one cannot but be struck by the fact that scenes
B and C never occur on the right hand side of the relief (on
Beck's hypothesis the evening/autumn/west side) and that the
scenes which follow from the death of the bull never appear
on the left hand side (the morning/spring/east side). And
perhaps that limitation, whatever its rationale, helps us to
understand the half-plausibility of the hypothesis of a
reading-order: the movement from left panel to right panel
parallels the movement of the main scene.
  Whatever the force of conceivable objections to this hypothesis, in its acceptance of the obvious differences between
the panelled monuments, it seems to me potentially more
interesting than the usual attempts to explain away the
evidence, as L. does when, on p. 503, he remarks: 'Peut-être
attachons-nous ... trop d'importance à la logique et à la
clarté de representations qui avaient en elles-mêmes assez
de pouvoir évocateur pour pallier les flottements et les
disparités dans l'enchaînement des épisodes', to say nothing
of his notion (p. 502) that the 'incohérences' of the Italian
monuments are to be explained by an uncomprehending borrowing
of side-scenes from the *limes*-area. Do we have to be so contemptuous of the inhabitants of the ancient world that we can
believe them not to have understood the rationale of their
own mysteries? It is not they who are at fault, but our own
preconceptions (12).
  4. My final point concerns the relation between these complex panelled reliefs and other monuments. For most of this
discussion I have been content to confine myself to Will's
choice of problematic; but we may welcome L.'s decision to
include in his discussion not only the panelled reliefs of
Italy but also those with a predella (556, 693, cf. 350) (13),
and the two monuments with a single additional scene (736 and
435). For in terms of the continuum between silence and garrulity all of these monuments may be classed towards the pole

of garrulity. But the decision fits ill with L.'s formal
preoccupations, since there is evidently no *formal* connexion
between these different options. And the decision to include
these monuments opens a Pandora's box of problems of which he
seems to be unaware. Why does L. include only these monuments in his category of 'reliefs with multiple scenes'?
While the predella of 693 seems to contain the feast-scene
on the left (the three reclining figures are unique, though
note 782 Emerita, with Kane, 1975: 318 n. 14), it also shows
'Oceanus' apparently approached by a putto driving a triton-
car (14), which reminds us not only of the Oceanus at Santa
Prisca (Vermaseren-van Essen, 1965: 131-33) but of the similar figure on the lost painting in the Casa di Tito (337) and
the head of Oceanus on the lower right of the Capua fresco
(181). This latter also has the head of 'Tellus' on the
lower left, and 598 (probably from Rome) has a complete
reclining 'Tellus' with a basket of fruits beneath the bull
(15). Why should these conventions be ignored?
    I have already suggested that the use of the reverse has
close connections ritually with the side-scenes. The most
notable Italian reverse (it has a socket for a round peg at
the bottom) is the Fiano Romano relief (641), and there are
two others, 635 (Brontoön; probably late) and the equally
fragmentary 397 (Rome). On this appears a figure with the
head of a raven, which itself occurs on a panel-scene (Dura,
scene V) [cf. Kane, 1975: 345-48]. And each of the panelled
reliefs in the Trento museum has a reverse: 723 probably a
feast-scene with a hunt-scene above (the boar at least is
visible), like Heddernheim and Rückingen; 729 is too broken
for decision, but it carried at least an altar and a raven,
and may therefore have borne another feast scene.
    One of the less readily-intelligible side-scenes is the
lion (scene Z: Sarrebourg and Königshofen), which is also
found on two Roman monuments: on the bottom right of 339 (San
Clemente, altar) and beneath Sol on the highly original 'Triumph' relief 334. 339 also carries as akroteria representations of Winter (L.) and Summer (R.), which occur explicitly
on German panelled reliefs (Heddernheim, Rückingen) (16).
It is probable too that the small figures in the akroteria of
one of the monuments which L. discusses, 556 Vatican, represent Summer and Winter rather than Sol and Luna, who appear
already in the predella (interestingly reversed, perhaps because Cautopates is here on the left, Cautes on the right,
which emphasises their seasonal significance if Beck is
right) (17).
    These disparate additions of 'information' to the minimal
relief serve to illustrate the ill-advisedness of being controlled by an inappropriate typology: for there can be no
rationale for excluding them from consideration if not because of the demands of a formal typology. L. concludes
from his analysis that Italy 'rejected' the panel option

because of a tension between it and the Italian emphasis
upon the cave (pp. 500-01) (18). But this is to fall into
the trap of supposing that the Mithraists were concerned
with the same formal issues as modern scholars; does not
Marino offer a perfectly good example of integration between
panel and cave; and Barberini? Should we not rather observe
another interesting Italian exclusion, of small sculptures
representing the scenes also found as side-scenes? Rome
itself has yielded only eight (or ten) such statues, and all
the rest of Italy another two (or six) (19). Of course the
very occurrence of such separate statues or reliefs which
reproduce scenes which also appear on the panels helps to
strengthen the earlier argument that these scenes have a
ritual purpose: they are elements of the highly articulated
espace religieux of the *mithraeum*. It can hardly be a
coincidence that so few have been found in Italy where
there are also few panelled reliefs; and it is surely that
double exclusion we have to explain.

It seems to me that the opposition between 'silence' and
'garrulity' in Mithraic art reveals a tension within the
mysteries which is characteristic of complex religious systems, which one might describe as a tension between 'essence'
and 'adequacy'. The precariousness and difficulty of any
religious view of the world, but especially of a novel cult,
necessitates the deployment of various strategies of legitimation, both of content and mode. And in the Roman world
the creation of characteristic images was one such mode.
Precisely because the religious image is a means of legitimation, it must be stereotyped, reproducible: in an important
sense divinity exists as image not as idea, as theological
statement. For a world which saw god constantly in dreams
and visions, the *form* of god is primary. And it was perhaps
this pressure towards 'essence' which produced the simple
but dramatic, memorable, image of Mithras as bull-killer in
the Mysteries, the stereotype of which is attended by a number of 'failed experiments'. Not only, though, is that
stereotype an aspect of the need for legitimation: it is
also a device which resists the erosion of oblivion, a
mnemonic device which can be read at many different levels,
which meet only in the artefact itself. But although the
simple image of the god is necessary, it is also inadequate.
The image of Mithras as bull-killer is merely an element in
a complex symbolic universe, the *mithraeum*, though it is
also *opposed* to that universe (in its directional symbolism,
for example) in some ways. In order to be more adequate to
the complexity of the symbolism of the Mysteries, the links
between image and temple must also be represented on the
image itself, links at the level of proposition and of ritual
action. And within the context of that pressure towards an
adequate representation of the complexity of the mysteries,
we can discern a similar tension between 'essence' and

'adequacy', registered on the one hand by the stereotyping
of certain scenes (the 'reproducibility' of the 'common'
scenes is remarkable) and on the other by the variety of
unique or rare scenes. Yet even this variety in no sense
exhausts the possibilities for representation, as the wall-
paintings at Santa Prisca, the bench-paintings at Capua,
the mosaics at Ostia betray in their different ways. And
surely the point to remark about the Mithraic art of Italy
(and those three last examples are all Italian) is not the
'failure' of the complex panelled relief there, but the
variety and imaginativeness of the Italian attempts adequately
to respond to the density, in symbolic and human terms, of the
Mysteries of Mithras.*

*I wish to thank Trevor Kain for figs. 1 and 2.

NOTES

1 Note the strictures of Bianchi Bandinelli, 1966: 261-74 and 1961: 3-45,
   and M. I. Finley's review (1976: 79-95) of Metzler, *Porträt und Gesellschaft* and Bammer, *Architektur und Gesselschaft in der Antike*.
2 As it is by Turcan in his exemplary study of the Mauls relief (*CIMRM*
   1400), 1976: 68-76, which prompted many of the points elaborated in
   this paper. I hope shortly to publish a version of my lecture at the
   1975 Lancaster IAHR Congress on the deficiencies of Campbell's typology.
3 L. accepts the priority of the Northern monuments over the Italian
   ones almost without discussion: 'Il faut penser ... que le type à
   piliers ne se developpe que tardivement en Italie (pas avant le fin
   du deuxième siècle, comme le montre nos exemples), sous l'influence
   des regions du *limes*, mais sans pouvoir atteindre dans l'organisation
   des épisodes une véritable cohérence' (p. 502, cf. 499). But this is
   a *suggestio falsi* by vague reference: by 'the end of the second century' L. on his own showing actually means a period at least as early
   as his date for Marino (160-170) and the Nersae relief (c. 172). Can
   there really be any confidence that any of the German reliefs are
   earlier? Hatt's date for the Königshofen monument is notoriously too
   early (Turcan, 1976: 75 n. 22), and there are no convincing grounds
   for dating any others earlier than the late Antonine period. On present evidence there is no serious case for accepting, let alone for
   assuming, that the Rhine complex panelled reliefs are earlier than the
   Italian ones, different though they may be.
4 All the earliest reliefs of this type seem to be late Antonine. I am
   sceptical, for reasons that will become evident, of any simple diffu-
   sionist hypothesis. There is a rather similar puzzle in explaining
   the sudden rash of *mithraea* — the very earliest excavated *mithraea* —
   around 150 AD, in widely separated sites, and none of them in Rome.
   Is it convincing to attempt to trace them either to a single source?
   I doubt it.
5 Except the Quadraro relief (321), since I have found it impossible to

decide whether there is a reading order or not. The following monuments are excluded because they are too fragmentary: Val di Non (729), Stockstadt I (1161a), Mainz (1225), Holzern (1294), Besigheim a and b (1301), Konigshofen (1359), Ptuj II (1510), Ptuj III (1579). Only the left panel of Castello di Tueno (723) survives; the left panel of Virunum (1430) is less well preserved, and smaller in its present state, than the right.

6   The two monuments from Besigheim should probably be added (1301), since the fragments seem to be lintels broken on the right; and the Hölzern monument (1294) whose scenes from left to right are:' water-miracle '; ?Mithras walking + something else; *'transitus dei'*; Mithras entering Sol's quadriga. This may mean that the first scene lost to the right was Luna, as at Heddernheim and Neuenheim, and that the lintel held originally 8 scenes, being just short of two metres long.

7   Cf. Cumont, 1899: 218; Saxl, 1931: 28; 34; 52; Will's position is difficult to make out (I am not sure whether p. 386 n. 2 is supposed to be part of Saxl's argument or Will's own comment, and his remarks on p. 397 are less than clear on the subject of intention). L. remarks (p. 499): 'Il ne fait pas de doute que ce tableau (what he calls the Initiation of Sol by Mithras; my scene S in the key to fig. 2, p. 216 below) ne soit la transposition d'une des phases de la cérémonie d'initiation réelle au cours de laquelle le myste, agenouillé devant le *Pater* était intronisé dans la communauté, avant de partager le banquet sacré à l'image de son dieu...En Italie, la prédilection pour les tableaux de caractère liturgique est à mettre en rapport avec le goût si marqué des romains pour l'observation d'un rituel....Rome reçoit une imagerie déjà traditionelle...mais sa marque se traduit par une insistance sur certains scènes où la légende tient moins de place que la cérémonie.' Although in a sense I have some sympathy for the point being made, this form of it involves more problems than it should: what exactly is meant by 'transposition'?; what grounds are there for supposing that the Italian reliefs are characterised by such scenes to a greater extent than the Northern ones? (from fig. 2, I would say none); what relation between 'legend' and 'ceremony' is being argued for? What are the implications for the whole issue of side-scenes?

8   A list has already been drawn up by Will, 1955: 376-384, though it presupposes a reading order, and conceals important difficulties of location and relation of scenes. I would also observe that there is a constant temptation to attach to a given scene an apparently technical name, as though we understood the significance of it. I have been deliberately as neutral as possible in describing each scene: there is nothing to be gained by concealing our ignorance.

9   Perhaps with excessive caution, I have selected a new symbol for a small number of scenes which may simply be variants of scenes ordinarily (or also) represented differently. Those to note are the following:
Scene N (723, top left), a draped figure standing to the front with a staff in his right hand, pointing down, may be a version of scene A (Dura, centre top).
Scene M on 723 (Sol and bearded figure) might be a version of scene J

(Sarrebourg). HH (Dieburg) may be a version of OO (Ptuj II). UU (Quadraro) perhaps ought to be included simply as C_2 (a variant on C). PP
(Ptuj III) may be an expanded version of the same scene, C_1, at Die
burg ('Saturnus' sitting on a rock). I have found Rückingen the most
difficult monument to divide into scenes. With some hesitation I have
divided DD from EE, on the grounds that they are too far apart to be
connected; if they are to be taken together, they would become a
variant of scene BB or scene FF. Though fragmentary, the relief
offers at least 6 unique scenes, including the only German representation of the planets (extreme right edge of third register, left part
of bottom register: scene TT). To accept all these identities would
reduce the total of scenes represented to 40.

Where I am reasonably certain that one scene is a version of
another, I have indicated that judgement with a lower case numeral,
e.g. X_1, E_2, and included such scenes in the totals without ado.

10   This is certainly the case with Heddernheim, Rückingen, Fiano Romano
(641), and Konjić (1896); and probably with 397, 635, 723, 729 (all
Italy). I have suggested elsewhere that the reverse of 1161 (Stockstadt I) may have represented another 'Phaethon' scene (1976: 183 n.
47), like Dieburg.

11   As it apparently is by L. (see above, n. 7).

12   L.'s inability to resolve the tension between the assumption of a
narrative purpose and the obvious differences in order and choice
could not be more clearly illustrated than by a sentence on p. 499:
'Dans le diffusion de l'imagerie mithriaque, on peut penser qu'il y a
une vulgate faite de scènes canoniques exactement recopiées, mais que
chaque "église" est libre de mettre l'accent sur les représentations
qui touchent davantage la sensibilité religieuse de ses fidèles'. Did
that freedom then extend to altering the *order* of the 'canonical
scenes'? - an odd sort of canonical narrative indeed.

13   For completeness' sake, L. properly mentions 469 (with a photograph,
p. 487, fig. 3), a stela-type almost certainly imported from the
Danube. It is striking that this model made absolutely no impression
on the Roman iconography. Perhaps one might suggest more generally
that innovation in the iconography of the mysteries was hardly ever
from other Mithraic monuments directly but from the wider set of craft
possibilities available within a given locality. Mithraic monuments
constitute a series only for us, not for their makers or users.

14   L. (p. 488) takes these as three scenes, and the putto as Sol in his
chariot, following *CIMRM*, where Vermaseren writes: 'He wears a flying
shoulder cape and on his back a quiver is visible or is it part of a
person behind him [Sol in his chariot?]'. In his discussion of these
Italian monuments, Will writes (p. 397) that in this Apotheosis 'le
cocher semble être ici un petit Eros élevant une couronne'. But a
closer look reveals that the chariot has no wheels and the 'horses'
no hind-legs; and that there is a continuous line between 'Oceanus'
and the car.

15   'Saturnus' and 'Tellus' appear together on the right hand panel of the
Virunum monument (1430: scene LL).

16   Cautopates is on the left of 339, Cautes on the right: on Beck's
theory these positions stress the seasonal aspect of the torch-

bearers, and the monument thus registers all four seasons.
17 To this list of different types of additional 'information' on
Italian reliefs we should of course add sequences of altars; of
altars and trees; of vases (in a predella: 670); and small oddities:
a leaping ox (552); craters (204; 530); an ant (542; ?334); an owl
(S. Stefano Rotondo, unpublished main relief). Of course these are
not 'side-scenes', but my point is that there are many types of additional 'information', some of which appear on the bull-killing scene
itself, and some outside; but the content of that 'information' is
often identical, so that there is no point in highlighting merely
formal aspects of its presentation.
18 His emphasis on such a tension is certainly misplaced, as I observe in
the text below. And his arguments are flimsy. No conclusion can be
drawn from the fact that the proportion of complex reliefs to simple
ones in Italy (1:9) is smaller than that for the 'rest of the Empire'
(1:4) (p. 496). First, 'the rest of the Empire' is no sort of category - how many complex panelled reliefs are there in Spain, Gaul,
North Africa, Syria, even in Germany? The complex relief is *standard*
only in the Danube area. L. would have to find similar tensions in
all those areas to sustain his case. Second, we clearly have to do
not with a problem of 'rejection' or even of 'preference' but with a
matter of the number of competing options locally available. Italy
presents us with the largest number of original schemes (of all
types) as well as with the largest range of 'common' types - inevitably, I think, because the iconographical 'tool-box' was more extensive there than elsewhere in the Roman world.
19 Reliefs are also included under the term 'statues'.
Rome: 344 (petragenes: S. Clemente); 353 (petragenes) and 354 (Sol
with globe and whip: both Piazza Dante); 428 (petragenes: S. Lorenzo
in Damaso); 462 (?petragenes, the rock with snake alone surviving:
Terme di Caracalla); 490 (?petragenes) and 491 (snake-legged giant:
both Santa Prisca); 590 (petragenes; possibly from near the Capitol);
599 (petragenes); 612 (petragenes, incomplete). Perhaps we should
add the lion-headed god to this list?
Rest of Italy: 260 (?petragenes: Palazzo 'Imperiale', Ostia); 291
(?*dodekatheon* on a vase; Sette Porte, Ostia); 666 (petragenes with
'Oceanus' below; now in Uffizi, Florence); 679 (??petragenes; Spoleto);
694 (Cautopates with crater, crescent and corn?: Bologna); 720? (base
with L. Jupiter and giant and R. ?Oceanus with giant; perhaps not
Mithraic: Angera).

BIBLIOGRAPHY

Beck, R.L. 1977. Cautes and Cautopates: some astronomical considera-
tions. *JMS* 2, 1, 1-17.
Bianchi Bandinelli, R. 1961. *Archeologia e cultura*. Milano/Napoli.
Bianchi Bandinelli, R. 1966. Quelques réflexions à propos des rapports
entre l'archéologie et l'histoire de l'art. *Mélanges offerts à K.
Michałowski* (ed. M.-L. Bernhard) pp. 261-274. Warszawa.
Campbell, L.A. 1954. A typology of Mithraic tauroctones. *Berytus*, 11,
3-60.

Cumont, F. 1899. *Textes et monuments relatifs aux mystères de Mithra.* Vol. I. Bruxelles.

Finley, M.I. 1976. In lieblicher Bläue. *Arion,* NS 3.1, 79-95.

Gordon, R.L. 1976. A new Mithraic relief from Rome. *JMS,* I, 2, 166-186.

Kane, J.P. 1975. The Mithraic cult-meal in its Greek and Roman environment. *Mithraic Studies,* II, pp. 313-351 (ed. J.R. Hinnells). Manchester.

Saxl, F. 1931. *Mithras, typengeschichtliche Untersuchungen.* Berlin.

Sontag, Susan. 1967. *Against interpretation and other essays.* London.

Turcan, R. 1976. The date of the Mauls relief. *JMS* I, 1, 68-76.

Vermaseren, M.J. & van Essen, C.C. 1965. *The excavations in the Mithraeum of the Church of Santa Prisca in Rome.* Leiden.

Will, Ernest. 1955. *Le relief cultuel gréco-romain.* BEFAR 183. Paris.

Plate II Complex panelled relief from Osterburken, *CIMRM*
1292 (photo: Badisches Landesmuseum, Karlsruhe)

Plate III Complex panelled relief from Dieburg, *CIMRM* 1247, face A (photo: Stadtmuseum Dieburg/Schloss Fechenbach)

Plate IV Complex panelled relief from Sarrebourg, *CIMRM* 966 (photo: Musées de Metz/ Musée archéologique)

Plate V Complex panelled fresco, Barberini Mithraeum, Rome, *CIMRM* 390. Note the extensive decay, by comparison with fig. 112 in *CIMRM*.

Plate VI Fragments of the Virunum complex panelled relief, *CIMRM* 1430 b,c (photo: Landesmuseum, Klagenfurt)

ADDITIONS AND CORRECTIONS

I: The Real and the imaginary

There is a fine account of divine statues in the Classical and Hellenistic periods in B. Gladigow, 'Präsenz der Bilder – Präsenz der Götter' in *Visible Religion* 4/5 (1985/6), 114–33.

p.9: On the assumptions of the Hellenistic account of the trajectory of naturalism, see now Stephen Bann, *The True Vine: Visual Representation and Western Tradition* (Cambridge, 1989), chap. 1; cf. J. Elsner, *Art and the Roman Viewer* (Cambridge, 1995), 15–17.

p.9f.: On Hellenistic Greek words for statues, see now K. Höghammar, *Sculpture and Society* BOREAS 23 (Uppsala, 1993), chap. 4.

p.10: With his customary brilliance, J. Svenbro has explored in *Phrasikleia: An Anthropology of Reading in Ancient Greece* (Ithaca, 1993), chap. 1, a quite different form of enlivening interaction between statue and viewer/reader.

p.11: The tastes and attitudes of Roman private collectors (at a more humble level) have been discussed recently by E. Bartman in *AJA* 92 (1988), 211–25 and in E.K. Gazda (ed.), *Roman Art in the Private Sphere* (Ann Arbor, 1991).

p.12: Intriguing light on the institutionalization of Homer and other epic has been shed by Gudrun Ahlberg-Cornell's study of Archaic representations of epic (and myth) down to 600 BC: *Myth and Epos in Early Greek Art* (Jonsered, 1992). Panhellenic sanctuaries are another obvious type of Archaic gesture towards inter-communal solidarity, cf. Catherine Morgan, 'The origins of panhellenism', in N. Marinatos and R. Hägg (eds.), *Greek Sanctuaries* (London, 1993), 18–44. A much less obvious one is the type of convergent patterning of civic temples – if it is not a mirage – suggested by A. Schachter in *idem* (ed.), *Le sanctuaire grec* Entretiens Hardt, 37 (Vandoeuvres, 1992).

p.12: The archaeology of early cult statues is presented exhaustively in I.B. Romano, *Early Greek Cult Images* (Ann Arbor, 1982).

p.13: B. Gladigow, 'Epiphanie, Statuette, Kultbild', in: H-G. Kippenberger (ed.), *Genres in Visual Representations* (= *Visible Religion* 7) (Leiden, 1990), 98–121 at 102, has observed that attributes are omitted from accounts of epiphany, which tends to confirm the point that they are a specifically iconic device. p.13: Brunhilde Ridgway deals with the statue of Athena *hygieia*, and the anecdote of the *technitês*, in her discussion of the statues of Athena on the Acropolis in Jenifer Niels (ed.), *Goddess and Polis: the Panathenaic Festival in Ancient Athens* (Princeton, 1993), 119–42. There is much material on the rôle of art – in this case vase-painting – in realizing the divine world in ever-new ways in K.W. Arafat, *Classical Zeus* (Oxford, 1990).

p.14: On the size of heroes, in the context of the famous *kouros* of the Sacred Way, cf. H. Kyrieleis, 'The Heraion of Samos', in Marinatos & Hägg, *Greek Sanctuaries* (see above on p.12), 125–53 at 150–52. E. Bartman discusses the Heracles *epitrapezios* of Martial in her *Ancient Sculptural Copies in Miniature* (Leiden, 1992), 147ff. in the context of a study of the ironic and playful intentions of such miniaturization.

p.16: The ambiguity of the divine statue between thing and divinity was also played upon in investiture rituals, especially of small moveable statues: cf. Gladigow, 'Epiphanie . . . ' (see above on p.13), who splendidly evokes the passage between statue and the subjective experience of epiphany. H. Versnel, 'What did ancient man see when he saw a god?' in Dirk van der Plas (ed.), *Effigies Dei* (Leiden, 1987), 42–55 at 46f., notes the relevance here of the emperor's statue used as a locus of asylum, and of the movable divine statue being used as a form of oracle while on its peregrinations.

p.20: The taxonomy of power has of course also a topographic aspect, which I ignored: cf. S.E. Alcock and R. Osborne (eds.), *Placing the Gods* (Oxford, 1994) – though it is a pity that the book is so focused upon F. de Polignac's *La naissance de la cité grecque* (Paris, 1984); note esp. Alcock's own contribution on Pausanias; and cf. J. Elsner (see above on p.9), *Roman Viewer*, chap.4.

p.21: On the restricted, though genuine, freedom of the maker in the case of fifth-century Athens, see D. Castriota, *Myth, Ethos and Actuality* (Madison, 1992).

p.22: For the rôle of 'high' images in relation to 'lower' ones, cf. B. Alroth, *Greek Gods and Figurines* BOREAS 18 (Uppsala, 1989). Gladigow usefully draws in the Weberian theme of the deliberate restriction of access to the holy implied by the creation of 'high' images (p.106).

II: The moment of death

Whatever their individual merits, the interpretative contributions to Robin Hägg (ed.), *The Iconography of Greek Cult in the Archaic and Classical Periods* Kernos Suppl. 1 (Athens and Liège, 1992) suggest that the dominant archaeological value of iconographic evidence remains documentary. But, as it happens, the entire issue of Archaic and Classical sacrificial imagery, including reference to choices and silences, has now been fully discussed by F.T. van Straten, *Hierà kalá* (Leiden, 1995). On the rôle of altars in the iconography, see J-L. Durand, 'Images pour un autel,' in R. Étienne and M-Th. Le Dinahet (eds.), *L'Espace sacrificiel* Bibliothèque Salomon-Reinach, 5 (Lyons-Paris, 1991), 41–55.

p.569: On sacred groves, see D. Birge, 'Sacred groves in the ancient Greek world', Ph.D diss. Berkeley, Calif. 1982 (Univ. Microf.).

p.569: On votive reliefs, see again F.T. van Straten, 'Votives and votaries in Greek sanctuaries', in Albert Schachter (ed.), *Le sanctuaire grec* (see above on I p.12), 247–84.

III: Mithraism and Roman society

C.R. Phillips, 'The sociology of religious knowledge in the Roman Empire to 284 AD', *ANRW* II 16,3 (1986), 2677–2773, argues at length for a Weberian approach to religious change in the Empire. Ramsay MacMullen, *Paganism in the Roman Empire* (New Haven, 1981), 124, with his bluff good sense, will have no truck with Weber: conscious satisfactions are the only ones the historian may entertain, and Mithraism was hardly more than an occasion for a barbeque. Moreover, MacMullen has little time for conclusions about social catchment based on epigraphic evidence (compare M. Rainer,

'Die Mithrasverehrung in Ostia'. *Klio* 66 (1984), 104–113 at 104–8); the archaeological evidence he ignores. But his sharp, sceptical look at the whole notion of 'oriental cults' has been immensely salutary. For Reinhold Merkelbach, *Mithras* (Königstein, 1984), 153–88 Mithraism was even more markedly than in my view a religion of conformism, mirroring in its organisation and value-structure the asymmetrical reciprocity characteristic of Roman society. The 'glue that held the Empire together' was the imperial administration, and the *familia Caesaris* in particular; and he goes so far as to suggest that the religious genius who, on Martin Nilsson's view (*Geschichte der griechischen Religion*[2] [Munich, 1967], 675f.) must have founded the mysteries of Mithras, was a member of the imperial household in Rome. Much the most complete survey of the epigraphic evidence for the social catchment and spread of Mithraism is Manfred Clauss, *Cultores Mithrae* (Stuttgart, 1992), an expanded version of his *Mithras* (Munich, 1990), 31–50, who likewise believes that the cult spread from Rome and Ostia. It was brought to the Rhine-Danube provinces by the army and members of the *portorium* system, but then rapidly spread into the civilian population. He places much less weight on the *familia Caesaris* than Merkelbach; his conclusions about the cult's appeal broadly agree with mine; cf. M. Meslin, 'La symbolique des cultes de Cybèle et de Mithra', in *Le symbolisme dans le culte des grandes religions* (Louvain, 1985), 173–85; Per Bilde, 'The meaning of Roman Mithraism', in J. Podemann Sørensen (ed.), *Rethinking Religion* (Copenhagen, 1989), 31–47; J.H.W.G. Liebeschuetz, 'The expansion of Mithraism among the regious cults of the second century', in: J.R. Hinnells (ed.), *Studies in Mithraism* (Rome, 1994), 195–216.

p.95: The contrast between the earliest inscriptions and the earliest mithraea is no longer tenable: closer attention to coarse-ware found in the newly-discovered temples at Caesarea Maritima in Palestine (e.g. K.G. Holum et al., *King Herod's Dream* [New York, 1988], 148–53) and Pons Aeni (the crossing of the Inn) in Noricum (J. Garbsch, *Bayerischer Vorgeschichtsblätter* 50 [1985], 355–462, and re-consideration of the hitherto neglected fourth and third mithraea at Heddernheim in Germania Superior (I. Huld-Zetsch, *Mithras in Nida-Heddernheim* Archäologische Reihe, 6 [Frankfurt-am-Main, 1986], 43–45) have made it highly likely that all four date from the late first century AD and thus long antedate any archaeological (though not epigraphic) evidence yet discovered in Rome and Ostia (cf. my review article 'Who worshipped Mithras?', *Journal of Roman Archaeology* 7 (1994), 459–7 4 at 461).

p.95: W. Burkert, *Ancient Mystery Cults* (Cambridge, Mass., 1987) also draws a relatively sharp contrast between Mithraism and other mysteries, though in rather different terms.

p.96: M. Clauss has persuasively urged that the Mysteries' emphasis upon the sun, the same as Mithras yet somehow different from him, played an important familiarizing rôle in the spread of the cult: 'Sol Invictus Mithras', *Athenaeum* 78 (1990), 423–50.

p.97: Whereas Merkelbach, perhaps inspired by some earlier work of Istvan Tóth, *Arheološki vestnik* 28 (1977), 385–92, tried to read the grades even into the Mithraic cult-relief and thus underpin their universality in the cult (*Mithras*, 77–129), Clauss has argued that they were sub-divisions of a priestly rank, and that the great majority of Mithraists held no grade (*Zeitschrift für Papyrologie und Epigraphik* 82, 1990, 183–94; *Cultores* 275–77). This seems to me highly unlikely; but the fact remains that the epigraphic testimony for grades is geographically uneven.

p.114, n.22: Restoration work in 1978 on the paintings in the Santa Prisca mithraeum showed that Vermaseren's *eternali* is impossible; but *et nos servasti... sanguine fuso* is reasonably secure (cf. S. Panciera, 'Il materiale epigrafico dallo scavo del mitreo di S. Stefano Rotondo', in U. Bianchi (ed.), *Mysteria Mithrae* (Leiden, 1979), figs. 12, 13).

p.99: On Tertullian *Adv. Marcionem* 1.13.4 see now Robert Turcan, *Mithra et le mithriacisme*[2] (Paris, 1993), 135–8.

p.101, n.50: F. Mitthof, 'Der Vorstand der Kultgemeinden des Mithras', *Klio* 74 (1992), 275–90, represents a welcome attempt to sort out the relation between Fatherhood and sacerdotal authority, though I cannot agree with all his conclusions.

p.109: Of more recent work on Ostian Mithraism, J.T. Bakker, *Living and Working with the Gods* (Amsterdam, 1994), 116–20 is more plausible than Rainer (see above, III introduction).

IV: Authority, salvation and mystery

p.73 n.14: It was the word λεοντίῳ on a scrap of codex from Hermupolis (*PBerol.* 21196) containing a series of enigmatic questions and answers that suggested to W. Brashear, *A Mithraic Catechism from Egypt* Tyche Suppl. 1 (Vienna, 1992), that it was Mithraic in origin. His thesis has been greeted mostly with scepticism (e.g. Chr. Harrauer, *Chronique d'Égypte* 68 [1993], 280f.; Turcan, *Mithra*[2] pp.152–56). It seems to me entirely possible however that at least in some temples catechetical texts were in use and that this simultaneously expressed and encouraged theological elaboration of the kind we find in the literary sources; cf. my 'Mystery, metaphor and doctrine in the Mysteries of Mithras', in J.R. Hinnells (ed.), *Studies in Mithraism* (Rome, 1994), 103–24.

V: Reality, evocation, and boundary

This article has been amusingly savaged by N.M. Swerdlow, 'On the cosmical mysteries of Mithras', *Classical Philology* 86 (1991) , 48–63 at 50f. (in the course of a wholly justified criticism of D. Ulansey, *The Origins of the Mithraic Mysteries* [New York, 1989, 1992[2]]). It had not occurred to me that citing Lewis Carroll would cause such offence, as implying, I suppose, constructionism; but of course I am no sort of constructionist. Swerdlow's own starting-point – he evidently adopts Cumont's views wholesale – is now wholly eccentric; and, like Cumont, he has nothing himself to offer on the choice of animal names for the grades in the Mysteries. But I would concede that the article exaggerates the Mysteries' opposition between life and death, which I now understand as complementary emphases.

p.35f.: Merkelbach, *Mithras* p.79, brilliantly suggested that the sistrum in the Leo frame at di Felicissimo denotes the date of the Nile flood, and thus alludes indirectly to the heliacal rising of Sirius, when the sun enters Leo. I refer to this association in n.32, but did not see that the sistrum most likely then stands for an interesting leonine date.

p.48f.: Merkelbach has urged that *nymphus* relates to the meaning of *nymphê* 'bee' and means something like 'männliche Puppe' (p.88). W. Fauth, *Göttingische Gelehrte Anzeigen* 236 (1984), 36–50 at 47f., finds this as implausible as I do.

p.55f.: My account of the *de fluviis* passage ignores both the analogies with, inter alia, the myth of Ullikummi (W. Burkert, 'Von Ullikummi zum Kaukasos: die Felsgeburt des Unholds', *Würzburger Jahrbücher* 5 [1979], 253–61) and the literary problems of the tract itself (F. Jacoby in *Abhandlungen zur gr. Geschichtsschreibung* [Leiden, 1956], 359–422).

p.77, n.30: the article on 'virus' remains unpublished.

VI: Sacred geography

The section on the mithraeum in L. Michael White, *Building God's House in the Roman World* (Baltimore, 1989), 47–59 rather oddly ignores the Mithraic interpretation of the mithraeum entirely in favour of social considerations.

p.122: A new Schlangengefäß that has come to light in Mainz clearly implies the rôle of water in Mithraic ritual: one face represents the scene of the 'water-miracle', the other four individual initiates: H-G. Horn, *Mainzer archäologische Zeitschrift* 1 (1994), 21–66; cf. the comments of R. Merkelbach, *Zeitschrift für Papyrologie und Epigraphik* 108 (1995), 1–6.

pp.134–38: I no longer think it likely that the mithraeum was commonly conceived as subdivided in these ways: I was rather carried away by the speculative chase.

p.139: On the rationale of the Mithraic order of the planets, see R.L. Beck, *Planetary Gods and Planetary Orders in the Mysteries of Mithras* (Leiden, 1988), 1–11, 85–88.

pp.140–42: Roger Beck, 'Sette Sfere, Sette Porte, and the spring equinoxes of AD 172 and 173', in *Mysteria Mithrae* (see above on III p.114 n.22), showed that these planetary positions cannot denote the *thema mundi* but in all probability refer to specific, unusual planetary configurations in those years, which were doubtless the (re)foundation-dates of these mithraea.

p.162, Bibliography: Part II of R.L. Beck's study of the Ponza zodiac appeared in *JMS* 2.2 (1977), 87–147.

VII: CIMRM 593

p.159: the date of CIMRM 23 (now *MAMA* X 449) is not 'second century BC' but most likely 'first century AD' (77/78), if we suppose the use of the Sullan era rather than that of Actium.

p.160: on the tantalising first-century AD inscription from Sarıhüyük in N. Galatia mentioning Mithrés and feasting κατὰ μάγους (S. Mitchell, *Inscriptions from N. Galatia* [Oxford, 1982] #404), see my review article in *JRA* 7 (1994), 470 (above, III p.95).

p.161 top: It is now certain that the mithraeum existed before 100 AD as an organized architectural space (above, III Introduction).

p.161: On Statius *Theb.* I.719f., see R. Turcan, *Mithra*[2] 127–34.

p.165, n.8: The suggestion that C. Sacidius Barbarus might have to be down-dated to the Antonine period is surely baseless: there is no reason to oppose the consensus that his inscription must date from before 114 AD.

p.172, Bibliography under Beskow, P. 1978: To read: 'The routes of early Mithraism', *Études mithriaques* (ed. J. Duchesne-Guillemin), pp. 7–18. Acta Iranica 17, series 1, part 4. Leiden.

IX: Panelled complications

This article has evoked an interesting piece by Stephen Zwirn, 'The intention of biographical narration on Mithraic cult images', *Word and Image* 5 (1989), 2–18, who distinguishes between the 'theophanic' quality of the central image and the various forms of commentary, both narrative (i.e. based on the deeds of Mithras) and theological, to be found on the complex reliefs.

GENERAL INDEX

Abstraction: I 19f.
Absurd claims, in religion: V 22f., 38f., 48, 55, 68
L. Accius: I 15
adikoi, at Dura: V 42
Adonis: V 45f.
agalma: I 30 n.23
Agorakritos: I 11, 16
Alexander of Abonouteichos: V 26
akeraios, at Dura: V 82 n.48
Alimentary rules: I 18; V 62f., 67
Alkamenes: 1 16
Allegory: V 87 n.83
Amphiaraus: II 569; IV 68
Androgyne: V 49
Animals, 'good to think with': V 24–38, 44–7, 57–62, 66–8
Apelles: I 23f.
Aphrodite: I 11, 15
apogenesis: IV 56, 58; V 31, 40, 47, 62; VI 127f., 133
Apollo: I 16; V 26f.; VII 162
Aquarius: V 78 n.32
Aquileia: IX 203
Arcturus: V 31, 73 n.14
Ares (planet): VI 124
Argentarii, arch of: IV 65
Arimanius/Ahriman: IV 73 n.15; V 62; VI 154 n.54
Aristonides: I 29 n.18
Armenia: V 55f.
Aromatics: V 79 n.38
Artemis: I 14, 16; II 563
Asclepius: I 15, 32 n.52
Asia Minor: III 96; IV 48, 60, 78 n.78; V 56f.; VII *passim*; VIII 169
Astrology/astronomy: IV 50–60; VI 126–42
Atalanta: V 46
Athena: I 13, 14, 16, 32 n.52
Attribute, divine: I 13; VI 129f.
Authority: IV 48, 50
Autochthony: V 56

Bacchanalia: III 93
Barley-corns: II 570; IV 66
Bierbach: IV 64

Bi-sexual principles: V 51f.
Biton: IV 61
bouklopos theos: IV 76 n.53 V 53
Boundaries defined: IV 69f.; V 40–68
Bourdieu, P.: I 25, 33 n.56, 69, 85; V 90 n.105
Bricolage: VII 149
Brightness, of god: I 13
Breath, of lion: V 35
Brown, P.: VIII 183 nn.37, 49
bucranion: II 569
Bull, Mithraic, iconography of: VII 161; VIII *passim*
Butcher, sacrificial: II 568; IV 65f., 68

Cacus: IV 61
Calendar, ritual: I 18; VI 120
Campanian terracottas: VIII 180 n.15
Cassowary: V 22
Catasterisms: V 26f., 32, 33
Chaeremon: IV 72 n.2
Chaldaean Oracles: VIII 171
Chorography: VI 142–45
Cockerel: V 74 n.16; VI 153 n.50; VII 154
Cold: VI 128f., 130
consecranei: III 107; IV 67
Cooking, of meat: II 570; V 62, 90 n.103
Commemoration: II 568–70
Commensality: IV 71
Corax (*Raven*), as bird: V 25–32, 43, 44–6 as grade: V 32
Corn, origin of: V 63
Cosmos: IV 53; VI 120, 126, 145, 153 n.49
Craft-production: I 20f.; II 568
Crown, Mithraic: V 24
cryphius: V 82 n.47

Daedalus: I 8f., 16
Dagger, Mithraic: IV 69; VI 124f., 142; VIII 166
Demeter: I 15
Demiurge: III 114 n.20
Detienne, M.: V 45, 55, 62, 78 n.37, 82 n.51, 91 n.111
Deviant religion: II 568; IV 49f.
Dionysus I 16, 18; II 568; IV 79 n.89, 82 n.51; VIII 172f.

INDEX OF SELECTED MITHRAIC MONUMENTS

References to M.J. Vermaseren, *Corpus Inscriptionum et Monumentorum Religionis Mithriacae*, 2 vols, The Hague 1956–60, unless otherwise indicated

INDEX OF SELECTED TEXTS